The Law of Landlord and Tenant

The Law of Landlord and Tenant

Sixth Edition

P F Smith BCL, MA

Reader in Property Law, The University of Reading

OXFORD

UNIVERSITY PRESS

*This book has been printed digitally and produced in a standard specification
in order to ensure its continuing availability*

OXFORD
UNIVERSITY PRESS

Great Clarendon Street, Oxford OX2 6DP
Oxford University Press is a department of the University of Oxford.
It furthers the University's objective of excellence in research, scholarship,
and education by publishing worldwide in
Oxford New York
Auckland Cape Town Dar es Salaam Hong Kong Karachi
Kuala Lumpur Madrid Melbourne Mexico City Nairobi
New Delhi Shanghai Taipei Toronto
With offices in
Argentina Austria Brazil Chile Czech Republic France Greece
Guatemala Hungary Italy Japan South Korea Poland Portugal
Singapore Switzerland Thailand Turkey Ukraine Vietnam

Oxford is a registered trade mark of Oxford University Press
in the UK and in certain other countries

Published in the United States
by Oxford University Press Inc., New York

ISBN 978-0-406-94679-9

Preface

Since 1997, when the last edition of this book appeared, there have been major changes in many parts of the law of landlord and tenant, not to mention a crop of law reform projects. As a result, the text of this book has been substantially revised. The book retains its style and objects from previous editions. However, old-style statutory protection is falling out of vogue. There is a penchant for litigation, reflected in the large number of recent cases, as well as a pre-occupation with human rights and consumerism. This shift in attitudes has, I hope, also been reflected in the text.

It is becoming a tradition to make use of Prefaces as a review of the main changes in the law. Accordingly, one should note two important statutes. The Commonhold and Leasehold Reform Act 2002 creates commonholds. This is a new type of tenure for flats and office units. Commonholds will be mainly available for new developments. We note the main aspects of the commonhold scheme so as to compare it with leaseholds. Long leases will probably die out slowly. The 2002 Act reforms the system for enfranchising houses and flats held on long leases, as well as imposing a battery of new controls on the levying of service and other charges. It also further clamps down on forfeiture abuses in the residential sector. These changes are noted where needed, I hope. The other major enactment, the Land Registration Act 2002, reforms the land registration system and affects leaseholds. When in force, it will thus lower the minimum threshold for registration of leaseholds separately from the freehold title and change the rules applying to adverse possession claims to remove the secrecy of acquisition of a squatter's title. These and other relevant aspects have been inserted where needed. The relevant text has been written as though both Acts were in force, although they are in fact to be brought into force by statutory instruments, which may be made on different days for different Parts of each Act.

Reform of some technical details of business tenancy renewal was recommended long ago by the Law Commission. At the time proofs were read, it was understood that the government was framing a draft Deregulation Order, which would put the relevant reforms into place on an adjusted basis – following a round of consultations. The main aspects of the anticipated reforms have been noted where relevant.

Many aspects of the common law of landlord and tenant have seen important new cases - notably, with regard to classification of leases and tenancies, enforcement of leasehold covenants, implied covenants, consents to assignment of tenancies, repairing obligations and forfeiture of leases. There have also been cases concerned with many aspects of re-possession of secure tenancies, business tenancy renewal and even some decisions on previously unresolved issues concerned with the Rent Acts. I hope these many faceted aspects have been duly reflected in the text.

Law reform projects abound. A Law Commission review of residential tenancies is currently under way. Just before the book went to press, the Commission published its Consultation Paper "Renting Homes: I: Status and Security". Phase II of this reform project will, it is understood, examine harassment and unlawful eviction and succession to tenancies. The 2002 Consultation Paper raised issues of importance and general interest, which are noted in Chapter 13 of this book. The Lord Chancellor's Office is promoting reform of the law of distress, although, it seems, reform will come only as part of an overhaul of the civil enforcement procedure as a whole. These and other reform proposals are noted in the relevant places.

This book has struck out in new directions. With the enactment and commencement of the Human Rights Act 1998, the effects of human rights claims in the field of public sector tenancies repossession, in particular, are now being felt and had to be taken into account, particularly with regard to secure tenancies. The book now critically examines selective comparative law aspects in fields such as rent revision and repairing obligations, to name two areas where such an exercise seems to have some merit, if only to assess our own system.

In conclusion, thanks are due to my colleagues Professor PR Ghandhi, Mrs E Cooke and Dr C Barker and Dr V Munro for giving me the benefit of their expertise in the fields of human rights, land registration and Scots law respectively. However, any misconceptions about these areas and indeed elsewhere are my sole responsibility. Thanks are also due to the staff at Butterworths Tolley for their kind consideration and for preparing the Tables and Index to this book. The text attempts to reflect the law as it was believed to be at April 2002, when the book went to press, but certain minor further adjustments were possible at proof stage.

PF Smith

Reading

July 2002

Contents

PART B

Principal rights and obligations of the parties to a lease or tenancy

CHAPTER 5

Covenants generally   89

CHAPTER 9

Repairing obligations 201

CHAPTER 10

Liabilities to third parties   255

PART C

Termination of tenancies

CHAPTER 11

Introduction 269

CHAPTER 12

Termination of leases and tenancies at common law

PART D

Residential tenancies

CHAPTER 13

Introduction to residential lettings   313

CHAPTER 14

Rent Act tenancies   325

CHAPTER 17

Protection from illegal eviction and other rights of residential tenants   451

CHAPTER 18

Long leasehold enfranchisement   469

PART E

Business tenancy renewal rights

CHAPTER 19

Introduction to statutory business tenancy renewals 499

CHAPTER 20

Application of the Landlord and Tenant Act 1954, Pt II 505

CHAPTER 21

Restrictions on contracting out   519

CHAPTER 22

Continuation and termination of business tenancies   523

CHAPTER 23

Grounds of opposition   537

CHAPTER 24

Dismissal of tenant's application   549

CHAPTER 25

Court order of a new tenancy   553

PART F

Agricultural tenancies

CHAPTER 26

Outline of old-style agricultural tenancies regime   565

CHAPTER 27

Farm business tenancies   573

Abbreviations and bibliography

Statutory abbreviations

AHA 1986	Agricultural Holdings Act 1986
ATA 1995	Agricultural Tenancies Act 1995
CLRA 2002	Commonhold and Leasehold Reform Act 2002
HA 1985	Housing Act 1985
HA 1988	Housing Act 1988
HRA 1998	Human Rights Act 1998
LPA 1925	Law of Property Act 1925
LP(MP)A 1989	Law of Property (Miscellaneous Provisions) Act 1989
LRA 1967	Leasehold Reform Act 1967
LRA 2002	Land Registration Act 2002
LRHUDA 1993	Leasehold Reform, Housing and Urban Development Act 1993
LTA 1954	Landlord and Tenant Act 1954
LTA 1985	Landlord and Tenant Act 1985
LTA 1987	Landlord and Tenant Act 1987
LTA 1988	Landlord and Tenant Act 1988
LT(C)A 1995	Landlord and Tenant (Covenants) Act 1995
RA 1977	Rent Act 1977

Periodical abbreviations

CL	Current Law
CLY	Current Law Yearbook
CLJ	Cambridge Law Journal
CLP	Current Legal Problems
Conv	Conveyancer
Conv (NS)	Conveyancer (New Series)
JHL	Journal of Housing Law

L & T Rev	Landlord and Tenant Review
LS	Legal Studies
MLR	Modern Law Review
NLJ	New Law Journal
PLJ	Property Law Journal
RRLR	Rent Review and Lease Renewal
SJ	Solicitors' Journal

Bibliography

The following are the principal works referred to in the text of this book.

Cheshire and Burn *Modern Law of Real Property* (16th edn, 2000) Butterworths, London

Clarke and Adams *Rent Reviews and Variable Rents* (1990) Longman, London

Code Civil (annually, latest edition 2002) Dalloz, Paris

Davey *Residential Rents* (1990) Sweet & Maxwell, London

Gordon *Scottish Land Law* (1989) W Green & Son, Edinburgh

Hague *Leasehold Enfranchisement* (3rd edn, 1999) Sweet & Maxwell, London

Hanbury and Martin *Modern Equity* (16th edn, 2001) Sweet & Maxwell, London

Luxton & Wilkie *Commercial Leases* (1998) CLT Professional Publishing, Birmingham

McAllister *Scottish Law of Leases* (1989) Butterworths, Edinburgh

Matthews and Millichap *A Guide to the Leasehold Reform Housing and Urban Development Act 1993* (1993) Butterworths, London

Megarry *The Rent Acts* (11th edn, 1988) Stevens, London

Megarry and Wade *The Law of Real Property* (6th edn, 2000) Sweet & Maxwell, London

Paton and Cameron *The Law of Landlord and Tenant in Scotland* (1967) W Green & Son, Edinburgh

Plucknett *A Concise History of the Common Law* (5th edn, 1956) Butterworths, London

Precedents for the Conveyancer (looseleaf) Sweet and Maxwell, London

Privity of Contract: A Practitioners' Guide (1995) College of Law, Guildford

Rodgers *Agricultural Law* (2nd edn, 1998) Butterworths, London

Smith, ATH *Property Offences* (1995) Sweet & Maxwell, London

Sparkes *A New Landlord and Tenant* (2001) Hart Publishing, Oxford

Sydenham & Mainwaring *Farm Business Tenancies* (1995) Jordans, Bristol

West and Smith's *Law of Dilapidations* (11th edn, 2001) Estates Gazette, London

Woodfall *Law of Landlord and Tenant* (looseleaf) Sweet & Maxwell, London

Wylie *Landlord and Tenant Law* (2nd edn, 1998) Butterworths, London

Table of statutes

ﬁﬂ

List of cases

G

Leases and tenancies: basic principles

Chapter 1

Introduction

1 GENERAL

The law of landlord and tenant deals with the rules of law applicable to leases. In this chapter we are going to look at some of the general themes of the subject.

1 Under a lease, an owner of land permits another person, a tenant, to occupy the land exclusively for a period which is determined by agreement, in return for regular payments of rent.[1] One of the advantages of granting a lease from a freeholder's point of view is that he does not forever give up the right to resume possession of his land: at the expiry of the lease, at common law, the freeholder is entitled to resume possession. A person may take a lease for many reasons, for example where he has a short-term use for land that he has no wish to own. Freehold and leasehold interests alike are capable of being investments, whose value will be governed, in part, by the length of the term granted by the lease.

2 The terminology of this subject can cause confusion, if only because the law of landlord and tenant sits uneasily, for reasons to be examined, between the boundaries of contract and property law.[2] Thus we find the owner who grants a lease described variously as a 'lessor' and a 'landlord', whereas his or her counterpart is sometimes referred to as a 'lessee' but sometimes carries the label 'tenant' or 'leaseholder'. It may be that the words 'tenant' and the description of the relevant instrument under which that person occupies or 'holds' the land as 'tenancy agreement' or 'tenancy' is today seen as most appropriate to a short-term occupation agreement. 'Lease' and 'lessee' suggest a substantial proprietary right for a period in excess of 21 years. Equally, it may seem rather heavy-handed to talk of the 'assignment' of a weekly council tenancy whereas that expression

---

1 *Ramnarace v Latchmann* [2001] UKPC 25, [2001] 1 WLR 1651.
2 The Law Commission Consultation Paper No 162 (2002) 'Renting Homes: 1 Status and Security' suggested terminological changes: such as that rather than 'dwelling-house' the term 'home' be used; and replacing rent with 'rent' in inverted commas (paras 9.62 and 9.74).

fits a formal transfer on sale in return for the payment of a large capital sum or 'premium' much more easily.

3   This book follows a traditional pattern and so divides its examination of the law of landlord and tenant into its 'common law' and 'statutory' elements. It does this because the common law regulates all general aspects of leases or tenancies, such as their form, classification, obligations and termination. Legislation affects specific aspects of particular types of leases: there is one set of rules for leases of business premises, there are three sets of rules for residential tenancies, and two sets of legislative rules for agricultural land and premises.

4   The modern law of landlord and tenant is a patchwork quilt comprising many different elements. This is because it caters for many different types of need. Let us review some of these needs in broad terms. At the one end of the scale, we find long residential leases, which may have been granted for periods of 99 or even 999 years, so as to enable the mutual enforcement of covenants to repair and maintain houses which had been subdivided into smaller units, or flats, at a time when, if the units or flats had been held subject to freehold tenure, there would have been grave if not insurmountable difficulties with enforcement (a problem met to some extent by the arrival of commonholds). However, many of these long leases were granted late in the nineteenth century, or early in this century, and are approaching their expiry, leading to serious problems: the lease may not be easy to sell or mortgage, and the leaseholder regards the premises as his or her home. Hence, with the passing of the Leasehold Reform Act 1967, it has been possible for leaseholders of houses to buy out their freeholder, subject to the latter receiving compensation in the form of a share of the value of the premises. In 1993, the right to enfranchise was extended to long leaseholders of flats in the Leasehold Reform, Housing and Urban Development Act 1993 (hereinafter LRHUDA 1993), an Act of some complexity, which has very recently been simplified somewhat. The amendments, it is hoped, will make freeholder obstruction of the enfranchisement process harder, while not depriving him of what is thought to be just compensation, in the form of a share in the marriage value in the case of enfranchisement of shorter terms, for loss of the freehold.[3]

5   At the other end of the spectrum, there are short-term tenancies granted to the occupiers of business and residential premises. It appears that short leases now dominate the business tenancy sector, at any rate for the purpose of small business tenants who seek renewal of their tenancies, where average lease lengths are said to be for a period of less than five years.[4] One of the commonest current varieties of tenancy in the private residential sector is the assured shorthold tenancy granted under the Housing Act 1988. This form of tenancy is insecure from the point of view of the tenant, who may have as little as a single period of six months before having to quit the premises. The arrival of tenants' charters within the social landlord sector (that is in cases where the landlord is a registered housing

3   LRHUDA 1993 as amended by the Commonhold and Leasehold Reform Act 2002 (hereinafter CLRA 2002).
4   Crosby and Murdoch 'Decoding Lease Structures' *Estates Gazette*, 20 May 2000, p 153.

association for example) has gone some way to mitigating this particular problem, with a statement that ordinarily, once the first year of an assured shorthold tenancy has expired, the tenancy will be changed to an assured tenancy.[5] But this is not necessarily a legally enforceable right, unless incorporated into the tenancy agreement.[6] Moreover, assured shorthold tenants have no real protection against overcharging resulting from the market rent for their house or flat being inflated by a scarcity of accommodation in the locality. This feature used to be part of Rent Act tenancies until the present dominance of assured shortholds forced rents of the first-mentioned tenancies up, when they were revised to such an extent that the government capped the full extent of the increase.[7]

6   Assured shorthold tenancies came into existence with the political decision of the then Conservative government in 1988 (a decision that has not been seriously called into question by their Labour successors since 1997) to deregulate residential rents as from 15 January 1989. Since then it is not possible, in principle, to create new tenancies governed by the Rent Acts. [8] The greater proportion of housing in England and Wales is held by owner-occupiers. Perhaps for this reason, short-term residential tenancies are considered the best form of private sector tenancy.[9] The government figure for the end of 1997, for example, was that 68% of all dwellings were owner-occupied, as opposed to 11% being privately rented and 16% rented from local authorities and 5% from housing associations.[10] But the rented sector remains important in numerical terms.[11] One-third of households lived in rented accommodation, a good part of it from social landlords under the auspices of the Housing Corporation or from local authorities – hardly in the same class as some Rachmanite landlords of the 1960s, but whose premises, especially if older than 50 years, may suffer from serious problems of disrepair.[12]

7   The law concerning residential tenancies may alter once a reform process in which the Law Commission is engaged is completed – provided the necessary legislation

---

5   Shorthold Tenant's Charter (Housing Corporation, 1998) p 5. However, such would not apply to those landlords renting purely for profit.

6   For an example of incorporation of Charter rights see *North British Housing Association Ltd v Sheridan* [1999] 2 EGLR 138.

7   See further ch 14 of this book.

8   Housing Act 1988, s 34. In *White v Waring* [1992] 1 EGLR 271 it was said that even then, almost all cases coming to the county court concerned statutory tenancies.

9   According to the Law Commission Consultation Paper No 162 (2002) 'Renting Homes I: Status and Security' para 1.23, private sector landlords provided accommodation to 'niche sectors of the market who in general fall outside the scope of social housing and many of whose tenants are not seeking to be housed on a long-term basis'.

10   DETR figures (July 1999) in [1999] Conv 450. There has been a doubling of houseowners since 1938.

11   According to the Law Commission's Consultation Paper No 162 (2002), para 1.66, the only group in England where the number in rented accommodation exceeds that in owner-occupied accommodation, however, is lone parents with dependent children. Overall, they say, the size of the private rented sector has held 'remarkable steady' over the 20 years from 1982-2002 (para 1.72).

12   *Housing Green Paper* (2000) pp 7ff.

is passed. The process had reached the stage, at the time this book went to press, that a Consultation Paper had appeared.[13] The Law Commission was asked to consider the law relating to existing forms of housing tenancies in the rented sector and their creation, terms and termination, with a view to simplification and reform.[14] Phase one of the project is the current phase.[15] It aims to develop two agreements: Type I and Type II tenancies. These would replace the current battery of tenancies (such as assured, assured shorthold, and secure tenancies). The first type would confer substantial security of tenure. It would be aimed primarily but not exclusively at the social rented sector. Type II tenancies would be a modernised form of assured shorthold tenancy. It appears that as things stand at present, the Law Commission would like to get rid of any Rent Act 1977 tenancies, which they regard as a residual category, in being once any new legislation comes into force. The Law Commission has dismissed the idea of including a 'right to housing' based on, for example, the Universal Declaration of Human Rights.[16] They did, however, think that the reform exercise had to consider social policy issues. They identified four policy issues: (1) guaranteeing security of tenure; (2) possession proceedings and the need (having regard to human rights considerations) for due process; (3) bringing a consumer perspective to bear on housing law; and (4) human rights.[17] The Commission point out that there is already an element of consumer law in the law of residential landlords and tenants (one could cite service charges controls and management controls imposed by legislation), not to mention unfair contract terms regulation (both discussed later in this book). But they wish to simplify the law and make it clearer. Hence their proposal that most terms of Type I and Type II tenancies will be laid down by legislation. Residential tenancy agreements would, the Commission provisionally suggest, have three parts. Part A would form the core part of the agreement: the subject matter and the parties and the length of the term, as well as the rent. Part B would include all terms required by law – ie security of tenure and currently implied terms. Part C would set out the rest of the agreement. Default terms would apply if not covered by the express agreement of the parties or where the latter were unfair.[18]

13   Law Commission Consultation Paper No 162 (2002) 'Renting Homes I: Status and Security'.
14   Law Commission Consultation Paper No 162 (2002), para 1.8.
15   This phase is likely to be completed with the appearance of a Final Report and Draft Bill in the summer of 2003 (Consultation Paper No 162 (2002), below, para 1.11). Matters such as transmission of agreements will be covered by a second Consultation Paper in the summer of 2002 (para 1.11). Consultation Papers will then, it seems, follow dealing with harassment and unlawful eviction and succession to tenancies.
16   By Article 25(1) of this document everyone has the right to a standard of living adequate for the health and well-being of himself and his family 'including ... housing ...'.
17   Consultation Paper No 162 (2002), para 1.19.
18   Consultation Paper No 162 (2002), para 1.39.

Brief historical perspective

The law governing leaseholds was not part of the law of real property. Logically, therefore, it is unnecessary in relation to landlord and tenant to outline the feudal system of land tenure, because it did not recognise leaseholds as real property, as they were classified as personal property along with chattels and labelled 'chattels real'. In consequence, leaseholds were purely contractual relationships, under which the landlord merely hired his land to the tenant for a limited period, in return for the payment by the tenant of rent. The remedies of a freeholder who was wrongfully dispossessed from land were real or *in rem*; in contrast, a tenant in occupation was denied any real remedies for the recovery of the land following wrongful eviction by the landlord. Later, the position of tenants was improved. It appears that during the thirteenth century a special writ in trespass was introduced: *de ejectione firmae*, under which a tenant wrongfully ejected from his land could first claim damages and eventually recovery of the term, against his landlord and the latter's successors in title.[19] With this remedy, a tenant's right to recover his lease or term was protected; but, as a non-freeholder, he never had *seisin* or possession of the land itself, and as has been pointed out,[20] the real actions (the writ of right and the possessory assizes) were never made available to him.

As to the reasons why leaseholds were treated as chattels real, one may have been economic pressure. In any case, a leasehold was regarded as a valuable investment, as where a tenant with no sufficient capital of his own was able to work another's farm land; a lease also provided a means of evasion of the usury laws so that a debtor would lease land to his creditor at a nominal rent, and the creditor would draw the rents and profits from the land.[21]

Certain advantages were apparent from the general classification of leaseholds as personal property: first, that leaseholders were exempted from the burdensome system of feudal incidents; secondly, leaseholds, unlike real property, could be freely disposed of by will; and thirdly, though the action for ejectment was originally limited to actions by the tenant against the landlord and his successors in title, it was later expanded to allow actions against any wrongful dispossessor of the tenant, and was so efficacious that freeholders in due course elected for it because of the (by then) more cumbersome and formalised (real) actions available to them: they did this by pleading the fiction that they held a leasehold.[22]

Nonetheless, possession remained with the landlord not the tenant. As time progressed, the law deliberately assimilated many, but not all, of the rules applicable to leases, as chattels real, and real property. It is also an irony that, after the reforms of the 1925 property statutes, all forms of tenure were abolished except one (socage tenure, the

19 See Plucknett, pp 373ff.
20 Cheshire & Burn, ch 1, p 35.
21 See further Plucknett, pp 571-574.
22 The enactment of the Common Law Procedure Act 1852 rendered the pleading of this fiction unnecessary.

standard freehold tenure). Indeed, by the Law of Property Act 1925, s 1(1) one of the two legal estates in land is a 'term of years absolute', which in turn is widely defined by the Law of Property Act 1925, s 205(1)(xxvii) as including both leases for a fixed term of any length (be it for one year or 999 years) as well as tenancies of an informal nature, such as one-year written tenancy agreements, not to mention 'periodic' tenancies. An example of the latter is an agreement in writing, or even orally, under which a tenant has exclusive possession of the premises of another for a period of one month or one week.

Within the 1925 legislation it is possible not only to create a legal lease or tenancy (which save in the case of a lease for a period of years or 'term' not exceeding three years at a market rent with the right to immediate possession requires a deed to pass a legal estate)[23] but also a lease or tenancy valid in equity, as where a written contract is entered into to grant a tenant a lease for a period exceeding the maximum period allowed for the informal creation of a legal lease. In principle, the substantive rights of the parties under an equitable lease are almost identical to those of the parties to a legal lease. Either party can obtain specific performance against the other party of the right to grant or obtain a lease, equity looking on that as done which ought to be done and treats the parties as though they were to all intents and purposes landlord and tenant.[24] Equity is impatient with form,[25] and holds an equitable tenant by assignment bound by the burden of a leasehold obligation to the same extent as he would have been if the tenancy had been in due form.[26]

Yet the tenure that results, upon a traditional analysis, from the granting and acceptance of a lease has been stated[27] to be fundamental to the relationship of the parties to a lease. So, a tenant who purported to grant a sub-lease for a longer period then the length of his own lease caused his own lease to be assigned by operation of law.[28] The 'sub-tenant' held direct from the landlord for the residue of the former tenant's lease; and the latter became a stranger to the land.

23   Law of Property Act 1925, ss 52 and 54.
24   *Walsh v Lonsdale* (1882) 21 Ch D 9, CA; this is thought to be so despite dicta that the substantive law of common law and equity has been 'fused' since the Judicature Acts of 1873 and 1875 (see *United Scientific Holdings Ltd v Burnley Borough Council* [1978] AC 904 at 925; but see also *Tinsley v Milligan* [1994] 1 AC 340 at 371). The remedy of specific performance is discretionary and not automatic in availability and would be refused to a tenant who was in serious breach of obligation: *Coatsworth v Johnson* (1885) 55 LJQB 220, CA. See Sparkes (1987) 16 Anglo-American LR 160 (who holds this case to be fundamentally flawed).
25   As pointed out by Hanbury and Martin *Modern Equity* (16th edn, 2001) p 30, equity does not ignore form but looks to the substance.
26   *Boyer v Warbey* [1953] 1 QB 234. This principle is also recognised by the Landlord and Tenant (Covenants) Act 1995.
27   *Milmo v Carreras* [1946] KB 306, [1946] 1 All ER 288, CA.
28   See also *Stretch v West Dorset District Council* [1996] EGCS 76.

Thus leases, as chattels real, though in origin personal property, have been said to be part property, part contract and so hybrid in nature,[29] although one writer has contended that contractual principles govern the interpretation of leases as a whole.[30] This raises the knotty question, which is still unresolved, as to whether leases are contractual agreements or proprietary estates.

Contract principles in leases

For the purposes of their formal classification within both the scheme of the property legislation and conveyancing matters, notably where relevant registration[31] and assignments,[32] all leases and tenancies are governed by the rules governing real property. Thus the Law of Property Act 1925, ss 1 and 205(1)(xxvii) recognise that leasehold interests, irrespective of their initial length, may constitute legal estates in land. With the grant of any lease or tenancy for however short a period, there is a kernel of an estate which has to pass from the landlord to the tenant in order to justify the existence of the hallmark of exclusive possession. The latter badge is what the House of Lords has held marks out a tenancy from a mere contractual licence.[33] Thus Nourse LJ said[34] that:

'a lease of land, because it originates in a contract, gives rise to obligations enforceable between the original landlord and the original tenant in contract. But because it also gives a tenant an estate in the land, assignable, like the reversion, to others, the obligations ... assume a wider influence ... . Thus landlord and tenant stand in one or other of two distinct legal relationships. In the first, it is said that there is privity of contract between them, in the second privity of estate'.

Nourse LJ was speaking in the context of the enforcement of covenants or obligations between landlord and tenant to an 'old tenancy', ie one granted before the reforms to the enforcement of leasehold obligations made by the Landlord and Tenant (Covenants) Act 1995, which do not draw a distinction between personal and proprietary obligations (Landlord and Tenant (Covenants) Act 1995, s 3). However, his remarks were approved by Lord Templeman in the House of Lords as being 'impeccable'.[35]

---

29 *Linden Gardens Trust Ltd v Lenesta Sludge Disposals Ltd* [1994] 1 AC 85, 108H, [1993] 3 All ER 417 at 432.

30 Pawlowski [1995] Conv 379.

31 Leases for a term exceeding seven years unexpired must be registered separately from the freehold title: Land Registration Act 2002, s 3.

32 To be valid at common law an assignment of a lease must be by deed even if the original term of the lease did not exceed three years, so allowing it to be validly created in writing: see *Crago v Julian* [1992] 1 All ER 744.

33 *Street v Mountford* [1985] AC 809.

34 In *City of London Corpn v Fell* [1993] QB 589.

35 [1994] 1 AC 458 at 465 (Lord Templeman); also per Millett LJ in *Bruton v Quadrant Housing Association* [1998] QB 834, CA.

The House of Lords has not been content to let matters rest at this point. In *Bruton v London and Quadrant Housing Trust*,[36] they moved to a more radical view: that a lease, in Lord Hoffmann's words, 'describes a relationship between two parties'. Moreover, he said, a lease was not concerned whether the question of whether the agreement creates an estate or other proprietary interest which may be binding on third parties. 'It is the fact that the agreement is the lease which creates the proprietary interest'. As has been pointed out,[37] these remarks were incidental. The decision in that case, on the facts, could have been arrived at by holding that the landlord having purported to grant the occupier a tenancy with exclusive possession, could not now be allowed to turn round and point to its own lack of capacity to grant tenancies under the agreement it itself held over the land concerned, as a ground for only conferring on the occupier a licence. The position is further complicated by the fact that the statements of Lord Hoffmann are difficult, if not impossible, to reconcile with the result in an earlier House of Lords decision.[38] There, a person occupying a room in a hostel, with apparent exclusive possession, lacked a tenancy because of a term in his agreement to occupy under which the management could move him into a different room if it judged this course of action appropriate. The term amounted to a clear indication that no exclusive possession, the traditional badge of a tenancy, was conferred on the occupier, as it is open to any owner of premises to withhold exclusive possession and so, with that, to withhold the grant of any property right to the occupier.[39]

Overall, it now seems that leases and tenancies retain a proprietary character[40] but are increasingly subject to an infusion of contractual principles. These plainly govern the interpretation of leasehold obligations. The following general observations of Neuberger J[41] seem in point. He said that the provisions in a contract (including in a lease) must be determined by the words the parties used in the provision concerned, the terms of the contract as a whole, its commercial purpose, and the surrounding circumstances when the contract was entered into, at least in so far as these circumstances were known to the both parties. The court would be cautious before relying on other cases concerned with the construction of similarly or even identically worded provisions in other contracts. However, while this latter principle is sometimes

---

36   [2000] 1 AC 406, [1999] 3 WLR 150.

37   Routley (2000) 63 MLR 424; for further comment see Rook [1999] Conv 517; Morgan [1999] Conv 493; PF Smith [2001] RRLRYB 259.

38   *Westminster City Council v Clarke* [1992] 2 AC 288.

39   For a clear example of this process in relation to business premises see *Shell-Mex and BP Ltd v Manchester Garages Ltd* [1971] 1 All ER 841.

40   Otherwise, apart from the fact that the Law of Property Act 1925 has not been repealed, the reasoning in eg *R v Tower Hamlets London BC, ex p Van Goetz* [1999] QB 1019 (where 'owner's interest' within housing legislation was held to comprise both that of a legal and an equitable owner) would make little sense.

41   In *Westside Nominees Ltd v Bolton MBC* [2000] L & TR 533 at 537 (rent reviews); also *Holding & Barnes plc v Hill House Hammond Ltd* [2000] L & TR 428 at 433 (repairs).

invoked in the context of repairing obligations, it is also important, as Neuberger J recognised, to strive for some consistency of interpretation so that landlords and tenants and their advisers know where they stand.

Certain general principles of contract law also govern specific aspects of the landlord and tenant relationship, such as the determination of periodic joint tenancies,[42] the principles under which terms may be implied into leases and tenancies,[43] and the rights and remedies of the parties, such as a landlord's right to rescind a tenancy for fraud or a tenant's right to accept a landlord's repudiation by conduct of a short residential tenancy on account of disrepair.[44] The House of Lords has, by invoking wide contractual principles, overturned the former principles applying to notices, seemingly of all kinds, served by landlords on tenants and vice versa.[45]

II SCOPE OF THIS SUBJECT

Main methods of creation of leases

Leases and tenancies arise in a number of different ways, which are explored in chapter 2 below. For present purposes, they may arise in the following two ways, at common law:

1 by express agreement, as where L demises land to T1 for a 21-year fixed term; and
2 by implied agreement, as where T2 enters L's land with L's consent, has exclusive possession and pays a weekly rent. T2 is weekly periodic tenant of L even though there may be only an oral agreement between the parties.

In the case of periodic tenants, T2 in the above example has a legal estate in land, derived from his exclusive possession and the payment and acceptance of rent for a periodic term. This is as much a legal estate as that demised to a tenant holding under a 999-year fixed-term lease.

Complex chains of assignments and also of sub-lettings can arise where there is a head lease which has a substantial number of years to run. Thus at least two different leasehold estates can exist over the same land and premises. Take the following illustration:

---

42 *Hammersmith & Fulham London BC v Monk* [1992] 1 AC 478, HL; also *Newlon Housing Trust v Alsulaimen* [1999] L & TR 38 at 40 (Lord Hoffmann).
43 See eg *Barrett v Lounova (1982) Ltd* [1990] 1 QB 348, CA; *Eyre v McCracken* (2000) 80 P & CR 220, CA.
44 See eg *Killick v Roberts* [1991] 4 All ER 289 (rescission for fraud of statutory tenancy); *Hussein v Mehlman* [1992] 2 EGLR 87.
45 *Mannai Investment Co Ltd v Eagle Star Life Assurance Co Ltd* [1997] AC 749.

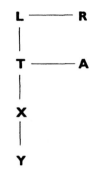

The freeholder, L, granted a 99-year lease to T in 1995. T granted a sub-lease to X in the following year for a period or 'term' of 50 years. In turn, X sub-under-let the whole premises to Y for one year in early 2002. Meanwhile L assigned his freehold reversion (viz, the freehold subject to the lease of T) to R in 1998, and T assigned his own leasehold reversion to A in return for payment in 2000. In the case of a short-term residential tenancy, as with an assured shorthold tenancy for an initial period of six months, the tenancy may well be incapable of being assigned or sub-let.

Outline of effect of private sector statutory regimes

Parliament has not been content to leave the regulation of the law of landlord and tenant to the common law, even at the price of complexity. For example, there is a long history of legislative control of the exercise of landlords' remedies. The law of distress for unpaid rent has been subject to statutes regulating this self-help remedy for at least 300 years. Statute conferred an automatic right for tenants to obtain relief against forfeiture for non-payment of rent in 1852. Recent legislation is more detailed and specific. The Landlord and Tenant Act 1987 confers remedies, such as the appointment of a manager, against recalcitrant landlords of a particular type of lessee, long residential lessees, of one type of premises, flats. Legislation to create a statutory form of compensation for improvements to agricultural tenants was first enacted in 1875,[46] and these tenants are subject for the future, if they hold 'farm business tenancies', to the Agricultural Tenancies Act 1995.

During the twentieth century, Parliament first intervened so as to protect residential tenants against what appeared to be oppressive and, in war-time conditions, politically inexpedient evictions, and then, once the immediate cause of the protecting legislation was at an end, made the legislation permanent. As a result that there came into being a code, the Rent Act 1977, for the protection and rent control of the occupation of most residential tenants despite the termination of their tenancies. The Law Commission recently pointed out that the protection given by the Rent Acts was not comprehensive, and indeed as from 1974 Parliament devised means (such as a resident landlord exclusion

---

46 Agricultural Holdings (England) Act 1875.

from protection) to encourage private landlords to let free from the security regime.[47] In any case, the Rent Act 1977 cannot apply to most residential tenancies entered into on or after 15 January 1989. These are subjected to the Housing Act 1988, Pt I, which creates assured and assured shorthold tenancies. The general balance between the competing parties has been adjusted almost as firmly in the landlord's favour as it had been tilted in the tenant's by the old rent restriction legislation. Thus, an assured shorthold tenant has no right to an automatic renewal of his tenancy once it has ended, and he has to pay whatever the landlord feels able to extract from him, unless the amount is wholly excessive by comparison to comparable rents in the local vicinity. The rent is to be paid no matter what the state and condition of the property.[48] Although it is commonly supposed that commercial or business tenants are well able to fend for themselves, Parliament has intervened to confer a qualified right to renewal of business tenancies, albeit at a market rent (Landlord and Tenant Act 1954, Pt II). Council tenants were granted security of tenure only by the Housing Act 1980, which has been replaced by the Housing Act 1985.[49] It has already been mentioned that a large reform project is currently under way by the Law Commission. If eventually implemented, it could see the end of the way Parliament has traditionally dealt with residential tenancies. At present, these are left to be negotiated (in theory) between the parties, with statutory control of security and succession superimposed. The new regime might lay down the standard terms of tenancies, allowing much less room for bargaining, as well as conferring varying degrees of security on tenants.

As things stand, however, Parliament differentiates between three different types of tenancies, depending on whether the premises are residential, business or agricultural. Most of the relevant 'codes' allow the tenant, instead of having to quit the premises when his lease runs out, to remain in occupation against the landlord's wishes unless and until the landlord is able to terminate the tenancy within the relevant statutory rules. As a general principle, the more recent the enactment, the easier such termination is likely to be. Thus, an assured tenancy is easier to terminate for non-payment of rent than is a Rent Act-protected or statutory tenancy. A 'farm business tenancy' is not renewable under statutory rights (as opposed to by agreement) in the way a business tenancy may be, even if the parties cannot agree to a renewal. Thus measures for substantial security of tenants in the private sector have increasingly been replaced by legislation dealing with matters of form, such as notices, but not of substance.

---

47   Law Commission Consultation Paper No 162 (2002), para 2.38.
48   It appears that in Scots law the tenant can in some cases withhold rent where the landlord is in material breach of his obligations, such as to repair: Paton & Cameron *Landlord and Tenant* (1967) pp 141-142.
49   According to the Law Commission Consultation Paper No 162 (2002), para 2.41, council tenancy provision rose from just over 5 million dwellings in 1920 to 17.6 million by 1980.

III   COMMONHOLDS

Introduction

Owing to the fact that positive covenants do not run with freehold land, there is no reliable method of ensuring to that successive owners and occupiers of freehold land which is in multiple occupation, such as a block of flats, observe covenants which involve spending money such as to repair or to pay for repairs. Accordingly, where blocks of flats have been developed, it has been the practice to grant to the occupiers long leases, taking advantage of the rules governing the transmission of positive covenants. However, in recent times, the long leasehold method has given rise to dissatisfaction on the part of lessees. Some landlords, with the obligation to keep the premises housing the flats concerned in proper repair and condition, have failed to comply with their responsibilities, either by neglecting to undertake any necessary work, or by failing to collect service charges from lessees to pay for the cost of works. There have been complaints of overcharging by unscrupulous landlords, as well as of landlords who buy up freeholds solely for the purpose of enforcing large arrears of service charges in the hope that they will be able to terminate the leases. As the term of a long lease diminishes, it becomes difficult or impossible to secure mortgage finance to purchase the residue of the lease, so rendering certain long leases unassignable.

Parliament has enacted a range of legislation in the field of landlord and tenant which tries, at the price of complexity, to address the problems of overcharging for repairs, neglect of maintenance and other abuses by landlords of long residential lessees, as well as enabling tenants of flats to buy out the freeholder or to extend their individual long leases. This legislation is examined in Part D of this book. However, in the view, not least of the Lord Chancellor's office, the time has come for more radical reform. We have now seen the enactment of commonhold legislation.[50]

The commonhold idea originated in the report of a working group of the Law Commission.[51] That group referred to some of the problems perceived with long leases and also noted that, as there was no standard form of lease, buying and selling leases might also be more complex and expensive than a freehold sale would be.[52]

Outline of commonhold ownership

This book is not the place for an examination of commonhold except in so far as it affects leases, but an outline of the principles of commonhold is called for.
1   The basis of commonhold ownership as proposed in 1987 was that it would be a system for freehold ownership 'where the emphasis is on co-operation between

---

50   CLRA 2002. It is understood that the commonhold legislation and final regulations will not be brought into force until at least one year from the passing of the 2002 Act. However, the text of this book is written as though the Act as a whole was in force.

51   Cm 179 (1987).

52   Cm 179 (1987) para 1.4.

owners living within a defined area'.[53] The government Consultation Paper of 1996 argued that, if most European, American and Commonwealth countries have similar schemes to commonhold, it is deficient of English law not to have 'an adequate system for the ownership of freehold flats'.[54] The revised scheme, and the present legislative package, envisage the application of commonhold both to developments of flats and also to commercial developments where there were multiple units, as with a business park or block of offices. The commonhold legislation was preceded by a government Consultation Paper[55] in which the aim of commonholds was thus lucidly described:

> 'Each separate property in the commonhold development will be called a unit. It might be a flat, a house, a shop or a light industrial unit. The owner will be called a unit holder. The body which will own and manage the common parts and facilities of the development will be called the commonhold association. The commonhold association will be a private company limited by guarantee, whose membership will be restricted to all the unit-holders within the development. The commonhold association will be registered at Companies House in the usual way ... all the unit holders in a development will have two interests in the property of the commonhold: a direct interest in the unit or units that they own and an interest in the commonhold association which owns the common parts.'

2   One of the advantages claimed for commonhold (as against long leases) is that the unit holders in a commonhold development would be able themselves to manage the arrangements for the repair and maintenance of the building, through a commonhold association, without the presence of a superior freehold interest. Rules, in what would be intended to be a standard form governing the extent of the association's liabilities and related matters, would be made: these would assist efficient management of the development. Commonholds owe a great deal to similar schemes in other countries such as parts of the USA. However, owing to the 100% threshold required for long lessees to convert, following the exercise of collective enfranchisement, from long leasehold to commonhold,[56] it is likely that commonhold developments will be of new schemes only. That said, commonholds may be established both with regard to residential developments and also business developments as well as in cases of a mixture of both types of development.

53   Cm 179 (1987) para 1.10.
54   Consultation Paper Cm 1345 (1996), para 1.1.
55   Commonhold and Leasehold Reform – Draft Bill and Consultation Paper (2000) Cm 4843 para 1.3; see Kenny [2001] Conv 1.
56   Under CLRA 2002, s 3 the consent of all registered long lessees is required to register the land concerned as commonhold land. This would be important where a majority but not all of the long leaseholders have bought out the freehold, leaving a minority of non-participating long leaseholders in the development. All these persons, as well as all the participating long leaseholders holding the freehold will have to consent to a commonhold registration under CLRA 2002, s 9.

Principal impact on leases of commonholds

The owner of freehold land (such as a developer) may apply to the Land Registry to register the land as a commonhold. The application must be accompanied by a commonhold community statement in which the rights and duties of the commonhold association and of the unit holders are set out.[57] There may be cases where the land in question is subject to long leases. A commonhold registration application may be made, by or on behalf of the long leaseholders of land who also hold the freehold because they have enfranchised the freeholder, but in this case, the consent of all long leaseholders – those with leases exceeding 21 years – is required.[58] Thus any long leaseholder who did not take part in the enfranchisement process can veto the application by disagreeing to it being made.

Tenants of commonhold units will be bound by the commonhold community statement. They will also be liable to pay charges to the commonhold association, with a right to recoup these out of rents.[59] A commonhold unit holder of a residential unit will only be allowed to create leases of up to a duration fixed by regulations. It is understood that the maximum duration to be allowed will be up to seven years.[60] The idea is to prevent a mixture of commonhold and long leasehold tenure in a commonhold development.

Once the first commonhold unit is disposed of to a unit holder by a developer who has registered the land concerned as commonhold land, the commonhold development is activated. At that point it is, somewhat abruptly if not harshly, provided that: 'any lease of the whole or any part of the commonhold land shall be extinguished by virtue of this section'.[61] It may well be in the absence of any authority that the effect of the specific provisions of CLRA 2002 overrides most, if not all, tenant protection legislation, otherwise the concept of extinguishing tenancies could have no sensible meaning. Any lease of less than 21 years of commonhold land is thus statutorily ended, and with it, statutory continuation rights that attach to it.

Under the Rent Act 1977, protected or statutory tenancy can only be terminated by means of a court order. Such order can only be made, notably, if suitable alternative accommodation is available to the tenant, or one of a number of discretionary grounds for possession apply.[62] In the case of an assured tenancy, there are similar provisions requiring an order of the court, which cannot be made except on grounds set out by

---

57   CLRA 2002, ss 3 and 31.
58   CLRA 2002, s 3.
59   CLRA 2002, s 19. Regulations will fill out the details of these matters.
60   CLRA 2002, s 17. In the case of commercial commonhold units, no such statutory ceiling applies (CLRA 2002, s 18) but the commonhold community statement may contain letting restrictions.
61   CLRA 2002, s 7(3)(f). The same harsh result follows where, following, say, a conversion from long leasehold to commonhold, the title is registered as commonhold land (CLRA 2002, s 9(3)(d)). Compensation is payable under CLRA 2002, s 10, ordinarily by the holder of a superior long lease who consented to the application for commonhold registration.
62   Rent Act 1977, s 98(1) and Sch 15. See further ch 14, below.

statute.[63] A Rent Act-protected tenancy, which one can appropriately label as a 'lease', will apparently be automatically destroyed once the first commonhold unit is disposed of, without any right to claim security under the Rent Act 1977. Much the same fate appears to await assured tenancies under the Housing Act 1988. However, it arguably cannot have been the intention of Parliament to disapply the statutory requirement that where a tenancy held by a residential tenant or indeed any residential occupier has 'come to an end', a court order is required to evict the former tenant if they remain in occupation of the premises.[64]

The case of Rent Act statutory tenancies presents some difficulty. A statutory tenancy, which came into existence following a protected tenancy which ended before the first commonhold unit disposal began, is arguably outside the extinguishing effects of CLRA 2002. That legislation refers to a 'lease'. This seems hardly an appropriate expression for a purely personal right of occupation – the label traditionally put on statutory tenancies by the courts.[65] On this basis, even if a commonhold developer, for example, has started to dispose of units to individual unit-holders, any statutory tenant in the building before the development process began might be able to claim to retain the protection of the Rent Act 1977 unless grounds for possession can be made out against him. The contention that any existing statutory tenancies at the time of the triggering of the commonhold rules lie outside the effects of the statutory extinction of leases is supported by the fact that continuation business tenancies are evidently caught by CLRA 2002 rules, since these are simply an extension of the common law lease or tenancy. On the other hand, a Rent Act statutory tenant has a right to possession valid against all the world, which ends only if the right is put to an end by the court, as well as rights to assign his tenancy.[66] From this, the courts may conclude that the provisions of CLRA 2002 extinguish statutory tenancies as well as protected tenancies without further ado.

Where there is a business tenancy of commonhold land to which the Landlord and Tenant Act 1954, Pt II applies, the specific CLRA 2002 extinguishment provisions necessarily appear to disapply the general rules of the later Act. Ordinarily, a tenancy within the business tenancies legislation is only capable of being terminated in accordance with the provisions of the Landlord and Tenant Act 1954, Part II.[67] However, a continuation tenancy, which arises on the termination of the previous contractual (common law) tenancy, has been held to be a mere extension of the contractual term, with a variation by statute of its mode of termination.[68] That being so, once CLRA 2002

---

63 Housing Act 1988, ss 5, 7 and Sch 1. Assured shorthold tenancies may only be terminated by court order but they expire on termination with no right of renewal (Housing Act 1988, s 21) and no security thereafter. See ch 15, below.
64 Protection from Eviction Act 1977, s 3(1).
65 *Keeves v Dean* [1924] 1 KB 685, CA; *Jessamine Investments Ltd v Schwartz* [1978] QB 264, [1976] 3 All ER 521, CA.
66 For these and other matters see Hand [1980] Conv 351.
67 Landlord and Tenant Act 1954, Pt II, s 24(1).
68 See eg *GMS Syndicate Ltd v Gary Elliott Ltd* [1982] Ch 1, [1981] 1 All ER 619; also *City of London Corpn v Fell* [1994] 1 AC 458 at 463, [1993] 4 All ER 968 at 971.

extinguishes the contractual tenancy, no continuation is possible, even though no specific exception on account of commonhold land has been carved out of the Landlord and Tenant Act 1954. If the tenancy is a continuing tenancy, the same result must await it as for the contractual tenancy to which it owes its existence.

IV THE HUMAN RIGHTS ACT 1998

The Human Rights Act 1998 (hereinafter HRA 1998) came into force on 2 October 2000. It is a major constitutional innovation. The following is intended as a note as to its possible impact on landlord and tenant.[69]

Primary and secondary legislation must be read by the courts, as public bodies, in such a way that it is compatible with the European Convention on Human Rights ('the Convention' or 'ECHR') – this is required by HRA 1998, s 3. The courts (by which is meant the High Court, the Court of Appeal, the House of Lords and the Judicial Committee of the Privy Council) cannot strike down legislation incompatible with the Convention. However, they are empowered to declare that the legislation concerned is incompatible with a particular Convention right (HRA 1998, s 4). The courts are not likely to make a declaration of incompatibility. Instead, they may adopt what is sometimes called a 'beneficial' or 'purposive' construction to legislation. If unavoidably a declaration of incompatibility has to be made, Lord Nicholls said that the courts should identify clearly the statutory provision said to be inconsistent with the ECHR .[70]

The courts are empowered by HRA 1998 to strike down delegated legislation if it is incompatible with Convention rights (HRA 1998, ss 3 and 6) unless the incompatibility is the direct result of primary legislation (HRA 1998, s 4). They may equally make a declaration of incompatibility.

HRA 1998 has an immediate impact on any 'public authority' such as a local authority, rent officer, or leasehold valuation tribunal (HRA 1998, s 6(3)).[71] No public authority is permitted to act in a way which is incompatible with a Convention right (HRA 1998, s 6(1)). 'Act' includes a failure to act (HRA 1998, s 6(6)). The 'victim' of the act or failure to act may bring legal proceedings against the public authority within one year of the act or neglect complained of or within such longer period as the court allows (HRA 1998, s 7(5)). Moreover a 'victim' can rely on the Convention as a defence in any proceedings – thus it could be prayed in aid in possession proceedings alleged to violate the Convention. Local authorities have already faced claims by aggrieved

---

69 See Harpum (2000) 4 L & T Rev 4 and 29; Halstead [2002] Conv 153.

70 *Re S (Children: care plan)* [2002] UKHL 10, [2002] 2 All ER 192, paras 37 and 41. It was also accepted that since HRA 1998 is retrospective, not all statutory provisions can be rendered consistent with the Convention.

71 The concept also included a charitable housing association, which had close links to a local authority, in relation to its lettings to tenants: *Poplar Housing and Regeneration Community Housing Association v Donoghue* [2001] EWCA Civ 595, [2002] QB 48. But taking rent from tenants does not ipso facto make the recipient body a public body: ibid. In any case, all the relevant circumstances of the case will have to be taken into account in deciding whether a registered housing association is or is not a public authority for human rights purposes: ibid.

tenants based on supposed violation of ECHR rights in the field of introductory tenancies and re-possession. By contrast, private landlords are only indirectly at risk from the Convention, owing to the statutory rubric enjoining courts to construe legislation so as to be consistent, where possible, with the ECHR.

The courts of England and Wales must take into account the 'jurisprudence' of the European Human Rights Court which sits at Strasbourg in determining questions relating to Convention rights (HRA 1998, s 2).

A Convention right which seems directly to concern landlord and tenant law is Article one of the First Protocol. This states that every natural or legal person is entitled to the peaceful enjoyment of his possessions. No one is to be deprived of his possessions except in the public interest and subject to the conditions provided for by law. The State's right to enforce such laws as it deems necessary to control the use of property in accordance with the general interest is unimpaired.

In disputes between private landlords and tenants, this article cannot be directly used (HRA 1998, s 6(5)) but it is possible that it has indirect effect since the courts must be satisfied as a public body that Convention rights have been complied with.[72] It is in relation to legislation such as the Leasehold Reform Act 1967, which allows for the buying out against his will of a freeholder of a long lessee of a house, that this article might be invoked. To some, this Act involves a taking of the possessions of the freeholder so as to violate Convention rights. The Strasbourg court has ruled that the 1967 legislation struck a fair balance between the demands of the general interest of the community and the fundamental rights of the individual freeholder.[73] This was so even though there was no right in court to challenge the basic operation of the enfranchisement legislation (a feature which did not infringe Article 6 of the Convention). More generally, there is a 'margin of appreciation', which the court allowed the UK government in the dispute over the Leasehold Reform Act 1967. The UK government was best placed to make judgments about the public interest. The court will review the means chosen to pursue the aim of the government, having regard to its established principle that there must be a 'reasonable relationship of proportionality between the means employed and the aim sought to be achieved'.[74] The Strasbourg court has, however, objected to provisions in legislation affecting private property rights which have the automatic effect of excluding an owner from enjoying his property,[75] especially when the provisions discriminated against smaller owners and not those with larger

---

72 A possibility envisaged by in *R (McLellan) v Bracknell Forest BC* [2001] EWCA Civ 1510, [2002] 1 All ER 899, para 42.
73 *James v United Kingdom* (1986) 8 EHRR 123. The Court expressly took into account the aim of the Leasehold Reform Act 1967, which it saw as implementing a legitimate social and economic policy (promotion of home ownership).
74 *James v UK* (1986) 8 EHRR 123, para 50.
75 Thus one might argue that the extinction of pre-existing leases under CLRA 2002, ss 7 and 9 as it is automatic, violates the ECHR, despite the compensation provisions of CLRA 2002, s 10. Provisions which discriminate against a tenant on an unlawful, technical ground would almost certainly do so: see *Larkos v Cyprus* (1999) 7 BHRC 244 (Article 14 violated).

landholdings.[76] If the proper procedures within legislation are not followed by a public body, then the 'victim' would also have grounds for a challenge under HRA 1998.[77] Presumably the same would follow in the case of a private landlord who neglected to follow the relevant procedures to gain a particular result, such as possession.

Challenges under Article 1 to the First Protocol might be made to the security of tenure provisions of the Rent Act 1977, on the basis that these limit the common law right of a landlord to regain possession of his own premises. A challenge to the generality of Austrian rent control legislation failed. One ground was that the landlord did not have his property transferred without compensation: the Austrian State was entitled to control his property in the general public interest and hence limit the maximum amount of rent the owner could charge his tenant for using it.[78]

Distress for unpaid rent might be vulnerable to a challenge under Article 6 of the Convention,[79] which guarantees access to a fair hearing in the courts, as well as under Article 8, which refers to the respect for privacy and home.[80] It appears that this includes an implied requirement that if a decision of a public body is attacked in court, the court has to conduct more than a routine review of the grounds for that body's decision.[81] Distress is a self-help remedy under which the landlord seizes goods on the premises and sells these so as to pay rent arrears. The vulnerability of distress to a human rights challenge lies in the absence of any right in the tenant to a hearing prior to the distress being levied. If the distress is by a local authority or other public body then the tenant or third party who was not duly notified under HRA 1998 could mount a direct attack on the lawfulness of the procedure.

The right to respect for private and family life might perhaps be said to be infringed where a local authority lets premises to a tenant which are unfit for human habitation. While a claim of this kind failed in relation to damp premises whose condition affected the health of the tenant's children, owing to procedural defaults in the way the claim was made the door was left just ajar by the Court of Appeal for a future claim to be considered.[82] However, the Court of Appeal was mindful of the fact that it was for Parliament and not the courts to make decisions as to resource allocations and no general and unqualified obligation is to be implied on local authorities with regard to their housing stock.

---

76   *Chassagnou v France* (1999) 7 BHRC 151 (also held that the legislation concerned, aimed at limiting hunting rights, violated Article 14 of the Convention, which outlaws discrimination).

77   Cf *A-G of Lesotho v Swissborough Diamond Mines (Pty) Ltd* (1997) 1 BHRC 383.

78   *Mellacher v Austria* (1989) 12 EHRR 391. It was otherwise with procedures which were so dilatory that the owner was greatly, and in the court's view with no justification, hindered in his legitimate claim for recovery of a rented flat: *Scollo v Italy* (1995) 22 EHRR 514.

79   See Walton [2000] Conv 508.

80   *Fuller v Happy Shopper Markets Ltd* [2001] 1 WLR 1681.

81   See *Terra Woningen v Netherlands* (1996) 24 EHRR 456 (reduction of rent by a rent board not properly reviewed by court; Article 6 of Convention thus violated).

82   *Lee v Leeds City Council* [2002] EWCA Civ 06, [2002] 1 WLR 1488. Severe pollution from neighbouring premises would appear to violate the ECHR, Art 8.

If an assured or assured shorthold tenant has failed to pay rent lawfully due (a ground for possession under Housing Act 1988, s 7(4)), Convention rights are relevant but their effect seems so far to be to require that the procedures laid down by the relevant legislation are followed. Where a tenant has seriously defaulted with his rent, it could also be argued that to deny the landlord possession would interfere with his Convention right to enjoyment of his possessions. The Court of Appeal have held that the mandatory re-possession procedures which apply to assured shorthold tenancies[83] do not infringe Article 8 (respect for family life) of the ECHR.[84] Parliament's views must be given deference in the housing field. It preferred to give preference to the needs of those dependent on social housing as a whole over individuals faced with loss of their home. The limited powers to stop re-possession within the relevant scheme were both legitimate and proportionate.

---

83 Ie Housing Act 1988, s 21(4).
84 *Poplar Housing and Regeneration Community Association v Donoghue* [2001] EWCA Civ 595, (2001) 33 HLR 823, [2001] EWCA Civ 595. ECHR, Art 8 is relevant to secure tenancy repossessions (as where possession is sought after a joint tenant's notice to quit): *Harrow London BC v Qazi* [2001] EWCA Civ 1834, [2001] All ER (D) 16 (Dec). See ch 16, below, however.

CHAPTER 2

Relationship of landlord and tenant

I NATURE OF THE RELATIONSHIP

Orthodox principles hold that where a tenancy is granted conferring exclusive possession on the tenant,[1] he obtains an estate in the land until the lease expires by effluxion of time or as from the expiry of a landlord's notice to quit. The tenant holds a proprietary right. If the due form for passing the legal estate to him is observed, where required, then the tenant holds a legal estate. If not, as where a written agreement for a lease for a term exceeding three years is entered into, then the grantee holds an estate in equity in the land. This confers on the tenant an equitable 'term of years', which ordinarily can be perfected into a legal title by the remedy of specific performance, equity looking on that as done which ought to be done.[2] The tenant and landlord were once said to hold under leasehold tenure: indeed the Court of Appeal ruled that without such tenure, the parties could not even be landlord and tenant.[3]

The House of Lords[4] has rejected the universality of the notion that a lease or tenancy must confer proprietary status on a tenant. They ruled that a lease or tenancy is a contractually binding agreement, not referable to any other relationship between the parties, under which the landlord gives the tenant the right to exclusive possession of land for a fixed or a renewable period. In return, the tenant pays money payments, ordinarily at regular intervals. The right to exclude the landlord from possession during the agreement is not, it now seems, a hallmark of a proprietary right. On the facts of that case, the agreement could not, on any view, have conferred any estate on the tenant. This was because his landlord (the trust) held under an express contractual licence from a local authority owner, under which the trust could not grant tenancies. However,

1   *Ramnarace v Lutchman* [2001] UKPC 25, [2001] 1 WLR 1651.
2   *R v Tower Hamlets London BC, ex p Von Goetz* [1999] QB 1019, CA.
3   *Milmo v Carreras* [1946] KB 306, [1946] 1 All ER 288 CA; also *Bruton v London and Quadrant Housing Trust* [1998] QB 834, CA, per Millett LJ.
4   *Bruton v London and Quadrant Housing Trust* [2000] 1 AC 406.

the occupier had exclusive possession of the premises he occupied, and was held to be a tenant despite the trust's lack of capacity to confer any leasehold estate on him. Lord Hoffmann regarded the fact that the grantor of the right to occupy could not pass any estate or title to the occupier as not relevant to the issue of whether a lease or tenancy had come into existence. The House of Lords approved a previous Court of Appeal ruling,[5] in which a public-sector occupier was held to have a tenancy notwithstanding the fact that the owner retained a duplicate set of keys and had probably intended the conferral of a licence to occupy on the tenant.

This House of Lords decision has been criticised.[6] Their Lordships paid little regard to the language of the agreement between the landlord and the occupier, which purported to be a licence to occupy. The decision could be confined to the special facts and circumstances, the provision of social housing – even so, the rulings will make it more difficult to grant short-term occupation agreements in the form of licences to temporary occupiers. The result of their Lordships' reasoning is that a person with no estate or interest in land may still grant a valid tenancy binding only on the parties. Third parties will not be bound by this type of tenancy, as it is not proprietary. This species of tenancy would presumably be non-assignable and could not be the subject of a proprietary sub-letting.

Leases and tenancies are hybrids, both proprietary in nature and also contracts.[7] Outside the narrow new class of a 'non-proprietary lease', they are Janus-faced. Leases and tenancies are proprietary rights, even if sometimes, as in the case of residential assured shorthold tenancies, or short duration business tenancies, the property content is of much less importance to the parties than the contractual obligations may be. A proprietary content in all leases and tenancies is part of the 1925 property legislation.[8] The contrast with civilian systems is apparent. In France, for example, almost all leases or *baux* are merely contractual agreements, as shown by the fact that, exceptionally, only two types of long lease are expressly regarded as conferring real rights on the lessee.[9]

Where a lease is granted by a landlord with an estate in the land concerned, there will be two concurrent estates, one held by the tenant, which ends with expiry of the lease, and the other by the landlord. Leases and tenancies are subject to the requirement that their duration is certain, a principle which we discuss later in this chapter. Most leases

---

5   *Family Housing Association v Jones* [1990] 1 WLR 779.
6   See citations in ch 1, above and also Pawlowski (2000) Nottingham LJ 85.
7   *Linden Garden Trust Ltd v Lenesta Sludge Disposals Ltd* [1994] 1 AC 85 at 108, [1993] 4 All ER 437 at 432, HL. For some general examples of contract principles affecting leases, see chs 1 and 5 of this book.
8   Eg Law of Property Act 1925, ss 1, 52, 54, and 205(1)(ii), (ix) and (xxvii), such that tenancies for one week can subsist as legal estates.
9   These are long agricultural leases (see Mazeaud, Mazeaud et Chabas *Leçons de Droit Civil* (8th edn, 1994) Vol II, Nos 1692ff) and construction leases (ibid, No 1697-2 – 1697-5). The former leases are said to be derived from Justinian: Jolowicz *Historical Introduction to Roman Law* (1939) p 283.

or tenancies are capable of being assigned or transferred to another person by the current tenant, as any property right is freely transferable: however, the terms of the agreement may, and frequently do, expressly restrict the right of the tenant to assign his lease or tenancy. The same principle applies to sub-lettings: the creation of a lease for a shorter period than the remaining period of the tenancy.

While ordinarily the tenant must vacate the premises once the period fixed for his occupation has arrived, some tenancies continue after the contractual expiry date owing to statute, as where a business tenant is entitled to a statutory continuation tenancy or a residential tenant holds over on expiry of an old-style Rent Act-protected tenancy.[10] However, in the private residential sector, with the dominance of insecure assured shorthold tenancies, the common law principle is not interfered with by statute, which contents itself with imposing formal notice procedures on the landlord to recover possession, as well as requiring him to make use of the courts if re-possession is resisted (see chapter 15 of this book).

II   SUBJECT MATTER

All land and interests in land lie in grant[11] and so may be leased. 'Land' is defined by the Law of Property Act 1925, s 205(1)(ix) (hereinafter LPA 1925), as including:

'land of any tenure, and mines and minerals, whether or not held apart from the surface, buildings or parts of buildings (whether the division is horizontal, vertical or made in any other way) and other corporeal hereditaments; also a . . . rent and other incorporeal hereditaments, and an easement, right, privilege, or benefit in, over, or derived from land; but not an undivided share in land . . . .'

Corporeal hereditaments consist of the land itself (including mines and minerals) and permanent structures on the land, such as buildings parts of buildings and fixtures. Incorporeal hereditaments are rights issuing out of land, and include rights of way, easements generally, sporting rights and other profits à prendre, tolls, commons and estovers and so on: all these may be leased but a deed is required to pass the legal estate.[12]

If a lease of a right of way over land adjoining the tenant's premises is expressly granted, the grantor is not obliged by the Landlord and Tenant Act 1954, Pt II to renew the lease on its expiry, since the tenant is not in occupation for statutory purposes.[13] If the tenant entitled to the lease of a right of way also holds a lease of adjoining premises protected by the Landlord and Tenant Act 1954, Pt II, then the relevant holding for statutory purposes includes the lease of the right of way.[14]

10   See Landlord and Tenant Act 1954, Pt II (business tenancies) and Rent Act 1977, ss 2 and 3 (old-style statutory protection).
11   Law of Property Act 1925, s 51(1).
12   LPA 1925, s 52(1). An equitable lease of an incorporeal hereditament may be validly granted.
13   *Land Reclamation Co Ltd v Basildon District Council* [1979] 2 All ER 993, CA.
14   *Nevill Long & Co (Boards) Ltd v Firmenich & Co* (1983) 47 P & CR 59, CA.

Goods and chattels cannot be let as such. Plant and machinery may be leased by a separate agreement to that leasing the land where they are situated. If chattels and land are let in the same agreement, as with furnished lettings, the rent issues out of the land as a whole and so the whole rent (including any part payable for the use of the furniture) is distrainable.

Easements in a lease

A tenant may obtain the benefit of easements in the lease, by express or implied grant, or express or implied reservation. For present purposes 'easement' means: 'a right attached to a particular piece of land which allows the owner of that land (the dominant owner) either to use the land of another person (the servient owner) in a particular manner . . . or to restrict its user by that other person to a particular extent . . . '.[15] However, one lessee cannot acquire easements prescriptively by common law, lost modern grant or, it seems, statute, against a neighbouring lessee;[16] nor may he prescriptively acquire easements for his sole benefit against neighbouring land, whether it is held by his landlord or any other person.[17]

The extent of any particular grant or reservation of an easement in favour of a tenant is a matter of construction.[18] The question of whether the rights so conferred have been interfered with is a question of fact.[19] In the case of the right to erect signboards, these are generally construed as capable of passing, if at all, as an easement,[20] but the right to erect a signboard may be spelt out of a demise 'with appurtenances'.[21]

The tenant may in the absence of express grant or reservation obtain certain easements by implication under one of four headings.

1 An easement of necessity. This is limited in principle to a right of access over the landlord's retained land (if any) if at the time of the demise there was no other means of access to the demised premises, however inconvenient: an easement of necessity is limited to the purposes of the lessee at the date of the demise.[22]

---

15   Cheshire & Burn, p 568. For further details, see Cheshire and Burn, ch 18, Part II; Megarry and Wade, ch 18, Pt II.

16   *Kilgour v Gaddes* [1904] 1 KB 457; *Simmons v Dobson* [1991] 4 All ER 25, CA.

17   *Gayford v Moffatt* (1868) 4 Ch App 133.

18   See eg *Paragon Finance plc v City of London Real Property Co Ltd* [2002] 1 EGLR 97.

19   See eg *Celsteel Ltd v Alton House Holdings Ltd* [1986] 1 All ER 608 (interference with access rights thanks to proposed construction by landlord of a car-wash on adjoining premises); *Saeed v Plustrade Ltd* [2000] EGCS 143 (reduction by landlord of rights to park cars in allotted spaces).

20   In *Francis v Hayward* (1882) 22 Ch D 177, CA, signboards were construed as part of the demised premises, but this was a very special case.

21   *William Hill (Southern) Ltd v Cabras Ltd* (1986) 54 P & CR 42, CA. Such right may not be construed out of a qualified prohibition against putting up signboards, ibid.

22   *Pinnington v Galland* (1853) 9 Exch 1; *Titchmarch v Royston Water Co Ltd* (1899) 81 LT 673; *Nickerson v Barraclough* [1980] Ch 325, [1979] 3 All ER 312.

2 Intended easements. These are readily implied into leases to enable the purposes of the tenant, if known to the landlord, to be effectually carried out, as where a tenant was held entitled to install a ventilation system in the basement kitchen of a restaurant, let as such.[23]

3 Continuous and apparent quasi-easements. These implied under the rule in *Wheeldon v Burrows*[24] but they must be continuous and apparent; necessary for the reasonable enjoyment of the demised premises; and used by the landlord up to the date of the grant of the lease, for the benefit of the demised land or premises. It was, for example, held that this rule enabled the equitable lessee of a house to use an unmetalled way over the landlord's land as a means of access to and from the house.[25]

4 LPA 1925, s 62(1). Any lease by deed automatically passes to the tenant a long list of easements, rights and reputed rights, 'at the time of conveyance demised, occupied or enjoyed with, or reputed or known as part or parcel of or appurtenant to the land or any part thereof'. The scope of any easements or rights passed by LPA 1925, s 62 is a question of fact.[26] This is supposed to be merely a word-saving provision in relation to leases and other conveyances. In fact where land is demised to a tenant and he under the lease enjoys a precarious right, such as to use a coal-shed on the landlord's land, and the lease is renewed, the right, unless expressly and clearly excluded on renewal,[27] is converted into a full easement.[28] A precarious easement not known to the law will not pass under LPA 1925, s 62, such as a right to a supply of hot water and central heating.[29] Subject to that, any right de facto enjoyed with the demised premises at the date of renewal of the lease, such as a way, or a right to park a car on a forecourt, will pass automatically on renewal under LPA 1925, s 62.[30]

---

23 *Wong v Beaumont Property Trust Ltd* [1965] 1 QB 173, [1964] 2 All ER 119, CA. The ventilation system, which had to be built against the landlord's back wall, was essential if public health regulations were to be complied with and in this sense 'necessary'.

24 (1879) 12 Ch D 31, CA.

25 *Borman v Griffith* [1930] 1 Ch 493.

26 See *Handel v St Stephens Close Ltd* [1994] 1 EGLR 70 (car-parking).

27 The grant of a lease 'with appurtenances' is insufficient to exclude LPA 1925, s 62: *Hansford v Jago* [1921] 1 Ch 322.

28 *Wright v Macadam* [1949] 2 KB 744, [1949] 2 All ER 565, CA. This rule applies to a licence to use a right of way or other advantage granted to a tenant let into occupation prior to the granting of a lease: on grant, the right becomes a full easement unless LPA 1925, s 62 is excluded: *Goldberg v Edwards* [1950] Ch 247, CA.

29 *Regis Property Co Ltd v Redman* [1956] 2 QB 612, [1956] 2 All ER 335, CA; nor a right to have one's flank outside wall proofed against the elements: *Phipps v Pears* [1965] 1 QB 76, [1964] 2 All ER 35, CA; nor a right to unlimited grazing: *Anderson v Bostock* [1976] Ch 312, [1976] 1 All ER 560.

30 *International Tea Stores Co v Hobbs* [1903] 2 Ch 165 (way); *Hair v Gilman* [2000] 3 EGLR 74 (car-parking).

III THE PARTIES

General capacity principles

Any person may, in principle, grant or accept a lease or tenancy. However, statute expressly prohibits any discrimination against potential lessees on the grounds of race and sex.[31] Although statute may impose specific disabilities on various types of landlord, which prevent them from granting leases or tenancies at all or above a certain duration,[32] it now appears that a landlord who cannot under the terms of his own occupation of land grant a lease may still grant a non proprietary tenancy to a tenant, although the tenancy will not bind third parties even if they have notice of it.[33]

Statute may impose disabilities on certain types of tenants. Thus if a legal lease is granted to a minor alone, the lease operates as a declaration that the land in question is held on trust for the minor.[34] Specific statutory rules also make provision for cases where the landlord or tenant as the case may be is a mental patient or is bankrupt.[35]

Turning to general disabilities, firstly, two persons may not validly grant a lease to themselves of property of which they are owners.[36] A single individual cannot grant a

31 Race Relations Act 1976, s 21(1); Sex Discrimination Act 1975, s 30(1).
32 Under CLRA 2002, s 17, regulations are to be made under which it is expected that no unit-holder will be able to grant a residential lease for a term exceeding seven years. The policy of this draconian restriction (not encountered in France for example) is apparently to avoid a mixture of long leasehold and unit-holder occupation in commonhold developments. It is the government's belief that active participation in commonhold management will be aided by this type of restriction. In France, unit-holders are often inactive in any case, thus calling into question this aspect of the proposed regulations. See *Le Monde* 14-17 March 1984.
33 *Bruton v London and Quadrant Housing Trust* [2000] 1 AC 406. Where a requisitioning authority confers an occupation right on someone, yet lacks capacity to grant leases, until *Bruton*, it was thought, following *Street v Mountford* [1985] AC 809, that the occupier was a licensee. This is probably still the case, although if the approach of Lord Hoffmann in *Bruton* to tenancies by estoppel is extended to statutory incapacity, a tenancy of a non-proprietary character might be said to have arisen. However, *Lewisham London BC v Roberts* [1949] 2 KB 608 CA, holding the contrary, was not overruled in *Bruton*.
34 Trusts of Land and Appointment of Trustees Act 1996, Sch 1, para 1(1). Where a lease is granted to a minor and an adult person jointly, the premises are deemed to be vested in the adult person on trust for that person and the minor (Trusts of Land and Appointment of Trustees Act 1996, Sch 1, para 1(2)). Although Sch 1 to the 1996 Act speaks of 'conveyance', this term includes 'lease' (Trusts of Land and Appointment of Trustees Act 1996, s 23(2)).
35 Mental Health Act 1983, s 93 (patients); Insolvency Act 1986, ss 306 and 284 (bankruptcy). The position where the landlord or tenant has died is governed, as regards the period of administration of their estate, by Administration of Estates Act 1925, s 39 (vesting full leasing powers in the estate administrators, subject to the concurrence of all such if more than one to the granting of a lease: Administration of Estates Act 1925, s 2(2)); see also *Harrison v Wing* [1988] 2 EGLR 4.
36 *Rye v Rye* [1962] AC 496, [1962] 1 All ER 146, HL; (1962) 78 LQR 175 (PVB); (1962) 78 LQR 177 (REM). Lord Simonds cited *Grey v Ellison* (1856) 1 Giff 438 to the effect that a notion of a lease by a man to himself was 'somewhat whimsical'.

lease to himself,[37] but a nominee may lease back land to his principal.[38] This is because a person cannot carve out of land he owns a lesser estate: the latter would be merged with the former automatically. Two persons cannot jointly grant to themselves, eg as partners, a lease of land of which they jointly own the freehold, as two individuals cannot carry out something which a single individual cannot do. Also, the notion of a person enforcing covenants in the lease against himself will not bear serious consideration. By reason of LPA 1925, s 72(3), tenants in common of land are enabled validly to lease land, by deed, to themselves in another capacity. But in such a case they accept the lease in that different capacity, as where the grantors are co-owning trustees of the legal estate and the persons accepting the lease are trust beneficiaries.

A tenant cannot grant to any other person a greater right to the premises than he himself has under his own agreement. Hence, where the tenant of a flat whose tenancy expired on 28 November 1944 granted to another person by a written agreement the right to occupy his flat for one year from 1 November 1944 and thereafter quarterly, he had granted a minimum period of some 15 months, which he had no capacity to do. The agreement took effect as an 'assignment by operation of law', passing to the occupier the whole of the erstwhile tenant's interest in the land, but no more.[39] The former tenant's claim for possession therefore failed. He was a stranger to the land. Likewise, in the context of business premises, a tenant whose tenancy was contracted out of statutory renewal rights could not confer on a new occupier for a period exceeding that of the tenant any right to renew their tenancy as against the landlord.[40]

Trustees of land

In the case of land jointly or successively owned or subject to will trusts, the law was radically reformed by the Trusts of Land and Appointment of Trustees Act 1996,[41] and for this reason calls for some slightly more detailed examination of the position. The 1996 Act created a unified system, the trust of land. For the purpose of exercising their functions, trustees of land have, in relation to all the land subject to the trust, the powers of an absolute owner (Trusts of Land and Appointment of Trustees Act 1996,

---

37 Such a lease might be treated as being a sham: see *National Westminster Bank plc v Jones* [2000] EGCS 82.

38 *Ingram v IRC* [1999] L & TR 85. There, property could apparently have been conveyed to family trustees with an obligation on them to lease it back to the deceased (a course of action evidently not favoured owing to the taxation implications).

39 *Milmo v Carreras* [1946] KB 306, [1946] 1 All ER 288, CA. The document seems to have been home-made.

40 *Parc (Battersea) Ltd v Hutchinson* [1999] L & TR 554. The intention of the parties might have been to create a sub-tenancy, but this made no difference, although a legal estate passed to the occupier automatically or by operation of law. Cf *Stretch v West Dorset District Council* (1997) 75 P & CR D26, where the tenant retained no part of the premises.

41 The Act came into force on 1 January 1997 (SI 1996/2974) and was passed to implement Law Com No 181; see Pottage (1989) 53 MLR 683.

s 6(1)).[42] The trustees may therefore grant leases of any length to any person, including an adult beneficiary of the trust (Trusts of Land and Appointment of Trustees Act 1996, s 6(2)). However, the Act allows these powers to be expressly restricted or limited by the relevant will or trust (Trusts of Land and Appointment of Trustees Act 1996, s 8). In addition, the trustees must, if they grant a lease, observe any relevant rules of statute, of law and of equity (Trusts of Land and Appointment of Trustees Act 1996, s 6(6)). Thus they would be bound by such rules as the formal requirements of contracts for a lease and the rule of equity that requires them to take reasonable care in their exercise of trust powers.

The exercise of the trustees' leasing powers may also be limited by the Trusts of Land and Appointment of Trustees Act 1996, s 11. Any adult trust beneficiary with an interest in possession in the land concerned has a statutory right to be consulted by the trustees, so far as practicable. Indeed, so far as is consistent with the general interest of the trust, the trustees must give effect to their wishes, or to those of a majority of beneficiaries, unless and to the extent that the disposition under which they hold excludes the consultation duty (Trusts of Land and Appointment of Trustees Act 1996, s 11(2)).

If a person takes a legal lease of unregistered land from trustees of a private trust of land who have failed to consult beneficiaries where required, the lessee, as a 'purchaser', is not concerned to see that the requirement has been complied with (Trusts of Land and Appointment of Trustees Act 1996, s 16(1)). His title is unaffected by the trustees breach of duty. This rule does not apply to registered land. If a trust beneficiary is in occupation of registered trust land pursuant to his statutory right of occupation (Trusts of Land and Appointment of Trustees Act 1996, s 12) his occupation rights would presumably override the registered title to the freehold and could be discovered by prior inspection of the land.

Mortgagors and mortgagees

Owing to the fact that a legal mortgagor by demise has no legal estate in possession out of which to grant a tenancy, it has been said that a tenancy granted after the execution of the mortgage deed is not binding on the mortgagee.[43] To overcome this problem, LPA 1925, s 99 confers a power of leasing on the mortgagor. This power may well be expressly excluded or curtailed by the mortgage deed (LPA 1925, s 99(13)).[44]

---

42 It is provided by Trusts of Land and Appointment of Trustees Act 1996, s 6(6) that the trustees must not exercise their powers in contravention of statute, nor of any rule of common law or equity.

43 *Carroll v Manek and Bank of India* (1999) 79 P & CR 173. A mortgagor by charge is in no better a position: ibid.

44 No exclusion or curtailment is allowed in the case of mortgages of agricultural land after 1 March 1948, which fall within the Agricultural Holdings Act 1948, nor in the case of mortgages of a new business tenancy under the Landlord and Tenant Act 1954, Pt II (Landlord and Tenant Act 1954, s 36(4)). There is no corresponding statutory prohibition in the case of

Where this is the case, the terms of the lease may allow a letting with the consent of the mortgagee. If the terms of a mortgage expressly prohibit the granting of any tenancies, then if the landlord grants a tenancy nevertheless, while it will bind the parties under the doctrine of estoppel, it cannot bind the mortgagee, who will be able to regain possession free of the tenancy if the mortgagor defaults.[45] By contrast, where an owner of registered land granted a protected tenancy to tenants and then raised money on the security of a legal charge, the rights of the tenant overrode the legal title, not being mentioned on the Register, and bound the subsequent mortgagee. Nor did it make any difference that the tenants had signed a statement agreeing to be postponed to the mortgagee, since they could not contract out of the jurisdiction of the court in respect of orders for possession under statute.[46]

With a view to promoting the easy flow of credit, the courts have so far not interfered with the right of a mortgagee to turn down a mortgagor's application for consent to a letting. Thus, the requirement of mortgagee consent is not at odds with the European Union principle of free movement of labour.[47] There is also no implied duty on a mortgagee to act reasonably in refusing his consent to the grant of a proposed tenancy by the mortgagor, at least in the absence of proof by the borrower of dishonesty or an improper motive on the mortgagee's part.[48] As was pointed out, the extent of any such implied duty would be difficult to frame, given that there may be a conflict between the interests of the two parties to the mortgage deed, and given that the mortgagee is entitled to favour its own interests in such a case. Concerning the statutory power, where it applies, the following should be noted.

1   It enables a mortgagor in possession (LPA 1925, s 99(1)) to grant leases or agreements for a lease, which will bind the mortgagor and mortgagee, of the whole or any part of the land in question. Only two kinds of lease are allowed:
   (a)   agricultural or occupation leases for up to 50 years; and
   (b)   building leases for up to 999 years.
2   Leases under the statutory power must comply with four formalities:
   (a)   the lease must take effect in possession not later than 12 months after its start date (LPA 1925, s 99(5));
   (b)   it must reserve the best rent reasonably obtainable in all the circumstances and no premium is allowed (LPA 1925, s 99(6));

---

farm business tenancies, so that LPA 1925, s 99 may be excluded (Agricultural Tenancies Act 1995, s 31(4)). The statutory power may be extended by express agreement whether in the mortgage deed or collateral to it (LPA 1925, s 99(14)).

45   *Dudley and District Benefit Building Society v Emerson* [1949] Ch 707, [1949] 2 All ER 252, CA; *Bolton Building Society v Cobb* [1966] 1 WLR 1. But where a tenancy was created which preceded the due registration of the mortgage charge at the Land Registry, the tenancy, protected by the Rent Acts, having been granted in 1988, bound the mortgagee: *Pourdanay v Barclays Bank plc* [1997] Ch 321.

46   *Woolwich Building Society v Dickman* [1996] 3 All ER 204, CA; Morgan [1997] Conv 402.

47   *Citibank International plc v Kessler* [1999] Lloyd's Bank LR 123.

48   *Starling v Lloyds Bank plc* [2000] 1 EGLR 101, CA.

(c)   the lease must contain a covenant by the lessee for payment of rent (LPA 1925, s 99(7));[49] and

(d)   a counterpart of the lease must be executed by the lessee and delivered to the lessor (LPA 1925, s 99(8)) and also, any counterpart of a lease granted by the mortgagor must, within one month of its making, be delivered to the mortgagee or first mortgagee (LPA 1925, s 99(11)).[50]

These formalities probably do not apply to oral tenancies;[51] they appear to apply to written agreements for a lease. As with leases by a tenant for life under a settlement, which are not formally valid, if the lack of formality is the sole reason for the invalidity, then the lease may be saved and take effect in equity under LPA 1925, s 152(1).[52] A lease which is not authorised by LPA 1925, s 99, or granted by a mortgagor whose statutory power of leasing is excluded or curtailed, binds the lessor and lessee by estoppel but not a prior legal mortgagee who is entitled to assert his legal interest against both parties. The lessee will lack the protection of the Rent Act 1977 as against the mortgagee.[53] Should the mortgagee or his receiver accept rent from the tenant, a new tenancy, binding on the mortgagee, may be created by implication of law,[54] but only if the circumstances warrant this inference, which is not automatic.[55]

Receivers

Receivers appointed by the High Court have no powers of leasing, without the authority of the court. It is not usual for the court to insert, in the order appointing a receiver, a general authority to grant leases: as a rule each individual proposal for a lease must be considered by the court on its merits.[56] If a receiver is appointed by a mortgagee under LPA 1925, s 101, all leasing powers of the mortgagor are thereby vested in the mortgagee (LPA 1925, s 99(19)), and are only exercisable by the receiver with his written authority; and the lessee will not obtain a legal estate unless the legal owner is a party to the lease.

---

49   The lease must contain a condition for re-entry for non-payment of rent within a time of up to 30 days: LPA 1925, s 99(7).

50   The lessee is not concerned to see that this is complied with: LPA 1925, s 99(11).

51   *Rhodes v Dalby* [1971] 1 WLR 1325 at 1331.

52   The onus is then on the lessee to show that, apart from non-compliance with the statutory power, the lease is otherwise valid: *Davies v Hall* [1954] 2 All ER 330, [1954] 1 WLR 855, CA.

53   *Dudley and District Benefit Building Society v Emerson* [1949] Ch 707, [1949] 2 All ER 252, CA; the same might apply to the protection of the Housing Act 1988. Cf Smith (1977) 41 Conv (NS) 197.

54   *Chatsworth Properties Ltd v Effiom* [1971] 1 WLR 144, CA.

55   See eg *Javad v Aqil* [1991] 1 All ER 243 at 251-253, CA.

56   Leases will be granted in the name of the estate owner and the best terms must be obtained: *Wynne v Lord Newborough* (1790) 1 Ves 164.

The Crown

By virtue of the Crown Estate Act 1961, s 1 the Crown Estate Commissioners may lease any part of the Crown Estate at the best rent obtainable, for any term not exceeding 100 years. A lease must take effect in possession not later than 12 months after its date, or in reversion after a lease having at that date not more than 21 years to run; and no option or contract may be made for a lease to commence more than 10 years from the date of contract, unless the rent under such lease is left to be fixed as at the commencement of the term in such a manner as in their opinion is calculated to ensure the best consideration reasonably obtainable at that date. They may, with the Royal Assent, under the Sign Manual grant leases, either gratuitously or at such rent as they think fit, of land for development, improvement or general benefit of the Crown, if it is to be used for any of the purposes specified in the Crown Estate Act 1961, s 5, or for any public or charitable purposes connected with Crown Estate Land, or tending to the welfare of persons residing or employed on it (Crown Estate Act 1961, s 5).

Government departments authorised to acquire land from time to time for public purposes are generally given power to lease any part of it which is not required for that purpose immediately. Their powers of leasing in such cases are limited strictly to the terms of the enabling Act.[57] Whether they can claim Crown privilege or not, eg whether such a lease is subject to the Rent Act 1977, depends upon whether they can be regarded as acting as agents of the Crown, or merely servants of the Crown; in the latter case they do not enjoy Crown privilege.

Corporations

A corporation is an artificial person, whose legal personality is unchanged. The leasing powers of corporations depend on whether and to what extent they are empowered to grant leases by their constitutive instrument (eg in the case of a company, its memorandum of association). The grant of a lease by a corporation must generally be by deed to pass the legal estate in the land.[58] In the case of a company incorporated under the Companies Acts, the same formalities apply to the granting of legal and equitable leases by it as apply to an individual, in the absence of a contrary intention in the company's memorandum of association.[59] A person who enters possession of corporate land under an unsealed lease may, it seems, still become a tenant from year to year at law.[60] The powers of a statutory corporation will be governed by the statute which creates it.[61]

---

57 As in Civil Aviation Act 1982, s 41.
58 A lease is executed by a company by the affixing of its common seal, but this is not necessary, provided that Companies Act 1985, s 36A is complied with.
59 Companies Act 1985, s 36.
60 *Ecclesiastical Comrs v Merral* (1869) LR 4 Exch 162.
61 See eg Iron and Steel Act 1982, s 14(1); New Towns Act 1981, ss 17, 37 (as amended by SI 1998/2871) and 64.

Local authorities

As to the leasing powers of local authorities, statute confers a general power on them to grant leases,[62] so that, for example, county councils, district councils and London Borough councils generally have power to grant leases of any length. If the consideration is less than the best rent that can reasonably be obtained, a lease cannot be granted except with the consent of the Secretary of State. Excepted from this latter requirement are short tenancies. If a local authority grants an option to renew a lease, such was not equated with a power to grant a lease, even if the result is that the option is void for lack of capacity.[63]

IV TYPES OF LEASES AND TENANCIES

If a lease is to exist as a legal estate, it must fall within the statutory definition of 'term of years absolute'.[64] If the lease is not a legal estate, as where it does not comply with the requirement of a deed, it may, if in writing, exist in equity.[65] The definition of terms of years absolute is wide[66] as can be seen from the following:

1 'A term of years (taking effect either in possession or in reversion whether or not at a rent) . . . subject or not to another legal estate, and either certain or liable to determination by notice, re-entry, operation of law, or by a provision for cesser on redemption or any other event'. This definition therefore includes leases for a fixed term of years, which may last for any length of time (whether for 1 year or 99 years) provided it is for less than perpetuity.[67] A lease may remain a term of years absolute though it expressly enables the landlord to re-enter or forfeit the term for breach of covenant. Several legal leasehold interests may exist concurrently in the same land, as where a lessee sub-lets the whole premises to a sub-lessee who in turn sub-under-lets.[68]

2 Under the definition clause, 'the expression "term of years" includes a term for less than a year, or for a year or years and a fraction of a year or from year to year'. All types of periodic tenancies are thereby included, whether they are weekly,

---

62   Local Government Act 1972, s 123 as amended; see *R v Hackney London BC, ex p Structuradene* [2001] 12 EG 168 (as to meaning of 'disposal' in the amended provision, which contains contradictory indications within itself).

63   *Stretch v West Dorset District Council* (1997) 75 P & CR D26.

64   LPA 1925, s 1(1)(b).

65   LPA 1925, s 1(3). In this case, an equitable term of years will be held to exist: *R v Tower Hamlets London BC, ex p Von Goetz* [1999] QB 1019, CA. If title is unregistered, the informal lease must be registered as a Class C(iv) land charge on pain of voidness against a purchaser for money or money's worth of the land (Land Charges Act 1972, s 4(5)); for the position where title is registered see ch 4 below.

66   LPA 1925, s 205(1)(xxvii).

67   See *Siew Soon Wah v Yong Tong Hong* [1973] AC 836, PC (tenancy described as 'permanent' held grant for longest period landlord had power to demise).

68   This is envisaged by LPA 1925, s 1(5).

monthly, quarterly or yearly. This is deliberate. It is permitted to create a legal periodic tenancy orally or in writing.

3 Certain types of lease are excluded from the statutory definition. A lease determinable on 'the dropping of a life, or the determination of a determinable life interest' cannot be a legal lease. A term of years 'determinable with life or lives or with the cesser of a determinable life interest' is also excluded from being a term of years absolute (and exists behind a trust). A lease created after 31 December 1925 which is 'not expressed to take effect in possession within twenty-one years after the creation thereof where required by this Act to take effect within that period' cannot be a legal lease.[69]

Concurrent leases

A concurrent lease is a term limited to commence before the expiry of an existing lease of the same premises. It operates as an assignment of part of the head landlord's reversion. The concurrent lessee becomes entitled to the rent payable and to enforce the tenant's covenants under the earlier lease.[70] For example, where X held a concurrent lease on a flat occupied by T, it was held that X was 'lessor' for the purpose of recovery from T of a proportion of a service charge.[71] There is no limit on the number of concurrent legal leases which may be granted. Each subsequent term operates as a reversion expectant on the term next preceding it. The subsequent term may be longer than the term next above it or it may be shorter, in which case the legal reversion lasts until expiry of the shorter term. All concurrent leases must be by deed to pass a legal estate.[72]

Reversionary leases

The statutory definition of a 'term of years absolute' includes a term taking effect in reversion, in other words at a future date. There is no requirement that a lease must take effect immediately. Reversionary or future leases are therefore permitted to take effect as from the date of grant. So, by LPA 1925, s 149(2), it is provided that leases are capable of taking effect from the date fixed for commencement, without actual entry, which latter was, until 1 January 1926, a condition precedent of the tenant's acquiring an estate in the land. By LPA 1925, s 149(3) some limits are imposed on the creation of reversionary or future leases: 'A term, at a rent or granted in consideration of a fine, limited . . . to take effect more than twenty-one years from the date of the instrument purporting to create it, shall be void, and any contract . . . to create such a term shall

---

69 The reason for this is to ensure that a leasehold estate in land is capable of taking effect in possession within a relatively short period of the grant of the term, in the interests of certainty.
70 *Re Moore and Hulm's Contract* [1912] 2 Ch 105.
71 *Adelphi (Estates) Ltd v Christie* (1983) 47 P & CR 650, CA.
72 LPA 1925, s 52.

likewise be void.' This provision was new in 1925.[73] A contract to create a lease which, when granted, will not infringe LPA 1925, s 149(3) is not invalidated by that provision, which only strikes down contracts to create leases which will infringe it when granted.[74] Otherwise a renewal option in any lease for over 21 years in duration would be invalidated by LPA 1925, s 149(3).[75] Because legislative policy is to discourage excessive renewals, any contract made after 1925 to renew a lease or sub-lease for over 60 years after the termination of the current lease is void.[76]

Leases for a fixed term

A lease for a fixed term is a lease of pre-defined length, such as for six months, one year, ten years, 99 years or 999 years.[77] The term created by such a lease must be expressed with certainty or by reference to something which can be rendered certain at the commencement of the lease, otherwise it is void for uncertainty: hence, a tenancy alleged to be a term certain for the duration of the Second World War was void as such.[78] A tenancy limited to continue unless ended by a month's notice on either side would likewise be invalid as a term certain.[79] Similarly, a term of uncertain maximum duration, which was to continue until the land was required by the landlord for a road-widening scheme, whereupon the lease was terminable on two months' minimum notice, was held to be void for uncertainty by the House of Lords.[80] In addition, applying that decision, a purported grant of a term certain determinable by an event within the control of both parties is invalid as a purported demise determinable on an uncertain future event: both conditions are repugnant to the nature of a term certain. Should both parties take care to map out in the operative part of the lease the maximum duration of the term, it seemingly is no objection that it may be determinable by one side or the other on the occurrence, within that period, of an uncertain future event: thus a term for five years certain may validly be determinable by the tenant if the War ends prior to the expiry of the lease or by the landlord if he wishes to redevelop the premises.

---

73 The rule against perpetuities does not preclude the granting of a lease to take effect at a remote future date.

74 *Re Strand and Savoy Properties Ltd, D P Development Co Ltd v Cumbrae Properties Ltd* [1960] Ch 582, [1960] 2 All ER 327, (1960) 76 LQR 352; *Weg Motors Ltd v Hales* [1962] Ch 49, [1961] 3 All ER 181, CA.

75 The renewal option in *Re Strand and Savoy Properties Ltd* [1960] Ch 582, [1960] 2 All ER 327, (1960) 76 LQR 352 was for one renewal of a 35-year term.

76 Law of Property Act 1922, Sch 15, para 7(2).

77 For a good example see *Re Bennington Road, Aston* (1993) Times, 21 July.

78 *Lace v Chantler* [1944] KB 368, CA.

79 *Onyx (UK) Ltd v Beard* [1996] EGCS 55.

80 *Prudential Assurance Co Ltd v London Residuary Body* [1992] 2 AC 386, [1992] 3 All ER 504, HL. It was held that there was an implied yearly tenancy, under which both parties had the unfettered power to determine it by six months' notice. See Bridge [1993] CLJ 26; Bright (1993) 13 LS 78; Sparkes (1993) 108 LQR 93; PF Smith [1993] Conv 461.

In order to measure the duration of the estate granted by a lease, a term certain is taken to commence as from the date of its execution,[81] but where a lessee takes possession under a prior agreement for a lease, the High Court has held that the date for measuring liability under covenants and for other purposes such as date from which the exercise of options runs, is that of the agreement.[82]

The period of letting need not be continuous.[83] A lease may validly prohibit personal occupation by the tenant at specified periods such as weekends. Time-share lettings are in principle valid: a person may be granted exclusive possession for one specified week in a specified number of years.[84] The fact that the period of the letting is short and discontinuous does not prevent the tenancy or lease from conferring proprietary rights on the tenant.[85] However, it may be that an occupation agreement for a very short period, even if apparently, exclusive possession has been conferred, will be construed as a licence to occupy.[86]

A periodic tenancy, such as from year to year, is saved from invalidity on the ground of uncertainty, according to the House of Lords, only because of the unrestricted power of either party to serve a notice to quit to terminate it at the end of any year. The term continues, however, until determined by notice as if both parties had made a new agreement at the end of each year for the ensuing year.[87]

A lease for a fixed term comes to an end automatically, and without any need for a landlord's notice,[88] when the term agreed expires: in other words, by effluxion of time. In addition, such tenancies may be made terminable before the expiration of the term on notice given by one party or the other to terminate the tenancy at given intervals during its currency (ie an option to terminate, or 'break-clause' as it is often called, expressed to be exercisable, for example, at the end of the seventh and the fourteenth years of a 21-year lease).

81 *Bradshaw v Pawley* [1979] 3 All ER 273 at 277-278; also *Liverpool City Council v Walton* [2002] 1 EGLR 149.
82 *Trane (UK) Ltd v Provident Mutual Life Assurance* [1995] 1 EGLR 33.
83 *Smallwood v Sheppards* [1895] 2 QB 627 (occupation for three successive Bank Holidays held agreement for single letting).
84 *Cottage Holiday Associates Ltd v Customs and Excise Comrs* [1983] QB 735. Query whether a time-share period exceeding 21 years would infringe LPA 1925, s 149(3).
85 *National Carriers Ltd v Panalpina (Northern) Ltd* [1981] AC 675 at 714.
86 *Krell v Henry* [1903] 2 KB 740; also *Boyland v Dublin Corpn* [1949] IR 60 (envisaging a tenancy granted for a few days or even a few hours); *Voli v Inglewood Shire Council* (1963) 110 CLR 74. See the discussion in (1998) 2 L & T Rev 131.
87 *Prudential Assurance Co Ltd v London Residuary Body* [1992] 2 AC 386, [1992] 3 All ER 504, HL; but see Wilde (1994) 57 MLR 117.
88 According to Lord Hoffmann in *Newlon Housing Trust v Alsulaimen* [1999] 1 AC 313 at 317, a periodic tenancy comes to an end also by effluxion of time, when the period or last period expires, for which the tenant (or the landlord) is willing for the tenancy to continue. That date is fixed by a notice to quit.

Leases for life or lives or until marriage

LPA 1925, s 149(6) provides that a lease or a contract for a lease at a rent or in consideration of a fine[89] 'for life or lives or for any term of years determinable with life or lives or on the marriage of the lessee' is automatically converted into a term of 90 years.[90] For example, a lease from a landlord to a tenant which comes to an end on the death of the tenant is caught by this provision, as is a lease to a tenant which ends on the marriage of the tenant, as is a lease to a person which comes to an end when some other named person dies. Also caught would be a lease to a tenant to end on the death of the survivor of the lessee and that of another named person.[91]

Such 90-year terms, which are legal estates by statutory conversion,[92] are determinable, by LPA 1925, s 149(6), on either side, where the relevant life is that of the original tenant, 'on the death or marriage (as the case may be) of the original lessee, or of his survivor', by at least one month's notice in writing given to determine the tenancy on one of the quarter days applicable to it, or if none, then on one of the usual quarter days. The notice is to be given in principle by the landlord or by his successor in title.

LPA 1925, s 149(6), as noted, applies to any term expressed to be determinable with any life or lives or on the marriage of the lessee,[93] whether the life is that of the landlord, the tenant, or the survivor of the tenant and some other person, no matter how short the term may be.[94] But LPA 1925, s 149(6) goes further: it also applies to any term of years determinable with life, as with a term granted by L to T for 21 years if he (T) so long lives. This will be automatically converted into a 90-year lease determinable at the earliest within one month of T's death.[95] The actual intentions of the parties therefore

89   'Fine' includes a benefit in the nature of a premium (LPA 1925, s 205(1)(xxiii)), so that the sale of a house at one-third of its value in exchange for a licence to occupy it for life conferred on the former owners was caught by LPA 1925, s 149(6), and bound a subsequent legal mortgagee of the premises: *Skipton Building Society v Clayton* (1993) 66 P & CR 223; Crabb [1993] Conv 478.

90   A contract for a lease within LPA 1925, s 149(6) is deemed to be a contract for a 90-year lease terminable by notice.

91   See *Bistern Estate Trust's Appeal* [2000] 2 EGLR 91 (the tenant and his wife). No notice could be validly served by the landlord on the death of the tenant's wife, while the tenant was still alive. The specific notice rule in LPA 1925, s 149(6)(c), which applies in such cases, was not 'topsy-turvy'. It did not invert the intention of the parties that this lease could only be terminated by the landlord after the death of the tenant and his wife.

92   The conversion is automatic, a feature which is criticised by Cheshire and Burn, p 386, who, citing from Hoffmann J in *Bass Holdings Ltd v Lewis* [1986] 2 EGLR 40, think that the automatic imposition of a 90-year term was a mistake. According to *Wolstenholme and Cherry's Conveyancing Statutes* (13th edn, 1972) p 278, this provision 'abolishes' leases for life.

93   Ie automatically on death (or marriage): *Bass Holdings Ltd v Lewis* [1986] 2 EGLR 40, CA.

94   However, in the case of a commercial lease for life of a residential commonhold unit, the maximum lease term is limited to the maximum limit allowed by regulations (expected to be for no more than seven years): CLRA 2002, Sch 5, para 3. In the case of a leases for life of commercial commonhold units, any restrictions in the commonhold community statement will apply and to that extent LPA 1925, s 149(6) will not apply: ibid.

95   The position if L at the date of the grant holds a leasehold reversion of (say) only 22 years is not solved by LPA 1925, s 149(6).

may count for little. However, LPA 1925, s 149(6) does not apply to a lease or tenancy determinable by notice after the dropping of a life or lives, such as a letting to T for three years with power in the landlord to terminate the tenancy by notice in the event of the death of the tenant during the currency of the term.[96]

Leases with a covenant or option for perpetual renewal

The lease may contain a covenant or option for renewal by the tenant. If the covenant or option is such that the right to renew must be reproduced perpetually in all further leases granted, perpetual renewal is created, with the following consequences. The grant of a term, sub-term or other leasehold interest which is perpetually renewable takes effect as a term of 2,000 years from the commencement date of the term, or a sub-term of 2,000 years less one day, calculated from the date of commencement of the head term out of which it was derived.[97]

Perpetually renewable leases or sub-leases take effect in substitution for the term originally granted. The rent, covenants and conditions of the substituted term are payable or enforceable during its 2,000-year span. Special provisions apply, of which the following[98] may be mentioned:

1   the lessee or underlessee may on giving written notice to the landlord at least ten days before the date on which the lease would, but for its conversion, have expired, determine the lease on such expiry date;
2   the lessee or underlessee must register all assignments or devolutions of the converted term with the lessor, his agent or solicitor within six months of the assignment; and
3   each lessee or underlessee, whether the original party or not, is only liable for rent accruing and breaches of covenant taking place while the lease or sub-lease is vested in him.

The object of Parliament was no doubt to prevent perpetual renewal, and the consequences of conferring perpetual renewal are draconian: for example the rent originally fixed remains for the whole 2,000-year span of the converted term.[99] The courts are reluctant to hold that perpetual renewal is intended. Hence, a covenant to renew at the 'like' rent and all covenants in the lease, did not create perpetual renewal.[100] The question whether a particular form of words confers a right to perpetual renewal is

96   *Bass Holdings Ltd v Lewis* [1986] 2 EGLR 40, CA.
97   Law of Property Act 1922, s 145 and Sch 15, paras 1 and 2. Identical provision is made for contracts for perpetual renewal: Law of Property Act 1922, Sch 15, para 7(1).
98   Law of Property Act 1922, Sch 15, paras 10 and 11.
99   In the case of a perpetually renewable lease of a commonhold unit, the drastic effects of the Law of Property Act 1922 are curbed. The lease is limited to the maximum term allowed for residential commonhold units (expected to be laid down in regulations as not exceeding seven years) or as permitted by the commonhold community statement in the case of commercial unit leases: CLRA 2002, Sch 5, para 1.
100 *Iggulden v May* (1804) 9 Ves 325.

one of construction and unambiguous language indicating an intention to include the entitlement to renewal in the terms of the renewed lease will be given effect to and perpetual renewal will be created: as with, for example, a covenant to renew 'on identical terms' as the present lease;[101] or to renew at the same rent and with the like covenants 'including the present covenant for renewal'.[102] The same result followed where the relevant words clearly indicated that the covenant to renew must be included in the terms of any renewed lease on every renewal, with the consequent conversion of a five-year term into a 2,000-year term at the same rent as that originally reserved.[103] A formula for renewal of a 21-year lease as often as every 11 years of the term expired was also held to create perpetual renewal.[104] The court may be able to decide what the parties' true intentions in the light of the surrounding circumstances were, and so it was held that words literally wide enough to confer perpetual renewal must be cut down to take these circumstances into account.[105] Where a renewal covenant in a seven-year lease provided that a renewed lease must contain a renewal covenant for a further seven-year term on expiry of the renewed term, the tenant was held entitled merely to a double renewal, this on the basis that an obligation for perpetual renewal must be expressly spelt out of the lease.[106] The safest course is to avoid any danger of perpetual renewal by providing expressly that renewal is to be on the same terms (for example) as the current lease excluding any further renewal covenant or option. However, in home-made agreements for a lease there is a danger that the parties will not be aware of the consequences of conferring what turns out to be a perpetual renewal, and it is suggested that the provisions under discussion should be revised so as to prohibit such renewals entirely.[107]

Periodic tenancies

The initial duration of a periodic tenancy is fixed by express or implied agreement of the parties at the commencement of the tenancy. The periods most commonly found are weekly, monthly, quarterly and yearly tenancies, and whatever period is employed is the minimum duration of the tenancy, though until notice of termination is given, its total duration will not be certain. As the tenancy progresses through one period and another, the tenancy is regarded as one continuous tenancy. In form, periodic tenancies

---

101 *Northchurch Estates Ltd v Daniels* [1947] Ch 117, [1946] 2 All ER 524.
102 *Parkus v Greenwood* [1950] Ch 644, [1950] 1 All ER 436, CA.
103 *Re Hopkin's Lease, Caerphilly Concrete Products Ltd v Owen* [1972] 1 All ER 248, [1972] 1 WLR 372, CA.
104 *Wynn v Conway Corpn* [1914] 2 Ch 705, CA.
105 *Plumrose Ltd v Real and Leasehold Estates Investment Society Ltd* [1969] 3 All ER 1441, [1970] 1 WLR 52 (the lease out of which the option derived was itself a once-only renewable lease).
106 *Marjorie Burnett Ltd v Barclay* [1981] 1 EGLR 41.
107 A contract for renewal which allows for a single renewal for a period over 60 years from the expiry of the lease is void: Law of Property Act 1922, Sch 15, para 7(2).

may well differ from fixed-term leases: periodic tenancies are likely to be in writing or even oral, with some written evidence of a tenancy.[108]

It is fundamental to periodic tenancies that both parties should be able to serve a notice to quit, which marks the end of the period of the tenancy. Any term which purports to preclude the landlord from serving a notice to quit as long as the tenant pays his rent and performs his covenants, might make it impossible for the landlord ever to serve notice, and is repugnant to the nature of a periodic tenancy.[109] The same result follows if a tenancy provides for service of a notice to quit only by the tenant, thus rendering it impossible at any time for the landlord to serve notice to quit.[110] A term which entitles the landlord to serve a notice to quit only if a predetermined but uncertain future event arises, such as an undertaking by the landlord of a weekly tenant not to give notice until the landlord required to pull down the demised buildings, is likewise void for repugnancy.[111] These principles were applied by the House of Lords to a tenancy which, in terms, was to continue until certain land might be required by the landlord for the purposes of a road-widening scheme. The landlords' successors in title were able to serve notice on the tenant even though they had no road-widening scheme, the term being construed as a tenancy from year to year, and so determinable on six months' notice by either side.[112] It was said to be of the essence of such a tenancy that both parties should be entitled to give notice to terminate it. This principle is qualified by the fact that it is open to the parties to grant a term from year to year with a fetter on the landlord's power to serve a notice to quit for a number of years determined in advance, thus saving a provision under which the landlord would not serve a notice on the tenant during the first three years of the tenancy.[113] The parties may also agree, for example, on the grant of a monthly tenancy subject to a fetter on the power of the landlord to determine it by notice to quit before a specified date.[114]

Yearly tenancies

Yearly tenancies (tenancies from year to year) may be created expressly or impliedly, and may be determined at the end of the first or any subsequent year by service of a valid notice to quit. In the absence of agreement to the contrary, six months' notice is required. Where rent is payable on the quarter days, and the tenant enters in the

---

108 In the case of a weekly residential tenancy, the landlord is bound by the Landlord and Tenant Act 1985, s 4 to provide the tenant with a rent book which notifies him of the landlord's name and address.

109 *Doe d Warner v Browne* (1807) 8 East 165.

110 *Centaploy Ltd v Matlodge* Ltd [1974] Ch 1, [1973] 2 All ER 720.

111 *Cheshire Lines Committee v Lewis & Co* (1880) 50 LJQB 121.

112 *Prudential Assurance Co Ltd v London Residuary Body* [1992] 2 AC 386, [1992] 3 All ER 504, HL.

113 Such a lease creates a determinable term of three years certain even if the landlord may, eg, serve a notice within that period on a stipulated event. Cf *Breams Property Investment Co v Stroulger* [1948] 2 KB 1, [1948] 1 All ER 758, CA.

114 *Parc Bettersea Ltd v Hutchinson* [1999] L & TR 554.

middle of a quarter, the courts will try to hold that the yearly tenancy commenced and is therefore terminable on a quarter day,[115] eg where on entry, the tenant pays a proportionate part of a quarter's rent, in respect of the period between the actual date of entry and the next quarter day.[116] A tenancy 'for one year, and so on from year to year' creates a fixed-term tenancy for one year, followed by a yearly tenancy; accordingly, it cannot be terminated before the end of the second year.[117]

A tenant holding over after the expiry of a fixed-term lease becomes a tenant at will or on sufferance. If he pays a yearly rent, a tenancy from year to year may arise, on terms not inconsistent with those of the previous lease, if the proper inference from the landlord's acceptance of rent coupled with the other circumstances is that both parties intend to create a tenancy.[118] Thus, if the landlord accepted the rent under a mistake, no implied grant of a yearly tenancy arises.[119] The question of whether an implied periodic tenancy is created is primarily one of the objective intention of the parties,[120] if stated, or of the proper inferences reasonably to be drawn from their conduct; the courts will adopt the same approach to this type of contract as they do in any other contract.[121] Hence, all the circumstances, including the payment of rent, which latter is an important factor, are taken into account.[122] It is easier to presume an intention to create an implied yearly tenancy where the tenant lacks any statutory protection, than when he is entitled to it. Yet no implied yearly tenancy arose where the landlord accepted, without more, two isolated payments of rent from an erstwhile service occupier (and licensee), as evidence of the real intentions of the parties is required.[123] Similarly, where a former secure tenant was allowed to hold over, after a suspended possession order had been made, he was held to have done so as the result of the course of the possession proceedings and there was therefore no intention to grant him by implication a new tenancy.[124]

If an acceptance of rent by the landlord is explicable on the ground that the tenant has statutory security of tenure, as with a business continuation tenancy or a Rent Act statutory tenancy, as a result of which the landlord may have no choice but to accept

---

115 *Croft v William F Blay Ltd* [1919] 2 Ch 343, at 357.
116 *Doe d Holcomb v Johnson* (1806) 6 Esp 10.
117 *Doe d Chadborn v Green* (1839) 9 Ad & El 658; *Addis v Burrows* [1948] 1 KB 444, [1948] 1 All ER 177.
118 *Vaughan-Armatrading Ltd v Sarsah* (1995) 27 HLR 631.
119 *Maconochie Bros Ltd v Brand* [1946] 2 All ER 778; *Sector Properties v Meah* (1973) 229 Estates Gazette 1097, CA.
120 *Sopwith v Stutchbury* (1983) 17 HLR 50 at 74, CA.
121 *London Baggage Co (Charing Cross) Ltd v Railtrack plc* [2000] L & TR 439.
122 *Javad v Aqil* [1991] 1 All ER 243, CA; *Brent London Borough Council v O'Bryan* [1993] 1 EGLR 59; also *Marcroft Wagons Ltd v Smith* [1951] 2 KB 496 at 506, CA.
123 *Thompsons (Funeral Furnishers) Ltd v Phillips* [1945] 2 All ER 49, CA; also *Dreamgate Properties Ltd v Arnot* [1997] EGCS 121 (computer-generated rent demand).
124 *Greenwich London Borough Council v Regan* [1996] EGCS 15, CA.

the rent, no automatic inference of a periodic implied yearly tenancy is made.[125] The courts take into account the fact that statutory security of tenure, where available, modifies the common law rule that a fixed term expires with no automatic implied right of renewal by effluxion of time, and the fact that the parties are taken to be aware of these rights.[126] However, the creation by statute of tenancies which lack security, such as residential assured shorthold tenancies or farm business tenancies, may well reduce the occasions in the future in which the common law inference of an implied new periodic tenancy is modified by the courts.

A person who goes into possession under a void lease or an agreement is, at common law, a tenant at will, but when he pays, or agrees to pay, rent in accordance with the intended lease, he may be a tenant from year to year depending on the facts, upon the terms of the intended lease. Thus, where guarantors of a company which had ceased trading occupied the premises and paid rent for a substantial period, at the same level as under a sub-lease held by the company, they were held to have been in possession as implied periodic tenants, much as would be a tenant holding over after a lease not protected by statute, paying rent.[127] A tenant may have rights in equity, however, for if he has a specifically enforceable agreement, he is treated as holding from the date of entry on the terms of the lease intended by the parties, as if it had been granted, under the doctrine in *Walsh v Lonsdale*.[128] However, the common law presumption of a new yearly tenancy is relevant where for some reason the remedy of specific performance is unavailable, such as failure by either party to perform a condition precedent.[129]

There must be clear evidence of an agreement for a tenancy (or a new tenancy, as the case may be), and payment of rent is not in itself decisive; nor is it even essential, if there is other evidence to support the implication. Conversely, the implication of a yearly tenancy may be rebutted by evidence to the contrary, eg by calculation[130] (though not necessarily payment) of the rent by reference to weekly sums.

Where a tenancy from year to year arises by implication, the tenant holds under such of the terms of the former (or intended) lease as are not inconsistent with those of a yearly tenancy, eg covenants to pay rent in advance,[131] to keep the premises in good tenantable repair,[132] provisos for re-entry by the landlord on non-payment of rent or on breach of other covenants.[133] No onerous covenants to do repairs are implied, which

---

125 *Cole v Kelly* [1920] 2 KB 106; *Longrigg, Burrough and Trownson v Smith* [1979] 2 EGLR 42, which may not be good law to the extent of suggesting that the common law presumption has been superseded: *Bennett Properties v H & S Engineering* [1998] CLY 3683.
126 *Cardiothoracic Institute v Shrewdcrest Ltd* [1986] 3 All ER 633 at 642.
127 *Walji v Mount Cook Land Ltd* [2002] 1 P & CR 163.
128 (1882) 21 Ch D 9.
129 *Coatsworth v Johnson* (1885) 55 LJQB 220, CA. According to Sparkes (1987) 16 Anglo-American LR 160, this case is incorrectly decided.
130 *Adler v Blackman* [1953] 1 QB 146, [1952] 2 All ER 945, CA; cf *Javad v Aqil* [1991] 1 All ER 243.
131 *Lee v Smith* (1854) 9 Exch 662.
132 *Richardson v Gifford* (1834) 1 Ad & El 52.
133 *Thomas v Packer* (1857) 1 H & N 669.

would not normally be done by yearly tenants,[134] such as to paint every three years,[135] or an option for renewal.[136] A notice to quit given to terminate a yearly tenancy must be expressed to expire at the end of any year of the tenancy. If it arose by reason of the tenant holding over, it is terminable on the anniversary of the termination, and not of the commencement of the original term,[137] unless a contrary intention can be inferred.

Periodic tenancies for less than a year

Periodic tenancies for less than a year may be created expressly, or may arise by implication, in the same way as tenancies from year to year. They include weekly, monthly, three-monthly, quarterly, six-monthly and half-yearly tenancies, and the only reason for treating them separately from yearly tenancies is that they are terminable on one full period's notice at common law, ie in the absence of any express agreement to the contrary, and therefore, unlike tenancies from year to year, they would not normally be terminable at the end of the first period. The period upon which a tenancy is based may be ascertained mainly by reference to the way in which the rent is calculated; thus, where the rent reserved is so much per year, a yearly tenancy will be implied, even though the rent is payable monthly. There is a distinction between a monthly or quarterly rent and monthly or quarterly instalments of a yearly rent;[138] and accordingly, where a tenant for a fixed-term at a weekly rent holds over and continues to pay the same weekly rent, the proper inference is that a weekly tenancy was intended.[139]

The difference between three-monthly and quarterly tenancies and between six-monthly and half-yearly tenancies relates to the date of their commencement, and hence to the dates on which they are terminable and the length of notice required. A tenancy commencing on one of the usual quarter days will normally be construed as a quarterly (or half-yearly tenancy) terminable on one quarter's notice on any quarter day (or on two quarters' notice, as the case may be, on either of the usual half-year days). Where such a tenancy commences in the middle of a quarter, it may be construed as a three-monthly or six-monthly tenancy, terminable on so many calendar months' notice[140] given to expire in the middle of a quarter or half-year, though this may be rebutted by payment of a proportionate part of a quarter's rent (ie from the date of entry to the next quarter day) with the result that the tenancy will be deemed to have commenced on the quarter day next after the tenant's entry.

---

134 *Bowes v Croll* (1856) 6 E & B 255.
135 *Pinero v Judson* (1829) 6 Bing 206.
136 *Re Leeds and Batley Breweries and Bradbury's Lease, Bradbury v Grimble & Co* [1920] 2 Ch 548.
137 *Croft v William F Blay Ltd* [1919] 2 Ch 343; *Addis v Burrows* [1948] 1 KB 444, [1948] 1 All ER 177, CA.
138 *Ladies' Hosiery and Underwear Ltd v Parker* [1930] 1 Ch 304, CA.
139 *Adler v Blackman* [1953] 1 QB 146, [1952] 2 All ER 945, CA.
140 'Month' means calendar month, in any agreement taking effect after 31 December 1925 (LPA 1925, s 61(a)): thus, a month's notice to quit served on 1 January expires on 1 February.

Tenancies at will

A tenancy at will arises where a person occupies land or premises with the express or implied consent of the owner, under a tenancy of indefinite duration.[141] The tenancy is terminable by a demand for possession, or by any act which is inconsistent with the landlord's continuing consent to the occupation of the tenant, such as the alienation of the landlord's interest with notice to the tenant,[142] or waste committed by the tenant.[143] The Protection from Eviction Act 1977, s 5 (see chapter 17, below) is inapplicable to tenancies at will.[144]

An implied tenancy at will arises if a tenant holds over rent-free at the end of his lease, with the implied consent of the landlord. It also arises where a tenant under a lease void at law,[145] or under an agreement for a future lease, enters into possession, rent-free. It may also exist where a person is let by the vendor into possession pending completion of a purchase.[146] There was held to be an implied tenancy at will where a person took possession during negotiations for a lease, though the occupier paid sums towards the rent, because the rent was not calculable by reference to a year, and no lease was ever entered into.[147] Where tenants held over on extensions of the last of a series of short-term tenancies intended to take effect outside the Landlord and Tenant Act 1954, Pt II, paying rent, pending abortive negotiations for a new lease, they were held to have done so as tenants at will only.[148] Where a person took possession of unoccupied premises, in anticipation of an agreement on the terms of a fixed-term lease, paying one quarter's rent in advance, thereafter two further quarter's interim rent, but the parties could not agree on the terms of the proposed lease, the occupier held as implied tenant at will rather than as a quarterly tenant.[149]

In the case of expressly created tenancies at will, rent may be payable under them. Its payment and acceptance will not necessarily convert the tenancy at will into a yearly tenancy.[150] Whether it does do so may depend on whether the tenancy at will is

---

141 *Ramnarace v Lutchman* [2001] UKPC 25, [2001] 1 WLR 1651.
142 Eg by mortgage, *Jarman v Hale* [1899] 1 QB 994.
143 Co Lit 57a; *Countess of Shrewsbury's Case* (1600) 5 Co Rep 13b.
144 *Crane v Morris* [1965] 3 All ER 77, [1965] 1 WLR 1104, CA.
145 *Dossee v Doe d East India Co* (1859) 1 LT 345, PC; *Meye v Electric Transmission Ltd* [1942] Ch 290.
146 *Wheeler v Mercer* [1957] AC 416 at 425, HL. This is thought to be unaffected by the dictum of Lord Templeman in *Street v Mountford* [1985] AC 809 at 820, [1985] 2 All ER 289 at 295, that the vendor-purchaser relationship involved a licence.
147 *British Railways Board v Bodywright Ltd* (1971) 220 Estates Gazette 651.
148 *Cardiothoracic Institute v Shrewdcrest Ltd* [1986] 3 All ER 633, [1986] 1 WLR 368.
149 *Javad v Aqil* [1991] 1 All ER 243, CA. The tenant was let into possession in anticipation of agreement on a fixed-term tenancy, as opposed to a person without statutory protection holding over after expiry of his lease: see *Walji v Mount Cook Ltd* [2002] 1 P & CR 163.
150 *Manfield & Sons Ltd v Botchin* [1970] 2 QB 612, [1970] 3 All ER 143.

genuine or not, given that tenancies at will lie outside the protection of the Landlord and Tenant Act 1954, Pt II.[151]

It is different where there is a non-business arrangement, as where a married couple was informally invited to live in part of a house, for so long as they wished, with the hope that it would be for the rest of their lives. This was held to create a tenancy at will, which was converted into a yearly tenancy on payment of rent.[152] In another case, by contrast, the owner allowed a family informally into occupation of his house and frequently visited them there. The occupiers were licensees: a result explicable today solely on the basis that there was no intention to create legal relations.[153] In the context of residential premises, if there is exclusive occupation rent-free for an indefinite period, this is taken to indicate an implied tenancy at will as opposed to a licence.[154] The title of the landlord is extinguished as from the expiry of 12 years uninterrupted rent-free occupation by a tenant at will. The 12 years run from the time when the tenancy at will comes to an end.[155]

Tenancies on sufferance

A tenancy on sufferance is said to arise where a tenant wrongfully holds over on termination of a previous tenancy, eg on the expiry of a fixed-term tenancy, without the landlord's consent, after surrender or on the determination of a tenancy at will. It is not really a tenancy at all, and is distinguishable from a tenancy at will by the lack of consent, express or implied, on the part of the landlord. There can then be no payment of rent under a tenancy on sufferance, but the landlord can sue to recover mesne profits. By acceptance of rent, however, or other acknowledgment the tenancy may be converted into a tenancy from year to year.

The landlord may sue the tenant for possession without demand, for though he entered lawfully, he becomes, in effect, a trespasser, by wrongfully holding over; and if his occupation continues uninterrupted for 12 years, he will acquire a good title as against his landlord, as a squatter. As against the Crown, however, no tenancy on sufferance can arise, for such a tenancy continues only by the *laches* of the landlord (ie his delay or negligence), and the Crown cannot be guilty of *laches*.

---

151 *Hagee (London) Ltd v Erikson and Larson* [1976] QB 209 at 216, [1975] 3 All ER 234 at 237, CA (Scarman LJ).
152 *Young v Hargreaves* (1963) 186 Estates Gazette 355.
153 *Heslop v Burns* [1974] 3 All ER 406, [1974] 1 WLR 1241, CA, as explained in *Street v Mountford* [1985] AC 809 at 824, [1985] 2 All ER 289 at 298.
154 *Ramnarace v Lutchman* [2001] UKPC 25, [2001] 1 WLR 1651.
155 Limitation Act 1980, s 15(6) and Sch I, para 5. See *Ramnarace v Lutchman* [2001] UKPC 25, [2001] 1 WLR 1651.

Tenancies by estoppel

Where a person who has no legal title to land grants a tenancy to a tenant, neither side is able subsequently to assert that the person granting the lease had no valid title. Estoppel precludes such unconscionable conduct. A valid tenancy as between the parties is assumed to have been granted.[156] The principle lasts for the whole period of the tenancy, and even after it has expired the former tenant cannot make use of a lack of title on his landlord's part as a defence in an action for rent or for damages for breach of covenant by the landlord.[157] The covenants in the tenancy by estoppel last during the whole period of the tenancy as between the parties.[158]

If the landlord who has no title assigns to a third party, and the latter claims rent, for example, the tenant is entitled to assert the new landlord's lack of title against the third party, provided he can prove a valid superior title, since the estoppel is only binding between the original parties to the tenancy.[159]

Lord Hoffmann has said that it is not the estoppel that creates the tenancy but the tenancy which creates the estoppel.[160] His Lordship rested the doctrine of a tenancy by estoppel on the principle that a person, having entered into an agreement which constituted a lease or tenancy, could not repudiate the ordinary incidents or obligations of the tenancy. These observations have been said to invert years of learning on the subject.[161] In the case in question, the issue could have been resolved simply by holding that the tenant could not have denied the landlord's lack of title and the landlord could not have denied that he granted a tenancy.

If the landlord (having granted a tenancy without having any title to do so) later acquires the legal estate in the land, whether title is registered or unregistered, then the estoppel is said to be 'fed' and the landlord's title as against the tenant is perfected. However, complications arose in the past where the landlord, in order to finance the purchase of his legal title, created a legal mortgage over the land and premises concerned. Where the landlord had previously to this transaction granted a tenancy to a tenant, without having then had a legal title to the land, it could be said that as soon as the landlord obtained the legal title, the estoppel was 'fed', so that the tenancy took priority to the legal mortgagee.[162] The House of Lords held that where a person obtains his registered title and on the same day charges it to a legal mortgagee, the whole process is part of one single transaction, so not allowing a gap or *scintilla*

---

156 *Wroe v Exmos Cover Ltd* [2000] EGCS 22, CA.
157 *Industrial Properties (Barton Hill) Ltd v Associated Electrical Industries Ltd* [1977] QB 580, [1977] 2 All ER 293, CA; *Newham London BC v Phillips* (1997) 30 HLR 859, CA; *St Giles Hotel Ltd v Microworld Technology* (1997) 75 P & CR D 380, CA.
158 *Cuthbertson v Irving* (1859) 4 H & N 742.
159 *National Westminster Bank Ltd v Hart* [1983] QB 773, [1983] 2 All ER 177, CA.
160 *Bruton v London and Quadrant Housing Trust* [2000] 1 AC 406 at 416.
161 Routley (2000) 63 MLR 424.
162 This was held to follow in *Church of England Building Society v Piskor* [1954] Ch 553, CA; also *Universal Permanent Building Society v Cooke* [1952] Ch 95. The result was that a protected tenancy within the Rent Acts might arise, in priority to the mortgagee.

temporis during which the prior tenancy by estoppel can be 'fed' or perfected as against the mortgagee.[163] On that basis the mortgage takes priority to the tenancy, which is important if the mortgagee wishes to sell the premises on the landlord's default with his mortgage. If and when electronic conveyancing is made optional, or even, possibly, obligatory, and once the reforms of the Land Registration Act 2002 are brought into force, registration gap problems of the kind which this last case dealt with are, it is claimed, likely to vanish.[164]

163 *Abbey National Building Society v Cann* [1991] 1 AC 56; Goldberg (1992) 108 LQR 380.
164 Law Commission Report No 271 (2001) 'Land Registration for the 21st Century' (eg paras 2.43-2.51).

CHAPTER 3

Leases and licences

I GENERAL PRINCIPLES

Introduction

Although leases are hybrids, part contract, part property, a lease or tenancy confers on the tenant the right to exclusive possession.[1] Save in the case of a non-proprietary lease, tenancies are distinguished from contractual licences to occupy by the fact that a tenant is entitled to peaceable enjoyment of the premises to the exclusion of the landlord and also of any third parties. This is thanks to the tenant's right to exclusive possession. However, if the occupier is granted a contractual licence to occupy the premises, his rights are purely contractual. The occupier has no exclusive possession of the premises. His rights do not, as purely contractual rights, ordinarily bind third parties, even if they have notice of the contractual licence.[2]

A sea change in the law

The House of Lords, in a decision in which 'orthodoxy was restored',[3] held in *Street v Mountford*[4] that if an agreement for the occupation of land confers exclusive possession on the occupier, for periodical money payments for a term, the agreement will in principle be a tenancy as opposed to a licence to occupy, even if it is labelled as a licence. The courts were there enjoined to ascertain the substance of the matter, and to go behind the form of the agreement. The House of Lords subsequently ruled that these principles applied with equal force to joint occupation agreements.[5] These must

1 *Street v Mountford* [1985] AC 809, [1985] 2 All ER 285, HL.
2 *Ashburn Anstalt v Arnold* [1989] Ch 1, [1988] 2 All ER 147, CA.
3 *Ramnarace v Lutchman* [2001] UKPC 25, [2001] 1 WLR 1651, para 15.
4 [1985] AC 809, [1985] 2 All ER 285, HL. See Anderson (1985) 48 MLR 712; Tromans (1985) CLJ 351; Bridge [1986] Conv 344; Clarke [1986] Conv 39.
5 *AG Securities Ltd v Vaughan; Antoniades v Villiers* [1990] 1 AC 417.

be objectively construed in the light of factors such as the surrounding circumstances, any relationship between the occupiers, the nature and extent of the accommodation, and the actual mode of occupation.

At one time, the courts took an approach to the construction of an agreement which one party claimed to be a lease or tenancy and the other a licence, which placed much more emphasis on the stated intentions of the parties. Typical was the result in a pre-1985 case,[6] since overruled.[7] It dealt with two separate occupation agreements allowing A and B to occupy a double bed-sitting room, whose plain object was to avoid the protection of the Rent Acts. The agreement formally denied any intention on the owner's part to confer exclusive possession on either A or B. The Court of Appeal ruled that there was nothing to prevent the owner granting licences to occupy if he so chose. The agreements were on their face genuine and the court would not assume from the intention to avoid Rent Act protection that they were a sham. The door was thereby opened to evasion of the Rent Acts by owners of residential property. It may be that in a case where there is no proved attempt to evade statutory protection, the courts will simply examine the terms of the agreement as a whole, and not simply ask if the three hallmarks of a tenancy are present.[8]

Genuine licences: some examples

The rulings in the House of Lords as to the construction of licences alleged to be tenancies do not preclude the use of a genuine licence to occupy. Such will have some or all of the following defining characteristics. The document will ordinarily be personal to the licensee, it may even be gratuitous,[9] and may be intended by both parties to be a temporary or holding device,[10] or may arise as the result of an act of generosity by the owner of the property.[11] The owner, as has sometimes happened with business premises, will genuinely retain exclusive possession of, or control over the premises,[12] as where an agreement entitled the owner and its servants or agents unrestricted and, in fact, genuinely needed, access to the premises for the purpose of its business.[13]

6   *Somma v Hazlehurst* [1978] 2 All ER 1011, [1978] 1 WLR 1014, CA.

7   By the House of Lords in *Antoniades v Villiers* [1990] 1 AC 417.

8   *Mehta v Royal Bank of Scotland* [1999] L & TR 340 at 350-351.

9   The fact that rent is not paid is not decisive: *Ashburn Anstalt v Arnold* [1989] Ch 1, [1988] 2 All ER 147, CA. Payments of household bills on a regular basis is not ordinarily equated to rent payments, an indicium of a tenancy, unless the parties clearly so intend: *Bostock v Bryant* [1990] 2 EGLR 101, CA.

10   As in *Venus Investments Ltd v Stocktop Ltd* (1996) 74 P & CR D23 (licence to occupy garage pending vacation of the premises after sale and stated to be personal did not create a tenancy). Compare *Vandersteen v Agius* (1992) 65 P & CR 266.

11   As in *Heslop v Burns* [1974] 3 All ER 406, [1974] 1 WLR 1241, CA.

12   Retaining a duplicate key is not necessarily a denial of exclusive possession: *Ward v Warnke* (1990) 22 HLR 496.

13   As in *Shell-Mex and BP Ltd v Manchester Garages Ltd* [1971] 1 All ER 841, [1971] 1 WLR 612, CA (where a garage forecourt was licensed to a licensee); also *Esso Petroleum Co Ltd v Fumegrange Ltd* [1994] 2 EGLR 90, CA (where the owner reserved control over the running

Another badge of a licence is where the owner of a business unit has reserved the right to move a unit-holder from one unit to another location if the owner deems it appropriate.[14] Such a right, if genuine, shuts out any claim to exclusive possession of the unit. The duration of an occupation agreement is not a decisive factor pointing against a licence. In one case, the courts held that a 21-year right, stated to be exclusive, to dump rubbish in excavated parts of a site where quarrying also continued was a licence: the licensee did not have exclusive control over the site.[15]

In the residential sector, where there have been a large number of claims, often with success, that a document stating that it is a licence amounts to a tenancy, the courts have accepted that there is a licence where, notably, no one of a number of occupiers has exclusive possession of any parts of a house or flat, but each occupier is sharing living accommodation with the others.[16] The nature and quality of the premises in issue is sometimes a factor pointing to a lease, as where the occupier has exclusive occupation of a house or flat with no interference by the owner. Equally, where the occupier of a room in an hotel claimed a tenancy, account was taken, in rejecting this claim, of the fact that the occupier had booked his room in an ordinary hotel with the presumed expectation of short-term permissive occupation.[17] Indeed, a person occupying an hotel room where services such as regular cleaning and changes of linen, not to mention breakfast, are provided, the occupier will ordinarily have a licence and may merely be regarded as a lodger, with no statutory protection even against eviction.[18]

Statutory background

Returning to the principles of construction of documents alleged by the owner to be a licence and by the occupier to be a tenancy, the background to such disputes is that

---

of the trade); and *National Car Parks Ltd v Trinity Development Co (Banbury) Ltd* [2001] 2 EGLR 43.

14 *Dresden Estates Ltd v Collinson* [1987] 1 EGLR 45; Bridge (1987) 50 MLR 655; PF Smith [1987] Conv 220. The same principle was held to apply to a hostel occupation agreement, where the owners could require an occupier, who was the sole occupant of a room, to move to a different room if the management of the premises required it: *Westminster City Council v Clarke* [1992] 1 All ER 695, HL.

15 *Hunts Refuse Disposals Ltd v Norfolk Environmental Waste Services Ltd* [1997] 1 EGLR 16, CA.

16 See eg *Parkins v Westminster City Council* [1998] 1 EGLR 22, CA (where the living accommodation in the flat as a whole was genuinely shared with two other persons authorised to do so by the owners, which authorisation ruled out exclusive possession).

17 *Brillouet v Landless* (1995) 28 HLR 836, CA. On the facts there was not even a licence to occupy and the Protection from Eviction Act 1977, s 3 did not, therefore, apply to the occupier.

18 *Appah v Parncliffe Investments Ltd* [1964] 1 All ER 838, [1964] 1 WLR 1064; *Luganda v Service Hotels Ltd* [1969] 2 Ch 209, [1969] 2 All ER 692, CA. In *Mehta v Royal Bank of Scotland* [1999] L & TR 340, an occupier of an hotel room on a 'long-term' basis where minimal services were provided was nevertheless a licensee, since both the owners and the occupier knew that the hotel was in receivership and up for sale as a going concern.

some, but not all, tenancies of residential and business premises are covered by statutory 'codes', which confer on the tenant after expiry of his or her lease varying rights to remain in occupation of the property. These statutes do not, generally, apply to licences,[19] and in the case of business and most residential tenancies, there is no specific legislation precluding landowners from conferring genuine licences to occupy on another person. For instance, genuine licences of residential accommodation lie outside the full protection of the Rent Act 1977.[20] Genuine licences are incapable of being assured, or assured shorthold, tenancies under the Housing Act 1988, and genuine licences of business premises are outside the protection of the Landlord and Tenant Act 1954, Pt II.[21]

The Rent Act 1977 ceased to apply to almost all tenancies of residential premises granted on or after 15 January 1989.[22] As a result, new residential tenancies created as from then do not enjoy anything like the same degree of security of tenure as formerly. Under an assured shorthold tenancy, the tenant has no statutory right to remain in possession of the house or flat let to him or her once the initial period of the tenancy expires. It is understood that these tenancies now dominate the private residential letting sector. That being so, the incentive may no longer exist for residential proprietors to confer licence agreements on those who might well otherwise have held tenancies: there is no security of tenure to avoid. However, owners of business premises may prefer to make use of licences to occupy, as a licensee cannot obtain a renewal or a continuation of his occupation once the agreement has expired (unless the owner agrees to this), whereas statutory continuation and renewal rights apply, unless expressly contracted out of,[23] to business tenants. Owners of business premises, by using licences in this way, run the risk of the licence, if challenged, being held to be a tenancy in disguise and so wholly within statutory renewal rights.

Some residential owners, attracted by the informal nature of licences, particularly where accommodation is to be shared between different occupiers, may procure the signature of an occupier on a document which asserts in terms that it is a licence, and which uses licence terms throughout, and attempts to avoid conferring exclusive possession on the occupier. One advantage for residential licensors as against residential landlords is that the former are not under any statutory repairing obligations as against their occupiers,[24] although the impact of this lacuna is mitigated by the fact that a

19 They may prevent an exclusive licence from being anything other than a tenancy, so as to protect social tenants against the misuse of licences: Housing Act 1985, s 79(3). Agricultural Holdings Act 1986, s 2(2)(b), is a similar type of deeming provision, but it only applies if exclusive possession is conferred (*University of Reading v Johnson-Houghton* [1985] 2 EGLR 113).
20 *Fordree v Barrell* [1931] 2 KB 257, CA.
21 *Shell-Mex and BP Ltd v Manchester Garages Ltd* [1971] 1 All ER 841, [1971] 1 WLR 612, CA.
22 Housing Act 1988, s 34.
23 A process which at present requires the approval of the county court (Landlord and Tenant Act 1954, s 38).
24 Landlord and Tenant Act 1985, s 11 only applies to residential tenancies.

licensor is under an implied duty to see to it that the licensed premises are reasonably fit for occupation for the licensee's purposes.[25] Thus, although some of the incentives for granting licences have been weakened,[26] their use in the future may continue.

II CONSTRUCTION OF 'LICENCE' AGREEMENTS

A significant change

In *Street v Mountford*,[27] an agreement for the occupation of land, was admitted to have conferred exclusive possession. The owner still contended that it amounted to a licence in view of the stated intentions of the parties. M agreed to occupy a furnished room in S's house at a weekly 'licence fee' of £37. The agreement, a 'personal licence', was non-assignable and avoided any overt suggestion of a tenancy. No services were provided by the owner and no onerous obligations placed on the occupier. At the foot of the agreement, there appeared a statement signed only by the occupier: 'I understand and accept that a licence in the above form does not and is not intended to give me a tenancy protected under the Rent Acts'. The House of Lords construed this agreement as creating a tenancy. The agreement admittedly conferred exclusive possession on the occupier, who paid a rent (or periodical payments) for a periodic term. The actual language in which the agreement was dressed up could not alter its true construction.

The House of Lords held that an agreement which one side claims to amount to a licence and the other asserts is a tenancy must be construed not in accordance merely with its formal language. It must be construed with regard to whether the agreement, express or implied, formal or informal,[28] confers exclusive possession on the occupier, in return for periodical payments, however labelled, for a term, fixed-term or periodic. 'If exclusive possession at a rent for a term does not constitute a tenancy then the distinction between a contractual tenancy and a contractual licence becomes wholly unidentifiable.'[29] These principles of construction apply whether or not the agreement relates to single or joint occupation. No one factor either in the agreement or in the surrounding circumstances, taken into account to assist in the construction of the agreement, is decisive. For example, where a homeless person was granted a written licence to occupy a flat and the only fact militating against the conferral of exclusive

25 *Wettern Electric Ltd v Welsh Development Agency* [1983] QB 796 (commercial premises but there is no reason why this principle should not apply to residential property).
26 The owner of premises held under a contractual licence which is not 'excluded' will still require court proceedings to evict the licensee after expiry of the licence (Protection from Eviction Act 1977, ss 3 and 3A (an example of an excluded licence would be a right to occupy an hotel room for an agreed period)).
27 [1985] AC 809, [1985] 2 All ER 289; Anderson (1985) 48 MLR 712; Tromans (1985) CLJ 351; Bridge [1986] Conv 344; Clarke [1986] Conv 39.
28 For an example of informal agreements see *Smith v Northside Developments Ltd* [1987] 2 EGLR 151, CA.
29 *Street v Mountford* [1985] AC 809, [1985] 2 All ER 285, HL, at 825 and 299 (Lord Templeman).

possession was that the owner retained a key for various purposes (such as to give access for repairs), the occupier was held to have a tenancy.[30]

The courts were invited by the House of Lords to be astute to detect and frustrate sham devices and artificial transactions whose only object is to disguise the grant of a tenancy and to evade the Rent Acts.[31] They may resort to this power, which entitles them to ignore a paper right of an owner to require the occupier to share with any person nominated by him, or a term denying the occupier the right to occupy the premises at a certain time of day, if the terms are suspect, the result being that, without them, the agreement may well confer exclusive possession and so a tenancy. This power may be mainly aimed at suspect terms in residential 'licences', but it applies equally to business premises. The power to ignore the stated intentions of the parties to create a licence has mainly been applied to suspect agreements, which are tenancies in licence clothing.

The House of Lords restored the traditional distinction between leases and contractual licences. The question of whether a lease or licence has been granted in a given case depends on the true construction of the agreement in the light of the surrounding circumstances. In the case of some business tenancies the indicia that may make it apparent that a residential occupier is a tenant may not be present,[32] so recognising judicially that agreements for the occupation of business premises may sometimes contain no obviously suspect terms, unlike in the case of residential premises.[33] If an agreement in reality creates a tenancy, the fact that it may contain paper denials of exclusive possession or be labelled as a licence will count for little.[34] It may be, at least where the court suspects an intention to evade statutory protection, that it will not merely pick its way through each term in an agreement:[35] it looks at the agreement as a whole.

Illustrations of the traditional approach

A number of cases illustrate the application of the approach required by the House of Lords, notably in relation to occupation agreements conferred on one person. Where a residential occupier had exclusive possession, and paid weekly sums for his occupation, and was not a service occupier, he was held a tenant despite an express denial in his agreement that he had a tenancy.[36] A houseparent who was accepted to have exclusive possession of a house owned by his employer, paying rent, under an

30   *Family Housing Association v Jones* [1990] 1 All ER 385, CA.
31   *Street v Mountford* [1985] AC 809, [1985] 2 All ER 285, HL, at 825 and 299; *AG Securities v Vaughan* [1990] 1 AC 417, 458.
32   See *Dresden Estates Ltd v Collinson* [1987] 1 EGLR 45, CA.
33   See eg *London and Associated Investment Trust plc v Calow* [1986] 2 EGLR 80; Bridge [1987] Conv 137.
34   See *Aslan v Murphy* [1989] 3 All ER 130, CA.
35   *Crancour v Da Silvaesa* [1986] 1 EGLR 80.
36   *Facchini v Bryson* [1952] 1 TLR 1386, CA.

informal agreement, was held to be a tenant.[37] So too a person taking possession of a house and paying weekly sums, to put the house into good order and then purchase it from the owner, was held in reality to have exclusive possession and so a tenancy, not a licence.[38]

By contrast, where a person occupied a self-contained bed-sitting room suitable for single occupation, in a supervised homeless men's hostel under an agreement containing a 'mobility clause' enabling the landlord to change his accommodation as it directed, he was in reality a licensee.[39] By further contrast, where a flat was suitable for use by a multiple and shifting population and was so used, with occupiers being entitled to give short notice (a right which was in fact exercised), there being no joint obligation to pay a single rent for the whole premises, there was a genuine licence.[40] That much depends on the facts and circumstances is shown by a further case where a couple was held to have exclusive possession of a three-bedroomed house despite formal terms entitling the owner to enter the premises at any time and accepting that the occupiers were licensees.[41]

In the context of business premises, an agreement for two years certain, relating to tennis courts, placing the 'licensee' under substantial repairing obligations and conferring exclusive possession on the grantee, because it reserved the owner a right to enter and inspect the premises, which was unnecessary if exclusive possession had not been conferred, was held to amount to a tenancy, despite its careful use of 'licence' labelling throughout.[42] Where the occupiers of a petrol-filling station agreed not to impede the owner's rights of possession and control, so as to enable the latter's servants to visit the premises when they chose, a genuine licence was created.[43] This decision was applied to three agreements for the exclusive use, subject to the overriding right of the owner to retain possession and control, of garage and shop land and premises: the agreements were construed as one.[44] A person who had been granted a series of 'licences' under the latest of which he used the main part of the land concerned exclusively as gallops, and had been required to accept the inclusion in the agreement of scrubland of no use to him, was held to have a business tenancy. The agreement entitled him to the exclusive right to exercise and train horses, and to a similar right to the unused land, despite its 'licence' terminology.[45]

37 *Royal Philanthropic Society v County* [1985] 2 EGLR 109, CA; PF Smith [1986] Conv 215; also *Postcastle Properties Ltd v Perridge* [1985] 2 EGLR 107, CA.
38 *Bretherton v Paton* [1986] 1 EGLR 172, CA.
39 *Westminster City Council v Clark* [1992] 2 AC 288, [1992] 1 All ER 695, HL.
40 *Stribling v Wickham* [1989] 2 EGLR 35, CA; also *Mikeover Ltd v Brady* [1989] 3 All ER 618, CA (separate obligations to pay share of rent indicated that two identical agreements were licences).
41 *Duke v Wynne* [1989] 3 All ER 130, CA.
42 *Addiscombe Garden Estates Ltd v Crabbe* [1958] 1 QB 513, [1957] 3 All ER 563, CA.
43 *Shell-Mex and BP Ltd v Manchester Garages Ltd* [1971] 1 All ER 841, [1971] 1 WLR 612, CA; also *National Car Parks Ltd v Trinity Development Co (Banbury) Ltd* [2001] 2 EGLR 43.
44 *Esso Petroleum Co Ltd v Fumegrange Ltd* [1994] 2 EGLR 90, CA: the degree of control over the conduct of the business at the service station was expressly taken into account.
45 *University of Reading v Johnson-Houghton* [1985] 2 EGLR 113; Rogers [1986] Conv 275.

Determining whether exclusive possession exists

The agreement to occupy in *Street v Mountford* was conceded to have conferred exclusive possession on the occupier. At least where they suspect that the 'licence' is a tenancy in disguise, the courts will tend to ignore paper denials of exclusive possession, as well as the stated intentions of the parties. If the owner has rights of entry, the courts may ask if he or she intends to and does exercise them: otherwise they may point to the conferral of exclusive possession.[46] In the case of joint residential occupiers, the court may have to decide, in determining whether exclusive possession has been conferred, issues of fact such as whether the occupiers are a cohabiting couple, or are independent persons; whether one person is liable for the whole payments for use and occupation, or each person pays only an agreed share of such sums, or different amounts are payable by different persons.[47] The course of the negotiations leading to the agreement may be relevant.

In construing any agreement, but especially for the occupation of residential premises, the courts detect and frustrate sham devices and artificial transactions that are designed to evade statutory protection conferred on tenants.[48] These principles were evolved against the background of the Rent Acts, which conferred rigid protection in favour of some tenants, so encouraging the grant of suspect occupation agreements. With the advent of assured shorthold tenancies, which confer almost no security on tenants, these principles may need less often to be invoked. Nevertheless the courts have resorted to their powers to treat a licence as a tenancy in disguise, as the following examples show.

A term entitling the owner to use a room in common with the occupier and permitting him to allow other persons to use the room together with the latter was held not genuine, as the room was to be occupied by an unmarried couple jointly.[49] By contrast, where four occupiers signed separate agreements to occupy at different dates and for different money payments, each occupier having to share with three others, with a system for re-allocating accommodation within the premises if any one occupier left, the House of Lords held that the occupiers were genuinely licensees sharing the premises.[50] Where an occupation agreement provided that the flat concerned could only be occupied between midnight and 10.30am and 12noon and midnight, and allowed

---

46   *Crancour v Da Silvaesa* [1986] 1 EGLR 80.
47   See *AG Securities v Vaughan* [1990] 1 AC 417, [1989] 3 All ER 1058, HL; Harpum (1989) CLJ 19; Baker (1989) 105 LQR 165; Hill (1989) 52 MLR 408; P F Smith [1989] Conv 128.
48   *Street v Mountford* [1985] AC 809, [1985] 2 All ER 285, HL; *AG Securities v Vaughan* [1990] 1 AC 417, [1989] 3 All ER 1058, HL.
49   *Antoniades v Villiers* [1990] 1 AC 417, [1989] 3 All ER 1058.
50   *AG Securities v Vaughan* [1990] 1 AC 417, [1989] 3 All ER 1058, HL. Also *Parkins v Westminster City Council* [1998] 1 EGLR 22, CA (where the flat to be occupied by the plaintiff with two other persons was living accommodation, capable if solely occupied of exclusive possession, but not the bedroom used by the plaintiff). Where there was a family sharing arrangement the court refused to hold that a lady co-occupier with the tenant held a sub-tenancy from him: *Monmouth BC v Marlog* [1994] 2 EGLR 68, CA (especially since the landlord was not in any contractual relationship with the lady in question).

the owner to remove furniture from the room as he wished, these arguably sham terms raised the question whether a licence was genuine.[51] By contrast, an agreement for the occupation by a person occupying under a 'licence' under which the landlord could change the accommodation offered was a licence in view of the other circumstances, including the fact that the landlord needed to exercise constant control over the occupiers.[52] The powers to go behind the form of an agreement have been exercised in relation to agreements to occupy business premises. Thus, a 'management agreement' in the form of a licence, admittedly designed to circumvent a prohibition on the creation of sub-leases in the grantor's own lease, which conferred exclusive possession and control on the occupier of a restaurant, was held to create a sub-tenancy.[53]

Exclusive possession but no tenancy

There are some circumstances where, though a grantee of occupation rights over residential property has exclusive possession, there is no tenancy. These circumstances were listed as follows in *Street v Mountford* by the House of Lords.

(i) No intention to create legal relations

If the circumstances and the conduct of the parties show that the occupier is to be granted a personal privilege, with no interest in the land, then he will be a licensee, even if apparently in exclusive possession.[54] However, this category is limited to family arrangements, or acts of friendship or generosity.[55] On these principles, a licence was created where an owner allowed a couple rent-free occupation as an act of generosity,[56] and also where there was occupation under what was, in substance, despite its tenancy labelling, an informal family arrangement.[57] A person who, under an oral agreement, renovated a dilapidated cottage and then resided there had a tenancy and not a licence.[58] There have been cases outside family and similar arrangements where licences have been held to exist simply because of the absence of intention to enter into legal relations. On this basis the occupier, apparently exclusively, of a room in an old people's home was held a licensee,[59] as was a war-time evacuee living in a house under informal arrangements with the owner.[60] A person, to whom no tenancy

51 *Crancour v Da Silvaesa* [1986] 1 EGLR 80, CA.
52 *Westminster City Council v Clark* [1992] 2 AC 288, [1992] 1 All ER 695, HL.
53 *Dellneed Ltd v Chin* [1987] 1 EGLR 75; Bridge [1987] Conv 298.
54 *Errington v Errington and Woods* [1952] 1 KB 290, [1952] 1 All ER 149, CA, applied in *Colchester Borough Council v Smith* [1991] 1 All ER 29.
55 *Ramnarace v Lutchman* [2001] UKPC 25, [2001] 1 WLR 1651.
56 *Heslop v Burns* [1974] 3 All ER 406, [1974] 1 WLR 1241, CA.
57 *Barnes v Barratt* [1970] 2 QB 657, [1970] 2 All ER 483, CA, also *Bostock v Bryant* [1990] 2 EGLR 101.
58 *Nunn v Dalrymple* (1989) 21 HLR 569, CA.
59 *Abbeyfield (Harpenden) Society v Woods* [1968] 1 All ER 352n, [1968] 1 WLR 374, CA.
60 *Booker v Palmer* [1942] 2 All ER 674, CA; also *Davies v Brenner* [1986] CLY 163.

had ever been granted, whose occupation was described as 'unlawful' in a letter sent to her by a local authority, could not claim to be a tenant as the authority on no view had consented to her being on the premises.[61]

Where parties negotiated for the grant of a lease 'subject to contract' but the negotiations broke down, it was held that the individual concerned was only a licensee. It was the mutual intention of the parties to enter into legal relations only if a lease was completed.[62] Indeed, if an occupier who is offered a tenancy refuses to fulfil conditions precedent, there may be no reason for conferring on him even a licence, and he will then be a trespasser, subject to speedy eviction.[63] Where the tenant died, leaving a daughter in residence, and the landlords only accepted rent from her for a short time while considering their position, it was held, on the special facts arising under residential succession provisions, that the landlords had not intended to contract with the daughter at all, and she was held a licensee.[64]

(ii) Exclusive possession exists but is referable to legal relations other than a tenancy

Exclusive possession is not decisive in all cases, because an occupier with exclusive possession is not necessarily a tenant. The occupier may be a lodger[65] or a service occupier. There may be other circumstances, as where the occupier is a fee simple owner, a person under contract to acquire a long lease,[66] a trespasser, a mortgagee in possession, or the object of charity.[67] Likewise, there was no tenancy where a former tenant against whom a possession order had been granted remained in occupation under a written agreement to pay off rent arrears at a regular rate.[68] A further example is where an owner, such as a requisitioning authority,[69] has no power to grant a

---

61   *Westminster City Council v Basson* [1991] 1 EGLR 277, CA. The occupier had been in a relationship with a joint-tenant husband whose wife had left him, the husband having also moved out after a few months.

62   *Isaac v Hotel de Paris* [1960] 1 All ER 348, [1960] 1 WLR 239.

63   As in *VG Fraulo & Co Ltd v Papa* [1993] 2 EGLR 99, CA.

64   *Marcroft Wagons Ltd v Smith* [1951] 2 KB 496, [1951] 2 All ER 271, CA.

65   However, where a tenant held a tenancy of a single, 72-square-foot, large furnished room, in an hotel but apparently to the exclusion of the landlord, the fact that he could not cook in his room did not prevent his having an assured tenancy: *Uratemp Ventures Ltd v Collins* [2001] UKHL 43, [2002] 1 AC 301.

66   As in *Essex Plan Ltd v Broadminster Ltd* [1988] 2 EGLR 73 (grant of option to take long lease on person who had entered occupation necessarily ruled out inference of a tenancy of premises, since the option gave the grantee an immediate equitable interest in the land).

67   As in *Gray v Taylor* [1998] 4 All ER 17, [1998] 1 WLR 1093, CA (where an almsperson had exclusive possession but their occupation was dependent on their status as a recipient of charity benefits).

68   *Leadenhall Residential 2 Ltd v Stirling* [2001] EWCA Civ 1011, [2002] 1 WLR 499.

69   *Finbow v Air Ministry* [1963] 2 All ER 647, [1963] 1 WLR 697; also *Lewisham London BC v Roberts* [1949] 2 KB 608, [1949] 1 All ER 815, CA. According to Lord Hoffmann in *Bruton v London and Quadrant Housing Trust* [2000] 1 AC 406, Denning LJ in the latter case was dealing with the issue of whether a tenancy binding on third parties could be granted by the authority.

tenancy. However, the House of Lords has ruled that a housing trust which had no power under the agreement conferring on it a right to occupy land had nevertheless granted exclusive possession and, with that, a tenancy, to a formerly homeless person. He did not share the accommodation with anyone else. The trust's lack of title was held to be irrelevant: the matter was not on the same footing as cases of a requisitioning authority incapable under its enabling statute to grant tenancies.[70] The extent to which this debatable decision reduces the scope of the present principle remains to be explored.

Service occupation A person is a service occupier where he is a servant in occupation of the house of his master in order to perform his services: the occupation must be strictly ancillary to the performance of the duties of the servant-occupier, and the servant's occupation in this case is deemed to be that of his master.[71] The test is objective: the fact that a particular employee is not in a position to better perform the duties required of him or that his occupation is in anticipation of such performance makes no difference; equally, if an employee's occupation is a fringe benefit or inducement to occupy in order to enable him to work better, he is a tenant, not a licensee.[72] In the former case, the possession is that of the master, the servant is a licensee, and no tenancy is created.[73] Examples of service occupation include: a surgeon whose post required residence within the hospital concerned,[74] a soldier required to occupy military quarters,[75] a chauffeur lodged in part of his master's premises,[76] and an hotel manager occupying rooms in the hotel premises.[77] However, the mere fact that the servant occupies the master's house rent-free as part of his remuneration will not of itself make him a service occupier.[78]

Occupation with services provided

In *Street v Mountford*[79] it was held that an occupier of residential accommodation is a lodger, a variety of licensee, who may hold no formal contract, only if the owner provides accommodation at a rent and, as part of the contract, be it express or implied, attendance or services which require the landlord or his servants to exercise unrestricted

---

70   *Bruton v London and Quadrant Housing Trust* [2000] 1 AC 406.
71   *Smith v Seghill Overseers* (1875) LR 10 QB 422; also *Redbank Schools Ltd v Abdullahzadeh* (1995) 28 HLR 431.
72   *Norris v Checksfield* [1991] 4 All ER 327, CA; *Redbank Schools Ltd v Abdullahzadeh* (1995) 28 HLR 431, CA.
73   *Mayhew v Suttle* (1854) 4 E & B 347, Ex Ch.
74   *Dobson v Jones* (1844) 5 Man & G 112.
75   *Fox v Dalby* (1874) LR 10 CP 285.
76   *Thompsons (Funeral Furnishers) Ltd v Phillips* [1945] 2 All ER 49, CA.
77   *Carroll v Manek and Bank of India* (2000) 79 P & CR 173. Even had there been a tenancy, it would have been excluded by Rent Act 1977, s 11 (tenancies of licensed premises).
78   *Hughes v Chatham Overseers* (1843) 5 Man & G 54; *R v Spurrell* (1865) LR 1 QB 72.
79   [1985] AC 809, [1985] 2 All ER 289 at 817-818 and 293, HL.

access to and use of the premises.[80] The view of Blackburn J[81] was adopted, according to which a lodger might have exclusive use of his room, in that no-one else was there, and he could stow his goods there; but the landlord retained for himself exclusive possession. In principle, if no services or attendance are provided by the owner, the occupier holds a tenancy, whether he is described in any agreement as a lodger or licensee or not. Accordingly, a person holding a licence of one room in a four-bedroomed flat, whose charge included a payment for services, was genuinely a licensee and not a tenant. The services (the provision of weekly cleaning and fresh linen) were such as genuinely to require unrestricted access by the landlord, using his own key, without needing the occupier's permission.[82]

Ruling out exclusive possession

It is possible for an owner of land genuinely to reserve rights that are sufficiently extensive to prevent the occupier from having exclusive possession. Whether this is in fact achieved by a particular form of words is a question of their construction in the circumstances. For example, a clause in a 'licence' agreement by which the licensees undertook not to impede in any way the officers, servants or agents of the licensor in the exercise of the latter's rights of possession of the premises deprived the licensee of exclusive possession.[83] It was the same with an agreement which entitled the owner to make a contemporaneous use of agricultural land with the occupier, so long as it did not interfere with the reasonable exercise of the latter's rights.[84] Likewise a 'milk-sharing agreement' which entitled the owner of agricultural land to alter the area of land and fields to which the agreement applied did not confer exclusive possession on the occupier.[85] Nor did a term in a 'licence' to occupy business premises under which the owner was entitled to require the occupier to transfer his occupation to other premises within the owner's adjoining property.[86] By contrast, more limited rights of entry or access may serve to emphasise the grant of exclusive possession.[87] Thus, where an agreement reserved rights of way over agricultural land in the owner's favour, that did not prevent a tenancy from being granted.[88]

---

80   See *Brillouet v Landless* (1995) 28 HLR 836, CA.
81   In *Allen v Liverpool Overseers* (1874) LR 9 QB 180 at 191-192.
82   *Huwlyer v Ruddy* (1995) 28 HLR 550, CA.
83   *Shell-Mex and BP Ltd v Manchester Garages Ltd* [1971] 1 All ER 841, [1971] 1 WLR 612, CA.
84   *Bahamas International Trust Co Ltd v Threadgold* [1974] 3 All ER 881, HL.
85   *McCarthy v Bence* [1990] 1 EGLR 1, CA; Rogers [1991] Conv 58.
86   *Dresden Estates Ltd v Collinson* [1987] 1 EGLR 45; Bridge (1987) 50 MLR 655; PF Smith [1987] Conv 220.
87   As in *Addiscombe Garden Estates Ltd v Crabbe* [1958] 1 QB 513; [1957] 3 All ER 563 (right to enter and inspect condition of premises).
88   *Lampard v Barker* (1984) 272 Estates Gazette 783, CA.

III CONCLUSIONS

The construction of agreements which one side alleges to be a tenancy and the other a licence is an uncertain business, and the result often depends on a detailed evaluation of factual considerations which vary with each case, despite the general rules of construction enunciated by the courts. Though common rules are supposed to apply to all classes of agreement, in reality differences of detail exist. If residential accommodation is scarce, this may enable owners to pressure occupiers into accepting any terms on offer. Hence, the requirement that the courts should look out for suspect terms or for whole agreements which are tenancies masquerading as licences. Should the parties succumb to the temptation to use sham terms, the courts will disregard these, once the criterion of a sham has been proved, and must discover the true effect of the agreement. If there is no proof, or suspicion, that the agreement is aimed at evading statutory protection, then the courts may simply construe the whole of the terms of the agreement and decide whether at the end of the day a licence or a tenancy was intended. The House of Lords, at a time when cast-iron residential security prevailed, noted that those who framed residential occupation agreements constantly attempted to circumvent statutory protection offered to tenants on termination of a lease, while still wishing to enjoy an income from the property.[89] This could not have failed to influence the approach of the courts to these agreements. Cast-iron security of tenure for residential tenants is a thing largely of the past. It may, however, have become almost impossible for social landlords to grant an occupier of self-contained residential premises a licence to occupy where the owner requires no unrestricted access for the purpose of providing personal services or attendance.[90]

---

89 *AG Securities v Vaughan* [1990] 1 AC 417 at 459 (Lord Templeman) and 466 (Lord Oliver).
90 Thanks to *Bruton v London and Quadrant Housing Association* [2000] 1 AC 406.

CHAPTER 4

Creation form and content of leases

I INTRODUCTION

An intending landlord and tenant may grant or accept a lease in due form without proceeding to enter into a contract for a lease. In some cases, such as the grant or assignment of a long lease, or of a building lease, the parties may well grant a lease by a two-stage procedure: entering into a contract for a lease and following this with the grant by deed of the leasehold estate in question. In any event, even in the case of a tenancy for a short period, a written tenancy agreement is usual.[1] It is necessary to note in this Chapter the principal rules governing the formation of a contract for a lease, as well as the formalities needed to create a legal lease. Since leases and tenancies are hybrid animals, part contract, part property, we need also to examine the question of rectification of leases and rescission, as well as the impact of consumer regulations and other principles on the contents of leases.

II CONTRACT FOR A LEASE

Introduction

If the parties decide to resort to two stages in the procedure leading to the formal grant of a lease, then even if the parties have agreed in principle about the terms of their agreement, the Law of Property (Miscellaneous Provisions) Act 1989, s 2 (hereinafter LP(MP)A 1989) imposes formal requirements on the formation of a binding contract for a lease.[2] It altered the rules governing the enforceability of contracts for the grant

---

1   As recognised in *Battersea Churches Housing Trust v Hunte* (1996) 29 HLR 346, CA. The Housing Corporation's Shorthold Tenant's Charter and their Secure Tenant's Charter both say that the tenant is entitled to a written tenancy agreement.

2   It will be appreciated that, on general principles, once a binding agreement for a lease has been reached, its terms will be specifically enforceable but, as with an agreement for a building lease,

of a lease, and repealed the previous legislative rules.[3] LP(MP)A 1989, s 2 does not apply to a contract to grant an oral lease for a term not exceeding three years.

The policy of this provision is to prevent disputes as to whether parties had entered into a binding agreement or over what terms they had agreed.[4] The need for certainty as to the formation of contracts of this type must outweigh the disappointment of those who make informal bargains in ignorance of the statutory requirement.[5] Hence the requirement that as a precondition of validity, a contract for a lease must be in writing and must contain all the agreed terms of the contract, which both parties must sign. However, once a formal deed embodying the agreement for a lease has been executed, the LP(MP)A 1989 ceases to apply to any agreement taken as one with the lease, as it only applies to executory contracts. So, a landlord who executed a lease, and who in a separate agreement undertook to pay the lessee for the cost of fitting-out works, could not rely on LP(MP)A 1989, s 2 as a ground for evading his obligation to pay, since the executed lease and the agreement were taken as one.[6] This saving of collateral agreements or 'side letters' is significant as these may bind third parties such as assignees of the landlord's reversion.[7]

Statutory requirements

The essential requirements[8] of LP(MP)A 1989, s 2 for the formation of a valid contract for a lease are as follows.

1   By LP(MP)A 1989, s 2(1), 'a contract for the sale or other disposition of an interest in land' (and thus a contract for a lease and for a surrender of a lease)[9] can only be made in writing. It must incorporate all the terms which the parties have expressly agreed in one document, or, where contracts are exchanged, in each.

2   The terms of the contract, or some of them, may be incorporated in a document either by being set out in it in full or by reference to some other document (LP(MP)A 1989, s 2(2)).

---

a claimant who has not performed a condition precedent (such as building a new house) cannot expect to obtain a formal lease: see *Rosen v Trustees of the Camden Charities* [2001] 1 EGLR 59.

3   LP(MP)A 1989, s 2(8) and Sch 2. In *McCausland v Duncan Lawrie Ltd* [1996] 4 All ER 995, CA, Neill LJ said at 1002 that the new rules were stated to be intentionally strict and to apply to variations in a contract as well as to its original terms. The rules applying until 27 September 1989 were in LPA 1925 s 40.

4   *Spiro v Glencrown Properties Ltd* [1991] Ch 537, [1991] 1 All ER 600.

5   *Yaxley v Gotts* [2000] Ch 162 at 175 (Robert Walker LJ).

6   *Tootal Clothing Ltd v Guinea Properties Management Ltd* [1992] 2 EGLR 80, CA.

7   As in *System Floors Ltd v Ruralpride Ltd* [1995] 1 EGLR 48, CA (where the commercial realities were taken into account).

8   See further Cheshire and Burn, pp 126-130; Megarry and Wade, paras 12-018ff.

9   *Commission for the New Towns v Cooper (Great Britain) Ltd* [1995] Ch 259, [1995] 2 All ER 929, CA.

3   The document incorporating the terms, or, where contracts are exchanged, one of the documents incorporating them (but not necessarily the same one) must be signed by or on behalf of each party to the contract (LP(MP)A 1989, s 2(3)).

Main effects of LP(MP)A 1989, s 2

1   Where the parties, as in the case of the intended grant of a building lease or other type of long lease, agree on a contract for the grant of a term exceeding three years, the contract must, by LP(MP)A 1989, s 2(1), be in writing or it will be invalid. The agreement must contain all the terms agreed. As a concession, if a document is referred to in the main contract, its terms will be incorporated into the main contract by reference (LP(MP)A 1989, s 2(2)). However, where it was claimed that the landlord of business premises had transferred a right, personal to the original tenant, to surrender the lease to his assignee, after an exchange of letters, it was held that since all the terms of the alleged contract to confer the surrender right or 'put option' had not been fully set out in one document as required by LP(MP)A 1989, s 2, there was no enforceable contract to confer the surrender right on the assignee.[10] Moreover, the omission even of a single term agreed between the parties, no matter how insignificant, from the contract would appear to render the entire contract a nullity.

2   It is essential to the validity of a contract for a lease that both parties should sign it. By 'sign' is evidently meant writing one's hand on the document; so, a prospective lessee must in that sense sign any letter signed by the intending landlord, which sets out the supposedly agreed terms of the lease.[11] The same principle would presumably apply to any letter containing draft variations of an existing tenancy. LP(MP)A 1989, s 2(3) allows for the signature by a duly authorised agent acting for either party.

3   A contract for an oral lease which is for a term exceeding three years is invalid. Equally, a lease by deed for such a period is valid provided the deed is signed and delivered; this allows the parties to proceed straight to the execution of a deed rather than making use of an agreement for a lease. An oral contract to grant a lease taking immediate effect in possession for a term not exceeding three years, which complies with LPA 1925, s 54(2), is exempt from the LP(MP)A 1989 requirement of writing. It is valid as an agreement for such a lease. But an oral contract for the eventual grant of a written term not exceeding three years appears to be struck down by LP(MP)A 1989, s 2, if this provision is read literally.

4   A contract for a lease for a term exceeding three years which does not comply with the requirements of LP(MP)A 1989, s 2 cannot be saved by equity except where a party might be able to claim rectification of the lease.

10   *Commission for the New Towns v Cooper (Great Britain) Ltd* [1995] Ch 259, [1995] 2 All ER 929, CA; also *Enfield London BC v Arajah* [1995] EGCS 164, CA.

11   *Firstpost Homes Ltd v Johnson* [1995] 4 All ER 355, [1995] 1 WLR 1567, CA.

5 If a tenant is entitled to claim an enforceable written contract for a lease, but the landlord fails to execute a deed, the tenant may assert that he holds a lease valid in equity, which entitles him to claim specific performance.

6 By contrast, if a contract for a lease is void for non-compliance with LP(MP)A 1989, s 2 but the person takes possession and pays regular money sums to the landlord, the common law would in principle recognise him as a periodic tenant by implication of law.

7 Where the parties or their solicitors each prepare draft contracts, these will not become binding unless and until they contain all the terms the parties have agreed and they have been signed by or on behalf of the parties. The practice of conducting all negotiations for a contract for a lease 'subject to contract', which has the effect of precluding any binding agreement,[12] may continue despite the enactment of LP(MP)A 1989, s 2.[13] However, an informal exchange of letters setting out the conferral of a 'put option' (or right to surrender) on an assignee by the landlord would, it was said, have been a sufficient note or memorandum to satisfy LPA 1925, s 40. It did not suffice to satisfy LP(MP)A 1989, s 2, which is much stricter.[14]

III FORMALITIES FOR THE CREATION AND ASSIGNMENT OF LEGAL LEASES

Creation of legal leases

Legislation imposes formalities for the grant of a lease or tenancy, in order for it to be a legal 'term of years absolute' within LPA 1925, s 1(1). The policy of these rules is to impose a requirement of a deed as a condition precedent of the valid creation of a legal lease, but to except the creation of short tenancies at a market rent from this requirement, thus allowing the valid oral creation of periodic tenancies.

1 In order validly to create a legal lease, a deed is required.[15] Otherwise the lease is void at law. Once the relevant sections of the Land Registration Act 2002 (hereinafter LRA 2002) are brought into force, a lease of registered land will only confer a legal

---

12 See eg *D'Silva v Lister House Development* [1971] Ch 17, [1970] 1 All ER 858. In such a case, the parties are only bound once the lease and counterpart have been exchanged.

13 As in eg *Enfield London Borough Council v Arajah* [1995] EGCS 164, and also in *Farah v Moody* [1998] EGCS 1, CA. See also *James v Evans* [2000] 3 EGLR 1, CA where both parties were aware that all negotiations for a tenancy agreement for ten years were subject to contract; the agreement was unenforceable as a result and on the facts was not saved by any proprietary estoppel, which would, if proved, displace the strict requirements of LP(MP)A 1989, s 2 owing to s 2(5), as to which see *Yaxley v Gotts* [2000] Ch 162; and also *Jones v Morgan* [2001] PLSCS 154 (as there is no 'no-go area' in LP(MP)A 1989, s 2 for estoppel).

14 *Commission for the New Towns v Cooper (Great Britain) Ltd* [1995] Ch 259, [1995] 2 All ER 929, CA.

15 LPA 1925, s 52(1); a lease is a 'conveyance' within LPA 1925, s 205(1)(ii). Note that an instrument can only be a deed if it is clear on its face that the parties intended it to be such, thanks to the Law of Property (Miscellaneous Provisions) Act 1994 , s 1(2). A lease by deed is in two parts, the lease and the counterpart.

title on the lessee once the formal grant of the lease has been registered (save in the case of short leases). Otherwise, the grant, transfer or creation of the lease is void for the purpose of passing a legal estate (LRA 2002, s 7(1)).

2 Where a lease takes effect 'in possession for a term not exceeding three years[16] (whether or not the lessee is given power to extend the term) at the best rent which can be reasonably obtained without taking a fine',[17] it may validly be created by a written or even an oral contract. To fall within the present exception a tenancy must confer an immediate right to possession, and not be a reversionary lease. Hence, a tenancy agreement under which a tenant took possession three weeks after signing an acknowledgment letter of the terms of his tenancy fell outside LPA 1925, s 54(2).[18] To fall within this exception, the initial duration of the lease is taken: it must be such that it is granted for a period not exceeding three years, even though it makes no difference that the tenant may have an option to extend the initial term beyond that period. A lease for a term exceeding three years which enables it to be determined within that time must be created by deed and if the title to the land is registered, registered if the lease period exceeds seven years.[19] Provided that the initial duration of a tenancy is not for a period exceeding three years, the fact that it may in due course exceed that period will not infringe the exception. Accordingly legal periodic tenancies may be created validly for any period, be it for a week, a month or a year.[20] They do not require registration even under the new rules.

3 The legislative exception for the valid creation of oral short leases is limited to terms which take effect in possession. This does not require physical possession, as it includes the receipt of rent and profits, or the right to receive them,[21] as from sub-tenants of the lessee. Since the lease must take effect in possession, a reversionary lease is excluded[22] and must if title is registered both be registered and granted by deed to be valid at law, no matter how short the term agreed. The word 'fine' means a premium, ie a capitalised rent. Thus, if any part of a market rent is taken from the tenant as a premium, the lease must be created by deed to be valid at law, notwithstanding the exception.

4 If a lease is created orally, but is required to be created by deed, it takes effect as a tenancy at will,[23] unless and until it is converted into a tenancy from year to year by operation of law. Equity is prepared to give effect to the intentions of the parties: a void legal lease may take effect in equity. No such lease is valid even in equity from 27 September 1989 unless it is in writing sufficient to comply with

16 Computed from the day the lease is made: *Foster v Reeves* [1892] 2 QB 255, CA.
17 LPA 1925, s 54(2).
18 *Long v Tower Hamlets London Borough Council* [1996] 2 All ER 683; the approach taken is that of *Foa* p 11, note (p) and is consistent with the fact that LPA 1925, s 149(3) restricts the ability to contract for reversionary leases.
19 *Kushner v Law Society* [1952] 1 KB 264, [1952] 1 All ER 404.
20 Cf *Re Knight, ex p Voisey* (1882) 21 Ch D 442 and the cases cited on periodic tenancies in ch 2, above.
21 LPA 1925, s 205(1)(xix).
22 See *Bush Transport Ltd v Nelson* [1987] 1 EGLR 71 at 73, CA.
23 LPA 1925, s 54(1).

LP(MP)A 1989, s 2.[24] In addition, unless a legal title is registered after the grant or assignment of lease of registered land for more then seven years unexpired, the lessee will only have a contract for a lease for that period. Registration alone confers legal title.

5 An oral lease validly created at law is not quite as good as a lease by deed because it is not a 'conveyance' within LPA 1925,[25] so that implied easements do not pass on its creation.

Registration rules

LRA 2002 was not in force when this book went to press[26] but once the relevant sections are brought into force, the principles governing registration of leasehold estates will be as follows and so it is inappropriate to consider the old regime. LRA 2002 applies the overall policy of making it necessary to register any substantial leasehold interest. Only once a leasehold title is registered can the legal title to the land be conferred on the lessee (LRA 2002, s 7(1)).

(i) Voluntary registration

The grant of a lease out of an unregistered freehold or long leasehold estate may be voluntarily registered, thanks to LRA 2002, s 3(3), where the lease in question is granted for a term of which more than seven years remain unexpired at the time of the registration application.[27] In the case of, notably, a time-share lease, where the right to possession of the lease is discontinuous, the lease may be registered voluntarily even if it has less than seven years to run (LRA 2002, s 3(4)). In the case of such leases it might be difficult for an intending purchaser to discover the existence of a tenant from an inspection of the land in question. A notice of a registrable lease will also be entered against the landlord's title.

(ii) Compulsory registration

The new rules (LRA 2002, s 4(1) and (2)) require that title to a leasehold estate must be registered when the lease is granted out of a registered freehold or leasehold estate and the lease has more than seven years to run at the time of grant or transfer (as by

---

24 This is without prejudice to LPA 1925, s 54(2) (LP(MP)A 1989, s 2(5)), see above.
25 *Rye v Rye* [1962] AC 496 at 512.
26 As to the Land Registration Act 2002 when at a late stage of its passage through Parliament see Cooke [2002] Conv 11. The Act was passed to implement, with changes in points of detail, Law Com No 271 (1998) 'Land Registration for the 21st Century'.
27 As a result of LRA 2002, s 3(7), where a tenant in possession has been granted a further lease to take effect in possession on, or within one month of the expiry of the first lease, and the terms together exceed seven years, the lease may be registered.

assignment for valuable or other consideration).[28] This marks a shift in the law, because under the old system only leases granted for a term exceeding 21 years were registrable. However, the policy of LRA 2002 is to make the registers of title as comprehensive as possible.[29] LRA 2002 carries the policy of making title depend on registration further. It is provided (LRA 2002, s 4(1)(d)) that a lease for 21 years or less which has not taken effect in possession after the period of three months from its date of grant must be registered.[30] This requirement is new. As pointed out in the Explanatory Notes to LRA 2002,[31] since the lessee under a reversionary lease for the permitted period of up to 21 years[32] will not be in possession, a purchaser of the land affected by it may not easily be able to find out about the existence of the lease.

(iii) Penalty for non-compliance

Failure to comply with the requirement of registration of a lease grant or assignment entails the penalty that the lease is void to the extent that it cannot transfer grant or create the legal estate (LRA 2002, s 7(1)). This penalty applies even if the formal requirement of making use of a deed has been complied with. LRA 2002 here applies the policy that title is only conferred by the fact of registration. However, an unregistered but registrable grant or assignment is not wholly without effect. The transaction takes effect as a contract for valuable consideration to grant or create the legal estate concerned (LRA 2002, s 7(2)). Thus it seems that the lessee holds a lease valid in equity only but without the ability to procure a valid legal title. In addition, the assignee of an unregistered transfer will be considered the assignee for all purposes, including the enforcement of leasehold covenants.

(iv) Additional points

The lessee or his successor in title is bound to apply for registration as proprietor of the estate, where it is compulsory (LRA 2002, s 6(1)). The application must be within two months of the date of grant or assignment of the lease (LRA 2002, s 6(4)), though this period can be extended by the Registrar. Where a lease is assigned or surrendered to the owner of the immediate reversion so that the lease is merged into the superior estate, there is no requirement to register the transaction (LRA 2002, s 4(4)). A leasehold estate granted for a term not exceeding seven years from the date of the grant is an

---

28 If the title to the superior freehold or lease is absolute, the lessee's title will be registered as absolute in view of the terms of LRA 2002, s 10. Otherwise he is registered with a good leasehold, qualified or possessory title.
29 The Lord Chancellor has the power under LRA 2002, s 5 to adjust by regulations the seven-year rule if he thinks fit.
30 Such a lease cannot override: LRA 2002, Sch 1, para 1.
31 (2002) p 10. The Notes do not of course form part of the Act but may be used as an aid to its interpretation.
32 LPA 1925, s 149(3).

unregistered interest which, if created according to the proper formalities where required, is a legal lease. This sort of lease overrides first registration of a freehold or long leasehold estate.[33]

Express assignment of legal lease

The main points to note are these.

1   Parliament makes no exceptions to the formal rules in the case of express assignments of a lease or tenancy[34] to correspond to those applicable to the creation of leases.[35] Any legal lease must be assigned by deed if the assignment[36] is to take effect as a valid legal assignment of the term: otherwise it is void at law.[37] Until a registrable transfer is registered within the time allowed, which is required if the unexpired term of the lease at the time of the assignment is over seven years, no legal title passes to the assignee.[38] No assignment of any legal lease, irrespective of its initial length, is valid even in equity unless it is in writing.[39] Hence, where a tenant orally undertook to assign a weekly periodic tenancy to his wife, but never assigned it by deed or in writing, no valid assignment had taken place at law or in equity and the tenancy remained vested in the husband.[40] This principle is not unqualified. It does not apply to the assignment of an informally-created tenancy which takes effect by operation of law[41] nor, apparently, to informal assignments of weekly (or seemingly other periodic) statutory tenancies under the Rent Act 1977.[42] It appears that an assignment of a secure tenancy may be informal owing to the overriding effect of the specific legislation applicable in this case.[43]

33   LRA 2002, Sch 1, para 1. A lease for a term not exceeding seven years will not override if it is to take effect more than three months after it is made. This is in accordance with the policy regarding reversionary leases.

34   Leases or tenancies may be assigned by operation of law, as where the tenant becomes bankrupt. If the lease contains a forfeiture clause, the tenant incurs a forfeiture; if not, by the Insolvency Act 1986, s 306 the lease will vest in the bankrupt's trustee in bankruptcy. The trustee may then for example disclaim the lease, if it is onerous (Insolvency Act 1986, s 315).

35   Where an enforceable contract to assign a lease is entered into, which is an alternative method of assigning a lease, it is subject to the same formalities as is a contract to grant a lease: see above; also *Parc Battersea Ltd v Hutchinson* [1999] 2 EGLR 33.

36   As opposed to an attempt to create a sub-tenancy of premises which was to be for a term exceeding the residue of the head-lease, which takes effect as an assignment by operation of law of the whole of the remaining period of the head-lease: *Parc Battersea Ltd v Hutchinson* [1999] 2 EGLR 33, following *Milmo v Carreras* [1946] KB 306.

37   LPA 1925, s 52(1); *Crago v Julian* [1992] 1 All ER 744, CA; *Camden London BC v Alexandrou* (1997) 74 P & CR D33; *Parc Battersea Ltd v Hutchinson* [1999] 2 EGLR 33. The exception in LPA 1925, s 52(1)(d) does not apply to assignments. See Sparkes [1992] Conv 252, 357.

38   Once LRA 2002, s 7 is brought into force.

39   LPA 1925, s 53(1)(a); *Botting v Martin* (1808) 1 Camp 317; *Crago v Julian* [1992] 1 All ER 744, CA.

40   *Crago v Julian* [1992] 1 All ER 744, CA.

41   LPA 1925, s 52(1)(g); *Milmo v Carreras* [1946] KB 306, [1946] 1 All ER 288, CA.

42   *Thomas Pocklington's Gift Trustees v Hill* [1989] 2 EGLR 97 at 100, CA.

43   *City of Westminster v Peart* (1991) 24 HLR 389, CA (Housing Act 1985, s 91(3)(c)).

2   At common law, the tenant is not bound to inform the landlord of an assignment.[44] The terms of the lease may expressly require him to do so, usually in writing, and often within a short time of the assignment having taken place. The process of making an assignment and the obtaining of a landlord's consent to that assignment are separate transactions.[45] If the tenant has assigned the lease in breach of a covenant which requires him first to obtain the consent of the landlord, the assignment transfers a title to the land to the new tenant, although the landlord may well be entitled to bring forfeiture proceedings against the latter.[46]

3   In the case of registered land, the same registration requirements will apply once the relevant sections of LRA 2002 are brought into force to assignments of legal leases as apply to the first grant of such leases. In one respect, the new Act may avoid a problem sometimes called the 'registration gap'. Under the regime of the Land Registration Act 1925, it was held that where there had been an assignment of a legal lease which had not been registered as required by that Act, the erstwhile lessee could continue to exercise a personal option to determine the lease.[47] The assignment was, however, effective in equity to pass an interest to the assignee. Under the new regime, the Land Registry will avoid a 'registration gap' between the disposition (in our case the assignment) and its registration.[48] Registration alone will confer title on all but an assignee whose lease is short enough to override the grantor's title.

IV   EQUITABLE LEASES

Where a binding contract for a lease has been entered into, but the lease is formally defective, and has under the new registration rules in the case of a grant out of registered land of a lease for over seven years, not been registered in timely fashion, so that the legal estate in the land is not passed to the tenant, but he takes possession and pays rent, the common law may imply that he holds as tenant from year to year. Equity treats the tenant, in these circumstances, as holding a specifically enforceable agreement for a lease, under which he may compel his landlord to grant him a deed, and thanks to which the landlord may compel the tenant to accept a deed. However, under LRA 2002 rules a tenant holding an unregistered lease for a term of over seven years holds an agreement for a lease only (LRA 2002, s 7(1)) without any prospect to require

---

44   In the case of perpetually renewable leases, the assignor is subject to an implied covenant to register every assignment with the landlord (Law of Property Act 1922, s 145 and Sch XV, para 10(1)(ii)).

45   *Sanctuary Housing Association v Baker* [1998] 1 EGLR 42, 30 HLR 809, CA (where a social landlord was held not entitled to avoid an assignment by way of exchange to which it was not a party).

46   *Old Grovebury Manor Farm Ltd v W Seymour Plant Sales and Hire Ltd (No 2)* [1979] 3 All ER 504; *Governors of the Peabody Donation Fund v Higgins* (1982) 10 HLR 82.

47   *Brown and Root Technology Ltd v Sun Alliance and London Assurance Co* [1997] 1 EGLR 39, CA. The position was held to be different in the case of unregistered land.

48   LRA 2002, s 7. Law Commission Report No 271 (2001) 'Land Registration for the Twenty-First Century' (2001) paras 2.48-2.58.

registration, as opposed to the grant of a deed. No legal title is conferred where the lessee fails to apply within the required or extended by the Registrar for registration (LRA 2002, s 6(1)).

In equity, each party to a void legal lease is treated as subject to the obligations of the lease, because equity treats that as done which ought to be done. In the main case in point, even though it was an interlocutory hearing,[49] a tenant held under a written lease of a mill for a seven-year term, and so held a lease which was void at law. The tenant took possession, despite not having a lease by deed. He fell into arrears with the rent, and the landlord, on his continuing default, exercised the legal remedy of distress. The tenant's claim that the landlord's use of this remedy was in itself illegal, as being limited to a case of a lease by deed, was dismissed. Equity regarded the tenant as entitled to hold in equity in accordance with the terms of his (void) legal lease.[50] Covenants to repair in an equitable lease were as much enforceable as they would have been in a formal lease by deed.[51] Where therefore a registrable lease is not registered in time, equity will enforce the obligation of the parties between themselves, but the lease void at law cannot override the landlord's registered title. In the case of an unregistered equitable lease of registered land for up to seven years, the lease will override as an occupation interest.[52]

Under recent legislation, covenants in tenancies granted on or after 1 January 1996 may be enforced by and against an equitable lessee in possession as much as if he were a legal lessee (Landlord and Tenant (Covenants) Act 1995, s 28(1)). This rule removes technical difficulties and inconsistencies in the previous law arising out of the doctrine of privity of estate. Indeed, the assignee of an informal tenancy granted prior to 1 January 1996 was bound by an undertaking to pay the landlord £40 towards redecoration of the premises immediately before the expiry of the tenancy. The fact that the tenancy was not by deed did not, after the Judicature Acts, bar enforcement of such a covenant.[53]

V RECTIFICATION AND RESCISSION OF LEASES

Rectification

The courts allow rectification of an executed, formal lease so that offending words are struck out of the lease or specific words inserted into it. Equity does not lightly allow such claims to succeed, as is shown by the fact that a high standard of proof is

---

49 *Walsh v Lonsdale* (1882) 21 Ch D 9, CA.
50 Owing to the fact that, after the enactment of the Judicature Acts 1873 and 1875, the equity rule prevailed over the common law rule, with which, in this case, it conflicted.
51 *Industrial Properties (Barton Hill) Ltd v Associated Electrical Industries Ltd* [1977] QB 580, [1977] 2 All ER 293, CA.
52 LRA 2002, Sch 3, para 2.
53 *Boyer v Warbey* [1953] 1 QB 234, [1952] 2 All ER 976, CA.

required: it has to be 'more than a 51:49 balance of probabilities'.[54] Otherwise it would be all too easy to strike a bad bargain and then later to ask the court to undo it, by re-writing parts of the lease the claimant did not subsequently appreciate the full effect of at the time he or she executed the lease. The commonest case of rectification arises where the written agreement is tainted by a mutual mistake. Exceptionally, rectification may be granted where one party alone has fallen into error. The latter is exceptional because the court construes contracts with regard to the objective intention of both parties and not the subjective intentions of one of them.[55] The following must be shown to found a claim to rectification.

1   The lease as it stands does not represent the common intention of the parties, when the lease was executed, but once it is rectified, it will do so.[56]
2   There was a mistake by the plaintiff in executing the deed, so that the deed does not translate that party's intention at the time of the execution of the deed.
3   There is no mistake by the other party, who intends the result in fact achieved and who, in fact, takes advantage of the mistake of the claimant party.[57] In this, it will suffice if the defendant or his agent, such as his solicitor, has wilfully shut his eyes to an obvious error by the claimant.[58]
4   The other party must be both aware of the claimant's mistake, and in not correcting it, his conduct must be unconscionable.[59] In effect, the defendant must be taking an unfair and unconscionable advantage of the other party's known error. It is not sufficient for a claimant merely to show that there has been a lack of care by the defendant or his solicitor, with the result that no inquiries had been made about a mistake of some kind.[60] Drawing the line between the making by the defendant of an innocent or careless mistake in not pursuing inquiries further and a dishonest failure to do so is no easy matter. It may involve the court making inquiries into the knowledge of the defendant along not dissimilar lines to those involved in the case of constructive trusts.
5   If both parties did not clearly intend to include specific words in the lease, such as to under-let premises at a rack rent, there is no common intention and so no case for rectification.[61]

---

54   *Coles v William Hill Organisation* [1998] L & TR 14 at 22.
55   *Commission for the New Towns v Cooper (Great Britain) Ltd* [1995] Ch 259, [1995] 2 All ER 929, CA.
56   See *Brimican Investments Ltd v Blue Circle Heating Ltd* [1995] EGCS 18.
57   *Templiss Properties Ltd v Hyams* [1999] EGCS 60.
58   *Coles v William Hill Organisation* [1998] L & TR 14.
59   *Kemp v Neptune Concrete Ltd* [1988] 2 EGLR 87, CA; *Oceanic Village Ltd v Shirayama Shokusan Co Ltd* [1999] EGCS 83; *Mace v Rutland House Textiles Ltd* (2000) Times, 11 January.
60   *Commission for the New Towns v Cooper (Great Britain) Ltd* [1995] Ch 259, [1995] 2 All ER 929, CA.
61   *Yorkshire Metropolitan Properties Ltd v Co-operative Retail Services* [1997] EGCS 57.

Rectification may be invoked to correct clerical mistakes, obvious slips, or the erroneous inclusion of a clause in the lease.[62] The court may, in its discretion, order rescission, as opposed to rectification, of a lease for mutual mistake, as where there is a misdescription of the premises to be let in the lease. Therefore, where by mistake a first floor was included in a lease, rescission was ordered and the tenant given an option to take a new lease without that floor.[63] Rectification may be ordered against an assignee of the lease with notice of the mistake,[64] seeing that a right to rectify may run through successive ownerships, as where a landlord was entitled to claim that the rent in a lease which had been assigned to the defendants had been misstated.[65]

As noted, if the claimant has simply made a bad bargain, forgetting a material matter in negotiations, rectification is out of the question.[66] Or, as was put in another case, a party who has merely been tough and successful does not have to fear a claim to rectification, provided he has not conducted himself unconscionably, by a party who has been unwise or who has made a bad bargain.[67]

Rectification of an executed lease is exceptionally possible where only one party is mistaken. Because the courts are loath to rectify a lease to reflect the intentions of one party alone, there must be additional circumstances which render it unconscionable for the party who wishes to stand by the written terms to rely on them. These requirements are satisfied by proof of fraud or undue influence. More generously, however, an equity of rectification of a contract for a lease was held to arise where A intends B to misconstrue a document by diverting B from discovering his own mistake by making false and misleading statements. Where, in negotiations with a landlord, a tenant diverted attention from a personal surrender or 'put' option by statements which raised only his interest in exercising a different option in the lease, impliedly representing that the tenant was not interested in exercising the 'put' option, the landlord was held to have been induced to contract on this basis. He was entitled to rectification of the contract so that the tenant could not surrender the lease.[68]

---

62 See eg *Coles v William Hill Organisation* [1998] L & TR 14 (where landlords in error had inserted a tenants' break clause); also *Stavrides v Manku* [1997] EGCS 58 (where rent review dates had been left out of a lease).
63 *Paget v Marshall* (1884) 28 Ch D 255.
64 *Equity and Law Life Assurance Society Ltd v Coltness Group Ltd* [1983] 2 EGLR 118.
65 *Ramsden (DB) Ltd v Nurdin & Peacock plc* [1999] 1 EGLR 119 (the claim failed on the facts).
66 *Harlow Development Corpn v Kingsgate (Clothing Productions) Ltd* (1973) 226 Estates Gazette 1960.
67 *Oceanic Village Ltd v Shirayama Shokusan Co Ltd* [1999] EGCS 83.
68 *Commission for the New Towns v Cooper (Great Britain) Ltd* [1995] Ch 259, [1995] 2 All ER 929, CA.

Rescission

Rescission, an equitable remedy, entails the cancellation of a lease or tenancy no matter how long or short.[69] It may be sought despite the execution, and in that sense performance, of the lease or tenancy.[70] The person claiming rescission must show that he would not have signed the lease save in reliance on the truth of the statement, which thus formed part of the contract.[71] Once the claimant becomes aware of the falsity of the statement, he must seek rescission promptly. There are a number of discretionary bars to relief, such as the conduct of the claimant,[72] or that possession has been taken under the lease for sufficiently long to rule out a claim, thus on the ground of acquiescence.[73] It now appears that where a claim may be made under a specific statute to a remedy, that will rule out a claim to the additional remedy of rescission.[74]

1   Rescission may be claimed where a prospective assignee of a long lease relies on one of the standard conditions of sale, which allows him to terminate the contract if the assigning tenant fails, three days before the completion date, duly to obtain the consent of the landlord to the assignment.[75]

2   Rescission is also available where a person has been induced to sign a lease or tenancy by a fraudulent statement made by the other party. Fraud unravels everything. For example, a Rent Act protected tenancy could have been rescinded by a landlord owing to a fraudulent misstatement by the tenant that he was having a house built elsewhere, which he would be able later to occupy. As a result that the statutory tenancy which arose once the protected tenancy had ended was set aside.[76] Similarly, where a landlord had informed a prospective tenant of a house that the drains were in order, a statement which was known to be false when made, the tenant was entitled to rescind the tenancy he signed on the faith of this collateral warranty.[77]

3   A party is entitled to rescind a tenancy on account of a negligent misrepresentation owing to a statutory reform extending the reach of this remedy beyond its original

69 Thus in *Nutt v Read* (1999) 32 HLR 761, rescission for mutual mistake was allowed in relation to an assured shorthold tenancy; in *Aubergine Enterprises Ltd v Lakewood International* [2001] EGCS 29, rescission was sought in relation to the assignment of a 125-year lease. Estoppel (a further equitable relief in such a case) may preclude a party from setting up a tenancy agreement if it has misled the owner of the premises: see *Bhopal v Walia* [1999] L & TR 461, CA.
70 Misrepresentation Act 1967, s 1.
71 See *Inntrepreneur Estates (CPC) Ltd v Worth* [1996] 1 EGLR 84.
72 See *Butler v Croft* (1973) 27 P & CR 1.
73 *Butler v Croft* (1973) 27 P & CR 1; also *Bridgegrove Ltd v Smith* [1997] 2 EGLR 40 (where it was held reasonable for a business tenant to hold over after expiry of a six-month fixed term tenancy having sunk its money into the business concerned).
74 *Rushton v Worcester City Council* [2001] EGCS 41 (right to buy legislation).
75 See *Aubergine Enterprises Ltd v Lakewood International Ltd* [2001] EGCS 29 (condition 8.3.4.)
76 *Killick v Roberts* [1991] 4 All ER 289, CA.
77 *De Lassalle v Guildford* [1901] 2 KB 215.

basis of fraudulent statements.[78] For example, where a landlord stated that certain premises were 'ideally suitable' for car repairs, when in fact they could not be used for paint spraying, a finding of negligent misrepresentation was held to be justified.[79]

4   As an alternative to rescission, damages may be sought. These are computed, without regard to remoteness rules, on the basis of all losses suffered by the claimant until the date that he found out that he had been misled.[80]

VI CONTENTS OF LEASES

Traditional view and the advent of charters and codes

The contents of a lease or tenancy[81] whether formal or informal are, in principle, for the parties to agree upon, subject to certain minimum requirements of the common law, as regarding certainty of the term granted. There are, strictly speaking, no standard forms, as opposed to precedents, for leases. Parliament last attempted to standardise leases generally in 1845.[82]

With the advent of charters of one kind or another, however, we have seen some attempts at informal, de facto but revocable, standardisation of certain residential tenancies by the backdoor (in other words without making use of general, primary, legislation). The Housing Corporation, a public sector body that oversees the activities of registered social landlords,[83] has produced both a Secure Tenant's Charter and an Shorthold Tenant's Charter. The contents of these Charters do not, strictly, have to be incorporated into tenancies granted by, for example, a registered housing association; but it seems that 'performance standards' of the Housing Corporation require that registered social landlords 'give their residents ... more rights than the law demands'.[84]

78 Misrepresentation Act 1967, s 2.
79 *Bridgegrove Ltd v Smith* [1997] 2 EGLR 40, CA.
80 *Bridgegrove Ltd v Smith* [1997] 2 EGLR 40, CA.
81 Which is not a sham, in which case no part of the agreement has any validity against a landlord or any third party: see *Bhopal v Walia* [1999] L & TR 461, CA.
82 In the Leases Act 1845, which for example gives an 81-word standard covenant to repair; but the Act was largely neglected according to the Law Commission: Law Com No 162 (1987) paras 3.8-3.10. The Royal Commission on Legal Services (1979) Cmnd 7648, Annex 21.1, para 13, supported standardisation, especially with regard to residential premises.
83 Under Housing Act 1996, Pt I.
84 Secure Tenant's Charter (1998) p 1; Shorthold Tenant's Charter (1998) p 1. As examples of the additional rights: a shorthold tenant is entitled to advice from the landlord as to alternative accommodation when his tenancy ends (p 7) and to a 'responsive' repairs service (thus once notified, 24 hours for emergency repairs, seven calendar days for urgent repairs and 1 calendar month for routine repairs). The latter also applies to secure tenants within their Charter (p 11), but in view of the greater security of tenure, the right to advice as to alternative accommodation is not mentioned. There are dissonances between shorthold and secure tenants, and the success of Scottish social landlord and tenant Charters in dealing with these is analysed in Mullen, Scott, Fitzpatrick & Goodlad 62 MLR 11. It goes without saying that none of these Charter 'rights' apply to private sector shorthold tenants.

A further example of informal attempts at standardisation, or at least informal explanation, of some aspects of leases was a voluntary commercial leases Code of Practice, which explained the basic terms of a commercial lease, the risks of taking an upwards-only rent review clause, and which encouraged 'good practice' such as settling disputes by agreement rather than by litigation.[85] These are no doubt useful aims, but whether in the heat of litigation they would be adhered to is not clear, even though recent procedural reforms aim to encourage settlement out of court rather than litigation.[86]

Specific contents of leases

A formal lease by deed must state the names of each party, the duration of the term certain, the premises granted, and the covenants of the lease. In the case of a written lease or tenancy agreement these features will ordinarily be present also.

(i) Duration of lease

After the date of the lease, a statement as to its duration (giving a commencement date and a termination date) is obligatory, on pain of voidness, in the case of any lease for a term certain. The date of commencement may precede the date of execution of the lease, as where the tenant has taken possession under an agreement for a lease.

A lease stated to commence 'on' a specified date is presumed to commence as at that date.[87] By a curious rule of construction, should a lease commence 'from' a specified date, say 1 January, it is taken not to commence on that day, but on the day following. However, this rule readily yields to any contrary indications which demonstrate that the parties intended the lease to commence on the stated day, as where rent is payable in advance on 1 January, 'from' which date the term is stated to run.[88] The High Court has ruled that a lease expressed to run from 24 June 1984 until 24 December 2003, ie from one specified date to another, ran as from 24 June 1984, so rebutting the presumption just mentioned.[89]

---

85 A new Code of Practice was launched in late April 2002. See Organ (2002) Estates Gazette, 27 April, p 146 .

86 See CPR 1998, Pt I (active management of cases by court) and CPR 1988, Pt 24 (procedure for settling a dispute without a trial); also Hindle (2000) Estates Gazette, 22 January, p 124; but for a critique see Herbert and Martin (2000) Estates Gazette, 5 February, p 139.

87 *Sidebotham v Holland* [1895] 1 QB 378, CA.

88 *Ladyman v Wirral Estates Ltd* [1968] 2 All ER 197; *Whelton Sinclair v Hyland* [1992] 2 EGLR 158, CA (where the parties were mistaken as to the correct commencement date of a renewed lease so that the application of the presumption would have left the premises undemised for one day).

89 *Meadfield Properties Ltd v Secretary of State for the Environment* [1995] 1 EGLR 39, thus rendering invalid a lessee's notice to terminate to expire on 23 June 1994, and so within ten years of the date of demise.

(ii) The premises

Premises demised by the lease will be defined, it is hoped clearly, and there may be a related statement as to the permitted use of the premises. Any ambiguities or uncertainties are resolved by the courts. Thus, a lease of 'land', which includes premises, will normally also include the outside of external walls. Where a long lease demised buildings and premises, it was held that the roof passed with the demise.[90] The question of the scope of any particular demise is one of fact.[91] In the case of flats, the demise of a flat is presumed to include the external walls enclosing it[92] but not the external walls of other flats in the same building.[93] A demise may also include any void spaces between the actual and 'false' ceilings of a sub-divided house.[94] It is presumed that a demise will include everything below ground level in a vertical line, such as a cellar, in the absence of specific words of exclusion.[95] In a lease 'with appurtenances', 'appurtenances' includes only such things as outhouses, yards and gardens.[96] If an upper floor of premises is demised separately from lower floors, the use of staircases passes (in principle) as an appurtenance to the upper floor tenant, on the basis of necessity if the staircase is the sole means of access as at the date of the demise.[97] A right of way in favour of the demised premises will pass as an 'appurtenance' if enjoyed at the date of the lease.[98]

Some leases, especially for a long term, contain exceptions and reservations.

1 Exceptions. A lease of land is presumed to include everything above and beneath the surface but the landlord may limit the physical extent of his grant by expressly excluding from it some part of the land such as a field, a building, or mines and minerals, or sporting rights.[99]

2 Reservations. These are new rights created in the lease in favour of the landlord subject to which the tenant will take the property, as with the landlord reserving himself a right of way over the demised premises, or reserving a right to build to any height on adjoining land notwithstanding that the buildings may obstruct any light on the demised premises.[100] Any reservations must be expressly made in the lease,[101] except in the case of a way of necessity.[102] Reservations are construed against the

---

90 *Straudley Investments Ltd v Barpress Ltd* [1987] 1 EGLR 69, CA.
91 *Douglas-Scott v Scorgie* [1984] 1 All ER 1086, [1984] 1 WLR 716, CA.
92 *Sturge v Hackett* [1962] 3 All ER 166, [1962] 1 WLR 1257, CA.
93 *Campden Hill Towers v Gardner* [1977] QB 823, [1977] 1 All ER 739, CA.
94 *Greystone Property Investments Ltd v Margulies* (1983) 47 P & CR 472, CA.
95 *Grigsby v Melville* [1973] 3 All ER 455, [1974] 1 WLR 80, CA.
96 *Trim v Sturminster RDC* [1938] 2 KB 508, [1938] 2 All ER 168, CA.
97 *Altmann v Boatman* (1963) 186 Estates Gazette 109, CA.
98 *Hansford v Jago* [1921] 1 Ch 322.
99 See eg *Mason v Clarke* [1955] AC 778, [1955] 1 All ER 914, HL.
100 *Foster v Lyons* [1927] 1 Ch 219.
101 *Re Webb's Lease* [1951] Ch 808, [1951] 1 All ER 131, CA.
102 *Liddiard v Waldron* [1934] 1 KB 435, CA.

landlord.[103] Thus a wide reservation entitling the landlord to do acts which would otherwise constitute a nuisance or an interference with easements was construed as being subject to an implied limitation that the lessees would not be deprived of all access.[104]

(iii) Other parts of lease

Any lease would be expected to reserve a rent payable by the tenant, by an initial formula which indicates the annual amount payable in sterling, and the intervals at which the rent is payable, which may be half-yearly, quarterly, monthly or weekly, and in principle on a given day in the month. Many modern leases make provision for the landlord's privilege of a rent review, under which the rent is to be revised upwards, or even downwards, at fixed intervals agreed in advance, say every five years.

Properly-drawn leases contain express covenants or obligations undertaken by both the landlord and tenant. These deal with every aspect of the relationship of the parties, and are discussed in Part B of this book. Thus the landlord may covenant for quiet enjoyment by the tenant, and undertake to insure the premises. As well as being liable for rent, the tenant may undertake to use the premises in only a specified manner, not to alter them, and to keep them in repair. If the landlord wishes to be able to forfeit (or terminate early) a lease for breaches by the lessee of his covenants, he will have to insert a proviso for re-entry or forfeiture.

The lease may also contain *options* by the tenant to purchase the reversion or to renew, and options by the landlord or tenant to break the lease during the term certain. Some leases provide that it is a *condition* of the lease that the tenant does not become insolvent or bankrupt, so terminating the lease on either event. Leases may contain *schedules*, which, as noted, make detailed provisions for general matters specified in the lease, such as rent review procedures or detailed repairing obligations. There may also be a schedule of fixtures, notably where the premises are let with fixtures or furniture, as well as a schedule of condition, which gives the condition of the premises at the date of the lease so that, if this deteriorates due to the tenant's failure in breach of covenant to repair, the landlord may more easily establish his right to forfeiture or damages.

Freedom of contract

In the traditional view of the common law, freedom of contract prevails in the negotiation and fixing of leasehold obligations. This view may be realistic in the case of some

---

103 *St Edmundsbury and Ipswich Diocesan Board of Finance v Clark (No 2)* [1975] 1 All ER 772, [1975] 1 WLR 468, CA; as in *Trailfinders Ltd v Razuki* [1988] 2 EGLR 46.
104 *Overcom Properties Ltd v Stockleigh Hall Residents Management* [1989] 1 EGLR 75. See also *Paragon Finance plc v City of London Real Property Co Ltd* [2002] L & TR 9, [2002] L & TR 139.

business leases although as we have seen, a different climate may be taking hold in the case of some residential tenancies. In the field of rent review, although standard forms are produced by the Law Society and RICS, some parties prefer to use their own, specifically negotiated terms, at the risk of uncertainty of interpretation. Some variety in clauses may be inevitable, if only because premises differ in their nature. On the other hand, certain types of covenant, as in the case of quiet enjoyment or limiting assignments or alterations, because they have similar overall aims irrespective of detailed differences in the type of premises, may not necessarily differ greatly as between different types of lease or premises.

Unconscionable bargains

The common law traditionally holds that, while a party to an executed lease may later find its terms onerous or even harsh, the only ground for rescission of such a lease is fraud or negligent misstatement. Equity is prepared to go further than this. The Privy Council has held that an executed lease may be set aside if it appears that the terms of the lease have been imposed by one party on the other in a morally reprehensible manner so as to affect his conscience.[105] Accordingly, a renewed lease was set aside because the tenant had taken an unconscionable advantage of the age, poverty and ignorance of the landlord, facts known to the tenant at the date of renewal, to secure an advantageous renewal for herself. The Privy Council, however, rejected the notion that an executed lease could be set aside by equity on the ground that the landlord and tenant had unequal bargaining strength, or that the terms of the lease had been harsh, foolish or even unreasonable. The basis of this doctrine is similar to that applying to rescission – unconscionable behaviour and the taking advantage of another party's known vulnerability. It was the unconscionable use by the tenant of the disabling circumstances of the landlord which raised an equity against the tenant in that case.

Non-application of the Unfair Contract Terms Act 1977 to leases

The High Court has twice held that the Unfair Contract Terms Act 1977 does not apply to the covenants of a lease, and its exclusion is not confined to the words of demise.[106] These rulings were approved without any demur in the Court of Appeal in relation to a clause in a lease forbidding the use by the tenant of the equitable right of set-off.[107] Hence, the courts cannot subject any of the terms of a lease to the statutory unfairness test. This seems difficult to justify in an age of consumerism, although in the context of the rulings, which dealt with business leases, it could be argued that there is no

---

105 *Boustany v Piggott* (1993) 69 P & CR 298; Pawlowski [1995] Conv 454.
106 *Electricity Supply Nominees Ltd v IAF Group plc* [1993] 3 All ER 372; *Star Rider v Inntrepeneur* [1998] 1 EGLR 53.
107 *Unchained Growth III plc v Granby Village (Manchester) Management Co Ltd* [2000] L & TR 186. This result is a good example of the continuing vitality of the proprietary approach to leases although the ruling was in terms justified by 'commercial reality'.

special need to protect tenants.[108] The Law Commission are working on a reform package as discussed below.

Impact of Unfair Terms in Consumer Contracts Regulations 1999, SI 1999/2083

(i) Background

On 22 July 1999, Regulations, in force from 1 October 1999, were promulgated to give effect to a European Union directive.[109] In essence, if these Regulations apply to residential as opposed to business leases, then some of these may be subject to a test of unfairness, so opening up a wide and uncharted field of challenge for tenants.

(ii) Comments

The common law regards a lease, because it passes an estate in land, as one consistent whole, which is why neither its operative words of demise nor its terms are not subject to the Unfair Contract Terms Act 1977. Hence, as a matter of first impression, these Regulations, which speak of a 'supplier', rather than 'landlord' and a 'consumer' rather than 'tenant', would seem not appropriate to leases or at their terms, save by adopting a strained interpretation of their language.[110] Nevertheless, these Regulations, however ill-suited to traditional views of the matter, probably apply to residential tenancies, if these are in truth mere 'land contracts'.[111] The Office of Fair Trading assumes that the Regulations apply to assured and to assured shorthold tenancies.

(iii) Basic requirements

The Regulations require that 'a seller or supplier' (the landlord) must ensure that any written term of a contract is expressed in 'plain, intelligible' language (Unfair Terms in Consumer Contracts Regulations 1999, SI 1999/2083, reg 7(1)).[112] If the contract is

---

108 However, the assumption that all business tenants without distinction can look after themselves, at a time when so many lessors are large corporations, is open to doubt: see *Reste Realty Corpn v Cooper* 3 ALR 3d 1341 at 1348 (1969) (New J Sup Ct).

109 Unfair Terms in Consumer Contracts Regulations 1999, SI 1999/2083. See Bright 20 (2000) LS 331. It is understood that the Law Commission will be consulting as to a more comprehensive measure: Law Commission Annual Report (2000) (No 268) p 24.

110 The Regulations seem applicable to certain types of licence to occupy, as these are, on first principles, contractual in nature even though a person who licences another to occupy a room or rooms in his house or flat, whilst still residing there, might not necessarily be 'acting' for purposes related to his profession.

111 Bright and Bright (1995) 111 LQR 655 (on the previous version of the Regulations).

112 The phrase 'this does not affect your statutory rights' would seem to be within the purview of this regulation: see Bulletin No 4 (1997) issued by the Office of Fair Trading; also Adams [1999] Conv 8. Thus a reference to landlords' obligations 'under the Landlord and Tenant Act 1985, s 11' might also be caught.

capable of continuing without the unfair term it continues to bind the parties (Unfair Terms in Consumer Contracts Regulations 1999, SI 1999/2083, reg 8(2)). Thus if anti-set-off clauses in a secure or an assured or assured shorthold tenancy were thought to fail the fairness test, and to be void, the tenant would presumably have to go on paying rent at the rate originally agreed. A new feature of the Unfair Terms in Consumer Contracts Regulations 1999, SI 1999/2083 when compared to the previous version is the sweeping powers in the Director General of Fair Trading, reflecting determination of Brussels to promote what it sees as consumer protection.[113] For example, the Director has power to apply for an injunction against any person who is using or appearing to him to be using an unfair term drawn up for general use in contracts concluded with consumers (Unfair Terms in Consumer Contracts Regulations 1999, SI 1999/2083, reg 12). Thus if the Director decided, that an anti-set off clause fell foul of the fairness test, he could not only prevent its use in the residential tenancy concerned but apparently in residential tenancies generally. What is more, certain qualifying bodies such as the Consumer Association have the same right to ask for an injunction as the Director. Both may publish guidance for the use of consumers and suppliers (Unfair Terms in Consumer Contracts Regulations 1999, SI 1999/2083, reg 15) and both have sweeping powers to obtain documents and information (Unfair Terms in Consumer Contracts Regulations 1999, SI 1999/2083, reg 13).

(iv) Limits to scope of Unfair Terms in Consumer Contracts Regulations (SI 1999/2083)

Despite their width, there are some limits to the scope of the 1999 Regulations:

1   only *residential tenancies* would be caught, and only those tenancies granted by such bodies as companies, local authorities, housing associations or Government departments. This is because the 'consumer' (including, doubtless, a tenant) must act for purposes outside his business; but the 'supplier' (so including a landlord) must grant the agreement for the purposes of his trade or business, including the activities of local authorities and the like (Unfair Terms in Consumer Contracts Regulations 1999, SI 1999/2083, reg 3). The terms do not apply to any contractual term that reflects a mandatory statutory or regulatory provision (Unfair Terms in Consumer Contracts Regulations 1999, SI 1999/2083, reg 4(2)), such as under the Rent Act 1977. However, they do require that the terms of the tenancy are in plain, intelligible language. The Unfair Terms in Consumer Contracts Regulations 1999, SI 1999/2083 do not apply to terms which have been individually negotiated. However, it is understood that the Law Commission will be recommending that the Regulations should extend to individually negotiated terms;[114]

---

113 It is not clear if an individual tenant can enforce the Regulations directly.
114 Law Commission Consultation Paper No 162 (2002) 'Renting Homes' para 6.48. At the time this book went to press, the Law Commission Report on Unfair Terms in Contracts had not appeared.

2 the main *effect* of the Regulations is that any term which has not been individually negotiated is regarded as unfair, if contrary to a requirement of good faith,[115] it causes a significant imbalance in the parties' rights and obligations to the detriment of the 'consumer' (Unfair Terms in Consumer Contracts Regulations 1999, SI 1999/2083, reg 5(1)). We then discover that a term is always regarded as not individually negotiated,[116] raising the prospect of its being unfair, if it is drafted in advance and the 'consumer' cannot influence its substance (Unfair Terms in Consumer Contracts Regulations 1999, SI 1999/2083, reg 5(2)). Therefore, if a residential lessee is presented with a term which is in a standard-form tenancy agreement presented to him for signature, he may be able to argue that he is not bound by it simply for that reason, provided the 'imbalance' test is satisfied. In addition, however, even if any term is individually negotiated, the Regulations may still apply if an overall assessment of the 'contract' indicates that it is a 'pre-formulated standard contract' (Unfair Terms in Consumer Contracts Regulations 1999, SI 1999/2083, reg 5(3)). Fairness within the 1999 Regulations itself suggests that a term is not to be unfairly imbalanced against the tenant (an example being an absolute prohibition on assignments, which can prevent a residential tenant from assigning the tenancy to an equally good assignee, so locking the tenant into the tenancy until it terminates). Forfeiture clauses for minor breaches of covenant would seem to be another example of a disproportionate and so unfair clause; and

3 these rules do not apply to any term which 'defines the main subject-matter of the contract' or which concerns the adequacy of the price or remuneration, as against the goods sold or supplied, provided however that the requirement of plainness intelligibility of language is complied with (Unfair Terms in Consumer Contracts Regulations 1999, SI 1999/2083, reg 6(2)). This latter exclusion, on economic grounds, no doubt, is significant: it shows that a prime aspect of the tenancy bargain, the initial rent due, is unaffected by the Regulations. The operative words of a lease (such as the words of demise as well as, presumably, the reservation of rent clause or clauses defining the demised premises and rights attached to them) are not subject to the Regulations. These major exclusions limit the regulatory impact to matters of detail.

(v) Terms which might be caught

The Regulations may affect many specific terms of assured and assured shorthold tenancies. The Office of Fair Trading has recently produced guidance in this specific area,[117] with a long list of potentially unfair terms in such tenancies which it says it will object to, and which it expects those using standard-form tenancy agreements to

---

115 An assessment of good faith is to be made and requires regard to be had to a number of specified matters, such as the strength of the bargaining position of the parties.

116 The onus is on the 'supplier' to claiming that a term was individually negotiated to show that it was.

117 OFT 'Guidance on Unfair Terms in Tenancy Agreements' (2001).

adjust in the light of the guidance. The OFT explain that the good faith test means that not only should a term not be used in a deceitful way, it should not be capable of being used in that way. In addition, the landlord must not take advantage of the tenant's necessity for accommodation or lack of experience. The good faith requirement, to them, looks to good standards of commercial morality and practice.[118] Among terms which they say offend against the spirit of the Unfair Terms in Consumer Contracts Regulations 1999, SI 1999/2083 are the following:

1   a term ruling out any right by the tenant to resort to set off of rent, although a term discouraging a tenant from setting off excessively large sums would not be outlawed;[119]

2   rent review clauses which fail to specify the timing of the rent revisions and which fail to refer the rent review to an objective decision-maker such as an independent expert, or to a prices index;[120]

3   a term under which the tenant has to make a substantial prepayment or deposit, which cannot be refunded, before the tenancy is signed;[121]

4   a clause under which the landlord can make a windfall profit out of a security deposit, ie a profit over and above the reasonable costs of the landlord in rectifying the results of the tenant having failed to take reasonable care of the premises;[122]

5   a term requiring the tenant to pay interest much in excess of the base rate where rent arrears have accumulated;[123]

6   a term which misleadingly seeks to shift liability for structural and external repairs from the landlord to the tenant;[124] and

7   an absolute prohibition on assignments and sub-lettings (at least where not confined to the initial period of the tenancy) would offend, in the view of the OFT, the Unfair Terms in Consumer Contracts Regulations 1999, SI 1999/2083.[125]

118 OFT 'Guidance on Unfair Terms in Tenancy Agreements' (2001) p 3.
119 OFT 'Guidance on Unfair Terms in Tenancy Agreements' (2001) p 13.
120 OFT 'Guidance on Unfair Terms in Tenancy Agreements' (2001) pp 32-33 (thus there seem to be merits, after all, in the French and other systems of indexation: see ch 8, below).
121 OFT 'Guidance on Unfair Terms in Tenancy Agreements' (2001) p 17.
122 OFT 'Guidance on Unfair Terms in Tenancy Agreements' (2001) p 20. If, on this view, the defect is minor and easily put right, the clause would offend against the Unfair Terms in Consumer Contracts Regulations 1999, SI 1999/2083 because it is indiscriminate in its operation, the severity of the breach not being taken into account.
123 OFT 'Guidance on Unfair Terms in Tenancy Agreements' (2001) p 19; also prima facie unfair in the OFT view would be a clause entitling a landlord to recover all his legal costs and expenses, as opposed to those reasonably incurred. In both cases the financial sanction imposed on the tenant is excessive and contrary to the Unfair Terms in Consumer Contracts Regulations 1999, SI 1999/2083.
124 OFT 'Guidance on Unfair Terms in Tenancy Agreements' (2001) p 8; also, a term in a tenancy of furnished premises which purported to exclude the common law duty of landlords as to fitness for habitation at the start of the tenancy. These are unfair exclusions of landlord liability.
125 OFT 'Guidance on Unfair Terms in Tenancy Agreements' (2001) p 47. The OFT also list a range of other potentially unfair terms, such as an obligation to drain down appliances whenever

A term allowing one party only to exercise a right denied to the other party would also seem to fall foul of the spirit of the Regulations, such as a break clause conferring on the landlord a right to terminate the tenancy before its nominal termination date.

Consumerism invades residential landlord and tenant

The advent of the Unfair Terms in Consumer Contracts Regulations 1999, SI 1999/2083 shows that there is a shift towards treating tenants as the consumers of a service: the provision by the landlord of accommodation in return for payment. As is mentioned in relation to repairing obligations, this shift has been observed in some States in the US, where, as may be imagined, consumerism is a powerful trend. The Law Commission seem to approve of this approach and are suggesting its formal incorporation into new primary and delegated landlord and tenant legislation.

In a Consultation Paper published just before this book went to press,[126] the Law Commission expressly stated their policy: to develop a consumer approach to regulating the residential housing relationship. They suggest that the parties would have to draw up a written, comprehensive, plainly-written contract or agreement. The format of the written agreement would be laid down in delegated legislation. In effect, there would be a model agreement. The agreement would apply to any contract for rent for the occupation of the tenant or 'occupier's' home, so extending both to tenancies and licences. The duty to provide the written agreement would fall on the landlord.[127] Failure to provide a written agreement in a timely fashion would attract penalties. Thus, the tenant could withhold rent payments from a defaulting landlord. There might even be criminal penalties against such landlords. Rent payments ought to be recorded. Tenants would benefit from a proposed presumption of statute that rent had been paid making records of rent payments highly relevant.[128] The written agreement, suggested by the Commission, would have to contain certain core terms, notably, the names and addresses of the parties, the address and details of the property, the rent, and the commencement and termination date of any fixed term.[129] The agreement, as to whose details consultation with interested bodies is suggested, would also have compulsory terms, such as to security of tenure and legally implied terms (both as to

---

the premises are left vacant. This would be too indiscriminating. No objection will be taken by to OFT if the relevant term required the tenant to drain down appliances if absent for significant periods in winter (p 53). A similarly indiscriminate term would also be a general requirement to keep the property and furnishings clean and dusted at all times. A prohibition against having guests overnight as well as a term banning keeping pets are seen as unnecessarily restrictive (p 54).

126 Law Commission Consultation Paper No 162 (2002) 'Renting Homes'. The Commission intend to produce their Final Report and Draft Bill during the summer of 2003.
127 Law Commission Consultation Paper No 162 (2002) 'Renting Homes', para 6.75.
128 Law Commission Consultation Paper No 162 (2002) 'Renting Homes' para 6.85.
129 Law Commission Consultation Paper No 162 (2002) 'Renting Homes', para 6.101. Views were invited as to what other terms should be considered to be core terms.

repairs and quiet enjoyment). These could not be contracted out of.[130] In addition, the Commission are floating the idea, as part of this new package, of having a section in the model agreement for express terms. These alone could be freely negotiated. But there would also be default terms: the present suggestion of the Commission is that a list of default terms would be supplied by delegated legislation.[131] Default terms would take effect if, for example, an express term were held to be unfair.

130 Law Commission Consultation Paper No 162 (2002) 'Renting Homes' paras 6.108 ff.
131 Law Commission Consultation Paper No 162 (2002) 'Renting Homes' paras 6.112 ff.

Principal rights and obligations of the parties to a lease or tenancy

CHAPTER 5

Covenants generally

I INTRODUCTION

Most fixed-term leases and tenancies contain express covenants or obligations entered into by the landlord and the tenant: not many parties are content to allow their relationship to rest solely on implied obligations. The obligations entered into by a landlord and tenant are enforceable not merely between the original parties, but by and against any person who takes an assignment of the landlord's reversion or the lease. The benefit and burden of positive and negative covenants of a lease[1] are annexed to the demised premises and the reversion. The law governing the enforcement of leasehold covenants, which originates from the sixteenth century[2] has been recast and reformed by statute, as from 1 January 1996.[3] Much of this chapter is therefore devoted to a consideration of the way in which leasehold covenants may be enforced after an assignment of the lease or the reversion. No particular form of words is required to create a covenant and the question is one of construction in each case. Thus, a recent form of lease contains covenants by the tenant under the heading 'tenant's obligations' and states that, for example, the tenant 'is to pay' the rent, and 'is to comply' with certain user obligations.[4]

Dependent and independent covenants

Some covenants may contain two limbs, and others, such as those for repairs and to pay rent or service charges, are related. Disputes may arise as to whether a party can

---

1   In the case of an assignment of an equitable lease, the mutual obligations of the parties were almost certainly (see, however, RJ Smith [1978] CLJ 98) enforceable as if there had been a lease by deed. The point has been put beyond doubt by the Landlord and Tenant (Covenants) Act 1995, s 28(1).

2   As shown by the citations in *City of London Corpn v Fell* [1994] 1 AC 458, 464B-465C, [1993] 4 All ER 968, 972D-973D, HL.

3   Landlord and Tenant (Covenants) Act 1995 (hereinafter LT(C)A 1995).

4   Law Society Business Lease (Whole Premises) cll 1 and 3.

avoid performing his obligations if the other fails to perform his own. The question has sometimes arisen in relation to covenants to repair, where one party undertakes to repair and the other to pay or contribute to the cost, or where one party agrees to supply materials and the other to carry out repairs.

The courts distinguish between *dependent* and *independent* covenants. The former creates a condition precedent to compliance by the other party with his obligation. The latter covenant requires performance by a party irrespective of whether the other party has performed his part. The question of into which type a given covenant falls is one of construction, and, particularly in older cases, some seemingly inconsistent results have been reached.[5] As a general guide, the court is more likely to hold that a covenant is dependent where the parties have, as with landlords' works which may require the payment by lessees of service charges, laid down a detailed procedure for the resolution, before any works are begun, of disputes between the parties as to the proposed method and costs of carrying out the work. Thus, where a landlord undertook, before commencing any major or substantial repairs, to submit to the tenants a copy of the specification and estimates, after which the tenant had time to object, the landlord, who ignored these procedures and undertook works, failed to recover some £36,707 in service charges from the lessees. The consultation procedures were a condition precedent to recovery of the charges, because of the dispute resolution procedure.[6]

The court is entitled to take into account any results flowing from an opposite construction, as where the landlord of an agricultural holding had undertaken to carry out certain repairs by September 1, the tenant agreeing to pay an increased rent as from the previous March. The two obligations were independent and the tenant could not avoid liability to pay the overdue rent on account of any default by the landlord with his repairing obligations.[7] Likewise, prompt payment by the lessee of a flat of his maintenance obligation was held not to be a condition precedent of his landlord's obligation to provide hot water and central heating, owing to the fact that if it were otherwise, the landlords, who had their remedies, could claim to be freed of all their maintenance obligations if the tenant failed to pay promptly.[8]

Collateral contracts

Although the terms of an executed lease are taken to be a complete record of the agreement of the parties, this is not so if the landlord made a representation, prior to the execution of the contract for a lease, which induced the tenant to sign the deed or other instrument. If so, the statement will amount to a collateral contract, provided it

---

5 Compare, eg *Tucker v Linger* (1882) 21 Ch D 18, CA and *Westacott v Hahn* [1918] 1 KB 495, CA.
6 *Northways Flats Management Co (Camden) Ltd v Wimpey Pension Trustees Ltd* [1992] 2 EGLR 42; also *CIN Properties Ltd v Barclays Bank plc* [1986] 1 EGLR 59, CA.
7 *Burton v Timmis* [1987] 1 EGLR 1, CA.
8 *Yorkbrook Investments Ltd v Batten* [1985] 2 EGLR 100, CA.

was intended to have contractual effect, as where the landlord makes a representation to the tenant as to the state of repair or fitness of the premises; or as where he undertakes, prior to such execution, to put down rabbits,[9] or that the drains of the house are in order,[10] or that there was (contrary to the fact) the benefit of planning permission for the whole building,[11] or that a lease would not when granted contain a beer tie.[12]

A tenant seeking to establish a collateral contract must prove, first, that the statement, which will be ordinarily a representation of fact, preceded the grant of the lease, and that it was intended to have contractual effect; secondly, that he would have refused to complete unless the representation was true; thirdly, the representation must not contradict the terms of the lease itself.[13] If the parties conduct further negotiations after the statement has been made, it will be harder to infer that the statement was intended as a collateral warranty, owing to the assumption that the written lease is a complete statement of the agreement between the parties.[14] The lapse of time between the making of the statement and the making of the formal lease will be taken into account: the longer the interval, the less likely it is that the statement will be treated as a collateral warranty.[15] If a covenant in the lease deals with the matter inconsistently with the alleged statement, the lease will prevail unless the landlord has estopped himself from enforcing that covenant, at least for the time being. Accordingly, where a landlord induced most sitting flat-tenants to take 99-year leases with full repairing covenants by promising the tenants to pay for initial roofing repairs, the landlord was held unable to recover the cost of these repairs from any of the tenants or their assigns as a result.[16] The tenant does not have to prove that a collateral warranty complies with the formal requirements of LP(MP)A 1989, s 2 since it supplements a lease and does not create an interest in land.[17]

Direct action

Some tenants may be able to make use of the Contracts (Rights of Third Parties) Act 1999, applying to contracts as from 11 May 2000, as by seeking to claim damages for

9   *Morgan v Griffith* (1871) LR 6 Exch 70.
10   *De Lassalle v Guildford* [1901] 2 KB 215, CA.
11   *Laurence v Lexcourt Holdings Ltd* [1978] 2 All ER 810, [1978] 1 WLR 1128.
12   *A 1406 Pub Co Ltd v Hoare* [2001] 23 EG 154 (CS).
13   *De Lassalle v Guildford* [1901] 2 KB 215, CA (lease silent about the drains); *Henderson v Arthur* [1907] 1 KB 10, CA.
14   *Inntrepreneur Pub Co v East Crown Ltd* [2000] 3 EGLR 31.
15   *Inntrepreneur Pub Co v East Crown Ltd* [2000] 3 EGLR 31.
16   *Brikom Investments Ltd v Carr* [1979] QB 467, [1979] 2 All ER 753, CA (the costs were recoverable under the strict terms of the lease). For a case where deceit was proved see *Gordon v Selico & Co* [1986] 1 EGLR 71, CA.
17   *Lotteryking Ltd v Amec Properties Ltd* [1995] 2 EGLR 13.

breach of a term in a contract made between the landlord and a third person.[18] It must be shown that the contract expressly provides that the tenant may enforce it, or that the contract purports to confer a benefit on the tenant (Contracts (Rights of Third Parties) Act 1999, s 1(1)). Thus if a landlord and his contractor agreed in a contract to put up a new building for letting, and the terms of the contract are in terms enforceable by all future tenants, any lessee of the premises would be entitled to bring an action on account, say, of construction defects, to the same extent as if he were the landlord and also as if he were named in the contract. However, it is understood that, at least in the commercial world, advantage is being taken of the fact that the Contracts (Rights of Third Parties) Act 1999 can be contracted out of (Contracts (Rights of Third Parties) Act 1999, s 1(2)), so limiting its benefit. Subject to that point, the Act might, especially if mutual enforcement of leasehold covenants is expressly envisaged, allow a tenant of neighbouring premises to enforce directly a covenant by a neighbouring lessee with their common landlord not to commit a nuisance, or not to make use of their premises for a use competing with the claimant tenant's trade, or to keep their premises open for trading at reasonable hours of business. In addition, some new leases may contain terms which, taking advantage of the Contracts (Rights of Third Parties) Act 1999, allow head landlords to enforce sub-lessees' covenants with a head lessee direct.[19]

II   GENERAL INTERPRETATION OF LEASEHOLD OBLIGATIONS

The courts have been evolving the principles which they make use of in interpreting leasehold obligations. A summary of what are conceived to be the main lines of their current approach is as follows.

1   In the House of Lords,[20] when considering whether to uphold as valid a notice to determine a commercial lease which contained an obvious mistake, Lord Steyn stated that in determining the meaning of the language of a commercial contract, the law generally favoured a commercially sensible construction. Words were to be interpreted in the way in which a reasonable commercial person would interpret them. The standard of that person was hostile to technical interpretations and to

18   The Act was passed following Law Com No 242 (1996) 'Privity of Contract'; see Bright and Williams (1999) 143 Sol Jo 1082; Perks (2000) 4 L & T R 21. For a case in which a landlord was ordered by the court to take forfeiture proceedings so as to comply with his obligation in the lease concerned to enforce lessees' covenants for the benefit of the plaintiff tenant see *Britel Corp NV v Orbach* (1997) 29 HLR 883, CA.

19   Where such a clause is absent, there would be difficulties as to direct enforcement: see *Amsprop Trading Ltd v Harris Distribution Ltd* [1997] 2 All ER 990 (where an attempt to make use of LPA 1925, s 56 failed, since no direct benefit was conferred on the freeholder as against the underlessees). Even where the Contracts (Rights of Third Parties) Act 1999, applies, unless the covenant specifies the freeholder as a person who may sue, the requirement of direct benefit might still have to be shown by him: see Bright and Williams (2000) Sol Jo 1082. It would not, on this view, suffice for a freeholder to show that the covenant benefited him.

20   *Mannai Investment Co Ltd v Eagle Star Life Assurance Co Ltd* [1997] AC 749 at 771. Also Lord Hoffmann, especially at 774-75; also *Investors Compensation Scheme Ltd v West Bromwich Building Society* [1998] 1 WLR 896 at 912.

undue niceties of language. This 'purposive' interpretation was contrasted unfavourably by Lord Steyn with a 'rigid and formalistic' approach. However, it should be borne in mind that in that case the tenant had made an obvious blunder which any reasonable landlord would have been able to realise could not be interpreted at face value.

2   It has been claimed that the courts will now shift towards an approach which pays much less attention than formerly was the case to the precise words of obligation used by the parties to a lease.[21] This claim is (with respect) not well founded. The Privy Council has ruled that if a formal document uses ordinary words, these will be given their ordinary meaning provided it is clear and unambiguous.[22] The courts, it was said, must not have recourse to the principles applying where there is an ambiguity in a lease where the words of a document were clear and unambiguous. Or, as has been put by the High Court,[23] only if it is apparent from the circumstances or as a result of a particular construction that something must have gone wrong, can the court abandon the dictionary and re-write the document in issue. It is true that High Court has also said[24] that it was 'well established' that the construction of a provision in a contract (and so in a lease) is to be determined by reference to the words the parties have used, the terms of the contract as a whole, its commercial purpose and the surrounding circumstances existing when the contract was entered into, at least in so far as these were known to both parties. However, the courts are not seemingly any more willing today than formerly to rewrite clear words in a lease.

3   The courts claim to give effect to the commercial purpose of a leasehold obligation, at least where the words of a lease are unclear or ambiguous, because they presume that the parties would intend a sensible result. Rent review clauses have sometimes only been made sense of on the basis of not adhering to a literal interpretation, so giving effect to their underlying purpose of inflation-proofing rents.[25] Their interpretation has on occasions even required that 'radical surgery'[26] is applied, if sense is to be made of a rent review clause as a whole in the context of the rest of the lease, with which it is taken to be consistent. Indeed, if the court cannot make sense of the words used in any leasehold obligation, it is entitled to abjure strict grammar to give the words what it regards as their true meaning.[27] It is also entitled to modify the ordinary meaning of words to avoid absurdities.[28]

---

21   See Morgan (1999) 3 L & T Rev 88.
22   *Melanesian Mission Trust v Australian Mutual Provident Society* [1997] 2 EGLR 128 at 129. As to the effect of a purely technical omission, see *First Property Growth Partnership LP v Royal Sun Alliance Property Services Ltd* [2002] EWHC 305.
23   In *HSBC Bank plc v Liberty Mutual Insurance Company* (UK) Ltd (2001) Times, 11 June.
24   In *Westside Nominees Ltd v Bolton MBC* (2000) L & TR 533 at 537; also *Holding & Barnes plc v Hill House Hammond Ltd* (2000) L & TR 428 at 433.
25   *Basingstoke and Deane BC v Host Group plc* [1988] 1 All ER 824, CA.
26   As in *Pearl Assurance plc v Shaw* [1985] 1 EGLR 92.
27   *Gilje v Charlegrove Securities Ltd* [2000] 3 EGLR 89 at 92.
28   *Jollybird Ltd v Fairzone Ltd* [1990] 2 EGLR 55 at 58, CA; also *Stapel v Bellshore Property Investments Ltd* [2001] 20 EG 231 (both these cases were dealing with complex service charge clauses).

4   Because the parties to a business lease, in contrast to, say, a residential tenant for a short term, have or may be assumed to have had, access to legal advice, persuading a court to ignore the meaning of precise words used in a particular covenant will not be easy, as where a number of expressions were used in a landlord's maintenance obligation to take it beyond merely carrying out repairs. The court enforced the meaning of these additional words.[29] In any case, the parties to a lease may have good reasons for agreeing to a form of words which produced a result which others might find surprising.[30]

5   The courts do not initially approach the meaning of words used in a disputed obligation in a lease by reference to earlier cases which use similar or even identical words, if only because the circumstances of each lease may differ. Once the court has made up its mind initially as to the meaning of the words used, it may then look at other authorities to see if these assist it to assess the view it has already formed.[31] This principle, respecting the objective intentions of the parties, has to be balanced against the need for consistency and certainty in the law, which it is suggested the House of Lords may have underestimated in its recent utterances. At all events, it has been said that in the field of rent review (and we would also add repairing obligations) the courts should approach questions of construction in a consistent way where possible, and provided the language used by the parties allows such an approach.[32]

III   ENFORCEABILITY OF COVENANTS IN GENERAL

1 Introduction. There are currently two sets of rules which govern the enforcement of covenants in a lease. Tenancies granted as from the commencement of LT(C)A 1995, which came into force on 1 January 1996,[33] are governed by this new code. The Act was prompted by a wish mainly to ease the position of business tenants. In that connection, a tenancy which has been renewed by agreement or following statutory procedures will count within LT(C)A 1995 as a 'new tenancy' and be subject to the new rules. Thus, the rather archaic and technical rules governing enforcement of leasehold covenants for 'old tenancies' will be shrinking in significance.

2 Basis of old tenancy rules. The old rules are based on the notion that liability to perform leasehold covenants is governed by two principles. As between the original landlord and the original tenant, the parties are said to be in *privity of contract*. All

29   *Crédit Suisse v Beegas Nominees Ltd* [1994] 4 All ER 803.
30   *Holding & Barnes plc v Hill House Hammond Ltd* (2000) L & TR 428 at 433. This would not disentitle the court to depart from the primary meaning or effect of the words used, as it indeed did in that case, where a gap in repairing obligations had been left by the parties.
31   *Crédit Suisse v Beegas Nominees Ltd* [1994] 4 All ER 803. At the same time, when considering an expression which is well-worn, such as an obligation to 'keep in repair', the courts may well look at the authorities first as an aid to construction, especially in a non-commercial case: see eg *Eyre v McCracken* (2000) L & TR 411, CA.
32   *Westside Nominees Ltd v Bolton MBC* (2000) L & TR 533.
33   Landlord and Tenant (Covenants) Act 1995 Commencement Order 1995, SI 1995/2963.

covenants in the lease are enforceable against both parties. If the tenant voluntarily assigns the lease[34] then the assignee, not having originally entered into the lease, is not in privity of contract with the landlord. He holds by *privity of estate*, however, as having a leasehold tenure with the landlord. Consequently, any covenant which runs with the land, as with standard tenants' covenants, such as to pay rent or service charges, or to undertake repairs, or to use the premises only as permitted by the lease, is enforceable against an assignee by the landlord. Likewise, an assignee may enforce the burden of landlords' covenants which run with the land against the landlord, whether he is the original landlord or a person to whom the reversion has been assigned, on the basis of privity of estate (the direct relationship of landlord and tenant) between them. Once the current assignee in possession has re-assigned the lease, he loses privity of estate with the then landlord automatically. The new assignee is subjected to the burden and subject to the benefit of the tenants' and landlords' covenants of the lease. The erstwhile assignee is freed at common law from the burdens and cannot claim any benefits under the leasehold covenants, as from the assignment date. However, the landlord may procure from the assigning assignee a covenant to observe the covenants in the lease until the end of the term, despite his having lost possession of the premises.

3 Vulnerability of original tenants under old tenancy rules. An original tenant, because he personally covenanted to observe the covenants of the lease until its contractual expiry date, is subjected by the common law, in the absence of release by the landlord, to a continuing liability to observe the burden of tenants' covenants until that date, despite his having assigned the lease and lost the estate in the land.[35] During times of economic stability, the continuing subjection of an original lessee to the burden of having to pay rent or service charges owed by any assignee for the time being, or to pay the landlord damages on account of dilapidations caused by an assignee, might not have seemed oppressive, perhaps because the solvency of assignees generally was more secure. In times of economic uncertainty and with harsher expectations of profit security, some business landlords have pressed home claims against original lessees, as well as against any person guaranteeing the performance of the original lessee, where they could not recover rent and service charges from an insolvent or bankrupt assignee.

4 Reform proposals. The Law Commission examined the law.[36] It considered that 'a landlord or tenant of property should not continue to enjoy rights nor be under any obligation arising from a lease once he has parted with all interest in the property'. It also believed that a lease should be regarded as a single bargain for letting the property. A successor should fully take the place of his predecessor, whether as landlord or tenant, and the distinction between covenants which ran with the land, or which touched and concerned it, and those which did not, should be abolished.

---

34   As opposed to making an assignment by operation of law, notably in bankruptcy and insolvency.
35   Nicholls LJ in *City of London Corpn v Fell* [1993] QB 589, 603-604, approved [1994] 1 AC 458, 465, [1993] 4 All ER 968, 973E, HL.
36   Law Com No 174 (1988) 'Privity of Contract and Estate' especially paras 4.1 and 4.46.

5 A new Act. Reform, although not quite on the lines proposed by the Law Commission, came with the LT(C)A 1995. This Act removes the liability of an original tenant for any breaches of covenant committed by his assignee or any other assignee, but not, as envisaged by the Commission,[37] in relation to an assignment of a tenancy in existence when LT(C)A 1995 came into force as from 1 January 1996. LT(C)A 1995 did away, in relation to 'new tenancies', with the ancient doctrine of covenants touching and concerning land, replacing it with a new concept of landlord and tenant covenants. It also re-cast the general rules as to enforcement of leasehold covenants, so that, for example, the doctrines of privity of contract and of estate have been done away with. Thus, a mortgagee in possession of a landlord's reversion is as much entitled to enforce 'tenant covenants' as would have been the landlord himself (LT(C)A 1995, s 15(1)(b)).

6 Statutory checks and balances. LT(C)A 1995 contains a number of checks and balances so as to render the abrogation of the 'privity of contract' liability of a tenant more palatable to commercial landlords, who were said to regard the new rule with unease, as affecting the stability of their rental income. The price of these checks and balances is a rather involved statutory scheme. For example, Parliament imposes strict time limits on the recovery of rent and service charges on landlords (LT(C)A 1995, s 17). LT(C)A 1995 also allows a landlord on an assignment of a commercial lease to obtain a tenants' guarantee (an 'authorised guarantee agreement') of the performance of his immediate assignee's obligations (LT(C)A 1995, s 16). Modest safeguards have been evolved by the courts for assigning tenants, so as to prevent guarantee agreements being imposed willy-nilly by landlords. The life of an 'authorised guarantee agreement' is limited. It does not extend to any period after the assignee has re-assigned the lease. If the immediate assignee defaults, and the tenant has to pay the landlord money on that account, he may be granted a reversionary or 'overriding' lease of the premises, so that he is able to enforce performance against the assignee, or terminate his lease and re-let the premises or occupy them himself.

IV   ENFORCEMENT OF COVENANTS IN RELATION 'OLD TENANCIES'

1   Liability of original lessee and lessor

General principles

An original tenant is liable to perform all the covenants in a lease granted before LT(C)A 1995 commenced, whether these are capable of running with the land because they touch and concern it, or are purely personal obligations to the landlord. If the original lessee expressly assigns the lease, he remains personally liable at common law[38] for the performance of any covenant that touches and concerns the land, such as, notably, to pay rent, or service charges reserved as rent or for repairs.

37   Law Com No 174 (1988) 'Privity of Contract and Estate' para 4.60.
38   Unless the landlord releases him at the time of the assignment or later.

This liability of an original lessee to pay for the results of the failure of his or any later assignee is strict. It seems to be based on the idea that the landlord must have at least one person to whom he may ultimately look for performance of the leasehold covenants, especially that to pay rent, throughout the common law term of the lease. It is for this reason that an original lessee could not plead as a complete defence to liability that the assignee had surrendered part of the premises to the landlord.[39] An original tenant may face a claim for assignees' rent arrears not only from the original landlord, but from an assignee of the reversion.[40]

The severity of the so-called privity principle (seeing that the tenant has no control over the performance of his obligations by any assignee in possession[41]) has been recently limited in two ways. First, the personal liability of an original lessee to observe leasehold covenants despite his having assigned the lease, runs only until the expiry of the contractual term agreed for the lease. It therefore does not extend to any continuation term under the Landlord and Tenant Act 1954, Pt II.[42] This principle yields to contrary language in the lease, as where the tenant remains liable during the lease and any extension of it by statute or otherwise.[43]

Secondly, it was held that a lessee who had covenanted to pay an annual rent of £12,000 throughout the term of his lease was not liable to pay the full claim of £38,462 of rent arrears, where it appeared that the lessor and an assignee of the lease had varied the original rent reservation so as to require the payment of an annual rent of £35,000. The deed of variation created an obligation not contemplated by the original lease, as between the landlord and the assignee, altering the estate, but not the obligations of the original lessee.[44]

The common law is consistent: an original landlord is under a similar continuing liability to observe any landlords' real covenants in the lease.[45] It has been suggested that the original landlord may be liable, under a real covenant, direct to an assignee who became tenant after the assignment of the reversion.[46]

---

39 *Baynton v Morgan* (1888) 22 QBD 74, CA; nor that a voluntary arrangement has been made in respect of the tenant's assignee: *March Estates Ltd v Gunmark Ltd* [1996] 2 EGLR 38.
40 *Arlesford Trading Co Ltd v Servansingh* [1971] 3 All ER 113, [1971] 1 WLR 1080, CA.
41 This fact is no defence to liability: *Thames Manufacturing Co Ltd v Perrotts (Nicol & Peyton) Ltd* (1984) 50 P & CR 1; hence the overriding lease provisions of LT(C)A 1995.
42 *City of London Corpn v Fell* [1994] 1 AC 458, [1993] 4 All ER 468, HL.
43 Even so, a tenant was not liable for interim rent as opposed to the lesser contractual rent, as the lease concerned did not expressly render him liable to pay the former sum: *City of London Corpn v Fell* [1994] 1 AC 458, [1993] 4 All ER 468, HL.
44 *Friends' Provident Life Office v British Railways Board* [1995] 2 EGLR 55, CA; see Bright in Jackson and Wilde (eds) *Reform of Property Law* (1997) ch 6; also *Metropolitan Properties Co (Regis) Ltd v Bartholomew* [1996] 1 EGLR 82, CA (where a subsequent variation in a lessee's obligations did not affect an earlier liability of a surety); and *Beegas Nominees Ltd v BHP Petroleum* [1998] L & TR 190 (where a 'stepped rent' memorandum agreed between an assignee and the landlords did not bind the original lessee).
45 *Stuart v Joy* [1904] 1 KB 362, CA.
46 *Celsteel Ltd v Alton House Holdings Ltd (No 2)* [1987] 2 All ER 240 at 244, CA.

So as to try to cover himself against his continuing liability under the privity of contract rule, the original lessee may, on assigning the lease, take an *express indemnity covenant* from the assignee – and the assignee in turn may act similarly on re-assigning.[47] Where a chain of indemnity covenants has thus been set up, and an original lessee is made to pay rent or other sums by the landlord, because the assignee in possession has defaulted, he in turn may claim an indemnity (the whole sums paid) from the assignee in possession, or, at his option, the person, if different, to whom he originally assigned the lease. The original lessee's right of recovery is quasi-contractual in nature: he is recovering moneys paid under compulsion to the landlord.[48]

Statutory mitigations of the principles

LT(C)A 1995 has introduced three mitigations of the full impact of the privity of contract rule as it applies to 'old-style' tenancies granted prior to 1 January 1996.[49] These mitigations also apply to any 'new tenancy' (ie one granted after LT(C)A 1995 commences), as where an assigning 'new tenant' has entered into an 'authorised guarantee agreement' in relation to his immediate assignee. No doubt the main beneficiary of the rules will be an original tenant where the assignee in possession has defaulted; where an intermediate assignee has expressly covenanted to observe covenants until the expiry of the lease, and has re-assigned, he could also invoke these rules. The rules cannot be contracted out of in the lease or tenancy and any 'agreement relating to a tenancy' (such as a term in the tenancy or collateral to it or a variation agreement) which has effect to 'exclude, modify or otherwise frustrate' these provisions is void (LT(C)A 1995, s 25(1)).

The first, and important, mitigation relates to the *time for recovery* of 'fixed charges' and is designed to prevent the landlord[50] from inflicting stale claims for such matters as rent, service charges or pre-determined sums payable on account of dilapidations[51] owed by the current assignee in possession, on the 'former tenant' who assigned him the lease. The essential rule is that the former tenant is not liable to pay 'any amount in respect of any fixed charge payable under the covenant unless, within the period of six months beginning with the date on which the charge becomes due'[52] the landlord

47 Covenants of indemnity are implied by LPA 1925, s 77(1)(C) and (D) (unregistered land) and Land Registration Act 1925, s 24(1)(b) and (2), but, with the enactment of LT(C)A 1995, Sch 2, these provisions cease to have effect in relation to tenancies granted after the commencement of the 1995 Act (LT(C)A 1995, s 30(3)).

48 *Moule v Garrett* (1872) LR 7 Ex 101; *Re Healing Research Trustee Co Ltd* [1992] 2 All ER 481. An intermediate assignee may claim against any person to whom he assigned, if he was not responsible for the breach.

49 See Fancourt *Enforceability of Leasehold Covenants* (1997) chs 20, 21 and 22.

50 Including any person entitled to enforce payment of the 'fixed charge' (LT(C)A 1995, s 17(6)), such as a management company.

51 'Fixed charges' are defined in LT(C)A 1995, s 17(6) so as to embrace all three types of sum.

52 A fixed charge due as at the commencement of LT(C)A 1995 is treated, in principle, for notice purposes as due at that date, so that the six month period for claiming it runs as from then (LT(C)A 1995, s 17(5)).

serves on this former tenant[53] a statutory notice in the prescribed form or in a form substantially to the same effect, otherwise the notice is not effective (LT(C)A 1995, ss 17(2) and 27(4)).[54] The former tenant, which expression includes an assignee of the lease who is no longer the tenant, owing to a re-assignment, is indeed only liable as the result of a timely notice to pay, in respect of sums caught by LT(C)A 1995, s 17.[55] The notice must inform the tenant that the 'fixed charge' is now due and that the landlord intends to recover from him the amount specified in the notice and interest on a specified basis: if the latter is not specified, it cannot be recovered. The amount stated in the notice is, by LT(C)A 1995, s 17(4), generally the limit of any claim the landlord may make for fixed charges against the former tenant or any guarantor of his (to whom the benefit of this rule extends by LT(C)A 1995, s 17(3), entitling him to a separate notice).[56] If a LT(C)A 1995, s 17 notice claims sums a landlord is not entitled to, it will still be valid, provided the notice includes sums to which he is in fact entitled.[57] This is because, in LT(C)A 1995, s 17(4), the sums claimed are not to exceed the amount specified, so that Parliament envisaged that smaller sums might be recoverable from the tenant.

The second alteration of the common law rules as they must have been thought to be relates to post-assignment variations as from the commencement of LT(C)A 1995, of tenancies which might increase the liability of the former tenant. Thus the demised premises might be changed, or their permitted user altered, or the amount of unit or shop floor space allotted to the current tenant might be varied by mutual agreement which becomes part of the lease. Any increased rent recoverable to the extent that it is referable to these types of variation cannot be recovered from the 'former tenant' (LT(C)A 1995, s 18(2)).[58] The scope of this relieving provision is narrow. Because it only applies to a variation which, at the time it was made, the landlord could have absolutely refused to allow (LT(C)A 1995, s 18(4)(a)), rent reviews are excluded from it.[59] Thus, a tenant who is under a continuing liability to pay rent until a tenancy

53   As to service see *Commercial Union Life Assurance Co Ltd v Moustafa* [1999] 2 EGLR 44 (service at last-known place of abode of tenant sufficient).

54   Ie Form No 1 of the forms prescribed in the Landlord and Tenant (Covenants) Act 1995 (Notices) Regulations 1995, SI 1995/2964.

55   *MW Kellogg Ltd v Tobin* [1999] L & TR 513. An assignee of the lease did not have to indemnify the tenant for two sums which could have been only claimed under a LT(C)A 1995, s 17(2) notice, had one been served in time. It was also held that s 17 did not apply to an indemnity covenant of an assignee of an 'old tenancy' as an indemnity covenant was purely personal.

56   If a landlord wishes to serve a LT(C)A 1995, s 17(3) notice he is not obliged to serve a LT(C)A 1995, s 17(2) notice on the former tenant as this step is not expressly required by the 1995 Act and would be otiose to imply into it: *Cheverell Estates Ltd v Harris* [1998] 1 EGLR 27.

57   *Commercial Union Life Assurance Co Ltd v Moustafa* [1999] 2 EGLR 44.

58   The benefit of this rule extends to a guarantor of the performance of the former tenant's obligations (LT(C)A 1995, s 18(3)).

59   As pointed out (*Privity of Contract* (1995) p 53), because of LT(C)A 1995, s 18(5) if an assignee carries out improvements within the Landlord and Tenant Act 1927 procedure, and an increase in rent resulted, a former tenant could not use LT(C)A 1995, s 18 to avoid paying that increase on the default of such assignee.

granted before the commencement of LT(C)A 1995 expires will still be subject to the risk of having to pay a rent inflated by an upwards review entered into between the landlord and an assignee, subject only to the notice requirements of LT(C)A 1995, s 17.

The third mitigation is that if a tenant or any guarantor of his obligations is subject to the privity of contract rule, he may, if, and only if, they pay all the moneys owed by any assignee as the result of a default notice under LT(C)A 1995, either may require the landlord by a 12-month-notice[60] to grant him an overriding lease under LT(C)A 1995, s 19.[61] If two persons have been served with a default notice, it seems that an overriding lease would be awarded to the first applicant (LT(C)A 1995, s 19(7)).[62] The landlord must comply with the request within a reasonable time of the request being received, on pain of breach of statutory duty (LT(C)A 1995, s 19(6)), unless the relevant tenancy has been determined (LT(C)A 1995, s 19(7)).[63] In principle the terms of the overriding lease are the same as those of the existing lease, although the parties may agree to make changes if they so wish. Purely personal covenants are, however, to be omitted.[64] With an overriding lease,[65] the legal costs of which are payable by the recipient of the lease, the erstwhile tenant or guarantor becomes the immediate landlord of the defaulting assignee for the term of his lease plus, in principle, three days (LT(C)A 1995, s 19(2)). He is then able to enforce his remedies against that person, including forfeiture of the lease and the re-possessing of the premises or granting a new lease to any other person.[66] These rules also apply to a tenant who holds a 'new tenancy' governed by the full benefit of LT(C)A 1995, if he has entered into an authorised guarantee agreement with the landlord as a condition of the assignment, and whose assignee has defaulted, leaving the former tenant with a liability to the landlord. An overriding lease must state which of the new or pre-1995 Act set of rules apply to it (LT(C)A 1995, s 20(1)). If an overriding lease is not within the reformed rules, the former tenant who holds it remains subject to the privity of contract rule vis-à-vis the head landlord, so placing him at a substantial potential disadvantage in the future if he cannot rid himself of the lease.

60   Given at the date of the payment or within 12 months of it (LT(C)A 1995, s 19(5)) but there is no prescribed form of notice. A written request would thus suffice.

61   See Elvidge and Williams *Estates Gazette* 23 November 1996, p 123.

62   Where an assignee of an old tenancy enters into a direct covenant with the landlord, on taking a lease, it undertakes to pay rent (in future) to the same extent as the original lessee: see *Beegas Nominees Ltd v BHP Petroleum Ltd* [1998] L & TR 190. If the assignee re-assigns, it is thus assumed that they could as appropriate claim an overriding lease.

63   Provision is made by LT(C)A 1995, s 17(8) for which of two or more competing requests for an overriding lease are to be acceded to by the landlord, where made on the same day.

64   No provision is made in LT(C)A 1995 requiring or dispensing with the consent of any superior landlord or mortgagee to the grant of an overriding lease.

65   Which binds any landlord's mortgagee, including chargee (LT(C)A 1995, s 20(7)), automatically (LT(C)A 1995, s 20(4)).

66   It has been said (*Privity of Contract* p 46) that if a landlord accepts rent arrears from a former tenant following a LT(C)A 1995, s 17 notice, that could waive (by conduct) a right to forfeit the occupation lease; if this is correct, and it is difficult to see how the landlord's waiver could bind the former tenant, then once the latter obtained an overriding lease, he would find that one of its purposes was frustrated.

Insolvency of assignee

Where, following the bankruptcy or insolvency of an assignee, the lease is disclaimed by the assignee's trustee in bankruptcy or liquidator, an original lessee remains, at common law, liable under the privity of contract rule, and so for unpaid rent to the landlord. Any guarantor of the original tenant is also liable. The disclaimer does not affect the right of the landlord, if a lease was granted before 1 January 1996, to have recourse to either party.[67] The original lessee may be as exposed in insolvency matters as elsewhere, since the assignee may alter his leasehold estate by entering into an arrangement with his creditors: the terms of the arrangement will bind the original lessee automatically, mitigated only by questions of construction as to the sums covered and the operative date of the arrangement.[68] In order to try to recoup his losses, the lessee is entitled to seek the restoration of a dissolved assignee company to the register of companies, so as to be able to claim an indemnity from him for moneys paid to the landlord.[69] A lessee or guarantor rendered liable in these circumstances could also seek to obtain an overriding lease under LT(C)A 1995, s 19.

Position of guarantors

If some person guarantees[70] or stands surety for the performance of an original tenant's or an assignee's obligation, his liability for breach of covenant,[71] although secondary, is co-extensive with the latter's liability. Indeed, the right of a landlord to enforce a covenant of guarantee passes automatically on any assignment by deed of the reversion.[72] Moreover, if a guarantor is released, this has no effect on the primary liability of the original tenant.[73] However, to avoid grave injustice, where a landlord received some £50,348 on account of rent due from a guarantor, whom he then released, he had to give credit for these sums against his claim for rent arrears from the original lessee.[74] If the lease has been disclaimed by the lessee's liquidator, the landlord may be entitled to require the guarantor to take a new lease, although if the requirement is made on or after 1 January 1996, the new lease will be subject to the 'new tenancies' covenant enforcement regime.[75]

---

67 *Hindcastle Ltd v Barbara Attenborough Associates Ltd* [1997] AC 70, [1996] 1 All ER 737, HL.
68 *Burford Midland Properties Ltd v Marley Extensions Ltd* [1995] 2 EGLR 15.
69 *Allied Dunbar Assurance plc v Fowle* [1994] 1 EGLR 122.
70 A written guarantee is not essential: this obligation may arise by implication, as in *Goodaston v FH Burgess plc* [1998] L & TR 46.
71 See eg *Knighton Estates Ltd v Gallic Management Co Ltd* [1998] EGCS 14 (where a release of a surety was not operative due to the lessee's failure to pay VAT).
72 *Kumar v Dunning* [1989] QB 193, [1987] 2 All ER 801, CA.
73 *Allied London Investments v Hambro Life Assurance* (1985) 50 P & CR 207, CA.
74 *Milverton Group Ltd v Warner World Ltd* [1995] 2 EGLR 28, CA.
75 See further Slessinger (2000) Sol Jo 725, noting that the guarantor will thus obtain an automatic release on assignment of the lease.

If, however, the terms of a lease are substantially varied so as to prejudice the guarantor, and his consent to the variation has not been sought,[76] the guarantor is released automatically at common law.[77] It is possible to avoid this result by clear language in the lease, but a statement in a surety covenant that any neglect or forbearance by the landlords in enforcing performance of a covenant against the lessee did not release the surety did not suffice to avoid an automatic release of the tenant's sureties, where the lease had been varied so as to allow the use of part of the premises as an off-licence.[78] Unfortunately for guarantors or sureties, once they have been forced lawfully to pay rent to a landlord, they cannot distrain for the rent nor bring forfeiture proceedings against the original tenant.[79]

2   Liability of assignees

We now discuss the common law principles on which leasehold covenants are enforceable by and against assignees of the reversion and of the lease. These apply to tenancies granted prior to the commencement of the LT(C)A 1995.

1   There must be *privity of estate* between the parties. In the present context, therefore, the parties must hold, directly, as landlord and tenant.[80] The assignee in possession is liable to perform and may enforce leasehold covenants, but once he parts with possession after a re-assignment, his liability to perform covenants ceases.

This doctrine has the effect that a person who does not directly hold a lease from a landlord might, but for statutory or equitable relaxations, be unable to enforce covenants against the landlord. However, owing to statute, a sub-tenant may claim the right to enforce a positive or negative covenant in the head lease against the head landlord, despite the lack of privity of estate between them.[81] Equity allows a head landlord to enforce directly the burden of a restrictive covenant contained in the head lease against a sub-lessee who has notice of it either by the covenant appearing in his sub-lease or owing to registration.

2   The covenant must be a real covenant: it must *touch and concern* the land. If this is not so, the covenant is a personal covenant and cannot be enforced by or against assignees, though it is enforceable between the original parties.

---

76   See generally HW Wilkinson (1995) 146 NLJ 1141.
77   See eg *West Horndon Industrial Park Ltd v Phoenix Timber Group plc* [1995] 1 EGLR 77.
78   *Howard de Walden Estates Ltd v Pasta Place Ltd* [1995] 1 EGLR 79.
79   *Re Russell* (1885) 29 Ch D 254 (distress); *BSE Trading Ltd v Hands* (1996) 75 P & CR 138 (forfeiture); see Mitchell [1998] Conv 133.
80   Therefore there must have been a legal assignment of the term; but equity has since *Boyer v Warbey* [1953] 1 QB 234, [1953] 1 All ER 269, CA, allowed the benefit (though apparently not the burden) of a lessee's covenant to pass on assignment of an equitable lease.
81   LPA 1925, s 78(1), which does not apply to tenancies granted after the commencement of the 1995 Act (LT(C)A 1995, s 30(4)).

Covenants touching and concerning land

The requirement that, to be enforceable by or against an assignee of the lease or the reversion a covenant must touch and concern the demised land, or, to use the language of statute, must have reference to the subject matter of the lease, is of ancient origin. The policy of this rule, which has become technical, is to limit the covenants that may be enforced against third parties, the right to enforce being itself a property interest. Covenants in a lease which directly affect the relationship of the parties as landlord and tenant, without regard to the personal identity of the particular parties concerned at any time, may be said to touch and concern the land, and so to run with it through successive assignments of the lease or the reversion. Thus, tenants' covenants to pay rent, insurance premiums, or service charges, as well as to repair, not to assign without consent,[82] not to make structural alterations and limiting the user of the premises will run with the land.

The House of Lords evolved four tests to be applied. A covenant will run with the land if:

1   it is beneficial to the owner of the land for the time being;
2   it affects the nature, quality, user or value of the landlord's land;
3   it is not in terms personal; and
4   the fact that a covenant is to pay a sum of money does not prevent it touching and concerning the land if (1) to (3) apply and the covenant is concerned with something to be done on, or in relation to the land.[83]

All implied covenants touch and concern land.[84] Conditions for re-entry for breaches of covenant which themselves touch and concern the land also do so.[85] Apart from these cases, there have been many examples of covenants which could have fallen into real covenants or personal covenants, and a few of these on either side may be given. A landlord's covenant for quiet enjoyment,[86] not to determine a quarterly tenancy during its first three years,[87] and to supply a housekeeper to clean flats[88] all touch and concern the demised land, as being of real value to any lessee. By contrast, a landlord's covenant to buy chattels, as opposed to fixtures at the end of the lease,[89] or to pay the tenant £500 unless the lease is renewed,[90] or to allow the tenant to display an advertising sign on other premises[91] were all classified as personal: one related to personal property, the other two did not have any direct bearing on the actual premises demised. More

82   As to which see *Goldstein v Sanders* [1915] 1 Ch 549.
83   *P & A Swift Investments v Combined English Stores Group plc* [1989] AC 632, [1988] 2 All ER 885, [1988] 3 WLR 313, HL.
84   *Wedd v Porter* [1916] 2 KB 91, CA.
85   See *Horsey Estate Ltd v Steiger* [1899] 2 QB 79, CA.
86   *Campbell v Lewis* (1820) 3 B & Ald 392.
87   *Breams Property Investment Co Ltd v Stroulger* [1948] 2 KB 1, [1948] 1 All ER 758, CA.
88   *Barnes v City of London Real Property Co* [1918] 2 Ch 18.
89   *Gorton v Gregory* (1862) 3 B & S 90.
90   *Re Hunter's Lease* [1942] Ch 124, [1942] 1 All ER 27.
91   *Re No 1 Albemarle Street W1* [1959] Ch 531, [1959] 1 All ER 250.

controversially, as showing the technical nature of the rule, it had been held that a landlord's covenant to return a deposit to the tenant at the end of the lease was personal and did not bind an assignee of the reversion,[92] whereas by contrast, a tenant's covenant to pay £40 towards redecoration on quitting ran with the land and bound his successor in title.[93]

A covenant by a surety of the tenant to accept a new lease from the landlord if the tenant became insolvent and his lease was disclaimed ran with the leasehold estate,[94] as of obvious value to any lessor, as did, for similar reasons, a covenant tying the lessees to petrol supplies of the lessor,[95] and a covenant from a third party to guarantee the performance of the tenant's obligations,[96] but not, for example, a tenant's covenant to repair chattels (not fixtures).[97]

Enforcement by and against assignees of lease

An assignee of the lease may sue (take the benefit) or be sued (be subject to the burden) of covenants in the lease which touch and concern the land, but, an assignee is liable only for breaches of covenant committed whilst there is privity of estate between himself and the landlord.[98]

In contrast to the original lessee, therefore, an assignee of the lease is not liable to the landlord for the time being[99] for breaches committed before the assignment, unless they are continuing breaches, as with a neglect to repair.[100] Nevertheless, it appears that if an original lessee has broken his covenant to repair, and assigns to a first assignee, who re-assigns to a second person, and the breach continued throughout, the second assignee (and ultimately the original lessee) are solely liable unless there is an express contrary stipulation when the lease was re-assigned.[101]

92 *Hua Chiao Commercial Bank v Chiaphua Industries Ltd* [1987] AC 99, [1987] 1 All ER 1110, PC; and equally curiously, a tenant's option to purchase is purely personal: *Woodall v Clifton* [1905] 2 Ch 257, as opposed to a landlord's covenant to renew, which is not: *Weg Motors Ltd v Hales* [1962] Ch 49, [1961] 3 All ER 181, CA.

93 *Boyer v Warbey* [1953] 1 QB 234, [1953] 1 All ER 269, CA.

94 *Coronation Street Industrial Properties Ltd v Ingall Industries plc* [1989] 1 All ER 979, [1989] 1 WLR 304, HL.

95 *Caerns Motor Services Ltd v Texaco Ltd* [1995] 1 All ER 247, [1994] 1 WLR 1249, even though successors in title were not mentioned.

96 *Kumar v Dunning* [1989] QB 193, [1987] 2 All ER 801, CA.

97 *Williams v Earle* (1868) LR 3 QB 739; nor a covenant to pay rates in respect of other land: *Gower v Postmaster General* (1887) 57 LT 527.

98 *Wharfland Ltd v South London Co-operative Building Co Ltd* [1995] 2 EGLR 21.

99 As against his potential liability to indemnify the original lessee or a previous assignee under covenants of indemnity.

100 *Granada Theatres Ltd v Freehold Investments (Leytonstone) Ltd* [1959] Ch 592, [1959] 2 All ER 176.

101 *Middlegate Properties Ltd v Bilbao* (1972) 24 P & CR 329.

An assignee of the lease is similarly not liable for any breaches of covenant committed by a person to whom he re-assigns the lease. This rule may be contracted out of by an express agreement, as where on taking an assignment the assignee covenants direct with the landlord to observe all the covenants in the lease and to pay the rent: in this case the assignee's liability for breaches of covenant commences with the date of the assignment and continues from then until the expiry of the term, co-extensively with the liability of the original tenant.[102] This process of direct covenanting with the landlord may take place each time the lease is assigned. Suppose that L grants a lease to T, who assigns to A, who in turn assigns to X, who assigns to Y, who is in default with rent payments. If L releases T on the assignment to A, this will not, in the absence of an express indication of intention to release X, automatically release X.[103]

Enforcement by and against assignees of reversion

Where the original landlord assigns by deed the reversion of a lease or tenancy granted before LT(C)A 1995 commences,[104] statute provides for the enforcement by and against the assignee of the freehold (or superior leasehold) reversion of the benefit and burden of the real covenants of the tenant and his assignee.[105]

Benefit of covenants. LPA 1925, s 141(1) (passing the benefit of landlords' covenants) provides that rent reserved by a lease, and the benefit of every covenant therein, having reference to the subject matter thereof,[106] 'shall be annexed and incident to and shall go with the reversionary estate in the land, immediately expectant on the term granted by the lease, notwithstanding severance of that reversionary estate . . .'.

A legal assignee of the reversion (ie a transferee out and out of the whole of the landlord's interest) obtains by LPA 1925, s 141(1) the right to enforce against the tenant in possession all the real covenants in the lease, to the exclusion of the original landlord. If, therefore, at the assignment date, there are outstanding and unclaimed rent arrears or damages for breaches of covenant, such as to repair, the assignee has the right to enforce these against the tenant, in addition to any further arrears or damages which may accrue during the post-assignment period.[107]

---

102 *Lyons & Co v Knowles* [1943] 1 KB 366, [1943] 1 All ER 477, CA; also *Estates Gazette Ltd v Benjamin Restaurants Ltd* [1995] 1 All ER 129, CA.
103 *Sun Life Assurance Society plc v Tantofex (Engineers)* [1999] L & TR 568; although as a matter of construction, the release of A was on the facts construed as an accord and satisfaction with X: see *Deanplan v Mahmoud* [1992] 1 EGLR 79.
104 It makes no difference whether the lease itself is by deed, or informal (see *Lotteryking Ltd v Amec Properties Ltd* [1995] 2 EGLR 13) or even, it seems, oral (LPA 1925, s 154).
105 Neither LPA 1925, ss 141 or 142 apply to tenancies granted after LT(C)A 1995 comes into force, unless the tenancy was granted under, in particular, a pre-commencement agreement (LT(C)A 1995, s 30(4)).
106 This is the statutory expression corresponding to the common law term 'touching and concerning', and has the same narrowing object: see above.
107 *Re King* [1963] Ch 459, [1963] 1 All ER 781, CA; *A and D London and County Ltd v Wilfred Sportsman Ltd* [1971] Ch 764, [1970] 2 All ER 600, CA.

Burden of covenants. LPA 1925, s 142(1) (transmitting the burden of real covenants) is, in its first part, cast in similar language to LPA 1925, s 141(1), but it further provides that the lessor's obligations 'may be taken advantage of and enforced by the person in whom the term is from time to time vested . . . .'

In contrast to LPA 1925, s 141, LPA 1925, s 142(1) does not in terms annex to the leasehold estate the right to take advantage of landlords' breaches of real covenant. It has therefore been held that an original landlord's liability for pre-assignment breaches to the tenant remains, and so a tenant of a flat, who had himself re-assigned his lease, recovered damages for breaches of a landlords' covenant to repair, from a former landlord, calculated down to the date of assignment of the reversion.[108] Equally, an assignee of the reversion who is sued for breaches of covenant to repair which continue into the post-assignment period cannot avoid liability unless he is able to show that the breach is spent.[109] The concept of a person who has assigned his whole interest continuing to be burdened by its covenants is not conducive of certainty and the LT(C)A 1995 provides for a procedure for releasing original and subsequently assigning landlords in these circumstances, but only where the tenancy was granted after the commencement of the 1995 Act.

LPA 1925, ss 141 and 142 apply 'notwithstanding severance of that reversionary estate' (ie where a part or parts of the reversion fall into separate hands), and apportionment of the benefits and burdens is provided by LPA 1925, s 140. A tenant who is served with a notice to quit in relation to a part of his land (after the reversion of that part has been severed) is given the option under LPA 1925, s 140(2) to quit the whole of the land if he so wishes, by serving a counter-notice within one month upon the reversioner in relation to the rest of the land.

Duty to notify tenants of dwellings of assignments

By the Landlord and Tenant Act 1985, s 3(1)[110] if the interest of the landlord of a tenancy[111] of premises consisting of or including a dwelling is assigned, the new landlord must give written notice of the assignment and of his name and address to the tenant not later than the next day on which rent is payable under the tenancy, unless that date is within two months of the assignment. In that case the period is the end of the period of two months. Failure without reasonable excuse to comply with this requirement is a criminal offence (Landlord and Tenant Act 1985, s 3(3)).

---

108 *City and Metropolitan Properties Ltd v Greycroft Ltd* [1987] 3 All ER 839, [1987] 1 WLR 1085.

109 See *Duncliffe v Caerfelin Properties Ltd* [1989] 2 EGLR 38.

110 As amended by the Housing Act 1996, s 93 (adding s 3A to the Landlord and Tenant Act 1985) to require the landlord of tenants who fall within the Landlord and Tenant Act 1987, Pt I to notify them of their right to acquire the freehold under the latter Act.

111 By the Landlord and Tenant Act 1985, s 3(4), 'tenancy' includes a statutory tenancy. However, the duty to notify does not apply to tenancies to which the Landlord and Tenant Act 1987, Pt II applies (LT(C)A 1995, s 32(1)).

If the above duty is broken, the old landlord remains liable, jointly and severally with the new landlord, to the tenant for any breaches of covenant until written notification is given to the tenant by the new landlord of the assignment and of the new landlord's name and address.[112]

V ENFORCEMENT OF COVENANTS IN RELATION TO LEASES OR TENANCIES GRANTED AS FROM 1 JANUARY 1996

I Introductory principles

LT(C)A 1995 reformed the law relating to the enforcement of covenants in 'new' tenancies, an expression which generally means tenancies granted as from the commencement of the Act (LT(C)A 1995, s 1(6)). The provisions of LT(C)A 1995 cannot be contracted out of (LT(C)A 1995, s 25) although it is provided that nothing in the Act prevents a landlord or tenant from releasing the other from a liability under the tenancy (LT(C)A 1995, s 26(1)).

The Law Commission had recommended that the reforms in the law it advocated should take effect as from the first assignment of any lease or tenancy.[113] However, the then government considered that, unless the new rules did not apply to tenancies in existence at the commencement of LT(C)A 1995, commercial landlords would not have supported the whole reform 'package' which the 1995 Act represents. Hence, the 1995 Act has checks and balances.

Nonetheless, the refusal of Parliament to extend the benefit of the abrogation of the 'privity of contract' rule to tenancies granted before LT(C)A 1995 but continuing after then may lame, and partly delay, the effectiveness of the reform and creates two classes of tenancy, subject to different sets of general enforcement rules, a reformed and an unreformed set (subject to the three mitigations already mentioned). Thus, although the long-term result may be to simplify the law, the short-term consequence of these reforms is to render it more complex.

LT(C)A 1995 supersedes the terminology and some of the principles of the common law, in the interests of promoting simplicity. Hence, by LT(C)A 1995, s 2(1), it applies to a 'landlord covenant' or a 'tenant covenant' of a 'tenancy':[114]

---

112 Landlord and Tenant Act 1985, s 3(3A) and (3B), which continue to apply to any tenancy granted as from the commencement of the 1995 Act: LT(C)A 1995, s 26(2).
113 Law Com No 242 (1996) 'Privity of Contract' para 4.59. For a review of these recommendations and of LT(C)A 1995, see Davey (1996) 59 MLR 1; also Bridge (1996) CLJ 313; Walter [1996] Conv 432.
114 'Tenancy' is widely defined so as to mean 'any lease or other tenancy' and includes both a sub-lease and an agreement for a lease but not a mortgage term (LT(C)A 1995, s 28(1)). 'Covenant' is also widely defined (LT(C)A 1995, s 28(1)) so as to include collateral agreements to the lease.

(a) 'whether or not the covenant has reference to the subject-matter of the tenancy'; and

(b) 'whether or not the covenant is express, implied or imposed by law'.

It will be seen that paragraph (a) supersedes the requirement that, to be enforceable as against assignees of the lease or the reversion, the covenant must touch and concern the land, because personal and real covenants of a tenancy are alike capable of being enforced. To that extent, LT(C)A 1995, s 2(1)(a) implements the view of the Law Commission. It said that all the terms of a lease should be regarded as a single bargain for letting the property. When the interest of one of the parties changes hands, the successor, they believed, should take his predecessor's place as landlord or tenant, without distinguishing between different categories of covenant.[115] Thus, the aim of simplification of the law is followed by LT(C)A 1995, s 2(1), as well as the related aim of certainty: the Law Commission considered that parties to a tenancy should know the extent of their obligations with certainty.[116]

2   New rules as to the transmission of leasehold covenants

Introduction

The reformed rules apply to legal and equitable leases without differentiation, as well as to sub-leases (LT(C)A 1995, s 28(1)). Technical difficulties in the way of enforcing the benefit and burden of leasehold covenants by and against informal lessees have been removed, as have those arising on the informal assignment of equitable, as opposed to legal, leases.[117] LT(C)A 1995 abolishes the privity of contract liability of an original tenant so that, once he has voluntarily assigned a tenancy, he ceases to be bound by its covenants (LT(C)A 1995, s 5). He also loses any right to enforce future performance of the covenants of the tenancy against the landlord. After he has assigned the reversion, the landlord is not automatically freed from the burden of his covenants, but may seek a release from them following a special notice procedure.

With the abolition of the doctrine of privity of estate, other difficulties cease to apply. As a result of LT(C)A 1995, s 15(1), both the freehold reversioner and the immediate landlord entitled to the rents and profits under the tenancy, if different, as well as a mortgagee[118] in possession of the reversion of the premises, may enforce the covenants of the tenant for the time being. Likewise, where any 'tenant covenant' is enforceable against the reversioner, it is expressly provided (LT(C)A 1995, s 15(2)) that it may be

---

115 Law Com No 174 (1988) 'Privity of Contract and Estate' para 4.1.
116 Law Com No 242 (1996) 'Privity of Contract' para 4.46.
117 Thus 'assignment' is defined in LT(C)A 1995, s 28(1) as including an equitable assignment.
118 Including chargee (but not a mortgagee by deposit of documents, which category has seemingly been abolished LP(MP)A 1989, s 2): *United Bank of Kuwait v Sahib* [1996] 3 All ER 215, CA.

enforced against any immediate landlord entitled to the rents and profits of the premises and a mortgagee of the reversion.[119]

A new code

1 Policy of rules. The governing provision, LT(C)A 1995, s 3, is designed to ensure that the recommendations of the Law Commission are properly integrated into the law of covenants.[120] LT(C)A 1995, s 3 restates for new tenancies the old rules for the transmission of the benefit and burden of leasehold covenants in a simple statutory code.[121] The Law Commission had recommended that the ancient distinction between personal covenants, which could not be enforced against any successor in title to the lease or reversion, and covenants touching and concerning land, which were capable of enforcement against third party assignees despite the lack of privity of contract between them, should disappear. The covenants in a 'new tenancy' will form the whole bargain between the parties for the time being to that tenancy, unless subsequently varied, binding on the current holders of the lease and reversion and mutually enforceable by them, however the obligations might previously have been classified.[122] However, owing to LT(C)A 1995, s 3(6)(a), covenants which are expressed to be personal to a party will not be enforceable under LT(C)A 1995 against any other person, so that it will still be possible for landlords to grant personal licences to tenants to use premises in a way not allowed by the lease.

2 Annexation of benefit and burden. By LT(C)A 1995, s 3(1):

'the benefit and burden of all landlord and tenant covenants of a tenancy:
(a) shall be annexed and incident to the whole, and to each and every part, of the premises demised by the tenancy and of the reversion in them, and
(b) shall in accordance with this section pass on an assignment of the whole or any part of those premises or of the reversion in them.'

There is no differentiation between positive and negative covenants, and so a single set of enforcement rules applies to both. It is provided in connection with covenants restrictive of the user or land contained in a tenancy or which the landlord has entered into that, as well as being capable of enforcement against an assignee, such covenants shall 'be capable of being enforced against any other person who is the owner or

119 Similar rules apply to a tenant's mortgagee, both as respects the ability to enforce and be bound by the tenant covenants of the tenancy (LT(C)A 1995, s 15(3) and (4)).
120 HL Committee on Landlord and Tenant (Covenants) Bill, 21 June 1995, col 355 (Lord Chancellor).
121 The aim of simplification is pursued further by getting rid of the technical distinction between things in esse and in posse (LT(C)A 1995, s 3(7)), as well as by the disapplication to new tenancies of both LPA 1925, ss 78 and 79 (LT(C)A 1995, s 30(4)(a)) as well as a similar disapplication of LPA 1925, ss 141 and 142 (LT(C)A 1995, s 30(4)(b)).
122 As to possible complications with LT(C)A 1995, s 3 in relation to agreements for a building lease, see Adams [1997] Conv 327.

occupier of any demised premises to which the covenant relates, even though there is no express provision in the tenancy to that effect' (LT(C)A 1995, s 3(5)). Therefore, where a sub-lessee occupies land which is subject to a restrictive covenant, he is bound by this provision to observe it, if enforceable, even if his or a head tenancy is silent as to the covenant. However, a restrictive view of the words 'any demised premises' was taken by the High Court.[123] It ruled that the words applied only to the premises in fact leased to the individual tenant in question. Hence, a business tenant could not make use of LT(C)A 1995, s 3(5) to enforce directly against another tenant in the relevant development a landlord covenant whose effect was to prevent other tenants from using their premises for use as a gift shop.

It will be seen also that LT(C)A 1995, s 3(1) draws no distinction between covenants which touch and concern the land and those which do not, so obviating the need to differentiate between purely personal covenants and those which affected the parties in their capacity as landlord and tenant. Nor does LT(C)A 1995, s 3 as a whole draw any distinction between rent and other covenants of a lease which might be enforceable by a landlord,[124] in contrast to the opening words of LPA 1925, s 141(1).[125] LT(C)A 1995, following the aim of promoting simplicity in this part of the law, makes no terminological distinction between the general rules governing the enforcement of landlord or tenant covenants. These are now in a single statutory code, in contrast to the previous rules, which are contained in statute for landlord and the common law for tenants.

The reference in LT(C)A 1995, s 3(1)(a) to: 'shall be annexed and incident to the whole, and to each and every part ...', is akin to the words in LPA 1925, s 141(1): 'shall be annexed and incident to ...', and the aim seems the same: to ensure that, on an assignment of the reversion or the tenancy, the full benefit and burden of the tenant covenants passes to the assignee, to the exclusion of the assignor. The words in LT(C)A 1995, s 3(1)(b): 'shall in accordance with this section pass on an assignment ...', emphasise that the transmission of the benefit and burden of leasehold covenants is automatic, without the need for any special or additional words in the instrument by which the assignment is carried out.

3 Assignment by tenant. It is provided by LT(C)A 1995, s 3(2) that:

> 'where the assignment[126] is made by the tenant under the tenancy, then as from the assignment the assignee:
>
> (a) becomes bound by the tenant covenants of the tenancy except to the extent that:

123 *Oceanic Village Ltd v United Attractions Ltd* [2000] 1 All ER 975; Draper 144 (2000) Sol Jo 638. The words 'any demised premises' taken by themselves would seem to allow direct enforcement by a tenant, but the High Court refused to read them in isolation from the rest of LT(C)A 1995, s 3.

124 Specific provision is made for the statutory transmission on assignment of the whole or any part of the reversion of the benefit of a landlord's right of re-entry in LT(C)A 1995, s 4.

125 Which is disapplied to new tenancies (LT(C)A 1995, s 30(4)).

126 An assignment of a tenancy is subject to the common law rules governing formal validity.

(i) immediately before the assignment they do not bind the assignor, or

(ii) they fell to be complied with in relation to any demised premises not comprised in the assignment.'

A tenant covenant would not bind the assignor immediately before the assignment if it has been released or waived by the landlord, unless the release or waiver has been expressed to be personal to the tenant (as envisaged by LT(C)A 1995, s 3(4)): there is thus a presumption that any waiver or release will not be personal.

By way of mirror provision, by LT(C)A 1995, s 3(2)(b), as from the assignment, the assignee 'becomes entitled to the benefit of the landlord covenants of the tenancy' subject to the same qualification as in LT(C)A 1995, s 3(2)(a)(ii) above. The same rules as to the taking of the benefit of landlord covenants and the subjection to the burden of tenant covenants applies where the landlord assigns the reversion to an assignee (LT(C)A 1995, s 3(3)). However, a if a covenant requires registration so as to render it enforceable against any third party assignee, the transmission rules of LT(C)A 1995 do not obviate the need for such registration (LT(C)A 1995, s 3(6)) whether under the Land Registration Act 1925 or the Land Charges Act 1972, depending on whether the title to the burdened land is registered or unregistered.

3 Abrogation of the privity of contract liability

Introduction

The Law Commission's examination of the law in 1988 led to a central recommendation. This was that 'when a tenant assigns the whole of the property demised by a lease ... his responsibility to comply with the covenants in the lease after the assignment should cease'. He should also cease to derive any benefit from the landlord covenants of the tenancy.[127] The Commission based their conclusion on considerations of equity in the general sense. 'It is intrinsically unfair that anyone should bear burdens under a contract in respect of which they derive no benefit and over which they have no control'.[128] LT(C)A 1995, s 5, which removes the privity of contract rule, so that the original tenant and any person to whom he assigns the lease are liable, in principle, to perform tenant covenants only during the period they hold the tenancy, provided it was granted as from 1 January 1996, must be seen against certain matters within the legislative reforms as a whole.

1 The landlord may be able to obtain from an assigning tenant a guarantee agreement within LT(C)A 1995, s 16, that his immediate assignee will perform the covenants of the tenancy. A difficulty may arise should the landlord insist that a surety or guarantor of the original tenant guarantees his performance of an authorised guarantee agreement. Such a requirement might perhaps contravene the

---

127 Law Com No 174 (1988) 'Privity of Contract and Estate' para 4.9.
128 Law Com No 174 (1988) 'Privity of Contract and Estate' para 3.1.

contracting out provision (LT(C)A 1995, s 25) of the 1995 Act. Equally, it is arguable that such an agreement is not a covenant, and that, applying LT(C)A 1995, s 24(2), any release of a tenant's guarantor is only co-extensive with that of the tenant himself, so that nothing in LT(C)A 1995 precludes the landlord from acting in this way against a guarantor.[129]

2   In connection with consents, the landlord of a commercial tenant (but not of a residential tenant) may make use of the Landlord and Tenant Act 1927, s 19(1A) so that, if the parties to the tenancy, at the time of the grant, or at the date of the assignment, so agree, consent may be given subject to a condition that the assigning tenant enters into an authorised guarantee agreement ('AGA') under LT(C)A 1995. Whereas at common law, an attempt in advance to lay down what conditions were to be deemed reasonable might have been risky, it is now intended by these amendments to avoid this particular ground for challenging guarantee conditions. However, at first, it seemed that the taking of AGAs by business landlords from assigning tenants and then from assigning assignees had degenerated into a routine practice, so risking undermining the benefit of the tenant release mechanism. In mitigation of this, it seems that if a lease has no provision that the tenant can be required to sign an AGA as a condition of his assigning the lease, then, where the lease enables the landlord only to refuse consent to an assignment if he has reasonable grounds to do so, the landlord cannot as an assignment condition, require an AGA unless the landlord is acting on reasonable grounds.[130] However, in that case, the reason why no provision for the taking of an AGA was made in the original lease was that it was an 'old tenancy' and the dispute arose in connection with the renewal of the tenancy as a 'new tenancy'. Nevertheless, the High Court drew attention to the fact that LT(C)A 1995, s 16(3)(b) renders a landlord's requirement for an AGA valid only if it is 'lawful' to impose it as a condition of a proposed assignment. Thus if the lease provides a 'fully qualified' or 'qualified' assignment covenant by the tenant, under which landlord consent can only be withheld on reasonable grounds, which the landlord must justify as such, it may even be that only if the proposed assignee is not as credit-worthy as the tenant could an AGA lawfully be imposed. Equally, if the lease absolutely prohibits assignments, an AGA can be 'lawfully' imposed no matter whether the landlord has reasonable grounds for doing so or not.

3   If part only of the demised premises is assigned, the liability of the former tenant of part may continue over the whole, where it is not possible to attribute a covenant to the part assigned.

4   The abrogation of the privity of contract liability of a tenant applies only where the assignment was voluntary as opposed to by operation of law. Assignments in bankruptcy or insolvency or which are in breach of covenant are excluded assignments (LT(C)A 1995, s 11(1)). The essential rule in these cases is that the

---

129   See Potter & Collins Estates Gazette 11 May 1996, p 118 and J E Adams Estates Gazette 10 August 1996, p 68; Dear Estates Gazette 21 October 2000, p 167.
130   *Wallis Fashion Group Ltd v CGU Life Assurance Ltd* [2000] 2 EGLR 49.

assignor tenant continues to be liable for post-assignment breaches of covenant. Only if at a subsequent stage the tenancy is voluntarily re-assigned does this continuing liability of the tenant come to an end (LT(C)A 1995, s 11(2) and (3)).
5   The effect of LT(C)A 1995, s 5 is that not only an original tenant, but also, provided a purposive and not a literal interpretation is applied to the words of s 5(1) any subsequent assignee voluntarily re-assigning the tenancy will be automatically free from the burden of tenant covenants. Neither will after assignment be any longer able to claim the benefit of landlord covenants. In the case of assignees who re-assign, LT(C)A 1995 is consistent with the previous common law and may operate more strictly. This is because an assignee may have to undertake to guarantee the performance of the obligations of the person to whom he re-assigns, owing to the operation of a condition as pre-arranged in the circumstances laid down by the Landlord and Tenant Act 1927, s 19(1A).

Tenants' statutory release

1 General rule. It is provided that where a tenant[131] voluntarily assigns the premises demised to him under a tenancy, then:
(a) if he assigns the whole of the premises demised to him under a tenancy, he is released, as from the assignment, by LT(C)A 1995, from the tenant covenants of the tenancy (LT(C)A 1995, s 5(2)(a)); and
(b) he ceases, as from the assignment, to be entitled to the benefit of the landlord covenants of the tenancy (LT(C)A 1995, s 5(2)(b)).

In this way, the privity of contract rule is rendered inapplicable, although the original tenant, or any of his assignees who re-assign the tenancy,[132] cannot use his automatic statutory release as a defence to an action for any breaches of covenant occurring before the release (LT(C)A 1995, s 24(1)). The Act takes effect automatically, and as from the assignment date the assignee is solely liable to perform leasehold covenants. In addition, where an assigning tenant is released, then to the same extent any other person, such as a surety or guarantor of his, is automatically released as from the date of the tenant's release (LT(C)A 1995, s 24(2)).

Owing to this reform, the need for any implied indemnity covenants from an assignee was removed and the relevant provisions of LPA 1925 do not apply to a tenancy

131 Who need not necessarily be a tenant of the whole premises, as where he holds a sub-lease of part (LT(C)A 1995, s 5(4)).
132 An argument that an assignee of the original tenant who re-assigns a new lease cannot claim the benefit of an automatic release under LT(C)A 1995, s 5(1) because of the statutory reference to premises 'demised to him' is dismissed by Fogel Estates Gazette 10 August 1996, p 64, as manifestly absurd; but the material words of LT(C)A 1995, s 5(1) could be literally interpreted as confined to the original lessee and an assignee has no premises assigned, but only vested in him.

entered into on as from the commencement of LT(C)A 1995.[133] There are elaborate provisions designed to prevent landlords inserting provisions in the tenancy to circumvent the effect of the statutory release from performance of tenant covenants (LT(C)A 1995, s 25), such as by disguised or overt forfeiture or termination or surrender-back clauses. The right of the parties to tenancies granted at any date expressly to release a landlord or tenant from the covenants of the tenancy is preserved (LT(C)A 1995, s 26(1)). Special provision was thought necessary where a management company, with no legal estate vested in it in the premises, enters into 'landlord covenants' such as to keep in repair and maintain the premises, and the tenant assigns the lease. By LT(C)A 1995, s 12, the benefit of the landlord covenants passes to the assignee tenant, and so does the burden of tenant covenants such as to pay rent and service charges.

2 Assignment of part of premises. Where, however, part only of the premises is assigned, the releases mentioned earlier operate only to the extent that the covenant in question falls to be complied with in relation to that part of the demised premises (LT(C)A 1995, s 5(3)). Thus, subject to what follows, certain covenants may be attributed to part only of the premises, as with a lease of a shop and rooms above, and the tenant assigns the shop and retains the living accommodation, and the lease has separate user covenants for the shop and the living accommodation.[134] In such a case, the tenant would be released by LT(C)A 1995, s 5 from future observance of the user covenants in relation to the shop, which the landlord would have to enforce against the assignee, but not in relation to the living accommodation.

Some covenants cannot be attributed to any part of the premises, since they relate to the whole premises: covenants to pay rent, to decorate or to insure, or to give the tenant facilities separate from the demised premises fall into this category. Where this is so, after the assignment, both the assigning tenant and his assignee are liable jointly and severally to the landlord for the performance of these covenants (LT(C)A 1995, s 13(1)). However, the tenant and assignee may agree to an apportionment of liability. This agreement may exonerate one party, presumably the assignor-tenant, from all liability under the covenant specified in the agreement (LT(C)A 1995, s 9(1) and (3)).[135] The parties may apply for the apportionment agreement to be binding on, for example, a landlord of the whole premises, following a prescribed form notice procedure (LT(C)A 1995, ss 10 and 27(1)).

Landlords' statutory release mechanism

1 Principles of the reform. The landlord may seek a release from the burden of his covenants as at the date when he assigns the reversion in the whole premises; but if

---

133 LT(C)A 1995, ss 14 and 30(2).
134 Example of the Law Commission (Law Com No 174 (1988) 'Privity of Contract and Estate' para 4.32).
135 A similar principle applies where a landlord assigns the reversion in part only of the premises (LT(C)A 1995, s 9(2)).

he does not, he remains liable, in contrast to an assigning tenant, for performance of the 'landlord covenants' of the tenancy, and entitled to the benefit of the tenant covenants, until the end of the lease. He is, however, entitled to seek a release under LT(C)A 1995, s 7 either at the date he assigns the reversion or at any subsequent re-assignment of it by a successor in title.

The Law Commission did not regard landlords as in quite the same position to former tenants. They firstly used empirical arguments. There was 'less need for radical change' since 'in most leases, the landlord undertakes far fewer obligations then the tenant and landlords may not be troubled by the prospect of continuing liability'.[136] They also noted dangers of abuse: 'the landlord's liability would not be limited', they said, 'until the date of the next assignment'. This was necessary 'to avoid landlords arranging to escape liability by the stratagem of assigning first to a nominee who very shortly afterwards assigns the property again'.[137] A further judicial limitation on landlord release is that it was not available to an assigning landlord who had offered a tenant a personal collateral contract, which was thus not transmissible, in that case, with respect to building defects.[138] The Law Commission also pointed out that this escape route was not open, by contrast, to a tenant who had to obtain the consent of the landlord to each assignment. However, the Commission accepted that, because the notice procedure proposed by them and adopted in LT(C)A 1995 is voluntary, some landlords would continue to be liable to observe landlord covenants and others would not, and that where liability continued, it would be a full and not a guaranteeing liability. This latter principle was justified on the ground that a tenant cannot control the way the reversion is assigned, in contrast to landlords, who are able to do so by disposition covenants.[139]

2 Statutory notice procedure. The procedure by which an assigning landlord may seek a release from the landlord covenants of the tenancy follows the recommendations of the Law Commission. By LT(C)A 1995, s 6, a landlord who assigns the reversion of premises[140] of which he is the landlord under the tenancy is given the right to seek a release by notice from the landlord covenants of the tenancy. Any eventual release does not affect the liability of any person jointly and severally liable with the landlord (LT(C)A 1995, s 13(2)).

---

136 Law Com No 174 (1988) 'Privity of Contract and Estate' para 4.16.
137 Law Com No 174 (1988) 'Privity of Contract and Estate' para 4.23.
138 *BHP Petroleum Great Britain Ltd v Chesterfield Properties Ltd* [2001] EWCA Civ 1797, [2002] 1 All ER 821. Attention was drawn at first instance to the words of LT(C)A 1995, s 28(1) defining 'landlord covenant' as being a covenant to be complied with by the landlord *'for the time being'* entitled to the reversion expectant on the tenancy (emphasis supplied).
139 Law Com No 174 (1988) 'Privity of Contract and Estate' para 4.25. This type of argument was accepted during the passage of the Bill: 263 HC Official Report (6th series) col 1240. Hence also the joint and several liability of different landlords as provided for by LT(C)A 1995, s 13.
140 Irrespective of whether the landlord is landlord of the whole premises or part only (LT(C)A 1995, s 6(4)).

Thus, if the landlord has assigned the reversion in the whole of the premises of which he is landlord, the notice releases him from all of the landlord covenants. He ceases to be entitled to the benefit of any tenant covenants, as from the assignment date (LT(C)A 1995, s 6(2)). Where the landlord assigns the reversion of part only of the premises, he may apply to be similarly released from the landlord covenants of the tenancy 'to the extent that they fall to be complied with in relation to that part of the premises' (LT(C)A 1995, s 6(3)(a)). As envisaged by the Law Commission, a landlord who does not at any time utilise the release procedure remains jointly and severally liable to the tenant for the observance of landlord covenants with his successor in title (LT(C)A 1995, s 13(1)), unless he is able to procure a release under LT(C)A 1995, s 7.

3 Contents of notice. Since the notice is regarded as an important document, it must be in a prescribed form (LT(C)A 1995, s 27(1)), as envisaged by the Law Commission.[141] The notice must therefore give full information to the tenant, on whom it is served, notably that he must be informed that any objections to the proposed release must be made by written notice served within four weeks of the service of the main notice (LT(C)A 1995, s 27(2)). LT(C)A 1995, s 8, which governs landlords' release notices, requires that the notice must be served before the assignment or within four weeks beginning with the date of the assignment (LT(C)A 1995, s 8(1)). Thus, the tenant is informed of the assignment and the notice requests a release of the covenants. But the prescribed form does not require the landlord to identify the obligations from which a release is sought – a curious lacuna.[142] If no objection is made, LT(C)A 1995, s 8(2) releases a covenant to the extent mentioned in the notice. Any release relates back to the date of the assignment (LT(C)A 1995, s 8(3)).[143] The tenant has the absolute right to serve a written notice (which does not have to be in a prescribed form) on the landlord objecting to the release. It must be served within four weeks of the date of service of the landlord's notice (LT(C)A 1995, s 8(2)(a)). Despite having served such a counter-notice, the tenant may by a further notice consent to the release.[144] The landlord may, after receiving a tenant's notice of objection, apply to the county court and it may declare that it is reasonable for the landlord to be released (LT(C)A 1995, s 8(2)(b)).[145]

---

141 Law Com No 174 (1988) 'Privity of Contract and Estate' para 4.18. The form is in Landlord and Tenant (Covenants) Act 1995 (Notices) Regulations 1995, SI 1995/2964, Form No 3.

142 This is because a landlord can apparently choose to seek release from some or all of its obligations: *BHP Petroleum Great Britain Ltd v Chesterfield Properties Ltd* [2001] EWCA Civ 1797, [2002] 1 All ER 821. It may be, however, that Form No 3 assumes that landlords will seek blanket releases of the kind evidently sought in the *BHP* case itself. It seems from the Law Commission Report No 174 (1988) 'Privity of Contract and Estate' that the Commission may have been thinking, when the whole reversion is assigned, of a blanket release mechanism (paras 4.17 and especially 4.20, speaking of cancelling a landlord's continuing liability).

143 Thus where a former landlord applies for a release, as where L assigned to R and R wishes to re-assign, L cannot escape liability for breaches of landlord covenants down to the date of any re-assignment.

144 His consent notice must in terms state that any objection notice has been withdrawn; if not, presumably, the objection notice stands (LT(C)A 1995, s 8(2)(c)).

145 No guidance appears either in the Act or in the Law Commission's report (Law Com Report No 174 (1988) 'Privity of Contract and Estate') as to what criteria are to be used in deciding on such reasonableness and so the issue seems to be entirely discretionary.

4 Authorised guarantee agreements by assigning tenants

It has already been observed that the abrogation of the privity of contract liability of an original tenant is not absolute, owing to the power of landlords to require the tenant to enter into a guarantee of the performance of the person to whom the lease has been assigned. In such a case, the original (or any later assigning tenant) remains secondarily liable to perform tenant covenants until the lease has been re-assigned.

1 Policy of the guarantee principle. The Law Commission recognised that there might, especially in the commercial field, be cases where the landlord was anxious to have the assurance of a continuing guarantee from his tenant and where it was objectively reasonable for him to do so.[146] Such a guarantee should be capable of being required only where the lease required the consent of the landlord to any assignment, so that where the lease had been granted for a long period at a low rent and at a premium, and the tenant was free to assign without restriction, no guarantee could be required from him. The Commission therefore recommended that 'a landlord whose consent has to be obtained should be able to impose a condition that the assignor guarantees the assignee's performance of the lease covenants'.[147] The continuing liability would last until the next assignment, whereupon it would come to an end. The assigning tenant had some control over the identity and attributes of his immediate assignee, but not over those of any subsequent assignee. However, it should be borne in mind, having regard to LT(C)A 1995, s 16, that if the immediate assignee is released from his obligations, so, in contrast to the common law, is the tenant-guarantor, as he would be by a material change in the obligations of the lease which was made without his consent.[148]

2 Authorised guarantee agreements. Where on an assignment, the original or any subsequent tenant by assignment is released by LT(C)A 1995 from a tenant covenant, the tenant may enter into an 'authorised guarantee agreement' with respect to the performance of that covenant by the assignee (LT(C)A 1995, s 16(1)). Under such an agreement the tenant must guarantee the performance of the relevant covenant to any extent by the assignee (LT(C)A 1995, s 16(2)(a)). Thus, a guarantee might extend only to the rent payable or it might extend to all the tenant covenants. Three conditions must be satisfied before an agreement amounts to an authorised guarantee agreement (LT(C)A 1995, s 16(3)):

1 by virtue of a covenant against assignment, the assignment cannot be effected without the consent of the immediate landlord ('the landlord under the tenancy') or some other person;[149]

---

146 Law Com Report No 174 (1988) 'Privity of Contract and Estate' para 4.10.
147 Law Com Report No 174 (1988) 'Privity of Contract and Estate' para 4.11.
148 Law Com Report No 174 (1988) 'Privity of Contract and Estate' para 4.11: 'this should avoid a former tenant finding himself responsible for obligations much more onerous than those he originally assumed'.
149 Whether the prohibition on assignment is absolute or qualified.

2   any consent is given subject to a lawfully imposed condition that the tenant is to enter into an agreement guaranteeing the performance of the covenant by the assignee; and
3   the agreement is entered into by the tenant under that condition.

The condition referred to in paragraph 2 may include a condition which has been agreed in advance, at the time the lease was granted, under which, if the lease is assigned by the tenant, the landlord, as a condition of the assignment, may require the assigning tenant to enter into an authorised guarantee agreement.[150] Whether a condition of this sort is reasonable may be judged in accordance with the general law. A good number of commercial landlords have evidently been imposing an automatic requirement, on assignments of new or renewed business leases, that the assignor-tenant enters into a guarantee agreement, tempered by an undertaking that, if the assignee satisfies financial criteria, such a requirement would be released.[151] Such a practice undermines the fundamental principle of LT(C)A 1995, which is to do away with the post-assignment liability of lessees. As seen, it is now only 'lawful' to impose an AGA where the original lease does not envisage this being done, if the landlord has reasonable grounds for his wish to impose an AGA on the tenant (at least where the lease does not totally prohibit assignments).[152]

There are certain safeguards within LT(C)A 1995 for assigning tenants, at the price of additional complexity in the law. A guarantee agreement cannot validly require the tenant to guarantee in any way the performance of the covenant concerned by any person other than the immediate assignee (LT(C)A 1995, s 16(4)(a)). It cannot impose on the tenant 'any liability, restriction or other requirement (of whatever nature)' in relation to any time after the assignee is released from the covenant under the Act on re-assignment or otherwise (LT(C)A 1995, s 16(4)(b)). This is not to prevent the landlord from obtaining a further guarantee agreement from such assignee on the re-assignment of the lease.

On the other hand, it is provided that a guarantee agreement may impose liabilities on the tenant as sole or principal debtor in respect of the assignee's obligations (LT(C)A 1995, s 16(5)(a)) but his obligations must be no more onerous than if he were liable as sole or principal debtor (LT(C)A 1995, s 16(5)(b)), so, arguably, precluding a landlord from claiming an additional rent, agreed or determined with an assignee, as after a rent review, from the assignor-tenant in default. He may be required by the agreement, as where an assignee goes bankrupt or becomes insolvent and there is a disclaimer of the lease, to enter into a new tenancy of the premises whose term expires no later than the term of the tenancy assigned, with tenant covenants no more onerous than those of

---

150 Thanks to the Landlord and Tenant Act 1927, s 19(1A), inserted by LT(C)A 1995, s 22, such a condition will not ipso facto be unreasonable merely because it is envisaged by the parties' agreement as reasonable.
151 See *Fogel* Estates Gazette 10 August 1996, p 64; also *Acheson* Estates Gazette 18 January 1997, p 132.
152 *Wallis Fashion Group Ltd v CGU Life Assurance Ltd* [2000] 2 EGLR 49.

the tenancy (LT(C)A 1995, s 16(5)(c)). The object of this latter provision seems to be to protect the landlord against a tenant who has assigned to a weak assignee and is visiting the consequences on the landlord. In order further to protect landlords in bankruptcy or insolvency cases and where an assignment is made in breach of covenant, it is provided that on the occasion of the first voluntary assignment after the involuntary assignment, when the former tenant will be released, he may at that stage be required by the landlord to guarantee the performance of the current assignee of his covenants (LT(C)A 1995, s 16(6)(a)).[153]

Since a tenant who assigns the lease and guarantees the performance of his immediate assignee is vulnerable to reimburse sums not paid to the landlord by the assignee or to pay him damages on account of the latter's breach of covenant, he is entitled, if his liability materialises, to demand an overriding lease from the landlord (LT(C)A 1995, s 19) as discussed earlier. In addition, he is entitled to a six-month warning notice of intention to recover fixed charges and to the other safeguards already discussed.

153 This applies even though the assignor may have entered into a guarantee agreement with the landlord.

Chapter 6

Implied covenants

I   BASIS OF IMPLYING COVENANTS INTO LEASES

Traditional basis

The traditional basis under which the courts imply covenants into a lease is to do so only if business efficacy requires it. The test is narrow. It involves asking whether the lease would be unworkable without the implication of the term contended for. Hence, where leases of flats would have been useless without implied covenants granting access to the flats via stairs, such rights, in the nature of easements, were implied into leases that did not expressly confer them.[1] A covenant may also be implied to correlate to an obligation imposed by an express term in the lease. Where a tenant undertook to pay charges in respect of a particular service (provision of a housekeeper), it was held that the landlord would be under an implied obligation to provide the service.[2] Where a statutory tenant under the Rent Acts was under an express obligation to repair the interior of a house, the landlord was held to be under a correlative implied obligation to repair the exterior, which was allowing damp penetration.[3] The tenant could not comply with her repairing obligation in these circumstances and the landlord was the appropriate person to carry the more onerous repairing obligation of the two parties.

Traditionally, courts decline to imply covenants into a lease in order to fill gaps left by the parties, or to remedy defects in a lease. Where statute provided a remedy (at the time, the appointment of a manager) in support of the landlord's repairing obligations, this was held a ground for refusing to imply a term that, if a landlords' managing company defaulted, the landlord of long residential lessees had a duty and not just a

---

1   *Liverpool City Council v Irwin* [1977] AC 239, HL.
2   *Barnes v City of London Real Property Co* [1918] 2 Ch 18.
3   *Barrett v Lounova (1982) Ltd* [1990] 1 QB 348, [1989] 3 All ER 351, CA; also *Edmonton Corpn v WM Knowles & Son Ltd* (1961) 60 LGR 124.

discretion to intervene.[4] The fact that it might reduce a tenant's costs to imply a term into a lease is not, of itself, sufficient to satisfy the test of business efficacy, so that no term was implied into a lease that the landlord would arrange insurance of the premises at the lowest possible cost to the tenant.[5]

Is change under way?

There have been indications that the narrow approach of the courts may be changing, at least in the case of repairing obligations where a lease imposes express and apparently comprehensive obligations on both parties. The court leant in favour of a construction which resulted in there being a complete code so far as repairs were concerned. It was prepared to fill a gap in the landlord's repairing obligations, so that these applied to the structure and exterior of the subject building as a whole, and were not confined to its foundations and the roof.[6] However, this reasoning may well be confined to business leases.[7]

The Court of Appeal refused to imply any obligation on a landlord of long leases of flats to carry out any work of repair which went beyond the terms of an insurance policy, where the leases made detailed and specific provisions for the management and repair of the flats concerned, at the lessees' expense.[8] Indeed, a case[9] in which a residential landlord was held to be under an implied obligation to carry out repairs to the exterior of a house so as to cure dampness, was said to rest on its special facts. Moreover, the common law, in Lord Hoffmann's words, takes 'a bleak laissez faire approach' to the question of implying into a lease or a tenancy any obligation by the landlord to keep the premises in repair or in a state for human habitation or for the use of the premises by the tenant.[10] As a result, their Lordships refused to impose any obligation on a council landlord to upgrade the sound-proofing of two flats. They declined to interpret the common law implied covenant for quiet enjoyment as requiring the landlord to pay for such work. The sound-proofing, even though not in accordance with modern standards, had been up to standard when installed. Hence, while apparently comprehensive leases of commercial premises may apparently be construed as not intending to leave gaps in the provision for repairs, tenancies of residential premises remain subject to a narrow presumption against implying terms. This seems anomalous.

4   *Hafton Properties Ltd v Camp* [1994] 1 EGLR 67.
5   *Havenridge Ltd v Boston Dyers Ltd* [1994] 2 EGLR 73, CA.
6   *Holding and Barnes plc v Hill House Hammond Ltd* [2000] L & TR 428, aff'd on appeal [2001] EWCA Civ 1334.
7   Thus in *Ratcliffe v Sandwell MBC* [2002] EWCA Civ 06, [2002] 1 WLR 1488, February, the test of business efficacy was applied without demur to deny a residential tenant any implied term that his landlord should cure condensation resulting from an inherent defect in the premises.
8   *Adami v Lincoln Grange Management Ltd* [1998] 1 EGLR 58.
9   *Barrett v Lounova (1982) Ltd* [1990] 1 QB 348, [1989] 3 All ER 351, CA.
10   *Southwark London BC v Mills* [1999] 4 All ER 449 at 453, HL. This problem may be in due course addressed by government plans to impose 'individual fitness rating standards' on residential property but at the date this book went to press matters were in abeyance.

Many residential tenants are in a vulnerable position, and often occupying old premises, in poor condition.[11] Business tenants may also have access to legal advice, but the same may not be presumed in the case of residential tenants holding short-term tenancies.

In any case, if a lease contains an express covenant in any form which covers the same subject matter as that sought to be dealt with by an implied covenant for quiet enjoyment, the express covenant will rule out any implied covenant in the same matter.[12] The limits of the implied obligation for quiet enjoyment and its possible relationship to the protection of possessions and privacy under human rights legislation remain to be fought out.[13]

II   LANDLORD IMPLIED COVENANT FOR QUIET ENJOYMENT

Scope of covenant[14]

An implied covenant by the landlord for quiet enjoyment arises from the relationship of landlord and tenant, however created, whether by deed, in writing, or orally.[15] It entitles the tenant to be put into possession.[16] It follows that it is also a breach of this obligation for a landlord to interfere with the tenant's access to the premises.[17] The landlord impliedly covenants that he has title at the commencement of the tenancy. The covenant extends to unlawful acts of the landlord and to lawful acts of other persons claiming under the landlord by way of entry, eviction, or interruption of the tenant's peaceful enjoyment of the land during the tenancy. It protects the tenant from acts which cause substantial interference with the tenant's ordinary use of the premises, whether those acts are done on the premises or not, and from any conduct of the landlord or his agent interfering with the tenant's freedom of action in exercising his rights as tenant.[18]

The covenant is narrow in scope. In particular, it does not apply to things done before the grant of the tenancy, even if they have continuing consequences for the tenant.

---

11   See eg Housing Green Paper (2000) para 2.7 ('the highest proportions of poor housing exist in the private rented sector and in local authority housing').

12   *Duke of Westminster v Guild* [1985] QB 688, [1984] 3 All ER 144, CA.

13   An unreasonable failure by a 'social' landlord such as a local authority or registered housing association to prevent harassment of a claimant tenant by other tenants of theirs could, perhaps, violate the latter's human rights under EHCR, Art 8. This is because under the HRA 1998, there is not only a duty on public sector landlords to act, but a failure to act violates the legislation (HRA 1998, s 6(6)). See *Hussain v Lancaster City Council* [2000] QB 1.

14   See passim Davey [2001] Conv 30.

15   *Kenny v Preen* [1963] 1 QB 499, [1962] 3 All ER 814, CA.

16   *Miller v Emcer Products Ltd* [1956] Ch 304, [1956] 1 All ER 237.

17   *Hilton v James Smith & Sons (Norwood) Ltd* [1979] 2 EGLR 44, CA.

18   *McCall v Abelesz* [1976] 1 All ER 727 at 730-731, CA; *Kenny v Preen* [1962] 3 All ER 814 at 820, CA.

The tenant takes the property in the physical condition in which he finds it.[19] Thus, conversions were carried out of a house into small flats. The sound-proofing gave no (or very little) protection to tenants against any sound which was the result of ordinary domestic living, causing annoyance to the tenants. The House of Lords refused to require the landlords to upgrade the sound-proofing to modern standards. The conversions were carried out in accordance with the then applying building regulations (but not in accordance with those now current). Their Lordships said that if expensive obligations were to be imposed on social landlords,[20] only Parliament could change the law. Only it could make the policy decisions and decide on the financial consequences. Both an implied and an express covenant for quiet enjoyment are covered by the principle (related to implied repairing obligations) under which it is fundamental to a lease that the landlord gives no implied warranty as to the condition or fitness of the premises. The covenant for quiet enjoyment cannot, it seems, be extended to apply to disturbance or inconvenience or any other damage attributable to the condition of the premises.[21]

Because an implied covenant for quiet enjoyment will only protect ordinary reasonable use of the premises by the tenant, it does not protect his privacy or amenities. In addition, when a landlord grants a lease, he does not by this accept any limits on use of neighbouring or adjoining land which he retains: the lessee can, on this view, always obtain an express covenant to give him any further protection he seeks.[22] Where, therefore, the landlord erected an iron external staircase that passed the tenant's bedroom window, destroying her privacy, she had no claim under the covenant.[23] On the other hand, where the entrance to the tenant's shop was barred by scaffolding erected by the landlord, damages were recovered for loss of custom.[24] There had been a direct physical interference that had damaged the tenant's trade. The House of Lords have now indicated that a breach of covenant may arise if there is no physical interference, as where there is regular excessive noise emanating from the premises next door held by another tenant of the same landlord.[25]

Harassment and related conduct

Harassment of a tenant may, at common law, constitute a breach of the present covenant, as where the landlord, without invading her rooms, sent a tenant threatening letters

---

19 *Southwark London BC v Mills* supra.
20 Which, according to Lord Hoffmann in *Southwark London BC v Mills* supra at 458 amounted to an improvement to the premises and so outside the express or implied covenant for quiet enjoyment.
21 *Southwark London BC v Mills* supra at 456 (Lord Hoffmann).
22 *Browne v Flower* [1911] 1 Ch 219, 226 – 227; also *Romulus Trading Co Ltd v Comet Properties Ltd* [1996] 2 EGLR 70.
23 *Browne v Flower* [1911] 1 Ch 219.
24 *Owen v Gadd* [1956] 2 QB 99, [1956] 2 All ER 28, CA.
25 *Southwark London BC v Mills* [1999] 4 All ER 449 at 453, HL.

and otherwise intimidated her by banging on the door and shouting abuse.[26] Landlords who cut off gas and electricity supplies,[27] or who entered the premises and removed the doors and windows[28] had both broken this covenant. Their conduct had rendered it impossible for the tenant to enjoy the possession of the premises granted them. It was not necessary to prove that the landlord had in fact offered violence to the tenant.

A minimal level of tenant protection

The limits of the protection offered by an implied covenant for quiet enjoyment to a tenant are, as we have seen, minimal, as emphasised by the following additional aspects.

1   The covenant extends only to the acts of the landlord and to his other tenants in which the landlord actively participates. The fact, therefore, that a tenant causes a nuisance to an adjoining or neighbouring tenant does not of itself trigger a landlord's liability. Where a tenant of an upper flat produced excessive noise, and flooding in the complainant's flat from overflowing taps, the landlord was not liable merely because of his knowledge of these events.[29] Nor does the implied covenant cover disturbance by 'title paramount', as where a sub-tenant finds that he is subject to a restrictive covenant in the head lease, of whose existence he may not know.[30]

2   The implied covenant terminates with the landlord's interest, so that where a tenant with eight and half years to run under his own lease, mistakenly granted a sub-lease for ten and a half years, the sub-tenant had no remedy when evicted by the superior landlord at the end of the eight and a half years.[31] On the other hand, the covenant includes an obligation to put the tenant into possession, so that if the previous tenant wrongfully holds over, the new tenant may sue the landlord.[32]

3   While an implied covenant for quiet enjoyment covers all unlawful acts of the landlord on the premises, acts done pursuant to rights under the lease cannot constitute a breach of covenant, such as forfeiture for breach of covenant or condition or entry to inspect the condition of the premises. Where a landlord, after having granted a long lease to T1, carried out faulty alterations to the floor of the flat above, let to T2, and the use of T2's flat inevitably interfered with the reasonable enjoyment of T1's premises below, the landlord was, exceptionally, in breach of covenant.[33]

26   *Kenny v Preen* [1963] 1 QB 499, [1962] 3 All ER 814, CA.
27   *Perera v Vandiyar* [1953] 1 All ER 1109, [1953] 1 WLR 672, CA.
28   *Lavender v Betts* [1942] 2 All ER 72.
29   *Mowan v Wandsworth London BC* (2000) 33 HLR 616. It may be otherwise in Queensland: *Aussie Traveller Pty Ltd v Marklee Pty Ltd* [1998] 1 Qd R 1.
30   *Jones v Lavington* [1903] 1 KB 253, CA; see also *Celsteel Ltd v Alton House Holdings Ltd (No 2)* [1987] 2 All ER 240, CA (dealing with the express covenant for quiet enjoyment).
31   *Baynes & Co v Lloyd & Sons* [1895] 1 QB 820.
32   *Miller v Emcer Products Ltd* [1956] Ch 304, [1956] 1 All ER 237, CA.
33   *Sampson v Hodson-Pressinger* [1981] 3 All ER 710, CA. In *Southwark London BC v Mills* [1999] 4 All ER 449 at 456 (Lord Hoffmann) this case was confined to its special facts. It could not have been intended that the upper flat of T2 would be used in such a way as to break the implied covenant for quiet enjoyment.

4   An implied covenant for quiet enjoyment extends to lawful acts of neighbouring tenants of the same landlord (ie acts which they may undertake under their own leases), as with mining operations by a tenant causing the land under another lessee's house to subside.[34] The acts of these tenants must be 'lawful' in the sense explained and the landlord is not liable if the offending tenant exceeds any limits imposed by his lease. Thus, where the defendants let farms to A, B and C, and A suffered damage from the flooding of drains on B and C's land, the landlords were held liable only for C's proper use of defective drains, in the sense of being authorised by his lease, but not for B's excessive ('unlawful') use of drains which were in good order.[35]

5   The covenant does not extend to things done before the tenancy was entered into: it is only prospective in nature. Thus, where a pipe had burst before the grant of a tenancy, causing flooding and damage to the premises, the landlord was not liable to the tenant for the result, as the events had preceded the tenancy.[36] The principle of tenant beware seems to be fully alive in this field, and was accepted by the House of Lords.[37]

Damages

The measure of damages for breach is the loss to the tenant resulting from it.[38] This includes removal expenses, damages for inconvenience and shock where appropriate, and legal costs.[39] If all that the tenant is able to prove is trespass, he cannot recover for loss of profits under a separate head.[40] A lessee of a flat who could not let it due to substantial interference caused by the landlord in the course of work to other parts of the premises, was able to recover loss of estimated rental income.[41]

If the landlord commits a tort, such as trespass or nuisance, then an additional separate claim may be framed by the tenant in tort.[42] Where the claimant can prove that there has been exceptionally bad conduct which causes serious injury to his feelings, accompanied with mental distress, he may be able to frame a claim for aggravated

---

34   *Markham v Paget* [1908] 1 Ch 697.
35   *Sanderson v Berwick-upon-Tweed Corpn* (1884) 13 QBD 547. According to Lord Millett in *Southwark London BC v Mills* [1999] 4 All ER 449 at 469, the landlord was liable for the breach of covenant committed by his grantee-tenant, who was under an obligation to maintain, which caused damage to the plaintiff tenant.
36   *Anderson v Oppenheimer* (1880) 5 QBD 602; also *Lyttleton Times Co Ltd v Warners* [1907] AC 476.
37   In *Southwark London BC v Mills* [1999] 4 All ER 449 at 453, HL.
38   *Sutton v Baillie* (1891) 65 LT 528.
39   *Grosvenor Hotel Co v Hamilton* [1894] 2 QB 836, CA; *Giles v Adley* [1987] CLY 2121.
40   *Lawson v Hartley-Brown* (1996) 71 P & CR 242, CA (where on account of trespass one-and-a-half years' rent was awarded for loss of trade).
41   *Mira v Alymer Square Investments Ltd* [1990] 1 EGLR 45, CA.
42   As in *Guppys (Bridport) Ltd v Brookling* (1983) 14 HLR 1, CA, where the landlords cut off all water supplies and sanitation as part of their redevelopment of premises.

damages on account of an illegal eviction.[43] If the conduct of the landlord has been particularly outrageous, exemplary damages may, exceptionally, be awarded. An example is where the landlord deliberately ignores the tenant's legal rights.[44] It is not necessary for the tenant to allege trespass as a condition precedent to an award of exemplary damages.[45] Nor is it necessary to show that the landlord made a profit or aimed at one.[46] There are, unhappily, many recent examples of claims against landlords who use forcing tactics to evict their tenants.[47] Where damages are awarded for a common law claim these must be set off against any damages awarded under a claim made under statute.[48]

III NON-DEROGATION FROM GRANT

Nature of obligation

The landlord is subject to an implied covenant not to derogate from the grant of the lease, or, in effect, not to take away with one hand what he has given with the other. The basis of this obligation rests on fair dealing between the parties rather than on a restrictive straitjacket of individual restrictions.[49] If a landlord, L, grants T1 a lease for a purpose known to both L and T1 (say for use as a gift shop) and L then grants T2 a lease of a neighbouring shop, and T2's use of these premises makes it impossible for

43 As in *Mehta v Royal Bank of Scotland* [1999] L & TR 340 (£10,000 awarded under this head in a case involving a licensee).
44 See eg *Drane v Evangelou* [1978] 2 All ER 437, [1978] 1 WLR 455, CA (£1,000 award upheld).
45 *Drane v Evangelou* [1978] 2 All ER 437, [1978] 1 WLR 455, CA. Also *Breeze v Elden and Hyde* [1987] CLY 2120 (Cty Ct).
46 *Amrani v Oniah* [1984] CLY 1974; cf *Ramdath v Daley* (1993) 25 HLR 273, CA; also *Burchett v Vine* [1997] CLY 3284.
47 See, eg *Abbott v Bayley* [1999] L & TR 267; also *Lord v Jessop* (21 April 1999, unreported) (awards on account of 'disgraceful, self-interested and bullying' conduct by a landlord); *Brown v Mansouri* [1997] CLY 3287 (awards of general damages plus damages for wholesale loss of goods of tenant as well as aggravated damages); *Perry v Scherchen* [2001] EWCA Civ 1192, (2002) 1 P & CR DG 8 (a commercial lessee in whose case the award of general damages fell within the acceptable limits); *Pillai v Amendra* LAG Bulletin, October 2000, p 24 (a bad case of blatant illegal eviction); *Biga v Martin* LAG Bulletin, June 2001, p 25 (criminal entry by landlord and assault on tenant justifying awards of general and exemplary damages). If the premises have not been re-let, an injunction allowing the tenant to regain possession could be awarded: see *Love and Lugg v Herrity* (1990) 23 HLR 217.
48 *Mason v Nworkorie* [1994] 1 EGLR 59 (where the tenant did not have a Rent Act tenancy, but was awarded £4,500 statutory damages): thus the principle would still apply to illegal evictions of assured shorthold tenants, despite the reduction in the level of damages awards under Housing Act 1988, ss 27 and 28 observable in respect of claims by such tenants.
49 *Chartered Trust plc v Davies* [1997] 2 EGLR 83 at 85, CA; *Harmer v Jumbil (Nigeria) Tin Areas Ltd* [1921] 1 Ch 200, CA. Images of 'parchment and sealing wax' and of 'copperplate handwriting' and of 'fusty title deeds' (per Nicholls LJ in *Johnston & Sons Ltd v Holland* [1988] 1 EGLR 264 at 267) may be dismissed from the mind, despite the name of the obligation.

T1 to run his business, L has committed a breach of this covenant. L will also be in breach if he retains land next door which he uses in such a way as to make T1's use of his own premises impossible for the known purpose. Thus if L lets a building to T1 for use as an hotel, and L on neighbouring land carries out building work which undermines the stability of the hotel, L is in breach of this implied duty. The principle extends to a case where T2 or L use their land or premises in such a way as to make T1's premises materially or substantially less fit for use for the known purpose of T1.[50] Both L and T1 must have contemplated the relevant purpose at the time the lease was granted,[51] as where the purpose is stated in a user clause in the lease. If the landlord does not know, when granting the lease, that the tenant intends to make use of the land for a specialised purpose, then the landlord cannot be liable for making use of the neighbouring premises for a purpose which prevents that particular use: if the tenant wishes, for example, to store sensitive paper, as opposed to ordinary paper, on his premises, he must notify the landlord at the time of the lease being taken of his intentions.[52]

A landlord can now break this covenant by deliberate omissions. To take a recent example: a tenant (T1) of a shopping mall took a lease of a shop unit, paying service charges. The landlord (L) had powers to make rules for the benefit of the development as a whole, which it could enforce. The promotion literature of the development suggested that the mall shops would only be let to high-class retail units. T's shop sold puzzles and executive toys. A neighbouring unit was in fact let to a pawnbrokers (T2) whose conduct of their business amounted to a nuisance, driving away T1's custom, so that her business was ruined. The failure of L, despite T1's requests, to enforce the house rules against T2, where the nature of the grant of the lease to T1 depended on the proper management of the shopping 'mall', amounted to a repudiatory breach of obligation by L.[53]

A repudiatory breach entitles the tenant to put an end to the lease. Hence, it must be shown that the tenant was deprived of substantially the whole benefit of his contract, as in the case just mentioned, where T1's passing trade was driven away by the customers of T2. Where a tenant's right to exclusive parking in front of his unit was seriously interfered with by two adjoining tenants, the fact that the landlord did nothing about the problem, although a breach of (express) covenant not to derogate from grant, did not repudiate the lease of the claimant.[54] Nor is a landlord under an implied

---

50   'The camel with the broken back is entitled to complain about the last straw' (Hart J in *Petra Investments Ltd v Jeffrey Rogers plc* [2000] 3 EGLR 120 at 127D).

51   *Johnston & Sons Ltd v Holland* [1988] 1 EGLR 264.

52   *Robinson v Kilvert* (1889) 41 Ch D 88.

53   *Chartered Trust plc v Davies* [1997] 2 EGLR 83 at 85, CA; also *Yankwood Ltd v Havering London BC* [1998] EGCS 75. The necessary implication from the circumstances in the former case was that the landlord would indeed act to enforce these house rules.

54   *Nynehead Developments Ltd v RH Fibreboard Containers Ltd* [1999] 1 EGLR 7. Damages would have been the appropriate remedy. The landlord had also failed contrary to covenant to promote the efficient management of that industrial estate.

liability to shield tenants from every possible adverse effect of taking a lease: in general, it is not a breach for a landlord to let an adjoining unit, for instance, to a competing tenant so that the complainant tenant's trade becomes less profitable. It was thus not a breach to have let a unit in a shopping mall to a major non-retail tenant whose entry into the development had an adverse effect on the claimant tenant's profits.[55] If the landlord has expressly or by necessary implication undertaken in a development not to alter the retail 'mix' of the shop units, doing so might break the covenant against derogation from grant, as the development would then, presumably, lose its original character. If the landlord of a residential estate allows a nuisance to take place on his land, in the form of severe racial harassment of a tenant by other tenants, this may amount to a breach of the present obligation.[56]

Further examples of breach

1 A breach occurred where an assignee of the landlord built on adjoining land in such a way as to obstruct the flow of air to the drying sheds in the tenant's timber yard, the premises having been let for that purpose.[57]

2 A tenant held a lease of land expressly for the purpose of storing explosives, and the defendant held a lease of adjoining land from the same landlord, with a view to working minerals, and the defendant built too near the plaintiff's magazine, so jeopardising the latter's statutory licence. The plaintiff obtained an injunction to restrain the breach.[58]

3 Endangering of the stability of the tenant's adjoining premises by vibration from heavy machinery on the landlord's premises broke the covenant, [59] as did a landlord who built against an external wall of the tenant's premises, using them as a party wall and blocking off the tenant's right to light.[60]

---

55 *Petra Investments Ltd v Jeffrey Rogers plc* [2000] 3 EGLR 120 (where the tenant settled with the landlord; but Hart J thought that it was an implied term of the substantial leases of this shopping centre that the landlord would not alter or use the common parts so as to deprive the centre of its character as a shopping mall).

56 See *Page Motors Ltd v Epsom and Ewell BC* (1981) 80 LGR 337; in *Hussain v Lancaster City Council* [2000] QB 1, the nuisance did not emanate from the landlord's estate so that the action failed.

57 *Aldin v Latimer Clark, Muirhead & Co* [1894] 2 Ch 437; also *Platt v London Underground Ltd* [2001] 20 EG 227 (CS); [2001] L & T R D 22 (closure of exit of tube station, costing kiosk tenant's trade).

58 *Harmer v Jumbil (Nigeria) Tin Areas Ltd* [1921] 1 Ch 200, CA.

59 *Grosvenor Hotel Co v Hamilton* [1894] 2 QB 836, CA.

60 *Betts Ltd v Pickford's Ltd* [1906] 2 Ch 87; similarly, an interference with a right to airspace of adjoining land granted to the tenant for advertising purposes: *Johnston & Sons Ltd v Holland* [1988] 1 EGLR 264; as well as interference with a tenants' profit à prendre: *Peech v Best* [1931] 1 KB 1, CA; and an unjustified reduction in a defined parking space: *Saeed v Plustrade Ltd* [2001] EWCA Civ 2011, [2002] 02 EG 102 (CS).

What is not a breach

In addition to the matters already noted, if the only complaint is of interference with the tenant's privacy,[61] or that adjoining premises have been let for a competing trade,[62] or that the insurance risks, such as for fire, have been increased by a letting of adjacent premises,[63] there is no breach of the present obligation. In one case,[64] the authorities were reviewed. The established principle that, express covenant apart, it was no breach of a covenant not to derogate from grant for a landlord to have let neighbouring premises for a competing trade to that of the tenants (in that case a banking business) was held to be correctly-based; no principle of alleged unfairness required it to be modified. However, the High Court has now restricted this principle in the case of a letting of a purpose-built gift shop selling aquarium related (and so specialist) products, where the successful complaint was that the landlord proposed to allow exactly these products to be retailed from adjoining premises.[65]

IV USUAL COVENANTS

1 Introduction. Where the parties make use of an agreement for a lease, to be followed by a formal deed, and the contract fails to specify the terms which will be inserted in the lease, it is implied that the lease will contain the usual covenants. The question of whether a particular covenant is 'usual' is one of fact. Evidence of conveyancers is taken into account.[66] The court will look at the nature of the premises, their situation and locality, the purpose for which they are being let, and the length of the term, and it may look at lists of what have been held to be 'usual' covenants in precedents. The word 'usual' means 'occurring in ordinary use', so that if it is found that in nine out of ten cases a covenant of a particular sort would be in a lease of premises of a given nature and district, the covenant may be 'usual'.[67]

2 Examples. The following have been held to be usual covenants: a covenant by the landlord for quiet enjoyment,[68] and the following covenants by the tenant: to pay tenants' rates and taxes; to keep the premises in repair and to deliver them up in repair at the end of the term; not to alter or add to the demised premises without the landlord's consent; not to stop up, darken or obstruct windows or light belonging to the demised

---

61   *Browne v Flower* [1911] 1 Ch 219.
62   *Port v Griffith* [1938] 1 All ER 295. A landlord cannot be impliedly prevented from putting up additional flats on his adjoining land: *Hannon v 169 Queen's Gate Ltd* [2000] 1 EGLR 40. It might have been different if there had been a letting scheme limited to a given number of flats: see *Devonshire Reid Premises Ltd v Trenaman* [1997] 1 EGLR 45.
63   *O'Cedar Ltd v Slough Trading Co Ltd* [1927] 2 KB 123.
64   *Romulus Trading v Comet Properties* [1996] 2 EGLR 70; HW Wilkinson (1997) 147 NLJ 93.
65   *Oceanic Village Ltd v Shirayama Shokussan Co Ltd* [2001] L & TR 478.
66   *Chester v Buckingham Travel Ltd* [1981] 1 All ER 386; Woodman (1981) 97 LQR 385; Crabb [1992] Conv 18.
67   *Flexman v Corbett* [1930] 1 Ch 672 at 678-679.
68   *Hampshire v Wickens* (1878) 7 Ch D 555.

premises; not to permit easements to be acquired against the demised premises; not to permit the demised premises to be used for specified purposes; a condition of re-entry for non-payment of rent; and a proviso for re-entry for breach of covenants other than to pay rent.[69] Certain covenants are *onerous or unusual,* such as: to insure;[70] to repair and rebuild;[71] not to assign or sub-let without consent; or not to exercise a particular trade.[72]

69 *Chester v Buckingham Travel* [1981] 1 All ER 386.
70 *Cosser v Collinge* (1832) 3 My & K 283.
71 *Doe d Dymoke v Withers* (1831) 2 B & Ad 896.
72 *Chester v Buckingham Travel* [1981] 1 All ER 386.

CHAPTER 7

Covenants in leases other than to pay rent and to repair

I INTRODUCTION

Since the covenants implied into a lease are the minimum necessary to enable the lease to function, a properly drafted lease will contain a number of express covenants. The parties are free, subject to statutory restrictions (such as those governing repairing obligations) and to consumer regulations of unfair contract terms, to insert covenants in whatever terms they think fit, and there is a wide range of forms and precedents to assist them in their task.[1] In the residential sector, however, particularly in the case of assured shorthold tenancies, there is a degree of standardisation of terms.

In this book we do not set out all possible varieties of all leasehold obligations. We concentrate on those obligations most commonly found in leases and tenancies, notably:
1 covenants limiting the right of the tenant to assign or sub-let the premises;
2 tenant obligations not to alter or improve the premises;
3 restrictions on the use the tenant may make of the premises;
4 obligations by the tenant to pay rent and to accept rent reviews; and
5 repairing and maintenance obligations of landlords and tenants.

Some leases contain an obligation by the tenant, as occupier, to pay rates and council tax as appropriate.[2] In the case of a business tenancy or a long residential lease, there may be an express covenant by the landlord to keep up insurance on the premises against damage or destruction of the premises from certain risks such as fire, flood,

---

1 See, eg Law Society Business Lease; also precedents in *Precedents for the Conveyancer*; also Luxton & Wilkie *Commercial Leases*.
2 In any case by Local Government Finance Act 1992, s 6, tenants of domestic premises, if resident, are liable to pay council tax. Liability for other assessments such as water rates is governed by statute (eg Water Industry Act 1991, ss 142 and 144).

earthquake, subsidence and vehicular and malicious damage.[3] Although the landlord is not liable at common law to re-instate the property if an event insured against materialises,[4] an express obligation may be imposed in the lease, although if re-instatement is not possible, the lease may provide for the way the insurance money is dealt with as between the parties.[5] Some leases provide an express landlord covenant for quiet enjoyment, but the protection to the tenant of this covenant may differ from that of the implied obligation, if it does not in terms extend to persons claiming under the landlord, such as his or her other lessees.

II DISPOSITION COVENANTS

General points and statutory background

At common law, the tenant may assign or sub-let the premises demised by the lease to any person or company he thinks fit. Many commercial leases, at any rate, seek to limit the disposition rights of the tenant, as by stating that the tenant cannot assign, sub-let or part with the possession of the demised premises without the consent of the landlord,[6] such consent[7] is not to be unreasonably withheld. Short residential leases may go further and completely prohibit any right to assign or sub-let the tenancy (in which case there would seem to be a violation of consumer regulations: see ch 4 above). Because an absolute prohibition on dispositions may deter business tenants from taking any other than a short tenancy, it seems that disposition covenants in the business sector will ordinarily be fully qualified. That is to say, the tenant undertakes that he will not assign, sub-let or part with the possession of the demised premises or any part of them without first asking for the landlord's written consent, which consent will not be unreasonably withheld. The purpose of a disposition covenant has been said to be to protect the lessor from having his premises used and occupied in an undesirable way by an undesirable tenant or assignee.[8]

---

3 The tenant may have to repay the landlord for the cost of the premiums: in this connection, the landlord is not under an implied duty to secure the cheapest possible insurance: see eg *Havenridge Ltd v Boston Dyers Ltd* [1994] 2 EGLR 73, CA. However, special information rights are conferred on residential tenants of flats by Landlord and Tenant Act 1985 Sch. Long lessees of houses may, subject to CLRA 2002, s 164, make their own insurance arrangements.

4 *Bullock v Dommitt* (1796) 6 Term Rep 650. There is a statutory requirement to re-instate in the case of fire destruction: Fires Prevention (Metropolis) Act 1774, s 83.

5 *Re King* [1963] Ch 459.

6 Sometimes reference may be made to the 'licence' of the landlord: as to this see eg *Cerium Investments Ltd v Evans* [1991] 1 EGLR 80.

7 As to 'consent' in the context of a dispute between an assigning lessee and its assignee see *Aubergine Enterprises Ltd v Lakewood International Ltd* [2001] 3 EGLR 71.

8 *Ashworth Frazer Ltd v Gloucester City Council* [2001] UKHL 59, [2002] 1 All ER 377, para 61.

Questions have arisen as to what types of transaction may be caught by disposition covenants. As to form, a covenant referring to an assignment is taken to refer to a legal assignment during the life of the assigning tenant[9] of the whole of the remainder of the lease which complies both at the contract and transfer stages with the statutory form required.[10] Similarly, a covenant against sub-letting is broken if the tenant creates a legal sub-tenancy over the whole or, if the covenant expressly refers to this, of part of the premises.[11] Only once the assignee has been registered at the Land Registry with a leasehold title, may he or she be considered to be the legal assignee of the lease.[12]

Disposition covenants vary in form. Some may refer to assignment, sub-letting[13] and a parting with the possession[14] of the demised premises or any part. If the tenant legally assigns the whole premises, he or she automatically parts with possession.[15] If, by contrast, the tenant is absent only for relatively short periods and retains exclusive possession, then there is no parting with possession in the prohibited sense.[16] The same result follows if the tenant allows someone to share the premises with him, without renouncing control over the premises.[17] But where a lessee formed a company which paid its own rent, made its own supply arrangements for electricity and water, and otherwise took over the control of the premises, possession was parted with in the sense that the tenant became a stranger to the land.[18] Where a tenant sub-lets first most of the premises and then the rest to a different person, a covenant against sub-letting the whole premises is broken.[19] It is not settled whether a covenant only

9   See Barnsley (1963) 27 Conv (NS) 159, as to the effect of a disposition by a tenant of his lease by will.
10   Thus, any contract to assign must comply with LP(MP)A 1989, s 2 and so be in writing and set out all the terms agreed. A deed must be employed to pass the legal title to the lease, no matter how short the residue of the term to be assigned: LPA 1925, s 52. This rule applies even if the original term was created orally or in writing: *Crago v Julian* [1992] 1 All ER 744, CA. In addition, once LRA 2002 comes into force, legal title can only be conferred in principle by registration.
11   *Serjeant v Nash, Field & Co* [1903] 2 KB 304 (thus extending to creating a legal mortgage by sub-demise; to prohibit creating a legal charge express language would be required: *Grand Junction Co Ltd v Bates* [1954] 2 QB 160, [1954] 2 All ER 385).
12   At least where the leasehold estate is registrable: LRA 2002, s 4. See ch 4 above.
13   For a case where a disposition covenant required the sub-letting to comply with specific requirements or 'provisos' such as to the payment of a full market rent by the sub-tenant and requiring covenants in the same form as in the head lease, see *Allied Dunbar Assurance plc v Homebase Ltd* [2002] L & TR 1.
14   A parting with possession refers to parting with the legal right to exclusive possession vested in the tenant by a lease: *Stening v Andrews* [1931] 1 Ch 470.
15   See *Marks v Warren* [1979] 1 All ER 29. An assignment of the whole premises inevitably involves parting with the possession of all parts of the premises, so that a prohibition only on assigning any parts of premises applied to an assignment of the whole: *Field v Barkworth* [1986] 1 All ER 362, [1986] 1 WLR 137.
16   *10A Challis Avenue Pty Ltd v Seddon* [1962] NSWR 653.
17   *Stapleton Enterprises of Manitoba Ltd v Bramer Machine Shop Ltd* [1978] 1 WWR 297.
18   *Lam Kee Ying Sdn Bhd v Lam Shes Tong* [1975] AC 247, JCPC.
19   *Yorkshire Metropolitan Properties Ltd v Co-operative Retail Services Ltd* [2001] L & TR 26, [2001] L & TR 298, following *Chatterton v Terrell* [1923] AC 578.

prohibiting underlettings would also catch assignments. An Irish case held that such covenant indicated by necessary implication that all disposals of the premises would be caught,[20] but this may give insufficient weight to the principle that a landlord covenant such as disposition covenants should be read against the interests of the party benefiting from it. An assignment in breach of covenant transfers a title to the assignee, but it is vulnerable to forfeiture if the landlord could reasonably have withheld his consent to it taking place.[21] As to whether a company tenant who amalgamated with another company would commit a breach of a covenant not to assign the lease, it has been held in Canada that a breach would be constituted, on the ground that after the amalgamation the lessee company would cease to exist.[22]

Absolute prohibitions on assignments or sub-letting have never been formally outlawed by legislation. On their face, they seem to impose an unbalanced fetter on a tenant's common law rights, even though the landlord may, if it chooses, licence a particular proposed disposition.[23] Pushed to extremes, an absolute prohibition may lock a tenant who cannot assign into the tenancy. It is therefore disappointing that the recommendation of the Law Commission, made as long ago as 1985, to abolish absolute prohibitions on dispositions of a lease (save in the case of short residential tenancies)[24] has not been enacted.

Legislation has affected the disposition covenants for over 70 years. If a disposition covenant is merely qualified (ie that it only allows the tenant to assign or sub-let the premises with the landlord's prior consent), that covenant is rendered fully qualified by legislation.[25] This means that a disposition covenant in any commercial or residential lease[26] is treated as though it read that the landlord will not unreasonably withhold his consent.

20 *Re Doyle* [1899] 1 IR 113.
21 *Old Grovebury Manor Farm Ltd v W Seymour Plant Sales & Hire Ltd (No 2)* [1979] 3 All ER 504.
22 *Crescent Leaseholds Ltd v Gerhard Horn Investments Ltd* [1983] 1 WWR 305.
23 LPA 1925, s 143 limits any licence in such a case to the particular disposition to which it relates.
24 Law Com No 141 (1985) 'Covenants Restricting Disposals, Alterations and Changes of User' paras 7.4-7.24.
25 Landlord and Tenant Act 1927, s 19(1)(a). This provision does not apply to a tenancy of an agricultural holding or to a farm business tenancy (Landlord and Tenant Act 1927, s 19(4) as amended). Landlord and Tenant Act 1927, s 19(1)(a) was held to be avoided, despite the fact that it cannot in terms be contracted out of, by a surrender-back clause. Such a clause, at issue in *Adler v Upper Grosvenor Street Investments Ltd* [1957] 1 All ER 229, approved in *Bocardo SA v S & M Hotels Ltd* [1979] 3 All ER 737, CA, allows the landlord prior to consenting, to require the tenant to offer it a surrender of the lease. In *Homebase Ltd v Allied Dunbar Assurance plc* [2002] EWCA Civ 666, compliance by a lessee with all provisos of a disposition covenant was required before any question of landlord consent could arise. One proviso in this case, which had been flouted, was that an underlease had to be granted at a market rent – a matter of obvious concern to the landlord.
26 A special rule (Landlord and Tenant Act 1927, s 19(1)(b)) applying to commercial building leases (granted for a term of more than 40 years), was abrogated by Landlord and Tenant Act 1927, s 19(1D), inserted by LT(C)A 1995, s 22. The special rule, which allows limited freedom

At this point it is instructive to note the position in Scots law, whose evolution has been somewhat different to that of English law. Although contractual rights in Scotland are freely assignable in principle, leases are governed by the principle of *delectus personae*, because a lease involves more than payment or delivery of a thing.[27] Thus a lease which does not expressly provide that the property may be assigned or sub-let by the tenant with the landlord's consent, such consent not to be unreasonably withheld,[28] cannot be assigned or sub-let. There are a number of exceptions to this rule, notably in the case of a lease of urban subjects.[29] However, where the main rule applies, the landlord can refuse consent to an assignation of the lease on any grounds even if these are unreasonable,[30] much as a landlord in England is able to do where the lease absolutely prohibits assignments and sub-lettings. Where a Scots lease provides for what in English law would be treated as a fully qualified disposition covenant, recent Scots authority suggests that the courts there are deciding issues of the reasonableness or otherwise of a landlord's refusal of consent along similar, but not identical, lines to their English counterparts, as by adopting a test of whether a reasonable landlord would have acted as did the landlord in question. Thus, a landlord who tried to obtain an advantage from consent, which the lease did not provide for, in the shape of a large premium, was held to have unreasonably withheld consent.[31] By contrast, a landlord which sought a guarantor of a tenant's obligations, where the tenant sought to assign the lease from a partnership to herself as sole tenant, had imposed a reasonable condition.[32]

Some differences exist as to the juridical nature of a covenant not to assign or sub-let the demised premises without the landlord's consent, such consent not to be unreasonably withheld. Traditionally, the covenant was a qualification on the tenant's undertaking not to assign or sub-let. This tradition is reflected in the terminology, which still refers to 'fully qualified' disposition covenants. On the other hand, in

---

to assign or sub-let, subject to a notice requirement, which still governs old tenancies, and old and new residential leases as defined in the Landlord and Tenant Act 1927, s 19(1E), was not thought appropriate for new commercial building leases.

27 Gloag and Henderson (10th edn, 1995) 41.18 and 41.19; Walker, Vol III, Book v, pp 215-16. See *Brador Properties Ltd v British Telecommunications plc* 1992 SC 12.

28 Or which provides, in what seems to be the more traditional form of words, that assignation of the lease is excluded except with the consent in writing of the landlord, such consent not to be unreasonably withheld. It will be appreciated that in Scotland there is no equivalent to the Landlord and Tenant Act 1927, s 19.

29 Rankine *Leases* p 175; also leases of rural subjects where these are of 'extraordinary duration': Rankine, p 173. It is probable that the exception for urban subjects does not extend to furnished lettings (Walker, Vol III, Book v, pp 215-16).

30 See *Marquis of Breadalbane v Whitehead & Sons* (1893) 21 R 138, CS. Even in the case of a fully qualified covenant, it was held in *Lousada & Co Ltd v JE Lesser (Properties) Ltd* 1990 SC 178 that if the landlord did not give reasons for refusing consent, the court would not assume that it had no valid reasons. The Landlord and Tenant Act 1988 does not apply to Scotland.

31 *Scottish Tourist Board v Deanpark Ltd* 1998 SLT 1121; also *Renfrew District Council v AB Leisure (Renfrew) Ltd* 1988 SLT 635n (where the landlords without justification sought to introduce, as conditions of consent, four new elements into the lease such as a full repairing obligation and more frequent rent reviews).

32 *Scotmore Developments Ltd v Anderton* 1996 STC 1304.

Canada it has been held that, owing to the modern view that a lease is a contract, the covenant that the landlord would not withhold consent unreasonably is a landlord covenant, which, if broken, can be enforced in damages by the tenant.[33]

No fine or sum of money in the nature of a fine (essentially no lump sum) is to be paid for the landlord's consent to an assignment or sub-letting (LPA 1925, s 144). However, this provision presents difficulties. It can be contracted out of in the lease. Also, a reasonable sum can be required by the landlord in respect of legal or other expenses in relation to any licence or consent: presumably what is reasonable is an issue of fact. It might have been better to do away with this provision and simply to outlaw the payment of all lump sums in these circumstances, as otherwise the landlord can abuse his or her position to extract a financial advantage from the tenant.[34]

Authorised guarantee agreements

When the law governing the enforcement of leasehold covenants was reformed by LT(C)A 1995, the liability of an original tenant to perform covenants was abolished by LT(C)A 1995, s 5, on an assignment of the lease. However, in the interests of commercial landlords, a form of guarantee is provided for in LT(C)A 1995, so as to compensate landlords for the loss of the financial security entailed in not being able to bring an action until the expiry of the lease against the original lessee for breaches of covenant, where the latter had assigned the term. The government feared that, but for these changes, landlords might seek to impose absolute prohibitions on assignment.[35]

LT(C)A 1995 therefore amends the Landlord and Tenant Act 1927 in such a way as to allow a commercial landlord to extract from an assigning commercial lessee an 'authorised guarantee agreement' (hereafter 'AGA') provided that certain conditions are met. The assigning lessee can then be made liable to pay rent arrears accumulated by its immediate, but not by any further, assignee, if the latter fails to remedy its default, under an AGA. The method used to achieve this result is, in essence, to allow the landlord to insert into a commercial lease a requirement, provided that it is lawful, that on assigning the lease, the assignor-tenant would sign an AGA for the benefit of the landlord.[36]

33 *Cudmore v Petro Canada Inc* [1986] 4 WWR 38; indeed, in *Lehndorff Canadian Pension Properties Ltd v Davis Management Ltd* [1989] 5 WER 481, the British Columbia, CA ruled that a refusal of consent on no valid grounds amounted to a repudiatory breach by the landlord, entitling the tenants to quit the premises and to cease to pay rent. This issue is not settled by the enactment of the Landlord and Tenant Act 1988 because this statute confers a remedy in tort on the tenant, not in contract.

34 See Crabb [1993] Conv 215.

35 HL Report of Landlord and Tenant (Covenants) Bill, *Hansard*, 5 July 1995, col 385.

36 At common law the principle is established that any attempt in the lease to set out in advance the grounds or conditions on which a landlord may grant or refuse consent to a proposed assignment cannot avoid the right of the court if asked to rule that any pre-set grounds or conditions are unreasonable: *Creery v Summersell & Flowerdew & Co Ltd* [1949] Ch 751. This principle still governs residential and agricultural tenancies, where the right to extract an AGA from an assigning lessee is not conferred.

The parties to a commercial lease may accordingly specify by agreement any circumstances (not just AGAs therefore) in which an immediate landlord may reasonably withhold his or her licence or consent to an assignment of the whole or any part of the demised premises. The parties may also specify any 'lawful' conditions subject to which any such licence or consent is to be granted. The landlord is not regarded as automatically unreasonably withholding his licence or consent to any such assignment if he withholds it on the pre-set ground or circumstance, and the circumstances exist (LT(C)A 1995, s 19(1A)). The insertion in the lease when drafted of pre-set terms or conditions or both will not be taken of itself to make them unreasonable. The onus of proof on the landlord of showing that the terms or conditions are reasonable,[37] if these are attacked by the tenant when it wishes to assign, is probably unaffected by LT(C)A 1995 reforms. However, as has been noted,[38] it is now possible for landlords to insert pre-set conditions into commercial leases as to the financial status or strength of proposed assignees, such as measured by their net profits, or by a multiplier of the annual rent or their asset value.

Thus, in a 'new' commercial tenancy (ie one granted or renewed on or after 1 January 1996) a requirement may lawfully be imposed when the tenancy is granted, that it will be a condition of any assignment that the tenant is to enter into an AGA under LT(C)A 1995, s 16. In addition, the landlord may require an assigning tenant to enter into an AGA at any time before an application to assign is made, as where no such condition had been pre-specified in the lease when drafted or in any document attached to it (LT(C)A 1995, s 19(1B)).

The requirement that the condition as to an AGA must be 'lawfully imposed' has now been considered by the High Court, which adopted a wide meaning of this expression.[39] The landlords of a lease being renewed under the Landlord and Tenant Act 1954, Pt II (and thus a 'new tenancy' within the meaning of LT(C)A 1995) sought to include a new term as to the assignment of the premises. This was that any assignment of the whole premises could be subject to a landlords' condition that the assigning tenant entered into an AGA with the landlord. It was noted that where, as in this case, the lease did not originally state that a tenant who assigned could be required by the landlord to enter an AGA, the landlord could only insert such a requirement if it was 'lawfully imposed'. The latter expression was synonymous with the word 'reasonable'; if a landlord was reasonable in seeking to impose an AGA, then the demand was lawfully imposed. If it had been unreasonable to make the demand, then it was not lawfully imposed.

This ruling has no direct application to a covenant taken from the lessee at the time of the grant of the lease that the landlord can impose an AGA on the assigning tenant.

---

37 Under the Landlord and Tenant Act 1988, s 1(6)(a).
38 *Acheson* [1997] 03 EG 132. In addition, landlords may insert a clause that, for example, envisages a condition that the premises will be in good repair when assigned, or will be put in repair by the proposed assignee.
39 *Wallis Fashion Group Ltd v CGU Life Assurance Ltd* [2000] 2 EGLR 49; Haley [2000] Conv 566.

However, the fact that the taking of an AGA is pre-set in the original lease terms will not of itself mean that the landlord can automatically impose an AGA on any assignment. He or she can only do so if it is reasonable to do so, and there may be circumstances in which, when a proposed assignment is being considered, the landlord would not be acting reasonably in imposing a pre-set AGA on the tenant.

Landlord and Tenant Act 1988

The Landlord and Tenant Act 1988 (hereinafter LTA 1988) is a procedural measure. It was passed to improve the speed of landlord decision-making on relation to disposition covenants. The landlord is under a statutory duty to give consent. Imposing a condition on consent, which condition is not reasonable, does not satisfy the statutory duty (LTA 1988, s 2). Thus, the landlord is guilty of breach of statutory duty and exposed to an action in damages (LTA 1988, s 4) if he unreasonably refuses his consent to written request to carry out a proposed assignment or sub-letting, or imposes an unreasonable condition, unless he can produce reasonable grounds for doing so. If the landlord refuses consent in circumstances outside the limits of any provision specifying the circumstances in which consent will be given or refused he or she will also be in breach of statutory duty (LTA 1988, s 1(5)).[40] It seems that the action of the tenant is in tort and not on the disposition covenant, thus excluding claims against a landlord who has assigned the reversion.

The landlord of any tenant, except a secure tenant, is under the statutory duties in relation to applications in writing for consent[41] to an assignment, under-letting, charging or parting with possession. Since the landlord is not given much time by LTA 1988 in which to make up his mind, he is not impliedly required by it to justify the factual basis of each of his assertions.[42]

Where the tenant serves on the landlord, or other person who may consent, a written application for consent or licence (LTA 1988, s 5(1)) the 1988 Act is triggered. The landlord, by LTA 1988, s 1(3), owes the tenant a duty, within a reasonable time:
1   to give consent, except where it is reasonable not to do so; and
2   to serve on the tenant written notice of his decision whether or not to give consent.[43]

In view of the short time allowed to the landlord in which to make up his mind, the landlord is entitled to decide on the basis of facts available at the time of the decision.

---

40   This provision is seemingly directed at a covenant by a landlord that he will not refuse consent to an assignment to a respectable and responsible person, treating his refusal of consent for an assignment to such a person as unreasonable.
41   As opposed to an oral application. It could be argued that the Electronic Communications Act 2000 treats e-mail and web-based applications for consent as being in writing.
42   *Air India v Balabel* [1993] 2 EGLR 66; but see below.
43   Once consent is given, its withdrawal will seemingly render the landlord liable for statutory damages: *Aubergine Enterprises Ltd v Lakewood International Ltd* [2001] EGCS 29.

A decision will not be invalidated by subsequent events that might falsify it, such as a later production of a good set of accounts.[44] A landlord's decision notice must, however, specify any conditions attached to consent, or the reasons for withholding it (LTA 1988, s 1(3)).

LTA 1988 applies neither to an absolute prohibition on assignments underletting or parting with the possession of premises (LTA 1988, s 1(1)(a)) nor to covenants not to change the user of the premises. It does not affect the law governing covenants against the making of alterations to the demised premises.

If a landlord receives a written consent application, where, in addition to his own consent, the consent of a superior landlord (or, say, mortgagee) is required, the recipient is bound to take reasonable steps to secure the receipt, within a reasonable time, of a copy of the application by that person (LTA 1988, s 2(1)). The superior landlord then comes under a mirror duty to that of the mesne landlord under LTA 1988, s 1 (LTA 1988, s 3).

The landlord must show, if challenged by the tenant, that he gave a consent within a reasonable time. LTA 1988 does not lay down any particular period of time as being reasonable. In ordinary circumstances, with no special difficulty, this period is not likely to exceed a few weeks.[45] Likewise, the onus is on the landlord to show that any condition is reasonable, where LTA 1988 applies, and if consent is refused, the onus is on the landlord to show that a refusal of consent was reasonable (LTA 1988, ss 1(6)(c) and 3(5)(a)). The onus is also on the landlord to show that he served his decision notice within a reasonable time (LTA 1988, s 1(6)).

The High Court ruled that if a landlord had a ground for refusing consent, which operated on his mind at the expiry of the time allowed for his decision notice under LTA 1988, he must place that ground in his decision notice. If he failed to do so, he would not be able to rely on the ground in later proceedings.[46] The House of Lords has refined this approach. Once a landlord has stated in writing the ground on which he refuses consent, he cannot, it was said, rely on any other ground. However, 'that does not mean to say that, when seeking to show that it was reasonable for him not to consent on the stated ground, he is confined to what he has said in his letter'.[47]

---

44 See *CIN Properties Ltd v Gill* [1993] 2 EGLR 97.
45 In *Dong Bang Minerva v Davina* [1995] 1 EGLR 41, 28 days sufficed on the facts. Time runs from the date of a tenant undertaking to pay the landlord's costs in considering the application: *Dong Bang Minerva v Davina* on appeal [1996] 2 EGLR 31. In *Venetian Glass Gallery Ltd v Next Properties Ltd* [1989] 2 EGLR 42 it was held that for a tenant to have made an application for consent and then within five days to follow it up with proceedings was not on the facts reasonable; also *Midland Bank plc v Chart Enterprises Inc* [1990] 2 EGLR 59 (10 weeks' inadequately explained delay unreasonable on facts).
46 *Footwear Corpn Ltd v Amplight Properties Ltd* [1998] 3 All ER 52; *Norwich Union Life Assurance Society v Shopmoor Ltd* [1998] 3 All ER 32. However, the inclusion of a bad ground in a decision notice will not invalidate the whole notice if there are also valid grounds.
47 *Ashworth Frazer Ltd v Gloucester City Council* [2001] UKHL 59, [2002] 1 All ER 377 para 75 (Lord Rodger, speaking for the whole House).

The landlord's decision will be but a short time from the tenant's written consent application, for (as already noted) LTA 1988 was passed specifically to force landlords to give reasons[48] and to speed up their decisions.[49] It is also aimed at preventing landlords from prevaricating on applications for consent they could not very well turn down, hoping the proposed assignment would not take place.[50] For these reasons, a landlord who has asked for information about a proposed assignee and who has not been supplied with it cannot delay making a decision, but equally is entitled to base the grounds of a decision on the factual material available at the time of the decision, so that the tenant cannot, presumably, be heard to complain if the landlord, without specific materials at his or her disposal at the time for decision, such as accounts, makes a decision which these materials would have affected.[51]

Reasonableness of refusal of consent – preliminary

LTA 1988, as noted, is a procedural statute. It does not regulate the substantive law affecting the issue of whether consent has been reasonably refused by the landlord.[52] However, it casts the onus of proving that consent to a proposed assignment or sub-letting was reasonably refused on the landlord. The question arises as to whether a landlord has unreasonably refused consent[53] to a proposed assignment or sub-letting. However, if the landlord has undertaken not to refuse consent to an assignment to a respectable and responsible person, and a proposed assignee satisfies that test, the landlord must consent to the proposed disposition.[54]

The date on which the reasonableness of a refusal of consent is decided upon is the date of the landlord's decision, as opposed to that of any subsequent proceedings between the parties.[55] Therefore, facts which might have swayed the landlord either way which appear after his decision cannot be relevant to its reasonableness, having regard to the short time allowed for a decision where LTA 1988 applies.[56]

---

48   At common law, there was no general duty on a landlord to give reasons: *Young v Ashley Gardens Property Ltd* [1903] 2 Ch 112, although if a landlord gave an obviously bad reason for a refusal of consent, the courts could assume that he or she had no good reasons to advance (*Lovelock v Margo* [1963] 2 QB 786, a case on forfeiture).
49   As to the pre-1988 difficulties see, eg *29 Equities Ltd v Bank Leumi (UK) Ltd* [1986] 1 WLR 1490 at 1494 (Dillon LJ) 'what so often happens is that landlords take a very long time before giving their minds to the matter'.
50   As judicially recognised in *Norwich Union Life Assurance Society v Shopmoor Ltd* [1998] 3 All ER 32 at 45.
51   See *Daventry Holdings Pty Ltd v Bacalakis Hotels Pty Ltd* [1986] 1 Qd R 406 at 411-12 (Thomas J) emphasising the need for fair dealing between both parties.
52   *Ashworth Frazer Ltd v Gloucester City Council* [2001] UKHL 59 [2002] 1 All ER 377.
53   Consent vitiated by fraud is no consent but the landlord may have to proceed against the assignee to forfeit the lease (as opposed to the assigning tenant): *Sanctuary Housing Association v Baker* (1997) 74 P & CR D 28.
54   *Moat v Martin* [1950] 1 KB 175, [1949] 2 All ER 646, CA.
55   *Bromley Park Garden Estates Ltd v Moss* [1982] 2 All ER 890, [1982] 1 WLR 1019, CA.
56   *CIN Properties Ltd v Gill* [1993] 2 EGLR 97; *Air India v Balabel* [1993] 2 EGLR 66.

The fact that consent could not reasonably be withheld does not exclude the tenant's obligation to apply for consent to the landlord.[57] A landlord whose consent is not sought may bring forfeiture proceedings, but relief may be granted if no damage is caused to his reversion, provided he could not reasonably have withheld consent.[58] A tenant may claim tort damages under LTA 1988 on account of breach of statutory duty for an unreasonable withholding of consent. He may, alternatively, carry out the transaction concerned and risk a forfeiture.[59]

Assessing 'reasonableness' of a refusal of consent

The House of Lords has recently revisited the general approach to be adopted to the question of whether a landlord has reasonably refused consent to a proposed assignment (or sub-letting).[60] Lord Rodger, giving the leading speech, said that the reasonableness test prevented the law from becoming unduly rigid. Thus reasonableness must be read in a general sense. The approach of Lord Denning MR[61] was approved.[62] Lord Denning MR said that cases dealing with the issue of reasonableness did not lay down propositions of law. When the words 'such licence shall not unreasonably be withheld' come to be applied to a particular case, the court could not determine by strict rules the grounds on which a landlord may or may not reasonably withhold his consent. The landlord was not limited by the contract to any particular grounds. The courts should not limit him. Lord Denning MR pointed out that 'the landlord has to exercise his judgment in all sorts of circumstances'. It was impossible for him, or the courts, to envisage them all.[63] Thus the issue of judging reasonableness was akin to that where statute gave the court a discretion. Strict rules could not fetter this discretion. A further statement by Balcombe LJ[64] was also approved by their Lordships. He said that 'it is in each case a question of fact, depending on the circumstances, whether the landlord's consent to an assignment is being unreasonably withheld'.

Hence, care must be taken not to turn a decision made on particular facts into a proposition of law of general importance.[65] If a refusal of consent is challenged by the

57 *Barrow v Isaacs & Sons* [1891] 1 QB 417, CA; also *Wilson v Fynn* [1948] 2 All ER 40.
58 *Scala House and District Property Co Ltd v Forbes* [1974] QB 575, [1973] 3 All ER 308, CA.
59 He may also apply to the county court under Landlord and Tenant Act 1954, s 53 for a declaration that consent was unreasonably withheld.
60 *Ashworth Frazer Ltd v Gloucester City Council* [2001] UKHL 59, [2002] 1 All ER 377.
61 In *Bickel v Duke of Westminster* [1977] QB 517 at 524.
62 *Ashworth Frazer Ltd v Gloucester City Council* [2001] UKHL 59, [2002] 1 All ER 377, para 67.
63 Thus no landlord when granting a long lease in 1947, as in *Bickel*, could have foreseen that by 1967 Parliament would allow an assignee to buy out his freehold.
64 In *International Drilling Fluids Ltd v Louisville Investments (Uxbridge) Ltd* [1986] Ch 513 at 521.
65 *Ashworth Frazer Ltd v Gloucester City Council* [2001] UKHL 59, [2002] 1 All ER 377, para 4 (Lord Bingham).

tenant, the landlord is bound only to show that his conduct was reasonable, not that it was right or justified. If the circumstances which caused the landlord to refuse consent were such that a reasonable man in the circumstances might reach the same conclusion, the landlord is not required to prove that his conclusions were justified.[66]

Some limitations of a general nature appear to have remained intact: notably, that a landlord is bound to base his refusal of consent to a proposed disposition on grounds which relate to the premises demised by the lease. General policy grounds applying to the whole of the premises which the landlord owns, where the demised premises are only part of these, appear not to be capable of grounding a reasonable refusal. An example was where a landlord refused consent to a proposed assignment of a residential lease because it had a general policy of obtaining surrenders of all leases in the block concerned. It was held that the ground advanced was unreasonable.[67] Similarly, a landlord who claimed that if he consented to the proposed transaction, he would lose a tenant in other premises of his had refused his consent on unreasonable grounds.[68]

Interaction with user covenants

If the landlord is asked to consent to a proposed assignment or sub-letting, and the result will necessarily be that the assignee or sub-lessee will break a user covenant in the lease, the landlord is reasonably entitled to refuse his consent.[69] If the landlord reasonably thinks that an assignment (or sub-letting) is probably going to result in a breach of a user covenant by the assignee or new sub-lessee, he is in principle entitled to refuse his consent. 'In deciding whether to withhold consent reasonable landlords need not confine their consideration to what will necessarily happen ... they may have regard to what will probably happen'.[70] The policy of this ruling is that a landlord would not necessarily wish to be saddled with a new tenant who would be likely to fail to comply with the user covenant, or who might seek to challenge it before the Lands Tribunal.[71] In addition, one might add, the new, less strict test means that landlords are not being forced to accept a real and uncovenanted change in the circumstances of the letting. However, as pointed out in the House of Lords, their rejection of the principle that a landlord who could not show that breach of a user covenant was inevitable as a result of the assignment could not refuse his consent reasonably on

---

66   *Pimms Ltd v Tallow Chandlers Co* [1964] 2 QB 547 at 564.
67   *Bromley Park Garden Estates Ltd v Moss* [1982] 2 All ER 890, [1982] 1 WLR 1019, CA.
68   *Re Gibbs and Houlder Bros Co Ltd's Lease* [1925] Ch 575, CA.
69   *Packaging Centre v Poland Street Estate Ltd* (1961) 178 Estates Gazette 189 (where the proposed sub-lease contained a covenant requiring use by the sub-tenant of the premises as offices alone, whereas the head lease referred to offices and showrooms). Also *Granada TV Network Ltd v Great Universal Stores Ltd* (1962) 187 Estates Gazette 391, and *Crown Estate Comrs v Signet Group plc* [1996] 2 EGLR 200.
70   *Ashworth Frazer Ltd v Gloucester City Council* [2001] UKHL 59, [2002] 1 All ER 377, para 70 (Lord Rodger). Also ibid para 6 (Lord Bingham).
71   Under Law of Property Act 1969, s 84 as amended.

that ground alone[72] must not be overrated. It may not always be reasonable to refuse consent merely because it is likely that the new tenant will break the user covenants in the lease. Everything will depend on the circumstances of the case. It may be that if the tenant could prove that unless a different user was made by the assignee of the premises, the premises could be sterilised for the rest of the lease, the landlord could not refuse consent reasonably.[73]

Examples of reasonable and unreasonable withholding of consent

The following are examples of cases where the landlord has been held reasonably to have refused consent to a proposed assignment or sub-letting, and also of the converse.

REASONABLE REFUSALS

Many reasonable refusals had in common the fact that the landlord legitimately resisted having an undesirable occupier, or that the proposed assignee would gain rights not vested in the current tenant, so producing an unforeseeable and detrimental change in circumstances for the landlord not envisaged when the lease was granted.

It was reasonable to refuse consent because of real fears[74] as to the future rent-generating capacity of premises,[75] as well as where the landlord had serious doubts as to the ability of the proposed assignees to pay the rent or concerning the assets or financial strength of the proposed assignee.[76] Similarly, a landlord who gave the original lessee a personal privilege of a right to end the lease reasonably refused consent to a re-assignment to that lessee, the sole purpose of it being to allow the latter to end the lease and with it, all liability for future rent.[77] Where the effect of a proposed disposition would be to give an assignee a right to enfranchise which the current tenant did not have, or to confer a protected sub-tenancy on a sub-tenant for the first time, it was reasonable for the landlord to refuse his consent as the original basis of the lease would have been altered to his disadvantage.[78]

72 As stated in *Killick v Second Covent Garden Property Co Ltd* [1973] 2 All ER 337, CA.
73 *Sportoffer Ltd v Erewash Borough Council* [1999] 3 EGLR 136.
74 As opposed to imaginary ones: *Rayburn v Wolf* (1985) 50 P & CR 463, CA.
75 *Re Town Investments Ltd Underlease* [1954] Ch 301, [1954] 1 All ER 585 (where a sub-lease was proposed at a low rent and a premium). Also *Blockbuster Entertainment Ltd v Leakcliff Properties Ltd* [1997] 1 EGLR 28 (where on the facts the landlord was not entitled to require a rent over the current open market level).
76 *British Bakeries (Midlands) Ltd v Michael Testler & Co Ltd* [1986] 1 EGLR 64; *Kened Ltd v Connie Investments Ltd* [1997] 1 EGLR 21; also *Footwear Corpn Ltd v Amplight Properties Ltd* [1998] 3 All ER 52 (but no rule of thumb existed that a proposed assignee's finances must be such that its net profits after tax equal three times the rent payable).
77 *Olympia & York Canary Wharf Ltd v Oil Property Investments Ltd* [1994] 2 EGLR 48, CA.
78 *Bickel v Duke of Westminster* [1977] QB 517, [1976] 3 All ER 801, CA; *Leeward Securities Ltd v Lilyheath Properties Ltd* [1984] 2 EGLR 54, CA; *West Layton Ltd v Ford* [1979] 2 All ER 657, CA.

A landlord who had reasonable suspicions as to the manner a proposed assignee would conduct his business had reasonably withheld his consent,[79] such fears relating to the 'personality' of the proposed assignee. A lessor whose tenant had been seriously in breach of his covenant to repair, and where there was no definite prospect that the assignee would remedy the breaches was held also to have refused consent reasonably.[80] A landlord genuinely believed that if it consented to a proposed assignment, the assignee would obtain planning permission for use of its own premises as a supermarket. This would then interfere with development plans of a competing supermarket company which was under contract to buy an adjoining site from the landlord. The landlord was entitled to refuse consent (and to pay due regard to its own interests in doing so, which landlords are entitled to do, and which the court extended to include the interests of a prospective purchaser of the landlord's reversion).[81]

UNREASONABLE REFUSALS

The grounds on which a landlord may reasonably withhold consent have been limited under the general law by two principles: first, that he must confine his reasons to the actual demised premises, and secondly, he cannot plead in aid general matters of good estate management. Therefore, a refusal of consent because it might be difficult to re-let premises of the landlord which were currently occupied by the proposed assignee was unreasonable,[82] as was a refusal based on the policy of the landlord of recovering vacant possession of flats by means of a surrender where the existing tenants left.[83] However, it was also held that a landlord of a major shopping mall was entitled to follow a policy that involved making use of a disposition covenant, so as to ensure continuity of diversity of unit occupation in the mall by permitted trade, which excluded that of the proposed assignee.[84]

A refusal of consent has also been held unreasonable for a variety of reasons, as shown by the following examples, which have little in common on the facts. A refusal was thus unreasonable where the aim of the refusal was to obtain possession,[85] or where the landlord tried to obtain a result not contemplated by the parties at the date of the relevant assignment, as where he refused to agree to an assignment to B until the tenant agreed to execute an earlier licence to assign to A.[86] Likewise, consent was

---

79 *Rossi v Hestdrive Ltd* [1985] 1 EGLR 50.
80 *Orlando Investments Ltd v Grosvenor Estate Belgravia* [1989] 2 EGLR 74, CA; PF Smith [1989] Conv 371. In *Straudley Investments Ltd v Mount Eden Land Ltd* [1997] EGCS 175, it was held that the assignment of a long lease would not prejudice future action on the covenant to repair, especially as the assignee was not unlikely to remedy matters.
81 *BRS Northern Ltd v Templeheights Ltd* [1998] 2 EGLR 182.
82 *Re Gibbs and Houlder Bros' Lease* [1925] Ch 575, CA.
83 *Bromley Park Garden Estates Ltd v Moss* [1982] 2 All ER 890, [1982] 1 WLR 1019, CA.
84 *Moss Bros Group plc v CSC Properties Ltd* [1999] EGCS 47. The proposed assignee was an electronic games retailer (the current tenant was a men's fashion shop). The lease envisaged that the landlord would act as it did.
85 *Bates v Donaldson* [1896] 2 QB 241, CA.
86 *Jaison Property Development Co Ltd v Roux Restaurants Ltd* (1996) 74 P & CR 357, CA.

unreasonably withheld where the reason was not bona fide,[87] or where, although the tenant was in breach of covenant, the disrepair was not very serious and the assignee intended to spend a considerable sum on repairs.[88] A refusal of consent for capricious reasons is unreasonable,[89] as where the ground was that a proposed assignee had diplomatic immunity.[90] If the court regards the landlord's fears as unreasonable, it will dismiss them. Thus a landlord who had no reasonable ground to suppose that a subsidiary company to whom the parent company wished to assign the lease would default was not entitled to require that the assigning tenant company guarantee the performance of its subsidiary.[91]

III COVENANTS AGAINST ALTERATIONS

Introduction

1 General aspects. The lessee may undertake not to make structural alterations to the premises; sometimes he may undertake not to alter the external appearance of the building. The question of whether particular work amounts to a breach of covenant may be a question of degree. Anything which significantly alters the form and construction of the building amounts to an 'alteration': in one case, it was held that making holes in an external wall, taken with additional work, amounted to a breach of covenant.[92] Similarly, where the structure of premises was changed by converting a house into flats, a breach of covenant was committed.[93] On the other hand, it was held that a lessee who had attached a clock to the outside wall of his premises had not carried out an alteration.[94] In the latter case, the work was found to be reasonably incidental to the trade of the lessee. If such a finding is made, small-scale works of this

---

87 *Lovelock v Margo* [1963] 2 QB 786, [1963] 2 All ER 13, CA; and a refusal based on the possibility of a superior landlord's refusal is unreasonable: *Vienit Ltd v W Williams & Son* [1958] 3 All ER 621, [1958] 1 WLR 1267.

88 *Farr v Ginnings* (1928) 44 TLR 249.

89 As to the meaning of an obligation not to refuse consent 'arbitrarily', this apparently means 'wholly unreasonably' whereas 'capriciously' directs attention to the motivation of the landlord: see *Secured Income Real Estate (Australia) Ltd v St Martins Investments Pty Ltd* (1979) 144 CLR 596 at 609 (Mason J).

90 *Parker v Boggon* [1947] KB 346, [1947] 1 All ER 46; and a refusal based on grounds of race or sex is automatically unreasonable by statute: Race Relations Act 1976, s 24; Sex Discrimination Act 1975, s 31.

91 *Storehouse Properties Ltd v Ocobase Ltd* (1998) Times, 3 April.

92 *LCC v Hutter* [1925] Ch 626.

93 *Duke of Westminster v Swinton* [1948] 1 KB 524, [1948] 1 All ER 248; *Iperion Investments Corpn v Broadwalk House Residents Ltd* [1992] 2 EGLR 235.

94 *Bickmore v Dimmer* [1903] 1 Ch 158. In *LCC v Hutter* [1925] Ch 626 the lessee put up T irons and brackets which were not reasonably incidental to his trade.

kind may not amount to a breach of covenant, provided that they can be removed without causing lasting damage to the premises.[95]

2 Absolute prohibitions. Some leases may require the tenant to submit to the landlord drawings and specifications of any work he or she proposes to carry out so that the landlord may grant a licence (or consent).[96] We consider fully qualified covenants below, but the wording of the covenant may be such that all alterations of a specified nature are absolutely prohibited.[97] The covenant may be qualified or fully qualified, as with disposition covenants. If an absolute prohibition against the making of structural alterations is broken by the tenant, the landlord is entitled to seek relief in the form of a mandatory injunction, provided the breach has not been waived and provided he or she makes the claim promptly. The extent of the breach is seemingly immaterial. Thus where a tenant had, during certain works, deliberately lowered the height of a parapet wall by some 12 inches, in breach of a covenant not to cut or injure the main walls of the premises, a mandatory injunction was granted to the landlord to compel the tenant to reinstate the wall to its former height.[98]

Statutory limits on absolute prohibitions

It will be appreciated that an absolute prohibition on the making of structural alterations gives the landlord substantial rights to protect the original appearance of the premises. At the same time it may work oppressively to tenants. As a result, statute has outlawed such prohibitions in the case of protected and statutory tenancies under the Rent Act 1977.[99] It could be argued that the consumer regulations which subject standard form clauses to an unfairness test have put in jeopardy all absolute prohibitions in residential tenancies (see ch 4 of this book).

The county court is empowered to vary an absolute prohibition on structural alterations to residential premises held on a long lease, as where it is proposed to create smaller units in the premises, which could break the covenant.[100] This power is exercisable in

---

95 *Joseph v LCC* (1914) 111 LT 276 (where the alteration, aimed at advertising the lessee's trade, was easily removable); also *Heard v Stuart* (1907) 24 TLR 104 (where the covenant extends to alterations to the appearance of the demised premises, then a breach would be committed even by putting up easily removable items such as advertisements).

96 Where a landlord grants a licence to the tenant to carry out alterations, the wording of the licence may, if appropriate, be conditional: see *Prudential Assurance Co Ltd v Mount Eden Land Ltd* [1996] EGCS 179. If the wording of the covenant is absolute, then the grant of a licence to carry out specific work is not in itself an abandonment of a right to enforce the covenant in future.

97 For an example see *Precedents for the Conveyancer* 5-83, Sch 4, Part II, para 1(7).

98 *Viscount Chelsea v Muscatt* [1990] 2 EGLR 48.

99 Housing Act 1980, ss 81-83 as amended. The Disability Discrimination (Amendment) Bill 2002, if enacted, will, by cl 12, override an absolute prohibition on structural alterations sought by a disabled person placed at a substantial disadvantage by a physical feature on the premises.

100 Housing Act 1985, s 610.

the public interest, so overriding the wishes of the landlord. One means of invoking it is to prove that there have been changes in the character of the neighbourhood, so that the relevant premises cannot be readily let as a single dwelling house, but could be let for occupation if converted into, say, flats.[101] However, it was held that a scheme to divide adjoining terraced houses into flats extending for the width of the former houses fell outside the scope of this legislation.[102] The Law Commission recommended that this anomaly be cured by amending legislation,[103] but since the recommendation was made, nothing has come of it.

The Disability Discrimination Act 1995, Pt III comes into force on 1 October 2004.[104] The delay in commencement is no doubt to allow time in the interim for lessees to comply. Absolute (as well as fully qualified) alteration covenants will then be affected. The policy of this legislation is to put disabled persons on the same footing with regard to access to premises as those without a disability. A disabled person is not denied equality of access to goods, facilities or services provided by, notably, traders and other business persons. A tenant of business premises is required by the Disability Discrimination Act 1995 to take reasonable steps to remove or alter any physical feature which makes it 'impossible or unreasonably difficult' for a disabled person to make use of the service in question (Disability Discrimination Act 1995, s 21(2)). Thus a lessee might be forced by the legislation to widen doors, or to provide lifts, or ramp access, depending on the circumstances.[105] If the lease contains an absolute or fully qualified prohibition on the making of alterations, the net effect of the Disability Discrimination Act 1995, s 27 is that, notwithstanding the terms of the lease, the lessee is entitled to carry out the work of alteration to comply with the Act. Indeed if he fails to comply with the Disability Discrimination Act 1995, the lessee would be open to a complaint under the Act from a disabled person. The lessee may apply in writing to the landlord for consent to the work. If the latter refuses consent or imposes an unreasonable condition on his or her consent, the tenant may refer the matter to the county court, which is empowered to make rulings whether the landlord's refusal or conditions are reasonable (Disability Discrimination Act 1995, Sch 6, para 4).[106]

Qualified and fully qualified covenants against alterations

Where a covenant against the making of alterations provides that the alterations cannot be done except with the consent or licence of the landlord, statute provides

---

101 See *Alliance Economic Investment Co v Berton* (1923) 92 LJKB 750 (on a predecessor provision to Housing Act 1985, s 610).
102 *Josephine Trust v Champagne* [1963] 2 QB 160, CA.
103 Law Com No 141 (1985) 'Covenants Restricting Disposals, Alterations and Changes of User' para 9.15.
104 Disability Discrimination Act 1995 (Commencement No 9) Order 2001, SI 2001/2030.
105 The statutory duty is not absolute: thus, in particular, if equivalent access can be provided, the statutory duty would be complied with.
106 Regulations are envisaged: these will set out the circumstances in which a landlord can reasonably refuse consent or impose conditions.

that the landlord will not withhold his consent unreasonably to work of alteration which amounts to an improvement.[107]

The landlord is given the following compensating rights (Landlord and Tenant Act 1927, s 19(2)). He may validly, as a condition of giving consent, require the lessee to pay him a reasonable sum in respect of any damage to or diminution in the value of the premises or any neighbouring premises resulting from the alteration. Thus, the landlord is able to recover money compensation for an improvement of a short-term nature that will not benefit him or her when the reversion on the lease falls in. The landlord may also require the tenant to pay him his legal or other expenses (such as surveying costs) properly incurred in connection with the licence or consent. If the improvement does not add to the letting value of the holding, the landlord may, when giving licence or consent, require as a condition that the lessee reinstates the premises to the condition they were in before the improvement. Such a requirement must, however, be reasonable.

The courts have long held that the test of whether a proposed structural alteration is an 'improvement' within the Landlord and Tenant Act 1927 is dependent on whether the premises will be improved from the point of view of the tenant rather than the landlord. For example, a tenant's proposal to open apertures in the party wall between their premises and adjoining premises, in both of which the tenant traded, amounted to an improvement within the Landlord and Tenant Act 1927.[108] Similarly, it was an improvement in the statutory sense to convert a roof space into a dormer window.[109] In what is still the leading case,[110] tenants of a shop wished to enlarge their premises, by pulling down a rear wall and connecting up their shop with adjoining land they held on a different lease. The work was an 'improvement' within the Landlord and Tenant Act 1927. It benefited the tenants' business. The fact that it was not beneficial to the landlord made no difference. The tenant failed, however, to prove that the landlord, who initially demanded £7,000 for its consent, had unreasonably withheld consent. Unfortunately for the landlord, he then refused consent and consequently did not ask for reinstatement. In a second case,[111] the tenant proved that consent had been withheld unreasonably. The Court of Appeal held that a landlord could advance aesthetic,

---

107 Landlord and Tenant Act 1927, s 19(2). This provision does not apply to a tenancy of an agricultural holding nor to a farm business tenancy (Landlord and Tenant Act 1927, s 19(4)). Rent Act 1977 protected or statutory tenancies are governed by specific provisions (Housing Act 1980, ss 81-83) to the exclusion of the Landlord and Tenant Act 1927. Because the Landlord and Tenant Act 1927, s 19(2) does not apply to absolute prohibitions, it can be readily avoided by taking such a covenant from the tenant, although direct contracting out of the Act is not permitted.

108 *Lilley and Skinner Ltd v Crump* (1929) 73 Sol Jo 366.

109 *Davies v Yadegar* [1990] 1 EGLR 71. However, if the only way the work can be carried out is by trespassing into the landlord's adjoining land or airspace, he can reasonably refuse his consent for that reason: *Tideway Investment & Property Holdings Ltd v Wellwood* [1952] 1 All ER 1142; *Haines v Florensa* [1990] 1 EGLR 73, CA.

110 *FW Woolworth & Co v Lambert* [1937] Ch 37.

111 *Lambert v FW Woolworth & Co (No 2)* [1938] Ch 883, CA. But as to the difficulties facing the landlord see *McCulloch v Elsholz* (16 January 1990, unreported) (landlord failed to show that

historical or even personal grounds for refusing consent, but given that the landlord in question had given a blanket refusal of consent, none of these issues were relevant to the dispute.

The tenant is bound to ask for consent, if required by the covenant: failure to do so risks forfeiture. Relief would only be granted if consent could not have been reasonably withheld. If the tenant wishes to claim that consent has been unreasonably withheld, or that a condition of consent is unreasonable, he or she has the right to apply to the court for a declaration.[112] An alternative, which risks a forfeiture claim[113] if the landlord has good grounds, is to carry out the work in any case.[114] A landlord who fails to give any reason for a refusal of consent has no right later, if his attitude is held unreasonable, to impose reinstatement on the tenant.[115] Giving no reasons is practically equivalent to giving an obviously bad reason. A landlord might therefore be held to refuse consent, if there are no valid grounds at the time of his decision for his refusal of consent or for the imposition of the condition complained of.[116]

IV USE OF PREMISES

General principles

At common law, the tenant, in the absence of any contrary covenant, may use the demised premises for any lawful purpose. Even without any covenant restricting the use of the premises, the tenant is prohibited from actively damaging them, by the doctrine of waste. In this section, we examine the way in which user covenants, especially of a negative nature, are construed by the courts and affected by legislation.

Some leases contain restrictions on the user allowed in relation to the premises. The EU has also intervened, owing to Articles 81 and 82 of the EC Treaty, which have led to the passing of the Competition Act 1998. Leases are within the scope of the Act as 'land agreements', so affecting user and related covenants. However, the government

---

objections to the tenant building a shed, extending a patio and building a retaining wall were well founded). Also eg *Balls Bros v Sinclair* [1931] 2 Ch 325 (where the landlord could not reasonably object to the tenant moving a staircase to facilitate his sub-lessee's business).

112 Landlord and Tenant Act 1954, s 53.

113 If the breach is flagrant, relief may be refused: see ch 12 below. The landlord may claim instead reinstatement and damages: see eg *Mosley v Cooper* [1990] 1 EGLR 124.

114 *Railway Comrs v Avrom Investments Pty Ltd* [1959] 2 All ER 63, [1959] 1 WLR 389, PC.

115 *Lambert v FW Woolworth & Co* [1938] Ch 883, CA at 906 (Slesser LJ).

116 *Lovelock v Margo* [1963] 2 QB 786, CA, but the reasoning of Lord Denning MR was criticised by Mason J in *Secured Income Real Estate (Australia) Ltd v St Martins Investments Pty Ltd* (1979) 144 CLR 596 at 611. In the case of covenants against alterations, there is no statutory duty on a landlord to give reasons. Giving no reason might cause an inference that a refusal was capricious. At the same time, in *Lousada & Co Ltd v JE Lesser (Properties) Ltd* 1990 SC 178 the court refused to assume that a landlord who had failed to given reasons had no valid reasons to advance. If a clearly bad reason is given to a lessee for a refusal or a condition, the courts might not allow the landlord to advance better reasons at any subsequent hearing.

has promulgated delegated legislation under which leases as land agreements are exempted, in principle, from the prohibitions of the Competition Act 1998, Chapter 1,[117] with the result that most user and restrictive covenants in leases appear to be excluded from the Act's controls. To qualify for exemption from the Competition Act 1998, the user restriction must benefit the party to the agreement in its capacity as the holder of an interest in the land which is the subject of the agreement. It has been argued that if a landlord wishes to impose a restriction on the trades carried on by all other tenants than one in a shopping centre, he may find that the exemption will not apply as it is not beneficial to him as landlord of the other leases.[118] At the same time it seems that most restrictions in leases will not infringe the Competition Act 1998 even if this argument is correct, although those landlords with a high regional or national market share could be at risk where their leases lie outside the 2000 regulatory mechanism.

The scope of any particular user covenant is for the parties to decide on. The onus of proving that a breach has taken place is on the landlord.[119] It would seem that any user covenants in a sub-lease should be construed independently of those in the head lease.[120] User covenants may specify that only a given type or range of user is permitted, such as use only as a private residence, or user only for certain types of trade or business. Equally, certain types of specified user may be prohibited or restricted, as where a flat was not to be used except as a single residence in one occupation,[121] or where the premises cannot be used otherwise than as a private dwelling house,[122] or only for the business of a named lessee.[123] A positive obligation to use the premises in a particular way may be imposed, at least in theory, but very clear language is required to achieve that result, and a positively-phrased obligation to use premises either for a given trade or for other purposes was insufficient to do so.[124]

---

117 Competition Act 1998 (Land and Vertical Agreements Exclusion) Order 2000, SI 2000/310, in force from 1 March 2000.

118 Shaw and Thompson Estates Gazette 1 April 2000, 184. See also Woolich Estates Gazette 24 June 2000, 135; Reuben and Tyler Estates Gazette 7 March 1998, 150.

119 *Basildon Development Corpn v Mactro Ltd* [1986] 1 EGLR 137, CA; also *McDonnell v Griffey* [1998] EGCS 70 (concerning the words 'in single occupation' with regard to a flat). Attempts have been made by tenants to enforce landlord user covenants against neighbouring lessees. Where a tenant of a shop had actual or constructive notice of a landlord's covenant preventing the use of premises save those let to the complainant as a restaurant, it was held liable to the complainant for breaking this covenant: *Walker v Arkay Caterers Ltd* [1997] EGCS 107. However, in *Oceanic Village Ltd v United Attractions Ltd* [2000] 1 EGLR 148, it was held that a tenant could not enforce landlord covenants in this sort of way owing to LT(C)A 1995, s 3(5). The position is thus unclear but the second ruling at least gives some content to the 1995 Act, which would otherwise be redundant.

120 *Atwal v Courts Garages* [1989] 1 EGLR 63, CA.

121 *Falgor Commercial SA v Alsabahia Inc* [1986] 1 EGLR 41, CA.

122 As in *Caradon District Council v Bussell* (2000) 33 HLR 360, CA (occupation by holiday tenants sufficed to break the covenant).

123 See eg *Granada TV Network Ltd v Great Universal Stores* (1962) 187 Estates Gazette 391; also *Law Land Co Ltd v Consumers' Association Ltd* [1980] 2 EGLR 109, CA.

124 *Montross Associated Investments SA v Moussaieff* [1990] 2 EGLR 61, CA.

Some user covenants are absolute, so that the lessee may only change the user of the premises if the landlord is prepared to agree to vary the lease or waive the breach for his benefit. Other user covenants may be either qualified or fully qualified, by analogy with disposition covenants. The Law Commission did not recommend that absolute user covenants should be made fully qualified, owing in part to the danger that this might raise rents, at least in the business sector where user covenants tended to be more specific, tying the tenant to specific uses within categories.[125]

Qualified covenants

Where the user covenant permits the tenant to alter the use of the premises with the landlord's consent,[126] the landlord is entitled to refuse his consent to a proposed change of user on any grounds, reasonable or not.[127] This means that, if the tenant cannot change the permitted user of the premises, and the user covenant is absolute, he may have to pay any sum demanded by the landlord for his consent to such change. Legislation does not imply any proviso that the landlord's consent cannot unreasonably be withheld: if this requirement is to exist, it must be expressly mentioned in the covenant itself.[128]

Legislation alleviates the position slightly: it applies both to qualified and fully qualified user covenants, except in the case of leases of agricultural holdings, farm business tenancies and mining leases. By the Landlord and Tenant Act 1927, s 19(3) if the proposed change of user does not involve any structural alteration of the premises, the covenant is deemed, notwithstanding any express provision to the contrary, to be subject to a proviso that no fine or sum of money in the nature of a fine, whether by way of rent increase or otherwise, is to be payable for any licence or consent of the landlord to that change.[129] The landlord is not precluded from requiring the payment of a reasonable sum in respect of any damage or diminution in the value of the premises or any neighbouring premises belonging to him. He may also require the payment, as part of this sum, of his legal or other expenses. If the tenant disputes the reasonableness

125 Law Com No 141 (1985) 'Covenants Restricting Disposals, Alterations and Changes of User' paras 4.32-4.53. However, it could be argued that an absolute user covenant in a residential lease would infringe the unfairness tests in the 1999 consumer regulations referred to in ch 4 of this book, because they seem to offer no balancing advantages to tenants (unless it is argued that without such covenants the rent of the subject premises would be higher).
126 A letter stating that a landlord had no objection to a proposed change in user from a retail shop to a restaurant subject to various conditions of a formal nature amounted to a consent under a user clause in the relevant lease, albeit personal to the tenant: *Rose v Stavron* [2000] L & TR 133.
127 *Guardian Assurance Co Ltd v Gants Hill Holdings Ltd* [1983] 2 EGLR 36.
128 The Law Commission recommended ending the privileged position of qualified user covenants (Law Com No 141 (1985) 'Covenants Restricting Disposals, Alterations and Changes of User' paras 6.14-6.16) which would leave a clear line between absolute and fully qualified user covenants, as exists in the case of assignments.
129 If a fine is actually paid before the licence is granted, it is irrecoverable: see *Comber v Fleet Electronics Ltd* [1955] 1 WLR 566.

of any sum demanded by the landlord as the price of his licence or consent, the court has power to declare that a given sum is reasonable in amount. If this is done, the landlord is bound to consent to the change in user, on being paid that sum. While an offer of consent on payment of money is not a consent, the Landlord and Tenant Act 1927, s 19(3) does not prevent a landlord refusing consent, offering to accept a surrender of the lease, and to re-grant a new lease on terms more advantageous to himself.[130]

Fully qualified covenants

The user covenant may provide that the landlord's consent to a change of use is not to be unreasonably withheld. In general, the reasonableness of any refusal of consent is judged in much the same way as in the case of assignments[131] except that the onus of proving unreasonableness of any refusal falls on the tenant.[132] Where a landlord sought to exploit the user covenant to attempt to maximise the rents of surrounding premises, his refusal of consent to a change of user for that reason was unreasonable.[133] At the same time, a landlord was held entitled to take into account considerations affecting property of his own, whether let or not, and whether or not in existence at the date of the lease. Thus where a proposed change of use might reasonably be thought by the landlord to involve competition with his own premises, that was a relevant matter in his deciding whether or not to consent.[134] If the tenant can prove that the premises would be sterilised for the remainder of the lease unless consent to the proposed change of user is given, the landlord might not be able reasonably to withhold consent,[135] but proving so extreme a case would not be easy.[136] In contrast to the position with consents to proposed assignments, which are affected by statutory restrictions on landlords' rights, a landlord is apparently entitled to advance reasons for refusing consent in proceedings even if these were not communicated to the tenant at the time of the refusal.[137] At the same time, if the landlord gives no reason for his refusal, the court will more readily infer that he has no valid grounds for refusing consent.[138]

130 *Barclays Bank plc v Daejan Investments (Grove Hall) Ltd* [1995] 1 EGLR 68.
131 See *Sood v Barker* [1991] 1 EGLR 87, CA; also *Hillgrove Developments Ltd v Plymouth City Council* [1997] EGCS 115.
132 *Hillgrove Developments Ltd v Plymouth City Council* [1997] EGCS 115; *Luminar Leisure Ltd v Apostole* [2001] 3 EGLR 23 at 25.
133 *Anglia Building Society v Sheffield City Council* [1983] 1 EGLR 57, CA.
134 *Sportoffer Ltd v Erewash Borough Council* [1999] 3 EGLR 136.
135 This might be an example of the application of the broad reasonableness test as laid down by *Ashworth Frazer Ltd v Gloucester City Council* [2001] UKHL 59, [2002] 1 All ER 377 discussed earlier in this chapter.
136 *Sportoffer Ltd v Erewash Borough Council* [1999] 3 EGLR 136.
137 *Kalford Ltd v Peterborough City Council* [2001] EGCS 42. However, the materials supplied to the landlord were held in any event insufficient to enable it to make an informed decision. The view of McCombie J in *Kalford* conflicts with dicta in *Tollbench Ltd v Plymouth City Council* [1988] 1 EGLR 79 at 81, which, however, was decided before LTA 1988 came into force.
138 *Tollbench Ltd v Plymouth City Council* [1988] 1 EGLR 79, CA

The user covenant may, however, provide that consent to a change of use is not to be withheld unreasonably and then restrict this by stating that, if consent is withheld on specified grounds, it will not be treated as having been unreasonably withheld. In such cases, because the second part of the clause cuts down its first part, the excepting part risks being narrowly construed.[139]

If the landlord demands an excessive sum in respect of his consent in relation to a matter set out in the Landlord and Tenant Act 1927, s 19(3), the tenant may apply to the court for a declaration as to what sum is reasonable. On payment of that sum, consent must be granted. If the landlord demands a fine or other sum as the cost of his consent, it may be that the Landlord and Tenant Act 1927, s 19(3) permits the tenant to treat the demand as an unreasonable refusal of consent. Where the landlord refuses his consent, or imposes an unreasonable condition, the tenant may apply to the county court for a declaration, in the same way as in the case of assignments.

Examples of certain types of use restriction

In leases of residential property, tenants sometimes covenant to use the premises as a private residence only, or not to use them for the purpose of any trade.[140] Such a covenant would be broken by the erection of a studio and classroom for pupils,[141] the presence of a notice signifying that the premises included an office,[142] the taking in of lodgers or paying guests,[143] or the garaging of a taxi which was used by the tenant in his business.[144] A covenant for private residence in the occupation of one household only, has been held not to be broken where one paying guest was taken in as a member of the family.[145]

In business leases, covenants against particular trades or for no trade other than a particular trade may be found, but the latter does not oblige the tenant to carry on that trade. The prohibited businesses or trades may be specific or the covenant may prohibit only noisy, offensive or dangerous trades, or it may disallow the sale of certain types of product, such as goods not usually sold in a food supermarket.[146] The onus of proving a breach will be on the landlord.

---

139 See *Berenyi v Watford Borough Council* [1980] 2 EGLR 38, CA.
140 Some leases require the tenant not to cause a nuisance to the landlord, his tenants and to adjoining occupiers: if the covenant extends to 'annoyance' it is much wider than a common law nuisance: see *Tod-Heatly v Benham* (1888) 40 Ch D 80; *Chorley Borough Council v Ribble Motor Services Ltd* [1996] EGCS 110, CA.
141 *Patman v Harland* (1881) 17 Ch D 353.
142 *Wilkinson v Rogers* (1863) 3 New Rep 145.
143 *Thorn v Madden* [1925] Ch 847.
144 *Jones v Christy* (1963) 107 Sol Jo 374.
145 *Segal Securities Ltd v Thoseby* [1963] 1 QB 887, [1963] 1 All ER 500; also *Falgor Commercial SA v Alsabahia Inc* [1986] 1 EGLR 41, CA.
146 *Basildon Development Corpn v Mactro Ltd* [1986] 1 EGLR 137, CA.

Keep open covenants

The enforcement of clauses in leases of shops which require the tenant to keep the premises open for trade throughout the lease has recently arisen. In one case,[147] the tenant of a supermarket in a precinct closed down its supermarket, in breach of covenant to 'keep the demised premises open for retail trade during the usual hours of business'. The tenant claimed that it was losing money from this outlet. The House of Lords held that its settled practice was not to grant specific performance to compel the tenant to carry on its business, even if damages were not an adequate remedy. The remedy of specific performance was exceptional. Moreover, if an order was made, the courts would then have to decide whether the terms of an order had been broken by the tenant, perhaps on more than one occasion. Notice was taken of the fact that disregard of an order for specific performance was a contempt of court. Repeated litigation rather than a once and for all damages inquiry was not to be encouraged. In addition, in effect, ordering the tenant to carry on trading at a loss would be oppressive.

The House of Lords emphasised that it was the cumulative effect of the reasons just given which led them to refuse specific performance in the case concerned, in agreement with the High Court. This could leave it open to a court specifically to enforce a keep open obligation, if say an 'anchor' tenant in a shopping precinct who was making profits decided to close its retail outlet because it was not making a sufficiently high level of profits. The Court of Session takes a different approach.[148] Scots law, based on Roman commentators and established precedent,[149] holds that if the tenant fails to do something which he has undertaken to do, the landlord can choose whether to seek specific implement or damages. Scots law had stood for over 300 years and would not be upset. The Court of Session thought that the supposed problem of a need continuously to supervise any order to a tenant to carry out its undertakings would not cause problems in Scotland. The position is not free from difficulty. One possibility of reducing the difficulty of enforcing compliance with a keep open covenant might be for landlords to insert in leases a higher rent level if the tenant does not continue trading and a lower one if it does. If trading ceases, damages could be agreed in advance.[150]

---

147 *Co-operative Insurance Society Ltd v Argyll Stores (Holdings) Ltd* [1998] AC 1, [1997] 3 All ER 297; Tettenborn [1998] Conv 23.

148 *Highland & Universal Properties Ltd v Safeway Properties Ltd* [2000] 3 EGLR 110.

149 Stair's Institutions 1.17.16, based on Justinian's Digest 42.1.13.1; *Stewart v Kennedy* (1890) 17 R (HL) 1 at 9-10.

150 McDonald (1997) 141 Sol Jo 771; also Luxton [1998] Conv 397. The landlord may wish to insert a covenant requiring the shop windows to be properly dressed (as was done in the *Argyll* case). Luxton suggests inserting a clause allowing the landlord to sub-let if the tenant ceases to trade.

Tying covenants

Mention must be made of tying covenants. These are undertakings by the tenant of a public house or petrol station to sell only the beer or petrol (and perhaps related products) supplied by the landlord brewer or petrol company. Subject to the regulation of the length of the tie, which is governed by the doctrine of restraint of trade, a tying covenant is enforceable at common law against the lessee currently in occupation.[151] An attempt to have a provision which precluded any right of set off in a lease also containing a tying covenant declared contrary to the Unfair Contract Terms Act 1977 failed. The anti-set off provision was concerned with the rent amount and was an integral part of the agreement by the landlord to grant a lease. The agreement for a lease was a contract for the creation of an interest in land and fell within the relevant exclusion of the Unfair Contract Terms Act 1977.[152]

A tying covenant relating to beer products is at risk of voidness, owing to the principles of the Treaty of Rome, Art 85.[153] This provision prohibits all agreements which affect trade between EU member states which have as their objective or effect the prevention, restriction or distortion of competition within the Common Market. Some landlords have been letting public houses on relatively long leases (say for ten years) with tying covenants. Some of these have been challenged under the EU legislation, with so far less than clear results.[154] A beer tie which is inconsistent with Article 85 is automatically void without any need for a decision of the EU commission or the courts.[155] The Court of Appeal ruled that Article 85 was not infringed by a particular tying covenant in a tenancy owing to the fact that, seemingly, competition in the sense intended by the EU Treaty was not injuriously affected by the beer tie.[156] The Court of Appeal gave weight to the view of the EU Commission, which was that there were on the facts no grounds to think that Article 85 had been infringed. More generally, the court followed European Court of Justice jurisprudence. This holds that a beer tie will fall foul of Article 85 if it is difficult for competitors who could enter the national market or who could increase their market share to gain access to the national market for beer distribution and the sale and consumption of drinks. However, in the case in question the market share of the landlords was small. The Court of Appeal referred a tying covenant in a different

151 *Cleveland Petroleum Co Ltd v Dartstone Ltd* [1969] 1 All ER 201; *Total Oil Great Britain v Thompson Garages (Biggin Hill)* [1972] 1 QB 318, [1971] 3 All ER 1226, CA.

152 *Star Rider Ltd v Inntrepeneur Pub Co* [1998] 1 EGLR 53. The exclusion is the Unfair Contract Terms Act 1977, Sch 1, para 1(b).

153 See Perks (1999) 3 L & T Rev 80. If the tenant is released from a brewery tie, the lease may then provide for payment of additional rent (as on a review): see *Inntrepreneur Pub Co (CPC) Ltd v Price* [1998] EGCS 167 (where any illegality in the beer tie was held not to preclude the implementation of a rent review).

154 There is a block exemption from article 85 (2790/1999), whose interpretation is for the English courts: *Byrne v Inntrepreneur Beer Supply Co Ltd* [1999] EGCS 86, CA and *Whitbread plc v Falla* [2000] EGCS 136.

155 *Passmore v Morland plc* [1999] 1 EGLR 51, CA.

156 *Gibbs Mew plc v Gemmell* [1999] 01 EG 117. The tenancy was at will. The landlords held only a small share of the market in the UK.

lease to the European Court of Justice, while refusing to imply a term into this lease that the prices charged to the tenant for liquor supplies must be reasonable, or that the price level must not render the tenant's business uncompetitive.[157] In addition, a beer tie can be caught by the EU prohibition and during the lease cease to be caught by it, as circumstances (such as those of the landlord for the time being) change.[158] It was accepted that this phenomenon could well cause uncertainty to the parties, especially having regard to the power of the EU Commission to issue exemptions from time to time, and because the tying agreements themselves change from time to time. That uncertainty was an inevitable result of Article 85, and the difficulties it poses should not be overestimated.

V   OPTIONS IN THE LEASE

Principles common to options

Leases may allow the tenant an option to renew,[159] to terminate the lease early or to purchase the landlord's reversion.[160] Some principles are common to these options.[161] The exercise of the tenant's privilege of exercising any of these three options is normally[162] dependent on his serving a prior written notice of exercise on the landlord, normally a given number of months before the expiry date of his lease. Options to renew and to purchase may well specify that unless such a notice is served strictly within the time allowed (such as within the last six months of the term) the option is not exercisable. The landlord may, however, be estopped from insisting on due service or waive the requirements.[163]

Options to renew and to purchase are, for the purposes of LP(MP)A 1989, s 2, a conditional contract in the lease. The lessee may convert the option into a concluded contract by means of his notice of exercise, provided he has complied with any conditions precedent to exercising his rights. The landlord does not have to sign this notice, since LP(MP)A 1989, s 2 cannot be construed as having impliedly imposed so strange an additional formality on the parties.[164] The most common of these conditions

---

157   *Courage Ltd v Creehan* [1999] 2 EGLR 145, CA (the implied term would be inconsistent with the express terms of the lease, notably the tenant obligation to buy at the best price).

158   *Passmore v Morland plc* [1999] 1 EGLR 51, CA; also *Barrett v Inntrepreneur Pub Co (GL)* [1999] EGCS 93.

159   Available to the lessee provided he or she has not been dispossessed by a squatter: see *Chung Ping Kwan v Lam Island Development Co Ltd* [1997] AC 38, PC.

160   Assuming that the premises are still in existence (see *Tomlinson v Millins* [1998] EGCS 178, where the premises burnt down and a right to purchase the landlords' reversion became, on the facts, inoperative despite a limited re-instatement requirement in the lease).

161   Questions of construction as to the circumstances of particular options may arise: for a recent example see *Nocturn Ltd v Water Hall Group plc* [1997] EGCS 97.

162   For a case where the right to renew was not dependent on prior notice see *Gardner v Blaxill* [1960] 2 All ER 457, [1960] 1 WLR 752.

163   See *Multon v Cordell* [1986] 1 EGLR 44.

164   *Spiro v Glencrown Properties Ltd* [1991] Ch 537, [1990] 1 All ER 600.

is a requirement that the tenant has paid the rent due and is not in breach of covenant at the date of service of his option notice or the date of expiry of the lease, as the case may be.

Options for renewal

Where a tenant seeks during the lease[165] to exercise an option to renew, if, as is commonly the case,[166] it is a condition precedent that at the relevant date he must not be in breach of covenant, any subsisting breach at or by the date when the option is exercisable by the tenant debars the tenant from obtaining renewal, unless it is waived.[167] This is because the tenant has a conditional privilege of renewal, not a right.[168] If the breach is spent (ie it lies at some time in the past history of the lease), the tenant will still be entitled to renew, as where in the past a tenant had twice withheld rent but owed none at the end of the lease.[169] This rule applies to all breaches of covenant, be they positive or negative.[170] It is no alternative to compliance with a pre-condition by a party who has not complied with the pre-condition that the condition is trivial and that the court should overlook his failure to comply.[171]

The severity of these principles, which are applied in the absence of waiver or estoppel by the landlord,[172] is illustrated by the effect on renewal rights of breaches of covenant to repair. In one case the tenant, at the operative date, had failed to carry out repairs costing a small amount of money, which would have been easy to execute, but lost the

---

165 A tenant holding over as a yearly tenant may seemingly exercise an option to renew: *Moss v Barton* (1866) LR 1 Eq 474.
166 As recognised in *Dun and Bradstreet Software Services (England) Ltd v Provident Mutual Life Assurance Association* [1998] 2 EGLR 175, at 180, CA.
167 *West Country Cleaners (Falmouth) Ltd v Saly* [1966] 3 All ER 210, [1966] 1 WLR 1485, CA; also *Commercial Union Life Assurance Co Ltd v Label Ink Ltd* [2001] L & TR 29, [2001] L & TR 580: rent not paid by 1 January, but a very few days late, deprived the tenant of a right to break its lease).
168 However, a condition that renewal depended on the parties agreeing a business plan did not prevent a lessee not in breach of his leasehold obligations from renewing: *Little v Courage* (1994) 70 P & CR 469, CA. In addition, a condition requiring a tenant of a public house to take a minimum gallonage of liquor from the landlord has been held to breach the Supply of Beer (Tied Estate) Order 1989, SI 1989/2390, art 7 (*Plummer v Tibsco Ltd* [2000] ICR 509). Such could presumably not be invoked so as to preclude the tenant from exercising a lease option.
169 *Bassett v Whiteley* (1982) 45 P & CR 87, CA. In this case 'the Court of Appeal had no difficulty in holding that the tenant had behaved reasonably, even if he had not complied with the obligation to pay rent': Jacob J in *Reed Personnel Services plc v American Express Ltd* [1997] 1 EGLR 229 at 230.
170 *Bass Holdings Ltd v Morton Music Ltd* [1987] 2 All ER 1001, CA.
171 *Reed Personnel Services plc v American Express Ltd* [1997] 1 EGLR 229 at 230.
172 See above. Estoppel was unsuccessfully raised in *Dun & Bradstreet Software Services (England) Ltd v Provident Mutual Life Assurance Association* [1998] 2 EGLR 175. No clear representation had there been made by the landlord that a penalty rent of some £322,173 need not be paid on time as required by the lease. Estoppel by convention did not arise.

ability to renew.[173] Likewise, a tenant who had failed to complete certain interior decorations as required, by the end of the lease, costing about £800, could not renew.[174] The High Court relaxed the rule. It held that a tenant who carried out regular checks at intervals but who had failed to cure some disrepair before the end of the lease would not lose the right to renew as he was not in breach until he failed, within a reasonable time, to remedy the breach.[175] However, where a tenant had twice withheld rent to put pressure on his landlord to carry out repairs, but owed no rent by the end of the term and was not otherwise in breach of covenants, the right to renewal at the expiry of the term was held unaffected.[176]

In the absence of express terms of renewal, the new lease will generally be for the same period and upon the same terms as the current tenancy. The parties may agree on the rent payable under the new lease. If they do not, the rent will probably be the same as the old rent. The parties may agree that the new rent is such as to be agreed by two valuers, one appointed by each party. If one party tries to frustrate the machinery agreed, then the court will determine what is a fair and reasonable rent.[177] Whether the parties' formula enables an arbitrator to include rent reviews in the new term is entirely a matter of construction.[178] Where an option to renew was at a rent not exceeding a specified sum, it was proper to imply a term that a fair rent was to be agreed, with the specified sum as an upper limit.[179]

Options to determine

(i) Introduction

A fixed term lease may enable the landlord or tenant to determine the term prior to its original expiry date, by notice served at some specified time. So as to limit their scope, some options to determine are expressed as exercisable only by the original, named lessee: hence, where MF, so named, assigned its lease to X and later obtained a re-assignment of the term to itself, MF's right to determine, construed as personal, did not survive the assignment to X.[180] The court refused to construe this lease as creating

173 *Finch v Underwood* (1876) 2 Ch D 310. This case was followed recently in *Commercial Union Life Assurance Co Ltd v Label Ink Ltd* [2001] L & TR 29, [2001] L & TR 380.
174 *Bairstow Eves (Securities) Ltd v Ripley* [1992] 2 EGLR 47, CA. See also *Reed Personnel Services plc v American Express Ltd* [1997] 1 EGLR 229, where the tenants failed to carry out repairs required within an eight-week timescale by a landlords' notice and lost their right to determine the lease.
175 *West Middlesex Golf Club Ltd v Ealing London Borough Council* (1993) 68 P & CR 461.
176 *Bassett v Whiteley* (1982) 45 P & CR 87, CA.
177 *Sudbrook Trading Estate Ltd v Eggleton* [1983] 1 AC 444, [1982] 3 All ER 1, HL; also *ARC Ltd v Schofield* [1990] 2 EGLR 525, CA.
178 *National Westminster Bank v BSC Footwear* (1980) 42 P & CR 90, CA.
179 *Corson v Rhuddlan Borough Council* [1990] 1 EGLR 255, CA.
180 *Max Factor Ltd v Wesleyan Assurance Society* [1995] 2 EGLR 38, affd on appeal [1996] EGCS 82.

a right running with the lease which was incapable of exercise after assignment even though it could be exercised on a re-assignment to the original lessee.

(ii) Validity of option notices

Until 1997, it had been held that a notice to exercise an option to determine was not consensual but a type of unilateral privilege and should be exercised strictly within any time-limits laid down for its exercise, otherwise it was not validly exercised and the lease continued.[181] A divided House of Lords has overturned this principle, which was thought both rigid and inappropriate. A new test was put forward. If, objectively, it would be obvious to a reasonable recipient of the notice with a knowledge of the lease and the relevant dates for exercise of the option that the person serving the notice had fallen into error and did not literally mean what was said in the notice as to the date of termination, the error would not affect the validity of the notice. According to Lord Steyn, this could be done provided the notice was 'sufficiently clear and unambiguous to leave a reasonable recipient of the notice in no reasonable doubt as to how and when [the notice] intended to operate'.[182] Both Lords Steyn and Hoffmann moved from strict, technical constructions of commercial documents to broader, purposive constructions. However attractive the majority's liberal approach to the construction of option notices may be, as pointed out by Lord Goff, it fails to take into account the bargain made by the parties: notices must be served as laid down in the lease or not at all. On the facts, the House of Lords held that a notice to determine a lease on 12 January of the correct year instead of 13 January (which was the correct anniversary day) was valid. The error in the date of the month was obvious and a reasonable person receiving the notice would have known that something was amiss.

(iii) Limits of ruling

The limits of the new rulings are being tested. The recipient of the notice is taken to have knowledge of the lease. He may be expected to read the notice in its immediate context. If another document, such as a letter, accompanies the notice, the recipient is apparently to read both together. If these leave him in no reasonable doubt about the correct termination date, the court may well overlook an error in the termination notice.[183] The High Court ruled that where a notice to determine made an error in the description of the tenant, this mistake could also be overlooked, as being trifling or immaterial, and the notice upheld.[184] In these cases, the courts were at pains to stress that the

---

181 *Hankey v Clavering* [1942] 2 KB 326, CA.
182 *Mannai Investment Co Ltd v Eagle Star Life Assurance Co Ltd* [1997] AC 749; see Wilkinson (1997) 147 NLJ 1187; PF Smith [1998] Conv 327.
183 As in *Garston v Scottish Widows' Fund* [1998] L & TR 230, where there was a notice to determine and a request for a new business tenancy.
184 *Havant International Holdings v Lionsgate (H) Investment* [2000] L & TR 297.

understanding of the landlord in question was not the issue: the question was how any reasonable landlord would have read the notice.

Once matters go beyond obvious slips on the face of a notice to terminate, especially where the notice is served under one or other of the many prescribed forms required, the courts are more hesitant about allowing the new test for validity to be used as an excuse for sloppiness. The new test indeed extends to notices, such as those served under business tenancy renewals[185] as well as to assured shorthold tenancy notices.[186] The court will however look at the particular statutory provisions and identify its requirements[187]; after all, certainty and clarity are of importance in such cases. Hence, it was held that a reasonable tenant could not be assumed to have known that a notice was served on behalf of his landlord.[188] Equally, a notice served under long lease procedures which failed to state that the landlord admitted the right to a new lease was invalid.[189] Similarly, a landlord could not reasonably be taken to know that the person serving a notice was the tenant or his assignee, where the description on the notice itself was wholly unclear as to the identity and quality of the notice server.[190] This information could not be extracted or reasonably inferred from the face of the notice. If that is all the material to hand at the time of service, the person receiving the notice does not have to make further inquiries beyond the documents supplied at the time of the service of the notice.[191] If a notice fails to supply the core information required, it will fail. In addition, where a notice is clear and unambiguous, the courts will give effect to the words used and will not search for ambiguities where there are none.[192]

---

185 *Sabella v Montgomery* [1998] 1 EGLR 65.
186 *Manel v Memon* [2000] 2 EGLR 40.
187 *Speedwell Estates Ltd v Dalziel* [2001] EWCA Civ 1277, [2002] 02 EG 104. Thus, a notice served under the Leasehold Reform Act 1967 which failed to give any particulars of the tenant's periods of occupation of the house in question, which was held to be core information, was invalid. This case was not so much an example of an error requiring small-scale correction but of wholesale material omission of material which no reasonable recipient could supply.
188 *Stack England Estate Co v Rendell* [2000] 2 CL 374. The notice (under the Agricultural Holdings Act 1986 Case F) was 'confusing and ineffective'.
189 *Burman v Mount Cook Land Ltd* [2001] EWCA Civ 1712, [2002] 1 All ER 144. A notice addressed to B was not deemed served on F (who was not addressed by name or status): *R v London Rent Assessment Committee* [2002] EWCA Civ 276, [2002] 24 EG 149.
190 *Lemmerbell Ltd v Britannia LAS Direct Ltd* [1999] L & TR 102, CA (break clause notice).
191 See *Clickex Ltd v McCann* [1999] 2 EGLR 63 (where a notice served to create an assured shorthold tenancy differed so much from the tenancy agreement that no reasonable tenant could have treated it as obviously having the effect intended by the landlord). An obvious mistake in a notice served under Housing Act 1988, s 20 was condoned in *York v Casey* [1998] 2 EGLR 25 (the termination date given was later than that of the commencement of the tenancy). In *Keepers and Governors of John Lyon Grammar School v Secchi* [1999] 3 EGLR 49 an error in an enfranchisement notice was not obvious and could not be treated as immaterial having regard to the importance of the statutory time-limits for service of further notices.
192 *Hart Investments plc v Burton Hotel plc* [2002] L & TR 6, [2002] L & TR 93.

(iv) Technical points

If an option is exercisable only by a written notice, an oral notice will not suffice. Especially where the option is exercisable by the landlord, it may be available only in specified circumstances, such as for the landlord's own purposes, or for redevelopment or reconstruction: whether an event falls within specified circumstances is a matter of construction.[193] Where a landlord proved that he required possession at some time after the date for exercise of the option but before the original expiry date of the term, this entitled him to exercise the option. He only had to establish that he required to occupy part of the premises, as against the whole, as he could not occupy any part without exercising his option.[194]

(v) Relationship to business tenancies legislation

Where the tenancy is one to which the Landlord and Tenant Act 1954, Pt II applies, it will end at common law at the date specified in the notice, although the tenancy then continues under the Landlord and Tenant Act 1954, s 24.[195] The landlord may serve a notice to determine the tenancy under the Landlord and Tenant Act 1954, s 25 which will take effect, if clearly so intended, as a common-law notice of determination under an option to determine.[196]

Options to purchase

Options to purchase the reversion are a separate agreement by the parties, which is collateral to the lease. Accordingly, an option to purchase needs to be protected against third party assignees of the reversion by registration (as noted earlier). The tenant may be unable to exercise an option to purchase if its terms provide that he must have performed the covenants of the lease. Normally, the tenant is to exercise the option by a written notice. The terms of the option may state the price payable, or they may provide, for example, for a formula, as where the price is to be a fair and reasonable price to be agreed by the parties or determined by arbitration. In one case, the parties agreed that the price was to be agreed by two valuers, one appointed by each party. However, the landlords refused to make an appointment. The options concerned had been duly exercised, and the House of Lords ordered an inquiry into the fair value of the reversion concerned, refusing to allow the landlords to frustrate the determination machinery provided by the lease.[197] The terms of the existing lease cease, in equity, to

193 *City Offices (Regent Street) Ltd v Europa Development Group plc* [1990] 1 EGLR 63, CA.
194 *Parkinson v Barclays Bank* [1951] 1 KB 368, CA.
195 *Weinbergs Weatherproofs Ltd v Radcliffe Paper Mill Co* [1958] Ch 437.
196 *Keith Bayler Rogers & Co v Cubes* (1975) 31 P & CR 412.
197 *Sudbrook Trading Estate Ltd v Eggleton* [1983] 1 AC 444, [1982] 3 All ER 1.

be enforceable once the relationship of vendor and purchaser has come into existence between the parties, as where the conditions precedent for exercise of the option to purchase have been satisfied and the price has been agreed.

CHAPTER 8

Rent and rent reviews

This Chapter examines the basic principles which govern the nature of rent, notes the remedies available to landlords for non-payment of rent, and then deals with the important topic (at least for commercial leases) of rent review.

I   NATURE AND CLASSIFICATION OF RENT

Rent as a contractual sum

One of the usual but not essential[1] badges of a lease or tenancy is that ordinarily rent is payable by the tenant to the landlord. Rent, as opposed to a premium,[2] is a regular, contractual, sum of money which the landlord is entitled to receive from the tenant in return for the tenant using and occupying the land and premises let by the lease.[3] The courts when defining the nature of rent now emphasise its contractual nature, rather than the more traditional definition of rent as an 'incident of tenure'. The lease may provide for rent to be payable in advance. If it does not do so, the common law rule

---

1   *Ashburn Anstalt v Arnold* [1989] Ch 1, [1988] 2 All ER 147 (holding that rent is not an essential element of a tenancy, as, after all, no rent is payable under a tenancy at will).
2   A premium is a capital or lump sum payable on the grant of a long lease or when it is assigned. Sometimes landlords in the residential sector have been able to take a premium from a tenant holding a short lease, the premium in this case being the rent for the lease 'capitalised' into a lump sum. There is nothing in the Housing Act 1988, which governs post-Rent Act tenancies, to counteract this practice. Sometimes the landlord may take a rent deposit on account of dilapidations; and also a right to deduct unpaid rent out of a rent deposit, as happened in *Obaray v Gateway (London) Ltd* [2000] EGCS 149 (where the right was wide enough to cover breaches of the tenancy and insolvency events).
3   *CH Bailey Ltd v Memorial Enterprises Ltd* [1974] 1 All ER 1003, [1974] 1 WLR 728, CA; *Standard Life Assurance Co v Greycoat Devonshire Square Ltd* [2001] L & TR 25, [2001] L & TR 290 (so that gross rents did not include a large lump sum payable on account of dilapidations).

applies: the rent will then be payable only in arrear.[4] The lease or tenancy will no doubt specify the dates on which rent is payable to the landlord. This might be on a specified day of the week or the month. The lease may require payment on the 'usual quarter days', by which is meant 25 March, 24 June, 29 September and Christmas Day.[5] In the case of a periodic tenancy, it is assumed that rent is payable for the same periods as those of the tenancy.

Rent is payable to the landlord

Rent is to be paid to the landlord or to his duly authorised agent.[6] Where the landlord has assigned the reversion, legislation protects residential tenants against having to pay rent to the wrong person. By the Landlord and Tenant Act 1985, s 3(1), where a landlord of premises consisting of or including a dwelling-house assigns his interest, the new landlord is required to give written notice of the assignment and of his name and address to the tenant. This must be done not later than the next day on which rent is payable, or if that is within two months of the date of the assignment, the end of two months. It is an offence not to comply with this requirement without reasonable excuse. In addition, the previous landlord remains under a continuing liability for breaches of covenant from the date of the assignment until due notification. However, the tenant is not excused from paying any of the rent due to the assignee, once notice is given, even that arising prior to any notification but after the assignment.

There is further protection under the Landlord and Tenant Act 1987, ss 47 and 48. These apply to premises which consist of or include a dwelling: thus to houses, flats and farmland which includes a dwelling,[7] as well as flats over commercial premises held on the same lease where the predominant user of the property as a whole is intended as residential.[8] By the Landlord and Tenant Act 1987, s 47(1) as amended, any demand for rent, service charges or administration charges (an example of the latter is a sum payable in respect of a landlord's consent to a proposed assignment) must contain the name and address of the landlord.[9] The sanction of not complying with this requirement is that the rent or service charge is treated for all purposes as not

---

4   *Coomber v Howard* (1845) 1 CB 440.
5   The lease may however not specify the usual quarter days, but require quarterly rental payments, as was traditional with annual tenancies. In that case the quarters are calculated from the date of the agreement: 2 Roll 450.
6   However, where the rent of an immediate tenant is in arrears, the superior landlord may require a sub-lessee to pay him the rent direct (until the arrears are paid off) following notice: Law of Distress Amendment Act 1908, s 6. See *Rhodes v Allied Dunbar Pension Services Ltd* [1989] 1 All ER 1161, CA. The under-lessee has a right under the Law of Distress Amendment Act 1908, s 3 to deduct the sums paid from any rent due to his immediate landlord.
7   *Dallhold Estates (UK) Pty Ltd v Lindsey Trading Properties Inc* [1994] 1 EGLR 93, CA.
8   Lettings of business premises within the Landlord and Tenant Act 1954, Pt II are excluded (Landlord and Tenant Act 1987, s 46(1)).
9   If the landlord's address is not in England and Wales, an address in England and Wales must be given at which all notices may be served on the landlord. Landlord and Tenant Act 1987, s 48

being due from the tenant until the Act is complied with (Landlord and Tenant Act 1987, s 47(2)).[10]

Rack or market rent

Most leases require the payment of a 'rack rent' for the premises.[11] That is to say, the tenant pays what the parties think is the full annual market value of the premises,[12] no doubt taking into account rents charged for comparable recent lettings in the locality. In the case of assured shorthold tenancies in the private residential sector, where no security within the Housing Act 1988 is conferred on the tenant, there are no significant legislative controls on the maximum amount of rent that may be charged to a tenant. On the other hand, a clause in the form of a rent review, in an assured tenancy, providing for a very large, if not exorbitant, increase in rent, was treated as a device to allow the landlord to regain possession of the premises without having to go to court, and so unenforceable.[13]

Personal liability of tenant for rent

The tenant is personally liable for rent due. It is no doubt usual to provide that a proportion of the rent is due as from the date of the lease, or the date the tenant takes possession, if sooner than that.[14] Even if the tenant holds a legal lease only as a trustee, and so not beneficially, he is personally liable for the whole rent due. If there are not enough trust funds to pay the rent, a trustee-tenant will be personally liable to the landlord to the extent of the deficit.[15]

---

requires that a landlord of any dwelling in England and Wales supplies the tenant with a name and address in England and Wales for service on him of any notices, subject to the same penalty of non-recovery of rent, etc as applies to the Landlord and Tenant Act 1987, s 47. Sufficient for the Landlord and Tenant Act 1987, s 48 is a statement of a name and address in the tenancy: a separate notice is not then required: *Rogan v Woodfield Building Services Ltd* [1995] 1 EGLR 72, CA.

10 However, Landlord and Tenant Act 1987, s 47 does not apply where there is a receiver or manager appointed whose functions include receipt of service charges (Landlord and Tenant Act 1987, s 47(3)).

11 As opposed to a *peppercorn rent*, which is often so low that it is not collected. Note that in the case of a mining lease the rent may comprise a *dead rent* (at a fixed level) and a fluctuating rent, or royalties, which depend on the value of the minerals worked.

12 Cf *Compton Group Ltd v Estates Gazette Ltd* (1977) 36 P & CR 148.

13 *Bankway Properties Ltd v Penfold-Dunsford* [2001] EWCA Civ 528, [2001] 2 EGLR 36, CA (this clause envisaged an increase in the annual rent from £4,680 a year to £25,000 and was treated as an invalid attempt to contract out of the provisions of HA 1988, whose scheme was mandatory).

14 Luxton & Wilkie, p 209. Apportionment may be provided for where a lease is terminated during a rent period but if not the Apportionment Act 1870 applies (subject to the serious limitation that it does not apply where rent is payable in advance).

15 As in *Perring v Draper* [1997] EGCS 109.

Rent has special characteristics

Lord Millett recently said that rent was not a simple debt. It was consideration for the right to remain in possession.[16] This remark emphasises that although the modern view of rent is that it is a contractual payment for use and occupation of land, rent retains some special characteristics. In particular, rent is traditionally 'reserved' in a lease 'out of land'. The significance of this is that if the buildings on the land are destroyed or damaged, the tenant continues to be liable in full for the rent due, for the whole of the remainder of the lease.[17]

Is rent always due?

(i) Cesser of rent

To counteract the harsh effects of the principle that rent is due from the tenant even if the buildings on the land have been destroyed, the lease may contain a 'cesser of rent clause', under which if a specified event, such as fire destruction of the premises, takes place, then all liability to pay rent is suspended until a further event takes place. This might be the rebuilding of the premises, using any insurance money released by the event in question.[18] The period of suspension is for the parties to select. A rent suspension clause which referred to the 'rent hereby reserved' did not apply to additional rent due on account of insurance premiums and service charges, since continuity of payment would be expected in relation to these payments.[19]

(ii) Frustration

Frustration of a lease, if shown, puts an end to all liability of the tenant to pay rent. However, the frustrating event must be very grave: it must prevent any substantial use being made of the premises for the purposes contemplated by the parties or permitted by the lease.[20] However, severe dislocation of the tenant's enjoyment of the premises is outside the doctrine of frustration.

16 *Christopher Moran Holdings Ltd v Bairstow* [1999] 1 EGLR 1 at 4, HL.
17 *Redmond v Dainton* [1920] 2 KB 256.
18 See, eg the wording of the clause in Luxton & Wilkie, p 203, which refers to destruction and damage by fire or other insured risk. This clause envisages that if the premises are not completely unusable, the tenant will have to pay a fair proportion of the rent.
19 *P & O Property Holdings Ltd v International Computers Ltd* [1999] 2 EGLR 17.
20 *National Carriers Ltd v Panalpina (Northern) Ltd* [1981] AC 675, [1981] 1 All ER 161, HL. Until these rulings, it was held that frustration could not apply to a lease, applying the traditional view that no estate in land could be frustrated.

Service charges as rent

Leases of flats and of commercial units sometimes reserve service charges (which are tenant contributions to repairing and maintenance work) and insurance payments as rent. This has the advantage from the point of view of the landlord that the moneys concerned, as recurring payments, are subject to the same remedies against the land as apply to non-payment of rent, if the money is not paid by the tenant. Thus a landlord can seek distress (subject to strict conditions) and forfeiture against a tenant who fails to pay service charges at all or in a timely fashion. The courts do not ask for a special form of words to achieve this. In one case it was held that the expression 'yielding and paying' reserved service charges as rent.[21] There are some controls on the recovery of service charges both in the case of business and residential tenants: these are discussed later in this book.

Certainty of rent

At one time, the rent level had to be fixed throughout the lease in order to be capable of being recovered. This rule was based on the idea that no distress for rent (a process of seizing the tenant's goods up to the rent owed and then selling them) was not possible otherwise.[22] The certainty rule precludes fixing a 'rent' based on as many hours a landlord may require from time to time as services from the occupiers of premises.[23] However, rents of a basic amount with, in addition, a portion based on the percentage turnover of the tenant's business, are 'certain' enough for the purposes of the certainty rule.[24] It is understood that such rents sometimes occur with trading units in shopping malls. The advent of rent review clauses has meant that the old principle of certainty has been abandoned to the extent that it is no longer required that a lease reserve a rent for the whole of the lease. A reservation for a part of the lease, such as for the first five years, followed by a statement that the rent for the next period of time will be that agreed as the market rent or ascertained by an arbitrator or expert, suffices for the revised certainty rule.[25]

---

21 *Royton Industries Ltd v Lawrence* [1994] 1 EGLR 110.
22 *Walsh v Lonsdale* (1882) 21 Ch D 9. There were two rents in that case, one fixed and one fluctuating. However, once the fluctuating rent had become ascertained, by reference to the tenant's profits, it would be certain and so distrainable for.
23 *Barnes v Barratt* [1970] 2 QB 657, [1970] 2 All ER 483, CA.
24 *Smith v Cardiff Corpn (No 2)* [1955] Ch 159, [1955] 1 All ER 113. For a recent example of turnover rents see *Heathrow Airport Ltd v Forte (UK) Ltd* [1998] EGCS 13 (6% of the gross turnover of the tenant, the tenant failing to show an abuse of power under EU rules by the landlord in not reducing the rent).
25 *Brown v Gould* [1972] Ch 53, [1971] 2 All ER 1505. The parties may agree that notwithstanding any rent review, the rent level fixed at the commencement of the lease is the minimum rent payable (so that the landlord is guaranteed a minimum rent level): see *New Zealand Post Ltd v ASB Bank Ltd* [1995] 2 NZLR 508.

Other rent payments

Apart from the 'rack rent', which is the commonest type of rent payment, it is possible to reserve the payment of a ground rent, and a variable or sliding scale rent. A ground rent is reserved in the case of a long lease: if it is not paid the landlord can institute forfeiture proceedings (subject to safeguards as discussed in ch 12, below). We shall discuss variable rents further under 'Rent reviews'. Rent is ordinarily payable in full, without deductions, to the landlord. Sometimes the tenant may claim that he can set off against the rents sums on account of, notably, dilapidations which the landlord, in breach of covenant, has failed to put right. To exclude this right, the lease will need to provide a statement that the rent is payable without any right of deduction or set off in law or equity. It was held insufficient simply to require payment of a rent 'without any deductions'.[26]

Position if tenant holds over

If the tenant holds over, or remains in occupation, at the end of his lease, the question arises as to his liability to pay for his continuing occupation. Two possibilities may be considered, assuming that the tenant's continuing in possession is not against the wishes of the landlord.

1   The parties may impliedly agree that the tenant, who may have held a fixed-term lease, is to remain as a periodic tenant at the same rent as that payable for the last period of the previous tenancy. This calls for no further comment, except to note that if the landlord decides to treat the tenant as a trespasser, and claims possession, he cannot thereafter recover payments for use and occupation.[27] In such a case, the former tenant must pay mesne profits to the landlord. These sums of money are compensation to the landlord, and are based on the letting value of the property. This may be the previously-payable rent, but the court may make a finding as to what is a reasonable rent for the wrongful use of the landlord's land by the trespassing occupier.[28] In this, the fact that the landlord might not have let the property to anyone else makes no difference, since the landlord is entitled to compensation for the wrongful use of his land by the trespasser.[29] At any rate, where the previous tenancy rent was not at a commercial rate, the compensatory principle requires a close examination of the facts. Thus, where a service tenant's deserted wife remained in occupation of Ministry of Defence property awaiting a repossession order so that she might be rehoused by a local authority, the sums due from her were those payable for comparable local authority housing accommodation. This sum was more than the concessionary rent but less than the abstract market value figure the landlords produced, which was rejected.[30]

26   *Connaught Restaurants Ltd v Indoor Leisure Ltd* [1994] 4 All ER 834, CA.
27   *Birch v Wright* (1786) 1 Term Rep 378.
28   See *Inverugie Investments Ltd v Hackett* [1995] 3 All ER 841, JCPC.
29   *Inverugie Investments Ltd v Hackett* [1995] 3 All ER 841, JCPC.
30   *Ministry of Defence v Ashman* [1993] 2 EGLR 102, CA; see Cooke (1994) 110 LQR 420; also *Lewisham London BC v Masterson* [2000] 1 EGLR 134.

2   The tenant may be holding over after expiry of a fixed-term lease with no agreement between the parties as to a new tenancy. The landlord may have served a notice to quit on the tenant, who, having held a periodic tenancy, however, remains in occupation until evicted. In both cases the landlord brings a claim for use and occupation.[31] This action is also available against a tenant who had sub-let the premises, so abandoning possession, where the sub-tenant wrongfully held over at the expiry of his sub-lease.[32] 'Wrongfully' does not include a holding over by a sub-tenant who is entitled to remain in possession thanks to, for example, residential security of tenure statutes.[33] The claim by the landlord is in essence for *damages*. Broadly, these are computed on the basis of the letting value of the premises. The court will have regard to the cost to the tenant of comparable accommodation, at least where he had enjoyed a preferential rent as a service occupier.[34] However, the rent payable under the previous tenancy may be used as evidence of the rental value of the premises. This level would not be relevant once one of the parties proposes a higher rent, as the parties are no longer in agreement that the old rent should continue to be payable.[35]

Position if tenant ceases to pay rent and remains in occupation

The position where a tenant ceases to pay rent and remains in exclusive possession against the landlord's wishes and so in adverse possession of unregistered land must also be noted. During the lease or tenancy, the tenant[36] has exclusive possession with the consent of the landlord, which precludes any claim by the tenant that his possession is adverse. Where the tenant holds under a lease in writing,[37] and fails to pay rent, once six years have expired from the date the payment is due, recovery of that sum is statute-barred.[38] Where the rent is £10 a year or more and it is paid to a third person for

31   The action may also be brought where the tenant holds over as a tenant at will (and so rent-free) pending a new tenancy, or as a tenant by estoppel.
32   *Ibbs v Richardson* (1839) 9 Ad & El 849.
33   See eg *Watson v Sanders-Roe Ltd* [1947] KB 437. The advent of assured shorthold tenancies in the private residential sector has reduced the significance of this point.
34   *Ministry of Defence v Thompson* [1993] 2 EGLR 107, CA.
35   *Dean and Chapter of the Cathedral of Christ Church Canterbury v Whitbread plc* [1995] 1 EGLR 82.
36   Other than a person with a personal right to occupy land following the tenancy, such as, notably, a statutory tenant under the Rent Acts, who can acquire title by adverse possession through non-payment of rent: see *Jessamine Investment Co v Schwarz* [1976] 3 All ER 521; also *Price v Hartley* [1995] EGCS 74.
37   An old fashioned expression which follows the language of the Statute of Frauds 1677, s 3 (in contrast to the rather more recent language of LPA 1925, ss 52 and 53, which follows the wording of the Real Property Act 1845, s 3). A rent book is not a lease in writing: *Moses v Lovegrove* [1952] 2 QB 533, [1952] 1 All ER 1279. Nor was a letter, signed by the tenant, that he intended to abide by the terms of a periodic tenancy. Time ran from 1977, when the tenant ceased to pay rent, not from 1984, when a landlord's notice to quit was served: *Long v Tower Hamlets London BC* [1996] 2 All ER 683.
38   Limitation Act 1980, s 19.

12 years or more, the title of the ertswhile landlord will be statute-barred as against the third person.[39] If a periodic tenant or a yearly tenant who holds without a lease in writing pays no rent to the landlord, time begins to run against the landlord as from the end of the first year or other period of the tenancy, and as from 12 years from that time, the effect of the statute is much harsher than in the case of a lease in writing, since the landlord's right to recover the land from the tenant will be statute-barred.[40] If the occupier is a licensee, time cannot run against the landlord since the licensee has no exclusive possession.[41]

II   REMEDIES FOR NON-PAYMENT OF RENT

There are three remedies for landlords where rent arrears have built up. These are: an action to recover the rent, distress and forfeiture.

Action for unpaid rent

The details of the reformed procedure to be taken in an action for unpaid rent lie outside the scope of this book,[42] but the county court now has an unlimited jurisdiction with regard to claims for rent arrears. In the residential sector, the landlord must precede any action with notices under statutory provisions which are considered when discussing Rent Act tenancies, assured and assured shorthold tenancies and secure tenancies. In principle, the action is taken in the county court for the district in which the land is situated. Once the landlord has forfeited the lease, or re-let the premises (a process called 'constructive re-entry'), an action for future rent from the ertswhile tenant cannot be maintained.[43]

If the tenant has overpaid rent in the past under a mistake of law or fact, he is entitled to set off in equity the amount of any past overpayments against the rent arrears claimed.[44] This is because equitable set-off is a cross-claim arising out of the same transaction (the lease) so that it is unconscionable for the landlord to insist on being paid rent arrears without giving credit for the claim made by the tenant. Thus where a tenant had paid two quarters rent under a mistake, he could set these payments off against a much larger claim for rent arrears, without having to make any prior demand to the landlord.[45]

39   Limitation Act 1980, s 15(6) and Sch 1, para 6.
40   Limitation Act 1980, s 15(6) and Sch 1, para 5.
41   *BP Properties Ltd v Buckler* [1987] 2 EGLR 168.
42   See CPR 1988, Pt 55 and Practice Direction 55, summarised by Webber (2001) 5 L & T Rev 102. The revised rules came into force on 15 October 2001.
43   See *Cromwell Developments Ltd v Godfrey* [1998] 2 EGLR 62.
44   *Eller v Grovecrest Investments Ltd* [1995] QB 272, CA.
45   *Fuller v Happy Shopper Markets Ltd* [2001] 2 EGLR 32.

Actions for unpaid rent are subject to a period of limitation. An action for unpaid rent as well a claim to distrain for unpaid rent are barred after the expiry of six years from the date when the arrears became due.[46] This limitation period applies, subject to the qualification that time runs only as from the date when the landlord demands payment, where the landlord is claiming unpaid rent against a guarantor of the tenant's obligation to pay rent. Although the statute does not expressly mention guarantors or sureties, the statutory expression 'damages in respect of arrears of rent' is used, and this is precisely what the landlord is claiming from a tenant's guarantor.[47]

Distress for unpaid rent

Distress for rent is a harsh, perhaps anachronistic,[48] yet effective self-help remedy.[49] Where available, it entitles the landlord to seize and in due course sell goods found on the tenant's premises so as to pay off rent arrears. Where service charges and insurance premium payments from a tenant are reserved as rent, then distress becomes available to enforce payment of these sums. Supposing that the rent is overdue, the landlord seizes relevant goods of the tenant as well as those of a third party, which can be carried out by his certificated bailiff labelling the goods on the premises and leaving them there. At the time the distress takes place, the tenant must be given a notice of distress. If within five days of this seizure, the rent remains unpaid, the goods may be sold off to pay the arrears. Although the landlord may distrain personally, many landlords employ a certificated bailiff to carry out distress. Indeed a company landlord must employ such a person.[50] If the tenant interferes with seized goods then this is a pound-breach, entitling the landlord to treble damages.[51] But if distress is illegal, as where no rent is due, or privileged goods such as tenant's fixtures or tools and implements of the tenant's trade, are seized, then the tenant may rescue the goods (in effect take them back). He may alternatively sue for their recovery prior to sale in the county court. Statute requires a landlord to obtain leave of the county court for a distress against the tenant of a dwelling house let on an assured or an assured shorthold tenancy.[52]

46 Limitation Act 1980, s 19. However, there is a difference between a landlord failing to collect rent and his agreeing not to do so, being estopped from resuming his contractual right to payment. In the latter case the possession of the tenant would be not adverse: see eg *Smith v Lawson* (1997) 75 P & CR 466.

47 *Romain v Semba TV Ltd* [1996] 1 EGLR 102 at 105B (Evans LJ). See *Moschi v Lep Air Services Ltd* [1973] AC 331 at 347-49 (Lord Diplock).

48 *Fuller v Happy Shopper Markets Ltd* [2001] 25 EG 159 at 164. 'The human rights implications of levying distress must be in the forefront of the mind of the landlord before he takes this step' (Lightman J).

49 See Walton 'Landlord's Distress' [2000] Conv 508. It was recognised in *Wharfland Ltd v South London Co-operative Building Co Ltd* [1995] 2 EGLR 21 at 22 that the remedy was back in vogue with commercial landlords.

50 Law of Distress Amendment Act 1888, ss 7 and 8; Distress for Rent Rules 1999, SI 1999/2360 as amended.

51 Distress for Rent Act 1689, s 3.

52 Housing Act 1988, s 19; a similar rule applies to distress against a protected or statutory tenant: Rent Act 1977, s 147. It is understood that distress is but seldom levied in either set of cases.

The goods of a third party such as a hire company which has hired goods to the tenant on hire or hire-purchase are at risk from distress. Statute[53] allows a third party to make a prescribed form written declaration to the landlord or certificated bailiff once distress is threatened. This is to the effect that the tenant has no beneficial interest in the goods, an inventory being required. Once this declaration is served, the third party can protect his goods against distress, with remedies for illegal distress against the goods concerned.

According to the Lord Chancellor's Department,[54] the commercial property sector relies heavily on distress. At least 20,000 cases were commenced to September 2000, although in only 2% of cases was there an actual, as opposed to a threatened, distress. A number of objections of principle can be made against this archaic remedy, whose abolition was proposed by the Law Commission in 1991.[55] As it is extra-judicial, it deprives the tenant of the possibility, before its exercise, of a court hearing. English law is now becoming unusual in retaining this remedy. As has been noted,[56] most American states have got rid of distress. In Australia, the States of New South Wales, Western Australia and Queensland, have abrogated it.[57]

In addition, serious doubts exist as to the compatibility of distress with HRA 1998. Distress might breach both ECHR, Art 6 and also the First Protocol of the Convention, Art 1. The tenant has almost no opportunity before a distress claim to challenge its validity. In a recent case[58] the Court of Appeal held that distress might break EHCR, Art 8, which speaks of respect for the tenant's family and home, in the context of a shop and residential accommodation let with the shop. The landlord had to take care to see to it that the tenant had no claims by equitable set-off against the rent arrears allegedly entitling the landlord to distrain. A third party who cannot rely on the protection of legislation of 1908 already mentioned could claim a violation of his human rights under the First Protocol of the Convention, Art 1 as he is at risk of losing his property without any sufficient redress.

Reform of the law of distress is being considered at the time of writing, but, so far, not its wholesale abolition. This would take place only for residential tenants. The current reform process has gone to two phases. There was first an independent review[59] followed by a Consultation Paper from the Lord Chancellor's department.[60] Both suggested keeping distress for commercial premises. The independent review advocated setting out the procedures clearly and rendering them effective; it also aimed to give 'debtors' protection from undue economic hardship and personal distress. The

53 Law of Distress Amendment Act 1908, ss 4 and 4A.
54 Distress for Rent Consultation Paper (2001), para 8.
55 Law Com No 194 (1991).
56 See eg Osowski (1993) 10 Alaska Law Rev 33.
57 Landlord and Tenant Amendment (Distress Abolition) Act 1930 (NSW); Distress for Rent Abolition Act 1936 (WA); Property Law Act 1974 (Qd).
58 *Fuller v Happy Shopper Markets Ltd* [2001] 2 EGLR 32.
59 Independent Review of Bailiff Law (2000) (www.open.gov.uk/lcd/enforcement/beatson.pdf).
60 Distress for Rent Consultation Paper (2001) (www.open.gov.uk/lcd/consult/distress). The responses to consultation (May 2002) may also be viewed on the Lord Chancellor's Office website.

independent review did not think, perhaps questionably in view of what has been said earlier, that the process of distress was inconsistent with the ECHR. What is clear is that distress is a complex and technical subject. The independent review recommended[61] therefore that clarity on the law should be the aim and also that that the right of the tenant and of any third party to challenge distress should be set out clearly so as to encourage consistency and certainty. The goods that were excluded from distress should be defined clearly, in a statute. Remedies for wrongful distress should be set out clearly, again in legislation.[62]

The Consultation Paper rejected the abolition of distress for commercial properties, where it was a cost-effective means of pursuing rent arrears.[63] However, if retained, distress for commercial properties would need to be modified. There would need to be a new regime, brought in once the review of enforcement law was at an end. It would, according to the Consultation Paper, set out clearly what the landlord was entitled to do. The new distress rules would have safeguards for tenants. Thus, the procedure would be open to challenge, this proposal having one eye on HRA 1998, no doubt.[64] Under this review's proposed rules, there would be many new restrictions on distress being levied, all with a view to drawing some of its sting without disarming it completely. It was for instance envisaged that the right of a landlord personally to distrain, already curtailed, would be dropped.[65] Only a certificated bailiff would be able to distrain. No distress would take place on Sundays.[66] An important change suggested was that the tenant would be entitled to 72 hours' formal notice that failure to pay outstanding rent might trigger a distress.[67] The tenant would then be able to apply to the court to challenge the validity of the threatened distress. The tenant whose goods were seized would also become entitled to 14 days' notice of intent to sell the goods at issue.[68] The Consultation Paper of 2001 favoured solving the problem of third party goods by totally excluding these from distress.[69]

---

61 Independent Review of Bailiff Law (2000) (www.open.gov.uk/lcd/enforcement/beatson.pdf), para 2.27. It also recommended giving sufficient time to the tenant or third party to apply to the court to prevent a sale of the goods.
62 Independent Review of Bailiff Law (2000) (www.open.gov.uk/lcd/enforcement/beatson.pdf).
63 Distress for Rent Consultation Paper (2001) (www.open.gov.uk/lcd/consult/distress), ch 2, para 12.
64 Distress for Rent Consultation Paper (2001) (www.open.gov.uk/lcd/consult/distress), ch 3, para 2.
65 Distress for Rent Consultation Paper (2001) (www.open.gov.uk/lcd/consult/distress), ch 3, para 8.
66 Distress for Rent Consultation Paper (2001) (www.open.gov.uk/lcd/consult/distress), ch 3, para 12.
67 Distress for Rent Consultation Paper (2001) (www.open.gov.uk/lcd/consult/distress), ch 3, para 25. However, to some business landlords such a warning might hobble the efficiency of the remedy, as it is understood that fear of distress taking place without warning is often enough to induce payment of the arrears in question.
68 Distress for Rent Consultation Paper (2001) (www.open.gov.uk/lcd/consult/distress), ch 3, para 29.
69 Distress for Rent Consultation Paper (2001) (www.open.gov.uk/lcd/consult/distress), ch 3, para 35.

Forfeiture for non-payment of rent

The landlord has the option to re-enter and so forfeit the lease on account of non-payment of rent. The effect of forfeiture, if successful, is that the court orders the tenant to give up possession of the premises to the landlord. The right to forfeit a lease is subject to a number of restrictions in the residential sector (as to which see Part D of this book) but it is relatively uninhibited in the commercial sector, a fact which has been judicially recognised.[70] The landlord cannot claim re-entry and forfeiture unless the lease expressly entitles him to do so on account of non-payment of rent. In addition, there are restrictions on a landlord's right to forfeit on account of small amounts of unpaid rent or service charges in particular.[71] At common law, no right of re-entry or forfeiture for non-payment of rent can be exercised unless a formal demand has been made for the rent, by the landlord or his agent. Formal demands for rent are normally expressly dispensed with in leases.[72] If the premises are occupied or are residential, the landlord must commence proceedings with a claim form; service of the claim form does not, however, it now seems, put an end automatically to the lease, nor to any sub-lease granted by the tenant.[73] This is owing to the fact that if the tenant (or sub-tenant) apply for and obtain relief, 'the right of re-entry for forfeiture is got rid of'.[74] The status of the tenant as from service on the tenant of the claim form seeking forfeiture is not clear. One view is that a forfeiture is notionally incurred as from the date of such service, subject to relief being granted (though relief is an integral part of the whole forfeiture process) and the landlord has unequivocally elected to treat the lease as being at an end. If relief is not granted, the lease will be forfeited retrospectively as from the date of service of the claim form.[75] On the other hand, the Court of Appeal also held that in relation to the County Courts Act 1984, s 138, the effect of service on the tenant of the landlord's claim form was not to place the lease in a state of suspended animation. The lease would continue to exist so that rent was payable until such time,

70 *Kataria v Safeland plc* (1997) 75 P & CR D30, CA.
71 By CLRA 2002, s 167 the landlord of a long lease of a dwelling (ie a lease for a term certain exceeding 21 years) cannot exercise a right of re-entry or forfeiture on account of unpaid rent, service charges or administration charges (such as fees for consents) if, in particular, the unpaid amount is below the prescribed sum, which cannot exceed £500.
72 The demand must be made at the place specified for payment in the lease, or otherwise on the land, and before and until sunset, on the last day for payment and for the sum in the last rental period. Once half a year's rent is in arrears and there is no sufficient distress on the premises to satisfy the demand for rent arrears, a formal demand is dispensed with by statute: County Courts Act 1984, s 139(1) (also Common Law Procedure Act 1852, s 210 in the case of High Court actions).
73 *Ivory Gate Ltd v Spetale* [1998] L & TR 58, CA.
74 *Dendy v Evans* [1910] 1 KB 263 at 269 (Cozens Hardy MR).
75 *Ivory Gate Ltd v Spetale* [1998] L & TR 58, CA. These technicalities do little credit to the law (thus in *Meadows v Clerical Medical and General Life Assurance Society* [1981] Ch 70 at 75 it was admitted that the status of the lease remained uncertain until the result of any relief application, having a 'trance-like existence' meanwhile).

if any, as the landlord became entitled to possession of the premises under the court order for possession.[76]

The landlord's right to re-enter and forfeit a lease of commercial premises was described as a proprietary remedy. Hence, a landlord who had assigned the reversion on the premises but who had also retained the right to re-enter and forfeit the lease on account of rent arrears could forfeit the lease.[77] One option available to the landlord of commercial premises is to re-enter peaceably the premises (a matter discussed further in ch 12, below). It is understood that this remedy is still popular with some commercial landlords, where the premises are vacant, if only because it is extra-judicial and cheap, but owing to the operation of statute[78] it is not lawful to use force to regain possession by means of re-entry. The landlord's right of re-entry or forfeiture is, however, at all times subject to the jurisdiction of the court to grant relief. In the case of county court actions, which will no doubt account for most cases, the jurisdiction is statute-based and depends on suspended possession orders (see below). In the case of the High Court, the jurisdiction to grant relief is based on ancient principles of equity,[79] according to which the right of re-entry clause is merely a security for the payment of rent and related sums such as service charge payments. Hence, equity will be disposed to grant relief (with the result that the tenant is re-instated as if no forfeiture had taken place) if the tenant is able and willing to repay the rent arrears owed and the landlord's (reasonable) costs.[80] This principle also explains why the equity jurisdiction, where applicable, extends to mortgagees and under-lessees alike,[81] as well as to a person holding a charging order.[82] The principle also extends the equity jurisdiction beyond rent to related periodical sums, such as service charge payments, provided these are reserved as additional rent.[83]

The landlord cannot forfeit a lease if he has waived the breach of covenant to pay rent. Waiver is discussed in ch 12, below, but in this context it is to be noted that a covenant to pay rent imposes a continuing obligation on the tenant. Thus if the landlord waives a right to forfeit on account of rent arrears by accepting rent due on a given occasion, his right to forfeit revives if the tenant fails to pay rent due on a future quarter.

Most if not all actions to forfeit a lease on account of non-payment of rent will now be taken in the county court of the district in which the land is situated. The grant of relief

---

76   *Maryland Estates Ltd v Bar Joseph* [1998] L & TR 105.
77   *Kataria v Safeland plc* (1997) 75 P & CR D30, CA.
78   Criminal Law Act 1977, s 6.
79   Which, although superseded by the provisions of LPA 1925, s 146(2) in relation to forfeiture for breaches of covenant other than to pay rent, are affirmed in the case of covenants to pay rent by the Supreme Court Act 1981, s 38.
80   *Ladup Ltd v Williams and Glyn's Bank plc* [1985] 1 WLR 851, [1985] 2 All ER 577.
81   *Belgravia Insurance Co Ltd v Meah* [1964] 1 QB 436, 443; *Billson v Residential Apartments Ltd* [1991] 3 All ER 265, 276.
82   *Croydon Unique Ltd v Wright* (1999) 32 HLR 670, CA (under statute: County Courts Act 1984, s 138(9C) but the same principle would surely apply to the equity inherent jurisdiction).
83   *Escalus Properties Ltd v Robinson* [1996] QB 231, CA. This principle of leaning against forfeiture is strengthened by the statutory restrictions on forfeiture on account of unpaid service charges (ch 12 below).

is pivotal to the tenant being able to retain his lease. The jurisdiction to grant relief in the county court is entirely based on statute, which is exclusive of the ancient equity principles applying, with some statutory modifications, to High Court actions.[84] Owing to recent legislation passed with the express aim of preventing unscrupulous landlords from using forfeiture for non-payment of rent, service charges and the like, no forfeiture or re-entry can be practised against a long lessee of a dwelling where the sum of money claimed is less than prescribed amounts.[85]

In essence, the governing principle of the County Courts Act 1984, s 138 as amended is to allow the tenant or other applicant such as a mortgagee to save the lease provided that all arrears of rent or service charges are paid off reasonably promptly. The forfeiture clause in the lease is thus treated as a security to enforce performance of the covenant to pay rent. The purpose of the County Courts Act 1984, s 138 is to grant relief to the tenant.[86] The 1984 Act therefore allows a number of opportunities to the applicant to obtain relief.

If the tenant or any mortgagee or underlessee[87] pays off the rent arrears or any sums payable as additional rent such as service charges, into court not less than five clear days before the return day for the tenant's defence, then under the County Courts Act 1984, s 138(2), the applicant is entitled to relief automatically. The proceedings end.[88] The tenant or other applicant may not avail themselves of this opportunity for an automatic stay to proceedings, which has, since 1852, been a feature of High Court proceedings.[89] In such a case, the county court's power to grant relief against forfeiture is based on the making of suspended possession orders. By the County Courts Act 1984, s 138(3), if the court is satisfied that the landlord is entitled to forfeit the lease, it must order possession to be given not less than four weeks from the date of the order. However, the court may at discretion suspend the operation of the order for a longer period, and if, during that period, the tenant or other applicant pays off the rent arrears

---

84 *Di Palma v Victoria Square Property Ltd* [1986] Ch 150, [1985] 2 All ER 676, CA.
85 CLRA 2002, s 167. Long lessee means essentially one holding a lease granted for a term exceeding 21 years. It appears (HC Debates, *Hansard*, 13 March, col 960) that the government envisages a prescribed floor of £350. In addition, no forfeiture can be exercised in respect of small sums outstanding unless these have not been settled within the prescribed period, expected to be three years. Under CLRA 2002, s 166, a long lessee of a dwelling is not liable to pay rent unless the landlord has given him notice of at least 30 days to pay. 'Rent' excludes service charges: this provision aims at ground rents.
86 *Maryland Estates Ltd v Bar Joseph* [1998] L & TR 105, CA.
87 The latter two classes of applicant are within County Courts Act 1984, s 138 by necessary implication: *United Dominions Trust Ltd v Shellpoint Trustees Ltd* [1993] 4 All ER 310, CA.
88 However, County Courts Act 1984, s 138(2) does not apply where the landlord is claiming forfeiture on other grounds beside non-payment of rent.
89 Under Common Law Procedure Act 1852, s 212. The tenant may thus pay into court all rent arrears and landlords' costs at any time, in this case, before judgment is given. However, in contrast to the county court rule, s 212 only applies if there is half a year's rent, or more, in arrear (*Standard Pattern Co v Ivey* [1962] Ch 432, [1962] 1 All ER 452), but, again in contrast to the position with the 1984 Act, Common Law Procedure Act 1852, s 212 may be made use of even if the landlord is also claiming forfeiture for other breaches, and is also available where the landlord has peaceably re-entered (*Howard v Fanshawe* [1895] 2 Ch 581).

and costs into court, the order will not take effect. By 'all rent in arrears' is meant all sums, rent or for use and occupation, due to the landlord at the time the court states in its order that possession is to be given up, on the assumption that all sums due to the landlord by then will be paid by the tenant.[90] The applicant will, if such arrears are paid off, obtain relief and holds the lease without any need for a new lease. The court, moreover, may, on the application of the tenant or other applicant such as a mortgagee, extend the time of suspension of the possession order. It may do this more than once if appropriate (County Courts Act 1984, s 138(4)). The tenant or applicant may then avert forfeiture by paying off the rent arrears and costs in question (County Courts Act 1984, s 138(5)). Once again, relief is automatic: the tenant holds the land under the lease as though no forfeiture had been commenced. The lease is wholly re-instated.[91]

On the other hand, the court must enforce the order for possession, if, during the original period of its suspension or any subsequent extension of that time, the tenant or other applicant fails to pay off the rent arrears and costs in question (County Courts Act 1984, s 138(7)). Once the order for possession has been enforced, the tenant, or other applicant such as a mortgagee, is then 'barred' from any further relief.[92] The point of this is that there is no right in the tenant or other applicant to ask the county court to grant relief in equity where under the County Courts Act 1984 any right to seek relief cannot be claimed. Otherwise, there would be nothing to prevent further litigation where the tenant had failed for no good reason to make use of the County Courts Act 1984 rights. Hence, where a lease had been forfeited for service charge arrears of some £299, and the tenant did not avail herself of the opportunities of the County Courts Act 1984, to obtain relief, it was held that the 1984 Act was a self-contained code. Hence, the tenant was barred from any further relief in the county court and had no right to apply to the High Court to exercise its inherent equity jurisdiction.[93] The tenant or any mortgagee or underlessee has one further chance to save the lease, owing to the County Courts Act 1984, s 138(9A) and (9C). The applicant has a six-month period as from the date of recovery of possession to apply to the court for relief.[94]

By way of comparison, it is useful to note the principles on which the High Court jurisdiction in equity to grant relief against forfeiture is exercised in the case of non-

---

90 *Maryland Estates Ltd v Bar Joseph* [1998] L & TR 105, CA.
91 *Maryland Estates Ltd v Bar Joseph* [1998] L & TR 105, CA.
92 *United Dominions Trust Ltd v Shellpoint Trustees* [1993] 4 All ER 310, CA (where a mortgagee who was duly notified of the forfeiture failed to apply within the parameters of County Courts Act 1984, s 138 and so was not entitled to apply outside them).
93 *Di Palma v Victoria Square Property Ltd* [1986] Ch 150, [1985] 2 All ER 676, CA. As noted elsewhere, an application to Strasbourg to declare that this result infringed ECHR, Art 6 failed. Especially with the further amendments to County Courts Act 1984, ss 138(9A)-(9C) there seems to be sufficient proportionality for the 1984 Act provisions to resist an attack under HRA 1998. Under CLRA 2002, s 167 the sum concerned in *Di Palma* would probably have fallen below what the anticipated amount is before landlords may as from the commencement of this provision forfeit.
94 See *Bank of Ireland Mortgages v South Lodge Developments* [1996] 1 EGLR 91.

payment of rent. The tenant or other applicant must apply within six months of the landlord's actual entry into the premises under an order for possession.[95] If the landlord makes use of peaceable re-entry, so avoiding a court order, the six-month time-limit is applied but not strictly as equity will not object to a few days' delay which can be explained by the applicant.[96] The court has a discretion in equity to grant or refuse relief and declines to lay down precise or rigid guidelines as to the way it may act. However, because equity regards the re-entry clause as merely a security for enforcing covenants to pay rent, relief is only exceptionally refused where all the rent arrears and costs are repaid by the tenant, especially where the tenant undertakes as a condition of relief to perform the covenants in the lease.[97] This is because the object of relief is to put the landlord and tenant back into the same position they would have been in if no forfeiture had taken place.[98] This explains why the lessee must, as a condition of relief, pay the lessor's properly incurred costs.[99] Indeed, if the lease has a rent review clause operative after the forfeiture date, but prior to the date of relief, the effect on rent of any sums payable by the lessee or other applicant must be taken into account so that the lessor is not adversely affected.[100] One of the conditions of relief will be payment of the relevant arrears and costs within a prescribed time-limit. If the parties have agreed on a time-limit for the repayment of arrears, it seems that, while the court may, under the new Civil Procedure Rules, override the parties' agreement having regard to the requirement to deal with a case 'justly', the court will, when dealing with an application to extend the agreed time for repayment, only exceptionally depart from the parties' agreement.[101] If, however, the landlord has re-let the premises to a third party, having obtained possession, this is a factor which will disincline the court to grant relief to the former tenant,[102] although the court might perhaps be prepared to consider the grant to the applicant of a reversionary lease if the landlord had acted precipitately.

Underlessees and mortgagees are entitled to apply for relief in the equity jurisdiction as much as are lessees. They must do so within the six-month time-limit already mentioned for lessees. If relief is granted to a mortgagee applicant, the head lease is revived.[103] Hence, the applicant must pay to the landlord all the rent arrears but is not

95   Common Law Procedure Act 1852, s 210.
96   *Thatcher v CH Pearce & Sons (Contractors) Ltd* [1968] 1 WLR 748. In this case, the delay was owing to the fact that the tenant was in prison.
97   *Public Trustee v Westbrook* [1965] 3 All ER 398, [1965] 1 WLR 1160, CA; also *Bland v Ingram's Estates Ltd (No 2)* [2001] EWCA Civ 1088, [2002] 1 All ER 244.
98   *Bland v Ingram's Estates Ltd (No 2)* [2001] EWCA Civ 1088, [2002] 1 All ER 244.
99   Ibid. If the lessor has increased his costs by unnecessary opposition to relief, he will have to pay the lessee's or other applicant's costs on the standard basis.
100 *Bland v Ingram's Estates Ltd (No 2)* [2001] EWCA Civ 1088, [2002] 1 All ER 244.
101 *Ropac Ltd v Inntrepreneur Pub Co (CPC) Ltd* [2001] L & TR 10. The requirement to deal with a case 'justly' was treated by the High Court as virtually a public interest factor.
102 See, eg *Silverman v AFCO (UK) Ltd* [1988] 1 EGLR 51, CA.
103 *Escalus Properties Ltd v Robinson Robinson* [1996] QB 231, CA.

liable to pay mesne profits (even if these might exceed the current rent, owing to rises in the value of the rental value of the premises). Underlessees and mortgagees have also a parallel right to ask for a vesting order of the lease under LPA 1925, s 146(4),[104] but to do this they must apply, in this case to the High Court or, more likely, the county court, before the landlord physically regains possession under the court order.[105] On the other hand, so as to deter the use of this uncivilised remedy, the courts have indicated that where a landlord peaceably re-enters premises, the applicant is not bound by this particular time-limit.[106] If an application under LPA 1925, s 146(4) is not possible, as where the landlord has deliberately not informed a mortgagee of the forfeiture claim, then there is no reason why the courts would not be able to invoke their ancient inherent equity jurisdiction to consider a relief application outside the statutory provisions and limits of time.[107]

III   RENT REVIEWS

Introduction

(i)   Purpose of rent review clauses

A lease of business property for any period of five years or more is likely to contain a formula under which an initial rent is payable only for the first period of five years.[108] After that initial period, the lease may well provide that the rent for the premises is to be fixed by a rent review formula, which may be of some complexity.[109] The main aim of these formulae, many of which have been fought out in litigation over the last 30 years or so, is not in serious doubt. It is to give the landlord the benefit of regular reviews to the current market rental value which the premises would command if let on the same terms on the open market at the date of rent review,[110] so as to prevent the value of the rent payable initially being eroded seriously as the lease continues. If, for some reason,

---

104 *Escalus Properties Ltd v Robinson Robinson* [1996] QB 231, CA; *Target Home Loans Ltd v Iza Ltd* [2000] 1 EGLR 23 (where it was pointed out that while relief under LPA 1925, s 146(4) could only take effect under the discretion of the court, it was automatic under County Courts Act 1984, s 138).
105 *Rogers v Rice* [1892] 2 Ch 170, CA.
106 *Billson v Residential Apartments Ltd* [1992] 1 AC 494, [1992] 1 All ER 141 (dealing, however, only with LPA 1925, s 146(2), so that the analogy with LPA 1925, s 146(4) may not be appropriate).
107 *Abbey National Building Society v Maybeech Ltd* [1985] Ch 190. Equity will not, after all, allow a statute to be used as an instrument of fraud, in this case, the stealing of a march by the landlord on the mortgagee.
108 See 'Monitoring the Code of Practice for Commercial Leases'(2000) DETR, para 3.3.
109 Since a lease is workable without a rent review clause, none can be implied in the absence of express provision or a successful claim for rectification: see *Crawford v Bruce* 1992 SLT 524.
110 *British Gas Corpn v Universities Superannuation Scheme Ltd* [1986] 1 All ER 978 at 980-81; *Ashworth Frazer Ltd v Gloucester City Council* [1997] 1 EGLR 104, CA.

the rent review procedure is inoperative, as where it is not invoked by the landlord,[111] then the lease may provide that the current level of rent up to the date for rent review will continue to be payable.[112] Most rent review clauses in England and Wales are of the 'upwards-only' variety,[113] so that it will never be possible for the tenant under a rent review to pay less than the rent payable just before the date of review. In New Zealand, the courts have been faced with 'ratchet clauses', whose effect has been held to provide a floor below which the rent cannot fall,[114] so protecting the landlord who deliberately decides in a falling market not to operate a rent review clause, producing the same effect as our upwards only clauses. No doubt many rent review clauses operate well and reported cases may reflect only anomalies. The courts may initially assume that the terms of rent review clauses are comprehensive and consistent within themselves, and with the rest of the lease.[115] Often enough, that initial assumption has to be revised.

(ii)   Interpreting rent review clauses

The courts apply a 'presumption of reality'[116] or of 'business common sense'[117] in order to try to reduce the scope of disputes about interpreting rent review clauses. They recognise that rent review clauses operate in the real commercial world.[118] Rent

---

111   In *Sunflower Services Ltd v Unisys New Zealand Ltd* (1997) 74 P & CR 112, the Privy Council declined to imply a term that the landlord was on the facts obliged to initiate a rent review where the rent review was to 'take effect' from a certain date. But where only one party could serve a trigger notice, the High Court held that the rent review must be implemented: *Addin v Secretary of State for the Environment* [1997] 1 EGLR 99. In any case, ordinarily, if a landlord fails to serve a notice to review the rent the tenant can serve a notice requesting him to do so or, failing this, the right to review will be deemed lost on that occasion.

112   Where no rent was reserved for a post-review period, the court exceptionally implied a term that the reviewed rent was to be the fair market rent of the premises at the review date: *Beer v Bowden* [1981] 1 All ER 1070, CA. However, this was a claim for rectification, and business efficacy dictated that both parties would have agreed to the term in the circumstances.

113   The government has from time to time indicated unhappiness with this feature of rent review clauses. According to the *Financial Times* 22 April 2002, a new Code of Conduct was by then signed so as to allow for greater flexibility in the design and terms of commercial leases. See also Organ [2002] Estates Gazette, 27 April, p 146. It seems that alternatives to upwards-only rent review should be offered (see also Macfarlane [2002] Estates Gazette, 22 June, p 148). Legislation may follow if this Code is ignored.

114   See eg *Board of Trustees of the National Provident Fund v Brierley Investment Ltd* [1997] 1 NZLR 1, JCPC.

115   *Postel Properties v Greenwell* [1992] 2 EGLR 130 (where, however, internal inconsistencies had to be resolved to reach a sensible result).

116   Per Hoffmann LJ in *Co-operative Wholesale Society Ltd v National Westminster Bank* [1995] 1 EGLR 97 at 99J.

117   *Bailey v Supasnaps Ltd* [1995] EGCS 89, CA.

118   *Dukeminster (Ebbgate House One) Ltd v Somerfield Properties Co Ltd* [1997] EGCS 126 (a clause which 'tested to the utmost the ability of the court to find a commercial solution').

review clauses are interpreted in the context of the lease as a whole.[119] The courts also bear in mind the overriding objective of a rent review clause, which is to bring the rent up to date: if there are some technicalities or intricacies which need to be stripped away in a rent review clause to enable that objective to be attained, these will be overridden,[120] unless the clause clearly requires otherwise. The courts are not therefore prepared to make artificial assumptions about the way a rent review is to operate unless these are unavoidably required by clear language. They set their faces against assumptions which artificially inflate the rent or confer extra benefits or windfalls to the landlord,[121] beyond a rent uplift to current market levels at the date of rent review, owing to some factor which has nothing to do with the actual subject premises. Thus, the Court of Appeal recently held that the new rent was to be ascertained on the assumption that the tenant was entitled to a 35-year-lease from the date the lease was granted and not for some notional period of 35 years from the date of rent review.[122] On the other hand, the courts have to follow the language of a clause which produces a clear result,[123] even one which is artificial or even unfair to one party, such as making an assumption for review purposes which conflicts with the actual lease terms, for instance, that the tenant is entitled to use the premises for any purpose after the rent review date, whereas the lease restricts user, or that the demised land is still not developed when in fact there are buildings on it.[124]

(iii)   Importance of rent reviews

The importance of rent reviews to landlords was early on recognised by the House of Lords, which thought that without a regular review of rent, the landlord would not have been prepared to grant a lease for a substantial period.[125] Their Lordships then deduced from this belief the *non sequitur* that equity required[126] that a lax construction be given to provisions in the rent review clause which entitled the landlord to commence

---

119 *Standard Life Assurance v Unipath Ltd* [1997] 2 EGLR 121, CA (where contentions that the landlord could obtain the benefit of property value increases generally were as much rejected as those of a tenant that the clause must be construed as allowing upwards and downwards review).

120 According to Woodfall, 8-018. See, eg *Law Land Co v Consumers' Association* [1980] 2 EGLR 109.

121 See *Brown v City of Gloucester Council* [1998] 1 EGLR 95, CA.

122 *St Martins Property Investments Ltd v CIB Properties Ltd* [1999] L & TR 1, CA.

123 *Melanesian Mission Trust Board v Australian Mutual Provident Society* [1997] 2 EGLR 128 JCPC.

124 As to the latter, see *Braid v Walsall Metropolitan BC* (1999) 78 P & CR 94, CA; or that an unrealistically high rent is payable: *Secretary of State for the Environment v Associated Newspaper Holdings Ltd* [1995] EGCS 166, CA.

125 *United Scientific Holdings v Burnley Borough Council* [1978] AC 904, [1977] 2 All ER 62.

126 At least this is the view of O'Higgins CJ in *Hynes Ltd v Independent Newspapers Ltd* [1980] IR 204 at 214-15, finding the reasoning in *Burnley* 'compelling'.

or 'trigger' a review of rent: viz, that the landlord could, unless clear contrary language was used in the lease, serve a notice requiring a rent review later than the time specified in the lease. This principle is, however, clearly embedded in the law and it has recently been followed without any demur.[127] Only legislation could remove it. In one sense, rent review clauses are wholly for the benefit of the landlord: once operated, the landlord recovers a higher rent and this at frequent intervals. The parties must clearly agree on the intervals for rent reviews: where a lease provided that the rent was to be agreed, this did not suffice to provide for a further rent review beyond that agreed by the parties.[128] There is no 'normal' pattern of rent reviews which can be assumed for valuation purposes. If a valuer has to decide on the reviewed rent for premises under a lease which fails to fix further clear rent review periods, he cannot assume that there will be a 'normal' pattern of five-yearly rent reviews for the purpose of fixing the new rent.[129]

(iv)   Complexity of the law

An unhappy aspect of rent review by contractual means is the sheer complexity of the law. While it is true that the parties may wish to make use of standard-form clauses produced by the professions, such as the Law Society/RICS Model Forms of rent review clause, in not a few reported cases the parties have seemingly used their own made-to-measure clauses. Unhappy results may follow, as one or other party seeks to squeeze out of a clause, which may be intricate if not technical, some advantage not immediately apparent to common sense. This situation poses dilemmas. There is a conflict between respect for the stated intentions of parties to a commercial lease and a desire to attain some level of predictability in the law. It was stated that a decision which interprets one given rent review clause is of no direct authority in the interpretation of a similar clause in a different lease of different premises.[130] On the other hand, we have already noted the importance of the presumption of reality, by which the courts seek, where the language of a given clause does not clearly militate against doing so, to give effect to the overriding purpose of rent review clauses. The tension between these two principles coupled with the complexity of some rent review clauses and assumptions drawn from them has ensured a large body of case law, of which the present analysis can necessarily only represent a selection.

---

127 *McDonald's Property Co Ltd v HSBC Bank plc* [2001] 3 EGLR 19 (where it seems that the wording of the clause at issue was identical to that in one of the joint appeals in the *Burnley* case).

128 *Stedman v Midland Bank plc* [1990] 1 EGLR 146, CA.

129 *National Westminster Bank Ltd v BSC Footwear Ltd* [1981] 1 EGLR 89.

130 *Equity and Law Life Assurance Society plc v Bodfield Ltd* [1987] 1 EGLR 124 at 125, CA.

Aspects covered in rent review clauses

A rent review clause may deal with at least the following matters.

The clause should specify a date as from which the rent is to be reviewed, which is likely also to be stated as the date as from which the new rent will be payable. However, assuming that the parties cannot agree on a new rent as from that date, and that the issue has to be resolved by an arbitrator or independent expert ascertaining the new rent, the new rent will not necessarily be determined until some time after the review date. If the lease does not expressly provide for the new rent to be backdated to that date, the court will presume, applying reality, that the new rent is only payable as from the next quarter following the award.[131] The rent review clause may also state a date at which the market value of the premises, on which the revised rent is to be based, must be ascertained. If no such date is specified, the courts will presume that the valuation date is the same as the date as from which the rent is to be reviewed.[132] This is a good example of the application of the presumption of reality: it is contrary to the whole purpose of a rent review for the court to fix by implication a date after the rent review date (such as the date at which the valuer makes his decision on the value of the premises).

Some clauses indicate the machinery which leads to the rent review process. One method is to provide that the landlord is entitled to serve a notice on the tenant a given number of weeks or months prior to the date of review, in which he initiates the review: a 'trigger notice'.[133] This notice may request the tenant to respond with a counter-notice, and a method of service may be indicated in the landlord's trigger notice.[134] As discussed below, these trigger notices, are in the absence of clear language stating that time is of the essence, or very clear indications that the time-limits are mandatory not merely indicative, considered to be mere machinery. They can thus be served later than the time prescribed for their service by the landlord, who can then still invoke a rent review. Questions may arise as to whether, in a falling market, the landlord can be required to initiate a rent review if he does not want to do so. It appears that the issue is resolved by allowing the tenant to serve a notice on the landlord requesting a rent review within a reasonable time, failing which the review cannot take place on that

---

131 *South Tottenham Land Securities Ltd v R & A Millett (Shops) Ltd* [1984] 1 All ER 614, [1984] 1 WLR 710.

132 *Glofield Properties Ltd v Morley (No 2)* [1989] 2 EGLR 118, CA.

133 Where a notice states that it is 'subject to contract' or 'without prejudice' and still purports to trigger a rent review it is a question of construction whether it is effective to do so. The test is as to how a reasonable recipient would construe it (*Shirlcar Properties Ltd v Heinitz* [1983] 2 EGLR 120, CA; also *Royal Life Insurance Ltd v Phillips* [1990] 2 EGLR 135). This point might affect the issue of whether a second and unambiguous trigger notice can be served: see *Norwich Union Life Assurance Society v Sketchley plc* [1986] 2 EGLR 126.

134 Eg by incorporating LPA 1925, s 196, as in *Stephenson & Son v Orca Properties Ltd* [1989] 2 EGLR 129. If such a provision were made in an assured tenancy rent review, it might conceivably offend against the 1999 consumer regulations (ch 4 above) as restricting the method of reply open to the tenant.

occasion.[135] This approach is by analogy, no doubt, with vendor and purchaser notices, seeing that time is presumed not to be of the essence in sale of land completions unless one of the parties by notice makes it so. In New Zealand, however, the issue depends on the wording of the rent review clause, as perhaps it would in England if the issue were to arise again. Where a clause stated that at any time not earlier than four months prior to the review date the landlord had to notify the tenant of its assessment of the current market rent, and failed to do so within 12 months of that date, time being of the essence, the landlord was held unable to require a review outside these periods of time.[136] By contrast where a clause stated that the landlord might give notice requiring a rent review, the word 'may' could only be read in a permissive sense and the landlord was not obliged to act.[137]

The landlord may be entitled to state by notice a rent which is proposed as the reviewed rent. In addition, the rent review clause may specify that unless the tenant replies with a counter-notice suggesting a new rent, the landlord's suggested rent will take effect and the tenant will be deemed to have agreed to pay this new rent. These clauses have caused difficulties, as typically happened in one case where a landlord suggested a new rent of £84,800 per annum and the tenant failed to serve a counter-notice contesting this rent within the 28 days allowed by the lease to do so. The Court of Appeal held that the deeming provision took full effect. As the tenant had failed to challenge the proposed new rent on time, the rent in the landlord's notice was the new rent payable.[138] This 'deeming provision' is harsh in its operation. It was noted by Arden LJ in this case that should such a term appear in a residential lease, and it turns out that the rent review clause was not individually negotiated, it could fall foul of the 1999 consumer regulations (as to which see ch 4, above).

Sometimes, the lease makes no mention of trigger notices and counter-notices and instead provides for an 'automatic' review machinery, as where the rent review clause states that the new rent is to be that agreed between the parties or as determined by an arbitrator at any time before the review date.[139]

Returning to clauses which provide for a notice mechanism to initiate the rent review process, the lease may envisage that once the landlord has served a trigger notice, there will follow a notice from the landlord or tenant to the other party which requests that an arbitrator or independent expert must ascertain the rent, where the parties have

---

135 *United Scientific Holdings v Burnley Borough Council* [1978] AC 904, [1977] 2 All ER 62, HL. See also *Barclays Bank plc v Savile Estates Ltd* [2002] EWCA Civ 589, [2002] 24 EG 152.
136 *Australasian Mutual Provident Society v Bridgemans Art Deco Ltd* [1996] 2 NZLR 263.
137 *Australasian Mutual Provident Society v National Mutual Life Association of Australasia Ltd* [1995] 1 NZLR 581.
138 *Starmark Enterprises Ltd v CPL Distribution Ltd* [2001] EWCA 1252, [2002] 2 WLR 1009. The Court of Appeal followed its own previous decision in *Henry Smith's Charity Trustees v AWADA Trading and Promotion Services* (1984) 47 P & CR 607. It held that its own later decision in *Mecca Leisure Ltd v Renown Investments (Holdings) Ltd* (1984) 49 P & CR 12, reaching the contrary result, was incorrect.
139 Law Society/RICS Model Clause Precedent 1.

failed within a specified time to agree as to the new rent. Thus an arbitration notice may envisage a request to the President of the RICS to appoint a valuer to act as an arbitrator. The appointment will no doubt be in accordance with the Guidance Notes published by the RICS.[140]

Rent review clauses often state in general terms the basis on which the premises are to be valued in order to ascertain the new rent. If it is intended to assume that the premises to be valued are not the same as the actual premises, this should be stated clearly, or the court will assume that the premises are the same at rent review as when the premises were let.[141] One general basis of valuation is the rent payable in the open market for the premises as between a willing landlord and a willing tenant, with an assumption of vacant possession. The presumption of reality requires that if any artificial assumption is to be made by the valuer about the period of the lease after the rent review date, or as to the hypothetical lease, such as to the length of the lease, vacant possession, compliance with tenant covenants or otherwise, or as to the permitted use of the premises, as well as whether there will be future rent reviews, these must be clearly stated in the rent review clause. Otherwise, applying the overriding objective of a rent review clause (which it will be remembered is to enable the landlord to obtain periodic revision of the rent to the level the premises would command if let on the open market) the terms of the hypothetical lease will be assumed to be the same as the actual lease granted to the tenant.[142]

Rent review machinery: time limits

(i)   General rule

The House of Lords ruled in the early days of rent review disputes that it was presumed that where a landlord was required to serve a trigger notice on the tenant, time was not of the essence. The trigger notice was mere machinery. The bargain between the parties was that the tenant accepted a rent review in return for the grant of a longer lease than would have been granted without rent review provisions.[143] Hence the landlord was entitled to request a rent review two months after the passing of the rent review date even though the lease envisaged that the landlord must serve a trigger notice before that date. Indeed, the fact that a landlord has delayed the service of a trigger notice for a significant period, such as three years,[144] will not of itself prevent

---

140 Minor deviations from these will not invalidate a genuine application: *Staines Warehousing Co Ltd v Montagu Executor and Trustee Co Ltd* [1987] 2 EGLR 130, CA.

141 *St Martins Property Investments Ltd v CIB Properties Ltd* [1999] L & TR 1, CA.

142 *Basingstoke and Deane Borough Council v Host Group Ltd* [1988] 1 All ER 824, CA; also *Westside Nominees v Bolton MBC* (2000) 81 P & CR 130, [2000] L & TR 533.

143 *United Scientific Holdings Ltd v Burnley Borough Council* [1978] AC 904, [1977] 2 All ER 62. For a critique see Goldberg and Smith (1992) 12 LS 349.

144 *Million Pigs v Parry (No 2)* (1983) 46 P & CR 333; also *H West & Son v Brech* [1982] 1 EGLR 113 (18 months); *Printing House Properties Ltd v JW Winston & Co Ltd* [1982] 2 EGLR 118 (23 months).

his initiating a rent review once time is not of the essence. However, the presumption that time is not of the essence in rent review procedures is strong and, if the lease does not expressly state that time is of the essence, the presumption will be disapplied only in the face of strong or compelling counter-indications in the lease.[145] The landlord cannot exercise a right to review when time is not of the essence if he has ignored a tenant's notice requiring a review within a reasonable time, or where he is estopped from exercising the right to review[146] or from seeking an arbitration.

Time is presumed to be of the essence, seemingly as a matter of law, however, in at least two situations. (1) The review notice is to be served no later than the last date on which the tenant can exercise a right to terminate the lease by notice. (2) Where the landlord triggers a rent review by notice, and there follows a period in which the tenant may decide whether or not to serve a notice ending the lease. Time is presumed to be of the essence in relation to triggering a review[147] owing to the fact that one factor in the tenant's decision to exercise a right to terminate the lease will be the level of the new rent.[148] On the other hand, a statement that an expert's valuation had to be given not less than 14 days prior to the relevant review date was not a compelling indication sufficient to displace the presumption that time is not of the essence in relation to rent review procedures.[149]

(ii)   Time of the essence

If time is to be of the essence in relation both to trigger notices, counter-notices and indeed in relation to arbitration notices, this requirement must be clearly specified in the lease in relation to each type of notice, otherwise the presumption that time is not of the essence will prevail in relation to the notice in issue.[150] This is because of the principle that rent review notices are considered as machinery. Indeed, even if time is stated to be of the essence with regard to one rent review period, it is not to be assumed that it will be of the essence with regard to any future rent review.[151] If the

---

145 *Phibbs-Faire v Malbern Construction Ltd* [1987] 1 EGLR 129. This case was doubted by the High Court in *Banks v Kokkinos* [1999] 3 EGLR 133; but see now *Iceland Foods plc v Dangoor* [2002] EWHC 107, [2002] 08 EG 161 (CS).

146 See *Esso Petroleum Co Ltd v Anthony Gibbs Financial Services Ltd* [1983] 2 EGLR 112, CA.

147 As opposed to asking for an arbitration, since by definition the time to be taken by the arbitrator is not within the control of the parties, the decision being after the review date: see *Metrolands Investments Ltd v JH Dewhurst Ltd* [1986] 3 All ER 659, CA.

148 *Central Estates Ltd v Secretary of State for the Environment* [1997] 1 EGLR 239, CA. If the tenant allows the rent review date to go by without exercising a contemporaneous right to break the lease, then in principle the landlord can invoke the right to a rent review: *Edwin Woodhouse Trustee Co Ltd v Sheffield Brick Co* [1984] 1 EGLR 130.

149 *McDonald's Property Co Ltd v HSBC Bank plc* [2001] 3 EGLR 19.

150 *Amherst v James Walker (Goldsmith and Silversmith) Ltd* [1983] Ch 305, [1983] 2 All ER 1067, CA. For a recent example, see *First Property Growth Partnership LP v Royal & Sun Alliance Services Ltd* [2002] EWHC 305.

151 *King's (Estate Agents) Ltd v Anderson* [1992] 1 EGLR 121.

parties do not state in so many words that time is deemed to be of the essence with regard to a given step, it was held to suffice to make time of the essence to state that the landlord could require arbitration by notice within three months from a trigger notice 'but not otherwise',[152] as where it was stated that if the landlord failed to apply for the appointment of an arbitrator, within a specified period, if the parties could not agree on the new rent, his trigger notice would be void.[153]

Basis of valuation

As seen, the principal object of a rent review clause is assumed to be that of giving the landlord the benefit of an open market rent for the premises let, so as to enable the rent to keep up with inflation. The courts decline to make artificial assumptions about the hypothetical lease (ie the lease period after the review date) unless these are expressly and clearly required by the terms of the clause at issue. All rent review provisions operate, it has been said, in a real world and not in one of fantasy: whether the valuation is to be of real or notional premises, the parties are assumed not to have agreed to a valuation which could not reasonably apply to the actual premises.[154]

Indeed, the principle of reality assumes that the parties intended that the notional letting postulated by the rent review clause is to be on the same terms as the actual lease, other than as to the amount of rent.[155] The letting is notional for valuation purposes because the valuation is ordinarily on the basis that there is no sitting tenant and that there are a number of potential bidders for a lease of the premises.[156] Thus it will be presumed, subject, as always, to any clear express terms of the lease, that there will be future rent reviews where relevant, and that the use permitted of the premises will be the same after the rent review as it was beforehand. It will also be assumed, unless the contrary is clearly required by a given rent review clause,[157] that the tenant will occupy the same premises after review as before, and that their state and condition will also be the same before and after review.[158] The valuer is assumed to be valuing the

---

152 *Drebbond Ltd v Horsham District Council* (1978) 37 P & CR 237.
153 *Lewis v Barnett* [1982] 2 EGLR 127; also *Darlington Borough Council v Waring & Gillow (Holdings) Ltd* [1988] 2 EGLR 159.
154 *Dukeminster (Ebbgate House One) v Somerfield Properties Ltd* [1997] 2 EGLR 125, CA (so that it was impermissible to take into account rents for any warehouse unit within a 35-mile radius of the subject premises, where such rents varied greatly: an implied requirement was imposed that the comparable premises rents must be of similar warehouses to the subject property).
155 *Basingstoke and Deane Borough Council v Host Group Ltd* [1988] 1 All ER 824 at 829, CA.
156 See *FR Evans (Leeds) Ltd v English Electric Co* (1977) 36 P & CR 185, where the actual tenant would have made no offer for a lease, as it would have preferred to leave.
157 As was the case in *Standard Life Assurance Co v Oxoid* [1987] 2 EGLR 140.
158 *Ravenseft Properties Ltd v Park* [1988] 2 EGLR 164; *Iceland Frozen Foods plc v Starlight Investments Ltd* [1992] 1 EGLR 126, CA.

whole premises.[159] If it is intended that the valuation is to be of the land, without any buildings which may have been erected by the tenant, this requirement must be clearly stated,[160] otherwise the value of the land plus the buildings will be taken into account.[161]

Open market rent

The dominant concept of most rent review clauses is that of an uplift of the current rent to the rent payable for the demised premises on the open market at the rent review date. Some formulae have required the ascertainment of, in terms, or by using equivalent expressions,[162] an open market rent for the premises as between a willing landlord and a willing tenant, with any assumptions to be made being stated. Other formulae have made use of the expression 'a reasonable rent for the demised premises'. Both these formulae refer to the demised premises and so require an objective assessment of the rent, without regard to the current tenant's ability to pay the new rent. The willing landlord and willing tenant formula, for example, is designed to produce an artificial situation in which the actual tenant's occupation is ignored, because it is assumed that vacant possession will exist at the review date. The tenant is assumed to be one of a number of (notional) bidders for a hypothetical lease as from the review date.[163] Specific circumstances affecting either the actual landlord or actual tenant are left out of account.[164] The valuer must reach a view as to the strength of the actual market for renting the premises at issue. Thus, where in fact a tenant had no access to a staircase, this fact was properly taken into account, even though the lease assumed that such access was available to tenants.[165] So strong is the requirement of a market valuation

159 For an example of contrary language see *Westside Nominees Ltd v Bolton MBC* (2000) 81 P & CR 130, a rent review clause in a long lease requiring an open market rent to be ascertained for the premises 'whether in whole or in parts' was held to require a rent to be ascertained for lettings on a re-organised basis of the premises in parts: two ground-floor retail units and five office units.

160 As in eg *Braid v Walsall MBC* [2000] L & TR 533, CA (where the lease was held clearly to differentiate between the 'demised premises' and the 'land', requiring the new rent to be based on the land as undeveloped). *Goh v Yap* [1988] 2 EGLR 148 was distinguished on the ground that there was a building on the land when the lease was granted (not the case in *Braid*) so that the rent had to be fixed by reference to the land and buildings.

161 See *Ipswich Town Football Club v Ipswich Borough Council* [1988] 2 EGLR 146; also *Braid v Walsall Metropolitan Borough Council* [2000] L & TR 533, CA.

162 Such as 'the full market rent': this was taken to impliedly import a reference to a willing landlord and a willing tenant: *Dennis & Robinson Ltd v Kiossos Establishment* [1987] 1 EGLR 133, CA.

163 The lease can expressly exclude the actual tenant from being a notional bidder: see *First Leisure Trading Ltd v Dorita Properties Ltd* [1991] 1 EGLR 133.

164 *FR Evans (Leeds) Ltd v English Electric Co* (1977) 36 P & CR 185. It could be argued that as a result the actual tenant's trading accounts should therefore be irrelevant, but apparently whether these are taken into account or not is a question of construction, as with premises with a specialist use such as a casino: see *Cornwall Coast Country Club v Cardgrange Ltd* [1987] 1 EGLR 146; *Ritz Hotel (London) Ltd v Ritz Casino Ltd* [1989] 2 EGLR 135.

165 *Jeffries v O'Neill* (1983) 46 P & CR 376.

which an open market formula in objective terms imposes on a valuer, that the courts have held that a personal user clause had to be remodelled for rent review purposes, since it had to be assumed that not only the actual tenant was a bidder to rent the premises, but that a number of persons would wish to do so (despite the fact that no-one other than the actual tenant could use the premises as they were in fact used).[166] On the other hand, if the formula refers to a reasonable rent as between the parties,[167] the reviewed rent may be treated as the rent the current tenant ought reasonably to pay, taking into account the tenant's circumstances.[168]

Assumptions and disregards

Despite the presumption of reality, many rent review clauses direct that specific assumptions or disregards should be made, and that the terms of the hypothetical lease will therefore be different to those of the actual lease. Even where the express terms of a lease require the presumption of reality to be departed from, the courts are reluctant to complicate matters unduly for valuers. Thus in one case,[169] the Court of Appeal refused to heap hypothesis on hypothesis, and dismissed a landlord's argument that the condition of notionally vacant premises for review purposes would have been improved by certain works which the landlord would, notionally, not actually, have carried out so as to improve their letting value.

Rent review clauses may thus state that it is assumed that the demised premises are available for letting with vacant possession; that the premises are fit for immediate occupation and use; the length of the lease is the unexpired portion of the lease. The terms of the lease after review may be assumed to be the same as those immediately preceding it, although rent review provisions will be assumed to exist in future (so as to prevent undue and once-and-for-all uplifts in the rent on the rent review in issue). The clause may state that the user of the premises after review is to be the same as it was beforehand and that it is assumed that the tenant has complied with leasehold obligations such as to repair. If the tenant had a rent-free period before the lease began (which is sometimes offered to lessees as an inducement to take a lease) the reviewed rent will not be reduced because of this.[170]

---

166 *Law Land Co Ltd v Consumers' Association Ltd* [1980] 2 EGLR 109, CA; also *James v British Crafts Centre* [1987] 1 EGLR 139, CA; *Orchid Lodge UK Ltd v Extel Computing Ltd* [1991] 2 EGLR 116, CA.

167 Where, however, an objective formula was provided for (under which a 'geared rent' related to the rent payable from a sub-lessee was to be ascertained) it was held that there was no room to imply a subjective formula such as payment after review of a fair rent to the tenant: *Coventry Motor Mart Ltd v Corner Coventry Ltd* [1997] EGCS 45.

168 *Thomas Bates & Son v Wyndham's (Lingerie) Ltd* [1981] 1 All ER 1077, CA.

169 *Iceland Frozen Foods plc v Starlight Investment Ltd* [1992] 1 EGLR 126, CA. To have acceded to the landlord's argument would have been to abandon or weaken the overriding principle already noted, and would have conferred windfall benefits on the landlord.

170 Indeed, it appears that in any event if a rent is produced for similar or 'comparable' premises to that let, and that rent reflects the fact that a rent-free period has been conceded to the

The express assumptions thus stated seem to reflect the approach of the courts even where these are not required to be expressly stated in the lease. Thus, even if there is no express provision as to fitness for occupation of the premises, it appears that valuers must assume that the premises are free from defects and ready for lessee use for the purposes of the business of the lessee, as well as being in a good state of repair and condition.[171] However, if the premises are in a poor state of repair or unsuitable condition for occupation, the tenant will have to pay an artificially inflated rent at rent review thanks to such assumptions. The courts have extended the principle of reality to future rent review clauses: even if there is no express statement that these are to be assumed, the presumption is that any future rent review provisions in the actual lease must be taken into account when assessing a reviewed rent,[172] so as to prevent the landlord gaining a windfall from a completely artificial assumption. This presumption would yield to clear contrary language.

The same process of reality applies to user of the premises and also with regard to the length of the term to be assumed after review. Thus unless there is express and clear contrary language, it is assumed that the user of the premises as permitted by the lease will be the same before and after the rent review.[173] This prevents an artificial reduction in the rent in case the tenant has a range of uses for the premises but only uses them for one purpose. Equally, to prevent an artificial inflation in rent levels, the courts refuse to assume that the current user restrictions of a lease will be relaxed unilaterally by the landlord: it is assumed that they will continue after review.[174] Regarding the length of the term to be assumed after rent review, in principle, once more recognising and applying reality rather than conjecture, the courts presume that the tenant will be entitled to a 'hypothetical lease' for the same remaining length as under the existing lease, as opposed to assuming, for example, that the 'hypothetical lease' is to run for the same period as the original term agreed for the lease.[175] This is because the court pays regard to the actually existing circumstances. The tenant has not in fact got a lease for the whole originally granted period once a rent review date arrives. Hence,

---

tenant in question, this rent cannot properly be used as a comparable with the rent review at issue, to inflate the new rent to the landlord's advantage: *Co-operative Wholesale Society Ltd v National Westminster Bank plc* [1995] 1 EGLR 97, CA.

171 *Pontsarn Investments Ltd v Kansallis-Osake-Pannki* [1992] 1 EGLR 148; *London and Leeds Estates Ltd v Paribas Ltd* [1993] 2 EGLR 149, CA.

172 *Arnold v National Westminster Bank plc* [1990] 1 All ER 529, CA; affd [1991] 3 All ER 41, HL.

173 *Basingstoke and Deane Borough Council v Host Group Ltd* [1988] 1 All ER 824, CA. If a lawful user alone is to be assumed, however, an express statement to this effect is required in the lease: see eg *Daejan Investments Ltd v Cornwall Coast Country Club* [1985] 1 EGLR 77; also *Tea Trade Properties Ltd v CIN Properties Ltd* [1990] 1 EGLR 155. This is presumably because the courts do not wish to read into clauses any more words than are necessary to make them work.

174 *Plinth Property Investments Ltd v Mott Hay and Anderson* (1978) 38 P & CR 361, CA; also *James v British Crafts Centre* [1987] 1 EGLR 139, CA; *SI Pension Trustees Ltd v Ministerio de la Marina de la Republica Peruana* [1988] 1 EGLR 119.

175 *St Martins Property Investments Ltd v CIB Properties Ltd* [1999] L & TR 1, CA; also eg *Lynnthorpe Enterprises Ltd v Sidney Smith (Chelsea) Ltd* [1990] 2 EGLR 131, CA.

where an ambiguous formula was used to describe the length of the lease assumed for valuation purposes, the court held that the rent review was to be on the basis of the residue of the actual term, invoking the principle that the purpose of a rent review clause was not to give a windfall to the landlord but to protect the rent level against inflationary pressures.[176] Clear language will displace this presumption.[177] Where the tenant is entitled to renew his tenancy under statute, a clear indication in the rent review clause that the common law term of the lease is alone to be taken into account for rent review purposes will be enforced,[178] otherwise the possibility of a statutory renewal may be taken into account.[179]

The tenant may, prior to the rent review date in question, have carried out improvements to the demised premises which increase their letting value. If an objective valuation of the premises is required, as with a requirement to ascertain a 'reasonable rent for the demised premises' then the effect of the tenant's improvements is to be taken into account in principle. The improvements become part of the premises.[180] As seen, an objective formula for ascertaining rent at review takes no account of subjective factors, even though the end result of this ruling is that the tenant paid twice for the improvement. There is a narrow escape exit from this principle. If the rent is to be reviewed on the basis of that agreed between the parties, without referring to the demised premises, then a subjective test applies. If the tenant wholly paid for or contributed to the improvements (as where these were carried out by a predecessor of the tenant's) the court will then disregard the effect of the work on the value of the premises.[181]

Not surprisingly, in view of the harsh effects of the common law rule, it sometimes abrogated or modified in leases. Thus a rent review clause may state that any increase in the rental value of the demised premises due to any improvement carried out by the tenant[182] or any sub-tenant before the review date and during the lease term, will be disregarded.[183] Disregard clauses do not always extend to cover work that the tenant

176 *St Martins Property Investments Ltd v CIB Properties Ltd* [1999] L & TR 1, CA (the formula was 'for a term equal in duration to the term hereby granted', which could have meant 35 years from the review date, or the whole original term of the lease).
177 *British Gas plc v Dollar Land Holdings plc* [1992] 1 EGLR 135.
178 *Toyota (GB) Ltd v Legal and General Assurance (Pensions Management) Ltd* [1989] 2 EGLR 123, CA.
179 *Pivot Properties Ltd v Secretary of State for the Environment* (1980) 41 P & CR 248, CA.
180 *Ponsford v HMS Aerosols Ltd* [1979] AC 63, [1978] 2 All ER 837, HL.
181 *Lear v Blizzard* [1983] 3 All ER 662 (an option clause case, but followed in *Jefferies v RC Dimock Ltd* [1987] 1 NZLR 419); *Dickinson v Enfield London Borough Council* [1996] 2 EGLR 88 at 91, CA.
182 According to *Durley House Ltd v Cadogan* [2000] 1 WLR 246, a case on the Landlord and Tenant Act 1954, s 34(2), 'carried out' requires no more than the tenant commissioning the works from a contractor. If a third party such as a manager commissions the work, the tenant must show some involvement in identifying or supervising the work.
183 Some clauses have stated that improvements within the terms of Landlord and Tenant Act 1954, s 34 are to be left out of account at rent review. The drawback here is that it may not be clear whether the original or the amended version of Landlord and Tenant Act 1954, s 34 is referred to: see *Brett v Brett Essex Golf Club Ltd* (1986) 52 P & CR 330, CA.

is obliged under covenant to execute.[184] However, where improvement work has been carried out prior to the grant of the lease, the question of whether the improvements in the pre-lease period are to be taken into account or disregarded at rent review is one of construction of the lease. This may cause uncertainty if the lessee takes possession shortly prior to a lease in order, for example, to fit out a shop unit.[185] Thus where a disregard clause spoke of improvements carried out during the term of the lease, it did not extend to works done under a licence preceding the lease.[186] There is little guidance from the courts as to the way a valuer is to operate a disregard clause of the type under consideration. The valuer may properly compare the state of the premises as they are at the date of review with some comparable but unimproved premises (although it is then hard to see how the premises can be said to be comparable). If there are no comparables, then the valuer is free to adopt any appropriate valuation method making due allowance for the effects of inflation and the passage of time.[187]

There is naturally a wide range of other matters which may, applying the principle of reality, be taken into account or disregarded in the absence of clear language in the lease. For instance, where an open market rent is to be ascertained, any effect of a tenant's breach of covenant to repair is to be left out of account.[188] Likewise, the existence of a discounted right to buy (in the case of a council tenancy) was ignored where a subjective rent review formula was used.[189] It was held inappropriate to take into account the fact that the lessee was under an obligation to reinstate the premises at the end of the lease.[190] Such an assumption would cause an artificial reduction in the reviewed rent. If the tenant installs tenant's fixtures, which are therefore removable at the end of the lease, reality requires any increase in value which comes about during the lease from such installation to be left out of account.[191]

184 See *Godbold v Martin the Newsagents Ltd* [1983] 2 EGLR 128; also *Forte & Co Ltd v General Accident Life Assurance Ltd* [1986] 2 EGLR 115 (work under a statutory obligation taken into account at review).

185 See *Panther Shop Investments Ltd v Keith Pople Ltd* [1987] 1 EGLR 131; *Hambros Bank Executor & Trustee Co Ltd v Superdrug Stores Ltd* [1985] 1 EGLR 99.

186 *Euston Centre Properties Ltd v H and J Wilson Ltd* [1982] 1 EGLR 57; it was held otherwise where a licence to improve was granted during the term of a lease: *Historic House Hotels Ltd v Cadogan Estates* [1995] 1 EGLR 117, CA.

187 *GREA Real Property Investments Ltd v Williams* [1979] 1 EGLR 121; *Estates Projects Ltd v Greenwich London Borough Council* [1979] 2 EGLR 85. The capital revaluation method was criticised in these cases, however.

188 *Harmsworth Pension Fund Trustees Ltd v Charringtons Industrial Holdings Ltd* [1985] 1 EGLR 97. But where a lessee was under an onerous repairing and rebuilding obligation, a downwards adjustment of some 27.5% in the reviewed rent was held justified: *Norwich Union Insurance Society v British Railways Board* [1987] 2 EGLR 137.

189 *Dickinson v Enfield London Borough Council* [1996] 2 EGLR 88, CA. Had an objective formula been made use of, it could be argued that the result might have been different, since a hypothetical new tenant might well be prepared to pay a premium rent for the prospect of keeping the valuable right to buy, which was introduced by Parliament with the express object of allowing sitting council tenants to buy their homes on advantageous terms.

190 *Pleasurama Properties Ltd v Leisure Investments (West End) Ltd* [1986] 1 EGLR 145, CA.

191 *Young v Dalgety plc* [1987] 1 EGLR 116, CA; *Ocean Accident & Guarantee Corpn v Next plc* [1995] EGCS 187.

Dispute resolution

The parties may be unable to agree as to the amount of the rent payable by the tenant as from the rent review date. In that case it is usual to find the rent review clause either requiring the rent to be ascertained by a valuer acting as an arbitrator, or as an independent expert. While the relevant law and procedure governing arbitrations and valuations lies outside the scope of this book, a brief note of these two methods of dispute resolution is included.

(i) Arbitrations

The lease may provide that if the parties cannot agree on a reviewed rent, the matter is to be referred to a valuer, by one or other party.[192] The valuer is then to act as an arbitrator. In such cases the Arbitration Act 1996 applies. Arbitrators act in a quasi-judicial capacity. It may well be that they are a 'public body' for the purposes of HRA 1998. Unlike a judge, an arbitrator is usually appointed for one single rent review dispute on an ad hoc basis, although selected no doubt from a panel of arbitrators by the President of the RICS. However that may be, arbitrators are bound by the rules of evidence and must act with fairness to both parties (so an arbitrator was not allowed to use a method of valuation not put in evidence).[193] If indeed any matter is likely to form part of the arbitrator's decision,[194] fairness requires that that matter be exposed to the submissions of both sides to the dispute.[195] On the other hand, an arbitrator is assumed to have professional expertise, so he is not bound slavishly to follow the precise calculations relating to comparable rents which both the parties[196] have put to him.[197] If the rent review clause permits this, or presumably also if both parties are advised of his wish to do so and they both consent, an arbitrator is entitled to receive

---

192 The High Court of Australia ruled in *Gollin & Co v Karemlee Nominees Pty Ltd* (1983) 153 CLR 455 that each party was under an implied obligation to give efficacy to the rent review by appointing a valuer as envisaged by the lease within a reasonable time when required to do so by the other party; hence appointments of valuers made without the knowledge of the other party were held void.

193 *Unit Four Cinemas v Tosara Investment Ltd* [1993] 2 EGLR 11. Nor may a valuation method not contemplated in the lease be made use of: see *Pupike Service Station Ltd v Caltex Oil (NZ) Ltd* [1995] ECGS 180, JCPC.

194 Such as his opinion of the rental value of the premises, according to Curtis (1999) L & T Rev 36.

195 See *Ravenseft Properties Ltd v Boots Properties Ltd* [1997] CLY 3326. It is not objectionable for an arbitrator to rely on his own expertise: ibid.

196 It is not proper for an arbitrator to rely on a point not raised by a party or to adopt an approach not explored by the parties in their submissions: *Ravenseft Properties Ltd v Boots Properties Ltd* [1997] CLY 3326. This differentiates the position of an arbitrator from that of an independent expert, who has much more leeway to make up his own mind.

197 *Lex Services plc v Orid House BV* [1991] 2 EGLR 126.

and consider rents agreed after the review date, the weight of such comparables being for the arbitrator.[198]

The High Court has powers to review the decisions of an arbitrator on a point of law. It has wide powers to confirm, set aside or vary the award, or to remit it for reconsideration to the arbitrator having regard to the court's opinion as to the point of law (Arbitration Act 1996, s 69). The leave of the court is required to appeal on a point of law, unless both parties consent. However, the leave gateways are deliberately narrow. Leave may be given if the court considers the determination of the point of law could substantially affect the rights of one or more of the parties (Arbitration Act 1996, s 69(3)). Leave will also only be granted if the court decides that the decision of the arbitrator is obviously incorrect, or is of general public importance and the decision is open to serious doubt. Either party to a rent review arbitration may also ask the court to interfere with an arbitrator's decision if there has been a serious irregularity affecting the arbitration, the proceedings or the award (Arbitration Act 1996, s 68). An example of misconduct under the pre-1996 Act regime, but which would seem to apply to post-Act cases, was a failure by the arbitrator to follow a procedure which he had laid down and informed the parties about.[199] The High Court has power to remove an arbitrator (Arbitration Act 1996, s 24) and made use of this power where it concluded that the association between an arbitrator and an associated company of the tenant (which had been instructing a partner of the arbitrator) was such as to amount to a real danger of bias, real danger meaning more than a minimal risk but less than a probability.[200]

The policy of the Arbitration Act 1996 is evidently to discourage appeals on trifling matters and to promote finality in arbitration decisions. To that end, the courts have interpreted the power under the Arbitration Act 1996, s 12 to extend time-limits for the service of notices in a narrow way. It appears that only if the failure to comply with a time-limit is outside the reasonable contemplation of the parties, or, in other words, is owing to something wholly exceptional and unforeseeable, will the court entertain an application to extend time-limits. Additionally, the Arbitration Act 1996 requires the court to be satisfied that it would be just to extend the time-limit or that the conduct of one party makes it unjust not to extend the time-limit. To show the strictness of the new regime, a tenant failed to serve a counter-notice contesting a landlord's rent notice within the time allowed, no time extension was granted. The tenant failed to respond in a timely fashion because of a mistake, but this was not enough to invoke the discretion of the court. The tenant would have to pay the rent stated in the landlords'

---

198 *Segama NV v Penny Le Roy Ltd* [1984] 1 EGLR 109. But it would be improper for an arbitrator to make use of evidence acquired by him in different proceedings to form his own judgment (*Top Shop Centres Ltd v Danino* [1985] 1 EGLR 9) unless, at any rate, the material was made available to both parties for their comments.

199 *Oakstead Garages Ltd v Leach Pension Scheme (Trustees) Ltd* [1996] 1 EGLR 26 (the arbitrator failed to inspect the premises, as he indicated that he would). Not obviously wrong was an allegedly ambiguous statement in past-award correspondence: *Checkpoint Ltd v Strathclyde Pension Fund* [2002] 13 EG 101 (CS).

200 *Save and Prosper Pensions Ltd v Homebase Ltd* [2001] L & TR 11, [2001] L & TR 107.

notice as a result.[201] In a subsequent case, it was said that the Arbitration Act 1996, s 12 contemplated that where parties agreed on a time-limit, they must have contemplated the consequences where there was an omission to comply with its provisions. Hence, in the absence of exceptional circumstances the claim to exercise a right out of time would fail and the court would not extend the time under the Act.[202] Thus where a rent review clause clearly or by necessary implication makes time of the essence in relation to a particular matter, it is not likely that the courts will allow the Arbitration Act 1996, s 12 to be used as a means of circumventing such agreements.

(ii) Independent expert

The rent review clause may state that if the parties cannot agree on a new rent, it is to be arrived at by a valuer or surveyor acting as an independent expert. The Arbitration Act 1996 does not apply. The main advantage of appointing an independent expert as opposed to an arbitrator is that this method of dispute resolution makes for cheapness, informality of procedure, and also finality, although it is now much more difficult to challenge decisions of an arbitrator than was formally the case. Where the landlord was entitled to apply for an independent expert, and deliberately abstained from doing so, fearing a lower rent, it was held that he could be compelled to do so, failing which there would be an inquiry as to the proper level of rent.[203] The terms on which the independent expert accepts his task may be agreed by the parties; the expert must then answer the questions to be decided on the basis of any contractual assumptions agreed by the parties and not go outside this remit, or the determination will be set aside.[204] The court is not usurping the decision-making power confided to the expert: it is simply holding the expert within the limits of what the parties who appointed him agreed upon. If these limits are not clear, then one or other of the parties can ask the court to determine them ahead of the determination by the expert.

Challenges on the merits of a decision of an independent expert which dissatisfy one of the parties are difficult to mount and do not often appear to have been crowned with success. This is owing to the fact that the court applies the standard of professional negligence. The question is whether the expert has arrived at a valuation figure which was one which a reasonably competent respected member of his profession might

---

201 *Fox & Widley v Guram* [1998] 1 EGLR 91.
202 *Harbour & General Works Ltd v Environmental Agency* [2000] L & TR 97 at 98-99; see Cheffings and Levy *Estates Gazette* 9 October 1999, p 187.
203 *Royal Bank of Scotland plc v Jennings* [1997] 1 EGLR 101, CA.
204 See *National Grid Co plc v M25 Group Ltd* [1999] L & TR 206, CA. In this case, the rent review clause directed the expert valuer to have regard to certain agreed contractual directions and disregards such as disregarding the occupation of the lessee, goodwill attached to the premises and certain improvements.

reasonably subscribe to. The test is not whether the figure would be arrived at by all similar experts or whether the complaining party disagrees with it.[205]

Comparison with rent indexation

(i) *Problems with contractual rent review*

Rent review under the contractual method has a number of advantages. It allows the parties to a commercial lease to decide freely on the method and details of rent revision suitable, at least in theory, for the specific premises at issue. It should guarantee institutional landlords, such as pension funds, a flow of inflation-protected income from commercial leases. Since most, if not almost all, rent review is upwards only, there is a floor sum below which the rent cannot fall. On the other hand, upwards-only rent review clauses have disadvantages. The presence of an upwards-only rent review clause might deter potential tenants from taking a lease in, say, shopping centres in times of recession,[206] unless offered inducements such as rent-free periods which then may cause complications at rent review. Upwards-only rent review clauses may seem unfair to tenants, who are subject to a floor of the current rent even if the letting value of the premises at the review date is less than this sum. If there is no reason why a landlord letting on a longer term should have to put up with the ravages of inflation, it might be asked why tenants should be forced to pay artificially high rents.[207] Rent review clauses may be complex in their operation and have generated much litigation, much of it about narrow, case-specific, technicalities. They place a narrow emphasis on rents of comparable properties. Arbitration provisions may be expensive to operate and may even encourage disputes, such as those relating to arbitration notices, allegations of bias or unfairness and so on. Hence it is of interest briefly to examine an alternative system of rent revision: indexation of rents. This is a system under which, broadly, the rent at the date of revision is increased if inflation has caused an upwards movement in the chosen index figure during the period leading up to the rent review.

---

205 *Zubaida v Hargreaves* [1995] 1 EGLR 127, CA; also *Currys Group plc v Martin* [1999] EGCS 115. It was there noted that valuation was an 'art not a science'. The expert in this case was, eg entitled to have regard to the fact that the landlord paid large incentives to tenants to induce them to take leases, keeping rents high.

206 According to Willett [1997] L & T Rev 90, rents based on a mixture of a fixed sum and a percentage of the turnover of the tenant are in use in some shopping centres. A typical proportion might be 80% of the rent fixed and the balance based on turnover. See also Heighton *Estates Gazette* 2 March 2002.

207 Were it not for the fact that the consumer regulations of 1999 (ch, above 4) do not have any impact on the price or consideration payable for the premises let, and thus, presumably, on rent review provisions, the ratchet feature of upwards-only rent review would risk falling foul of the fairness tests in the case of residential leases.

(ii)   Indexation of rent

Before the flood of rent review litigation began, some 30 years ago, the High Court held valid a clause in a commercial lease under which there was to be an annual, automatic revision of the rent payable based on movements in the Retail Prices Index.[208] Such a clause did not fall foul of the principle that a rent had to be certain.[209] The High Court held that the principle required either certainty of amount, or the provision of a formula under which a certain rent could be ascertained. Indeed, in a later case,[210] the possibility of making use of alternative indices was envisaged, such as the cost of living index and the Retail Prices Index, comparing the highest variation, in the chosen revision period, of both indices. With its traditional freedom of contract approach, the courts both in England[211] and also in Queensland, Australia,[212] had little difficulty in allowing the parties to select any published index they saw fit to adopt.[213] Much greater difficulty has been experienced, however, if one of the parties wishes, in the absence of an express term allowing him to do this, to rely at revision on a different index, or on a revised version of the chosen index, claiming that the index selected has become 'dated' by the time revision comes around.[214] However, although the system of indexation as a means of rent revision has been tried in common law jurisdictions at various times, the system seems not to be widespread in England.[215]

(iii)   Note of position in France

At first sight, given the apparent simplicity of the indexation system, its relative desuetude in England is surprising. Rent indexation is seemingly more in vogue in France than here, and it has the advantages of being automatic, objective and also more frequent than rent review at five-yearly intervals. It does not necessarily produce such sharp 'jumps' in rent for tenants. This book is not the place to examine the details of the French system: a few key aspects only are highlighted.[216] We note the system as

208 *Blumenthal v Gallery Five Ltd* (1971) 220 Estates Gazette 31.
209 In contrast to the use of 'gold clauses' which was condemned by the Court of Appeal on the ground of public policy: *Treseder-Griffin v Co-operative Insurance Society Ltd* [1956] 2 QB 127 (although this rigid approach may no longer be law, see *Multiservice Bookbinding v Marden* [1979] Ch 94).
210 *Bisset v Marwin Securities Ltd* [1987] 1 EGLR 115.
211 See *Standard Life Assurance Co v Oxoid Ltd* [1987] 2 EGLR 140.
212 *Re Ipswich Road Property Pty's Lease* [1974] Qd R 215 (the chosen measure being the relevant indexation date for prices published at Brisbane).
213 According to *Thompson on Real Property* (1994) Vol 5, p 438, the two measures most used in the US for calculating indexed rents are the price indices for All Urban Consumers and the Consumer Prices Index for Wage Earners and Clerical Workers.
214 See *Tanner v Stocks and Realty (Premises) Pty Ltd* [1972] 2 NSWLR 722 (where the court refused to allow the landlord to depart from a chosen index merely on the ground that it had been numerically rebased).
215 See Clarke and Adams ch 20; Adams [1979] Conv 236.
216 See further PF Smith [2000] RRLRYB 286.

it applies to the initially fixed rent of a lease. Ordinarily, sliding scale rents come into effect as from the first anniversary of the grant of the lease, and then annually. The object of rent revision by use of an index, usually that published by the INSEE,[217] is recognised as being to enable the landlord to inflation-proof the rent,[218] much as would be the case in England. A key aspect of rent revision by indexation, which distinguishes it from contractual rent review, is that the French system is said to be automatic in operation: the rent for the premises is adjusted, potentially both up or down, in so as to reflect movements in the index when compared with the previous year's values. The landlord is entitled to a revised rent without any need to serve a notice on the tenant.[219] There are, however, some legislative safeguards against excessive movements in the rent, defined as one-quarter either up or down, when compared to the current passing rent.[220] Where the legislation is invoked, the court bases the new rent on the letting value or 'valeur locative' of the premises. However, perhaps inconsistently with a prophylactic view of this rule, landlords as well as tenants can invoke the legislation: it might even be to a landlord's advantage to base the revised rent on the letting value of the premises rather than the indexed increase.[221] A tenant could presumably ask for some moderation in the indexed rent if a key player tenant left a development.[222] To this extent, the French system allows an escape from the automatic system into a regime akin to those at common law based on property values, with this difference: it is the court and not the parties, or a landlord's notice, which fixes the new rent level.

(iv) Conclusion

Despite the apparent simplicity and objectivity of rent indexation, it is not likely that its use in France will encourage its widespread importation to England. A principal stumbling block seems to be that the index chosen may not be directly related to the premises, and an inflation index may reflect a range of measures, some of which have nothing to do with letting values of premises.[223] Difficulties may be encountered if a chosen index 'dates' or its weighting is altered, where the lease fails to allow for this possibility. English institutional landlords are familiar with the contract-based review of rent system and would presumably be reluctant to abandon it in favour of a system which might allow rent revision downwards as well as upwards.

217 Not allowed by a *loi* of 9 July 1970, which imposes a principle of direct relationship between an index and the lease, are, eg the SMIC index or any related wages index.
218 Lyon, 9 July 1990, D. 1991.47.
219 Civ 3e, 2 October 1985, Loy et Copr 1986 No 33.
220 Decree of 30 September 1953, Art 28. However, turnover rents or 'clauses-recettes' lie outside the scope of this provision: Paris, 17 March 2000, D.AJ 497. This principle is controversial (see Duruppé, note to this ruling).
221 See Civ 3e, 6 January 1993, Gaz Pal 1993.I. 19.
222 Versailles, 11 March 1988, Rev Loy 1989.90.
223 Such, at least, is said to explain the reluctance of Eire to adopt widespread rent indexation: see Wylie *Landlord and Tenant Law* (2nd edn) p 256.

CHAPTER 9

Repairing obligations

Most leases for any length impose express obligations to repair or for work extending beyond repairs on either the landlord or the tenant. There have been cases where the lease is silent as to the repairing obligations of either party, and, particularly in the case of short residential leases, Parliament has intervened. This chapter examines both implied and express repairing obligations, and also the range of remedies available to both parties.[1] The chapter also examines the question of reform.

I   LANDLORD'S IMPLIED OBLIGATIONS

The common law refuses to imply any repairing obligations against a landlord who is not under any express obligations. It adopts, in the words of Lord Hoffmann, a 'bleak laissez faire' approach.[2] The House of Lords accordingly refused to imply any obligation on a council landlord to pay for the installation of new and improved sound-proofing in mature flats let to their tenants. The original sound-proofing had been to the standard then required by Building Regulations and did not have to be 'upgraded'. The non-liability rule is, in the view of the House of Lords, a fundamental principle: it is certainly of long standing. Under it, a landlord is not under any implied obligation to put the demised premises into repair at the commencement of the lease,[3] and the landlord is not impliedly bound to pay for improvements to the premises. The landlord offers no implied warranty to the tenant that the premises are, or will be kept, fit for human habitation or suitable for any other purpose at the commencement of, or during the term.[4] There is no implied contractual duty on a landlord to keep in repair any premises he retains adjoining the demised premises even though, if his premises are in disrepair,

1   See further West and Smith's *Law of Dilapidations*.
2   In *Southwark London Borough Council v Mills* [2001] 1 AC 1 at 8, [1999] 4 All ER 449 at 453.
3   *Gott v Gandy* (1853) 2 E & B 845.
4   *Hart v Windsor* (1844) 12 M & W 68; *Sutton v Temple* (1843) 12 M & W 52.

this may well damage those of the lessee.[5] The Court of Appeal has recently refused to imply any term requiring a landlord, already under a statutory obligation to keep the structure and exterior of a dwelling house in repair, to put the premises into good condition, so curing condensation, damp and mould.[6] To imply such an obligation would be to imply a bargain not undertaken by the parties.[7]

The harsh traditional rule was based on the notion that a lessee could inspect the premises prior to taking a lease and had to take them as he found them, which principle may owe something to the principle of buyer beware, which treats a lease or even a short-term tenancy as a property conveyance. In a statement approved by Lord Millett,[8] Martin B said that 'one who takes a house must be held to take the premises as they are, and cannot complain that the house was not constructed differently'. This principle casts the onus of inspections on the person least likely to be fully informed about the state of the premises, but in the same vein, Lord Goddard CJ said that a person 'takes the property as he finds it and must put up with the consequences. It is not to be supposed that the landlord is going to alter the construction, unless he consents to do so.'[9]

The no-liability rule has exceptions. The Court of Appeal once invoked the contractual principle of business efficacy so as to imply a term into a periodic statutory tenancy of a terraced house, the exterior of which the landlord was liable to repair. The tenant was under an express obligation to keep the interior in repair, which she could not sensibly perform, owing to extensive water penetration from the exterior.[10] This principle may be confined to defective residential leases. The case dealt with a statutory tenancy derived from a contractual tenancy entered into some 20 years before the imposition on landlords by statute of limited obligations to keep in repair. The Court of Appeal refused to imply any obligations by a landlord of a long lessee to carry out structural repairs, where it considered that the scheme of the long leases in question did not require any implication of terms. Of note was the fact that the term of the lease concerned was long, and also

5   *Tennant Radiant Heat Ltd v Warrington Corpn* [1988] 1 EGLR 41, CA. However, the landlord was liable in nuisance and negligence. There are exceptions to this rule. If the terms of a lease expressly reserve a landlord control of the fabric of the main parts of a building, and the design of the building is such that parts of the premises demised are protected by the retained property, the lease may be construed as requiring the landlord to keep the protecting parts of the retained property in repair: see eg *Hallisey v Petmoor Developments Ltd* [2000] EGCS 124 (where a roof terrace of flats on the top floor protected much of the area of flats below).

6   *Lee v Leeds City Council* [2002] EWCA Civ 06, [2002] 1 WLR 1488.

7   For an example of such an express obligation see *Welsh v Greenwich London BC* [2000] 3 EGLR 41.

8   In *Southwark London Brough Council v Mills* [2001] 1 AC 1 at 17, [1999] 4 All ER 449 at 461, the statement being in *Carstairs v Taylor* (1871) LR 6 Exch 217 at 222.

9   In *Kiddle v City Business Properties Ltd* [1942] 1 KB 269 at 274-75.

10   *Barrett v Lounova (1982) Ltd* [1990] 1 QB 348, [1989] 1 All ER 351.

that detailed provisions had been made for the repairing obligations of the lessees, who were expected to pay for the relevant works.[11]

One ground on which repairing obligations may still be implied is where the landlord should be placed under a correlative obligation to one already undertaken by the other party.[12] Statute imposes limited repairing obligations on landlords if the tenancy is residential and for less than seven years, so limiting the number of occasions of use of the power to imply repairing duties. Where statutory obligations govern the position, there is no scope for any common law implied obligations.[13] The courts are also assiduous in avoiding implying terms if some remedy is available under statute to a tenant: thus, no term could be implied into a lease of a flat where, should the managing company default in its obligations to repair, these must be taken over by the landlord. There was no necessity for the term, first, because the lease expressly provided that in the case of default, the landlord might intervene if it thought fit, and secondly, because the tenant could have invoked a statutory right to apply for the appointment of a manager.[14]

A different set of principles may govern commercial leases which contain express schemes for dealing with repairing obligations which are not capable of being literally construed as being comprehensive, so leaving gaps in the provision for repairs. The courts may now be inclined, if they think that the parties to a business lease intended the repairing obligations to form a comprehensive scheme, to adopt constructions of the language of the lease which require some words to be inserted. Thus, in construing a commercial lease so that certain words obliging a landlord to carry out roofing repairs were inserted, it was held that general principles of construction required the court to assume, unless the parties expressly and clearly provided the contrary, that the landlord was going to be liable to carry out roofing repairs.[15] Where no provision at all has been made for a repairing obligation, the Court of Appeal are prepared to envisage a commercial lease in which neither party is liable for repairs.[16] The principle invoked by the courts under the guise of commercial common sense could be merely a beneficial interpretation of the words used by the parties, rather then an example of filling in wholesale gaps in the provision for repairs. Nevertheless, if the parties have

---

11 *Adami v Lincoln Grange Management Ltd* [1998] 1 EGLR 58; see also *Duke of Westminster v Guild* [1985] QB 688, [1984] 3 All ER 144, CA (where the tenant had an express right of access over the landlord's land to repair a drain, and hence could not impliedly require the landlord to repair it for the tenant's benefit).

12 *Barnes v City of London Real Property Co* [1918] 2 Ch 18 (tenant undertook to pay a specified sum for repairs so impliedly obliging landlord to undertake these); also *Barrett v Lounova (1982) Ltd* [1990] 1 QB 348, [1989] 1 All ER 351.

13 See *Demetriou v Poolaction Ltd* [1991] 1 EGLR 100, CA (business premises and no correlative obligation on the landlord), a principle mentioned in *Lee v Leeds City Council* [2002] EWCA Civ 06, [2002] 1 WLR 1488, para 64 without any demur.

14 *Hafton Properties Ltd v Camp* [1994] 1 EGLR 67.

15 *Holding & Barnes plc v Hill House Hammond Ltd* [2001] EWCA Civ 1334.

16 In *Demetriou v Poolaction Ltd* [1991] 1 EGLR 100 at 104E.

not chosen to provide for a specific matter, the courts are likely to be careful to avoid wholesale adjustments to their agreement under the guise of a beneficial construction of the contract.[17]

There are a small number of established cases where the courts have implied repairing and related obligations against a landlord.[18]

Houses in the course of erection

In a lease of a dwelling house which is still in the course of erection at the date of the lease, there is an implied warranty that it will be built with proper materials in a workmanlike manner, and that when it is completed, it will be fit for human habitation.[19]

Landlord builder

If the landlord builds an unfurnished dwelling house or flat to his own design and specification (where it is a local authority), the landlord will be liable in negligence for dangerous defects causing personal injury to occupiers. The scope of the duty is to see that the occupiers, such as the tenant and his family, are reasonably safe when the premises are let from personal injury due to dangerous defects. The duty is not avoided by the mere fact that the person to whom it is owed knows of the danger, unless it would be reasonable to expect him to remove or avoid it.[20] The duty was broken where a defective glass panel had been installed in a flat designed by a local authority, where the internal wall at issue was defectively designed,[21] but not where the local authority concerned had installed window locks, with removable keys. The design of these windows was held not to have been defective, using the yardstick of a reasonably skilful window designer and installer.[22]

If the landlord is not the builder then there remains no liability at common law for dangerous defects.[23] In such cases, recourse must be had to the Dangerous Premises

---

17 As opposed to correcting obvious mistakes: *Holding & Barnes plc v Hill House Hammond Ltd* [2001] EWCA Civ 1334, para 21.

18 Conditions as to the fitness and suitability of houses are implied by the Landlord and Tenant Act 1985, s 8, but since the section operates on rent levels which have not been revised since 1957 (at which time rents were controlled) the provision is redundant: *Quick v Taff-Ely BC* [1986] QB 809 at 817, [1985] 3 All ER 321 at 324, CA. This provision may well be superseded by new health and safety fitness ratings if and when legislation is enacted.

19 *Perry v Sharon Development Co Ltd* [1937] 4 All ER 390, CA.

20 *Rimmer v Liverpool City Council* [1985] QB 1, [1984] 1 All ER 930, CA. Also *Targett v Torfaen Borough Council* [1992] 1 EGLR 275.

21 *Rimmer v Liverpool City Council* [1985] QB 1, [1984] 1 All ER 930, CA.

22 *Adams v Rhymney Valley DC* [2000] 3 EGLR 25, CA. The council were not negligent in not taking outside advice.

23 *Cavalier v Pope* [1906] AC 428, HL; *McNerny v Lambeth London Borough Council* [1989] 1 EGLR 81, CA; PF Smith [1989] Conv 216.

Act 1972, but liability under the Dangerous Premises Act 1972, s 4 depends on proof of disrepair by the tenant, which may leave him without a remedy if there is merely a design fault in the premises, but no disrepair. Nevertheless, s 4 is significant, as it reformed the common law,[24] and it is convenient to mention it here.

Defective Premises Act 1972

Under the Defective Premises Act 1972, s 4, where the premises are let on a tenancy which puts on the landlord an obligation to the tenant for the maintenance or repair of the premises, the landlord owes to all persons who might reasonably be expected to be affected by defects in the state of premises (thus the tenant but also members of his or her family) a 'duty to take such care as is reasonable in all the circumstances to see that they are reasonably safe from personal injury or from damage to their property caused by a relevant defect' (Defective Premises Act 1972, s 4(1)). A 'relevant defect' is a defect in the state of the premises existing at, in particular, the time the tenancy was entered into or after then, arising or continuing because of an act or omission by the landlord which amounts to failure by the landlord to carry out his obligations to the tenant for the maintenance or repair of the premises (Defective Premises Act 1972, s 4(3)). The concept is not unlimited since it does not require the landlord to lag water pipes.[25] The tenant does not have to give the landlord notice to the defect (Defective Premises Act 1972, s 4(2)): this provision contrasts with that under LTA 1985, s 11, where notice is required. By the Defective Premises Act 1972, s 4(4), where the premises are let under a tenancy which expressly or impliedly gives the landlord the right to enter the premises to maintain or repair them, then as from the time when the landlord first exercises, or by notice or otherwise can put himself in a position to exercise the right, he is for purposes of the Defective Premises Act 1972, s 4 treated as under an obligation to carry out the work in question.[26] If, therefore, the tenancy contains an express or implied right of entry to inspect and repair then liability under the Defective Premises Act 1972, s 4 is triggered if a relevant defect such as a defective gas fire,[27] or a damaged step[28] exists, even if the tenant has not informed the landlord. However, the Defective Premises Act 1972, s 4 is limited in its operation by the fact that the landlord is only liable if the 'relevant defect' is the result of a state of disrepair in breach of his

---

24 *Sykes v Harry* [2001] EWCA Civ 167, [2001] 1 EGLR 53, CA.
25 *Boateng v Camden London BC* Legal Action, July 2001, p 22. Thus the landlords were not liable for injuries caused to a child of the tenant by contact with hot water pipes.
26 There is an exception for defects caused by failure of the tenant to comply with the tenant's repairing obligations.
27 As in *Sykes v Harry* [2001] EWCA Civ 167, [2001] 1 EGLR 53, CA (where the tenant ought to have given notice, since he had immediate control of the premises, and damages were reduced to reflect this omission).
28 See *McAuley v Bristol City Council* [1991] 2 EGLR 64, CA (defective garden step did not fall within the landlord's statutory duty under Landlord and Tenant Act 1985, s 11 but since there was a right to enter to repair the step, it triggered liability under Defective Premises Act 1972).

tenancy obligations.[29] Thus the landlord was exonerated from having to remove a defective paving slab which was not within the demised premises and which had injured a small child.[30]

Furnished houses

There is an implied condition in a tenancy of a furnished house or flat that the premises are fit for habitation at the commencement of the tenancy.[31] If on the day the tenancy commences, the premises are not fit for human habitation, the tenant may repudiate the lease, or he may elect to keep the lease and sue for damages.[32] The implied condition is limited. It does not oblige the landlord to keep the premises fit for human habitation during the tenancy.[33] Infestation with bugs,[34] and defective drainage,[35] are examples of breaches of this implied condition.

Miscellaneous

There are a number of cases where an obligation to repair has been implied against a landlord because, without an implication, the lease would be unworkable. Where the landlord retained possession and control of the common parts of a block of flats, such as the common stairways, rubbish chutes, lifts and lighting, he was under an implied duty to take reasonable care in all the circumstances to repair and maintain these parts.[36] Similarly, where a tenant enjoyed a right of way over a path which she used as an essential means of access to the premises, the landlord was under an implied duty to maintain the path.[37] More generally, in relation to premises not let to the tenant, but whose maintenance in proper repair is necessary for the protection of the demised premises or the safe enjoyment of them by the tenant, there is an implied obligation of uncertain scope on the landlord to take reasonable care that these retained parts are not in such a state as to cause damage to the tenant or the premises.[38] Where the tenant had to pay for the cost of external repainting, which the landlord had not expressly undertaken to do, the landlord was under an implied obligation to do the work in question.[39] However, the Court of Appeal has recently indicated that a landlord

29 *Lee v Leeds City Council* [2002] EWCA Civ 06, [2002] 1 WLR 1488, paras 69ff. The right of entry conferred on the local authority was in terms limited to the purpose of carrying out repairs. Thus there was no liability on the landlords to cure condensation and other matters rendering the house unfit for habitation owing to design faults.
30 *Boldack v East Lindsey DC* (1999) 31 HLR 41, CA.
31 *Smith v Marrable* (1843) 11 M & W 5; *Collins v Hopkins* [1923] 2 KB 617.
32 *Wilson v Finch Hatton* (1877) 2 Ex D 336.
33 *Sarson v Roberts* [1895] 2 QB 395, CA.
34 *Smith v Marrable* (1843) 11 M & W 5.
35 *Wilson v Finch Hatton* (1877) 2 Ex D 336; also *Collins v Hopkins* [1923] 2 KB 617.
36 *Liverpool City Council v Irwin* [1977] AC 239, [1976] 2 All ER 39, HL.
37 *King v South Northamptonshire District Council* [1992] 1 EGLR 53, CA.
38 *Hargroves, Aronson & Co v Hartopp* [1905] 1 KB 472; *Cockburn v Smith* [1924] 2 KB 119.
39 *Edmonton Corpn v WM Knowles & Son Ltd* (1961) 60 LGR 124.

cannot be under an implied obligation to remedy unfitness as a correlative obligation to the requirement of a council tenancy on the tenant to live on the premises.[40]

Note on reform

The Law Commission has proposed the introduction of a new statutory implied obligation as to fitness for human habitation, which would apply to any lease of a dwelling house for a term of less than seven years, corresponding to the tenancies to which the existing statutory implied obligation to repair applies. The lessor would be subject to an implied covenant that the dwelling house was fit for human habitation at the commencement of the tenancy. He would have to keep it in that state during the lease.[41] The obligation would be subject to a requirement of notice (as with the present statutory obligation to repair) and so would not be absolute, although the fitness criteria would be updated. If this proposal is implemented, and it would be expensive as many short lettings are by local authorities,[42] tenants would benefit from an obligation to ensure fitness for habitation to correspond to the existing landlords' obligation to keep dwelling houses let on short leases in repair. Considerations of expense to local authorities may well entail the adoption of a different scheme: the enactment of individual health and safety ratings for dwellings.[43] At all events as things stand at present, where there is no landlord breach of an express or implied statutory obligation to repair, the matter has to be dealt with within the confines of environmental protection legislation.

II TENANT'S IMPLIED OBLIGATIONS

In the event of the lease or tenancy agreement failing to impose any express repairing or maintenance obligations on the tenant, there are circumstances in which he is subject to a liability not to commit waste (which may also be relevant where the lease fails to prohibit structural alterations). In addition, a tenant is subject to limited implied obligations to repair.

Waste

(i) Three types of waste

The object of waste was once said by an American reform body to be to allow a person who has a limited interest in property, such as a tenant, to carry out their reasonable

---

40 *Lee v Leeds City Council* [2002] EWCA Civ 06, [2002] 1 WLR 1488.
41 Law Com No 238 (1996) 'Responsibility for State and Condition of Property' para 8.35.
42 Even though the proposal would only apply to tenancies entered into after the new obligation came into force.
43 See 'Health and Safety in Housing' (2001) DETR.

desires to the greatest extent consistent with the protection of the interest of the other person.[44] This typically laissez faire principle understates the prophylactic nature of waste. The subject of waste is ancient,[45] and technical. The Law Commission have recommended the abolition of waste, noting that liability in waste overlaps with liability for tenant-like user.[46]

There are three types of waste. *Voluntary waste* is committed by any deliberate or negligent act of the tenant's which causes permanent damage, such as ploughing up pasture, felling or maiming trees or shrubs, overloading the floor of premises so as to cause it to collapse,[47] or altering or converting the premises without the landlord's prior permission.

Ameliorating waste[48] is waste which improves the value of the land, buildings or premises, at least from the lessee's point of view, such as by dumping waste on the land,[49] or carrying out alterations to the land, converting buildings[50] or extending premises, or improving the current use of the land.[51]

Permissive waste is based on allowing, by neglect, a building to fall down for lack of repairs. However, if a house is in a poor condition at the commencement of a lease, as where it has no roof, it was said that the tenant is not liable in permissive waste for allowing the house to collapse.[52]

A tenant's obligation not to commit waste is founded in tort, and is independent of any contractual obligation in the lease, whether express or implied. If the lease contains an express covenant to repair or against alterations, the landlord may still elect to sue in waste.[53]

---

44   Report of the Law Revision Commission, State of New York (1935), cited in Bathurst (1949) 13 Conv NS 278.
45   If not archaic: *Mancetter Developments Ltd v Garmanson Ltd* [1986] QB 1212, [1986] 1 All ER 449, CA.
46   Law Com No 238 (1996) 'Responsibility for State and Condition of Property'. They would replace waste and tenant-like user with a default obligation, ie one that could be contracted out of or modified in a tenancy agreement, based on fault, requiring a tenant to take proper care of the premises and to make good damage done wilfully or negligently by him or any other person lawfully in occupation of the premises during his occupation or possession (paras 10.31ff).
47   *Manchester Bonded Warehouse Co v Carr* (1880) 5 CPD 507.
48   See further (1900-01) 14 Harv LR 226 (for the view that a tenant should be hampered as little as possible in the use of the demised premises, so advocating a narrow view of ameliorating waste liability); also (1929-30) 43 Harv LR 1130.
49   See *West Ham Central Charity Board v East London Waterworks Co* [1900] 1 Ch 624.
50   As in *Doherty v Allman* (1878) 3 App Cas 709, HL. The breach was only technical.
51   As in *Meux v Cobley* [1892] 2 Ch 253 (conversion of arable land into market gardens).
52   Co Litt 53a.
53   *Mancetter Developments Ltd v Garmanson Ltd* [1986] QB 1212, [1986] 1 All ER 449, CA.

(ii) Liability for waste and remedies

Not all tenants are liable for waste or all kinds of waste. Tenants holding a lease for a term certain are liable both for voluntary waste and also for permissive waste. With regard to permissive waste, the principle of liability of fixed-term lessees was taken as established some 150 years ago,[54] and has been confirmed more recently by the High Court,[55] where the authorities going back to the middle ages were reviewed.[56] A periodic tenant from year to year and for a shorter period is liable for voluntary but not, it would seem, for permissive, waste,[57] except, perhaps, to the extent of keeping the premises wind- and water-tight. A weekly tenant is liable only for voluntary waste.[58] A tenant at will is not liable for either voluntary or permissive waste, but an act of voluntary waste terminates the tenancy and renders him liable in trespass.[59]

A tenant against whom an action for waste is brought has a defence if he shows that the damage resulted from the ordinary, reasonable and proper use of the premises,[60] or that the damage was caused by an Act of God, such as floods or lightning or fire.

If waste is proved, the landlord may claim damages or an injunction. The measure of damages is the loss in value to the landlord's reversion.[61] This may be the cost of making good the damage to the buildings or land concerned, as where a damages award was based on the cost of making good holes left in the building by a careless removal of tenant's trade fixtures.[62] In this case, the tenant was liable even though he was entitled to remove the fixtures, because he could not exercise that right without

---

54 See notably *Yellowly v Gower* (1855) 11 Exch 274. Parke B there placed the liability for voluntary and permissive waste of fixed term tenants and tenants for life on the same footing. This decision was accepted in the Canadian case of *Morris v Cairncross* (1906) 14 OLR 544 (where the wording of the Statute of Marlborough, as noted in that case, was revised by the Constitutional Act 1792 so as expressly to make lessees liable for permissive waste).

55 As well as by Foa *General Law of Landlord and Tenant* (8th edn, 1957), p 281 where it states that 'tenants for years are liable for permissive as well as for voluntary waste'.

56 *Dayani v Bromley London BC* [1999] 3 EGLR 144. The High Court, rejecting the 'considerable' doubts of Woodfall, 13.124, and relying on Littleton, section 71 and Blackstone, Book II, Ch XVIII, section V, noted that the judges who dealt with the issue at or shortly after the passage of the Statutes of Marlborough and of Gloucester, and who held tenants for a term certain liable for permissive waste, were best able to judge the intentions of Parliament. The later repeal of the Statute of Gloucester and the abolition of the writ of waste had no effect on permissive waste liability, as the action for such waste was on the case, and was a common law development.

57 *Torriano v Young* (1833) 6 C & P 8.

58 *Warren v Keen* [1954] 1 QB 15, CA.

59 *Countess of Shrewsbury's Case* (1600) 5 Co Rep 13b. A tenant at sufferance is liable for voluntary waste: *Burchell v Hornsby* (1808) 1 Camp 360. The liability of such a tenant for permissive waste is unclear but Megarry and Wade, 14-236 seem to think that such a tenant is not liable for this variety of waste.

60 *Manchester Bonded Warehouse Co v Carr* (1880) 5 CPD 507.

61 *Whitham v Kershaw* (1886) 16 QBD 613, CA.

62 *Mancetter Developments Ltd v Garmanson Ltd* [1986] QB 1212, [1986] 1 All ER 449, CA.

making good the damage to the building.[63] The landlord may claim damages despite the expiry of the lease,[64] and also where the tenant holds over.[65]

The landlord may sue for an injunction, as where he claims a negative injunction to restrain alterations to the building. An injunction is not considered appropriate if the acts of waste are too trivial to warrant the grant of this discretionary remedy.[66] On the other hand, the fact that an alteration might also amount to a breach of covenant in the lease is no absolute bar to relief.[67] An injunction might, at discretion, be appropriate to restrain the conversion of a house into a shop, so altering the whole character of the premises.[68] An injunction might also be granted to restrain further acts of waste (in such a case damages would not be an adequate remedy and could not be quantified, but damages could be awarded to compensate the landlord for any past injury).[69]

Tenant-like user

There is a limited implied contractual duty on a lessee to use the premises in a tenant-like manner, and to deliver up possession to the landlord at the termination of the tenancy in the same condition as when the tenant took them, fair wear and tear excepted.[70] The duty, sometimes referred to as an obligation to use in a tenant-like manner, is minimal. It does not oblige the tenant to carry out substantial repairs, as shown by the examples given in the leading case: if the tenant goes away in winter, he may, if this is reasonable, have to turn off the water and empty the boiler and do minor repairs. The tenant must not wilfully or negligently damage the house, neither must his family or guests, and he must replace any breakages. He is not bound to execute any repairs caused by items, such as windows, wearing out or decaying due to old age.[71] This obligation does not compel the tenant to lag internal water-pipes as a precaution against freezing in winter, nor to turn off the stop-cock or drain the water system, unless the circumstances, such as the severity of the cold, the conditions in the premises and the length of the tenant's absence, make it reasonable to expect this.[72]

Almost any properly-drafted lease or tenancy will make express provisions as to the repairing obligations of the tenant. However, a covenant to leave premises in repair

63 In *Mancetter Developments Ltd v Garmanson Ltd* [1986] QB 1212, [1986] 1 All ER 449, CA, a director of an occupying company, who had procured the removal of the fixtures, was personally liable to the landlords in damages.
64 *Kinlyside v Thornton* (1776) 2 Wm Bl 1111.
65 *Burchell v Hornsby* (1808) 1 Camp 360.
66 *Doherty v Allman* (1878) 3 App Cas 709, HL.
67 *Countess of Shrewsbury's Case* (1600) 5 Co Rep 13b.
68 *Marsden v Edward Heyes Ltd* [1927] 2 KB 1, CA.
69 See *West Ham Central Charity Board v East London Waterworks Co* [1900] 1 Ch 624.
70 *Marsden v Edward Heyes Ltd* [1927] 2 KB 1, CA.
71 *Warren v Keen* [1954] 1 QB 15, [1953] 2 All ER 1118, CA.
72 *Wycombe Health Authority v Barnett* (1982) 47 P & CR 394, CA (short absence, tenant not liable when pipe burst); cf *Mickel v M'Coard* 1913 SC 896 (long absence in mid-winter, tenant liable).

does not, apparently, exempt a tenant from an implied duty to use the premises in a tenant-like manner.[73]

The Law Commission considers that the current rules of waste and tenant-like user are inadequate and imprecise. They would, as we have noted, replace both sets of rules with a statutory duty, which would, in particular, require the tenant to take proper care of the premises and to make good any wilful damage to them.[74]

III LANDLORD'S STATUTE-IMPLIED OBLIGATION TO KEEP IN REPAIR DWELLING HOUSES AND FLATS

Since 1961 statute has imposed on landlords limited obligations[75] to keep dwelling houses and flats held on short leases in repair. At the time the original legislation was being promoted, the government indicated their view that it would not be reasonable to require a tenant holding a short-term tenancy to undertake major repairs. At the same time, the government wished to see that necessary repairs were done, noting that at the time some tenancy agreements made no proper provision for repairs at all.[76] Short-residential tenants are in a vulnerable position:[77] it would be unfair to expect such tenants, who have to pay a market rent, to live in premises which are out of repair, and unreasonable to require them to carry out remedial work to the premises at their own expense where they have only a limited interest. The statutory obligations of the landlord are not very onerous: they depend on notice of the want of repair. In addition, factors such as the age of the property are expressly relevant to the compliance with the statutory obligations (LTA 1985, s 11(3)).

Under the general law, the landlord cannot be required to cure unfitness which is not a disrepair. Thus, a house that had become uninhabitable owing to severe condensation was not out of repair because the metal frame windows, which the tenant sought to have replaced by the landlord with a view to easing the 'sweating' from these windows, were not in a state requiring any repairs. The windows were not physically damaged.[78] This harsh principle has been restated recently by the Court of Appeal.[79] They said that the ruling in the first-mentioned case was not inconsistent with principle or with earlier cases. In addition, the obligation on the courts imposed by HRA 1988, s 3 (to read obligations imposed by legislation as being consistent with ECHR rights) did not

73 *White v Nicolson* (1842) 4 Man & G 95.
74 Law Com No 238 (1996) 'Responsibility for State and Condition of Property' para 10.37.
75 See *Newham London Borough Council v Patel* (1978) 13 HLR 77 at 84.
76 637 HC Official Report (5th series) cols 974-75 (Mr Brooke). The problem of poor quality housing persists to this day, as admitted by the government's Housing Green Paper (2000), p 8.
77 As implicitly recognised by Law Com No 238 (1996) 'Responsibility for State and Condition of Property' p 64, note 36.
78 *Quick v Taff-Ely BC* [1986] QB 809, [1985] 3 All ER 321, CA.
79 *Lee v Leeds City Council* [2002] EWCA Civ 06, [2002] 1 WLR 1488.

require the court to look for some different meaning to the current interpretation of the LTA 1985, s 11(1)(a). The court was not disposed to confer greater rights on the tenant than Parliament had intended to confer. In any case, policy choices (such as allocation of council landlords' resources) were not really for the courts to undertake. It will be appreciated that HRA 1988 allows a wide margin of policy appreciation and decision-making to Parliament in housing matters.

However, where the landlord is subjected to the extended obligation in the case of flats (so that he has to keep in repair for example a common roof not demised to any tenant) his duty is absolute and does not depend on prior notice from lessees. Hence a landlord who failed to remedy a damaged roof which allowed water ingress into a top-floor tenant's flat was liable in damages as from the date the disrepair first caused damage, as opposed to the time at which he eventually put in hand repairs.[80] Moreover, although the LTA 1985, s 11 imposes limited repairing obligations on landlords, there is nothing to prevent individual tenancy agreements going further, and, if they do, the express wording will be enforced against the landlord concerned. For example, in a recent case,[81] the landlord of a secure tenant undertook in terms to 'maintain the dwelling in good condition and repair' with certain specific exceptions.[82] The flat was subject to damp and mould caused by condensation (the external walls were not thermally insulated or dry lined). Whereas such a condition would not necessarily trigger liability under statute, the Court of Appeal insisted that the reference to 'good condition' was intended to connote a separate concept to that of 'repair', so that failing to provide thermal insulation or dry lining to the external walls was a breach of obligation by the landlords for which they were liable in damages.

Application of 1985 Act

The Landlord and Tenant Act 1985, s 11 imposes repairing obligations on landlords of dwelling houses or flats, where the lease is for a term of less than seven years.[83] The Landlord and Tenant Act 1985 (hereinafter LTA 1985) thus applies to assured shorthold tenancies granted under the Housing Act 1988 as amended, to Rent Act protected or statutory tenancies where the protected tenancy from which they are derived is for a term less than seven years, to secure tenancies, to introductory tenancies and even to a person who holds a 'non-proprietary lease' from a landlord who holds no estate in the land from the owner.[84]

In terms excluded from LTA 1985 are any leases granted on or after 3 October 1980 to a local authority and certain other public sector bodies (LTA 1985, s 14(4)). Tenancies

80   *Passley v London Borough of Wandsworth* (1996) 30 HLR 165, CA.
81   *Welsh v Greenwich London BC* [2000] 3 EGLR 41, CA.
82   It will be appreciated that the (narrower) statutory obligation is deemed to be read into all relevant tenancy agreements even if not set out word for word.
83   Landlord and Tenant Act 1985, s 13(1). The date of grant must be on or after 24 October 1961.
84   *Bruton v London & Quadrant Housing Trust* [1999] 2 EGLR 59, HL.

to which the Landlord and Tenant Act 1954, Pt II applies are also excluded from LTA 1985 (LTA 1985, s 32(2)), as are leases granted to the Crown (LTA 1985, s 14(5)).[85] The statutory obligations are supplemented by a statutory instrument whose aim is to make sure that the gas appliances in the premises which are let to short term tenants are safe and where appropriate regularly inspected.[86]

A lease is caught by the Act where it is determinable at the landlord's option before seven years from the commencement of the term (LTA 1985, s 13(2)(b)).[87] If the lease contains a tenant's option to renew which, if exercised, would prolong the lease over seven years, the Act does not apply (LTA 1985, s 13(2)(c)). Any part of the term falling before the date of the grant of the lease is ignored in computing the statutory period which starts from the date of the grant or agreement for a lease (LTA 1985, s 13(2)(a)).[88] This is to counter artificial backdating of leases with a view to extending the term beyond seven years. If the landlord obtains a registered rent on the basis that he is responsible for structural repairs under LTA 1985, when in fact he is not, because the lease is for a term over seven years, provided he demands the full rent, he will be estopped from denying liability under LTA 1985.[89]

Scope of landlord's duty

LTA 1985, s 11(1) implies a covenant by the landlord:
(a)   to keep in repair the structure and exterior of the dwelling house (including drains, gutters and external pipes) (LTA 1985, s 11(1)(a)); and
(b)   to keep in repair and proper working order the installations in the dwelling house for the supply of water, gas and electricity, and for sanitation (including basins, sinks, baths and sanitary conveniences but not other fixtures, fittings and appliances for making use of the supply of water, gas or electricity) (LTA 1985, s 11(1)(b)) and installations for space heating and heating water (LTA 1985, s 11(1)(c)).

If the lease is of a flat (or any other ' dwelling house' forming part only of a building) the duty in LTA 1985, s 11(1)(a) extends to any part of the structure or exterior of the building in which the landlord has an estate or interest (LTA 1985, s 11(1A)(a)). An example would be the common parts or the roof, if these are not demised to the individual lessees.

---

85   Nor is the Crown bound by LTA 1985 where it is landlord: *Department of Transport v Egoroff* [1986] 1 EGLR 89, CA.
86   Gas (Installation and Use) Regulations 1998, SI 1998/2451 (see Driscoll (1998) 142 Sol Jo 1014). Note also the Electrical Equipment (Safety) Regulations 1994, SI 1994/3260.
87   *Parker v O'Connor* [1974] 3 All ER 257, [1974] 1 WLR 1160, CA (lease for over seven years with right to determine lease on death of landlord outside this provision as right to determine not unfettered).
88   *Brikom Investments Ltd v Seaford* [1981] 2 All ER 783, [1981] 1 WLR 863, CA.
89   *Brikom Investments Ltd v Seaford* [1981] 2 All ER 783, [1981] 1 WLR 863, CA.

In the case of installations, where the landlord lets only part of the building (again for example, where flats are let and the landlord retains the common parts and/or the roof), the landlord must keep in repair and proper working order an installation which directly or indirectly serves the flat. This is so, provided that the installation is in part of a building in which the landlord has an estate or interest or which is owned or controlled by him (LTA 1985, s 11(1A)(b)).

The extended obligations only apply if the disrepair or failure to maintain affects the tenant's enjoyment of the flat or common parts (LTA 1985, s 11(1B)).[90] If, in order to comply with the extended repairing covenant, the landlord needs to carry out works or repairs otherwise than in, or to an installation in, the flat concerned and has no sufficient right in the part of the building or installation concerned to enable him to carry out the required repairs, it is a defence for the landlord to prove that he used all reasonable endeavours to obtain such right as would be adequate to enable him to carry out the works or repairs, but he was unable to do so (LTA 1985, s 11(3A)).[91]

Any covenant by the tenant for the repair of the premises (including any covenant to put in repair or deliver up in repair, to paint, point or render or to pay money in lieu of repairs by the tenant or on account of repairs by the landlord) is nullified (LTA 1985, s 11(4)), in so far as it relates to matters covered by LTA 1985, s 11(1).

The statutory obligations are read into the relevant tenancy and are taken to form part of the contract between landlord and tenant.[92] These obligations are, it seems, frequently invoked. Exceptionally for an obligation to 'keep in repair', notice is required of the existence of a defect to the landlord from the tenant (as to which see below). However, contractual remedies are available to the tenant where the landlord is in breach of the statutory obligation, which is broken as soon as the premises fall out of repair, subject to his being given notice. Thus not only is the tenant able to claim damages,[93] but specific performance has an active role to play for tenants claiming in county courts against neglectful landlords.[94] Indeed, the remedy of repudiation is available to the tenant where there are gross and persistent breaches of statutory obligation. This may be important to assured shorthold tenants,[95] who have little

90   The definition of 'common parts' in Landlord and Tenant Act 1987, s 60(1) is expressly applied.
91   If the disrepair is in a flat adjoining that of the premises affected, a complainant could claim that under Access to Neighbouring Land Act 1992 the landlord could obtain an access order against the lessee of the flat to which he has no right of access under the lease concerned, so that the landlord could not then invoke the statutory defence.
92   *O'Brien v Robinson* [1973] AC 912 at 927 (Lord Diplock).
93   See further below; but for two among many examples: in *Switzer v Law* [1998] CLY 3624, where, to fulfil his statutory obligation, the landlord had to install extractor fans to rid the premises of moisture and also had to pay general damages of £5,500 to compensate a tenant (at a rent of £20 throughout) for some eight years of inconvenience and discomfort from the date of her claim; in *Coldbeck v Mohamed* [1999] CLY 1399 there was a 'handmade' tenancy agreement where the premises were in a 'dreadful' state and almost uninhabitable – again heavy damages were considered appropriate.
94   See Law Com No 238 (1996) 'Responsibility for State and Condition of Property' para 5.12.
95   As in *Hussein v Mehlman* [1992] 2 EGLR 87.

choice but to pay a market rent for premises in which, but for repudiation, they might find themselves having to pay for unsatisfactory accommodation.

Exceptions

LTA 1985, s 11(2) expressly absolves the landlord from liability:
(a) for repairs attributable to the tenant's failure to use the premises in a tenant-like manner;
(b) to rebuild, or reinstate the premises as a result of damage by fire, tempest, flood or other inevitable accident; and
(c) to repair or maintain any tenants' fixtures.

Thus, a liability to undertake responsibility for any of these matters, or to pay for their cost, may legitimately be cast on the tenant (LTA 1985, s 11(4)).

LTA 1985, s 11(3) provides that in determining the standard of repair required to satisfy the obligations, regard is to be had to the age, character and prospective life of the house and the locality in which it is situated.[96]

The landlord's obligation is coupled with a right of entry, conferred on the landlord or a person authorised by him in writing, to view the state of repair of the premises, exercisable at reasonable times of the day and on giving 24 hours' written notice (LTA 1985, s 11(6)). With this right there is also an implied right to enter and execute the required repairs. Only if the work goes outside the scope of what the statutory covenant requires will the landlord commit a trespass against the tenant.[97]

No contracting out

Covenants by the tenant which purport to apply to the tenant the landlord's statute-implied duties are of no effect (LTA 1985, s 11(4)). Accordingly, a covenant by the tenant to pay service charges or money in lieu of repairs[98] is nullified in so far as it relates to landlords' statutory obligations (LTA 1985, s 11(5)).[99] Express contracting out of the landlord's statute-implied duties is forbidden by LTA 1985, s 12(1), except under the procedure laid down in LTA 1985, s 12(2) by way of a joint application to the county court, prior to the granting of the lease. The court may, with the consent of the parties, authorise the inclusion in the proposed lease or in an agreement collateral

---

96   This adopts the standard of repairs in *Proudfoot v Hart* (1890) 25 QBD 42, CA; *Jaquin v Holland* [1960] 1 All ER 402, [1960] 1 WLR 258, CA; also *McClean v Liverpool City Council* [1987] 2 EGLR 56, CA.
97   *McDougall v Easington District Council* [1989] 1 EGLR 93, CA.
98   Including any express covenant to carry out exterior redecorations: *Irvine v Morgan* [1991] 1 EGLR 260.
99   Or a tenants' covenant to spend a stated sum annually on repairs and decorations, in so far as caught by LTA 1985, s 11(1): see *Moss' Empires Ltd v Olympia (Liverpool) Ltd* [1939] AC 544, [1939] 3 All ER 460, HL.

thereto, of agreements excluding or modifying these statutory obligations, if, having regard to the other terms of the lease (such as an adjustment in rent) and in all the circumstances of the case, it is reasonable to do so.

Meaning of structure, exterior and installations

(i)   Structure and exterior

The High Court has ruled that the 'structure' of a dwelling house consists of those elements of the house which give it its essential appearance, stability and shape. Windows are part of the structure even if not load-bearing. The expression 'structure' does not include fittings, decorations, an internal plaster finish and the like.[100] However, by extension, steps and a path giving access to the dwelling house concerned were held to be part of the exterior[101] but not a path at the back not giving access.[102] Any part of the structure[103] and exterior of a house which does not form part of the demise to the tenant, such as drains or gutters on adjacent land, lies outside the statute-implied obligations of the landlord and any obligations on him in relation to those parts must be expressly imposed if at all.[104] There may be circumstances in which the landlord, where disrepair affects the structure and exterior and also causes damage to the internal decorations, has to do work to prevent further damage to the latter.[105]

(ii)   Installations

Sanitary conveniences are 'installations' within LTA 1985, s 11(1).[106] Otherwise the term includes such things as pipes, radiators, boilers, or even refrigeration equipment. The landlord is bound to keep installations of the prescribed type in repair 'and proper working order' so that while he is not thereby obliged to lag water-pipes,[107] the landlord must see to it that the installation is in such condition that it works properly as an installation. Thus if a water cistern bursts and floods the premises, the landlord is bound to replace it and is liable in damages to the tenant.[108] However, the courts do not subject the landlord to an absolute obligation. Where the landlord had replaced the

---

100 *Irvine v Morgan* [1991] 1 EGLR 260.
101 *Brown v Liverpool Corpn* [1969] 3 All ER 1345, CA.
102 *Hopwood v Cannock Chase District Council* [1975] 1 All ER 796, [1975] 1 WLR 373, CA.
103 See *Irvine v Morgan* [1991] 1 EGLR 260.
104 *Peters v Prince of Wales Theatre (Birmingham) Ltd* [1943] KB 73, [1942] 2 All ER 533, CA. In the case of leases of *flats*, LTA 1985, s 11(1A), above, would appear to reverse this result, in relation to parts of the demised premises retained by the landlord in the same building, though not, presumably, in relation to adjoining land of his.
105 *Staves v Leeds City Council* (1990) 23 HLR 107 (damaged plaster was treated as part of the structure which was itself out of repair).
106 *Sheldon v West Bromwich Corpn* (1973) 25 P & CR 360, CA.
107 *Wycombe Health Authority v Barnett* (1982) 47 P & CR 394, CA.
108 *Liverpool City Council v Irwin* [1977] AC 239, [1976] 2 All ER 39, HL.

communal water pipes in a block of flats, and since then there had been regular interruptions to the water supply when the water pressure fell, the Court of Appeal held that the landlord did not have to provide installations which functioned regardless of the circumstances. Equally, the landlord could not supply installations which could accommodate no later changes in the character of supply. The installation had to function under supply conditions which it was reasonable to anticipate would prevail. Thus an unforeseen short-term event such as a drought, causing an interruption in water supply, would not be something the landlord would have to remedy: the cost of the work might be disproportionate.[109]

Limits on landlord's duty

In the case of lettings of flats, the landlord's obligation was at one time judicially limited. 'Exterior' referred to the exterior of the particular flat and not the exterior of the whole building. The same limit applied to 'structure'.[110] This has been reversed by statute (LTA 1985, s 11(1A)). Whether the roof of a top-floor flat falls within the landlord's obligation under LTA 1985, s 11(1) is a question of fact: if the ceiling and roof are an inseparable unit then they may well both be within LTA 1985, s 11(1).[111] If not, then LTA 1985, s 11(1A), would require the landlord to keep the roof of a building containing flats, where this was retained by the landlord, in repair in any case. A landlord's breach of the statutory covenant in relation to a common roof or external walls or common parts may be enforced, therefore, by any lessee of a flat within the building holding a short lease, provided, as seen, that the disrepair is such as to affect that lessee's enjoyment of their flat or common parts they are entitled to use (LTA 1985, s 11(1B)).

The landlord is not bound to undertake to insert any new thing, by way of an improvement, which was not there before, so that he is not liable under LTA 1985, s 11(1) to install a new damp-proof course where the ' dwelling house' never had one.[112] Nor is he bound to improve the design of the house, or to cure inherent defects, provided that the actual items which the tenant is trying to force the landlord to replace are themselves in repair: hence a local authority landlord was held not bound to replace metal windows nor to insulate lintels so as to cure severe condensation in a house where neither item was out of repair.[113] In this case, it had been conceded that the house was built according to the requirements of the then current building

109 *O'Connor v Old Etonians Housing Association* [2002] EWCA Civ 150, [2002] 14 EG 127.
110 *Campden Hill Towers Ltd v Gardner* [1977] QB 823, [1977] 1 All ER 739, CA.
111 *Douglas-Scott v Scorgie* [1984] 1 All ER 1086, [1984] 1 WLR 716, CA.
112 *Wainwright v Leeds City Council* (1984) 82 LGR 657, CA. However, the statute does not lay down limits to the common-law concept of repair. According to *Edwards v Islington London BC* Legal Action, July 2001, p 24, underpinning to prevent structural movement may in some circumstances constitute a repair.
113 *Quick v Taff-Ely Borough Council* [1986] QB 809, [1985] 3 All ER 321, CA; also *Lee v Leeds City Council* [2002] EWCA Civ 06, [2002] 1 WLR 1488.

regulations. By contrast, where a rotten door whose lack of repair had caused damage was replaced by a self-sealing aluminium door, this amounted to a repair and the landlord was liable for damage due to water penetration.[114] However, it was also said in this case that if the only defect in the door had been that it did not perform its primary function of keeping out the rain, and the door had otherwise been undamaged, that could not amount to a defect within LTA 1985, s 11. Under s 11, moreover, the landlord is not bound to advise the tenant about the effects of his use of particular parts of the premises. Thus where a tenant used a cupboard designed to store dry goods in order to dry out washing, contributing to a problem of damp, the landlord was not liable for the results of the tenant's misuse of this cupboard.[115]

The question of how much repairing work is required to satisfy LTA 1985, s 11 is thus a question of fact: in one case, piecemeal repairs to the roof of an old terraced house sufficed even though, no doubt, the whole roof might one day have to be replaced.[116] Where a landlord replaced the front and rear elevations of a house, and its roof structure and rainwater disposal system, at a cost of £10,718, extending its life by some 30 years, he was not bound to make good the interior decorations[117] because the work went beyond a repair.[118]

Notice requirement

Where a landlord has expressly covenanted to keep the premises, or the structure, exterior and main roof and walls of a building in repair, he is liable to put right any defect which falls within his covenant, as soon as physical damage manifests itself. Liability is strict,[119] the landlord having undertaken that the premises will not fall into disrepair. Advance notice from the tenant is not a condition precedent to liability to carry out the work or in damages, except in relation to a defect occurring in the demised premises themselves, in which case notice is required.[120] Therefore, where a landlord let parts of a house, but retained the remainder of the premises, and undertook to keep (in particular) the gutters in good tenantable condition, he was liable, without need for notice, for damages to the tenant caused by a roof gutter overflowing.[121]

It is, however, an implied condition precedent to a landlord's liability to keep in repair under LTA 1985, s 11, that he must have notice of the defect or want of repair, where the

114 *Stent v Monmouth District Council* [1987] 1 EGLR 59, CA.
115 *Southwark London BC v McIntosh* [2002] 1 EGLR 25.
116 *Murray v Birmingham District Council* [1987] 2 EGLR 53, CA.
117 For which, otherwise, he may be liable: see *Bradley v Chorley Borough Council* [1985] 2 EGLR 49, CA.
118 *McDougall v Easington District Council* [1989] 1 EGLR 93, CA.
119 *Bishop v Consolidated London Properties Ltd* (1933) 102 LJKB 257 (where the landlord carried out regular inspections).
120 *British Telecommunications plc v Sun Life Assurance Society plc* [1996] Ch 69, CA; PF Smith [1997] Conv 59.
121 *Melles & Co v Holme* [1918] 2 KB 100.

defect is located in the premises let to the tenant.[122] This condition is justified by a need to avoid the landlord having constantly to exercise vigilance over the property.[123] The fact that the tenant has exclusive possession of the house or flat has been also advanced as a reason for the condition, since the tenant is best able to report to the landlord about disrepair within the premises.[124] Yet the notice exception extends to defects in existence prior to the commencement of the term,[125] which are not likely to be known or discoverable by short-residential tenant. It makes no difference that the landlord has an implied right to inspect and so to enter and repair under LTA 1985, s 11(6).

The tenant must give the landlord such information as would make him, as a reasonable landlord, inquire into the position, whether by letter or report.[126] Provided the tenant states in general terms what is amiss, he is not required to give information as to the precise degree of disrepair.[127] The type of defect is irrelevant, be it patent or latent. In the case of latent defects, the result of the notice rule may be to deprive the tenant of damages owing to a defect suddenly manifesting itself without warning, so that where a ceiling fell in on the tenant, injuring him, owing to an unknown defect, the landlord, who had no notice, was not liable in damages.[128] Though at one time, it appeared that the tenant had to give notice personally, the rule has been relaxed so that notice may now be given by a third party such as a landlord's rent-collector (or agent) or officer or employee.[129]

Except in relation to any parts of premises not demised to the lessee but which fall within LTA 1985, s 11(1A), where his obligation to keep in repair is absolute, the landlord is only in breach of covenant under LTA 1985, s 11 if, after a reasonable time from his being given notice, he fails, following any necessary inquiries, to carry out the necessary works to cure any defects.[130] What is a reasonable time is a question of

---

122 *McCarrick v Liverpool Corpn* [1947] AC 219, HL; *O'Brien v Robinson* [1973] AC 912, HL. No notice is required where the disrepair and consequent damage to the tenant's premises arises in a part retained by the landlord: *Passley v London Borough of Wandsworth* (1996) 30 HLR 165, CA. Thus, where damage was caused to a tenant by a vandalised sewage stack, which was in a part of the premises retained by the landlord, the landlord was liable with no need for notice: *Bavage v Southwark LBC* [1998] CLY 3623.

123 See *McCarrick v Liverpool Corpn* [1947] AC 219, HL.

124 *Austin v Bonney* [1999] Qd R 114 at 119.

125 *Uniproducts (Manchester) Ltd v Rose Furnishers Ltd* [1956] 1 All ER 146, [1956] 1 WLR 45.

126 Eg a valuation report to the landlord: *Hall v Howard* [1988] 2 EGLR 75, CA. Notice does not have to take the form of a complaint by the tenant: ibid.

127 *Griffin v Pillett* [1926] 1 KB 17; *Al Hassani v Merrigan* (1987) 20 HLR 238, CA.

128 *O'Brien v Robinson* [1973] AC 912; [1973] 1 All ER 583, HL.

129 *McGreal v Wake* [1984] 1 EGLR 42, CA; *Dinefwr Borough Council v Jones* [1987] 2 EGLR 58, CA.

130 *Porter v Jones* [1942] 2 All ER 570, CA (landlord who failed for eight months from notice to remedy disrepair held liable in damages); also *Morris v Liverpool City Council* [1988] 1 EGLR 47, CA (a few days' wait for emergency repairs not on facts unreasonable).

fact and it will be short in the case of urgently required repairs.[131] However, attempts have been made in 'tenants' charters' to set out time-limits for carrying out repairs after the landlord has notice. For example, under the shorthold tenant's charter produced by the Housing Corporation, it is stated[132] that the landlord 'should have deadlines for dealing with repairs'. The response times should, it is said, be no more than 24 hours for emergency repairs, seven calendar days for urgent repairs and one calendar month for routine repairs.[133]

IV CONSTRUCTION OF EXPRESS COVENANT TO REPAIR

Scope of express covenants

It is in the interest of the landlord to see to it that his building or premises are kept in a proper state of repair and maintenance during the lease. Where special statutory rules do not apply, the allocation and extent of the liability for repairing and other work is for the parties to determine. Both factors may vary with the nature and intended use of the building. Thus, where there is a newly-built or mature office block or block of flats in the occupation of many tenants, it may be more convenient for the landlord to undertake liability for at least structural and major repairs and maintenance and for the tenants to contribute to the cost of the work,[134] so making the landlord's obligation a right of recovery.[135] In the case of a single building or unit such as a factory, the tenant may undertake a general obligation to repair the demised premises. The court will strive to avoid interpreting a lease so as to produce an overlapping repairing obligation as between the landlord and the tenant or tenants.[136]

Liability under a covenant to repair, or to keep in repair, runs as from the date of the lease. Therefore, if a head lease and subsequently granted sub-lease contain identical covenants to repair, the standard expected from the two leases may be different even

---

131 *McGreal v Wake* [1984] 1 EGLR 42, CA (eight weeks from repair notice held a reasonable time on facts).

132 At p 11. The Housing Corporation's Secure Tenant's Charter contains identical aspirations (because in the latter Charter it is admitted that the time-limits for repair after notice are no more than 'performance standards' as opposed to a 'right based in law').

133 If the reasoning in *Re S (Children: care plan)* [2002] UKHL 10, [2002] 2 All ER 192 is applied by analogy to the aspirations in the relevant Charters, their breach would not appear, ipso facto, to give rise to a cause of action by a tenant, since no express deadlines are given for curing disrepair by legislation.

134 There is a summary of the practice of commercial landlords and tenants in 'Monitoring the Code of Practice for Commercial Leases' (2000) DETR.

135 *Plough Investment Ltd v Manchester City Council* [1989] 1 EGLR 244 at 247. If the landlord carries out works (at his choice) to an unreasonably high cost, beyond what the tenants could reasonably be expected to pay, then the excess seemingly is irrecoverable at common law: see *Fluor Daniel Properties Ltd v Shortlands Investments Ltd* [2001] 2 EGLR 103.

136 *Petersson v Pitt Place (Epsom) Ltd* [2001] EWCA Civ 86, [2001] L & TR 21, [2001] L & TR 238 (where questions arose as to which party had to repair roof terraces, where the landlord had to repair the main structure of the building and the lessees each had to repair their flat).

if the language of each covenant is identical.[137] Liability is limited in the case of a tenant or sub-tenant to the exact premises let, which may raise issues of fact as to what precisely is covered, if the language of the lease is less than clear.[138]

It may still be the case, as a matter of general principle, that a landlord's covenant to keep in repair (or merely to repair) is construed in the same way as would be a tenant's obligation.[139] In the absence of a term in the lease rendering it unnecessary, no notice is required to the landlord before he is liable under a covenant to keep in repair, save in relation to the premises demised to the tenant.[140] The landlord is under an absolute obligation in relation to any non-demised premises. By contrast, where notice is exceptionally required, he is liable to the tenant in damages only if he fails within a reasonable time of notice to carry out the necessary work. However, some landlords' obligations may be construed more widely than similar obligations of tenants. Thus the landlord of a new office building who expressly undertook to 'maintain repair amend renew ... and otherwise keep in good and tenantable condition' certain exterior and structural parts of the building was obliged by this covenant to replace inherently defective external cladding, even though the work went well beyond repair.[141] By contrast, a mere obligation to keep in repair did not oblige a landlord to replace metal frame windows by wooden-frame windows, where the former were not damaged, in order to alleviate severe condensation in a house.[142] There was no condition of disrepair. Likewise, the tenants of an office building who were under a general covenant to repair, were held not liable to waterproof the basement, to protect it from its propensity, caused by an inherent design fault, to allow water penetration, where at the date of the hearing the basement was dry and apparently undamaged by an earlier entry of water. The fact that the basement suffered from an inherent design fault made no difference.[143] It appears therefore that a general covenant to repair does not require the tenant to improve the premises in any way, save in so far as incidentally required as part of a repair.

The courts in interpreting repairing and related obligations take into account the words used in the covenant in issue. They also take into account the surrounding circumstances and if there is some ambiguity in the covenant they will try to make

137 *Ebbetts v Conquest* [1895] 2 Ch 377, CA.
138 See eg *London Underground Ltd v Shell International Petroleum Co Ltd* [1998] EGCS 97 ('underside' of a floor did not include columns and girders). Also *Ibrahim v Dovecorn Reversions* [2001] 2 EGLR 46.
139 *Torrens v Walker* [1906] 2 Ch 166.
140 *British Telecommunications plc v Sun Life Assurance Society plc* [1995] 3 WLR 622, CA; see Wilkinson (1995) 145 NLJ 1793.
141 *Crédit Suisse v Beegas Nominees Ltd* [1994] 4 All ER 803.
142 *Quick v Taff-Ely Borough Council* [1986] QB 809, [1985] 3 All ER 321, CA (obligation under LTA 1985, s 11).
143 *Post Office v Aquarius Properties Ltd* [1987] 1 All ER 1055, CA; PF Smith [1987] Conv 224. As a result, no-one was liable at that stage to cure the defect. This was a 'remarkable case' where intellect may have taken precedence over any other process (per Harman J in *Minja Properties Ltd v Cussins Property Group plc* [1998] 2 EGLR 52 at 55). However, it was treated as sound law in *Lee v Leeds City Council* [2002] EWCA Civ 06, [2002] 1 WLR 1488.

commercial common sense of the wording of the obligation.[144] The Court of Appeal indicated that little assistance was to be obtained from looking (at least in the first instance) at the way covenants to repair in other leases had been construed since the court had to give a full meaning to each word of the covenant and proper and full effect to the context.[145] There are variations, after all, in the language used in repairing obligations. Thus a tenant may undertake to 'repair', which suggests a modest level of obligation, or the tenant may have to 'keep in good and substantial repair'. According to the Australian High Court, this obligation requires the covenantor to undertake a higher standard of maintenance 'such that the condition of the premises is both good and substantially sound' although the premises did not have to be put into 'mint condition'.[146]

The common law places limits on the scope of a tenant's general covenant to repair. As well as declining to hold a tenant liable for improvements to the premises,[147] it holds that he is only liable for subordinate renewal, and not for the complete rebuilding of the premises. Three questions have been posed by the Court of Appeal in determining on which side of this difficult dividing line work fell:

1   whether an alteration went to substantially the whole of the structure or only to a subsidiary part;
2   whether the effect of the alterations was to produce a building of a wholly different character to that let; and
3   as to the cost of the works in relation to the previous value of the building and their effect on its value and life-span.[148]

Implicit, however, in the concept of repair is the notion of replacing a damaged item with its exact or nearest modern equivalent. Thus a tenant who wished to replace an underfloor heating system (which in fact could have been brought into working order, albeit at some considerable cost) with night storage heaters, which were cheap to install, was not entitled to claim that such work would comply with its obligation to repair.[149]

In the end, much depends on the exact words of covenant and the precise factual context in which they appear, including the variety of tenancy or lease at issue. Thus, the tenant of a building with a rusty steel frame at the date of the lease was held not

144 *Holding & Barnes plc v Hill House Hammond Ltd* [2000] L & TR 428 at 432 -33; on appeal [2002] EWCA Civ 1334 paras 14-18.
145 *Fincar SRL v 109/113 Mount Street Management Co Ltd* [1999] L & TR 161, CA.
146 *Alcatel Australia Ltd v Scarcella* (1998) 44 NSWLR 349 at 354 (Windeyer J).
147 See eg *Mullaney v Maybourne Grange (Croydon) Management Co Ltd* [1986] 1 EGLR 70 (replacement windows not within tenant obligation to pay for repairs, where their cost was double that of repairing the existing windows); also *Minja Properties Ltd v Cussins Property Co Ltd* [1998] 2 EGLR 52 (where on the facts replacing worn-out window frames with windows of a different and better design was repairing and maintenance work, the element of improvement in design being seemingly dismissed as minimal).
148 *McDougall v Easington District Council* [1989] 1 EGLR 93, CA.
149 *Creska Ltd v Hammersmith and Fulham London BC* [1998] 3 EGLR 35.

liable to pay for the cost of extensive work to eliminate the rusting, but only to cure the immediate, visible, damage produced by that defect.[150] A statutory tenant holding a lease originally granted for a period of seven and a quarter years, who was expressly obliged to put the premises in good and substantial repair and to substantially repair and maintain them, was held not liable to pay for the installation of a damp proof course and to cure dampness at a total cost of some £15,000.[151] The Court of Appeal took into account the circumstances of the particular tenancy, and of the particular house: installing a new and comprehensive damp proof system was a different type of operation to simply dealing with the consequences of damp (which latter works would amount to a repair). The house never had a damp-proof course when built. By contrast, a lessee under a general covenant to repair was bound, as part of repairing defective stone cladding, to pay for the insertion of new expansion joints, as these formed a trivial part of the whole building and no competent engineer would have allowed the work to be done without these joints.[152] Where a lease in terms envisaged that the lessees of an office building would have to contribute to renewals or replacements as well as to repairs, a lessee could not escape paying his share of the cost of installing a new roof with a better, more storm-resistant design, merely on the ground that the design was an improvement on that of the old roof.[153]

Meaning of particular covenants

Some leases impose merely an obligation to repair on the landlord[154] or tenant. Others may go further and require the covenantor to put or keep the premises in repair or even in a specified condition. A breach of an obligation by a landlord, to keep premises not demised to the tenant in repair, has been held to take place as soon as the premises fall out of repair, so that damages were calculated as running from a date some two years before the repairs to cure disrepair to a floor of premises not demised to the tenant were put in hand by his defaulting mesne landlord.[155]

(i) To put in repair

A covenant by the tenant to put the demised premises into repair, at the commencement of the lease[156] or within a reasonable time thereafter, which is appropriate where the premises are dilapidated at the date of the demise, may specify a particular standard of

---

150 *Plough Investments Ltd v Manchester City Council* [1989] 1 EGLR 244.
151 *Eyre v McCracken* (2000) 80 P & CR 220, CA; PF Smith [2001] Conv 102.
152 *Ravenseft Properties Ltd v Davstone (Holdings) Ltd* [1980] QB 12, [1979] 1 All ER 929.
153 *New England Properties plc v Portsmouth New Shops Ltd* [1993] 1 EGLR 84.
154 According to Nicholls LJ in *British Telecommunications plc v Sun Life Assurance Society plc* [1995] 3 WLR 622 at 630, a landlord's obligation merely to repair premises is something of a rarity in modern leases.
155 *British Telecommunications plc v Sun Life Assurance Society plc* [1996] Ch 69, CA.
156 Ie within a reasonable time: *Doe d Pittman v Sutton* (1841) 9 C & P 706.

repairs. If not, the standard is that required to render the premises fit for the particular purpose for which they are let, and no more.[157] If the premises are dilapidated at the date of the demise, a covenant to keep them in repair impliedly involves a covenant first to put them into repair in any event.[158] In relation both to a covenant to put and to keep in repair, however, if the landlord cannot prove a condition of disrepair, ie deterioration from a former better condition, this particular rule has no application.[159]

(ii) To keep in repair

A covenant by the tenant (or a landlord) to keep premises in repair is an absolute covenant, and so presupposes that the premises have first been put by him, where they are dilapidated at the commencement of the term, into repair, and thereafter the tenant must keep them in repair throughout the term.[160] A covenant to keep in repair also necessarily requires the tenant to deliver up the premises in repair at the end of the lease. The standard of repairs is either that laid down in the lease, or that under the general law and if a Schedule of condition of the premises at the date of the demise is drawn up, it may be a guide to the required standard. Similar principles apply to a landlord who has undertaken to keep a building in a specified state and condition. He must undertake works required to put the premises in that condition, even if they have never been in that state, as where a landlord of an office building built with defective external cladding had to do the necessary works to prevent water ingress.[161]

(iii) To leave in repair

A separate obligation may be imposed on a tenant to leave the premises in repair, whether or not an obligation to keep in repair has been imposed. If only an obligation to leave in repair is imposed, then until the lease ends, the landlord cannot make any claim against the tenant for dilapidations.[162]

(iv) Fair wear and tear excepted

An exception for fair wear and tear is sometimes found in tenants' covenants to repair, particularly in short leases. This exception relieves the tenant from liability for disrepair arising both from the normal action of time and the elements, and from the normal and reasonable use of the premises by the tenant for the purpose for which they were let.[163]

---

157 *Belcher v McIntosh* (1839) 2 M & R 186.
158 *Proudfoot v Hart* (1890) 25 QBD 42, CA.
159 *Post Office v Aquarius Properties Ltd* [1987] 1 All ER 1055, CA.
160 *Proudfoot v Hart* (1890) 25 QBD 42, CA; also *Luxmore v Robson* (1818) 1 B & Ald 584.
161 *Crédit Suisse v Beegas Nominees Ltd* [1994] 4 All ER 803.
162 A breach of a covenant to leave in repair gives a separate cause of action to the landlord, even if the tenant covenanted to keep in repair: *Ebbetts v Conquest* (1900) 16 TLR 320.
163 *Terrell v Murray* (1901) 17 TLR 570; *Gutteridge v Munyard* (1834) 1 Mood & R 334.

An exception for fair wear and tear will excuse the tenant from liability for any repairs required solely due to the passage of time, but not from liability for repairs necessitated as the result of abnormal or extraordinary phenomena such as lightning, storm, flood, earthquake, fire or accident. An exception for fair wear and tear applies only to direct damage which the tenant proves is the result of the reasonable use of the premises and the ordinary operation of natural forces, and the tenant must see to it that the premises do not suffer more than the operation of time and nature would produce. If further dilapidations result from a cause which may ultimately be traceable back to fair wear and tear, the tenant is not excused from doing repairs necessary to cure the indirect damage.[164] Thus, while he might not be liable merely because a worn-out slate fell off the roof, he could not escape liability by pleading a fair wear and tear exception for water ingress into the premises through the resulting hole, and so his best remedy might be to replace the slate.

Standard of repair

The standard of repair required may be laid down in terms in the covenant to repair. The length of the lease is a relevant factor, and a lower standard of repairs may be expected under a short lease as opposed to a long lease. However, in one case, it was held that the tenant could not rely on his own neglect to comply with his repairing obligations so as to reduce the standard of repairs.[165] By contrast, a tenant's obligation to keep the interior of a flat held on a three-month protected tenancy obliged the tenant only to use the premises in a tenant-like manner.[166]

In the case of a *long lease*, the proper standard, if none is laid down in the lease, is that arrived at by assuming that the tenant has kept the premises in the same condition as a reasonably-minded owner would have kept them in, with full regard to the age of the building, its locality, the class of occupying tenant, and the maintenance of the property in such a way that an average amount of annual repair only was necessary.[167]

In the case of a *short lease*, the rule is derived from a case where a house was let for three years and the tenant was under an express obligation to keep the premises in good tenantable repair.[168] This required such repair as, having regard to the age, character and locality of the house, would make it reasonably fit for the occupation of a reasonably minded tenant of the class who would be likely to take it. It was said that the age of the house must be taken into account because a 200-year-old house would not be expected to be in the same condition as a new house. Its locality was relevant

---

164 *Haskell v Marlow* [1928] 2 KB 45, approved in *Regis Property Co v Dudley* [1959] AC 370, [1958] 3 All ER 491, HL.
165 *Ladbrooke Hotels Ltd v Sandhu* [1995] 2 EGLR 92 (rent review).
166 *Firstcross Ltd v Teasdale* (1982) 47 P & CR 228.
167 *Anstruther-Gough-Calthorpe v McOscar* [1924] 1 KB 716, CA.
168 *Proudfoot v Hart* (1890) 25 QBD 42, CA.

because houses in Grosvenor Square required a wholly different standard of repair to those in Spitalfields. The character of the house was relevant, because repairs appropriate for a palace would not be so for a cottage. If a reasonably minded incoming tenant would not require redecorations, then these need not be done; however, if damp had caused the paper to peel off the walls, it would have to be replaced. The quality of decorations need not be better than the original quality. The standard of repair imposed by this case is a subjective one,[169] in the sense that it may be that, during the life of the lease, the requirements of incoming tenants will be greater or lower than those prevailing at the start of the lease. This obligation only requires the court to 'have regard to' the matters mentioned and it does not directly relate the standard of repair to the intended use, if any, of the premises, and it requires the standard of repair to be decided as at the commencement, and not the termination, of the lease.

Interpreting covenants to repair

Compliance with a covenant to keep the property in repair, or to repair, will in principle involve work of subordinate renewal: replacing the damaged parts of the property with new, undamaged parts. The issue is whether the work is, as a matter of fact and degree, a repair or whether it involves substantially renewing the whole, or almost the whole, of the demised premises, in which case the work is outside a repairing covenant.[170] The circumstances to be taken into account in a particular case may, it has been held, include all or some of the following:

1   the nature of the building;
2   the terms of the lease;
3   the nature and extent of the defect;
4   the nature, extent and cost of proposed remedial works;
5   at whose cost the works are to be done;
6   the value of the building and its expected life-span;
7   current building practice;
8   the likelihood of a recurrence if one remedy rather than another is adopted; and
9   the comparative cost of alternative remedial works and their impact on the use and enjoyment of the building by the occupants.[171]

However, it should be borne in mind that much depends on the facts of each case and the wording of each covenant.

---

169 It does apply, however, to equipment such as air-conditioning plant (see *Land Securities plc v Westminster City Council (No 2)* [1995] 1 EGLR 245) or fire protection equipment (see *Shortlands Investments Ltd v Cargill* [1995] 1 EGLR 51).
170 *Ravenseft Properties Ltd v Davstone (Holdings) Ltd* [1980] QB 12, [1979] 1 All ER 929.
171 *Holding and Management Ltd v Property Holding and Investment Trust plc* [1990] 1 All ER 938, CA.

No liability to execute any remedial work can arise unless there is proved to be a condition of disrepair in the premises.[172] To overcome the general law, the parties may agree to exclude or limit any liability they might otherwise be under to cure inherent design faults in the structure of the premises, where newly-built: express words are required to achieve this.[173] Otherwise, liability to cure design faults is a question of interpretation of the particular covenant to repair. If a design fault produces a condition of disrepair, and the only sensible way of executing the work is, in the process, to cure the design fault, then a repairing covenant will require the party subject to it to pay for all the remedial work, although to some minor extent he is improving the design of the premises. Accordingly, a landlord was held liable to replace a worn-out (and originally defectively-designed) front door with a new one of a different design as the only sensible way of complying with his repairing covenant,[174] but not liable to replace metal-frame windows or to insulate lintels, neither of which items were out of repair, in order to cure a design fault in a council house, which produced severe condensation.[175]

The *method and extent of repairs* is a question of fact and degree. 'In the end', it was once said, '... the question is whether the ordinary speaker of English would consider that the word "repair" as used in the covenant was appropriate to describe the work'.[176] Sometimes, a repairing obligation will involve replacing the whole of the damaged article, say the whole roof,[177] but sometimes mere patching-up of an admittedly old roof or other item will suffice.[178] However, in a recent case it was held that a reconditioning of all affected heating and air-conditioning units was sufficient compliance with a lessee's repairing obligation.[179] Indeed, 'if there is more than one method of repair which a reasonable practical surveyor would support, then it is for the covenantor to choose which method of repair to adopt'.[180] It may be that a covenant extends beyond mere repairs to cover significant renewals, such as the replacement of an old roof which had been blown away in a severe storm with a new roof of a better design.[181]

172 Thus if a latent defect (which has not yet produced physical damage) threatens to one day cause a total collapse of the whole premises, the tenant is not liable to cure that defect: see *Clowes v Bentley Pty Ltd* [1970] WAR 24.
173 See eg *Precedents for the Conveyancer* Vol 1, pp 5-66. Also Taylor (2001) 5 L&T Rev 18, suggesting eg defining what is meant by 'defect'; inserting a landlord's obligation to rectify a defect and excluding liability on the lessee's part to carry out such work or to pay for it as a service charge.
174 *Stent v Monmouth District Council* [1987] 1 EGLR 59, CA.
175 *Quick v Taff-Ely Borough Council* [1986] QB 809, [1985] 3 All ER 321, CA.
176 Per Hoffmann J in *Post Office v Aquarius Properties Ltd* [1985] 2 EGLR 105 at 107C.
177 As in *Elite Investments Ltd v T I Bainbridge Silencers Ltd* [1986] 2 EGLR 43.
178 *Murray v Birmingham City Council* [1987] 2 EGLR 53, CA. Also *Scottish Mutual Assurance plc v Jardine Public Relations Ltd* [1999] EGCS 43 (where short-term repairs to a roof to plug leaks were held sufficient to last for the rest of the lease, and that it was not possible for the landlords to charge the lessees for work whose benefit would outlast the leases).
179 *Ultraworth Ltd v General Accident Fire and Life Assurance Corpn plc* [2000] L & TR 495.
180 *Ultraworth Ltd v General Accident Fire and Life Assurance Corpn plc* [2000] L & TR 495 at 504.
181 *New England Properties plc v Portsmouth New Shops Ltd* [1993] 1 EGLR 84.

Repair and renewal

Repair involves, in law, the renewal of subordinate parts of the premises so as to leave the damaged article so far as possible as though not damaged.[182] Repair therefore may involve replacing a worn-out or damaged article with one that is brand new, corresponding as closely as possible to the original. A tenant subject to a general covenant to repair is not required to give back at the end of the lease premises different in kind from the original subject matter of the demise, such as a house with properly-built foundations where it had poorly-built ones formerly. Equally, the mere fact that remedial work involves the replacement of a faultily-constructed subordinate part of the premises is no defence to liability to pay for the full cost of the remedial work.[183]

The exact scope of a general covenant to repair may be difficult to determine. For this reason, perhaps, some leases have attempted to set out in precise detail the obligations of the landlord or tenant, in such a way as to extend beyond the concept of repairs. Thus in one case the landlord undertook to 'maintain repair amend renew ... and otherwise keep in good tenantable condition' the structure of certain new office premises.[184] The result of the case has been noted earlier. The High Court refused, in holding the words to extend the landlord's obligations beyond mere repairs, to give anything other than a natural meaning to these (wide) words. It did not treat them as though contained in a standard form of covenant or contract.

Returning to a general covenant to repair, in relation to older premises, it has been held that a covenant to repair does not bind a party to give back totally new premises, but only premises in proper repair, allowing for the effects of time.[185] The terms of the covenant and the age of the premises are relevant factors.[186] If, therefore, the result of work of renovation would be to give the landlord premises totally different in kind from those let at the outset, such works lie outside the scope of repairs. This defence results from a case[187] where the tenants of a 100-year-old house on a seven-year lease covenanted that they 'when and where and as often as occasion shall require will sufficiently and substantially repair, uphold, sustain, maintain, amend and keep' the premises. The house was demolished at the end of the lease due to its dangerous condition. To have saved it would have required (in place of the old foundations which were a timber platform resting on muddy ground) underpinning of the house with new and proper foundations through 17 feet of mud to solid ground. The tenant

---

182 *Anstruther-Gough-Calthorpe v McOscar* [1924] 1 KB 716, CA. Thus, the replacement of electrical wiring fell within a lessee's covenant: see *Roper v Prudential Assurance Co Ltd* [1992] 1 EGLR 5.

183 *Ravenseft Properties Ltd v Davstone (Holdings) Ltd* [1980] QB 12, [1979] 1 All ER 929.

184 *Crédit Suisse v Beegas Nominees Ltd* [1994] 4 All ER 803, 817-18.

185 *Lister v Lane and Nesham* [1893] 2 QB 212 at 216-17, CA.

186 *Gutteridge v Munyard* (1834) 1 Mood & R 334.

187 *Lister v Lane and Nesham* [1893] 2 QB 212; also *Sotheby v Grundy* [1947] 2 All ER 761 and *Halliard Property Co Ltd v Nicholas Clarke Investments Ltd* [1984] 1 EGLR 45. These principles were recently followed in *Weatherhead v Deka New Zealand Ltd* [2000] 1 NZLR 23 (where in effect the materials used to build the premises had completely worn out).

was held not liable to pay for the costs of re-building the house. In no case, held the Court of Appeal, is a tenant bound under repair, to pay for work which would give back to the landlord a new and different thing from the premises as let at the start of the tenancy.[188]

Similarly, a landlord has been held not liable under repair, to rid an old house of damp, which was built without a damp course.[189] A tenant, likewise, was held sufficiently to have complied with a covenant to repair by replacing an elaborate but unsafe bay window with a new window, flush with the main walls: he was not obliged to provide new supports where the old were improperly built in the first place.[190] This is because, as noted, neither the landlord nor the tenant is bound, under a covenant to repair, to improve the design of the premises or items in it such as fixtures. Accordingly, a landlord who replaced wooden windows with double-glazed windows, where the old windows could, at half the cost, have been repaired, failed to recover any part of the cost of the work from the tenant.[191] If a covenant enables work going beyond mere repairs to be carried out, the basic design of the premises or part may be improved.[192]

Equally, the mere fact that remedial work is shown to involve substantial but subordinate renewal, will not of itself take the matter out of a general covenant to repair. Whether one is dealing with older or new premises, the issue is to be decided by taking into account the matters already discussed. This is ultimately a matter of fact and degree.[193] The view has been expressed that the cost of the work rather than the value of the building as repaired should be stressed if the two are seriously divergent.[194] Any repair involves subordinate renewal, and if at the completion of the work, what is done has left the premises substantially the same as when let, then the work normally falls on the repair side of the line. In a leading case,[195] the front wall of a 200-year-old house had to be demolished following a dangerous structure notice, and it was re-built from ground level, in compliance with modern requirements, but it was a similar wall to that it replaced. The tenants had to pay for the cost: what was done being the renewal or replacement of a defective part. The covenant in that case was very strong, requiring the tenant to repair and keep in thorough repair and good condition: this meant that if

---

188 There is no rule that the cost of underpinning may not have to be borne as part of a lessees' repairing covenant: see eg *Alexander v Lambeth London BC* [2000] CLY 3931.

189 *Pembery v Lamdin* [1940] 2 All ER 434, CA; also *Wainwright v Leeds City Council* (1984) 82 LGR 657, CA (council house); but cf *Elmcroft Developments Ltd v Tankersley-Sawyer* [1984] 1 EGLR 47, CA (defective damp-course to be replaced with proper course at cost of landlord under general covenant).

190 *Wright v Lawson* (1903) 19 TLR 510, CA.

191 *Mullaney v Maybourne Grange (Croydon) Management Co Ltd* [1986] 1 EGLR 70.

192 *Sutton (Hastoe) Housing Association v Williams* [1988] 1 EGLR 56, CA (old windows could be replaced, accordingly, with windows of a better design).

193 *Brew Bros Ltd v Snax (Ross) Ltd* [1970] 1 QB 612, [1970] 1 All ER 587, CA.

194 *Elite Investments Ltd v T I Bainbridge Silencers Ltd* [1986] 2 EGLR 43. This case was concerned with extensive roofing repairs.

195 *Lurcott v Wakely and Wheeler* [1911] 1 KB 905, CA.

need be, the tenant must replace part after part until the whole was, in due course, replaced.

Further, while the age and nature of a building may qualify the meaning of a covenant, of themselves they cannot relieve a tenant (or landlord) from his obligation. Where, however, a structure has been built for a special use, and is now obsolete, it has been said that the lessee could plead the Leasehold Property (Repairs) Act 1938 to avoid liability to repair it.[196]

The possible extent of liability is shown by the fact that a tenant under a general and unqualified covenant to repair was held liable to pay for the cost of replacing defective outside stone cladding with new and properly constructed stone cladding, the cost of this being only a small fraction of the total replacement cost of the whole building.[197] In addition, a long-lessee's repairing obligation was construed as not limited to work needed to preserve for the 15-year 'commercial life' a defectively-built structure, rather than much more costly work to provide for a properly-built edifice for the duration of the lease.[198] It may be possible for a tenant to escape liability by showing that the defectively-built part of the premises cannot be saved and that it is a separate entity, so that to rebuild it would lie outside the scope of his covenant, as where a tenant was held not liable to replace to correct standards an unstable and 'jerry-built' structure built after the main premises had been constructed, which had collapsed.[199]

In view of the financial risk to which tenants of new buildings are exposed, the tenant may wish to obtain a covenant from the landlord to remedy any inherent defect in the building, so limiting the repairing obligation, or a collateral warranty from the building contractor and all persons involved in the design and supervision of the work.[200] The benefit to a tenant of a landlord's express structural design guarantee was shown where the landlord of a restaurant covenanted to keep the main walls and roof in good structural repair and condition throughout the lease and to make good all defects due to faulty materials or workmanship. The foundations had been faultily built so that extensive remedial work became necessary, for which the landlord was liable under his unqualified obligation, the work being within the contemplation of the parties when the lease was entered into.[201]

Repair involving painting

The tenant may expressly undertake a separate obligation to repaint the exterior and interior of the demised premises, at say, five- or seven-yearly intervals, in the case of

196 *Ladbrooke Hotels Ltd v Sandhu* [1995] 2 EGLR 92.
197 *Ravenseft Properties Ltd v Davstone (Holdings) Ltd* [1980] QB 12, [1979] 1 All ER 929.
198 *Ladbrooke Hotels Ltd v Sandhu* [1995] 2 EGLR 92.
199 *Halliard Property Co Ltd v Nicholas Clarke Investments Ltd* [1984] 1 EGLR 45.
200 Whereupon the landlord could then agree with the contractor that the benefit of the warranty is to be sued on by the tenant for the time being, enabling successors to the lease to bring an action: Contracts (Rights of Third Parties) Act 1999, s 1.
201 *Smedley v Chumley & Hawke* (1981) 44 P & CR 50, CA.

long leases, or at the end of the term, in the case of short leases. An obligation to paint in a specific year operates as soon as that year commences.[202] Some leases may provide that the tenant is to keep the property in good decorative condition and to redecorate it in the last six months of the lease to the landlord's reasonable specification.[203]

Even where the tenant is not under a specific obligation to paint, but only a general covenant to keep in good tenantable repair (or some similar obligation), he will be obliged to carry out whatever painting is necessary to preserve the woodwork and decorations from decay, to a standard sufficient for the requirements of reasonably-minded incoming tenants, bearing in mind the standard of the locality of the premises.[204]

V PAYMENT FOR REPAIRS: CONTROL OF SERVICE CHARGES

Introduction

Where the tenant holds a lease of a unit or floor within a larger building, or is a long-lessee in a block of residential flats, the arrangement for repairs and maintenance may well be that the landlord will undertake an obligation to keep in repair and to maintain the structure and exterior of the relevant building, and to maintain the common parts and installations. In return, the landlord becomes entitled to recover service charges from each unit tenant. These sums may be reserved as rent, so that the landlord may be able to distrain for unpaid service charges, and in any case treat unpaid service charges as rent arrears. The whole subject of service charges is fraught with difficulty and technicality, if only because tenants may think that they may be in danger of being made to pay for work which is to an unnecessarily high standard, or which will outlast their period of leasing, or that the service charges would be reduced if the landlord carried out one method of repairs rather than another. In what follows, there is a necessarily brief examination of the principal safeguards available to tenants generally and also to residential tenants against misuse by landlords of service charges to make a profit or to overcharge lessees.

Controls at common law

(i) Recovery of overpayments

There must be clear words charging the tenant to pay service charges for the specific items claimed: if these are not present the landlord can only have charging words

---

202 *Kirklinton v Wood* [1917] 1 KB 332; assuming the EU regulations referred to in ch 4, above
 apply to residential leases, obligations to paint at specified times might be within their ambit.
203 See Taylor (2001) 5 L & T Rev 18.
204 *Proudfoot v Hart* (1890) 25 QBD 42, CA.

inserted if the lease can be rectified.[205] Moreover, if a service charges clause states that the sums due are to be paid in advance of the work being done,[206] and it then turns out that the landlord was not entitled to charge for the work (as where the work went outside the scope of a repairing and maintenance obligation) then the tenant can bring an action in restitution for recovery of overpaid service charges. Recovery is possible, therefore, provided there is a mistake of law or of fact. If the landlord has changed its position since the payment was made, this would act as a bar to recovery, but at present it is not clear what the landlord would need to prove to establish this. Time will run against the tenant from the time the mistake was discovered, or the time from which the mistake ought with reasonable diligence have been found out.[207] This may not be the same time as the payment was made, and could lead to the re-opening of stale claims some years after payments have been made. Claims could relate to one payment or to a series, depending on the circumstances. On the other hand, the policy of the law as re-examined by the House of Lords is that the landlord is not entitled to retain moneys to which he is not entitled, otherwise he would become unjustly enriched at the expense of the tenant. It has thus been held that where five overpayments of rent (the same would apply to service charges) had been made under a mistake of fact, these could be recovered from the landlords and so refunded to the tenants. It was no defence to the landlord that he honestly thought the sums were due, or that he was entitled to full amounts rather than some lesser sum.[208] It has been claimed[209] that recovery under this principle of restitution will now be possible if (in our context) service charges paid by a tenant to a landlord are held by agreement, or in court or a tribunal not to be due to the landlord, provided that the tenant can prove that when paying, they believed that they would obtain reimbursement if the sums concerned were held not to be due. Past accounts will therefore be examinable to see if erroneous payments have been made on this basis, given that time runs from discovery of the mistake, not the date of payment.

(ii) Interpretation of clauses

The landlord has a privilege of charging for work covered by service charges,[210] which he is entitled to carry out: clearly there is a danger of overcharging and of charging for items which fall outside the landlord's repairing and maintenance obligations. Although

205 *Reston Ltd v Hudson* [1990] 2 EGLR 51 (external windows not demised to lessees, hence no service charges on that account).
206 In *P & O Property Holdings v International Computers Ltd* [1999] 2 EGLR 17, it was noted that ordinarily service charge liability was not suspended by the operation of a rent suspension clause.
207 *Kleinwort Benson Ltd v Lincoln City Council* [1998] 4 All ER 513, [1998] 3 WLR 1095, HL. See Thompson [1999] Conv 40; also Lamont (1999) 3 L&T Rev 12.
208 *Nurdin and Peacock plc v DB Ramsden & Co Ltd (No 2)* [1999] 1 EGLR 15.
209 Brock *Estates Gazette* 6 March 1999, p 173.
210 Hence a claim to unpaid service charges can be subject to an equitable set off: see *Filross Securities Ltd v Midgeley* [1998] 3 EGLR 43, CA; also *Unchained Growth III plc v Granby Village (Manchester) Management Co Ltd* [2000] L & TR 186 (where set off was excluded).

the landlord is entitled to recover reasonably incurred expenditure to meet the maintenance costs concerned, so that underpayments of charges must in principle be made good to the landlord, even if the landlord undercharged in error, [211] the operation of service charges clauses contain dangers for lessees. To meet these, the courts construe service charge clauses strictly, although not to produce an absurd result,[212] and they disallow evasions of their jurisdiction.[213] There is, first, an overriding principle that requires that it is an implied term of all service charges clauses that costs must be reasonably and properly incurred: if they are not then the sums are irrecoverable.[214] If the original basis of calculation of a service charge was fair, but becomes unfair during the lease, the landlord can only recover up to what the court judges to be a reasonable sum from the tenant.[215] In addition to this overriding rule, service charge clauses, as landlords' clauses, are construed narrowly as respects items recoverable under them. Thus, a clause entitling a landlord to recover for legal and other costs incurred in obtaining service charges from any tenant, from lessees generally, was confined to costs incurred in litigation.[216] A clause which enabled the recovery of the costs of repairs did not entitle the landlord to carry out improvements to the design of certain windows and then to charge the tenants for the latter work.[217] Service charge clauses are construed with the rest of the lease, on ordinary contract principles. Thus, a clause was interpreted as allowing increased charges for heating only where there had been fuel cost increases as opposed to increases in central heating costs as a whole.[218] Service charge clauses which are taken to require consultation with lessees before any major work is embarked on by the landlord are likely to be held to involve the landlord first consulting (as by submitting estimates to the lessees for their comments) before doing the work, on pain of non-recovery of the charges.[219]

---

211 As in *Universities Superannuation Scheme Ltd v Marks and Spencer plc* [1999] L & TR 237.

212 See *Billson v Tristrem* [2000] L & TR 220, CA (where a clause was interpreted despite its wording as requiring lessees to contribute to charges for use of all common parts, not just those in fact used by an individual tenant); also *Gilje v Charlgrove Securities Ltd* [2001] EWCA Civ 1777, [2002] 16 EG 182.

213 Thus a term that a surveyors' or managing agents' certificate is conclusive as to the amount due is not capable of ousting the jurisdiction of the court or a tribunal to rule on the matter: *Re Davstone Estates Ltd's Lease* [1969] 2 Ch 378, [1969] 2 All ER 849; *Rapid Results College v Angell* [1986] 1 EGLR 53, CA.

214 *Finchbourne v Rodrigues* [1976] 3 All ER 581, CA.

215 *Pole Properties Ltd v Fineburg* (1981) 43 P & CR 121 (floor area basis had become unfair, so that tenant could only be charged for actual heating use).

216 *Morgan v Stainer* [1993] 2 EGLR 73.

217 *Mullaney v Maybourne Grange (Croydon) Management Co* [1986] 1 EGLR 70; however, express language can overcome this: see eg *Sutton (Hastoe) Housing Association v Williams* (1988) 20 HLR 321, CA.

218 *Jollybird Ltd v Fairzone Ltd* [1990] 1 EGLR 253.

219 See eg *Northways Flats Management Co (Camden) v Wimpey Pension Trustees Ltd* [1992] 2 EGLR 42; also *Yorkbrook Investments Ltd v Batten* [1985] 2 EGLR 100 and *CIN Properties Ltd v Barclays Bank plc* [1986] 1 EGLR 59.

Statutory controls for residential tenants

Parliament, as its suspicions of landlord malpractice have grown and its leaning towards tenants, perceived as consumers, has increased, has produced a battery of controls over service charges by landlords against tenants of houses and flats. These reflect the fact, judicially recognised, that it is of concern to tenants that they are not overcharged. Service charges can be a source of great friction between landlord and tenant.[220] The overall aim of the controls is, in the first place, to provide some protection, in the form of trust provisions, against insolvency or abuse of funds by the landlord leading to a loss of money supposed to provide for the maintenance of the property. Secondly, legislation entitles tenants on an individual basis to wide rights to be consulted and to information being provided about the service charges payable by them. Parliament also restricts the availability of forfeiture in the case of allegedly unpaid service charges[221] and also enables a manager to be appointed where there has been overcharging of tenants.[222]

1 Trust provisions. Service charges paid to the landlord or to some other person such as a managing agent must, together with all other service charges, be held by the payee as a single fund, or as separate funds, on trust to pay the matters covered and, subject to that, on trust for the contributing tenants for the time being.[223] In addition, to avoid two or more service charge funds being blended in one account,[224] the funds in question must be held in a separate account with a 'relevant financial institution', with tenant rights of account inspection, and there are criminal penalties for not complying with this particular requirement.[225]

2 Requirement of reasonableness. Residential tenants of houses and flats are given by legislation the right to resist excessive charges.[226] 'Relevant costs' (an expression which includes, notably, service charges and payments for insurance), cannot be recovered unless these have been reasonably incurred. In addition, the works or services in question must have been provided to a reasonable standard.[227] Both tenants

220 *Martin v Maryland Estates Ltd* [1998] 2 EGLR 81.
221 In relation to forfeiture, where premises are let as a dwelling, the landlord cannot forfeit the lease for non-payment of service or administration charges (such as payments towards landlord's costs) unless it has been finally determined by a leasehold valuation tribunal or a court that the amount in question is payable by the tenant (Housing Act 1996, s 81 as amended).
222 Under Landlord and Tenant Act 1987, Pt II, s 24, which applies where unreasonable service charges have been made or are proposed or likely, or where the trust and account provisions of Landlord and Tenant Act 1987, ss 42 or 42A are not complied with.
223 Landlord and Tenant Act 1987, s 42.
224 A problem which exercised the government: Commonhold and Leasehold Reform Consultation Paper (2000) Part II, Section 4, paras 9-12.
225 Landlord and Tenant Act 1987, ss 42A and 42B, added by CLRA 2002, s 154.
226 The definition of 'service charge' extends to improvements (LTA 1985, s 18(1)(a) as amedned by CLRA 2002, Sch 9, para 7). Such tenants have also a new right to refuse to pay an unreasonable 'administrative charge', such as a sum payable in connection with consents (CLRA 2002, Sch 11).
227 LTA 1985, s 19(1). What is 'reasonable' is a question of fact and degree: see eg *Wandsworth London BC v Griffin* [2000] 2 EGLR 105 (where it was reasonable for the landlord to have replaced certain windows with new double-glazed windows in the circumstances, eg that the lowest of six tenders had been accepted).

and also (as a precaution against future disputes) landlords have the right to apply to the leasehold valuation tribunal for a determination of whether 'relevant costs' on such matters as repairs, management or services have been incurred to a reasonable standard, and also whether, if certain such costs, again notably for repairs, management or insurance are to be incurred, they will have been incurred to such a standard.[228]

3 Consultation and information. Where there is a contract for specific works on a building or any other premises as well as for an agreement entered into by the landlord for a period of over 12 months, the latter type of agreement to be specified in regulations, the landlord can only recover service charges from tenants provided he complies with consultation requirements.[229] Where there is no long-term agreement with regard to charges, then if the amount concerned exceeds prescribed amounts from time to time in regulations, the excess over the prescribed amount cannot be recovered unless the consultation requirements have been complied with.[230] The extension of consultation requirements, which at one time only applied where amounts above prescribed amounts were at stake, is owing to the view of the government that long-term contracts or agreements for service provision of various kinds may have substantial cost implications for leaseholders even though the individual amounts of each head of charge may not exceed the prescribed amount. The government also thought that some landlords might deliberately manipulate work programmes so that no item triggered any requirement to consult.[231] In addition to these consultation requirements, each tenant who is liable to pay service charges is entitled to a statement of account within six months of the ending of the period of account concerned, which period cannot exceed 12 months.[232] If the tenant is not supplied with a statement of this kind in a timely fashion, the tenant has a statutory right to withhold service charges payments as specified.[233] Other rights of residential tenants with regard to service charges and

---

228 LTA 1985, s 19(2A) and (2B). See *R v London Leasehold Valuation Tribunal, ex p Daejan Properties Ltd* [2000] 3 EGLR 44. The High Court even ruled that a tenant can pay a sum which is disputed under protest, obtain a ruling and then recover that sum or part of it if the amount is held to be unreasonably incurred. However, this ruling was reversed on appeal [2001] EWCA Civ 1055 on the ground that once a charge had been paid, it was no longer 'payable' within LTA 1985, s 19(2A). Thus the section allowed an application with regard only to a current dispute. However, the latter ruling has been overturned by CLRA 2002, s 155, adding Landlord and Tenant Act 1985, s 27A.

229 LTA 1985, s 20 as substituted by CLRA 2001, s 151. The actual consultation requirements will be laid down in regulations. Consultation does not apply if the amount payable from any tenant for the works on a specific matter or under a long-term contract is below the sums specified in regulations. The consultation requirements may also be dispensed with following an application to the leasehold valuation tribunal: see *Wilson v Stone* [1998] 2 EGLR 155 (concerned with the original LTA 1985, s 20 but dealing with emergency repairs). Under the original s 20 'tenant' included a non-occupying intermediate tenant: *Heron Maple House Ltd v Central Estates Ltd* [2002] 13 EG 102.

230 LTA 1985, s 20(3) and (4).

231 Commonhold and Leasehold Reform Consultation Paper (2000) Part II, Section 3, Chapter v, para 21.

232 LTA 1985, s 21 as substituted by CLRA 2002, s 152.

233 LTA 1985, s 21A (added by ibid).

related payments include a wide right to inspect and to have copies made of accounts and related documents, and where a demand is made for payment of a service charge, it must be accompanied by a statement of the rights and obligations of tenants of dwellings in relation to service charges.[234]

VI LANDLORD'S REMEDIES FOR BREACH OF TENANT'S COVENANT TO REPAIR

The landlord has various remedies to enforce the tenant's covenant to repair, namely, entering and executing the repairs, forfeiture, and claiming damages.

Rights of entry to make landlord's repairs

There would be little point in statute conferring repairing obligations on, notably, landlords of short residential lessees, and not conferring correlative rights of entry, inspection and repair. For example, LTA 1985, s 11(6) implies a covenant by the lessee that a landlord who is subject to LTA 1985, s 11 may 'at reasonable times of the day and on giving 24 hours' notice in writing to the occupier, enter the premises ... for the purpose of viewing their condition and state of repair'.[235] The landlord of, notably, business or long residential tenants, has an implied licence, where he has no express right of entry and repair, to execute repairs for which he is liable.[236] This right is limited to what is strictly required to enable the work to be done, and no more. A right of entry to execute landlord's repairs is implied in the case of weekly tenancies,[237] because it must be in the contemplation of both parties that the tenant will not do such repairs; but in any case, a right of entry is implied if required to make the lease work, as where the landlord of a periodic tenant was held to have an implied right to enter and was thus, owing to the Defective Premises Act 1972, s 4, liable for the repair of a defective

---

234 As to inspection, see LTA 1985, Sch para 3 as substituted by CLRA 2002, Sch 11, para 9. While landlords can charge for copying, the charges, as administration charges, cannot exceed a reasonable amount: CLRA 2002, Sch 11). In addition, under LTA 1985, s 21B (inserted by CLRA 2002, s 153) a demand for payment of a service charge must be accompanied by a summary of the rights and obligations of tenants of dwellings in relation to service charges. The form and content of the summary is to be a matter for regulation. A tenant is entitled to withhold payment of a service charge if this requirement is not complied with and he cannot be subjected to forfeiture or other penalties while the statutory requirement is not complied with.

235 This carries with it an implied right to execute repairs. Rights of access and repair in the case of protected and statutory tenancies are conferred by Rent Act 1977, ss 148 and 3(2) and for assured tenancies by Housing Act 1988, s 16.

236 *Granada Theatres Ltd v Freehold Investment (Leytonstone) Ltd* [1959] Ch 592, [1959] 2 All ER 176, CA. In *Hammersmith London BC v Creska (No 2)* [2000] L & TR 288, the landlord had an express right of entry and repair on tenant default, but was refused a mandatory injunction in support of it, in discretion.

237 *Mint v Good* [1951] 1 KB 517, [1950] 2 All ER 1159, CA.

step.[238] The exclusive possession of the tenant is emphasised by the fact that an entry to carry out repairs which is not expressly or impliedly allowed, or permitted by statute, is illegal, even if the landlord himself could lose his own head lease if the repairs are not executed.[239]

Leasehold Property (Repairs) Act 1938

Special rules imposed by the Leasehold Property (Repairs) Act 1938 apply both to forfeiture actions and to damages claims against the tenant for breach of covenant to repair.[240]

The original object of the Leasehold Property (Repairs) Act 1938 was to prevent speculators buying up small property in an indifferent state of repair and serving Schedules of dilapidations on the tenants, with which the tenants could not comply. The Leasehold Property (Repairs) Act 1938 applies to most commercial and residential property, but it does not apply in four instances:

1 to a lease of an agricultural holding within the Agricultural Holdings Act 1986 or to a farm business tenancy (Leasehold Property (Repairs) Act 1938, s 7(1));
2 where the original length of the term is less than seven years (Leasehold Property (Repairs) Act 1938, s 7(1));
3 where at the date of service of the notice under LPA 1925, s 146(1), less than three years of the term are unexpired (Leasehold Property (Repairs) Act 1938, s 1(1)); and
4 to a breach of covenant or agreement which imposes on the lessee an obligation to put the premises into repair which is to be performed on the lessee taking possession or within a reasonable time thereafter (Leasehold Property (Repairs) Act 1938, s 3), so excluding an obligation to put into repair premises which are dilapidated at the commencement of the lease.

By the Leasehold Property (Repairs) Act 1938, s 1(1), where the landlord serves on the tenant a forfeiture notice under LPA 1925, s 146(1) which relates to a breach of covenant or agreement to keep or put in repair any of the demised premises, the tenant may within 28 days from that date serve a counter-notice on the landlord, claiming the benefit of the Leasehold Property (Repairs) Act 1938. At the date of service of the notice, three years or more of the term must remain unexpired.

Similarly, by the Leasehold Property (Repairs) Act 1938, s 1(2), a right to claim damages for such a breach of covenant cannot be enforced by action commenced at any time when the lease has an unexpired residue of three years or more to run, unless the landlord serves on the tenant not less than one month before the commencement of

238 *McAuley v Bristol City Council* [1991] 2 EGLR 64, CA.
239 *Stocker v Planet Building Society* (1879) 27 WR 877. Such entry may be restrained by an injunction: *Regional Properties Ltd v City of London Real Property Co Ltd* [1981] 1 EGLR 33.
240 See Blundell (1938/9) 3 Conv (NS) 10; PF Smith [1986] Conv 85.

the action a LPA 1925, s 146(1) notice. Again, the tenant may then by a 28-day counter-notice claim the benefit of the Leasehold Property (Repairs) Act 1938.

By the Leasehold Property (Repairs) Act 1938, s 1(4), in the case both of damages and forfeiture, the requisite LPA 1925, s 146(1) notice must, on pain of invalidity, contain a statement, in characters not less conspicuous than those used in any other part of the notice[241] to the effect that the tenant is entitled to serve on the landlord within 28 days of service of the s 146(1) notice, a counter-notice claiming the benefit of the Leasehold Property (Repairs) Act 1938; and the s 146(1) notice must also state a name and address for service of the counter-notice on the landlord.[242] The effect of service within the 28-day period of a counter-notice by the tenant is that no proceedings by action or otherwise may be taken by the landlord for the enforcement of any right of re-entry or forfeiture or for damages without the leave of the court (Leasehold Property (Repairs) Act 1938, s 1(3)). In the absence of any authority, it is believed that a notice served outside the 28-day period would be invalid as the Leasehold Property (Repairs) Act 1938, affects the landlord's substantive rights and is not simply procedural.

By Leasehold Property (Repairs) Act 1938, s 1(5), there are only five grounds under which leave may be given:

(a) that the immediate remedying of the breach is requisite for preventing substantial diminution in the value of the reversion, or that the value thereof has been substantially diminished by the breach;

(b) that the immediate remedying of the breach is required for giving effect in relation to the premises to the purposes of any enactment, or of any by-law or other provision having effect under an enactment, or for giving effect to any order of a court or requirement of any authority under an enactment or any such bylaw or provision as aforesaid;

(c) where the tenant is not in occupation of the whole premises as respects which the covenant or agreement is proposed to be enforced, that the immediate remedying of the breach is required in the interests of the occupier of those premises or of part thereof;

(d) that the breach can be immediately remedied at an expense that is relatively small in comparison with the much greater expense which would probably be occasioned by postponement of the necessary work; or

(e) special circumstances which in the opinion of the court render it just and equitable that leave should be given.

The terms of leave, if granted, are at the discretion of the court (Leasehold Property (Repairs) Act 1938, s 1(6)). The House of Lords has ruled that a landlord who applies for leave to proceed must prove his case to the ordinary civil standard of proof, that one (or more) of the leave requirements has been satisfied. Where, therefore, a landlord

---

241 Ie equally readable or equally sufficient: *Middlegate Properties Ltd v Messimeris* [1973] 1 All ER 645, [1973] 1 WLR 168, CA.

242 LPA 1925, s 196 applies to the service of a Leasehold Property (Repairs) Act 1938 counter-notice.

could not prove any substantial damage to his reversion, he failed to obtain leave, even though the premises, a redundant dock, were very seriously dilapidated. If the landlord cannot prove a ground within the Leasehold Property (Repairs) Act 1938, s 1(5), his application will be dismissed as of right and the threat of forfeiture will be removed. Should he establish a ground, the court may, at its discretion, adjourn or dismiss the application (again lifting the threat of forfeiture) on condition that the requisite repairs are carried out, under the Leasehold Property (Repairs) Act 1938, s 1(6), or grant relief on terms under LPA 1925, s 146(2) or forfeit the lease.[243] Thus the Leasehold Property (Repairs) Act 1938, is an integral part of the forfeiture process in the case of dilapidations and, according to the House of Lords, where leave is applied for, unless the parties otherwise agree, the forfeiture action is to be fought out under the 1938 Act, and any leave application by the tenant must thereafter be dealt with, where necessary. There are some limits to the scope of this Act.

1   Certain persons cannot claim the benefit of the Leasehold Property (Repairs) Act 1938, notably, legal mortgagees in possession or entitled to possession, or chargees of the lessee's interest in the premises.[244] However, an assignee in possession is entitled to claim the 1938 Act.[245]

2   A landlord's claim for costs and expenses in the preparation and service of a LPA 1925, s 146 notice is a claim for a contract debt, where the tenant is under express covenant to pay these costs, and is outside the Leasehold Property (Repairs) Act 1938.[246]

3   If the landlord has the right to enter and execute repairs under the lease, but no express right to charge the tenant with their cost, no part of the cost will be recoverable unless, prior to acting, the landlord serves a LPA 1925, s 146 notice on the tenant, which will allow him to claim the Leasehold Property (Repairs) Act 1938. This is because the landlord's claim is for damages.[247]

4   If the lease enables the landlord, following a notice to repair to the tenant, to enter, execute the work and charge the tenant with the cost, the costs of the repairs are in principle treated as contract debt, as the landlord may recover the costs without having to concern himself with the restrictions of the Leasehold Property (Repairs) Act 1938.[248] These potentially oppressive clauses are to be construed narrowly,

---

243 *Associated British Ports v CH Bailey plc* [1990] 2 AC 703, [1990] 1 All ER 930; PF Smith [1990] Conv 305.

244 *Church Comrs for England v Ve-Ri-Best Manufacturing Co Ltd* [1957] 1 QB 238, [1956] 3 All ER 777; also *Target Home Loans Ltd v Iza Ltd* [2000] 1 EGLR 23.

245 *Kanda v Church Comrs for England* [1958] 1 QB 332, CA.

246 *Bader Properties Ltd v Linley Property Investments Ltd* (1967) 19 P & CR 620, approved in *Middlegate Properties v Gidlow-Jackson* (1977) 34 P & CR 4, CA.

247 *SEDAC Investments Ltd v Tanner* [1982] 3 All ER 646, [1982] 1 WLR 1342; PF Smith [1983] Conv 72. The repairs were urgent, and the conclusion was reached with 'surprise and regret'.

248 *Jervis v Harris* [1996] 1 All ER 303, [1996] 2 WLR 220, CA. See Taylor (1998) L & TR 11. Sums payable under a recovery of costs clause may fall within Landlord and Tenant (Covenants) Act 1995, s 17(7)(c) so entailing landlord compliance with the relevant notice procedures if he is to recover against a former tenant or his guarantor.

and so the landlord cannot resort to an entry and repair clause in order to enter and then charge the tenant for any work not within the exact scope of his covenant to repair.[249] Also, if a landlord spent money on work of no use to him or the tenant, the cost of that work would fall outside a recovery of costs clause.[250]

5   The Leasehold Property (Repairs) Act 1938 applies only to repairing covenants, not, for example, to a covenant to cleanse,[251] nor to a covenant to lay out insurance moneys of the premises, if these are destroyed by fire.[252]

6   Because the courts strive where possible to uphold formal notices, a LPA 1925, s 146 notice which contains the statements required by the Leasehold Property (Repairs) Act 1938, s 1(4) will be valid even if it refers to alleged breaches of non-existent covenants.[253] If a s 146 notice is bad for want of compliance with the 1938 Act, but is good as respects other alleged breaches of covenant, it will be severed and valid as respects the latter breaches.[254]

LPA 1925, s 147

Where a LPA 1925, s 146 notice served on a tenant relates to internal decorative repairs, the tenant may apply to the court for relief, and if, having regard to all the circumstances, including in particular the length of the tenant's unexpired term, the court is satisfied that the notice is unreasonable, it may, by order, wholly or partially relieve the tenant from liability for these repairs.

If any of the four following exclusions apply, the relieving power of LPA 1925, s 147(1) is excluded. These are, by LPA 1925, s 147(2):
1   where the liability arises under an express covenant or agreement to put the property into a decorative state of repair, which has not been performed;
2   where any matter is necessary or proper for putting or keeping the property in a sanitary condition, or for the maintenance or preservation of the structure;
3   to any statutory liability to keep a house in all respects reasonably fit for human habitation; and
4   to any covenant or stipulation to yield up the house or other building in a specified state of repair at the end of the term.

Where LPA 1925, s 147 applies, the tenant may apply to the court immediately he receives the notice concerned, and the court may relieve him completely from liability for internal decorative repairs. LPA 1925, s 147 does not apply to a tenant's covenant to carry out regular exterior redecoration at stated intervals.

---

249 See *Amsprop Trading Ltd v Harris Distribution Ltd* [1997] 1 WLR 1025 at 1035.
250 *Jervis v Harris* [1996] 1 All ER 303, [1996] 2 WLR 220, CA.
251 *Starrokate Ltd v Burry* [1983] 1 EGLR 56, CA.
252 *Farimani v Gates* [1984] 2 EGLR 66, CA.
253 *Silvester v Ostrowska* [1959] 3 All ER 642, [1959] 1 WLR 1060.
254 *Starrokate v Burry* [1983] 1 EGLR 56, CA.

Damages

At common law, a lessee against whom the landlord brought an action for damages at the end of the lease was liable to pay for the reasonable cost of putting the premises into repair, so as literally to comply with his covenant to repair.[255] It made no difference that the landlord might, on regaining possession, wish to put the premises to a different use to that of the tenant.

The Landlord and Tenant Act 1927, s 18(1) limits the maximum amount of damages recoverable. It is not clear whether this provision is any more than declaratory of the present common law principle that damages are recoverable only for a party's actual loss.[256] At all events, the courts have striven to interpret the Landlord and Tenant Act 1927, s 18(1) in the main so as to produce this result though, as will appear, in some cases it has had the unhappy effect of fortuitously depriving a landlord of damages.

(i) General rule

By the Landlord and Tenant Act 1927, s 18(1):

'damages for a breach of covenant or agreement to keep or put premises in repair during the currency of a lease, or to leave or put premises in repair at the termination of a lease, whether such covenant is expressed or implied, and whether general or specific, shall in no case exceed the amount (if any) by which the value of the reversion (whether immediate or not) in the premises is diminished owing to the breach of such covenant or agreement'.

The Landlord and Tenant Act 1927, s 18(1) has no effect on the computation of damages, although it fixes a ceiling on the maximum amount recoverable.[257] Accordingly, a tenant could not set off against a damages award any sum to take into account the fact that the landlord had regained possession earlier than the original expiry date of the lease.[258] Yet the Landlord and Tenant Act 1927, s 18(1) may restrict a damages award where the landlord claims compensation during the lease, since it seemingly requires the court to assess the difference between the value of the landlord's reversion with the premises in repair and with them in a dilapidated state. The Court of Appeal have emphasised that where a landlord claimed damages for breaches of repairing covenant near the beginning or at the middle of the term of a long lease, if the landlord failed to produce evidence of a fall in value of his reversion, he runs the serious risk of the court concluding that there was no significant diminution.[259]

255 *Joyner v Weeks* [1891] 2 QB 31, CA.
256 Law Com No 238 (1996) 'Responsibility for State and Condition of Property' para 9.36ff think that Landlord and Tenant Act 1927, s 18(1) need not be altered as it is probably declaratory of the common law; for a review of the provision see DN Clarke (1988) 104 LQR 372.
257 *Shortlands Investments Ltd v Cargill* [1995] 1 EGLR 51.
258 *Hanson v Newman* [1934] Ch 298, CA.
259 *Crewe Services & Investments Corpn v Silk* [1998] 2 EGLR 1, CA (where a damages award of some £11,633 was reduced to £3,000 to reflect uncertainties as to whether, in relation to a

Where the landlord claims damages after the lease has expired, the basic measure of damages remains compensatory in nature, subject to the ceiling imposed by the Landlord and Tenant Act 1927, s 18(1). The cost of repairs may be the best evidence of loss to the reversion. Where a tenant left a house in a poor condition at the expiry of a short residential lease, the landlord was awarded £36 as the cost of putting the premises into a condition suitable to re-let them for the same purposes to a new tenant.[260] Similarly, a landlord had to pay an incoming lessee some £690,000 as an inducement to bring the premises into a standard of repair which met with the landlord's standards. The High Court held that the negative value of the reversion had been inflated by the former tenant's breach. Since the cost of repairs, as shown by a dilapidations Schedule, was the best guide to the assessment of damages, the lesser sum of £295,321 was awarded.[261] Where, however, a landlord proved that a market existed for his premises, which he sold out of repair at a reduced price, the loss to his reversion exceeded the cost of repairs, this latter sum was recoverable in full.[262] Even if there is no obvious market for the premises, the courts may find diminution on the facts. The High Court thus awarded some £40,000 in damages to a landlord. Although there might be no local market for the premises, which were redundant mill premises, the building out of repair would have attracted a discount when compared to its state in proper repair, in favour of the type of developer who, in the court's view, would be likely to buy this type of property.[263] However, where damage to the saleability of the reversion cannot be shown, the Landlord and Tenant Act 1927, s 18(1) may reduce any damages award to a nominal sum only, as where a landlord had been able to sell the premises for conversion into flats, for a good price, and could not prove that the price had been reduced because of the dilapidations.[264]

The Landlord and Tenant Act 1927, s 18(1) has operated to reduce or eliminate damages in other cases. For example, lessees who were entitled to obtain a renewal of their tenancies under the Landlord and Tenant Act 1954, Pt II had committed breaches of their covenants to repair, but no damages could be recovered since the reversion had

---

continuing agricultural tenancy, the landlord intended or was able to carry out remedial work, the cost of which is normally good evidence of the diminution in value to a reversion). With a view to insuring that both landlord and tenant keep each other informed of the case against him at an early stage and to encourage early settlement of disputes, the Property Law Association have produced a draft pre-action Protocol. This is accessible on their website (pla.org.uk). This document does not extend to damages claimed during the term of a lease. It also excludes claims for re-instatement on the apparent ground that Landlord and Tenant Act 1927, s 18(1) does not apply to these latter.

260 *Jones v Herxheimer* [1950] 2 KB 106, CA. If the incoming tenant is to use the premises for a different use, which requires a less extensive degree of repairs, this factor will impose a cap on the damages, under Landlord and Tenant Act 1927, s 18(1): see eg *Sun Life Assurance plc v Racal Tracs Ltd* [2001] 1 EGLR 138 (where the method of repairs deemed appropriate for future storage use of the premises was less than the cost of repairs claimed).

261 *Shortlands Investments Ltd v Cargill plc* [1995] 1 EGLR 51.

262 *Culworth Estates Ltd v Society of Licensed Victuallers* [1991] 2 EGLR 54, CA.

263 *Craven (Builders) Ltd v Secretary of State for Health* [2000] 1 EGLR 128.

264 *Landeau v Marchbank* [1949] 2 All ER 172.

not suffered loss, since a market rent was payable for the new tenancies under statute.[265] The rent had to be fixed on the assumption that the premises were in repair, otherwise the tenants could take advantage of their own wrong to reduce the rent.[266] Likewise, a landlord who re-let the premises concerned, which were badly out of repair, to a new lessee who undertook to carry out improvements failed to prove any loss to his reversion from the former tenant's breach and so failed in a claim to damages.[267]

Moreover, any damages otherwise recoverable by the landlord may be reduced if he does not intend to re-let the premises for the same purpose as those of the previous tenant, or where such re-letting is not, as where planning restrictions supervene, possible. In such a case the damages awarded will have regard to the intended or lawful future user of the premises.[268]

(ii) Demolition or alteration of premises

So as to reverse the common law, the Landlord and Tenant Act 1927, s 18(1) also provides that no damages shall be recovered for breach of any covenant to leave or put in repair at the termination of the lease, if it can be shown that the premises in whatever state of repair they might be, would at or shortly after the termination of the tenancy have been or will be pulled down or such structural alterations made as to render valueless the repairs in question. Where a local authority resolves before the end of the lease to acquire the premises compulsorily, the landlord cannot claim any diminution in value even though the compulsory purchase order is not made until afterwards.[269]

The date for determining the landlord's intention to demolish etc is the termination of the lease; and the intention must be definite and not conditional;[270] and if definite at the relevant time, it is irrelevant that the landlord's intention is later set at naught.[271] The second limb of the Landlord and Tenant Act 1927, s 18(1) contemplates a demolition rendering repairs nugatory, as opposed to acts by a tenant (and local authority) whose compulsory purchase of the premises could reward them for their breaches of covenant.[272]

265 *Family Management v Gray* [1980] 1 EGLR 46.
266 *Crown Estate Comrs v Town Investments Ltd* [1992] 1 EGLR 61, at 63.
267 *Mather v Barclays Bank plc* [1987] 2 EGLR 254. Likewise in *Ultraworth Ltd v General Accident Fire & Life* [2000] 2 EGLR 115, it was held that since the sale price of the premises was not affected by the disrepair, no damages were payable by the erstwhile lessee. No less than four methods of valuing the premises for statutory purposes were considered in this case.
268 *Portman v Latta* [1942] WN 97; also *Sun Life Assurance plc v Racal Tracs Ltd* [2001] 1 EGLR 138.
269 *London County Freehold and Leasehold Properties Ltd v Wallis-Whiddett* [1950] WN 180.
270 *Cunliffe v Goodman* [1950] 2 KB 237, [1950] 1 All ER 720, CA.
271 *Salisbury v Gilmore* [1942] 2 KB 38, [1942] 1 All ER 457, CA.
272 *Hibernian Property Co Ltd v Liverpool Corpn* [1973] 2 All ER 1117, [1973] 1 WLR 751.

244 Principal rights and obligations of the parties to a lease or tenancy

Some concluding points may be made. First, the date down to which damages for breaches by the tenant of his covenant to repair is measured is, in the case of forfeiture, the date of service of the writ claiming forfeiture, which effects notional re-entry, as opposed to the date when the landlord eventually recovers possession of the premises.[273] Secondly, the Landlord and Tenant Act 1927, s 18(1) does not apply to a covenant by the tenant to spend a stated sum on repairs, nor to a covenant to pay the landlord the difference between the stated sum and any amount actually expended.[274] Thirdly, the Landlord and Tenant Act 1927, s 18(1) only limits landlords' damages claims in relation to the covenant to repair: it does not affect the measure of damages in other cases, such as covenants not to alter the internal planning of the premises,[275] or building leases.[276]

Specific performance

At one time it was thought that, in contrast to the right of a tenant to seek specific performance of a landlord's obligation to repair, the landlord could not ask for this remedy as a matter of principle. This idea was based on an old case, which was seen by the Law Commission as being redundant.[277]

The High Court has now ruled that equity has a jurisdiction to order a tenant to comply with his repairing obligations by specific performance.[278] There were no constraints of principle or authority against such a ruling. Problems of supervision could be overcome by sufficiently defining the required work in the court's order. At the same time, the High Court indicated that an award of specific performance to a landlord would be made only with great caution, owing to the dangers of oppression to tenants and because of a policy of not harassing tenants, which lay behind the Leasehold Property (Repairs) Act 1938, which, however, does not apply to specific performance. Where forfeiture is open to the landlord, which it was not in the case in question, it may be that specific performance will not be available to landlords as they have a sufficient alternative remedy.

---

273 *Associated Deliveries Ltd v Harrison* (1984) 50 P & CR 91, CA.
274 *Moss' Empires Ltd v Olympia (Liverpool) Ltd* [1939] AC 544, [1939] 3 All ER 460, HL.
275 *Eyre v Rea* [1947] KB 567, [1947] 1 All ER 415.
276 *Lansdowne Rodway Estates Ltd v Potown Ltd* [1984] 2 EGLR 80.
277 The case was *Hill v Barclay* (1810) 16 Ves 402, which, however, was concerned with forfeiture; the Law Commission's views are in their Report (Law Com No 238 (1996) 'Responsibility for State and Condition of Property' paras 9.19-9.20).
278 *Rainbow Estates v Tokenhold Ltd* [1998] 2 All ER 860; see Wilkinson (1998) NLJ 9 October 1998, p 1475; Pawlowski & Brown [1998] Conv 495. Specific performance was ordered, because there were serious breaches costing some £300,000 to put right, and because the lease contained no re-entry clause and could not be forfeited.

VII TENANTS' REMEDIES FOR BREACH OF LANDLORD'S COVENANT TO REPAIR

Tenants have a wide range of remedies both at common law, such as damages, and in equity, such as to specific performance, against landlords in breach of their covenants to repair.

Damages

The aim of an award of damages is to restore the tenant to the position in which he or she would have been if the landlord had not broken his covenant.[279] The court compares the state of the premises during the period of the breach and the condition in which the premises ought to have been if the covenant had not been broken, but the way in which damages are worked out is not governed by any one formula. Liability runs as from the date of notice from the tenant if the disrepair exists within the confines of the premises demised to the tenant, on principles already discussed. If the disrepair is in part of the premises not let to the tenant, then where the landlord is under an obligation to 'keep in repair' liability in damages runs from the time the state of disrepair arises.[280]

There are numerous cases on the quantification of damages and the position is best summarised by noting that the Court of Appeal regards the actual amount of damages as primarily for county court judges: thus the whole area is fact-sensitive. Awards of damages will therefore only be upset on appeal if there is an error of principle.[281] The Court of Appeal does not like overall or 'global' calculations, however, and prefers to see calculations of individual head of damages. On the other hand there is seemingly no 'tariff' of damages awards, such as on account of discomfort or inconvenience, which landlords can parade before the county court so as to prevent an award being made above that figure.[282]

Tenants who remain in occupation[283] can claim damages under various heads, such as for loss of amenity, and for discomfort and inconvenience at having to live in premises which are in disrepair,[284] and for making good interior decorations on account of the

---

279 *Wallace v Manchester City Council* [1998] 3 EGLR 38, CA.
280 *Passley v Wandsworth London BC* (1996) 30 HLR 165, CA (where the damage was caused by burst pipes in a roof, which had not been demised).
281 *Brent London Borough Council v Carmel* (1995) 28 HLR 203.
282 See *Wallace v Manchester City Council* [1998] 3 EGLR 38, CA; the annual Current Law Year Books regularly set out county cases of damages awards, often for breaches of the landlord's statutory obligation under LTA 1985, s 11. See also, eg Madge NLJ 5 November 1999, p 1643.
283 Those who wish to dispose of their lease are entitled to the difference between the sale price realised and that which would, but for the disrepair, have been realised: *Wallace v Manchester City Council* [1998] 3 EGLR 38, CA. If the tenant has failed to sub-let owing to the state of the premises, he may claim the loss of potential rental income: ibid.
284 *McGreal v Wake* [1984] 1 EGLR 42, CA.

landlord's breaches of covenant.[285] Claims may also be made if the tenant's health has suffered or there has been a loss of personal comfort.[286]

Set-off of cost of repairs from rent[287]

Two claims may be made under set-off: at common law, and in equity.

(i) Common law

At common law,[288] where a landlord is in breach of covenant to repair and the tenant carries out the repairs, he may set off the cost of repairs against his future liability for rent. Where occupiers spent £630 on repairs for which the landlord was liable, it was held that they could recoup themselves out of future rents for the sum spent.[289] The right is narrow. Any sum must be certain for the right, which is at common law, to exist; and it must be unchallenged or unchallengeable, eg awarded in arbitration. Any excess over a proper amount will be disallowed. The sum must be spent only on matters falling within the landlord's covenant to repair, where he has notice and is in breach.[290] While it seems that common law set off is limited to breaches by an assignee of the reversion in the case of a tenancy granted prior to 1 January 1996, as opposed to his predecessor,[291] no such limit applies to 'new tenancies' granted after that date.

(ii) Equity

Equity, following the law, insists that there must be an existing debt or claim for an equitable right to set-off to arise.[292] But equity has relaxed the common law insistence that the relevant claim must be certain: the tenant may set off an estimated sum representing the cost of landlord's repairs as a defence to a landlords' claim for rent arrears against him. Moreover, in contrast to the common law rule, the tenant need not prove that he has spent any money of his own on repairs as a condition precedent to claim an equitable set-off.[293] Both these principles may be explained on the ground that the claim to set-off goes to the foundation of any claim to rent arrears: hence, a

---

285 *Bradley v Chorley Borough Council* [1985] 2 EGLR 49, CA.
286 As in eg *Switzer v Law* [1998] CLY 3624.
287 See Waite [1981] Conv 199; Rank (1976) 40 Conv (NS) 196.
288 Where set off is apparently derived from statutes of set-off of mutual debts: *Courage Ltd v Crehan* [1999] 2 EGLR 145, CA.
289 *Lee-Parker v Izzet* [1971] 3 All ER 1099, [1971] 1 WLR 1688.
290 *British Anzani (Felixstowe) Ltd v International Marine Management (UK) Ltd* [1980] QB 137, [1979] 2 All ER 1063; *Asco Developments v Gordon* [1978] 2 EGLR 41.
291 *Kemra (Management) Ltd v Lewis* [1999] CLY 3729.
292 *Barribal v Everitt* [1994] EGCS 62, CA.
293 *Melville v Grapelodge Developments Ltd* (1978) 39 P & CR 179.

landlord's bailiffs were restrained by injunction from executing a distress against a tenant claiming equitable set-off.[294]

Both the common law and equitable rights to set off against rent arrears may be excluded by a clause which in terms provides for payment of rent in full without any deduction or set off whatever, or by a provision in the lease requiring the tenant to pay rent by direct debit.[295] It was also held that such an 'anti set-off clause' was not subject to the test of reasonableness imposed by the Unfair Contract Terms Act 1977, s 3. The statutory exclusion of any contract 'so far as it relates to the creation … of an interest in land' (Unfair Contract Terms Act 1977, Sch 1, para 1(b)) was given a wide interpretation.[296] Nevertheless, the Court of Appeal has insisted that the equitable right of set-off is important. Clear words of exclusion are required to displace it: the expression 'without any deduction' did not suffice to do so since the word 'deduction' was ambiguous.[297]

Specific performance

(i) General equity jurisdiction

Subject to the overriding discretion of the court to refuse relief, the court may, in its equity jurisdiction, order a landlord who is in clear breach of a covenant to repair to comply with his covenant by carrying out the work specified in the order. Thus, a landlord was ordered to replace a balcony which he had covenanted to repair, but it was not demised to the tenants. It had partially collapsed. As there was no doubt as to the work to be done, and the breach was plain, the court's discretion would be exercised in favour of granting an order.[298] In one case an order of specific performance was made against a landlord, requiring him to keep lifts in working order, even though the landlord was insolvent.[299] An order was granted against landlords of a block of flats who had seriously neglected their obligations to repair the property, to such an extent that the tenants had been forced to leave the premises concerned.[300] The equity jurisdiction applies to all types of premises, although it is unclear whether it is superseded where the specific jurisdiction conferred by statute applies. It is also possible that, in contrast to the statutory jurisdiction, equity has no power to order specific performance (or for that matter a mandatory injunction) where the item sought

---

294 *Eller v Grovecrest Investments Ltd* [1994] 2 EGLR 45, CA.
295 *Gibbs Mew plc v Gemmell* [1999] 1 EGLR 43, CA. However, in the case of a residential lease or tenancy, an anti-set-off clause which was not previously negotiated with the tenant could well fall foul of Unfair Terms in Consumer Contracts Regulations 1999, SI 1999/2083.
296 *Electricity Supply Nominees Ltd v IAF Group Ltd* [1993] 3 All ER 372; approved in *Unchained Growth III plc v Granby Village (Manchester) Management Co Ltd* [2000] L & TR 186, CA.
297 *Connaught Restaurants Ltd v Indoor Leisure Ltd* [1994] 4 All ER 834, CA.
298 *Jeune v Queen's Cross Properties Ltd* [1974] Ch 97, [1973] 3 All ER 97.
299 *Francis v Cowlcliffe* (1976) 33 P & CR 368.
300 *Gordon v Selico Co Ltd* [1986] 1 EGLR 71, CA.

to be replaced is situated within the confines of the demised premises, as the landlord is excluded from these by the very fact of his having granted a lease. The equity and also the statutory jurisdiction may be exercised not only by the High Court but also by a county court judge sitting as a small claims arbitrator.[301]

If damages are an adequate remedy, then specific performance is debarred; but since the latter award ensures, seeing that it is a contempt of court for a landlord to refuse to comply with it, that the work will be done, it may be that this defence is not especially formidable an obstacle. It is probably no longer a bar to an award of specific performance that constant supervision by the court might be required to enforce the order.[302]

(ii)   Statutory jurisdiction

LTA 1985, s 17 confers a specific jurisdiction to award specific performance against a landlord of tenants of dwellings (which is defined so as to include houses and flats and premises ancillary thereto such as yards). The landlord must be in breach of his repairing obligation, which receives a wide definition in LTA 1985, s 17(2)(d).[303] The jurisdiction allows the court to make an order even where the disrepair relates to a part of the premises not let to the tenant, such as where a common roof to a number of flats has collapsed or is seriously damaged. The court is thus empowered to make an order against both landlords who are in breach of their statutory obligations to keep in repair, and those who have express obligations to repair and maintain a block of leasehold flats.

(iii)   Reform

The Law Commission, after an exhaustive examination of the position, have now recommended that specific performance should be reformed and based on a general statutory jurisdiction. The remedy should be stripped of technical defences such as the constant supervision rule, or the fact that landlords may doubtfully obtain it. The basis of the proposed new jurisdiction would be the discretion of the court, and so whether the remedy was appropriate.[304] Since, to judge by the Commission's findings, the courts already make considerable use of the current statutory jurisdiction under LTA 1985, s 17, this reform seems useful, as developing, simplifying and extending to non-residential tenancies an established practice.

---

301 *Joyce v Liverpool City Council* [1996] QB 252, [1995] 3 All ER 110, CA; and see SE Murdoch [1995] 29 EG 118.

302 See *Joyce v Liverpool City Council* [1996] QB 252, [1995] 3 All ER 110, CA, for an analysis of the means by which this supposed bar may be overcome.

303 The definition goes beyond repairs and includes a covenant to maintain, renew construct or replace any relevant property.

304 Law Com No 238 (1996) 'Responsibility for State and Condition of Property' paras 9.31ff.

Appointment of a receiver

Under the Supreme Court Act 1981, s 37, the High Court has a general jurisdiction to appoint a receiver in all cases where it appears just and convenient to do so. A receiver was accordingly appointed under this jurisdiction over residential blocks of flats, in one case, where the premises were seriously out of repair, due to the landlord's neglect to collect and apply to repairs service charges from the tenants, and in other cases, simply to support the covenant to repair, of which the landlord was in serious breach.[305] Such an order is capable of being protected by a caution against the landlord's title under the Land Registration Act 1925, s 54: a means, effectively, of blighting the landlord's ability to dispose of his interest in the premises while a receivership is in force.[306]

Appointment of a manager

Under the Landlord and Tenant Act 1987, Pt II, a manager[307] may be appointed by a leasehold valuation tribunal on the application of a tenant. The following deals with the position as amended by subsequent legislation. There must be a lease of residential flats (whether a purpose-built block with at least two flats or a house converted into flats). This specific jurisdiction, aimed at landlords who seriously neglect their repairing, maintenance and related obligations,[308] excludes that of equity (Landlord and Tenant Act 1987, s 21(6)). It was enacted as part of a more general policy of improving the remedies of tenants of residential flats against landlords who neglected their repairing and related obligations, such as in relation to insurance policies or the maintenance of the common parts. It was considered that the general equity jurisdiction was not sufficiently precise.[309] With regard to breaches by landlords or their managing agents of repairing and maintenance obligations the following matters may be noted.

1   The application must be against the immediate landlord or a person such as the landlord's managing agent. It may be made by one or more tenants. A management order may be made if, in particular the landlord is in breach of a management obligation or he would be in breach but for the fact that it has not been reasonably

---

305 *Hart v Emelkirk Ltd* [1983] 3 All ER 15, [1983] 1 WLR 1289; *Daiches v Bluelake Investments Ltd* [1985] 2 EGLR 67; *Blawdziewicz v Diadon Establishment* [1988] 2 EGLR 52.
306 *Clayhope Properties Ltd v Evans* [1986] 2 All ER 795, [1986] 1 WLR 1223, CA.
307 The manager is vested with managerial powers such as to let part of the premises and to spend money on them so as to enable them to be let: *Sparkle Properties v Residential Developments Ltd* [1998] EGCS 68.
308 Including also breaches of the landlord's obligations with respect to trusts of service charges accounts and of his obligation not to make unreasonable administrative charges (Landlord and Tenant Act 1987, s 24(2) as amended CLRA 2002, Sch 11, para 9). The leasehold valuation tribunal may also appoint a manager where satisfied that unreasonable administration charges have been made, are proposed or are likely to be made and that it is just and convenient to make the order (Landlord and Tenant Act 1987, s 24(2)(aba), added by CLRA 2002, Sch 11, para 9).
309 See Hawkins [1985] Conv 12 for a review of the background.

practicable for the tenant to give him the requisite preliminary notice (Landlord and Tenant Act 1987, s 24(2)(a)). In this case, it must be just and convenient[310] to make the order.

2   No order may be made unless the tenant or tenants have served on the landlord and his manager a notice which complies with the Landlord and Tenant Act 1987, s 22. A s 22 notice must specify the grounds on which an order is being requested. It must require the landlord or person upon whom the notice is served to remedy the breach within a specified and reasonable time, by specified steps. The degree of particularisation will seemingly be related to the terms of the lease: thus, if redecoration at intervals is required, it might suffice to say that the property was last redecorated in a given year. The amount of time to be allowed may be governed by the conduct of the landlord or other person to date. A landlord who showed no intention of complying with his obligations could not say that a 28-day period for compliance was too short.[311]

3   If the landlord or manager who has been served with a Landlord and Tenant Act 1987, s 24 notice remedies the breaches within the reasonable time allowed, this will avert the making of a management order. If made, an order displaces the landlord from the management of the property and, if the functions of a receiver are given to the manager, from the rent. While an order may be varied or even discharged on the application of the landlord or his manager, such an order may only be made if the applicant shows either that to accede to the application will not result in recurrence of the circumstances which led to the making of the order or it is just and equitable to vary or discharge the order (Landlord and Tenant Act 1987, s 24(9A)).

Repudiation

In a landmark county court decision,[312] tenants holding a three-year assured shorthold tenancy were entitled to accept a landlord's repudiatory breach of his statutorily-implied repairing covenants, by leaving the house concerned during the tenancy and giving back the keys. The landlord had refused to remedy serious disrepairs such as an uninhabitable bedroom due to a collapsed ceiling, rainwater penetration in the sitting-room, a damp hall wall and an unusable outside toilet. The tenants were awarded substantial general damages. The landlord's refusal to perform his implied repairing covenants, no doubt a primary obligation, could be said to have deprived the tenant of substantially the whole benefit which the parties intended him to obtain from the contract: a short tenancy of a house which he might expect would be kept in repair by

---

310 These words invite eg a consideration of such matters as whether delays in serving relevant notices or the onset of winter might preclude relief: see *Howard v Midrome Ltd* [1991] 1 EGLR 58.

311 *Howard v Midrome Ltd* [1991] 1 EGLR 58.

312 *Hussein v Mehlman* [1992] 2 EGLR 87; see Bright [1993] Conv 71; Harpum [1993] CLJ 212.

the landlord as required by statute. The doctrine of repudiation and its use by a tenant as a remedial device has taken its place in English law.[313]

VIII REFORM OF THE LAW

The position to date

There is no doubt that disrepair of property remains a serious issue. Thus the government has admitted that a sizeable minority of people had severe housing disrepair problems.[314] Various bodies charged with law reform have examined the present rules and have concluded that reforms are required. In 1992, the Law Commission published a Consultation Paper.[315] It suggested imposing on all landlords a duty to maintain demised premises by reference to the safe, hygienic and satisfactory use of the property for its intended purpose.

The Law Commission produced a final Report in 1996.[316] Some of the individual recommendations have already been noted in this chapter. The Report repays careful study. The thrust underlying the proposals as a whole, is to create a coherent and principled code regulating the responsibilities of the parties to a lease.[317] The Commission are not complimentary about the present law. To them, it provides a patchwork of private and public law remedies which overlap at times and which provide no remedies on other occasions (as where a house is unfit but not out of repair).

The Commission think that the parties to a lease must be compelled, in the public interest in seeing properly maintained leasehold property, to address the issue of liability for repairs when negotiating a lease. They propose a general implied but residual statutory covenant by the landlord to keep the demised premises, their common parts and any premises whose disrepair might affect the tenant's premises, in repair and to make and keep them fit for human habitation.[318] The covenant could be contracted out of, and would not apply to short residential leases, where specific compulsory obligations would be imposed. At the time of writing the future is not clear. This is owing to the fact that the government, as already noted, is likely to revise the way in which the public sector deals with health and safety of housing, which may entail in due course reforms of the private law affecting short-term residential leases along the lines proposed by the Law Commission, but only to complement these health and safety reforms. At the time this book went to press, it appeared that no primary

---

313 *Chartered Trust plc v Davies* [1997] 2 EGLR 83, CA.
314 Housing Green Paper 'Quality and Choice' (2000), p 8.
315 No 123 Responsibility for the State and Condition of Property; see PF Smith [1994] Conv 186.
316 Law Com No 238 (1996) 'Responsibility for State and Condition of Property'; as to the Report, see (1996) 146 NLJ 397; Bridge [1996] Conv 342; for some comparative perspectives, see PF Smith [1998] Conv 189.
317 Law Com No 238 (1996) 'Responsibility for State and Condition of Property' para 6.22.
318 Law Com No 238 (1996) 'Responsibility for State and Condition of Property' paras 7.7-7.10.

legislation, which will be needed for even these limited reforms to be passed, was contemplated in the 2001/2002 Parliamentary Session (which was thought to have been overloaded).

Comparative notes

In order to evaluate the current state of English law, it is useful to note the position as it is understood to be in Scotland and France, where the principles seem to lean more heavily in favour of requiring landlords to maintain let premises in a proper state of repair and maintenance.

The principles applying to Scottish secure tenants with regard to maintenance by their landlords of these tenants' homes are much more favourable to tenants than is the current English law. For example, a Scottish social landlord must provide the secure tenant with a house which is at the commencement of the tenancy, wind- and water-tight and in all respects reasonably fit for human habitation.[319] It must also maintain the house in a habitable condition during the tenancy period.[320] The landlord must, under its duty to maintain, take into account the extent to which the house, thanks to disrepair or sanitary defects, falls short of current building regulations.[321] Moreover, in relation to the specific problem of condensation dampness, while the current position in English law is that of no implied liability on the landlord, provided there is no disrepair *strictu sensu*,[322] matters are less restrictive north of the Border. This is owing to the fact that the statutory expression 'sanitary defects' in relation to Scottish secure tenancies expressly refers to dampness.[323] It would appear[324] that, at least in the case of Scottish secure tenants, the landlord must provide a house where, provided it is heated to a reasonable temperature and at a reasonable cost to the tenant, if condensation results, the landlord may have to cure it.[325] The law applying to Scottish secure tenants, which is said to reflect Scots common law, retains the concept of unfitness for human habitation. By contrast, as we have seen, it is possible that in future the government will get rid of this notion in England and Wales, and replace it with an individualised health and safety fitness rating, which could, if it degenerates into a cost-saving device, turn out to be a poor cousin of the more robust Scots law.

---

319 Housing (Scotland) Act 2001, Sch 4, para 1(a). The landlord is required, before the commencement of the tenancy, to inspect the house and to identify any work necessary to comply with its statutory duty. It must then notify the tenant of any such work (para 2).

320 Housing (Scotland) Act 2001, Sch 4, para 1(b).

321 Housing (Scotland) Act 2001, Sch 5. Also, eg Draft Model Scottish Short Secure Tenancy Agreement of January 2002, cl 5.7; and Model Scottish Secure Tenancy Agreement, cl 5.7.

322 See *Lee v Leeds City Council* [2002] EWCA Civ 06, [2002] 1 WLR 1488 (holding that while severe environmental pollution may affect an individual's well-being so badly as to violate ECHR, Art 8, unfitness due to condensation in a council house caused by a design fault cannot seemingly do so).

323 Housing (Scotland) Act 2001, Sch 4, para 6.

324 From Model Scottish Secure Tenancy Agreement and the Draft Short Scottish Secure Tenancy Agreement, note 5.6.

325 *Fyfe v Scottish Homes* 1995 SCLR 209.

The fact that Scots law also envisages that, in some cases, landlords of Scottish secure tenants may have to upgrade the standard of the homes concerned to modern building regulations exposes a further dissonance with English common law, which imposes no such requirement.[326]

In France, the basic rules applying to maintenance of tenanted premises also contrast with the current approach of English law. Essentially, a French landlord of any premises (business or residential) is bound under the general law to deliver the property to the tenant in a good state of repair and also to guarantee the freedom of the premises from latent defects.[327] Thus the landlord is bound to put and keep the premises in proper repair, the standard being the intended use by the tenant of the property in question. A landlord had to repair a roof which had been allowed to fall out of repair, and was required to keep up a central heating system:[328] both familiar problems on this side of the Channel, the difference being that the tenant could rely on the general law rather than the terms of the lease concerned. Under the general civil law obligations, it seems that landlords must also see to it that the premises are safe to use.[329] Landlords of commercial premises often contract out of the obligation of the French Civil Code, Arts 1719 and 1720 to deliver and then maintain the premises in a good state of repair. Some *doctrine* regards contracting out clauses as an abuse of superior landlord power.[330] This has not deterred landlords from contracting out whenever they lawfully can do so.[331] The French courts have upheld clauses such as one requiring the tenant to take the premises as they find them on letting.[332] A similarly successful contract-out clause was a statement in a lease that all liability for repairs except to the walls and roof fell on the tenant.[333] But even where not contracted out of, the general law obligations of French landlords are to repair and not to rebuild, so that, as would be the case in England and Wales, if the cost of the works exceed the value of the whole building, the courts classify the work as 'reconstruction' and not repair, so that it lies outside the landlord's general law obligations.

These comparative considerations seem to re-enforce the case for comprehensive legislative reform, as the task cannot now be carried out by the English courts. If the law is reformed as suggested by the Law Commission, there would be a two-tier system in England and Wales for dealing with repairing obligations. On the one hand,

---

326 *Southwark London BC v Mills* [1999] 4 All ER 449, HL.
327 Code Civil, arts 1719, 1720 and 1721. However, the guarantee of art 1721 against *vice caché* is limited, since it does not evidently apply to a fault the tenant could have found out about for himself prior to taking a tenancy. From Dalloz, *Code des Baux*, 2000, p 31, the sort of things falling within *vice caché* might include a roof falling in, collapse of sub-soil, or a staircase collapsing under the tenant, as well as carbon monoxide fumes from a defective chimney.
328 Paris, 15.12.1994, cited in Dalloz, Code Civil 1997/98, p 1311; Pau 4.5.1994 in ibid.
329 Dalloz, Code Civil 1997/9, p 1312.
330 Auque, *Baux Commerciaux*, No 102.
331 As admitted by Auque, *Baux Commerciaux*, No 99.
332 Juris Classeur, *Baux*, No 185. But the landlord may still have to maintain the premises during the lease.
333 Reims, 6.7.1979, D. 1979 IR 97 and see n 334, below.

landlords of business and also of residential lessees for terms exceeding seven years would be subject to a default obligation which they could easily contract out of by the simple expedient of shifting the burden to the tenant (as we have seen, this often happens with commercial leases in France).[334] It is also understood that this also often occurs with commercial leases in Scotland.[335] Those English landlords with short-term residential tenants would, if the Law Commission reforms ever reach the statute book undiluted, be subject to a more rigorous and comprehensive statutory obligation to repair and to keep in a state fit for human habitation not unlike the French requirements imposed on residential landlords under the guise of the minimum standards of habitability.[336] The Law Commission was not troubled by the prospect of contracting out where allowed, notably in the commercial sector. Indeed they anticipated it with business leases, almost as a matter of course, as their proposed basic rules aimed only to make sure that one party or the other to a lease was liable for repairs.[337]

334 See also *Code des Baux et de la Copropriété* (2000), notes to Code Civil, arts 1719 and 1720. However, from this, it is not enough for a tenant simply to agree to a term in a lease that he is taking possession aware of the state or condition of the premises.
335 McAllister *Scottish Law of Leases* (1989) pp 27-28; eg in *McCall's Entertainments (Ayr) Ltd v South Ayrshire Council (No 2)* 1998 SLT 1421.
336 Loi of 6 July 1989, Art 6 and Décret 2002-10 of 30 January 2002.
337 Law Com No 238 (1996) 'Responsibility for State and Condition of Property' para 7.9.

CHAPTER 10

Liabilities to third parties

In this chapter we examine the way in which a landlord's title, and thus right to resume possession at the end of a lease, can be affected by a third party removing him from his title. There is a basic examination of the liability of landlords and tenants in nuisance and negligence to third parties (mainly arising out of disrepair of the premises or injuries caused to a third party visitor). Both landlord and tenant may be subject to access rights from a neighbouring owner in order to carry out certain types of work to the latter's premises, and these rights are examined.

I   LOSS OF TITLE TO A SQUATTER: OLD REGIME AND REFORM

The tenant may lose title to premises owing to these having been in the adverse possession of a 'squatter' who has the necessary intention under the general law to dispossess the tenant.[1] The rules regulating squatters' acquisition by possession of a title to land were held consistent with human rights principles.[2] In what follows, we confine our remarks to registered land where the title to the lease is registered separately from the freehold title.

Until the relevant parts of LRA 2002 are brought into force, the position as regards registered land remains governed by the Land Registration Act 1925. In essence, under these latter rules, once a squatter has obtained, by adverse possession with the required intention to dispossess, a title to leasehold land, he is entitled to apply to the Land Registry to be registered with a title. The leaseholder's 'paper' title will, if the

---

1   For a recent example, see *Batt v Adams* [2001] 2 EGLR 92.
2   Limitation Act 1980, s 15. According to *JA Pye (Oxford) Ltd v Graham* [2001] EWCA Civ 117, [2001] Ch 804, limitation of title rules are not inconsistent with the ECHR, First Protocol, Art 1. They were a logical and pragmatic consequence of barring the right of the owner to repossess the land. Kerr LJ said that the 12-year period fell within the margin of appreciation allowed by Strasbourg jurisprudence in determining limitation periods.

successful squatter's application is accepted, be closed. Pending registration, the leaseholder holds the leasehold title on trust for the squatter, but without prejudice to the landlord's reversionary title.[3] The squatter obtains a title to the lease, not the reversion. Only once the lease expires will time start to run against the landlord for statutory purposes. At the same time, once a leaseholder's registered title has been closed by the Land Registry, and a title awarded to the successful squatter, the landlord cannot accept a surrender of the leasehold title from the leaseholder, as there is nothing to surrender.[4]

The new rules are part of the larger reform package as proposed by the Law Commission to the whole land registration system.[5] The report was hostile to the idea that squatters' claims against registered titles should be based on possession, as they are in the case of unregistered land. The Law Commission stated that all titles to registered land should be based on registration.[6] Those affected by adverse possession should also have a chance to stop a claim by a squatter before the claim became impossible to defeat by time running out. This approach places primacy of title over long possession. However, as noted by Mummery LJ,[7] limitation periods are in the public interest. They preclude the making of stale claims, so avoiding a real risk of injustice. They ensure certainty of title, and protect established and peaceable possession of property from stale claims. In view of the safeguards put in place by LRA 2002 for registered leasehold proprietors and their freeholders, the prospect of a successful human rights challenge to these rules by owners or lessees seems remote indeed.

The new legislative rules contain checks and balances, to avoid stale claims. The Land Registry is required to serve notice of claim, triggering a right to object (in effect) in landlords and tenants. A squatter in possession for however long a period cannot resist possession proceedings by the tenant or landlord if brought prior to his claim having been made known to them. It is the secrecy of adverse possession that has been struck at the roots by the reforms.

II NEW REGIME

The effect of the LRA 2002, once in force, on adverse possession claims to a registered leasehold title may be summarised as follows. Adverse possession of itself for however long a period will not confer a title on the squatter. Once a squatter[8] has been in adverse possession for a period of ten years ending with the date of the application,

---

3   Land Registration Act 1925, s 75(2).
4   *Spectrum Investment Co v Holmes* [1981] 1 All ER 6.
5   Law Com No 254 (1998) 'Land Registration for the Twenty-First Century' Cmnd 4027.
6   Law Com No 254 (1998) 'Land Registration for the Twenty-First Century' para 10.43.
7   In *JA Pye (Oxford) Ltd v Graham* [2001] EWCA Civ 117, [2001] Ch 804.
8   Or where relevant a series of squatters, since successors in title to the estate in adverse possession may claim (LRA 2002, Sch 6, para 11).

he may apply to be registered as proprietor of a registered estate.[9] No title is conferred on the squatter except by registration. The registrar is required to give notice of the application to the current tenant and the superior landlord.[10] Both the freeholder and his tenant may require that the application is to be dealt with under a specific set of rules, under which there is in effect a presumption that the applicant cannot be registered with a title.[11] The main effect of the application for registration after the 10-year period is therefore likely to be to enable the tenant and any superior landlord in particular to be notified by the Land Registry of the claim and to object to it with the period allowed by Land Registry Rules, which period is anticipated to be two months in duration. But the squatter cannot avoid making this application as no title is conferred on him save by registration. If a squatter's application is rejected, he may make a further application to be registered as the new proprietor of the leasehold estate if he is still in adverse possession of that estate from the date of the application until the last day of the period of two years beginning with the date of its rejection.[12] If there is an objection from the registered leasehold proprietor or his superior landlord, to an initial application, it is open to the squatter to resist the objection only on narrow grounds. He may prove that it is unconscionable, because of an equity by estoppel, for the registered proprietor to dispossess him. He must also show, in this, that the circumstances are such that he should be registered as proprietor.[13] For example, the squatter may have built on the disputed land in the mistaken belief that he owned it and the registered proprietor knowingly acquiesced in the error.[14] The squatter has also been given a defence based on an inconsistency between the boundaries to land on the ground and the Register entries, as where he has put up a fence in the place he thought correct having regard to the position on the ground.[15] But LRA 2002 is set out in such a way as to make applications for registration by squatters much more difficult than before. The element of secrecy in acquiring title is removed as the lessee and the freeholder must be notified of the application.

If the tenant or superior landlord make use of the suspension period following rejection of an application by the squatter based on 10 years' adverse possession to procure

9   If the lease is for a term of less than seven years, then title cannot be registered, but since the squatter's occupation must be apparent, the landlord will presumably have no difficulty in resisting it. It is understood (Colby *Estates Gazette* 17 July 1999, p 116) that adverse possession claims against short lessees are rare.
10   LRA 2002, Sch 6, paras 1 and 2.
11   LRA 2001, Sch 6, para 5. There are only narrow grounds on which the applicant can be registered with a title, notably, that it would be unconscionable for the registered proprietor to seek to dispossess the applicant (LRA 2001, Sch 6, para 5(2)(a)).
12   LRA 2002, Sch 6, para 6(1). There are provisions to ensure that if there are currently proceedings for possession under way against the squatter which involve asserting a right to possession to the land, or if judgment for possession has been given against him in the last two years, the application will fail, as also where the squatter has been evicted after a judgment for possession (LRA 2002, Sch 6, para 6(2)).
13   LRA 2002, Sch 6, para 5(2).
14   Example of the Explanatory Notes to LRA 2002, Sch 6.
15   LRA 2002, Sch 6, para 5(4). The squatter may also defend himself by proof that the registered proprietor led him to think that the boundary is where he now claims it to be.

the removal of the squatter on the ground that he has not been in adverse possession of the land for the full statutory period of 12 years, the squatter cannot ordinarily claim any registered title to the lease. If neither the lessee nor the superior owner evicts the squatter once the latter's application has been successfully objected to, the squatter has the right to re-apply for registration after two years have expired from the date of rejection of his first application. In that case, the application will succeed against the registered lessee, whose title will be superseded.[16] The previous 'title' of the squatter by adverse possession[17] will then be extinguished.[18]

Under the rules governing unregistered leaseholds of registered land, a squatter is only entitled to claim the title against which he squatted, ie the leasehold, not the freehold title.[19] This principle survives LRA 2002 with regard to the superior title, so, probably unavoidably, breaking with the principle that registration alone confers title. The adverse possessor applies, for example, once the two-year period is at an end, for registration as proprietor of the estate he has been in sufficient adverse possession against, which is the tenant's, not that of a superior landlord. When the latter's interest falls into possession at the end of the lease, he can still re-claim possession against the squatter. However, if the superior landlord does not object to a claim made to that estate after the 10-year period, he risks being saddled with the squatter as the new proprietor of the leasehold estate.[20] He cannot prevent this from happening by taking a surrender from the former tenant, after the squatter been entered as the new registered proprietor of the leasehold estate.

III   LANDLORD AND TENANT THIRD PARTY LIABILITY

Landlord liability in nuisance to third parties

The two principal sources of landlord liability in nuisance for present purposes arise out of the dilapidated state of the demised premises and out of claims by a tenant that

16   LRA 2002, Sch 6, paras 6 and 7. If the court has ordered the squatter to vacate the land under a judgment for possession given against him within the last two years, he cannot make the subsequent application (LRA 2002, Sch 6, para 6(2)). But, as noted by the Law Commission, the squatter must wait for two years in question before applying. It is possible that a squatter could abandon possession after the 10-year period and before the expiry of the 12-year period Law Com No 254 (1998) 'Land Registration for the Twenty-First Century' Cmnd 4027, para 10.49.

17   Which overrides as against third parties under LRA 2002, Sch 1, para 2 as an occupation interest. The trust provisions of Land Registration Act 1925, s 75 were deemed inappropriate to the new principles of LRA 2002. They have, subject to transitional provisions, been repealed by the 2002 Act.

18   LRA 2002, Sch 6, para 9. However, prior interests remain in force such as those of a person entitled to enforce restrictive covenants: ibid. This principle is carried forward from unregistered land: see *Re Nisbet and Potts' Contract* [1906] 1 Ch 386.

19   *Fairweather v St Marylebone Property Co Ltd* [1963] AC 510, [1962] 2 All ER 288, HL.

20   Under LRA 2002, Sch 6, para 9, while the estate is free of any registered charge affecting the estate immediately before registration (LRA 2002, Sch 6, para 9(3)) it is not provided that the adverse possessor is freed from performing leasehold obligations.

another tenant of the landlord is causing him a nuisance, which the landlord has adopted. The second of these sources is dealt with first.

(i) Landlord liability on account of conduct of other tenants

The conduct of a neighbouring or adjoining tenant or tenants may cause a complainant tenant a nuisance in accordance with general principles: matters such as harassment, racial abuse, deliberate damage to the neighbouring premises which impacts on the complainant tenant's use and enjoyment of his or her own premises. The issue here discussed is narrow: it relates to the extent to which the common law is prepared to hold the landlord liable in the tort of nuisance on account of the nuisances committed by another tenant. In a recent case,[21] liability of a landlord was denied. The tenants alleged that they had been the victims of a campaign of racial harassment from other tenants on the same estate. The tenants' complaint was that, knowing of these matters, the landlords did not take possession proceedings against the offending tenants or do anything else within their powers to put matters right. The principle was affirmed, approving a well-established case,[22] that ordinarily the person to be sued for nuisance was the occupier from whose premises the nuisance emanated: the tenant not the landlord in our case. Liability in nuisance cannot be based simply on the fact that the landlord may know of the nuisance committed by the tenant and has taken no steps to prevent it.[23] The landlord is only liable if he had authorised the tenant to commit the nuisance, as where the nuisance was expressly authorised in the lease, or the landlord has actively participated in the nuisance,[24] or a nuisance was the certain result of the purposes for which the property was let.[25]

(ii) Landlord liability arising from dilapidated adjoining premises

There are a number of circumstances in which a landlord may face liability in nuisance or negligence on account of the dilapidated state of the premises. These may be summarised as follows.[26]

---

21 *Hussain v Lancaster City Council* [2000] QB 1, [1999] 4 All ER 125, CA. See also *Mowan v Wandsworth London BC* (2000) 33 HLR 616 (landlord not liable in nuisance for bad behaviour of a mentally ill adjoining tenant). The claimant was not deprived of her right to a fair trial by the 'exclusionary' principle of nuisance: the rule was not a total exclusion and in any case there was no cause of action.

22 *Smith v Scott* [1973] Ch 314, [1972] 3 All ER 645, concerned with a letting to adjoining tenants on terms expressly prohibiting nuisance, who nevertheless committed numerous acts of nuisance, for which the landlord was not held liable.

23 *Malzy v Eicholz* [1916] 2 KB 308.

24 *Southwark London Borough Council v Mills* [1999] 4 All ER 449, [1999] 3 WLR 939, HL.

25 In *Page Motors Ltd v Epsom and Ewell BC* (1981) 80 LGR 337, business tenants proved that landlords adopted the nuisance behaviour of certain gypsies on land adjoining the demised premises, eg by continuing the gypsies' possession on the land on policy grounds, and then allowing them to make use of a water supply and skips supplied by the landlords.

26 See also West and Smith's *Law of Dilapidations* ch 13.

Where a lease expressly reserves a right to the landlord to enter and repair the premises, or where such a right is conferred on him by statute, and also where it is implied,[27] then if a third party is caused damage or injury by a defective condition in the premises, the landlord is liable to that person in nuisance. It is taken from the right of entry and repair that the landlord has sufficient control over the premises. Thus where premises had been let to yearly tenants, and the lease conferred on the landlord a right to enter, inspect and repair, the landlord was held liable to a passer-by who suffered injury when he fell down a light shaft with a defective cover.[28] The landlord cannot avoid liability in nuisance in such cases by pointing to a tenant's covenant to repair in the lease.

Where premises abut the highway, and they are in a dangerous or defective condition, the landlord may be liable to a third party whose adjoining premises are damaged or who suffers personal injury as a result of that condition, provided the state of the premises amounts to a nuisance. The landlord must have undertaken a duty to repair. This rule of strict liability extends to a case where the landlord did not know in advance of the danger.[29] If the lease has an obligation to repair by the landlord coupled with an express or implied or statutory right to enter and inspect the premises, this suffices to give the landlord sufficient control for the purposes of this rule. There are exceptions to the rule, notably, that there is no liability on the landlord if the condition of the premises was caused by an act of a trespasser or by some cause other than neglect to repair, such as a secret and unobservable process of nature such as subsidence. If a latent rather than a patent defect has caused the third party damage or injury, the onus lies on him to show that the landlord had actual or presumed knowledge of the defect and also that he then failed to take any reasonable steps to end the nuisance, with ample time to do so.[30] Thus, if damage suddenly manifests itself from a hidden, and until then unknown, latent defect, the landlord avoids liability. The strict liability rule is exceptional.[31]

The landlord may also be liable to a third party on account of the state and condition of premises[32] let to a tenant if the landlord licenses the tenant to commit a nuisance. The third party must show that the landlord let the premises knowing them to be in a dilapidated and dangerous condition, as where a landlord let premises which he knew

27 *Mint v Good* [1951] 1 KB 517, CA (weekly tenancy, where such a right was implied under the guise of business efficacy).
28 *Heap v Inde Coope and Allsopp Ltd* [1940] 2 KB 476, CA. The third party could have chosen to bring an action against the tenant: see *Brew Bros Ltd v Snax (Ross) Ltd* [1970] 1 QB 612, CA.
29 *Wringe v Cohen* [1940] 1 KB 229, CA. This principle was rejected in Canada (in *O'Leary v Meiltides and Eastern Trust Co* (1966) 20 DLR (2d) 258) and has been criticised as being inconsistent with principle (1940) 56 LQR 140)).
30 *Sedleigh-Denfield v O'Callaghan* [1940] AC 880, HL.
31 See *Southwark London Borough Council v Mills* [1999] 4 All ER 449, [1999] 3 WLR 939, HL.
32 As well as for an escape of fire from premises of which the landlord retains the common parts: see *Ribee v Norrie* [2001] L & TR 23, [2001] L & TR 259, CA.

at the time of the tenancy had insecure chimneys.[33] The landlord may be liable under this principle even if he has not undertaken any repairing obligations, provided that he has sufficient actual or presumed knowledge or control over the premises at the date of the letting. Thus a landlord who let premises known by him to be suffering from seepage under a flank wall which was tilting towards adjoining premises was liable to the neighbouring owner for damage caused.[34]

Where a landlord has let premises to a tenant and then lets adjoining premises to another tenant, and the first tenant complains that the use of the premises by the second tenant is a nuisance, the landlord is liable to the complainant only in exceptional circumstances. The House of Lords refused to hold a council landlord liable in nuisance where the complainant asserted that, owing to inadequate soundproofing in the flat concerned, all the noises of domestic living could be heard. There was no suggestion that the landlord had authorised the second tenant to commit a nuisance, and the normal user of a residential flat for living in could not amount to a nuisance to any neighbouring tenant of the same landlord. The landlord could thus not be required, under the guise of nuisance, to upgrade the sound-proofing concerned.[35]

Tenant liability in nuisance

Tenants are under a duty to highway users to ensure that no injury is caused to them from a defective condition of the premises.[36] Regular inspections should reduce the risk of liability but they cannot eliminate it completely, although if the defect concerned is secret and cannot be discovered by a reasonable inspection, the tenant is not liable (much as the landlord would escape liability in similar circumstances).[37] The strict liability rule, to which there are exceptions similar to those applying to landlords, covers only highway users, otherwise negligence by the tenant must be shown, which may not be an unduly heavy onus for a claimant to discharge.[38]

33 *Todd v Flight* (1860) 9 CBNS 377.
34 *Brew Bros Ltd v Snax (Ross) Ltd* [1970] 1 QB 612, CA. If the landlord does not have the requisite degree of knowledge, he is not liable: *St Anne's Well Brewery Co v Roberts* (1928) 44 TLR 703, CA.
35 *Southwark London Borough Council v Mills* [1999] 4 All ER 449, [1999] 3 WLR 939, HL. Compare *Sampson v Hodson-Pressinger* [1981] 3 All ER 710, CA, as explained by the House of Lords in the *Mills* case, where the only way an altered terrace over the complainant's flat could be used was in such a way as to cause a nuisance. This case was treated as exceptional in the *Southwark* case.
36 *Tarry v Ashton* (1876) 1 QBD 314. This case was concerned with a heavy lamp which fell on a passer-by. Proof of negligence was not required. See also *Wilchick v Marks and Silverstone* [1934] 2 KB 56 (where the tenants failed to recover their loss, as they could not prove an obligation to repair by the landlords).
37 See eg *Barker v Herbert* [1911] 2 KB 633.
38 See *Cunard v Antifyre Ltd* [1933] 1 KB 551, where damages were recovered from a tenant who failed to keep a gutter from falling into a condition where it fell into the premises occupied by the plaintiffs.

Liability of landlords and tenants as occupier

Landlords and tenants alike may be liable under statute, in negligence, to a third party injured on the premises where they are 'occupiers'.

The landlord may be an 'occupier' of premises if he has a sufficient degree of control over them, as where a landlord lets part of the premises and retains common parts such as an entrance hall, a staircase, lift, or forecourt. In these circumstances, the landlord is subject to the common duty of care. Where the whole or parts of premises are occupied by a tenant, the tenant is the 'occupier' of the whole or of the parts for statutory purposes. The duty extends to 'visitors' as opposed to 'persons other than visitors'[39] and is imposed by the Occupiers' Liability Act 1957, s 2. The common duty of care is to take such care as is reasonable in all the circumstances to see that the visitor will be reasonably safe in using the premises for the purposes for which he is there (Occupiers' Liability Act 1957, s 2(2)). The duty applies to the visitor's person and property.[40] The duty is not to ensure the visitor's safety, but to show reasonableness.[41] In determining the discharge of the common duty of care, regard is to be had to all the circumstances (Occupiers' Liability Act 1957, s 2(4)). The duty is subjective, because it is likely to be higher with children and elderly persons, and lower with a normally active adult. Two among many examples must suffice of the duty having been broken.[42] A landlord's failure to replace the glass in a school door broke the statutory duty,[43] and where a pathway regularly used for access by the elderly to certain premises became irregular, so that an old person fell on a projecting paving stone, liability was constituted.[44]

If there is a known defect on the premises, the landlord or tenant 'occupier' may be able to discharge his duty to the visitor by giving him adequate warning, as by using

39   In the case of the latter, still referred to as 'trespassers' (*Ratcliff v McConnell* [1999] 1 WLR 670) the relevant and lower duty (otherwise a burglar would enjoy a higher standard of care than a lawful visitor) is laid down by s 1 of the Occupiers' Liability Act 1984. See Buckley [1984] Conv 412. If a person enters premises to communicate with the occupier, then, whether or not he knows his entry is prohibited, that person is arguably not a 'trespasser': *Christian v Johannessen* [1956] NZLR 664. Query – whether this generous principle would extend to unwelcome persons such as 'competitive observers' (see *Chaytor v London, New York and Paris Association of Fashion and Price* (1961) 30 DLR (2d) 527).

40   The duty is subject to specific qualifications, so that notably the occupier is not under any obligation to the visitor with regard to risks voluntarily accepted by him as visitor (Occupiers' Liability Act 1957, s 2(5)); the degree of care, or want of it, ordinarily looked for in a visitor is a relevant factor in assessing the common duty of care (Occupiers' Liability Act 1957, s 2(3)); but an occupier must be prepared for children to be less careful than adults (Occupiers' Liability Act 1957, s 2(3)(a)): thus the occupier may have to remove obvious sources of danger to children from the premises.

41   *M'Glone v British Railways Board* 1966 SC (HL) 1 at 15 (Lord Guest).

42   In *Jolley v Sutton London BC* [2000] 1 WLR 1082 at 1089, it was said that occupiers' liability was a very fact-sensitive area. For this reason, a long list of examples would seem otiose.

43   *J v Staffordshire County Council* [1997] CLY 3783.

44   *Wright v Greenwich London BC* [1996] CLY 4474.

prominent notices, but a warning will not absolve an occupier from liability unless in all the circumstances it is enough to enable the visitor to be reasonably safe (Occupiers' Liability Act 1957, s 2(4)(a)). If a warning notice would have made no difference to the visitor's conduct, he cannot complain of its absence.[45] If the danger complained of was caused by an independent contractor employed by him, the occupier is treated as having discharged the common duty of care if he took such steps as would reasonably be expected of him to satisfy himself that the contractor was competent and that the work had been properly done (Occupiers' Liability Act 1957, s 2(4)(b)).[46]

Ordinarily it is the tenant, as having exclusive possession of the premises, who is the occupier of premises for statutory purposes, although there may be two occupiers where the landlord retains some part of the premises from the demise, such as staircases or entrances.[47]

Occupiers are free to restrict, modify or exclude the common duty of care, as by a prominent notice at the entrance to the premises to the effect that the visitor enters at their own risk. However, by the Unfair Contract Terms Act 1977, s 2(1), an occupier cannot restrict his liability for death or personal injuries resulting from negligence by any notice. In other circumstances than these, the exclusion or restriction must comply with statutory tests of reasonableness (Unfair Contract Terms Act 1977, s 2(2)). However, the limits on the freedom of an occupier to exclude or restrict liability only apply to his business liability (Unfair Contract Terms Act 1977, s 1(3)). This means that a domestic occupier[48] remains free to restrict or abrogate liability for negligence by notice or otherwise.[49]

IV   ACCESS ORDERS

(i)   Introduction

The common law provides only limited rights to an owner or tenant to obtain access to adjoining land for the purpose of repairs or maintenance work, where the neighbouring owner or tenant is not prepared to permit the access under licence. The neighbouring land may enjoy a right of access under an easement, but this may not be available. Thus if there is no easement and a licence is refused, or is only obtainable on unacceptable conditions, and there is no alternative means of access to the neighbour's

---

45 *Staples v West Dorset District Council* (1995) 93 LGR 536.
46 See *Ferguson v Welsh* [1987] 1 WLR 1553, HL (from which it appears that if the occupier had reasonable grounds to believe that the independent contractor was using an unsafe system, it might be reasonable to expect the occupier to supervise him).
47 *Wheat v E Lacon & Co Ltd* [1966] AC 552, HL.
48 As well as an occupier who permits access to the premises for recreational or educational purposes.
49 The borderline between domestic and business occupation may not be easy to fix, as where a domestic tenant takes in lodgers: see Mesher [1979] Conv 58.

property, until legislation was enacted, deadlock could result. As a result, an owner might find that, for example, a flank wall abutting on adjoining premises would simply go unrepaired, with resulting deterioration of the property. The Law Commission examined the position and concluded that it was not satisfactory.[50] In due course, Parliament enacted the Access to Neighbouring Land Act 1992, which applies to landlords and tenants alike.

(ii) Main principles of legislation

The overall purpose and effect of the Access to Neighbouring Land Act 1992 is to grant access rights (which must arise under a county court order) to neighbouring owners or lessees, for the purpose of carrying out 'basic preservation works' to the land in question. The order of the court may be subject to a number of safeguards designed to protect the respondent owner or lessee from undue interference with their use of the land, by means of access which may be intrusive and inconvenient. At the same time, the person gaining access will have proved that it is necessary for the works in question. The result of balancing the claims of neighbouring owners or lessees is a complex act.

(iii) Outline of operation of the Act

Both a landlord and a tenant may be subject to orders granting access rights under statute, and both may apply for such orders against a neighbouring owner or lessee. The Access to Neighbouring Land Act 1992 only applies if the neighbour refuses access. The applicant then seeks an access order from the county court. The court must be satisfied that access is needed to carry out 'basic preservation works' to the land, notably the 'maintenance, repair or renewal of any part of a building or other structure comprised in, or situate on, the dominant land' (Access to Neighbouring Land Act 1992, s 1(4)).[51] The applicant must prove that the works are 'reasonably necessary for the preservation of the whole or any part of the dominant land'. The works must be shown to be incapable of being carried out without entry to the servient land, or if this is not shown, the works must be 'substantially more difficult to carry out' without entry to the servient land (Access to Neighbouring Land Act 1992, s 1(2)). Once there is proved a need for works, then it is presumed that these are necessary to preserve the land (Access to Neighbouring Land Act 1992, s 1(4)). The access order must, so as to protect the respondent, specify the area of land to which access is required, and the date and period of entry (Access to Neighbouring Land Act 1992, s 2(1)(c)). Thus, the Access to Neighbouring Land Act 1992 does not seem

50 Law Com No 151 (1985) 'Rights of Access to Neighbouring Land'.
51 'Basic preservation works' also include – the clearance, repair or renewal of any drain, sewer, pipe or cable in or on the dominant land; the treatment, cutting back, felling, removal or replacement of any hedge, tree, shrub or growing thing in or on the dominant land; and the filling in or clearance of any ditch on the dominant land.

to allow an access order on the ground of mere convenience if the applicant can gain access to the part of their own premises needing work of preservation by some other, more expensive or inconvenient means. Moreover, the Act generally denies any right to an access order for improvement or alteration works, unless these are incidental to the work of preservation (Access to Neighbouring Land Act 1992, s 1(5)). These restrictions are important,[52] having regard to the intrusive nature of an access order. (In the absence of authority, they may suffice to prevent successful challenges to the Access to Neighbouring Land Act 1992 on the supposed basis that they might interfere with an owner's right to his possessions or privacy in the sense envisaged by HRA 1998.) In addition to these matters, an access order must specify the works in question and also contain conditions with which the applicant must comply. The applicant must also leave the land and make good any damage, once the period of access allowed is at an end (Access to Neighbouring Land Act 1992, s 3(3)(b)). On the other hand, an access order may entitle the owner to bring materials, plant and equipment onto the part of the premises to which access is permitted (Access to Neighbouring Land Act 1992, s 3(2)(b)), and to carry out the works, even if the respondent dissents. There are a number of bars to an access order being made, as where unreasonable interference with the occupation of the respondent is shown. Once made and registered, an access order binds both the tenant and the landlord of the land to which access is to be granted, provided the landlord has been joined in the application (Access to Neighbouring Land Act 1992, s 4(1)). An access order will bind, automatically, a person to whom the reversion on a lease has been assigned after the order has been made (Access to Neighbouring Land Act 1992, s 4(1)(b)). But if there are tenants in occupation of the 'servient land' over which access is sought, if the applicant wishes the current landlord to be bound by an access order, he must join him in the action.

(iv) Comments

The Access to Neighbouring Land Act 1992 goes less far in conferring access for the purpose of repairs and related work than it could have done,[53] but this may be as well having regard to the omni-present shadow of challenges under HRA 1998. The Access to Neighbouring Land Act 1992 contains the important safeguard to those who may have to put up with access to their land from a landlord or tenant that the terms of the access are defined by the court, which has a wide discretion. The right of access has been labelled as a form of short term and limited easement.[54] The right to apply to court cannot be contracted out of or restricted (Access to Neighbouring Land Act 1992, s 4(4)), so that if access is granted by licence for a sum of money which the requesting

---

52 As are those enabling the court to lay down the works, and also to avoid or restrict any loss of privacy to the respondent, not to mention the compensation provisions (Access to Neighbouring Land Act 1992, s 2)).

53 Compare the Property Act 1974, s 180 (Queensland), which confers a right of user in broad terms, in the form of an easement or licence, for a perpetual or fixed period if the servient owner has unreasonably refused such a right over his land.

54 Wilkinson [1992] *Conv* 225.

lessee or landlord is not prepared to pay, then an application to court for an access order may be made. Access might not just be sought in the case of landlord and tenant in order to enable compliance with a covenant to repair: it might be needed to enable the landlord to comply with public health legislation, for example. There are uncertainties in the Access to Neighbouring Land Act 1992. Access must be 'reasonably necessary', which presumably it would be in the case just mentioned, if the only way the work could be done was by access to the neighbouring land. The statutory term 'respondent' includes a landlord and tenant alike, but it is not clear whether it would include a licensee. The effect of an access order is evidently to confer immunity within the confines of the court order on the person obtaining it for the purpose of the relevant works to the land.[55] Failure by an entering lessee or landlord to comply with the terms of an access order would expose the person concerned to an action for breach of statutory duty.

---

55   'Land' is also not defined in Access to Neighbouring Land Act 1992 but it bears a wide meaning, because in *Dean v Walker* (1996) 73 P&CR 366, CA the expression was held to include a party wall.

Termination of tenancies

Chapter 11

Introduction

1 TERMINATION AT COMMON LAW

Part C of this book is concerned with an examination of the methods by which, at common law,[1] a lease or tenancy may be ended by the landlord or by the tenant.

According to Lord Hoffmann, both fixed-term leases and periodic tenancies end by effluxion of time, as where the termination date of a fixed-term lease arrives, or on the expiry date of a landlord's or tenant's notice to quit.[2] This is because in English law, rights of property are, in his view, four-dimensional. They were defined not only by the physical boundaries of the property but for the time the interests were to endure. When a fixed-term lease comes to an end, the tenant has no property to dispose of. The landlord's reversion falls in and he is entitled to regain possession of the property. In the case of a periodic tenancy, it comes to an end at the expiry of the last period for which the landlord or tenant have been willing for the tenancy to continue (that is, as stated in the relevant notice to quit). The form of termination in the case of a periodic tenancy is that of a notice to quit, which is unnecessary in the case of a fixed-term lease, where expiry comes about automatically at common law. However, to their Lordships, form must not be confused with substance.

Sometimes, fixed-term leases may be terminated before the arrival of the contractually agreed termination date. One of the most controversial landlord remedies for breach of tenant covenant is forfeiture. If the right to re-enter or forfeit a lease for breach of covenant is expressly reserved in the lease, the landlord can invoke forfeiture in a serious case of tenant breach. If the court is not disposed to grant relief to the tenant, so reinstating him, the lease terminates without compensation and the landlord

---

1   It will be appreciated that where a lease expires by time running out, or a tenancy ends by notice to quit, the tenant may be able under statute to retain possession either, as with business tenancies, pending renewal, if available, or, as with assured shorthold tenancies, pending eviction in proceedings, if the tenant is not willing to quit voluntarily.

2   *Newlon Housing Association v Alsulaimen* [1999] L & TR 38.

repossesses the premises. This remedy, no doubt mainly aimed at business or long residential lessees, is open to abuses by unscrupulous landlords. Thus, it has apparently been recently used as a means of trying to terminate long leases of residential flats for failure to pay ground rent or service charges.[3] In the past, some business landlords have made use of this remedy to try to end leases on account of relatively trifling dilapidations.[4] Still other commercial landlords have seized on the fact that it is possible to forfeit a lease of vacant commercial premises by means of 'peaceable re-entry'. This is a cheap method of putting an end to a lease outside the courts, which has been frowned on by the courts,[5] and which might infringe HRA 1998,[6] but which the Law Commission would like to codify.[7]

Termination of a lease or informal tenancy by the tenant may be achieved notably by the tenant surrendering the lease to the landlord, or by the tenant claiming that the landlord has by conduct repudiated the lease. If the landlord and tenant so conduct themselves that the only inference to draw is that neither is any longer bound by the lease or tenancy, it will be impliedly surrendered, even if no formal deed of surrender has been executed. Thus if a tenant leaves the keys to premises with the landlord and the latter re-lets the premises to a different person, the tenant is not allowed by equity to claim later that his tenancy is still operative.[8] Repudiation is, by contrast, related to frustration. If the landlord shows so complete a disregard of his fundamental obligations of the tenancy that the tenant is deprived of the whole benefit of the lease, as where he totally neglects in breach of covenant to carry out repairs so that the premises are uninhabitable, his repudiatory conduct may be 'accepted' by the tenant leaving the premises and refusing to pay rent in future.[9] It may be as well for tenants that the courts have adapted the contractual principle of fundamental breach to leases, since the Law Commission seem to have deferred, if not abandoned, their original, and useful, scheme for tenant termination orders against persistently bad landlords.[10]

II   FRUSTRATION

Frustration is one means by which an executed lease may be brought to an end, if a frustrating event takes place during the currency of the lease.[11] In the present context,

---

3   Hence the specific curbs placed on the use of forfeiture by eg Housing Act 1996, s 81 and extended to forfeiture notices against residential leases by CLRA 2002, s 168.

4   Hence Leasehold Property (Repairs) Act 1938 (see *National Real Estate & Finance Co Ltd v Hassan* [1939] 2 KB 61 at 78).

5   *Billson v Residential Apartments Ltd* [1992] 1 AC 494, HL.

6   See Bruce (2000) 150 NLJ 462.

7   Consultative Document 'Termination of Tenancies by Physical Re-Entry' (1998) and Press Release, 30 June 1999. Reform of the whole of forfeiture was proposed as long ago as 1985 (see ch 13 below) but at the time of writing no legislation had been passed although a new draft Termination of Tenancies Bill was awaited from the Law Commission.

8   *Proudreed Ltd v Microgen Holdings plc* [1996] 1 EGLR 89, CA.

9   As in *Hussein v Mehlman* [1992] 2 EGLR 87; also below.

10   The 1994 Termination of Tenancies Bill (LC No 221) omitted provision for such schemes.

11   For an exhaustive analysis see Treitel *Frustration and Force Majeure* (1994) ch 11.

frustration is some event, such as the total destruction of the land itself, or the rendering of the land totally or substantially unusable for a mutually contemplated purpose throughout the lease, which destroys the whole basis of the relationship of landlord and tenant.[12] Should frustration take place, the tenant is relieved thereafter from any liability to pay rent. The lease is terminated. It is not certain what events, other than perhaps an earthquake or flood which destroyed the demised land, might frustrate the estate granted to a lessee, because these events alone could be said to render the bare legal estate in the land useless, as opposed to making performance of the tenant's obligations less convenient or more expensive. It has therefore been said, in defence of a narrow doctrine of frustration, that in the case of a long lease, the lessee takes upon himself the risk, by accepting a long term, of changes in circumstances which he could not have foreseen at the date of the grant of the lease, even though the burden of his obligations may be thereby increased.[13]

The following events supervening after the grant of a lease have been insufficiently serious to frustrate it: destruction of buildings on the land; utter impossibility of building on the land due to wartime regulations;[14] the fact that some part of the land could not be used at all for quite a significant part of the lease, or that there will be severe disruption to the user of the demised premises for the purpose or purposes contemplated in the lease, for part of the term.[15]

The fact that a supervening event, such as temporary impossibility of building on land due to regulations, may suspend the performance of an obligation of a lessee cannot of itself mean that the whole lease is frustrated, at least where it was granted for a long term; however, the possibility has now been canvassed of 'frustratory mitigation'.[16] If this principle were to be invoked, it might temporarily relieve a lessee from the performance of a specific obligation, without freeing him from the need to comply with the rest of his covenants. Thus, a lessee who could not, due to planning restrictions not foreseen at the time the lease was granted, build on his land, might be able to avert forfeiture for non-compliance with that obligation (unless and until the planning position changed) but could not avoid paying rent.

III REPUDIATION

An assured shorthold tenant was held to have been entitled to accept his landlord's repudiation of the tenancy occasioned by the latter's complete and grave refusal to

---

12 *National Carriers Ltd v Panalpina (Northern) Ltd* [1981] AC 675, [1981] 1 All ER 161, HL. Frustration may also apply to a contract for a lease: *Rom Securities Ltd v Rogers (Holdings) Ltd* (1967) 205 Estates Gazette 427.
13 Treitel, para 11-008; but the application of this doctrine to say, a five-year tenant of furnished premises should these be destroyed is less easy to defend.
14 *Cricklewood Property and Investment Trust Ltd v Leighton's Investment Trust Ltd* [1945] AC 221, [1945] 1 All ER 252, HL.
15 *National Carriers Ltd v Panalpina (Northern) Ltd* [1981] AC 675, [1981] 1 All ER 161, HL.
16 See Morgan [1995] Conv 74, noting *John Lewis Properties plc v Viscount Chelsea* (1993) 67 P & CR 120.

comply with his repairing obligations.[17] Assuming that the party in breach has notified the innocent party that he does not intend to comply with an essential obligation of the lease, repudiation is operative, at the injured party's election, where a serious breach of that covenant is established. In the case of a landlord, his persistent refusal to comply with a statutory or express covenant to keep in repair is a candidate for the application of the doctrine, and it has been held that a very serious breach of covenant not to derogate from grant was repudiatory in nature.[18] In the case of tenants, a total abandonment of the premises without paying any further rent might suffice. However, the courts will not lightly allow the invocation of this principle. Thus, it was held that intensive parking of vehicles on the tenant's unit forecourt was not such as to repudiate the lease, as the tenants were not deprived of the whole benefit of the lease, but rather seriously inconvenienced.[19] The most appropriate remedy in this case would have been damages.

To justify applying the contractual principles of repudiation to contracts for leases and executed leases, we note that the House of Lords have more than once treated the interpretation of covenants in leases as being governed by contractual principles,[20] so that the legal estate created by an executed lease may be determined by repudiation as much as by frustration, as is now possible, albeit only in exceptional circumstances.

There is a limit. Repudiation of an executed lease would resemble forfeiture where relief was refused, in that it would only be in the case of a fundamental breach of the whole lease that it could be invoked as freeing the other party from his own obligation to perform all its covenants himself, allowing him to terminate the lease and sue for damages. This idea seems to be borne out in the authorities.[21] In a leading Canadian case, the tenant abandoned premises held on a 15-year lease, despite his covenant to carry on his business continuously for the whole lease. The precinct was adversely affected. The landlord was entitled to accept the tenant's repudiation of the contract and to sue for loss of future rent for the unexpired term of the lease, having mitigated his losses by re-letting to other tenants at lower aggregate rents than that reserved from the ex-tenant.[22] In this respect, repudiation, being anticipatory breach, because the injured party does not have to wait until the lease expires before bringing an action

---

17   *Hussein v Mehlman* [1992] 2 EGLR 87; Bright [1993] Conv 71; Harpum [1993] CLJ 212.
18   *Chartered Trust plc v Davies* [1997] 2 EGLR 83 (see ch 6, above). The tenant was driven to bankruptcy by the landlord's conduct.
19   *Nynehead Developments Ltd v RH Fibreboard Containers Ltd* [1999] 1 EGLR 7; see Pawlowski & Brown [1999] Conv 150.
20   See *United Scientific Holdings Ltd v Burnley Borough Council* [1978] AC 904.
21   For a recent example, see *Abidogun v Frolan Health Care Ltd* [2001] 45 EG 138 (CS), where it was held that in substance forfeiture not repudiation (which latter would avoid the need for a statutory notice) was being claimed.
22   *Highway Properties Ltd v Kelly Douglas & Co Ltd* (1971) 17 DLR (3d) 710. A landlord cannot, after forfeiture, claim damages for loss of rent for the rest of the forfeited term of the lease: *Jones v Carter* (1846) 15 M & W 718.

in respect of it, has advantages to landlords not present where they accept an implied surrender, where no similarly based claim could seemingly be formulated.

A further example, already mentioned, of breach of covenant serious enough to raise the application of repudiation would be a complete abandonment of the premises by the tenant,[23] or a tenant's outright refusal to pay any rent.[24] It is significant that the High Court of Australia has been reluctant to place a wide interpretation on the circumstances in which repudiation is available. It has thus held that even persistent breaches of a covenant to pay rent, in the absence of express stipulation, would not go to the root of the contract, at least where the tenant intended to pay in due course.[25] In a further decision, where the tenant holding an unregistered agreement for a lease failed to pay rent because of his baseless claim that the landlord had failed satisfactorily to complete certain works, the High Court of Australia did hold that the tenant had by conduct repudiated the lease, exposing him to a landlord's action for loss of rent.[26] However, the Court recognised that a lease was not an ordinary contract. It passed an interest in property. Therefore, an isolated or insignificant breach of covenant would not trigger a right of either party to claim that the whole lease had been repudiated. If the tenant repudiates his own essential lease obligations, and the landlord accepts this, as things currently stand, the landlord could regain possession of the premises without the restrictions applying in the case of forfeiture. Even if the law is reformed so as to require a termination order in the case of any termination by a landlord, including one after tenant repudiation of his lease, repudiation seems to be an exceptional remedy.

---

23 As in eg *Buchanan v Byrnes* (1906) 3 CLR 704 and as envisaged in *Kingston upon Thames Royal London Borough Council v Marlow* [1996] 1 EGLR 101.
24 As envisaged in *Hussein v Mehlman* [1992] 2 EGLR 87.
25 *Shevill v Builders Licensing Board* (1982) 149 CLR 620.
26 *Progressive Mailing House Pty Ltd v Tabali Pty Ltd* (1985) 157 CLR 17.

CHAPTER 12

Termination of leases and tenancies at common law

1   INTRODUCTION

A fixed-term lease expires by effluxion of time and so ends automatically, without the need for any proceedings by the landlord, at the date fixed for the expiry of the tenancy. A periodic tenancy continues unless or until either party decides to end it by notice to quit, on the expiry of which the tenancy expires by effluxion of time.[1] In this chapter, we examine the three main methods by which a lease or tenancy may be ended at common law, notice to quit, surrender or forfeiture.[2] The fact that the landlord may be able to terminate a tenancy at common law does not necessarily mean that he will be able as a direct result to obtain physical possession of the premises. Even in the case of assured shorthold tenancies, for example, where there is no right of renewal[3] after expiry of the tenancy, the landlord cannot obtain possession except with an order of court.[4] If the tenancy is 'excluded', notably where the landlord is a residential occupier sharing the premises with the tenant, no order of court is required in order to evict the tenant on termination of his or her tenancy.[5]

Once a head tenancy or lease has come to an end, and the head tenant has failed to remove any sub-tenant before the end of his or her own lease, then the tenant is liable, at common law, and in the absence of statutory protection for the sub-lessee, to the landlord for the latter's costs in removing the sub-tenant, and for lost mesne profits, as where the landlord had agreed to re-let the premises.[6]

1   *Newlon Housing Trust v Alsulaimen* [1999] L & TR 38 at 42.
2   Which is a method of termination which is expressly preserved against business tenants (Landlord and Tenant Act 1954, s 24(2)).
3   As opposed to the statement in the Housing Corporation Shorthold Tenants' Charter, p 6, which envisages landlords making 'every effort' to help the tenant stay in their home.
4   Protection from Eviction Act 1977, s 2.
5   Protection from Eviction Act 1977, s 3A.
6   *Henderson v Van Cooten* (1922) 67 Sol Jo 228.

Fixtures on the land

The tenant may have installed items, that were originally chattels, onto the land during the lease which have become part and parcel of the land[7] and so permanently attached to it, so that their removal would either destroy the item itself or permanently damage the land. This book is not the place for a detailed examination of the law governing the tests determining when a chattel becomes a fixture.[8] In essence, the courts look at the degree of annexation of the chattel, asking questions such as whether it rests on its own weight, so that it can be detached without injuring the land. Alternatively, the courts ask whether the item has been permanently attached to the land, in which case permanent damage to the land is likely to result if the item is removed.[9] If there is doubt from the degree of annexation or attachment test, the courts look at the intention of the tenant, or his predecessor, as the person who brought the chattel onto the land. The tenant may have intended to improve the land permanently. Alternatively, his intention might have been to enjoy the chattel as such. The courts have sometimes applied both tests. On this basis, a tenant who installed a greenhouse which was easy to detach from its supports and remove, had not installed a fixture.[10] But if the item concerned is an air-conditioning plant, it would be difficult for a tenant installing this into a building to argue that the plant was not a fixture.[11]

At common law, fixtures are part of the land. Fixtures which have been installed by a tenant will pass to the landlord at the end of the lease. The courts have long recognised that it would be damaging to the interests of tenants if they could not, at the end of the tenancy, remove trade fixtures, such as engines and boilers, petrol pumps and fittings in a public house.[12] The right of removal must be exercised at any time during the tenancy and also, where appropriate, during any statutory extension of the tenancy, but not once the tenancy has ended,[13] unless the landlord licenses the tenant to have access to the premises. Tenants are also entitled, at common law, to remove domestic and ornamental fixtures[14] but if irreparable injury would be caused to the fabric of the building itself as opposed to the decorations, then this privilege is not applicable.[15]

7   The expression of the House of Lords in *Elitestone Ltd v Morris* [1997] 2 EGLR 115; see Conway [1998] Conv 418.
8   See eg Cheshire and Burn, pp 151 – 157; Megarry and Wade 14 – 311 – 14 – 328; West and Smith, pp 279-81.
9   *Holland v Hodgson* (1872) LR 7 CP 328; *Reid v Smith* (1905) 3 CLR 656 and *Chelsea Yacht & Boat Co Ltd v Pope* [2000] 2 EGLR 23.
10   As in *Deen v Andrews* [1986] 1 EGLR 262. A similar result might follow with light office partitions which could be easily moved around: *Short v Kirkpatrick* [1982] 1 NZLR 358.
11   *Pan Australian Credits (SA) Pty Ltd v Kolim Pty Ltd* (1981) 27 SASR 353.
12   *Climie v Wood* (1869) LR 4 Exch 328, *Smith v City Petroleum Co Ltd* [1940] 1 All ER 260 and *Elliott v Bishop* (1854) 10 Exch 496, respectively. However, a substantial building which has become permanently attached to the land was not classified as a tenants' trade fixture: *Pole-Carew v Western Counties and General Manure Co Ltd* [1920] 2 Ch 97, especially at 121-22 (Warrington LJ); cf *Webb v Frank Bevis Ltd* [1940] 1 All ER 247.
13   *New Zealand Government Property Corpn v HM & S Ltd* [1982] 1 All ER 624, CA.
14   Such as tapestries, stoves, cupboards and bookcases fastened by ties to the wall.
15   *Spyer v Phillipson* [1931] 2 Ch 183. In this case Stuart period wood panelling had been attached by comparatively light ties to the walls of certain rooms by the tenant, who was held entitled to remove the panelling on expiry of his lease.

The tenant of an agricultural holding to whom the Agricultural Holdings Act 1986 applies has, under the Agricultural Holdings Act 1986, s 10, a right to remove fixtures[16] at the end of the tenancy or before the expiry of two months from the termination of the tenancy. No unavoidable damage must be caused by the tenant (Agricultural Holdings Act 1986, s 10(5)).[17] The right is barred if the tenant is in breach of his tenancy obligations (Agricultural Holdings Act 1986, s 10(3)(a)) and it is dependent on notice requirements (Agricultural Holdings Act 1986, s 10(3)(b)) which enable the landlord to elect to purchase a particular fixture or building (Agricultural Holdings Act 1986, s 10(4)). A fixture or building erected under an obligation to the landlord is outside the statutory right of removal (Agricultural Holdings Act 1986, s 10(2)(a)). Moreover, Agricultural Holdings Act 1986, s 10 may be contracted out of in the tenancy agreement.[18]

The tenant of a farm business tenancy, a creation as from 1 September 1995 of the Agricultural Tenancies Act 1995, has a right to remove fixtures and buildings which he or she installed under the Agricultural Tenancies Act 1995, s 8. In exercising this right of removal, the tenant must not cause any avoidable damage to the land and must make good all damage caused (Agricultural Tenancies Act 1995, s 8(3) and (4)). The right is wider in certain respects than that of the Agricultural Holdings Act 1986 so that, for example, it extends to any fixtures or buildings acquired by the tenant (Agricultural Tenancies Act 1995, s 8(5)). In addition, it is not expressly debarred where the tenant is in arrears with his rent. The right of removal excludes any common law right of removal (Agricultural Tenancies Act 1995, s 8(6)). The right to remove must be exercised during the continuance of the tenancy or at any time after termination of the tenancy if the tenant remains in possession as tenant. There is no right to an extension of time to remove fixtures and buildings if the tenant holds over under licence (unless presumably the landlord grants permission to the tenant to remove fixtures and buildings). In this latter respect the Agricultural Tenancies Act 1995 is stricter than the Agricultural Holdings Act 1986, which, as we saw, gives the tenant a two-month extension period to his removal right. If the fixture or building has been erected in place of a landlords' fixture or building then the statutory right of removal is excluded (Agricultural Tenancies Act 1995, s 8(2)(b)). This provision was said to amount to statutory confirmation of the common law.[19] The statutory right of removal

16 Notably by the Agricultural Holdings Act 1986, s 10(1), any engine, machinery, fencing or other fixture affixed for the purposes of agriculture or not, by the tenant to the holding, as well as any building erected by him on the holding. The statutory right goes beyond the common law concession for trade fixtures, as it applies to buildings.

17 He or she must make good any damage caused (Agricultural Holdings Act 1986, s 10(5)). This does no more than affirm the common law. A tenant who causes damage to the landlord's land in removing trade fixtures, for example, commits an act of waste: *Mancetter Developments Ltd v Garmanson Ltd* [1986] QB 1212, [1986] 1 All ER 449, CA. Damages would be the usual remedy but where a fixture had special qualities a mandatory injunction was ordered to force re-instatement: *Phillips v Lamdin* [1949] 2 KB 33, [1949] 1 All ER 770 (an Adam door, in a vendor-purchaser dispute).

18 *Premier Dairies Ltd v Garlick* [1920] 2 Ch 17 (dealing with Agricultural Holdings Act 1908, s 21).

19 House of Lords Committee of the 1995 Bill (*Hansard* 12 December 1994, col 1170). Mention was made of *Sunderland v Newton* (1830) 3 Sim 450 (a case of a tenant who replaced parts of the landlord's building and whose successors were restrained from removing the new parts in

is excluded where the tenant has received statutory compensation for the item (Agricultural Tenancies Act 1995, s 8(2)).

II NOTICE TO QUIT

General principles

A notice to quit is a statement, usually in writing, by either the landlord or the tenant that he has decided to put an end to a periodic tenancy at the date of termination given in the notice.[20] A periodic tenancy continues only for as long as both the landlord and the tenant or all joint tenants agree that it is to continue. A bilateral right to serve a notice to quit is therefore fundamental at common law to the validity of a periodic tenancy. If no notice to quit is served at the expiry of the period agreed for a tenancy, it will continue, at common law, for the same period as that originally agreed.

The parties to a periodic tenancy will have agreed on the length of the tenancy, either expressly or by implication. The tenancy may be for one week, one month, quarterly, for six months or yearly. Unless the parties otherwise agree, the *length* of a notice to quit must be the same as that of the initially agreed duration of the tenancy. Thus, a weekly tenancy requires a week's notice, a monthly tenancy a month and so on. In this, 'month' means a calendar month: a month's notice ends in the corresponding date in the appropriate subsequent month, no account being taken of the fact that some months are longer than others.[21] In the case of a yearly tenancy, six months' notice to quit is required, to expire on the anniversary date of the creation of the tenancy.

The length of notices to quit must be considered having regard to the intervention of statute. In the case of premises let as a dwelling, by the Protection from Eviction Act 1977, s 5(1), no notice by a landlord or a tenant is valid unless it is in writing and contains prescribed information.[22] Such notice must be given not less than four weeks before the date on which it is to take effect.

A valid notice to quit puts an end to the right to occupy of the tenant under that tenancy as from its expiry date. Statute may affect the validity of notices to quit, as by limiting the landlord to certain grounds (as with assured and protected tenancies and tenancies of agricultural holdings) or by only allowing him to serve a notice to terminate which complies with statute (as is the case with business tenancies). Where the landlord of a tenant of an agricultural holding made statements in his notice to quit, as to the

---

question). As with the Agricultural Holdings Act 1986, a fixture etc erected under a tenancy obligation is not removable under the Agricultural Tenancies Act 1995 and indeed not at all owing to the exclusivity of the statutory right.

20 There is nothing to prevent the landlord offering the tenant a new tenancy in a notice to quit: *Ahearn v Bellman* (1879) 4 Ex D 201.
21 *Dodds v Walker* [1981] 2 All ER 609, [1981] 1 WLR 1027, HL.
22 Ie as prescribed in Notices to Quit (Prescribed Information) Regulations 1988, SI 1988/2201.

falsity or truth of which he was reckless, the notice was vitiated by fraud and could not be relied on.[23]

At common law, where a periodic tenant serves a valid 'upwards' notice to quit on his landlord, the notice automatically puts an end to any sub-tenancy granted by the tenant. Any periodic sub-tenancy falls with the ending of the superior tenancy on which it depends.[24] The House of Lords have approved this principle, pointing out that otherwise a head landlord would be saddled with a tenant who was not of his choosing.[25]

At common law, a notice to quit does not have to exclude the date of the giving of the notice and the date of its expiry. However, the tenancy may specify that clear notice must be given. Unless this is so, a notice given to terminate a weekly tenancy which commences on, say, Saturday 1st of a month may be validly given to expire on Saturday 8th.

There are a number of technical rules governing the *expiry date* of a notice to quit. Even though a periodic tenancy strictly expires at midnight of the day before the anniversary, a notice will be valid if it is expressed to expire either on the anniversary of the commencement of the tenancy or on the previous day,[26] whether the tenancy is a yearly, monthly, or weekly tenancy.[27] A notice to quit at noon, however, is bad at common law, by virtue of the strict rule as to expiry.[28] Although a notice to quit should therefore expire on a rent day, the parties may contract out of this by sufficiently clear language.[29]

The courts try to avoid holding notices to quit void on technical grounds. Hence, a notice to quit need not specify the date of expiry, provided that the date is clearly identifiable, as for example 'at the expiration of the present year's tenancy'.[30] Moreover, if the date of the commencement of the tenancy is uncertain, it may be advisable for the notice not only to specify what is thought to be the proper date of expiry, but also to provide further that if that is not the proper date, the notice will expire on the first date thereafter upon which the tenancy could lawfully be terminated.[31]

23 *Rous v Mitchell* [1991] 1 All ER 676, CA. The same principle applies to business tenancies (see *Marks v British Railways Board* [1963] 3 All ER 28, [1963] 1 WLR 1008) and tenancies under the Rent Acts (*Lazarus Estates Ltd v Beasley* [1956] 1 QB 702, [1956] 1 All ER 341).
24 *Pennell v Payne* [1995] 2 All ER 592, CA.
25 *Barrett v Morgan* [2000] 1 All ER 481 at 488. See Dawson [2000] Conv 344.
26 *Sidebotham v Holland* [1895] 1 QB 378; *Yeandle v Reigate and Banstead Borough Council* [1996] 1 EGLR 20, CA; Cooke [1992] Conv 263.
27 *Crate v Miller* [1947] KB 946, [1947] 2 All ER 45.
28 *Bathavon RDC v Carlile* [1958] 1 QB 461, [1958] 1 All ER 801.
29 *Harler v Calder* [1989] 1 EGLR 88, CA.
30 *Doe d Gorst v Timothy* (1847) 2 Car & Kir 351.
31 *Addis v Burrows* [1948] 1 KB 444, [1948] 1 All ER 177 but see *P Phipps & Co (Northampton and Towcester Breweries) Ltd v Rogers* [1925] 1 KB 14.

Notice to quit by a joint tenant

We have seen that a notice to quit is a unilateral document: it does not require the consent of the recipient to be validly served nor to take full effect, assuming it is otherwise valid. The House of Lords has ruled that where a periodic tenancy is held by two or more joint tenants, any one of the joint tenants may serve a notice to quit on the landlord, without first obtaining the consent of any of the others.[32] In this case, cohabitees were granted a joint weekly tenancy of a council flat, but fell out and one of the pair then served a four-week notice to quit, as required by statute, on the landlord, without consulting the other ex-cohabitee. The notice was upheld. The House of Lords applied contractual principles and held that where joint periodic tenants had agreed to a tenancy for one year initially, thereafter from year to year unless terminated by notice, neither joint tenant had bound himself for more than one year. Hence, once the initial period of one week had expired in the present case, either joint tenant could put the tenancy to an end by serving a notice to quit on the landlord. Another way of putting the same point is that, if there is to be a renewal of any periodic tenancy, all parties must agree to it: so, by serving a notice to quit, one joint tenant makes it clear to the landlords and to the other joint tenants, who share the whole tenancy with him, that he does not consent to the renewal.[33] There is no reason why, therefore, a joint landlord cannot serve a notice to quit on the tenant without consulting his co-landlord.

This case has certain limits, owing to the danger of a landlord reaching an agreement with one joint tenant whose relationship with his partner may have broken down to accept a notice to quit served by him alone, so as to circumvent the protection of the Protection from Eviction Act 1977, s 5(1). This provision requires a minimum period of four weeks' notice from both landlord or tenant.[34] Where joint tenants were entitled to give a notice to terminate a tenancy agreement with immediate effect, a notice served by one alone, with a view to allowing the landlord to regain possession against the other joint tenant, was invalid, as the notice was not to quit, since the notice did not take effect at once.[35]

---

32   *London Borough of Hammersmith and Fulham v Monk* [1992] 1 AC 478, [1992] 1 All ER 1.
33   This principle enables a local authority to receive a notice to quit from say a joint tenant wife who is estranged from her joint tenant husband, so as to evict the husband and rehouse the wife, as in *Newlon Housing Trust v Alsulaimen* [1999] L & TR 38. See also *Harrow London BC v Johnstone* [1997] 1 All ER 929, HL; Thompson [1997] Conv 288. The enactment of Trusts of Land and Appointment of Trustees Act 1996, s 11 (duty of trustee to consult trust beneficiaries) has had no effect on these principles: *Notting Hill Housing Trust v Brackley* [2001] EWCA Civ 601, [2001] 35 EG 106. But see *Harrow London BC v Qazi* [2001] EWCA Civ 1834, [2001] All ER (D) 16 (Dec) (non-consenting joint tenant continued to occupy premises as his 'home', so that court must consider whether dispossession was justified under ECHR, Art 8(2).
34   And the service of prescribed information (Notices to Quit (Prescribed Information) Regulations 1988, SI 1988/2201).
35   *London Borough of Hounslow v Pilling* (1993) 25 HLR 305, CA.

Errors in notice to quit

A new, relaxed principle applies to notices to quit that contain errors, such as giving the wrong date of expiry. The House of Lords have ruled, in relation to option notices, that if a reasonable recipient of a notice is able to interpret it in the sense obviously intended, as where they must have realised that the notice contains an obvious error, then the notice will be effective.[36] The problem is to decide when a notice to quit contains an obvious error to a reasonable recipient. A misstatement of the year of termination would seem to be 'obvious' if, for example, a notice to quit gives the correct date of the month concerned, but a year which has not yet arrived.[37] Likewise, a notice to quit which contains a small error on a point of detail not material to the substance of the notice, such as where the notice misdescribes the premises, would be valid despite the error.[38] A notice to quit served on a business tenant which failed to identify the correct landlord would seem not to be valid, even today, since it misstates an essential piece of information for the tenant.[39]

Service of notice

A notice to quit may be given either by the landlord or by the tenant, or by their authorised agents. If served personally, it need not be directed to the party served, by name, and if sent to him, it may be addressed to him by description. It is sufficient to leave the notice with the addressee's wife or servant, provided that the recipient is made to understand that it should be delivered, whether or not it ever is.[40] A notice which is just left on the premises, eg under the door of the tenant's house, will be validly served if it can be shown that it came into his hands in time.[41]

Leases may incorporate the provisions of LPA 1925, s 196. A lease or tenancy may expressly provide for the omission of this special set of service rules, as allowed by LPA 1925, s 196(5). This particular method of service cannot be implied into a tenancy agreement, as where a weekly tenancy was silent as to service of notices and a notice to quit served on an absent tenant was invalid as it was not proved to have come to his attention.[42] LPA 1925, s 196, which is for the benefit of landlords, provides that a notice:

36 *Mannai Investment Co Ltd v Eagle Star Life Assurance Co Ltd* [1997] AC 749.
37 *Carradine v Aslam* [1976] 1 All ER 573 (1975 not 1973, for an option notice served in 1973).
38 See *Safeway Food Stores Ltd v Morris* [1980] 1 EGLR 59.
39 See *Divall v Harrison* [1992] 2 EGLR 64. Likewise, a date in a notice differing from that in a tenancy agreement would be invalid (*Clickex Ltd v McCann* [1999] 2 EGLR 63 (assured shorthold tenancy notice). Nor was a notice served on the original, not the current, tenant valid: *R (on the application of Morris) v London Rent Assessment Committee* [2002] EWCA Civ 276, [2002] 24 EG 149.
40 *Tanham v Nicholson* (1872) LR 5 HL 561.
41 *Lord Newborough v Jones* [1975] Ch 90, [1974] 3 All ER 17, CA.
42 *Wandsworth London BC v Attwell* [1996] 1 EGLR 57, CA; also *Enfield London Borough Council v Devonish* (1996) 29 HLR 691, CA .

1   must be in writing;
2   is sufficient if addressed by designation and not by name;
3   is sufficiently served if it is left at the last-known place of abode or business in the UK of the addressee, or in the case of notice served on the tenant, if it is affixed or left for him on the land or any house or building comprised in the lease;
4   is sufficiently served if sent by registered post or recorded delivery and not returned undelivered; and,
5   if so posted, is deemed to have been delivered at the time it would, in the ordinary course of post, be delivered.

III   SURRENDER

A surrender of a lease is essentially the giving up of the tenant's estate to the immediate landlord, which causes the lease to be destroyed.[43] The tenant's estate is absorbed into the landlord's reversion and is extinguished by operation of law. The tenancy ends in a manner not contemplated by the tenancy agreement terms. Surrender reflects the principle that a person cannot at the same time be a landlord and tenant of the same premises.[44] 'As soon as the tenancy and the reversion are in the same hands, the tenancy is merged, that is, sunk or drowned, in the reversion'.[45]

Express surrender

Any express surrender of a lease, no matter what its length, must be by deed, on pain of invalidity.[46] No particular form of words is required,[47] but 'surrender and yield up' or 'assign and surrender' suffice. An express surrender must operate immediately and cannot be expressed to operate in the future.[48] A future surrender may be treated as an enforceable contract to surrender, which is valid.[49]

43   Because the landlord's agreement is required (in contrast to the position where one joint tenant serves a notice to quit) a surrender of his rights by one joint tenant to the other has no effect on the liability of the person surrendering to pay rent to the landlord: *Burton v Camden London BC* (1997) 30 HLR 991, CA.
44   *Barrett v Morgan* [2000] 1 All ER 481, HL.
45   *Rye v Rye* [1962] AC 496, [1962] 1 All ER 146 at 513 and 155; Co Litt (19th edn, 1832) Vol II, p 337b.
46   LPA 1925, s 52(1); *Camden London BC v Alexandrou* (1997) 74 P & CR D33, CA. However, the parties may waive this requirement: *Inntrepreneur Pub Co (CPC) Ltd v Deans* [1999] CLY 3702.
47   *Weddall v Capes* (1836) 1 M & W 50.
48   *Doe d Murrell v Milward* (1838) 3 M & W 328.
49   Subject to compliance with LP(MP)A 1989, s 2.

Implied surrender

No deed is required for implied surrender, sometimes called surrender by operation of law.[50] In order for a landlord or tenant to rely on an implied surrender, it must be shown that possession is abandoned and that the conduct of both parties is unequivocal and inconsistent with a continuation of the tenancy. The tenant must have unequivocally offered to surrender and the landlord to accept that surrender, or vice versa. The law recognises that parties do not always observe the formalities required for a surrender, and that at some point it would be inequitable, having regard to their conduct, to allow one party to set up the absence of formalities as a ground for resisting the ending of the lease.[51]

A series of recent cases has confirmed that surrender by operation of law is not based on intention but rather on estoppel. There must be an unequivocal act by the tenant,[52] which is inconsistent with his retaining possession from then on under his lease. The landlord must accept the tenant's act. After this, both parties are prevented from going back on their conduct. Thus if a tenant gives up possession and returns the keys to the landlord, who accepts them and then re-lets the premises to a new tenant, neither party would be allowed to turn round and assert the continuing existence of the tenancy.[53] At the same time if one of the parties asserts expressly or by conduct that the tenancy is continuing, as where rent arrears are claimed by a landlord who is also complaining of a breach of tenant covenant,[54] no question of implied surrender can arise. Moreover, actions speak louder than words.

Where, for example, a tenant no longer lived permanently in the flat concerned, but returned regularly to feed her cats, and retained a key and her furniture there, the landlord could not claim that the fact that she was no longer permanently resident amounted to an implied offer of surrender. The conduct of both parties was too equivocal.[55] The same result followed where a landlord accepted the return of the keys to the premises for a few days but intended to accept a surrender of the tenancy only once a new lease had been granted.[56] Where the landlord changes the locks of the premises, this may or may not amount to an acceptance of a tenant's offer to surrender, depending on the facts. If the landlord is at the time intent on re-letting the premises, his changing the locks may estop him from asserting the continuing existence of the

50 LPA 1925, s 52(2)(c).
51 *Proudreed Ltd v Microgen Holdings plc* [1996] 1 EGLR 89, CA.
52 See eg *Newham London BC v Phillips* (1997) 30 HLR 859, CA (where a sole tenant had not unequivocally transformed her tenancy into a new joint tenancy with her sister on the facts, thus a notice to quit served by her sister on the landlords did not end the tenancy).
53 *Matthey Securities Ltd v Ervin* [1998] 2 EGLR 66, CA; *Gibbs Mew plc v Gemmell* [1999] 1 EGLR 43; *Zionmor v Islington London BC* (1997) 30 HLR 822; *Allen v Rochdale BC* [2000] Ch 221, CA.
54 As in *Charville Estates Ltd v Unipart Group Ltd* [1997] EGCS 36.
55 *Chamberlaine v Scally* (1992) 26 HLR 26, CA. A similar equivocation by the tenant was apparent in *Zionmor v Islington London BC* (1997) 30 HLR 822, where the tenant left his friend in occupation of his flat during what was apparently a temporary absence.
56 *Proudreed Ltd v Microgen Holdings plc* [1996] 1 EGLR 89, CA.

lease, but if he has changed the locks to protect the security of the premises, it may be otherwise.[57]

By contrast, where a council tenancy had been granted to the present occupier's cousins, but these had left permanently for Nigeria, and the occupier frequently and in writing claimed to the landlords that she held the tenancy, the latter accepting rent from her for some time, the only conclusion could be that a surrender of the former tenancy had been impliedly offered and accepted.[58] Similarly, where a lady left a house held on a weekly secure tenancy, returning the keys to the landlord, having been re-housed, the tenancy was impliedly surrendered. The landlords refused to release the tenant from her liability to pay rent until she had given up her first tenancy, and because of the fact that she had been rehoused.[59]

Where the parties agree to alter a term of an existing lease this may well amount to an implied surrender of the old tenancy and a re-grant of a new tenancy but whether this has occurred is a question of fact. For example, where a 1943 tenancy of an agricultural holding was varied in 1957 by a memorandum, so that as from then the tenancy was held jointly, the memorandum being sewn into and cast in the same formal language and terms as the current tenancy, save that the tenancy was joint and the rent increased, the High Court concluded that the 1943 tenancy had been varied, not impliedly surrendered.[60]

However, the parties may be taken to have agreed on the grant of a new lease, which is subject to the implied condition that it is valid,[61] at a higher rent on different terms, so surrendering the existing lease.[62] If so, the landlord has no power to grant the new lease except on the footing that the old lease is surrendered: by accepting the new lease the tenant is estopped from denying the surrender of the old one.[63] The difficulty is, as with implied surrender as a whole, not with this application of the doctrine of estoppel, but with applying it to particular facts.[64] For example, a tenant of business premises whose original tenancy was for seven years from 1977, at a fixed rent throughout, was found to have accepted an oral offer from his landlord of a term ending only in 1991, at the same rent, but with a rent review in 1984. The previous tenancy had been surrendered impliedly and a re-grant of a new tenancy had taken

---

57 *McDougalls Catering Foods Ltd v BSE Trading Ltd* [1997] 2 EGLR 65, CA; *Relvok Properties Ltd v Dixon* (1972) 25 P & CR 1; also eg *Buchanan v Byrnes* (1906) 3 CLR 704 at 721 (where the landlord took possession of an hotel to avoid the loss of the licence attached to it: there was no implied surrender of the tenant's lease on the facts, having regard to the nature of the premises).

58 *London Borough of Tower Hamlets v Ayinde* (1994) 26 HLR 631, CA.

59 *Sanctuary Housing Association v Campbell* [1999] 2 EGLR 20, CA.

60 *Francis Perceval Saunders Trustees v Ralph* [1993] 2 EGLR 1: hence, the succession provisions of the relevant legislation were not operated in 1957.

61 *Barclays Bank Ltd v Stasek* [1957] Ch 28, [1956] 3 All ER 439.

62 An alternative method of achieving the objective of varying a lease is to agree on the grant of a reversionary lease, to commence on the termination of the existing tenancy.

63 *Jenkin R Lewis & Son v Kerman* [1971] Ch 477 at 496, [1970] 3 All ER 414 at 419, CA.

64 See generally Dowling [1995] Conv 124.

place.[65] But there must be solid evidence of an agreement for a new tenancy, and sometimes the court may conclude that all that the parties have done is to agree on the implied surrender of the existing tenancy.[66] It appears to be a rule of law that an extension of the current lease by supplemental deed takes effect as an implied surrender of the current lease and the re-grant of a new lease.[67] This rule is narrow since where the landlord and tenant of two adjacent agricultural holdings, the second of which had been granted later than the first, agreed for the purpose of two successive rent reviews to treat the rent for the two holdings as a single rent, the underlying estates in the land were not thereby altered and the two separate tenancies continued, as the variation in rents did not, on established principles, ipso facto trigger a surrender and re-grant by operation of law.[68]

Difficulties have arisen, notably with council tenancies, where a tenant abandons possession of the premises and claims that this, coupled with his intention not to resume occupation, amounts to a surrender by operation of law of his tenancy. It appears that should the tenant leave owing substantial amounts of rent, after a long absence, the court may, depending on the facts, infer that his offer so to surrender the tenancy has been impliedly accepted by the landlords.[69] Such inference would be easier to make where the landlord changes the locks of the premises and re-lets them to a different tenant.[70]

There is no duty on a landlord claiming rent from a guarantor or surety to mitigate his losses by re-taking possession of the premises, or by taking a surrender of the lease: he is entitled to require the guarantor to comply with his obligations, who can, if the tenant is a company in liquidation, apply to the court to vest the tenancy in him, which he can then dispose of by sale of the tenancy or by a new letting.[71]

Operation of a surrender

The effect of a surrender is to transfer to the landlord the whole of the tenant's interest, but subject to any lesser interests which the tenant may have created, eg equitable charges.[72] He cannot prejudice the rights of any sub-tenants, for example, by surrender, any more than he could by an assignment of the lease, and in effect, by LPA 1925, s 139

---

65   *Bush Transport Ltd v Nelson* [1987] 1 EGLR 71, CA.
66   As on the facts of *Take Harvest Ltd v Liu* [1993] AC 552, [1993] 2 All ER 459, JCPC. See also *Tomkins v Basildon DC* [2002] EWCA Civ 876 (tenant did not intend to give up right under existing lease to use premises for business purposes so that old lease not surrendered at all).
67   *Re Savile Settled Estates* [1931] 2 Ch 210; *Baker v Merckel* [1960] 1 QB 657; see *Precedents for the Conveyancer* Precedent 5-92 for a precedent of a right to an extended lease following notice.
68   *JW Childers Trustees v Anker* [1996] 1 EGLR 1, CA.
69   *Preston Borough Council v Fairclough* (1982) 8 HLR 70, CA.
70   See *R v London Borough of Croydon ex p Toth* (1986) 18 HLR 493.
71   *Bhogal v Cheema* [1999] L & TR 59.
72   *ES Schwab & Co Ltd v McCarthy* (1975) 31 P & CR 196, CA.

the landlord is put in the position of an assignee of the sub-lease, for the purpose of preserving the rights and obligations under it. The purpose of LPA 1825, s 139(1) has been said to be to preserve the ability to enforce the covenants and conditions of the sub-lease for the benefit of the sub-lessee and the next vested right in the land but for the unexpired portion of the sub-lease only.[73] By LPA 1925, s 150(1) a lease may be surrendered with a view to the acceptance of a new lease, without any surrender of any underlease.

The effect of surrender upon liabilities for breach of covenant before the surrender is not without doubt. The tenant should remain liable for such breaches, even after surrender;[74] nevertheless, in the case of an express surrender, it would be advisable to put the matter beyond all doubt by express agreement in the instrument.

The tenant is not entitled to recover any part of any rent paid in advance.[75] The tenant remains liable for any arrears due before the surrender under any personal covenant, if any; if not, the landlord will be able to maintain an action for use and occupation.[76]

IV FORFEITURE

General aspects

(i) Preliminary

Where the tenant has committed a serious breach of covenant,[77] the landlord may try to bring the lease to an end prematurely, a process known as forfeiture. If he wishes to forfeit a lease for breach of covenant, the lease must contain an express right of re-entry or forfeiture entitling him to do so.[78] The effect of a breach of covenant is not, therefore, automatically to make the lease void. The landlord must take positive steps to bring the lease to an end. If the tenant commits a repudiatory breach of his lease, as by refusing to pay any rent for a long time, it is possible that the landlord could treat the lease as being at an end without going through the procedures which apply in the case of forfeiture. This remains to be settled but it would be unfortunate if landlords could circumvent the jurisdiction to grant relief to tenants by relying on repudiation.

In this section we examine forfeiture for breaches of covenant other than to pay rent. The rules have been described as a legal minefield.[79] The courts and statute lean

---

73 *Bromley Park Garden Estates Ltd v George* [1991] 2 EGLR 95, 96.
74 *Richmond v Savill* [1926] 2 KB 530; but see F E Farrer *Conveyancer* vol xi, pp 73, 81.
75 *William Hill (Football) Ltd v Willen Key and Hardware Ltd* (1964) 108 Sol Jo 482. Apportionment Act 1870, s 3 allows apportionment of rent accruing during a period which straddles that in which surrender takes place.
76 *Shaw v Lomas* (1888) 59 LT 477.
77 Some leases may draw a distinction between breaches of covenant or condition, as where it is a condition of the lease that the tenant does not go bankrupt or become insolvent.
78 This requirement is not necessary for breaches of condition: *Doe d Lockwood v Clarke* (1807) 8 East 185.
79 *Rexhaven v Nurse and Alliance and Leicester Building Society* (1995) 28 HLR 241 at 255.

against forfeiture, regarding it as a remedy of last and not first resort for landlords. The remedy is still, however, alive in the commercial and long residential sector. In the former case, forfeiture of a business lease will destroy any prospect of the tenant obtaining a renewed tenancy under statute.[80] In the case of long residential leases there is some evidence[81] that forfeiture is used by unscrupulous landlords as a means of pressuring tenants who fail to pay ground rent or service charges on time even though demands for these sums have not been presented to the tenants. Forfeiture is used by landlords of vacant commercial premises,[82] especially by means of the extra-judicial method of 'peaceable re-entry'.

(ii)   Human rights impact

HRA 1998 may be used as a challenge to forfeiture, especially where peaceable re-entry is made use of by the landlord, owing to the fact that the courts, as a public authority within the Act, must under HRA 1998, s 6(1) uphold Convention rights. There are a number of unresolved issues, given the generalised language of the Convention when compared to the technicalities of forfeiture. Take ECHR, Art 6. It speaks of a dispute. But in the case of a lawful physical re-entry by a landlord, as where he changes the locks of vacant commercial premises, so regaining control of the premises, it seems to strain language to speak of a 'dispute' since a forfeiture will have taken place.[83] Reference might be made to the protection of privacy as set out in ECHR, Art 8. It seems scarcely appropriate to regard the privacy of business lessees as being on a par with residential long lessees. It has been held in Strasbourg that it may not be realistic to split up the life of a person into professional and private areas for the purposes of ECHR, Art 8.[84] At the same time, Lord Nicholls stated recently[85] that the primary purpose of ECHR, Art 8 is to protect individuals against arbitrary interference by public authorities, which would seem to lessen if not eliminate the prospects of success of any challenge to forfeiture against a private landlord by aggrieved tenants. In any case, it could be said that there are enough safeguards, whether in the form of statutory notices or the relief jurisdiction, to render forfeiture human rights compliant.

(iii)   Exercise of a right of re-entry

If the landlord wishes to forfeit the lease for breach of covenant, he must, because the lease has been rendered voidable, take positive steps to show unequivocally that he

---

80   Owing to Landlord and Tenant Act 1954, s 24(2).

81   Commonhold and Leasehold Reform Consultation Paper (2000), Section 4.5.

82   Insolvency Act 1986, s 11(3)(ba) requires the leave of the court for forfeiture by peaceable re-entry or claim form where the tenant is insolvent, adding a further restriction to the landlord's ability to forfeit.

83   See Bruce (2000)150 NLJ 97.

84   *Niemietz v Germany* (1992) 16 EHRR 97, 16 December Series A No 251A.

85   *Re S (Children: care plan)* [2002] UKHL 10, [2002] 2 All ER 192, para 53.

intends to terminate the lease, as where a landlord entered into a new, reversionary, lease of premises vacated by the lessee's administrators.[86] His right of re-entry is exercisable either by taking possession peaceably, or by bringing an action for possession. Therefore, unless a tenant in occupation is prepared to give up possession voluntarily,[87] the landlord will be obliged to commence proceedings for forfeiture by claim form.

It is unlawful to enforce a right of re-entry or forfeiture otherwise than by proceedings in court while any person is lawfully residing on the premises or any part of them (Protection from Eviction Act 1977, s 2). Although it is a criminal offence for the landlord to threaten or use violence for the purpose of gaining entry to any building,[88] the landlord is able to gain entry lawfully by changing the locks to temporarily or permanently unoccupied premises,[89] which is 'peaceable re-entry', as this sort of violence to property is not contrary to this rule. The landlord must, however (except in the case of breaches of covenant to pay rent and sums expressly reserved as rent such as service charges), first serve a LPA 1925, s 146(1) notice on the tenant and allow a reasonable time for him to remedy the breach.[90] Some landlords have been quick to realise the advantages of this cheap, and rapid, method of forfeiting a lease. It was held by the Court of Appeal that where a landlord peaceably re-entered an unoccupied building early in the morning, following a LPA 1925, s 146(1) notice, the tenant not having by then applied to the court for relief against forfeiture, the peaceable re-entry put it out of the tenant's power to apply under statute and he could not apply in equity as there was no general inherent equitable jurisdiction to grant relief outside the statute.[91] This decision was reversed by the House of Lords on the narrow ground that a landlord's peaceable re-entry meant that he did not base his physical possession of the premises on an order of court, whose effect would, once actual possession was obtained, bar any application for relief by the tenant.[92] A landlord who used the uncivilised method of peaceable re-entry would face an application for relief by the tenant after regaining physical control of the premises. Unlike the position where he had chosen to proceed by the civilised method of serving a writ, there was no cut-off point, in theory, after which a tenant could not apply for relief (other than the discretion

---

86 *Re AGB Research plc* [1994] EGCS 73; also *Redleaf Investments v Talbot* [1994] EGCS 73.

87 There is no forfeiture by peaceable re-entry of a head tenant's interest where the landlord does not challenge the continuation of any sub-lease: *Ashton v Sobelman* [1987] 1 All ER 755, [1987] 1 WLR 177.

88 Criminal Law Act 1977, s 6(1).

89 Owing to the repeal of the statutes of forcible entry and detainer by Criminal Law Act 1977, Sch 13.

90 Otherwise the re-entry will be a trespass: see eg *Cardigan Properties Ltd v Consolidated Property Investments Ltd* [1991] 1 EGLR 64.

91 *Billson v Residential Apartments Ltd* [1991] 3 All ER 265; Goulding [1991] Conv 380; PF Smith [1992] Conv 33.

92 *Quilter v Mapleson* (1882) 9 QBD 672; *Rogers v Rice* [1892] 2 Ch 170, approved by the House of Lords, below, but confined to cases where the landlord proceeds by claim form.

of the court).[93] We note possible reforms to peaceable re-entry at the end of this chapter.

Once a claim form seeking forfeiture has been served on the tenant, then if possession is ordered unconditionally, the forfeiture is backdated to the date of the claim.[94] Curiously, once a claim form is served asking for forfeiture, then the landlord is entitled to mesne profits not rent until the date possession is ordered.[95] As from an unconditional possession order, the tenant covenants in the lease are put to an end.[96] The tenant holds a shadowy and ill-defined interest in the premises pending the making of an order for possession.[97] This is sufficient to enable him to claim relief against forfeiture and also to enable a sub-lessee to enforce tenant's covenants.[98] Inconsistently, perhaps, it appears that during the 'limbo period' between issue of a claim form and an order for possession or the grant of relief to the tenant, the landlord cannot enforce repairing covenants against the tenant.[99] The lease has a 'trance-lie' existence with somewhat obscure characteristics: thus the tenant's lease will be fully and retrospectively restored if relief is granted (provided he complies with any relief terms imposed on him).[100]

(iv) Waiver of forfeiture

A landlord loses his right to forfeit a lease if he waives the right to re-enter or forfeit. Waiver evolved as a common law doctrine at a time before the courts were conferred a statutory power to grant relief against forfeiture.[101] This is not an area where a rigid or precise taxonomy of principles is possible.[102] Waiver is related to estoppel. It would appear that the following strict principles are confined to cases of demand or acceptance of rent.[103] A landlord cannot blow hot and cold: he cannot take future rent, for example, once he knows of a breach of covenant serious enough to enable him to forfeit the lease. Waiver thus occurs where the landlord, with sufficient knowledge of the breach, communicates to the tenant his intention not to forfeit the lease or does some

93 *Billson v Residential Apartments Ltd* [1992] 1 AC 494, [1992] 1 All ER 141; PF Smith [1992] Conv 273.
94 *Ivory Gate Ltd v Spetale* [1998] 2 EGLR 43, CA; *Maryland Estates Ltd v Bar-Joseph* [1998] 2 EGLR 47, CA.
95 *Associated Deliveries Ltd v Harrison* (1984) 50 P & CR 91.
96 *Ivory Gate Ltd v Spetale* [1998] 2 EGLR 43, CA; also *Twogates Properties Ltd v Birmingham Midshires Building Society* [1997] EGCS 55 (sub-leases also covered by this principle).
97 *Liverpool Properties Ltd v Oldbridge Investments Ltd* [1985] 2 EGLR 111, CA.
98 *Peninsular Maritime Ltd v Padseal Ltd* [1981] 2 EGLR 43, CA.
99 *Associated Deliveries Ltd v Harrison* [1984] 2 EGLR 76, CA.
100 *Meadows v Clerical, Medical and General Life Assurance Society* [1981] Ch 70; *Ivory Gate v Spetale* [1998] 2 EGLR 43, CA.
101 By the Conveyancing Act 1881, s 14.
102 *Ballard (Kent) Ltd v Oliver Ashworth (Holdings) Ltd* [1999] 2 EGLR 23 at 27A (Robert Walker LJ).
103 *Yorkshire Metropolitan Properties Ltd v Co-operative Retail Services Ltd* [2001] L & TR 26, [2001] L & TR 298.

unequivocal act recognising its continuing existence.[104] As soon as he has the requisite degree of knowledge, which may be imputed to him from his servants or agents,[105] the landlord must elect whether to forfeit the lease or waive the breach. If he recognises the lease as continuing, the landlord must communicate his decision to the tenant,[106] as by a letter or by accepting rent due for a post-breach period.

The degree of knowledge is a question of fact: where relevant, as with illegal alterations, the landlord need not be aware of all the details of the progress of the work, provided he is aware that it is being carried out.[107] If the landlord communicates[108] to the tenant a fixed intention not to forfeit (express waiver), or should he perform some unequivocal act which is consistent only with the continued existence of the lease (implied waiver), then the landlord waives the breach.

An unqualified demand for rent falling due after the date of the breach,[109] or a similar acceptance of rent amount in law to implied waiver.[110] It makes no difference for the landlord to claim that his action is without prejudice to any right of his to forfeit.[111] Once the landlord has elected to forfeit, as by serving claim form for possession,[112] this is a conclusive decision to terminate the lease.[113] However, as service of a notice under LPA 1925, s 146(1) is merely a preliminary to forfeiture, it cannot operate as waiver.[114] An offer to purchase the tenant's interest, if made with the requisite knowledge of the breach, may, however, amount to waiver.[115] A mere entry into negotiations cannot do so, however.[116]

Implied waiver is judged objectively: the landlord's acts and not his words or intentions count. The landlord is exposed to the risk that his agent's acts, even if unauthorised,

---

104 *Matthews v Smallwood* [1910] 1 Ch 777, 786, approved by Lord Diplock in *Kammins Investments Co v Zenith Investments (Torquay) Ltd* [1971] AC 850, 883.
105 *Metropolitan Properties Ltd v Cordery* (1979) 39 P & CR 10, CA.
106 *Cornillie v Saha* (1996) 72 P & CR 147, CA.
107 *Iperion Investments Corpn v Broadwalk House Residents Ltd* [1992] 2 EGLR 235.
108 The silence of a landlord is not, however, waiver: *West Country Cleaners (Falmouth) Ltd v Saly* [1966] 3 All ER 210, [1966] 1 WLR 1485, CA.
109 There is no inconsistency and no waiver where a landlord demands or accepts rent due on or before the relevant breach: *Re A Debtor No 13A-10-1995* [1995] 1 WLR 1127.
110 *Central Estates (Belgravia) Ltd v Woolgar (No 2)* [1972] 3 All ER 610, [1972] 1 WLR 1048, CA; also *Welch v Birrane* (1974) 29 P & CR 102; *Van Haarlam v Kasner* [1992] 2 EGLR 59. If, as with a Rent Act statutory tenancy, the landlord has no choice but to accept rent tenders, then, exceptionally, whether there has been a waiver is a question of fact: see eg *Trustees of Henry Smith's Charity v Willson* [1983] QB 316, [1983] 1 All ER 73, CA.
111 *Segal Securities Ltd v Thoseby* [1963] 1 QB 887, [1963] 1 All ER 500.
112 By contrast, a landlord who issued a summons requiring access to certain flats once he knew of breaches of covenant waived the right to forfeit the leases: *Cornillie v Saha* (1996) 72 P & CR 147, CA.
113 *Expert Clothing Service and Sales Ltd v Hillgate House Ltd* [1986] Ch 340, [1985] 2 All ER 998, CA.
114 *Church Comrs for England v Nodjoumi* (1985) 51 P & CR 155.
115 *Bader Properties Ltd v Linley Property Investment Ltd* (1967) 19 P & CR 620 at 641.
116 *Re National Jazz Centre Ltd* [1988] 2 EGLR 57.

may be imputed to him, as where the landlord wished to forfeit a lease for a single but serious breach of covenant, but rent was accepted, in error, by an employee of the landlord's agent, so precluding any forfeiture for that breach.[117]

Cases of acceptance of rent may fall into a specific category. In some mitigation of the exact time at which waiver may take place, it was held that rent payable into a bank account was only impliedly accepted where the landlord became aware, from bank statements, that his account had been credited with payments: he did not waive a known breach unless, within a reasonable time of his awareness, he failed to repay the money.[118] It has been said that in cases other than payment or acceptance of rent, the court is free to look objectively at all the circumstances of the case, in order to decide whether a landlord's act amounts to waiver.[119] Hence, if, having become aware of circumstances which might entitle him to forfeit the lease, the landlord reasonably accepts an explanation from the tenant, his continued acceptance of rent will not prevent him from bringing a forfeiture based on the circumstances in question, if the tenant's explanation is false.[120]

Any actual waiver by a lessor is limited by LPA 1925, s 148(1), unless a contrary intention appears, to any breach 'to which such waiver specially relates' and is not to 'operate as a general waiver of the benefit of any such covenant or condition'. This provision affirms the common law, since the effect of waiver in a given case depends on the type of covenant broken. In the case of rent, a fresh cause of action arises each time an instalment falls due and seemingly not before then.[121] In the case of negative covenants, such as against assignments or under-lettings, a waiver of a given breach is final; but not in relation to any later breach, which gives rise to a separate cause of action. Where there is a breach of a continuing covenant, such as to repair or as to user, a continuing breach after a waiver gives rise to a fresh cause of action.[122]

The question as to at what point in time a waiver comes to an end and a fresh cause of action arises is one of fact.[123] Where a tenant was in breach of covenant to repair, and, following a LPA 1925, s 146(1) notice, the breach was waived, but the disrepair continued, no further statutory notice was required since the condition of the premises had not changed.[124]

---

117 *Central Estates (Belgravia) Ltd v Woolgar (No 2)* [1972] 3 All ER 610, [1972] 1 WLR 1048, CA.
118 *John Lewis Properties plc v Viscount Chelsea* [1993] 2 EGLR 77.
119 *Expert Clothing Service and Sales Ltd v Hillgate House Ltd* [1986] Ch 340, [1985] 2 All ER 998, CA.
120 *Chrisdell Ltd v Johnson* [1987] 2 EGLR 123, CA.
121 See *Re A Debtor No 13A-10-1995* [1995] 1 WLR 1127.
122 *Penton v Barnett* [1898] 1 QB 276, CA; also *Farimani v Gates* (1984) 128 Sol Jo 615, CA.
123 See *Cooper v Henderson* [1982] 2 EGLR 42, CA.
124 *Greenwich London Borough Council v Discreet Selling Estates Ltd* [1990] 2 EGLR 65.

Restrictions on and relief against forfeiture

While equity was prepared to grant relief from forfeiture for non-payment of rent, only in very limited circumstances could the courts grant relief in other cases.[125] The present-day restrictions on forfeiture and also the general power to grant relief against forfeiture are contained in LPA 1925, s 146, applying to all covenants other than that to pay rent. The policy of this provision, which must be complied with before a right of re-entry or forfeiture in a lease may be enforced by the landlord, is as follows.

1   to give the tenant warning of a breach of covenant;
2   to enable the tenant to have a reasonable opportunity to remedy the breach, where remediable;
3   to enable the court, at its discretion, which is very wide, to relieve the tenant from forfeiture; and
4   to give sub-lessees and mortgagees special protection against loss of their respective interests where the lease is forfeited.

Special requirement in case of long residential leases

However, in the case of attempts to forfeit long residential leases, ie terms which when granted exceeded 21 years, there is a further block in the path of a landlord who wishes to use the blunt instrument of forfeiture to enforce leasehold covenants. In essence, a landlord of a long-lessee of a dwelling cannot serve a LPA 1925, s 146 notice at once, even if he thinks he is entitled to claim forfeiture. The landlord must apply to the leasehold valuation tribunal for a determination, of a factual nature, that a breach of covenant or condition has occurred.[126] The landlord may only serve a LPA 1925, s 146 notice if it has been finally determined by the tribunal that such a breach has occurred. However, if the tenant admits the breach, there is no need for the landlord to apply to the tribunal. The government noted that in practice forfeiture of long residential leases, as opposed to its being threatened to scare tenants, is rare. There was a need for legislation to combat a practice of unscrupulous landlords. These, it was said, exploited leaseholders' fears about the costs of legal proceedings, when there had been only minor or even non-existent breaches of covenant.[127] The idea of having preliminary proceedings so as to make forfeiture more difficult is not new, as it is also made use of in connection with breaches of covenant to repair by the Leasehold Property (Repairs) Act 1938, which applies to most residential and business leases (as to which see ch 9 of this book).

125 See eg *Hill v Barclay* (1811) 18 Ves 56.
126 CLRA 2002, s 168(1) and (2). This provision cannot be contracted out of (CLRA 2002, s 169).
127 Commonhold and Leasehold Reform Consultation Paper (2000), Part II, Section 4.6.

LPA 1925, s 146

(i) General

LPA 1925, s 146 restricts a landlord's right of re-entry or forfeiture in various ways. Generally, compliance with s 146(1) is an essential preliminary to forfeiture.

LPA 1925, s 146 in principle applies to any lease which contains a right of re-entry or forfeiture under a proviso or stipulation for breach of any covenant or condition.[128] The right of re-entry or forfeiture is rendered unenforceable by action or otherwise unless and until the landlord serves a LPA 1925, s 146(1) notice on the tenant. The contents of this notice are discussed below. By LPA 1925, ss 146(12), any express stipulation to the contrary in the lease is overridden.

(ii) Exclusions of LPA 1925, s 146

LPA 1925, s 146 does not apply to forfeiture for non-payment of rent (LPA 1925, s 146(11)). Sub-lessees and mortgagees have the right to request a vesting order under LPA 1925, s 146(4) where a lease is forfeited for non-payment of rent, as well as in the case of breaches of other covenants and conditions.

LPA 1925, s 146 does not apply, by LPA 1925, s 146(9), to a condition for forfeiture on the bankruptcy of the lessee, nor on taking in execution of the lessee's interest if contained in a lease of:
1 agricultural or pastoral land;
2 mines or minerals;
3 a house used or intended to be used as a public house or beershop;
4 a house let as a dwelling-house, with the use of any furniture, books, works of art, or other chattels not being in the nature of fixtures; or
5 any property with respect to which the personal qualifications of the tenant are of importance for the preservation of the value or character of the property, or on the ground of the neighbourhood to the lessor, or to any person holding under him.[129]

LPA 1925, s 146 is also excluded, by LPA 1925, s 146(8), in two further specific cases:
1 where there was a breach of a covenant against assignment, sub-letting or parting with possession of the demised premises before the commencement of LPA 1925; and

---

128 This includes voluntary and involuntary acts by the lessee, and a lessee must be served with a LPA 1925, s 146(1) notice if his surety is bankrupt: *Halliard Property Co Ltd v Jack Segal Ltd* [1978] 1 All ER 1219, [1978] 1 WLR 377. Semble, LPA 1925, s 146 applies to breach of an implied condition or covenant: *British Telecommunications plc v Department of the Environment* [1996] NPC 148 (see *Commercial Leases* February 1997).
129 Cf *Earl Bathurst v Fine* [1974] 2 All ER 1160, [1974] 1 WLR 905, CA where relief against forfeiture was refused because the tenant had shown himself to be personally unsuitable.

2   in the case of a mining lease, to a covenant or condition allowing the lessor to have access to or inspect books, accounts, records, weighing machines or other things, or to enter or inspect the mine or its workings.

It appears that the second exception is justified by the fact that the rent payable under a mining tenancy is usually dependent on the amount of minerals produced by a mine.[130]

(iii) Partial exception in other cases of bankruptcy

LPA 1925, s 146 is partially excluded, where LPA 1925, s 146(9) does not apply, by LPA 1925, s 146(10), whose net effect is this. LPA 1925, s 146 applies for one year from the date of the tenant's bankruptcy or the taking in execution of his lease. If the tenant's interest is sold during the year referred to, the protection of s 146 continues without time limit for the new tenant. If the tenant's interest is not sold within the year, the protection of s 146 ceases completely.[131]

Restrictions on enforcement of right of re-entry: LPA 1925, s 146(1)

No right of re-entry or forfeiture for breach of any covenant or condition in the lease is enforceable by action or otherwise, unless and until the landlord has served on the tenant a notice[132] complying with LPA 1925, s 146(1). Section 146(1) provides that the notice must:
1   specify the particular breach complained of;
2   if the breach is capable of remedy, require the tenant to remedy the breach (a reasonable time must be allowed for a remedy); and
3   in any case, it must require the tenant to make compensation in money for the breach.

A letter containing the requisite points will suffice. A LPA 1925, s 146(1) notice is required whether re-entry is by service of a writ or peaceable, due to the words 'or otherwise' in s 146(1).[133] A s 146(1) notice operates as a necessary preliminary to actual forfeiture.[134]

---

130 Law Com No 142 (1985) 'Forfeiture of Tenancies' para 2.51.
131 The time-limit is strictly enforced as far as the tenant's interest is concerned, but it has no effect on any right of a mortgagee to apply for a LPA 1925, s 146(4) order outside the one-year period: *Official Custodian for Charities v Parway Estates Developments Ltd* [1985] Ch 151, [1984] 3 All ER 679, CA.
132 Service of the notice is governed by Law of Property Act 1962, s 196, with a special rule for breaches of covenant to repair (Landlord and Tenant Act 1927, s 18(2), requiring that the fact of the service of the notice is known to the tenant, although this requirement is complied with by service of registered post).
133 *Re Riggs, ex p Lovell* [1901] 2 KB 16; *Billson v Residential Apartments Ltd* [1992] 1 AC 494, [1992] 1 All ER 141, HL.
134 *Church Comrs for England v Nodjoumi* (1985) 51 P & CR 155.

Any attempt to avoid LPA 1925, s 146(1) will be invalidated by the courts, who are astute to detect disguised forfeiture clauses, and are jealous to safeguard their jurisdiction to grant relief to the tenant.[135] For example, a term under which, in the event of failure to comply with a covenant in the lease, the landlord could fill in the date on an undated deed of surrender previously executed, did not avoid the need to serve a LPA 1925, s 146 notice prior to forfeiture proceedings.[136] Similarly, a clause enabling the landlord to terminate the lease for breaches of covenant by a three months' notice served on the tenant did not preclude the court from exercising its jurisdiction to grant relief against forfeiture.[137] Not every term entitling the landlord to terminate a tenancy is a disguised forfeiture: for example a provision in a weekly tenancy agreement enabling either party to terminate it on four weeks' notice was not treated as a disguised forfeiture clause: however, the tenancy was a weekly tenancy terminable on a minimum four weeks' notice and no considerations of policy required the court to go behind the term.[138]

Since the primary aim of a LPA 1925, s 146 notice is for the landlord to see to it that the covenants of the lease are complied with, the notice must be served on the lessee in possession at the time of service.[139] Once that person has received the notice, he can make up his mind whether he is going to take action to avert forfeiture. The expression 'lessee' includes (LPA 1925, s 146(5)) an original or derivative under-lessee, where relevant; and all joint lessees, if any, must be served with a notice; as must any assignee, even where the assignment was in breach of covenant, as well as any mortgagee in possession.[140] If the landlord serves a LPA 1925, s 146(1) notice on the tenant which might be invalid, and serves a further notice, he is not obliged to await the determination of the validity of the first notice before serving the second.[141]

When preparing a LPA 1925, s 146(1) notice, the landlord has two predictions to make. If he gets either wrong, any proceedings based on his notice will fail. First, he must decide whether the breach in question (or, if there is more than one, then *each* breach in question) is capable of remedy. As a rule of thumb, positive covenants, such as to repair, are capable of remedy and negative covenants are incapable of remedy. There is no absolute rule and in marginal cases difficult questions of construction arise, there being no guarantee that the landlord will be correct in law. Where a breach is capable

---

135 See *Meadows v Clerical Medical and General Life Assurance Society* [1981] Ch 70, [1980] 1 All ER 454 (relief applications are part of the process of forfeiture).
136 *Plymouth Corpn v Harvey* [1971] 1 All ER 623, [1971] 1 WLR 549.
137 *Richard Clarke & Co Ltd v Widnall* [1976] 3 All ER 301, [1976] 1 WLR 845, CA.
138 *Clays Lane Housing Co-operative Ltd v Patrick* (1984) 49 P & CR 72, CA.
139 *Kanda v Church Comrs for England* [1958] 1 QB 332, [1957] 2 All ER 815, CA.
140 *Old Grovebury Manor Farm Ltd v W Seymour Plant Sales and Hire Ltd (No 2)* [1979] 3 All ER 504 (assignee): *Target Home Loans Ltd v Iza Ltd* [2000] 1 EGLR 23 (mortgagee in possession).
141 *Fuller v Judy Properties Ltd* [1992] 1 EGLR 75, CA. The tenant's relief application succeeded and it was granted a reversionary lease, the premises having been re-let.

of remedy and the landlord's notice fails to require one, it will be invalid.[142] Secondly, a reasonable time must be allowed from service of the notice for all breaches to be remedied; if the landlord issues a writ too soon then proceedings will fail.[143] The time for remedy must be allowed, even if it is an empty formality, as where it is plain that the tenant has no intention of doing anything. But a LPA 1925, s 146(1) notice is not invalid merely because it omits to require the tenant to pay the landlord compensation, as the latter need not touch the former's money if he does not wish to.[144]

(i)   Particular breach

In relation to certain covenants (eg against sub-letting) it is necessary for the landlord to indicate no more than the particular covenant which has been broken. Breaches of other covenants, on the other hand, should be specified in greater detail. In relation to breaches of repairing covenants especially is it necessary to identify the respects in which the covenant has been broken, as by a dilapidations schedule prepared by the landlord's surveyor.[145] It was held that a notice which mentioned repairs needed under various headings, such as 'roofs', was sufficiently informative in relation to a covenant to repair in a lease of a row of six houses, without indicating which house or houses were referred to.[146] After all, the means by which a remedy should be carried out is for the tenant to decide on.[147] Thus a notice which told a tenant that he had broken a covenant against alterations by turning one dwelling into two did not have to go further and become overburdened with details.[148]

(ii)   Special rules as to disputed service charges

A statutory rule exists in relation to service charges whose amount is disputed by the tenant of premises let as a dwelling or where a court or arbitral tribunal has to determine the amount of a service charge in relation to such premises. The restrictions are seemingly aimed at landlords who buy up the reversions of leasehold flats and then claim forfeiture for service charges arrears – perhaps where large outstanding repairs are said to be

---

142 As in *Expert Clothing Service and Sales Ltd v Hillgate House Ltd* [1986] Ch 340, [1985] 2 All ER 998, CA (failure to reconstruct premises by a certain date held capable of remedy and landlord's notice which failed to require remedy held bad).
143 As in *Horsey Estate Ltd v Steiger* [1899] 2 QB 79, CA (two days' time held insufficient).
144 *Rugby School Governors v Tannahill* [1935] 1 KB 87, CA.
145 Owing to the fact that under LPA 1925, s 146(3), the costs of preparation of such a schedule may only be recovered if the lessee obtains relief, some leases expressly enable the landlord to recover such costs whether or not relief is granted. However, such blanket clauses in a residential lease might offend against Unfair Terms in Consumer Contracts Regulations 1999, SI 1999/2083.
146 *Fox v Jolly* [1916] 1 AC 1, HL.
147 *John Lewis Properties plc v Viscount Chelsea* [1993] 2 EGLR 77, 83-84.
148 *Adagio Properties Ltd v Ansari* [1998] 2 EGLR 69, CA.

needed.[149] However, the new legislation cuts across the fact that separate rules exist for forfeiture for non-payment of rent and for breaches of other covenants. This may render the application of the new provisions less than easy, as covenants to pay service charges are not clearly on either side of this dividing line. On the one hand, some leases expressly reserve service charges as rent; some, however, do not. Yet it has been said that in the context of relief against forfeiture there is no difference between a covenant to pay rent and a covenant to pay service charges.[150] But the statutory references to LPA 1925, s 146(2) do not seem relevant where a landlord claims rent and service charges reserved as rent.

A landlord cannot enforce a right of re-entry or forfeiture where there is such a dispute or pending determination as to the amount of a service charge. He may only claim forfeiture after 14 days running from the date of final determination by, notably, a leasehold valuation tribunal, or if the tenant admits the claim.[151]

(iii) If the breach is capable of remedy

The general policy behind LPA 1925, s 146 is to give time to the lessee to remedy the breach. Breaches of a covenant against assignment or underletting are incapable of remedy[152] as are those of a covenant against illegal user of the premises.[153] To that extent there is a difference between breaches of positive and negative covenants, and where a breach is incapable of remedy, a LPA 1925, s 146(1) notice need not require a remedy.[154]

A breach of a covenant not to cause or permit immoral user of the premises is probably still incapable of remedy by mere cesser of the user, if the breach has cast a stigma on the premises, which is only removable by the eviction of the offending tenant.[155] The concept of a breach being incapable of remedy seems unnecessary since if the ground of complaint is irremediable damage to the landlord's interests, such considerations

---

149 A related legislative restriction applies to ground rent payable by long residential lessees. The tenant is not liable to pay ground rent, which may be a nominal sum but may rise during the term of the lease, unless the landlord complies with prescribed form notice requirements. These are laid down by CLRA 2002, s 166. The object of this provision is to preclude landlords from buying up reversions on residential blocks and then using forfeiture as a remedy for non-payment of ground rent.

150 *Khar v Delbounty Ltd* [1997] EGCS 183, CA.

151 Housing Act 1996, s 81(1) and (2) as amended. This restriction does not apply to business tenancies or to tenancies of agricultural holdings or farm business tenancies (Housing Act 1996, s 81(4)).

152 *Scala House and District Property Co Ltd v Forbes* [1974] QB 575, [1973] 3 All ER 308, CA.

153 *Hoffman v Fineburg* [1949] Ch 245, [1948] 1 All ER 592; *Van Haarlam v Kasner* [1992] 2 EGLR 59.

154 *Rugby School Governors v Tannahill* [1935] 1 KB 87, CA.

155 *Rugby School Governors v Tannahill* [1935] 1 KB 87, CA (user as a brothel); *Dunraven Securities Ltd v Holloway* [1982] 2 EGLR 47, CA; *British Petroleum Pension Trust Ltd v Behrendt* [1985] 2 EGLR 97, CA.

might properly go to the question of relief against forfeiture, where the court has a discretion, rather than to technical matters relating to the drafting of LPA 1925, s 146(1) notices.

It now appears that the courts are reluctant to discriminate between breaches of positive and negative covenants. If compliance by the tenant with a remedy required by a LPA 1925, s 146(1) notice, combined with payment of any compensation, puts right the harm suffered by the landlord then, save in the specific cases mentioned, a breach of a negative covenant may be remedied. It makes no difference that the precise status quo ante may not be capable of being restored. Thus, a LPA 1925, s 146(1) notice which complained that the tenant had broken a covenant not to put up signs or to alter the property without consent was invalid, as it failed to require a remedy from the tenant – which would have been simple enough in that case, seeing that the offending sign could have been removed.[156]

Where a lessee was personally innocent, and, at the date of service of the LPA 1925, s 146(1) notice, lacked any knowledge of the breach or breaches, and had not deliberately shut his eyes thereto, a prompt cesser of the breach, procured by his removal of offending sub-lessees, was in any case held to amount to a remedy on the facts and a LPA 1925, s 146(1) notice which failed to require a remedy was held bad.[157]

(iv) Requirement to remedy the breach

Since most breaches of covenant, positive or negative, are capable of being remedied by the tenant, so enabling him to avert dispossession, if the landlord, after service of his LPA 1925, s 146(1) notice, fails to allow the tenant a reasonable time to elapse in which to remedy the breach, any action based on his notice will fail. In the case of such few breaches of covenant as are as a matter of law incapable of remedy, no reasonable time at all need be allowed to elapse for any remedy and it was held in order for a writ to follow service of a LPA 1925, s 146(1) notice in 14 days.[158]

There is no hard and fast rule as to what exactly does amount to a reasonable time for the purpose of remediable breaches, but what is quite clear is that if there are a number of remediable breaches alleged in the notice, a reasonable time, sufficient to enable each breach to be remedied, must be allowed.[159]

---

156 *Savva v Hussein* [1996] 2 EGLR 65, CA. See Brown and Duddridge (1997) 1 L & T Rev 70.
157 *Glass v Kencakes Ltd* [1966] 1 QB 611, [1964] 3 All ER 807.
158 *Scala House and District Property Co Ltd v Forbes* [1974] QB 575, [1973] 3 All ER 308, CA (relief granted on facts).
159 *Hopley v Tarvin Parish Council* (1910) 74 JP 209. In *Bhojwani v Kingsley Investment Trust Ltd* [1992] 2 EGLR 70, three months was said to be adequate in the case of repairs, but it was also admitted that there were no hard and fast rules. A two-month period was held not to be sufficient on the facts.

Relief against forfeiture

(i) Jurisdiction to grant relief

Statute confers a jurisdiction on the court to grant relief against forfeiture. By LPA 1925, s 146(2): 'where a lessor is proceeding, by action or otherwise to enforce a right of re-entry or forfeiture, the lessee may, in the lessor's action, if any, or in an action brought by himself, apply to the court for relief'. The sub-section proceeds: 'the court may grant or refuse relief, as the court, having regard to the proceedings and conduct of the parties under the foregoing provisions of this section, and to all other circumstances, thinks fit'. Should the court grant relief, LPA 1925, s 146(2) provides that it may do so on 'such terms, if any, as to costs, expenses, damages, compensation, penalty, or otherwise, including the granting of an injunction to restrain any like breach in the future, as the court, in the circumstances of each case, thinks fit'.

The borderline between the scope of the present jurisdiction and that arising from equity of the High Court to grant relief in the case of rent default is not always easy to define, as shown by a case in which the lease did not reserve maintenance payments as rent, so that in the result the court had to consider relief under the statutory jurisdiction, whereas had the service charges been reserved as rent, the court's jurisdiction to grant relief would have presumably been based on equity.[160]

The courts are anxious not to allow the statutory jurisdiction to grant relief to be whittled down on technical grounds. So, for example, the power to grant relief arises as from the service of a LPA 1925, s 146(1) notice on the lessee, who may thereafter apply for relief.[161] Despite the fact that he is not, under common law rules, in privity of estate with the lessor, an equitable assignee of an underlease may apply under LPA 1925, s 146(2) for relief against forfeiture.[162] Similarly, the statutory jurisdiction is not excluded by the fact that the landlord chooses to forfeit the lease by the uncivilised method of peaceable re-entry, rather than by proceeding by claim form against the lessee, as 'proceeding' in s 146(2) includes out of court proceedings.[163] The court has, however, no power to grant relief once the landlord has obtained an order for possession forfeiting the lease and the order has been lawfully enforced against the tenant.[164]

Indeed, not only may a head tenant, but also, having regard to the width of the expression 'lessee' in LPA 1925, s 146(5),[165] a person holding a lesser estate by way of underlease and a mortgagee by sub-demise may both apply for relief under LPA 1925,

---

160 *Khar v Delbounty Ltd* [1996] EGCS 183, CA.
161 *Pakwood Transport Ltd v 15 Beauchamp Place* (1977) 36 P & CR 112, CA.
162 *High Street Investments Ltd v Bellshore Property Investments Ltd* [1996] 2 EGLR 40, CA.
163 *Billson v Residential Apartments Ltd* [1992] 1 AC 494, [1992] 1 All ER 141, HL.
164 *Quilter v Mapleson* (1882) 9 QBD 672; *Rogers v Rice* [1892] 2 Ch 170, as explained in *Billson v Residential Apartments Ltd* [1992] 1 AC 494, [1992] 1 All ER 141, HL.
165 As including 'an original or derivative underlessee' and, by analogy with LPA 1925, s 146(4), a mortgagee by underlease or by legal or equitable charge (as to the latter, see *High Street Investments Ltd v Bellshore Property Investments Ltd* [1996] 2 EGLR 40, CA). As observed in

s 146(2).[166] It makes no difference that neither party is, at common law, any more than is an equitable assignee of a lease referred to above, in privity of estate with the head landlord.[167] There may be advantages to mortgagees in applying for the court to exercise its discretion under LPA 1925, s 146(2) rather than LPA 1925, s 146(4). The effect of relief is to fully re-instate the lease as if it had been never forfeited, whereas the grant of relief under s 146(4) is effective only from the date of the court's order. Thus, while a landlord demanded mesne profits from a mortgagee from the date of issue of the writ (and of notional forfeiture) to that of the date of the order, the court, since the lease was granted at a premium, refused to make any such order against a mortgagee under a LPA 1925, s 146(2) relief application.[168]

If the tenant is able and willing to take effective steps within any time-limit specified in the court's order, which time-limit may be extended, in its discretion, once or more often by the county court,[169] to remedy the breach or breaches in question, forfeiture is not, ordinarily, ordered, provided the tenant complies punctually with any terms of relief. Thus, a tenant of an hotel who obtained a consent order in a landlords' forfeiture action in which phases of work were set out, which the tenant had to carry out to the premises (which had become seriously dilapidated), was denied relief on the basis that he seriously failed to adhere to the conditions of the consent order. On the facts, the court was sceptical about the tenant's ability to execute the necessary works.[170]

Escalus Properties Ltd v Robinson [1996] QB 231, [1995] 4 All ER 852, CA, this definition is wider than the definition of 'lessee' in the Conveyancing Act 1881, s 14(3). When the LRA 2002, s 23(1) comes into force, a registered owner will not be able to create mortgages by demise or sub-demise.

166 It is not clear whether an equitable tenant can apply for relief against forfeiture under statute: see *Sport International Bussum BV v Inter-Footwear Ltd* [1984] 1 All ER 376, from which it appears that the court cannot entertain relief applications by equitable tenants under County Courts Act 1984, s 138; see Pawlowski (1998) L & T Rev 53. From *Greenwood Village Property v Tom the Cheap (WA) Pty* [1975] WAR 49, it appears that that an equitable tenant may indeed invoke the relief jurisdiction applying in Western Australia. LPA 1925, s 146(5) could be construed as including an equitable lessee, who is in a different position to a charging order holder, as he has more than a mere equity in the land.

167 *Escalus Properties Ltd v Robinson* [1996] QB 231, [1995] 4 All ER 852. This was the first time the point had been decided but the Court of Appeal held that LPA 1925, s 146(5) had been drafted so as to overrule on that point *Nind v Nineteenth Century Building Society* [1894] 2 QB 226, holding the contrary; their interpretation of LPA 1925, s 146(5) is shared by Wolstenholme & Cherry, Vol 1, p 267.

168 *Escalus Properties Ltd v Robinson* [1996] QB 231, [1995] 4 All ER 852, CA.

169 See eg *Crawford v Clarke* [2000] EGCS 33 (where the county court ordered re-instatement of unauthorised alterations as a condition of relief, and allowed two applications by the tenant for a time-extension but not, exceptionally, a third application. This exercise of discretion was not upset on appeal).

170 *Fivecourts Ltd v JR Leisure Development Co Ltd* [2001] L & TR 5. Neuberger J there indicated that once a lessee had obtained relief on conditions, it could not expect further indulgence save on proof of good grounds.

A forfeiture clause is thus regarded as a security for the compliance by the tenant with his covenants.[171] For this reason, the grant or refusal of relief depends in the end on the way the court exercises its discretion in the particular case in question and no hard and fast rules can be laid down.[172]

The courts decline to grant relief if the tenant is not able and willing to remedy the breach, owing to the fact that the landlord should be put in the same position as if there had been no breach.[173] Often, therefore, whether the court will grant relief or not will depend on whether the tenant is prepared to accept any terms that the court imposes as a condition of the giving of relief: the court cannot force the tenant to accept relief on its terms.[174] Whether or not it grants relief to the tenant against forfeiture of his lease may also depend on the respective merits of the tenant and any sub-tenants involved in the proceedings.[175] The court has jurisdiction to grant relief in respect of part of the premises if physically separated from the remainder and a separately re-lettable unit.[176]

(ii) Relief in particular cases

If a covenant against immoral user is deliberately broken, generally, unless the breach is isolated, no relief will be granted.[177] Indeed, a deliberate breach of any covenant, especially a negative covenant, may prejudice the tenant's chances of relief.[178] The court looks at all the relevant factual circumstances. For example, where a tenant decided to assign a lease following a landlord's refusal on what would have been valid grounds to consent to the assignment, relief was refused on a number of grounds.[179] The tenant had never, seemingly, intended to ask the landlord's consent. A misleading letter which did not mention that a concluded contract to assign had been entered into was sent to the landlord about the assignment. A further example: where lessees by assignment, motivated by the wish to make a rapid profit out of short-term lettings of the altered premises, carried out flagrant breaches of a covenant against alterations, which work was also in breach of planning enforcement notices, all relief was refused

171 *Hyman v Rose* [1912] AC 623, HL; *Shiloh Spinners Ltd v Harding* [1973] AC 691, [1973] 1 All ER 90, HL; also *On Demand plc v Michael Gerson plc* [2001] 1 WLR 155; on appeal [2002] UKHL 13.
172 *Hyman v Rose* [1912] AC 623, HL; *Mount Cook Land Ltd v Hartley* [2000] EGCS 26.
173 See *Inntrepreneur Pub Co (CPC) v Langton* [1999] EGCS 124 (a case on non-payment of rent).
174 *Talbot v Blindell* [1908] 2 KB 114.
175 *Duke of Westminster v Swinton* [1948] 1 KB 524, [1948] 1 All ER 248.
176 *GMS Syndicate Ltd v Gary Elliott Ltd* [1982] Ch 1, [1981] 1 All ER 619.
177 *Borthwick-Norton v Romney Warwick Estates Ltd* [1950] 1 All ER 798, CA; *British Petroleum Pension Trust Ltd v Behrendt* [1985] 2 EGLR 97, CA.
178 *St Marylebone Property Co Ltd v Tesco Stores Ltd* [1988] 2 EGLR 40.
179 *Crown Estate Comrs v Signet Group plc* [1996] 2 EGLR 200. The landlord gained, as a result of its successful forfeiture, vacant premises free from renewal rights under Landlord and Tenant Act 1954, Pt II but this result was left out of account in deciding whether relief was appropriate.

despite the fact that the landlord's recourse to a 'dawn raid' might otherwise have prevented them from resisting the grant of relief.[180] In another case, the county court was held entitled to refuse relief to an applicant where it was not sure that he would comply immediately with a condition to put up a surgery which he had so far failed to do in breach of covenant.[181] The result of these cases well illustrates the way in which no one factor is relevant to relief applications: the attitudes of the parties as well as objective breaches may be relevant.

Nevertheless, weight may properly be attached to the financial losses which the tenant would suffer if refused relief: as noted, the wilfulness of a breach does not of itself preclude the court from granting relief.[182] This is especially so if no lasting loss or damage will result from the breach to the lessor,[183] provided that he can be adequately compensated, in money or in the terms of relief. Thus, where the tenant's sub-lessee and licensee permitted prostitution in their premises, which was contrary to covenant in the tenant's own lease, which required the use of the premises as a high-class restaurant or night club, relief was granted to the tenant, even though it was fixed with knowledge of the breach, because there was no lasting damage or stigma, as the offending occupiers had been removed, and if relief had been refused, the lessee, who held a valuable lease, would suffer a disproportionate financial loss.[184]

Two technical limits on applicants for relief are worthy of note. In the case of joint tenants, all must apply for relief.[185] A person holding a possessory title to unregistered land cannot apply for relief.[186]

(iii) Effect of relief

If relief is granted, the effect is as if there had never been a forfeiture of the lease, which will be fully restored, so that any sub-tenant will be unaffected by the proceedings.[187] However, should possession be granted by a court of first instance, and the Court of Appeal reverses the forfeiture (say by ordering relief to be granted to the tenant), the clock is not totally put back, because any acts of the landlord under the order for possession, until its reversal, are considered lawful.[188] If the court imposes time-limits

---

180 *Billson v Residential Apartments Ltd (No 2)* [1993] EGCS 155.
181 *Darlington Borough Council v Denmark Chemists Ltd* [1993] 1 EGLR 62, CA.
182 As in *Southern Depot Co Ltd v British Railways Board* [1990] 2 EGLR 39.
183 As in *Mount Cook Land Ltd v Hartley* [2000] EGCS 26 (where the landlord could not prove any loss itself from the sub-lettings in question and despite the 'sloppy practice' of one of the lessees in sub-letting without asking for landlord consent).
184 *Ropemaker Properties Ltd v Noonhaven Ltd* [1989] 2 EGLR 50.
185 *T M Fairclough & Sons Ltd v Berliner* [1931] 1 Ch 60. Law Com No 142 (1985) 'Forfeiture of Tenancies' recommended abolishing this rule: para 3.63.
186 *Tickner v Buzzacott* [1965] Ch 426 [1965] 1 All ER 131.
187 *Dendy v Evans* [1910] 1 KB 263; *Hynes v Twinsectra Ltd* [1995] 2 EGLR 69, CA.
188 *Hillgate House Ltd v Expert Clothing Service and Sales Ltd* [1987] 1 EGLR 65.

to comply with a condition of relief, it has an inherent jurisdiction to extend them.[189] If relief is not granted, and an order for possession is made, the lease will be treated as having been forfeited with effect from the service of the claim form.

(iv) Failure to apply for relief

If the tenant fails to apply for relief under LPA 1925, s 146(2), he cannot apply for relief in equity on any ground covered by statute, since the enactment of legislation has ousted any general inherent equity jurisdiction there might previously have been.[190] There appears, therefore, to be only a residual equitable jurisdiction in these circumstances to grant relief to the lessee applicable to cases of fraud, accident, surprise or mistake.[191] The position of under-lessees and mortgagees who do not avail themselves of LPA 1925, s 146(4) is unclear and is discussed below. The scope and basis of the relieving jurisdiction under LPA 1925, s 146(2) contrasts with the position with respect to non-payment of rent,[192] where the High Court's jurisdiction is based on equitable principles as modified by statute on points of detail (see ch 8, above).

(v) Costs

Under LPA 1925, s 146(3), the landlord is entitled to recover, as a debt due to him from the tenant, all reasonable costs he has properly incurred 'in the employment of a solicitor and surveyor or valuer, or otherwise', if the tenant is given relief, or if the breach is waived at the request of the tenant.[193] Consequently, if the tenant remedies

189 *Chandless-Chandless v Nicholson* [1942] 2 KB 321, [1942] 2 All ER 315 and cases discussed earlier.
190 *Shiloh Spinners Ltd v Harding* [1973] AC 691 at 725, [1973] 1 All ER 90 at 102, HL; also *Official Custodian for Charities v Parway Estates Developments* [1985] Ch 151 at 155, CA; *Smith v Metropolitan City Properties Ltd* [1986] 1 EGLR 52.
191 *Barrow v Isaacs & Son* [1891] 1 QB 417. In *Billson v Residential Apartments Ltd* [1992] 1 All ER 141, HL, Lord Templeman referred to this jurisdiction without specifically mentioning surprise, but surprise was mentioned in *British Telecommunications plc v Department of the Environment* [1996] NPC 148 (see *Commercial Leases* February 1997). The residual jurisdiction was considered in *Bland v Ingrams Estates Ltd* [2001] L & TR 13, [2001] L & TR 125, CA, but it did not there apply on the facts as relief had been sought by the persons otherwise eligible to apply. According to the High Court in this case, [1999] 2 EGLR 49 as an equitable chargee, the applicant held only as 'mere equity' within the sense of *Westminster Bank Ltd v Lee* [1956] Ch 7, and so outside a claim to relief in the inherent jurisdiction, which protects holders of proprietary rights only. However, there would seem to be nothing to prevent an equitable chargee from joining the tenant in the forfeiture action and then applying in that person's shoes. The inherent jurisdiction to grant relief is wider in the case of leases of personal property: see *On Demand plc v Michael Gerson plc* [2001] 1 WLR 155, CA, where the relevant principles were reviewed.
192 See also *Ladup Ltd v Williams and Glyn's Bank plc* [1985] 2 All ER 577, [1985] 1 WLR 851.
193 If the tenant claims the Leasehold Property (Repairs) Act 1938, the landlord requires the leave of the court to recover costs under LPA 1925, s 149(3) (Leasehold Property (Repairs) Act 1938, s 2); but recovery under an express term of the lease would be outside this, as a contract debt.

the breach on notice and there are no court proceedings, the landlord is probably not entitled to any costs incurred, for example, in the preparation of his LPA 1925, s 146 notice.[194] It may well be that the lease contains an express term allowing the landlord to recover these costs, whether arising in actual or contemplated proceedings.

Protection of sub-lessees and mortgagees

(i)   General principles

At common law, a sub-tenancy is destroyed automatically if the head tenancy is forfeited.[195] LPA 1925, s 146(4) enables any sub-lessee, and hence any legal mortgagee[196] of any part of the property to apply to the court for a vesting order, either in the forfeiture proceedings or a separate action. An order will, if granted, create a new tenancy and vest in the applicant the part of the property occupied by the sub-lessee for a term not exceeding the remaining term of the original sub-lease, the length of the term being, subject to that, at the court's discretion.

The conditions for the grant of a vesting order are at the court's discretion. LPA 1925, s 146(4) refers to the position immediately before forfeiture: if then a sub-lessee occupies the whole or part of the premises for business purposes, he will be entitled to a vesting order, not only in relation to the residue of his contractual term but also in respect of its continuation by the Landlord and Tenant Act 1954, Pt II, after expiry of the sub-term at common law, of appropriate length.[197] The subsection applies where the landlord is *proceeding* to enforce, by action or otherwise, a right of re-entry or forfeiture under *any* covenant, proviso, etc, in the lease, or, exceptionally within LPA 1925, s 146 *for non-payment of rent*, thus conferring a parallel statutory jurisdiction to that of equity.

A mortgagee by way of legal charge[198] is entitled to an order, as is a guarantor who has a right to call for a legal charge or mortgage.[199] If the words 'is proceeding' in LPA 1925, s 146(4) bear the same meaning as in LPA 1925, s 146(2), the fact that the landlord

---

194 *Nind v Nineteenth Century Building Society* [1894] 2 QB 226, which would appear not to have been overruled in *Escalus Properties Ltd v Robinson* [1996] QB 231, [1995] 4 All ER 852, on this point.

195 *Viscount Chelsea v Hutchinson* [1994] 2 EGLR 61, CA.

196 As opposed to an equitable chargee holding a charging order on the lessee's interest, who cannot invoke LPA 1925, s 146(4): *Bland v Ingrams Estates Ltd* supra (although it seems that such an application might have a 'strong case' for being eligible to apply for relief under County Courts Act 1984, s 138(9c) (non-payment of rent)).

197 *Cadogan v Dimovic* [1984] 2 All ER 168, [1984] 1 WLR 609, CA.

198 *Grand Junction Co Ltd v Bates* [1954] 2 QB 160, [1954] 2 All ER 385. An order will not ipso facto re-instate sub-lessees: *Hammersmith and Fulham London Borough v Top Shop Centres Ltd* [1989] 2 All ER 655.

199 *Re Good's Lease* [1954] 1 All ER 275, [1954] 1 WLR 309.

proceeds to forfeit by peaceable re-entry rather than by claim form should not exclude the statutory jurisdiction to grant relief to under-lessees and mortgagees.[200]

(ii) Discretion as to relief

In granting an order, on the application of a sub-lessee or mortgagee, the court has a discretion whether to grant relief,[201] and relief may be granted to an under-lessee or mortgagee where there is no jurisdiction to grant it to a lessee, as where the latter is bankrupt.[202] The terms of relief are at the discretion of the court.[203] As a general rule, relief will be granted provided the applicant pays off all rent arrears owing to date, undertakes to comply with the covenants in the head lease, pays off the landlord's costs, and remedies any outstanding breaches of covenant, in relation to the premises or part to which the application relates.[204] The idea is to put the landlord back into the same position as he was in before the forfeiture took place.[205] If this object cannot be achieved, and perhaps in any case, the jurisdiction to grant relief should, at least according to a recent High Court case, be exercised sparingly. The landlord is having a person thrust on him with whom he did not contract.[206]

If the circumstances warrant it, relief will be refused at discretion. For example, relief was refused where rent had not been paid to the head landlord for 22 years and it had been assumed that the sub-leases had gone.[207] The same result followed where a sub-lessee held only a monthly tenancy of a basement, which was badly out of repair: he refused to undertake admittedly onerous repairing obligations in relation thereto, which the head lease had cast on the lessee: if relief had been granted in these circumstances, the landlords would have had less extensive rights regarding repairs than originally.[208]

If the court makes an order under LPA 1925, s 146(4), its effect, in contrast to LPA 1925, s 146(2), is not retroactive. The forfeited interest is not revived. Any conditions attached to a vesting order are conditions precedent to actual vesting: hence, any

---

200 In *Billson v Residential Apartments Ltd* [1992] 1 AC 494, [1992] 1 All ER 141, this issue was not expressly dealt with. In *Gray v Bonsall* [1904] 1 KB 601 at 607, however, Conveyancing and Law of Real Property Act 1892, s 4 (the predecessor to LPA 1925, s 146(4)) was treated as a separate relieving provision. If so, the view in the text would not necessarily apply.

201 See eg *Matthews v Smallwood* [1910] 1 Ch 777.

202 *Wardens of Cholmeley School, Highgate v Sewell* [1894] 2 QB 906.

203 *Ewart v Fryer* [1901] 1 Ch 499.

204 *Belgravia Insurance Co Ltd v Meah* [1964] 1 QB 436, [1963] 3 All ER 828, CA; *Official Custodian for Charities v Mackey (No 2)* [1985] 2 All ER 1016, [1985] 1 WLR 1308; *Grangeside Properties Ltd v Collingwoods Securities Ltd* [1964] 1 WLR 139, CA.

205 *Chatham Empire Theatre (1955) Ltd v Ultrans* [1961] 2 All ER 381, [1961] 1 WLR 817.

206 *Duarte v Mount Cook Land Ltd* [2001] 33 EG 87 (CS). A new lease was in fact granted to a person whom the tenant (whose lease was forfeited) had allowed into occupation under a sham sale agreement. However, the landlord appeared to have been content with such a grant.

207 *Public Trustee v Westbrook* [1965] 3 All ER 398, [1965] 1 WLR 1160, CA.

208 *Hill v Griffin* [1987] 1 EGLR 81, CA. The applicant was not prepared to undertake onerous liabilities for repairs on a periodic tenancy, which was all the court could grant him.

rights accrued in the landlords prior to an order, such as to rent in the twilight period from service of the writ down to the date of a LPA 1925, s 146(4) order, are unaffected by the order.[209] For this reason, as indicated above, it may be advantageous for a legal mortgagee to apply for relief under LPA 1925, s 146(2). If, however, a receiver was in possession of the tenant's interest during the twilight period between notional and actual forfeiture, he is entitled to rents for that period to the exclusion of the landlord.[210]

(iii) Defects of LPA 1925, s 146(4)

Arguably, LPA 1925, s 146(4) suffers from certain defects, for example:

1   It does not enable the court to preserve existing tenancies, nor indeed may the landlord elect to do so. The effect of relief under LPA 1925, s 146(4) is to create a new tenancy, as is shown by the fact that if the successful applicant is a mortgagee, he holds a substituted security.[211]

2   Subject to special considerations applicable to business tenancies, the court can never grant to the applicant a new tenancy for a longer term than he had originally under his old sub-lease. As was seen, this may work harshly where the original sub-tenancy was merely periodic, or for a short fixed term.

3   The subsection contains no guidelines as to the rent payable under the new tenancy, but it has been held that the court has power to vary the rent.[212]

4   After the landlord has regained actual possession following an order of court forfeiting the lease, no applications under LPA 1925, s 146(4) may be entertained. A landlord must, in proceedings, set out a statement giving the name and address of any person, including a mortgagee, known to him.[213] There may, however, be sub-lessees and mortgagees unknown to the landlord; not a likely situation if the lease requires due notification of any sub-leases or mortgages to the landlord. These unknown persons, if such there be, may still not be notified of pending forfeiture proceedings, and the landlord is under no implied obligation to notify them.[214] In these exceptional circumstances it is possible that the court has an inherent jurisdiction in equity to accede to an application for relief even after it has ordered forfeiture.[215] As already mentioned, this inherent jurisdiction may still exist, although it is difficult to see how it could have survived the enactment of a statutory code, of which LPA 1925, s 146(4) is part, so ruling out any co-existing

---

209   *Official Custodian for Charities v Mackey* [1985] Ch 168, [1984] 3 All ER 689.

210   *Official Custodian for Charities v Mackey (No 2)* [1985] 2 All ER 1016, [1985] 1 WLR 1308.

211   *Chelsea Estates Investment Trust Co Ltd v Marche* [1955] Ch 328 at 339.

212   *Ewart v Fryer* [1901] 1 Ch 499, CA (higher rent commanded due to fact that premises ceased, with forfeiture of head lease, to be a tied house).

213   Practice Direction – Possession Claims (to CPR 1998, Pt 55) para 24. The particulars must be filed for service on that person.

214   *Egerton v Jones* [1939] 2 KB 702, [1939] 3 All ER 889, CA.

215   *Abbey National Building Society v Maybeech Ltd* [1985] Ch 190, [1984] 3 All ER 262. A sub-lessee may invoke equitable estoppel to save his interest: *Hammersmith and Fulham London Borough v Top Shop Centres Ltd* [1989] 2 All ER 655.

equity jurisdiction.[216] A mortgagee (or sub-lessee) may apply for an executed judgment for possession to be set aside, if he has grounds for relief. Only rarely would the court accede to the application, and merely forgetting to respond to a notification of a claim to forfeiture was not a case for relief.[217]

Reform

Reform of the forfeiture rules has been proposed more than once by the Law Commission.[218] They made an initial set of proposals in 1985. The main features of these proposals were as follows.

1 There should be brought into force, in place of the current systems, a new termination order scheme. It would apply to all breaches of tenants' covenants, whether non-payment of rent or all other breaches, and to insolvency events.

2 Certain archaic doctrines, which operate either harshly or capriciously, would be abolished. These include the doctrine of re-entry and waiver. The latter doctrine would be replaced by a new rule that the landlord would lose his right to forfeit only if his conduct would lead a reasonable tenant (and the actual tenant) to believe that he would not seek a termination order. (It might be noted that the doctrine of waiver antedates the availability of statutory relief and is a less flexible instrument designed to attain that object.) However, as we shall note, peaceable re-entry may well not be done away with in the light of consultations which took place in the late 1990s.

3 Rent would be due down to the date the court terminated the lease – not, as at present, down to the date of notional re-entry and no further.

4 The court would have power to grant either:
   (i) an absolute termination order, reserved for very serious and irremediable cases; or
   (ii) a remedial termination order, which would operate to end the tenancy unless the tenant took specified remedial action.

5 The power to save sub-leases and the interests of mortgagees would be retained and improved. For example, the landlord would be enabled to elect to retain some, or all, of any derivative interests in the premises.

The Law Commission's original scheme also proposed granting tenants a right to terminate their tenancies on the ground of landlords' breaches of covenant.

---

216 See eg *Shiloh Spinners Ltd v Harding* [1973] AC 691, HL; also *Official Custodian for Charities v Parway Estates Developments Ltd* [1985] Ch 151 at 155, CA.

217 *Rexhaven Ltd v Nurse* [1995] EGCS 125.

218 Law Com No 142 (1985) 'Forfeiture of Tenancies'; and see eg P F Smith [1986] Conv 165; Cherryman (1987) 84 LSG 1042; Adams (1991) 17 LSG 17; Luxton [1991] JBL 42. A special notice rule in cases involving repairs would, generally, be retained, though there would be modifications: *paras* 8.33ff.

These useful proposals never saw the light of day. In 1994, the Commission produced the Termination of Tenancies Bill.[219] The Bill deviated from the original proposals, as it failed to mention the proposed tenants' termination order scheme. No legislation followed even the truncated 1994 scheme. Then, during 1998 and 1999 the Law Commission published revised proposals to address the fact that commercial landlords did not, perhaps unsurprisingly, wish to see this cheap and effective remedy abrogated. The peaceable re-entry proposals derive from a Consultative Document, adjusted by a Press Release of June 1999. The essence of these proposals was to create a new statutory right of 'peaceable' re-entry available to commercial landlords alone. Thus the revised right would not apply to residential premises.[220] The proposals aimed to provide landlords of commercial premises with a 'management tool to protect both the value of their investment and their income stream' where the tenant had defaulted.[221] The right would not operate in such a way as unfairly to deprive tenants and owners of derivative interests of their right to apply for relief. The new right would have to be integrated with the 1985 termination order scheme. As a result, which would contrast with the present position, physical re-entry would not put an immediate end to the tenancy. It would operate as an irrevocable election by the landlord to terminate the tenancy within, ordinarily, a one-month period.[222] The period would take effect unless, in particular, the tenant applied for relief.[223] Under the 1998 proposals, the tenant would remain liable to pay rent and to observe lease covenants until the expiry of three months after the landlord had re-entered. At first sight, this proposal seems at variance with the idea that the landlord has irrevocably elected to end the lease, and so is having it both ways. The Law Commission insisted that the proposal was fair, citing for example the argument that the tenant's breach had caused the landlord to re-enter in the first place.[224]

---

219 Law Com No 221 (1994); see Peet (1994) 26 EG 132 and Wilkinson [1994] Conv 177.

220 For a comment on the 1998 proposals see Adams [1998] Conv 164. Safeguards in the form of a right to apply for relief, and so for a court hearing, are important if the revised scheme is to survive attack under HRA 1998.

221 Consultative Document (1998), para 3.16. If the lease had a significant capital value, the revised peaceable re-entry scheme would not be available to landlords, whereas it will be appreciated that peaceable re-entry, where at present allowed, is not limited to short tenancies. In their Press Release of 30 June 1999, the Commission suggested a test based on the length of the term of the unexpired tenancy and so unexpired terms of more than 25 years (para 16): 'standard' business tenancies would not be excluded by this test from the revised re-entry scheme.

222 While the 1998 proposals had floated the period of three months, the Commission then decided to reduce the period to one month (Press Release 30 June 1999, para 12).

223 Consultative Document (1998), para 3.17.

224 Consultative Document (1998), para 3.19. The 1998 proposals would, however, allow a tenant to apply for an order to restore him or her to possession (ibid); or the tenant could surrender the lease; in any case even if the liability proposal had not been made, the Commission noted that the tenant would have to pay damages for breach to the landlord; they also noted that the express liability proposal would prevent the doctrine of repudiation being used by landlords as a way round forfeiture procedures (Consultative Document (1998), para 3.19).

The statutory re-entry right would be exercisable only on compliance by the landlord with certain conditions, such as service on the tenant of a notice requiring the tenant to remedy the breach within a reasonable period:[225] the notice would have to be served within six months after the landlord had actual knowledge of the facts entitling him to bring the lease to an end.[226] As from the moment this notice had been served on the tenant, he or she could then apply for relief, as could any derivative interest holder, within a three-month period.[227]

At first sight it may seem odd that a self-help remedy which as we saw, the House of Lords stigmatised as being 'uncivilised' should be recommended as suitable for incorporation in a general statutory reform of the law applying to forfeiture. The Law Commission's deference to the view of its commercial respondents is to be noted. This is balanced by the continuing perceived need to remove this remedy in the case of residential premises, where the only proper course of action can be court proceedings. At least if peaceable re-entry is codified and limited, its application would be less unpredictable than at present. The next stage in the reform of forfeiture is understood to be the appearance of a further Draft Termination of Tenancies Bill.

225 In the case of non-payment of rent and irremediable breach the period proposed in the Press Release of 30 June 1999 would be seven working days (para 13).
226 Consultation Paper (1998), para 3.22. This proposal would represent an improvement on the present law by making for certainty. Actual re-entry would have to take place if at all within six months of the landlord's notice. Notice would have to be served on derivative interest holders as envisaged in Consultative Document (1998), para 3.23.
227 The Commission thought that it was 'uncommon for a tenant who has abandoned the premises to seek relief from forfeiture' (Consultative Document (1998), para 3.26). They therefore expressed the view that the tenancy would not have to be preserved for three months after physical re-entry to allow for relief applications, where the premises had been abandoned.

Residential tenancies

CHAPTER 13

Introduction to residential lettings

1   BRIEF HISTORY OF STATUTORY INTERVENTION

The common law does not seek to control the rent payable by tenants of private-sector landlords. Such security of tenure as the tenant has at common law is dependent on the agreement of the parties, who are free to agree on whatever length of tenancy suits them, and about renewal of the tenancy. Statute has been a feature of private-sector residential tenancies since 1915. The history of the field has been chequered. As the Law Commission put it, 'the principle that the State should guarantee tenants' security of tenure, irrespective of the terms of the contract, has become a central principle of housing law'.[1] They go on to note that security of tenure is not and has never been absolute. Indeed, as time has passed, the security offered to private-sector tenants has tended to shrink away. When legislative regulation first appeared,[2] it was designed to limit or freeze rent increases so as to prevent social unrest during the then prevailing war conditions.[3] The rent restriction legislation remained on the statute books. It may be that this was owing to the fact that once established, it was no easy matter to put the clock back, at a time when much of the population lived in rented accommodation.[4] Decontrol of rents was commenced by the Rent Act 1957, but this led to unpleasant cases of illegal pressures on protected tenants to leave their

1   Consultation Paper No 162 (2002) 'Renting Homes I: Status and Security'.
2   Increase of Rent and Mortgage Interest (War Restrictions) Act 1915.
3   The social background is set out by the Law Com Consultation Paper No 162 (2002) 'Renting Homes I: Status and Security' para 2.11. The early rent restriction legislation had two abuses to combat. One was excessive rent increases at a time of shortages of urban housing. The other was retaliatory eviction of tenants who sought to enforce their rights.
4   According to the Law Com Consultation Paper No 162 (2002) 'Renting Homes I: Status and Security' para 2.14, by 1953 it appears that at least 90% of all dwelling houses in England and Wales fell within the scope of the Rent Acts. By 2002, however, this figure had dwindled to such an extent that the Law Commission suggested that if their reform proposals were adopted, Rent Act tenancies should be done away with and converted into Type I occupation agreements (Law Com Consultation Paper No 162 (2002) para 14.43). There are precedents for this: by Housing Act 1980, s 64(1), any remaining controlled tenancies were converted into regulated tenancies.

accommodation.[5] Hence, in due course, came the enactment of statutory protections against illegal eviction and harassment, now embedded in the Protection from Eviction Act 1977.[6]

The legislation known as the Rent Acts was consolidated by the Rent Act 1977. Even before the advent of deregulation in the Housing Act 1988, the Rent Act scheme had by then allowed for a number of lettings of private-sector residential accommodation to be outside full protection. Thus, a house or flat let on a tenancy under which the rent included payment for board or substantial attendance falls outside the protection of the Rent Acts.[7] Lettings by owner-occupiers are subject to relatively easy or mandatory re-possession.[8] Lettings by resident landlords, a category created by the Rent Act1974, were not protected tenancies but were at most 'restricted contracts'.[9] However, according to the Law Commission,[10] the general expansion of the scope of the Rent Acts 'encouraged landlords to enter into agreements which they hoped might fall outside the scope of the legislation, so that their properties were not subject to rent regulation and their occupiers did not have long-term security of tenure'.[11] Much of the material discussed elsewhere in this book about the construction of written occupation agreements purporting to be 'licences' is the result of a series of attempts, some blatant, by owners, to evade the protection of the Rent Acts by using tenancies in disguise. The latter need to be distinguished both from genuine licences to occupy, not to mention from tenancies at no rent, service occupancies and family arrangements.

5   Law Com Consultation Paper No 162 (2002) 'Renting Homes I: Status and Security', quote from the Oxford Dictionary definition of 'Rachmanism', derived from the activities of a 'notorious private landlord' (para 2.18).

6   When the private residential sector was freed from the shackles of the Rent Acts by the Housing Act 1988, there were enacted specific provisions (Housing Act 1988, ss 27 and 28). These aim to combat landlords who tried to force out existing Rent Act protected or statutory tenants so as to replace them with much less secure assured shorthold tenants.

7   Rent Act 1977, s 7.

8   Rent Act 1977, Sch 15, Pt II, Case 11.

9   Rent Act 1977, s 12 as amended. Furnished lettings were not within the original Rent Act scheme until some protection came in thanks to the Furnished Houses (Rent Control) Act 1946, in the form of rent control through rent tribunals (see Megarry's *Rent Acts* ch 20). That separate regime was done away with by Rent Act 1974, s 1, and furnished tenancies fell within full protection. The policy of the law since then has been to differentiate between lettings by landlords who live in close proximity to tenants (as where the parties live in the same house and share the same staircase, so to speak) and those where the tenant has exclusive possession of his rooms, provided these form his dwelling: see *Uratemp Ventures Ltd v Collins* [2001] UKHL 43, [2002] 1 AC 301. The Law Commission, Consultation Paper No 162 (2002) is not suggesting removing the resident landlord exclusion. This would be maintained in the new suggested system subject to certain conditions (paras 9.109- 9.110).

10   Law Com Consultation Paper No 162 (2002) 'Renting Homes I: Status and Security' para 2.39.

11   Ie the so-called 'fair rent' regime ushered in by the Rent Act 1965, although old-style controlled tenancies were not abolished until the Housing Act 1980.

The Housing Act 1988 was enacted. It specifically aimed to deregulate rents. In that way it intended to increase the supply of private rented houses and flats. The Housing Act 1988 created two types of tenancy in the private rented sector: assured tenancies and assured shorthold tenancies. Assured tenancies have deregulated, and so open market, rents. However, as regards security of tenure and succession they are not unlike Rent Act tenancies. Assured shorthold tenancies are wholly insecure and most of these are of short duration. Tenancies under the Rent Act 1977 cannot, as from 15 January 1989, be created, except in exceptional cases. The Housing Act 1988 was followed by a further Housing Act 1996, which has resulted in the presumption that, as from the commencement of the 1996 Act, private-sector residential tenancies are assured shorthold tenancies.[12] As things now stand, the legislative framework for the latter tenancies does little to interfere with the common law, and provides a hollow shell, which is concerned mainly with the issue of termination of assured shorthold tenancies by notices leading to repossession proceedings. It is worth drawing specific attention to the fact that there is virtually no rent control[13] of the rent of an assured or an assured shorthold tenancy at all: the rent is that of the marketplace. Indeed, a market rent can in principle be charged even if the landlord is in serious breach of his statutory repairing obligations.[14]

It is understood that the average length of assured shorthold tenancies is about 15 months. These are the dominant private-sector tenancy today. There are currently estimated to be at most about 150,000 tenancies within the Rent Acts. This figure, which accounts only for some 6% of the whole private rented sector, is also a declining one.[15] In the private rented sector, there were (in 2000) said to be some 1,241,000 assured shorthold tenancies, which is about 54% of the whole sector. That compares with some 275,000 assured tenancies. That figure represents a modest 12% of the whole sector.

The balance of the field as between landlord and tenant has shifted away from tenant security, at least in the case of lettings by private landlords. The Rent Acts created a 'status of irremovability'[16] on a statutory tenant[17] once the common law or 'contractual' tenancy had expired, a feature which was disliked by landlords. They originally imposed

---

12 Housing Act 1988, s 19A.
13 Save for the narrow provision of Housing Act 1988, ss 13 and 14 (see ch 15, below).
14 Subject to the right of the tenant to treat the landlord's breach as repudiatory in nature (see ch 9 above).
15 DETR Housing Statistics (2000) Table 6 and following. Partington (2001) 5 L&TR 95 says that the rate of decline is around 25,000 to 30,000 a year. This may be owing to the fact that regulated fair rents for statutory tenancies, the main class of surviving Rent Act tenancy, are based on assured tenancy and thus open market comparables. It remains to be seen whether the cap on fair rent increases (see ch 14, below) affects the rate of decline or not.
16 *Keeves v Dean* [1924] 1 KB 685 at 686; also called '*monstrum horrendum informe ingens*' in *Marcroft Wagons Ltd v Smith* [1951] 2 KB 496 at 501, derived, it seems, from Virgil's sea-monster in the *Aenied*.
17 According to Megarry's *Rent Acts* (11th edn, 1988) p 251, the expression 'statutory tenancy' *did not appear in statute until the Housing Repairs and Rents Act 1954.*

controls on rents. These were eased with the progressive abolition of rent control as from 1957, the removal of controlled tenancies in 1980, and the alteration of the rent provisions in the Rent Acts to 'fair rent' provisions as from the Rent Act 1965. This feature still discouraged private landlords from letting.[18] Radical reform of the old system came in two waves. The first aspect was to allow landlords to let to tenants at market rents, but with the grant of security of tenure not dissimilar to that provided for Rent Act tenants, although opening up to landlords additional grounds for possession[19] where the court has no overriding discretion to refuse to order possession. The more radical part of the 1988 reform package was to create and then further encourage the creation of wholly insecure 'assured shorthold tenancies' as the prime private-sector residential tenancy. This was achieved by means of a statutory presumption that from 28 February 1997, a residential tenancy granted in the private sector was to be assured shorthold.[20] The government of the day seemed to have thought that the reforms of the Housing Act 1996 were simply a recognition of pre-existing reality. At a more technical level, until the 1996 Act regime came into being, an assured shorthold tenancy could only be created validly if a prior notice procedure, which was thought of as technical, was followed.[21] This procedure seems to have caught some landlords out, the erstwhile penalty being the deemed grant of an assured (and much more secure) tenancy.[22]

The effect of the changes has seemingly been to bring about a change in the attitude of landlords to letting residential premises. Thus from empirical research published by the government in 1996,[23] it appears that landlords[24] have much greater confidence about letting their property in the 1990s than in the 1980s. Landlords in the private rented sector were in the main satisfied both with their rent levels and with the fact that tenants had no security (or, as was put, that they were adequately protected against

---

18   Such was the firm belief of the Conservative government in 1987 (see 'Housing: the Government's Proposals', Cm 214).

19   As for example a mandatory redevelopment ground (Housing Act 1988, Sch 2, Ground 6) and a mandatory rent arrears ground (Housing Act 1988, Sch 2, Ground 8).

20   Housing Act 1996, s 96(1), adding s 19A to Housing Act 1988. In addition, certain social landlords such as housing associations may only let dwellings on assured or assured shorthold tenancies, not secure tenancies (Housing Act 1988, Chapter v, and Sch 18. The Law Com Consultation Paper No 162 (2002) 'Renting Homes I: Status and Security' para 2.102 notes that the change was not retrospective, adding to the complexity of the law. Some housing association tenants may still hold Rent Act tenancies as a result.

21   As laid down by Housing Act 1988, s 20 and regulations.

22   For examples see *Penayi v Roberts* [1993] 2 EGLR 51, CA and *Clickex Ltd v McCann* [1999] 2 EGLR 63, CA.

23   DETR 'Private Landlords in England' (http://www.housing.detr.gov.uk).

24   According to the DETR research cited in the previous note, 74% of private lettings are owned by landlords who let as a 'sideline' interest. Only 10% of such lettings appear to be by institutions. A similar conclusion was reached by DETR research 'Repairs and Improvements to Private Sector Dwellings in the 1990s' (http//www.housing.detr.gov.uk).

tenants not leaving the premises). In view of the shift of the balance of legislative advantage towards landlords since 1988, these findings are not surprising.[25]

There is also a social tenancies sector, once dominated by local authority landlords. It is now increasingly permeated by the voluntary sector, notably registered housing associations.[26] It was only thanks to the Housing Act 1980 that local authority and other public or quasi-public-sector tenants gained security of tenure for tenancies usually held on periodic tenancies. The security comes in two parts. The legislation (Housing Act 1985) confers protection from eviction from the tenant's home without an order of court, which cannot be made save on specific grounds. In addition, the tenant has the protection of the court's discretion. There is a right of succession on the death of a secure tenant to certain relatives and close family members. As seen, from the Housing Act 1988[27] housing association tenancies were taken out of the secure tenancy sector and put into the assured tenancy sector.

II THE REFORM AGENDA

The law is set for further change, which in its presently suggested form will incorporate some of the existing law, but under two umbrellas and with much simplification and, to some extent, building on the method used of the Housing Act 1988, which prescribes two basic statutory schemes. In 2001, the Law Commission published a Scoping Paper.[28] The Commission wished to alter the basis of the law to a consumer approach. A landlord is to be seen as a supplier of a service and the tenant as a consumer, as, one might add, is the case in some parts of the US.[29] The Commission were, and are, not disposed to adopt the explicit view that a tenant has a right to a place to live in.[30] The Law Commission thought at the preliminary stages of reform that they would like to

25 In order to counteract perceived abuses by some landlords in the management of their premises, the government is consulting on the question of imposing a licensing regime for landlords and/ or their managing agents, at least of leasehold flats and houses managed as part of an estate (DETR 'Improving the Standard of Residential Leasehold Management' (2002)).

26 If a housing association is not registered it will not qualify for Housing Corporation grants. According to the Law Com Consultation Paper No 162 (2002) 'Renting Homes I: Status and Security' para 2.106, public-sector loans are a significant element in the finance available to these hybrid bodies.

27 Housing Act 1988, Sch 18.

28 'Reform of Housing Law: A Scoping Paper'.

29 See eg *Javins v First National Realty Corpn* 428 F 2d 1071 at 1079 (1970) ('in the case of the modern apartment dweller, the value of the lease is that it gives him a place to live' so that he seeks a package of services: walls, ceilings and proper maintenance, inter alia).

30 As in France (Loi No 89-462 of 6 July 1989, Art 1). This, however, is in a jurisdiction where the right of ownership embedded in the French Code Civil, Art 544 is ordinarily considered to be primordial (Cons Const 16 January 1982 D. 1983.169). However, as with human rights cases in the UK (see eg *R v Bracknell Forest BC, ex p McLellan* (2001) 33 HLR 989), the French Constitutional Court recognises that the domestic legislature can validly impose fair limits on the extent of the ownership principle in the general social interest: Cons Const No 48-203 of 29 July 1998 D. 1999. 269.

see that any legislation complies with the Human Rights Convention. Their preliminary view in 2001 was that the essential structure of the new regime would, however, be based on the current law.

During April 2002, the Law Commission published their provisional proposals for the first part of their reform programme with regard to residential occupation agreements.[31] One aim is to promote simplification in the law. They make the point that to date we have simply seen layers of different specific legislation. They prefer to suggest a new set of schemes with the old or existing tenancies, in their words, 'mapped onto' the new regime.[32] The current Labour government sets its face against adjusting the current landlord slanted, assured tenancy regime. As a government reform body, the Law Commission provisional programme floated in 2002 does not, predictably, envisage a change in the broad thrust (as opposed to the details) of the current regime, either as it affects the private or, for that matter, the social, sector.[33]

The devil lies in the detail, however, and some valuable work is being done. The Law Commission adopt the provisional approach that residential home occupancy agreements should be written, and provided by the landlord, so as to make for certainty as to the terms of the agreement. This will also provide some measure of uniformity of rights and obligations as between the types of tenancy provisionally proposed.[34] Indeed, the Law Commission at present envisage that legislation would require the sub-division of any Type I or Type II agreement into three parts. Part A would consist of the core terms such as the parties, the premises, the rent and any term of the agreement. That could not be contracted out of. Part B would also have to be adopted by both parties. The terms would be the circumstances in which the landlord could seek possession by order of the court, and also any terms imposed by legislation (such as to keep in repair the structure and exterior of the premises). Only Part C would allow some flexibility to the parties. The Commission have suggested that delegated legislation would list the matters which Part C should contain, in default, such as break clauses. If express terms were not included in an occupation agreement, or were, if inserted, deemed to be unfair in the regulatory sense, the express terms would be disapplied and the default terms would become operational.[35]

---

31   Law Com Consultation Paper No 162 (2002) 'Renting Homes I Status and Security'.
32   Law Com Consultation Paper No 162 (2002) 'Renting Homes I Status and Security' para 3.6.
33   Law Com Consultation Paper No 162 (2002) 'Renting Homes I Status and Security' para 3.7.
34   This is the position, it would appear, with Scottish Secure Tenancies under the Housing (Scotland) Act 2001. The Law Commission expressly refer to this Act in the Law Com Consultation Paper No 162 (2002) 'Renting Homes I Status and Security' paras 4.4-4.44. They suggest (para 10.69) adopting into England and Wales the procedures of Scottish Secure Tenancies under the Housing (Scotland) Act 2001, s 12 with regard to landlords regaining possession of premises which it is believed the tenant has abandoned. As the Commission point out, the Housing Act 1985 contains no such provisions. Reliance has to be placed on the uncertainties of the doctrine of implied surrender.
35   See Law Com Consultation Paper No 162 (2002) 'Renting Homes I Status and Security' paras 6.89-6.121.

The provisional new tenancies are suggested to be landlord neutral: their new tenancy provisional proposals would be available to any landlord, private or social. A consumer approach is favoured, with emphasis on fairness between the parties (this approach is foreshadowed by the Unfair Terms in Consumer Contracts Regulations 1999).[36] Noting the impact of the European Convention on Human Rights thanks to the passing of HRA 1998, a key plank of the Law Commission's provisional proposals is to ensure that any new residential tenancy legislation is human rights compliant. These latter considerations may explain the fact that, for example, under the Type I agreement provisionally proposed by the Law Commission, the landlord would need an order for possession from the court to evict the occupier. Also, in this, the court would retain an overriding discretion to refuse to grant a possession order, with proper notification of the occupier in advance of the landlord's intention to seek possession.[37]

The provisional proposal of Law Commission as to the permitted new residential occupancy agreements in standard form, capable of some modification by the parties, is briefly as follows: there would be two types of agreement, under which rent was payable,[38] labelled Type I and Type II.[39] The limitation currently a feature of secure tenancies, that the home be the tenant's only or principal home, would be dropped. Any agreement conferring the right to occupy a home would fall within the scheme. Certain types of letting would fall outside the scheme, as they do the various present schemes, such as holiday lettings[40] (but not lettings to those residing in almshouses,[41]

36 Unfair Terms in Consumer Contracts Regulations 1999, SI 1999/2083, examined in ch 4 above, although as the Commission conceded, it is not fully clear whether these Brussels-originating regulations apply to landlords and tenants. If the 'landlord neutral' approach floated by the Commission in 2002 gains favour, and new style security and due process regimes apply to occupiers not tenants, this definitional problem would seem to be sidestepped.
37 Law Com Consultation Paper No 162 (2002) 'Renting Homes I Status and Security' paras 10.3-10.7 and 10.27-10.48 (thus it is suggested that landlords would have time-limits in which possession proceedings after a notice would have to be brought. Notices would have to comply with basic formalities such as giving reasons for seeking possession). Under paras 12.11-12.27 there are provisionally proposed new, 'structured' arrangements governing the exercise by the court of its discretion, based on the model of the Housing (Scotland) Act 2001, s 16(3). A 'structuring' approach could, however, risk putting the discretion of the court into a straightjacket which, as explained elsewhere in this book, is not a feature of the current law and is probably not even a requirement of compliance with the ECHR (see *London Borough of Lambeth v Howard* [2001] EWCA Civ 468, (2001) 33 HLR 636). The discretionary principle applying to discretionary grounds of secure tenancies for example necessarily involves the judge considering all relevant factors. Thus proportionality and legitimacy are seemingly ipso facto satisfied.
38 So that agreements at no rent would fall outside the provisional scheme (Law Com Consultation Paper No 162 (2002) 'Renting Homes I Status and Security' para 9.70).
39 Questions would arise as to whether any Rent Act tenancies still running at the time of any statutory reform to bring in Type I and II tenancies should be converted into Type I tenancies. The Commission suggested in 2002 that the advantages of the Type I scheme were sufficient to justify conversion, provided the fair rent system was retained (Law Com Consultation Paper No 162 (2002) 'Renting Homes I Status and Security' para 14.43).
40 Law Com Consultation Paper No 162 (2002) 'Renting Homes I Status and Security' para 9.95.
41 Law Com Consultation Paper No 162 (2002) 'Renting Homes I Status and Security' para 9.100. The Commission also wished to see all service occupancies protected by the Protection from Eviction Act 1977 (para 9.132).

which would alter the law). The new, provisional scheme would not apply if the lease were granted for a term certain exceeding 21 years in duration.[42] Both Type I, the more secure, and Type II, a reconstituted assured shorthold tenancy, would be available to public and private landlords alike (or be 'landlord neutral'). The Commission was aware that some social landlords are hybrid private-sector public-sector landlords: an example being non-registered housing associations. This would, for reasons advanced, represent a change in the law.

Type I agreements in the form currently under discussion, would, therefore, be the longer term and more secure tenancies. The Commission invited views as to whether the only type of tenancy available for this type of tenancy would be periodic tenancies.[43] That form of tenancy is, it is understood, the principal form of social landlord letting as things stand today. In the currently suggested model, replacing secure and assured tenancies, the Type I tenancy would have to set out all the grounds on which landlords could recover possession. These would be grouped into Occupier Default, Social Policy and Estate Management grounds. Under the first category would fall failure by the occupier to pay rent, or using the premises for immoral or illegal or immoral purposes (building on the present law). Anti-social behaviour and domestic violence would be included in the second set of grounds.[44] A feature of all Type I agreements, whoever the landlord might be, would, in the model floated in April 2002, be a right for landlords to seek possession on estate management grounds such as redevelopment or suitable alternative accommodation.[45] The latter are well known to Rent Act and assured tenancies, the former also is a feature of assured tenancies.

One of planks of the security to be conferred by the new legislation the Commission currently have in mind is that there would be no circumstances in which a court should mandatorily be required to make an order for possession of a Type I tenancy.[46] The Law Commission believe that owing to the effect of the ECHR, Art 8 (that evicting an

42   Law Com Consultation Paper No 162 (2002) 'Renting Homes I Status and Security' para 9.20. This adopts the approach of Housing Act 1985, s 115. However, the scope of the new scheme as suggested in 2002 would be determined outside the current lease and licence rules (para 9.42).

43   Law Com Consultation Paper No 162 (2002) 'Renting Homes I Status and Security' para 7.16.

44   Indeed, the Commission suggested that local authorities and registered social landlords alike ought to be placed under a specific duty to take action against anti-social behaviour (Law Com Consultation Paper No 162 (2002) 'Renting Homes I Status and Security' paras 13.30-13.31). Serious anti-social behaviour would be specifically defined and a new summary possession procedure was suggested to deal with it (paras 13.40-13.55).

45   Law Com Consultation Paper No 162 (2002) 'Renting Homes I Status and Security' paras 7.77-7.84. The differences between secure and assured tenancies would thus be smoothed out if this proposal is adopted in due course. The 'ghost' grounds for possession of Rent Act and assured tenancies, such as where a demolition or closing order have been made of the premises (Housing Act 1985, s 270), would be retained in the provisionally proposed new scheme. However, they would be enforceable by the relevant authorities, not the landlord (para 7.92).

46   Law Com Consultation Paper No 162 (2002) 'Renting Homes I Status and Security' para 7.26. Indeed the Commission suggest the conferral of an extended discretion on the court in discretionary repossession cases (para 12.10). This builds on the existing law (eg Rent Act

occupier from his home prima facie contravenes the requirement of respect for that person's home) the scope for making use of mandatory grounds for possession may have been reduced. A social landlord as a public body cannot act in a way which is incompatible with the occupier's human rights. The Commission thought that use of any mandatory ground could be challenged by tenants of bodies such as registered housing associations.[47] Thus all grounds for possession of Type I tenancies, the Commission thought, must be discretionary. The Commission considered at length the issue of whether there had to be a discretion even in the case where the tenant of the proposed Type I tenancy had accumulated serious rent arrears. They provisionally recommend that there should be a discretion in such cases also. One ground for their view is that the Commission claim they had been told by district judges that a common reason for rent default was problems with the administration of housing benefit.[48]

Type II agreements as suggested in 2002 by the Law Commission would be a much less secure form of agreement, and it would also be landlord neutral (in their words: available both to public and private landlords). Type II agreements would be presumed to apply to private landlords. Controversially, perhaps, the Law Commission suggested that social landlords could make use of Type II agreements.[49] The Type II agreement would be modelled around the existing assured shorthold tenancy. Type II agreements would not be for any long period. A new feature of this provisional proposal when compared to assured shorthold tenancies is that on expiry of a fixed-term Type II agreement, a periodic agreement would automatically arise, unless a new fixed-term agreement had been set up by the parties.[50] But each party could then terminate that periodic implied tenancy without having to give a reason. There would, in contrast to the position with Type I agreements, be circumstances in which the court could mandatorily order possession. Indeed landlords would be able to obtain possession without having to resort to a court hearing.[51] The agreement, which could be fixed term or periodic, as at present, would have to state that the landlord would be entitled to obtain possession from the court solely on the basis of a notice procedure, and it is possible that the six month 'moratorium' on repossession currently applying to assured

---

1977, s 100 and Housing Act 1985, s 85). There would also be a new requirement to consider whether evicting the tenant is proportional to the benefit obtained in not doing so. Reference would expressly be made to the effect of granting or refusing an order on the landlord and the general public.

47 Law Com Consultation Paper No 162 (2002) 'Renting Homes I Status and Security' paras 7.21-7.23.

48 Law Com Consultation Paper No 162 (2002) 'Renting Homes I Status and Security' para 7.40. Hence not to confer a discretion on the court in such a case would seem to the Commission to be harsh.

49 Law Com Consultation Paper No 162 (2002) 'Renting Homes I Status and Security' para 8.10. However, the Commission anticipate that local authorities would use Type II agreements, if they were indeed able to do so, in circumstances where at present they make use of introductory tenancies (see ch 16 below).

50 Law Com Consultation Paper No 162 (2002) 'Renting Homes I Status and Security' para 8.71.

51 Law Com Consultation Paper No 162 (2002) 'Renting Homes I Status and Security' paras 8.12-8.14.

shorthold tenancies would disappear, but at the time of writing the matter has been left open.[52] Once the occupier had accrued two months' rent arrears the landlord would be able to seek an order for possession and the court would, once the facts were proved, have no discretion to refuse to order possession.[53] The Law Commission justify this severe suggestion on the ground that:

> 'we want to encourage landlords to provide Type II agreements not simply on a periodic but also on a fixed term basis. Where an agreement has been provided on a fixed-term basis, then it becomes essential that – should the tenant start getting into rent arrears – the landlord can take steps to determine the agreement even before the fixed term has expired. We do not anticipate landlords being willing to let on fixed term Type II agreements without this'.[54]

They do not seem to note that some tenants may have temporary financial problems, especially where the tenant is benefit-dependent, which could be overcome by a discretion should matters go to court. However, forfeiture procedures should, say the Commission, be disapplied to fixed-term Type II tenancies, for the avoidance of doubt.[55]

A feature of both types of suggested scheme would be that landlords would have to obtain a court order for possession against any occupier not excluded from the

---

52 The arguments for and against the retention of the moratorium are canvassed in Law Com Consultation Paper No 162 (2002) 'Renting Homes I Status and Security' paras 8.24-8.26. Thus on the one hand it is a minimum and not long guaranteed period of occupation but equally it is apt to be inflexible. This could be overcome as far as tenants are concerned by a right to give one month's notice to terminate at any time, (as was the position with protected shorthold tenancies of up to two years in length under Housing Act 1980, s 53). Indeed the Commission float the idea of including two-way break clauses in fixed-term agreements (para 8.60-8.68).

53 Law Com Consultation Paper No 162 (2002) 'Renting Homes I Status and Security' para 8.41. This would, it was said, allow landlords who let on fixed term Type II tenancies to take action to stop the accumulation by tenants of heavy rent arrears, so encouraging lettings of this type (para 8.40). The law would be following the same principles as currently apply to Ground 8 applying to assured tenancies (see ch 15, below).

54 Law Com Consultation Paper No 162 (2002) 'Renting Homes I Status and Security' para 8.40. However, no other circumstances seemed to the Commission to justify entitling landlords to a mandatory possession order (para 8.42). If this proposal is adopted, then for example Housing Act 1988, Sch 2, ground 1, premises let which are the landlord's future or principal home, would vanish. However, the Commission claim that this ground is 'effectively redundant' (para 8.43). Their view of 2002 may owe something to nervousness about the HRA 1998 implications of mandatory grounds. As noted elsewhere in this book, the courts at present seem disposed to allow a wide margin of policy appreciation to the legislature and it is possible that the Law Commission are being over-cautious.

55 Law Com Consultation Paper No 162 (2002) 'Renting Homes I Status and Security' para 8.54. In any event it could well be that forfeiture clauses do not satisfy the test of fairness as laid down by Unfair Terms in Consumer Contracts Regulations 1999, SI 1999/2083 since they might having regard to the current and any future legislative structure be misleading. This is because the forfeiture clause suggests repossession without a court order, which, however, is not possible, for reasons explained elsewhere in this book.

schemes.[56] Occupiers under Type I and also those under periodic type II agreements would have a right, as at present, to give notice to quit of a minimum period of four weeks.[57] Open is the issue whether social landlords would be required to use only Type I agreements. If they were, then the Law Commission, borrowing from the introductory tenancy regime, provisionally recommend a probationary tenancy agreement for occupiers.[58]

If anything like the provisional reform proposals here outlined is adopted after the period of consultation and following the Final Report and Draft Bill expected during 2003, there would be knock-on effects on other parts of the law of landlord and tenant. Long leases (ie terms exceeding 21 years) would fall outside the provisionally suggested new scheme.[59] The Law Commission, more radically, suggest that the line between Type I and II schemes and excluded forms of occupation agreement should not be drawn by reference to the lease/licence distinction. Instead, the test for application of Type I or II occupation agreements would be whether there was a contract at a rent for the occupation by an occupier of premises as a home.[60] The Commission justify this shift in the law by the point that with the arrival of assured shorthold tenancies, landlords no longer have much incentive to contract out of the legislative scheme.[61]

---

56   Law Com Consultation Paper No 162 (2002) 'Renting Homes I Status and Security' para 10.7. The landlord would have, as is required with assured tenancies, to precede a demand for possession with a preliminary warning notice to the tenant (paras 10.10-10.11). Three months were suggested as a time period which would have to elapse from the service of this notice until proceedings were issued (para 10.29).

57   Law Com Consultation Paper No 162 (2002) 'Renting Homes I Status and Security' para 10.51. Immediate termination would take place if the landlord repudiated the contract by breach (para 10.61). An express surrender of a Type I or Type II agreement ought, the Commission suggested, to be in writing and not by deed. They also suggested (para 10.65-10.69) a procedure for dealing with abandoned premises modelled on Housing (Scotland) Act 2001, ss 17-19.

58   Law Com Consultation Paper No 162 (2002) 'Renting Homes I Status and Security' paras 11.26ff. But while at present challenges to the decisions of landlords go to the Administrative Court, the Commission suggests that these, under its new scheme, should go to the county court.

59   Law Com Consultation Paper No 162 (2002) 'Renting Homes I Status and Security' para 9.20. As noted at para 9.19, this is in effect the current position. Reference maybe made to eg Housing Act 1985, s 115.

60   Law Com Consultation Paper No 162 (2002) 'Renting Homes I Status and Security' paras 6.8 and 9.21. The Commission seem to agree with the view of eg Lord Millett in *Uratemp Ventures v Collins* [2001] UKHL 43, [2002] 1 AC 301 that 'home' is a more appropriate term these days than 'dwelling house' (which expression goes back to the Rent Acts). They are opposed at present to imposing a requirement of occupation as one's only or principal home, perhaps owing to current trends of social mobility (paras 9.79ff). They would drop the requirement of eg Housing Act 1988, s 3(1) and also, not mentioned by them, Rent Act 1977, s 1 that the 'home' is let as a separate dwelling (paras 9.84-9.89). This if adopted would follow the approach of the House of Lords in the *Uratemp* case.

61   Law Com Consultation Paper No 162 (2002) 'Renting Homes I Status and Security' para 9.27. They also think that the lease/licence distinction is not understood by the public at large (para 9.39). To them, licences and tenancies are contracts and their provisional scheme is contract

We would add the obvious point that that scheme is after all landlord slanted: it allows charging a market rent, even where the premises are in disrepair, and ease of landlord repossession. But some exclusions from the provisional new statutory scheme would be retained from the present law as a matter of policy, eg rent-free occupation,[62] as well as holiday lets.[63]

The initial overall impression of the provisional package of reforms is that they would not seem to represent a very radical break with the regimes actively operating today. No cast-iron security of tenure has been conferred on residential tenants for at least 30 years either, it seems, in practice or under newer legislative regimes. The new suggestions reflect this reality and are welcome to that extent. It is hard to dispute the need to try to simplify the law. Whether this is best done by prescribing permitted terms is a matter around which there may be some debate, but the process of laying down compulsory legislative frameworks in this field was started as long ago as 1980 with protected shorthold tenancies.[64] It may be that in the residential field, this type of legislative prescription is the best way of trying to avoid the consequences of the landlord/tenant bargaining imbalance. Bringing in consumerism in a formal sense to control unfair contract terms in tenancies as provisionally proposed seems to reflect the reality that we live in a consumer era. But the approach has its limits: it does not appear to preclude rent review in principle, even if it is upwards-only. If the use of plain language in tenancy agreements reduces, rather then increases disputes, this can only be welcomed. Disappointing was the exclusion from the provisional scheme of any further consideration of reform of the current inadequate statutory repairs regime affecting residential tenancies.

---

based (so that to continue basing the application of statutory schemes on lease/licence issues would be presumably artificial).

62 Law Com Consultation Paper No 162 (2002) 'Renting Homes I Status and Security' para 9.70. This would reflect the current law that family arrangements cannot amount to tenancies.

63 Law Com Consultation Paper No 162 (2002) 'Renting Homes I Status and Security' paras 9.94-9.95: after all these are commercial short-life activities. However, it is doubtful whether an express exclusion is required: cf *Walker v Ogilvy* (1974) 28 P & CR 288, although the provisionally proposed removal of any residence requirement might require an express exclusion *ex abundanti cautela*. By contrast, agreements for the occupation of almshouse residents would fall, it was suggested, within the new scheme (paras 9.9ff) even though they, as licensees, cannot hold assured or assured shorthold tenancies under the Housing Act 1988. Resident landlords would continue to be able to let free from the security rules proposed (paras 9.109-9.110). All service occupiers (currently licensees) would be brought within the Protection from Eviction Act 1977, and not be excluded as at present (paras 9.129ff).

64 Housing Act 1980, ss 51-55; PF Smith [1982] Conv 29.

CHAPTER 14

Rent Act tenancies

I POLICY OF RENT ACT PROTECTION

Introduction

Private sector residential tenancies of houses and flats were first subjected to statutory controls in the emergency legislation of 1915. The legislation, known as the Rent Acts, which still confers a form of rent regulation and security of tenure on certain residential tenants,[1] is considered to originate with the Increase of Rent and Mortgage Interest (Restrictions) Act 1920. That Act imposed rent controls and created statutory tenancies, arising once the original contractual tenancy expired, so enabling the 'statutory' tenant to hold over despite such expiry, but solely by virtue of statute. Since then, no less than 26 Acts in this field have been passed. The Rent Act 1977 (hereinafter RA 1977) is a consolidation of this 'remarkable sequence of enactments'.[2] Subject to transitional provisions, it is no longer possible to create new tenancies within RA 1977. New private sector residential tenancies granted as from 15 January 1989 fall under the assured tenancies scheme.[3] Statutory tenancies arising out of tenancies which were, when granted, fully protected by the Rent Acts, survive. They continue to generate

---

1   Protection along the same lines as that conferred on residential private tenants was conferred on agricultural workers by Rent (Agriculture) Act 1976, as a result of which there may be statutory tenancies as well as successions to statutory tenancies. To qualify under the 1976 Act, the claimant has to be, in principle, a qualifying worker currently or formerly employed in agriculture or forestry. The qualifying conditions and security of tenure apparatus under the 1976 regime is, in the main, the same as under RA 1977. The 1976 Act regime was replaced at the same time as that of the Rent Acts with the advent of assured agricultural occupancies under the Housing Act 1988, Pt I, Chapter III.
2   *Cadogan Estates Ltd v McMahon* [2000] 4 All ER 897 at 901 (Lord Hoffmann).
3   As are tenancies granted by housing associations, owing to the abrogation of 'housing association tenancies' by the Housing Act 1988, s 35. There are apparently some 70,000 new such lettings each year (Hughes and Lowe *Public Sector Housing Law* p 173).

issues, especially with regard to rent regulation, re-possession and succession rights.[4] For this reason, an examination of the not yet defunct Rent Act regime is retained in this book.[5] This system is, however, withering away as the new century advances. It has been claimed that there might be some 150,000 Rent Act protected or statutory tenancies in existence. Their number is seemingly falling at an annual rate of between 25,000 and 30,000 a year.[6]

The original object of the Rent Acts was to prevent the tenant from having the rent raised against him, as well as to preclude his eviction after the contractual expiry date of his tenancy.[7] The feature of retaining security of tenure despite the termination of the original tenancy remains to this day. The House of Lords has now punctured the security umbrella somewhat, by holding that a statutory tenant who was made bankrupt on account of non-payment of a judgment debt lost his tenancy, even though his daughter had paid the rent due to the landlords.[8] As to the former policy of rent control, it was abandoned in fits as from 1957 onwards.[9] All surviving Rent Act tenancies are 'regulated tenancies' within the so-called 'fair rent' system. That regime allows landlords to procure regular revisions of the rent. With the advent from 1989 of deregulated assured tenancy rents, some regulated rents payable by Rent Act statutory tenants have shown a tendency to rise steeply, since regulated rents must be compared with rents for similar premises let under the assured tenancies scheme. This has led to government intervention with a view to limit these: a partial return, during the twilight years of the Rent Act system, to a form of rent control.

RA 1977 offers differing levels of protection, depending on the nature of the tenancy. Full protection is conferred on protected and statutory tenants, although the exact degree of protection depends on the nature of the tenancy itself.[10] The main surviving Rent Act tenancy is, for reasons given, that creature of statute, the statutory tenancy.

4   In *White v Wareing* [1992] 1 EGLR 271 it was said that most county court cases were concerned with statutory as opposed to protected tenancies.

5   The warning of Brooke LJ in *North British Housing Association v Sheridan* [1999] 2 EGLR 138 at 143 against excessive citations comes to mind here.

6   Partington (2001) 5 L & T Rev 95. There was a lower estimate in *Cadogan Estates Ltd v McMahon* [2000] 4 All ER 897 at 911: Lord Millet thought that there were 'more than 100,000' statutory tenancies still in existence at that time.

7   *Remon v City of London Real Property Co Ltd* [1921] 1 KB 49 at 57.

8   *Cadogan Estates Ltd v McMahon* [2000] 4 All ER 897. A wide view was placed on the expression 'obligation' of the statutory tenancy in RA 1977, Sch 15, Pt I, case 1. In a convincing dissent, Lord Millett noted that a statutory tenant has no interest in the premises. Extending the 'obligations' of the tenancy within Sch 15, Pt I, case 1 to breach of a bankruptcy condition was in his view incorrect. The succession provisions of RA 1977 suggested that higher priority was given to the security of the family than to a landlord's rent security.

9   The decontrol process commenced with the Rent Act 1957, but was finally only completed on 28 November 1980 (Housing Act 1980, s 64).

10 In particular, there is a class of tenancy known as restricted contracts, which cannot be created as from 15 January 1989. The following pre-15 January 1989 tenancies are restricted contracts – tenancies granted by a resident landlord within RA 1977, s 12; a tenancy governed by the board or substantial attendance provisions of RA 1977, s 7; in addition to this, a licence where furniture or services are provided.

Criticisms of the Rent Acts

The Rent Acts have been criticised for inadequate definition, hidden meanings, missing principles, incautious superimposition and plain mistakes.[11] The courts have therefore been left to make what they can of the Acts, which is accepted were passed in haste and which have caused problems of interpretation to the courts. It was not long before it was held that courts should interpret the Rent Acts in a reasonable and common sense way.[12] The Rent Acts cannot therefore be interpreted in the same way as ordinary legislation. Since the Acts are enacted without much regard to common law principles, and cut across them as a result, the courts tend to limit the effects of the Acts where possible to the smallest necessary extent.[13] If there is a real difficulty which the court cannot resolve without going back through the antecedents of the legislation, it will have to perform this task, even though RA 1977 is taken at least in part, to be a consolidating Act.[14] At the same time, RA 1977 must be interpreted in accordance with broad policy considerations.[15] These tensions show the difficulty presented by this legislation.

The courts have also been warned not to undertake routine investigations of the legislative antecedents of a provision in the Rent Acts, especially if the issue turns on a single word or provision.[16] Difficulties may be impossible to resolve, by means of ordinary interpretation, so as to put the court in the draftsman's chair and interpret the provision in the social or factual context when it was enacted.[17] If this happens, and the court cannot gain anything from recourse to the antecedents of the provision, it may refer to Parliamentary debates, provided that is that a clear statement may be found by the sponsor of the legislation.[18] As to the compatibility of the Rent Acts with human rights principles, reference should be made to ch 1, above.

11 Megarry *The Rent Acts* p 15. Also p 14. The editors condemn the use by the draftsman of 'language which resembles the art of popular journalism rather than the terms of art of conveyancing'. These observations were quoted by Lord Hoffmann in *Cadogan Estates Ltd v McMahon* supra to justify adopting a broad, non-technical approach to the Rent Acts.
12 *Remon v City of London Real Property Co Ltd* [1921] 1 KB 49, CA.
13 *Landau v Sloane* [1981] 1 All ER 705, HL; *Wilkes v Goodwin* [1923] 2 KB 86, CA.
14 *Farrell v Alexander* [1977] AC 59, HL.
15 *Cadogan Estates Ltd v McMahon* [2000] 4 All ER 897 at 902; also *Read v Goater* [1921] 1 KB 611 at 615 (a 'broad, common sense manner so as to give effect to the intention of the Legislature').
16 *R v Secretary of State for the Environment, Transport and the Regions, ex p Spath Holme Ltd* [2001] 1 All ER 195 at 204-5 (Lord Bingham).
17 *R v Secretary of State for the Environment, Transport and the Regions, ex p Spath Holme Ltd* [2001] 1 All ER 195 at 204-5 (Lord Bingham).
18 *Pepper v Hart* [1993] AC 593, HL – this is a point applicable to any statute, though the occasions when the power might be used remain to be seen. The county court resorted to this power in *Goringe v Twinsectra* [1994] CLY 2723.

Replacement of Rent Acts

The legislature made a fundamental shift in its policy in relation to tenancies granted in the private residential sector by private landlords and other bodies such as housing associations, when it created, as from 15 January 1989, assured and assured shorthold tenancies. These are the only two forms of residential tenancy which may ordinarily be granted as from then on.

There are some limited transitional rules, whose main effect is as follows. Where any of the following narrow exceptions applies to a private sector residential tenant, RA 1977 will apply and not the Housing Act 1988, Pt I, even though the date of the new tenancy is on or after 15 January 1989.

1 The tenant was a protected or statutory tenant whose tenancy was originally granted before 15 January 1989. The tenant has died, before that date, leaving a surviving spouse or family member, either of whom is entitled to claim a statutory tenancy by succession.

2 The protected or statutory tenant died on or after 15 January 1989, leaving a surviving spouse, who, in contrast to a family member, has the privilege of being able to claim a statutory tenancy by succession.

3 Where transitional provisions apply to the tenancy. In particular, where it was granted to a person (alone or jointly with others) who, immediately before the tenancy was granted, was the protected or statutory tenant. The tenancy must have been granted by the person who was either the landlord, or one of the joint landlords, under the previous protected or statutory tenancy.[19] This rule is aimed at preventing a tenant who has voluntarily surrendered a previous protected or statutory tenancy in exchange for a new tenancy from losing the protection of RA 1977 in relation to the new tenancy.[20] It was not clear from the literal wording of the legislation whether the premises under the new tenancy had to be the same as those previously held. It was held in the county court that the premises under the new tenancy do not have to be the same or substantially the same as those held under the previous protected or statutory tenancy.[21] This principle has been twice adopted by the Court of Appeal.[22] This would seem correct. It would

---

19 Housing Act 1988, s 34(1)(b), subject to s 34(2). A related rule: where the court has ordered possession on the ground of suitable alternative accommodation being available for a former protected or statutory tenant, and considers that the grant of an assured tenancy would not afford the tenant the required security of tenure, it may direct that the tenancy is to be a protected tenancy (Housing Act 1988, s 34(1)(c)).

20 *Laimond Properties Ltd v Al-Shakarchi* (1998) 30 HLR 1099, CA.

21 *Goringe v Twinsectra* [1994] CLY 2723, where the county court had regard to the intentions of the promoters of the transitional provisions of the Housing Act 1988. See Walden-Smith (1994) 29 Estates Gazette 114.

22 *Laimond Properties Ltd v Al-Shakarchi* (1998) 30 HLR 1099, CA, where, however, the Housing Act 1988, s 34(1)(c) was applied, on the ground that an assured tenancy of a similar flat would confer equivalent security. Also *Arogol Co Ltd v Rajah* [2001] EWCA Civ 454, [2001] 29 EG 119 (CS), so that a protected tenant of a back room who moved into the whole floor retained Rent Act protection in respect of the whole floor.

otherwise be all too easy to evade this particular rule, which is to protect pre-1989 tenants against abuse, by the simple expedient of persuading a statutory tenant to accept a new tenancy of the existing premises minus a room not used by him.

4 There is no time-limit for the period that must elapse before a new tenancy lying outside the protection of RA 1977 is granted to the tenant. Where a protected tenant faced with a possession order agreed to accept a new protected shorthold tenancy (which has no security after expiry) and to leave the flat concerned for 24 hours, he could not later claim that his new tenancy was protected by the Rent Act.[23] The same result might have been reached if the tenant had voluntarily surrendered an earlier protected or statutory tenancy and in such a case it is seemingly unnecessary for the tenant to remove himself physically from the premises.[24]

II PROTECTED TENANCY DEFINED

General principles

RA 1977, s 1 provides that: 'a tenancy under which a dwelling house (which may be a house or a part of a house) is let as a separate dwelling is a protected tenancy.' A protected tenancy remains protected only during the contractual period of the tenancy, whether this is for a term certain or periodic. The impact today of this provision is reduced by the fact that it is not generally possible to create a protected tenancy of residential premises on or after 15 January 1989. Also, for some years before that date, it must surely have been unusual for a landlord knowingly to grant a protected tenancy unless he was able to rely on a mandatory ground for re-possession of the tenant after expiry of the contractual term (as where the landlord was an owner-occupier). There are still a substantial number of statutory tenancies, as noted. A statutory tenancy arises only if a protected tenancy was created originally, and after that tenancy has expired or was terminated. Statutory tenancies are, as their name implies, the sometimes disliked creature[25] solely of statute. They confer on the 'tenant' a purely personal right of occupation, despite the fact that his previous protected tenancy has expired,[26] rather than an estate in land.[27]

---

23 *Bolnore Properties Ltd v Cobb* [1996] EGCS 42, CA.
24 Cf *Dibbs v Campbell* [1988] 2 EGLR 122, CA.
25 In *Marcroft Wagons Ltd v Smith* [1951] 2 KB 496 at 501 Evershed MR referred to statutory tenancies as a '*monstrum horrendum informe ingens*' or a 'statutory right of irremoveability'.
26 *Remon v City of London Real Property Co* [1921] 1 KB 49, CA.
27 *Jessamine Investment Co v Schwartz* [1978] QB 264, [1976] 3 All ER 521, CA; also *Johnson v Felton* [1994] EGCS 135, CA. However, a statutory tenant is apparently entitled to maintain an action of trespass: *Marcroft Wagons Ltd v Smith* [1951] 2 KB 496.

The qualifying conditions

RA 1977, s 1 has traditionally been broken down as follows into its various component parts in order to make sense of it. If any of the following elements are not present, there can be no protected and so no statutory tenancy.

(i)   Tenancy

There must be a contractual tenancy for there to be full protection. 'Tenancy' expressly includes a sub-tenancy (RA 1977, s 152(1)). If it is assigned, a protected contractual tenancy remains protected. If it is terminated by forfeiture or notice to quit, it loses protected status and becomes a statutory tenancy (RA 1977, s 2(1)(a)).

RA 1977, s 1 applies to any kind of tenancy. The class of tenancy does not matter and s 1 may apply both to fixed term and to periodic tenancies of any length; and equally, it may subject legal and equitable tenancies alike to RA 1977.

RA 1977 deals with premises of which the person is genuinely a tenant of a landlord, as opposed to cases where the tenancy is a device to enable some other sort of relationship to come into existence, and so a prospective purchaser going into possession pending completion is not a protected tenant: it makes no difference that sums labelled as rent are payable.[28]

A genuine licence to occupy is outside RA 1977. Problems still arise with this principle. In a recent case,[29] a person who had managed an hotel occupied certain rooms there (in which he lived) rent-free: indeed at a later stage his contract of employment required such occupation. Not surprisingly, he was held to hold a licence because he was a service occupier, and could not claim Rent Act protection.[30] The courts are, however, assiduous in detecting and frustrating artificial devices and sham transactions whose only object is to disguise the grant of a tenancy and to evade RA 1977 (see further ch 3 above). By contrast, provided the agreement is genuine and not shown by the occupier to be a sham, a tenancy may legitimately be granted to a company, even one specially bought 'off the shelf', which licenses or authorises an individual to occupy a house or flat. On the termination of the contractual or protected tenancy, the company tenant, provided that it genuinely performs the obligations of the tenancy, enjoys no further security as statutory tenant since it cannot comply with the residence requirement of RA 1977, s 2.[31] The occupier, as its licensee, is in no better a position:

28   *Hopwood v Hough* (1944) 11 LJCCR 80; cf *Bretherton v Paton* [1986] 1 EGLR 172, CA.
29   *Carroll v Manek and Bank of India* (1999) 79 P & CR 173. In any event even if there had been a tenancy, it was held that RA 1977, s 11 would have ruled out protection.
30   Had it not been for the fact that the occupier was a service occupier, he might but for RA 1977, s 11 have held a tenancy within the Rent Acts, provided that the rooms he occupied were his home: *Uratemp Ventures Ltd v Collins* [2001] UKHL 43, [2002] 1 AC 301 (a case on assured tenancies).
31   *Hiller v United Dairies (London) Ltd* [1934] 1 KB 57, CA; also *Carter v SU Carburetter Co* [1942] 2 All ER 228, CA.

the fact that the letting is to a company so as to avoid RA 1977 does not of itself entitle the court to hold that the whole arrangement is a sham device.[32]

(ii) Dwelling house let as a separate dwelling

'Dwelling house' in RA 1977, s 1 includes entire houses and self-contained flats;[33] and any permanent buildings designed or adapted for living in are capable of being a dwelling house for present purposes. A house cannot be a 'dwelling house' if it is constructed to consist of a number of units of habitation, all of which are to be sub-let.[34] The question of whether given premises are a 'dwelling house' is one of fact, and where premises had been converted from a warehouse into a garage with living rooms above, the living rooms fell within the Act.[35] A tenant of a houseboat would not be within the Rent Acts as the houseboat is not a permanent structure.[36]

The premises need not comprise a single unit: two or more physically separate units, demised together, may constitute a separate dwelling.[37] Likewise, where a house, cottage and land attached thereto were demised in one lease, the combined unit was a separate dwelling within RA 1977, s 1.[38]

If the tenant is granted a lease which envisages that the premises are going to be used both for business and for residential purposes, then the statutory requirement of a letting as a separate dwelling is not satisfied and the tenancy cannot be a protected or statutory tenancy.[39] The expression 'let as a separate dwelling' has contracted in scope since it was first used. At that time, a mixed user letting was capable of being a controlled tenancy. With the abolition of controlled tenancies and the conversion of any remaining such tenancies into regulated tenancies,[40] the sole legislation which is capable of applying to a pre-1989 mixed user tenancy is the Landlord and Tenant Act 1954, Pt II.

If the tenant holds different parts of the same house under different lettings from the same landlord, and carries on some of his living activities in one part of the house and

---

32 *Hilton v Plustitle Ltd* [1988] 3 All ER 1051, CA; Rogers [1989] Conv 197; *Estavest Investments Ltd v Commercial Express Travel Ltd* [1988] 2 EGLR 91, CA; *Kaye v Massbetter Ltd* [1991] 2 EGLR 97, CA. Nor was a tenancy granted to a company so as to procure tax deductions for that reason a sham: *Eaton Square Properties Ltd v O'Higgins* [2001] L & TR 165, CA.

33 The dwelling house must not be outside certain rental value limits as specified by RA 1977, s 4. The limit in the case of a tenancy entered into after 1 April 1990 is £25,000 a year. In the case of a tenancy entered into before then, there is a set of rateable value limits applying.

34 *Horford Investments Ltd v Lambert* [1976] Ch 39, [1974] 1 All ER 131, CA.

35 *Gidden v Mills* [1925] 2 KB 713.

36 *Chelsea Yacht & Boat Co Ltd v Pope* [2000] 2 EGLR 23 (assured tenancies).

37 *Langford Property Co Ltd v Goldrich* [1949] 1 KB 511, [1949] 1 All ER 402 (two separate flats let together); also *Grosvenor (Mayfair) Estates v Amberton* (1982) 265 Estates Gazette 693.

38 *Whitty v Scott-Russell* [1950] 2 KB 32, [1950] 1 All ER 884, CA.

39 *Henry Smith's Charity Trustees v Wagle* [1989] 1 EGLR 124, CA.

40 By Housing Act 1980, s 64.

the remainder of them in the other part of the house, neither tenancy will be protected. If there is a single composite letting of the two parts as a whole, then the tenancy may well be protected, but the difference between the two results is one of fact and degree.⁴¹ Moreover, if all parts of a house, consisting of single rooms and a flat, were let by the tenant to other persons, the tenant has no protected tenancy since 'let as a separate dwelling' is confined to the singular.⁴² On the other hand, a sub-letting of part of the premises by the tenant of the whole did not deny the tenant protection of the whole, since he was entitled to possession of the sub-let part.⁴³

If part of a house is let, the part need not necessarily be self-contained for there to be a 'dwelling house' and so a protected or statutory tenancy. The premises must be the home of the tenant, or the 'place where he moves and has his being'.⁴⁴ The tenant must have the exclusive right to use living rooms, which may include the kitchen. 'Sharing' of other accommodation with the landlord, but which is visited only for specific purposes, such as a bathroom or toilet, does not deprive the tenant of protection.⁴⁵ But where a tenant had exclusive possession of two rooms only in a house and shared the kitchen and other living accommodation with the landlord, he fell outside the protection of the Rent Acts.⁴⁶ Indeed it may be doubted whether this tenant held a tenancy.

At all events, in the context of assured tenancies, but in reasoning applying to the Rent Acts, the House of Lords has ruled that there is no reason why a tenant exclusively occupying an hotel room should not fall within the 1988 Act scheme.⁴⁷ The tenant regarded his room, in which he was able to live and sleep, as his home. The House of Lords condemned the 'heresy'⁴⁸ of some earlier dicta,⁴⁹ that it was a pre-requisite of statutory protection for a tenant to be able to cook meals in the premises. Indeed, it was not even essential for the premises to possess all the features sometimes found in dwelling houses for the tenant to have a 'dwelling house' in the statutory sense. As was pointed out, the 1977 and 1988 statutory schemes dealt often with property at the lower end of the housing market. Their Lordships also pointed out that there had been major social changes in relation to life habits in the last 40 years. There were more

41   *Hampstead Way Investments Ltd v Lewis-Weare* [1985] 1 All ER 564 at 568, HL; also *Kavanagh v Lyroudias* [1985] 1 All ER 560, CA.
42   *Horford Investments Ltd v Lambert* [1976] Ch 39, [1974] 1 All ER 131, CA.
43   *Regalian Securities Ltd v Ramsden* [1981] 2 All ER 65, [1981] 1 WLR 611, HL.
44   *Curl v Angelo* [1948] 2 All ER 189 at 190H (Lord Greene MR).
45   *Cole v Harris* [1945] KB 474, CA.
46   *Neale v Del Soto* [1945] KB 144, [1945] 1 All ER 191, CA.
47   *Uratemp Ventures Ltd v Collins* [2001] UKHL 43, [2002] 1 All ER 46; PF Smith [2002] Conv 285.
48   The word 'heresy' is, however, a curious use of language. The Greek word αἱρέσις means 'choosing', 'choice' (Sauter's *Pocket Lexicon to the Greek New Testament*, p 8).
49   Notably in *Wright v Howell* (1947) 92 Sol Jo 26 ('dwelling included all the major activities of life, particularly sleeping, cooking and feeding'). 'Sleeping' is however doubtfully described as an activity: *Curl v Angelo* [1948] 2 All ER 189.

single households, and a mushroom growth in fast-food outlets, so that people did not necessarily need to cook meals in their homes.

In many cases where part of a house has been let, prior to the assured tenancy regime, the landlord will be able to show that he satisfies the residence tests posed by the 'resident landlord' exemption from full protection.[50] In such a case, the tenant would hold only a restricted contract.[51] Where this is not the position, as where the landlord and the tenant do not have separate dwellings in the same building, the court will have to ascertain whether the occupier has exclusive possession of the premises with no sharing of living accommodation with the landlord. If at the date of proceedings for possession, the house is the tenant's home, it will fall within the basic scheme of RA 1977, s 1. If the tenant is entitled to shared use of living rooms with the landlord, then the intrusion into the landlord's privacy is such that the tenancy cannot be protected (or statutory).[52] But if the tenant has limited access only to a living room, such as a right to draw water in the landlord's kitchen,[53] the tenant is not denied security of tenure merely for that reason.[54]

Tenancies excluded from protection

There are a number of exclusions from RA 1977 protection umbrella. Two of these, concerned with holiday lettings and resident landlords, are also a feature of the exclusions from assured tenancy status. These exemptions are therefore examined in a little more detail. Other exclusions from full protection are noted here for the sake of completeness.

(i) Holiday lettings

By RA 1977, s 9, which has an equivalent exemption in the case of assured tenancies,[55] a tenancy is not a protected tenancy if the purpose of the tenancy is to confer on the tenant the right to occupy the dwelling house for a holiday.[56] It is questionable whether a holiday exemption was needed, having regard to the fundamental significance of the requirement of a 'dwelling house' by RA 1977, s 1.[57] Out of season lettings are protected,

---

50   RA 1977, s 12 and Sch 2.
51   Restricted contracts were phased out by the Housing Act 1988, s 36, as from 15 January 1989.
52   The resident landlord exception would not apply in such a case: *Lyons v Caffery* [1983] 1 EGLR 102.
53   As in *Hayward v Marshall* [1952] 2 QB 89.
54   *Uratemp Ventures Ltd v Collins* [2001] UKHL 43, [2002] 1 All ER 46.
55   Housing Act 1988, Sch 1, para 9.
56   See Lyons [1984] Conv 286.
57   *Caradon District Council v Paton* [2000] 3 EGLR 57 at 59 ('the concept of using a property as a ... dwelling house involves the use of it, in some way, as a home'). Also *Walker v Ogilvy* (1974) 28 P & CR 288 at 293 (a holiday tenant could not comply with the requirement of residence attached to a statutory tenancy).

but possession is recoverable after termination of these under a mandatory ground.[58] The policy of RA 1977, s 9 is to deny Rent Act protection to lettings of holiday homes or flats.

There is no statutory definition of 'holiday'. In one case,[59] a dictionary definition was accepted. 'Holiday' was taken to mean a period of cessation of work or period of recreation. The question is how far the courts are prepared to accept at face value, both under RA 1977, s 9 and in relation to the assured tenancies scheme, a statement of purpose such as that 'it is mutually agreed that the letting hereby made is solely for the purpose of the tenant's holiday in the London area'. Such a statement is evidence of the purpose of the tenancy, and takes effect unless the tenant proves that the statement is a sham.[60] Thus, where a landlord was proved by the tenants to have known that, despite a statement that there was a holiday letting, the tenants in fact intended to occupy the premises as students, and so for work, the letting fell outside RA 1977, s 9.[61] By contrast, where the tenant held under a three-month tenancy which stated that it was for the purpose of the tenant's holiday in the London area, the statement had not been proved to be untrue by the tenant, so that it was taken to be genuine, and the agreement therefore stood at face value.[62]

(ii) Resident landlords

A tenancy granted by a resident landlord which falls within RA 1977, s 12 is not a protected tenancy and cannot give rise to a statutory tenancy, but will be a restricted contract, if any of these latter survive.[63] The policy of this exclusion is to enable an owner of a house or flat to let rooms in a separate part of the premises without conferring any security on the tenant.[64] The landlord has an assurance of being able to recover vacant possession at the end of the contractual tenancy, as with a view to selling his home with vacant possession.[65] Only individual landlords and not companies benefit

---

58   RA 1977, Sch 15, Pt II, Case 13.
59   *Buchmann v May* [1978] 2 All ER 993 at 995, CA; also *Francke v Hackmi* [1984] CLY 1096 (no necessary implication that there is a period of recreation).
60   *Buchmann v May* [1978] 2 All ER 993, CA.
61   *R v Rent Officer for London Borough of Camden, ex p Plant* [1981] 1 EGLR 73.
62   *Buchmann v May* [1978] 2 All ER 993. Thus, that the flat is in a place not usually considered to be a holiday resort will not disentitle the landlord to rely on a statement that the letting is for the tenant's holiday unless the statement is proved to be false: see *McHale v Daneham* (1979) 249 Estates Gazette 969; also *Ryeville Properties v Saint-John* [1980] CLY 1598.
63   There is a similar exclusion from assured tenancy status where the landlord is resident (Housing Act 1988, Sch 1, para 10) and the discussion in the next pages would seem relevant thereto. In this case, the tenancy may also be an excluded tenancy (ie excluded from Protection from Eviction Act 1977, s 3 by Housing Act 1977, s 31) in which case the tenant has no security of tenure at all.
64   *Cooper v Tait* (1984) 48 P & CR 460, CA.
65   *Barnett v O'Sullivan* [1995] 1 EGLR 93, CA.

from RA 1977, s 12. If the landlord shares living accommodation with the tenant,[66] RA 1977, s 12 does not apply, and the question, as adumbrated earlier, is then whether the tenant's exclusive accommodation is his home.[67] If it is, then he may fall within the Rent Acts if his tenancy was granted prior to 15 January 1989.

THE RULE

The exemption operates within a narrow time frame. A tenancy of a dwelling house granted[68] on or after 14 August 1974 but only until 15 January 1989 (the advent of assured tenancies) is not a protected tenancy if three conditions apply:

1 The dwelling house forms part only of a building and, except where the dwelling house also forms part of a flat, the building is not a purpose-built block of flats.
2 The tenancy was granted by a person who, at the time when he granted it, occupied as his residence another dwelling house:
   (a) where part of a flat is let, the part occupied by the landlord forms part of the flat; or
   (b) in any other case, it also forms part of the building.
3 At all times since the tenancy was granted the interest of the landlord under the tenancy has belonged to a person who, at the time he owned that interest, occupied as his residence another dwelling house which:
   (a) is either part of the same flat in which the tenant resides; or
   (b) is part of the same building in which the tenant resides.

The last two conditions are not construed too narrowly, having regard to the policy of RA 1977, s 12. Where a tenant holding a tenancy within RA 1977, s 12 moved into new accommodation nearby, into which the landlord and his family followed him, a matter of weeks after, the new tenancy was as much subject to s 12 as was the previous one, as there had been, in substance, a concerted move by all parties, despite the time-interval between the actual moves.[69]

'BUILDING"

The word 'building' is not defined[70] but the question of what is the same building is one of fact. There must be one building at the time of the grant and termination of the tenancy, so that any conversion works to a building during the tenancy must not achieve a separation of the building into two entities.[71] If the landlord lives in an

---

66 A concept which, in the context of shared use of a bedroom, was construed by the House of Lords in *Goodrich v Paisner* [1957] AC 65, to involve alternating use by each party, reasonable conduct by both being assumed.
67 *Uratemp Ventures Ltd v Collins* [2001] UKHL 43, [2002] 1 All ER 46.
68 Excluded is a tenancy granted to a sitting protected or statutory tenant, which remains fully protected or statutory as the case may be: RA 1977, s 12(2).
69 *Barnett v O'Sullivan* [1995] 1 EGLR 93, CA.
70 Any more than it is in the case of the assured tenancy exclusion.
71 *Lewis-Graham v Conacher* [1992] 1 EGLR 111, CA.

extension to the house where the tenant lives, which is separate from the house, having no internal communication with it, and its own separate entrance, the landlord does not live in the same building as the tenant.[72] The mere fact that there may be a continuous roof common to a number of separate units of dwelling does not of itself mean that the units all form one building. If the appearance of the property is that it is one large continuous building with various extensions in which the landlord and tenant reside, these may be one building, at least if there is no lack of internal communications within the entity.[73] Where two flats had the appearance of being part of the same building, albeit with separate entrances, a ruling that the landlord was resident in the same building was not upset on appeal.[74]

PURPOSE BUILT BLOCK OF FLATS

A building is a purpose-built block of flats if as constructed it contained and contains two or more flats.[75] Thus a two-storey building with a shop on the ground floor and a flat above is not within the term 'purpose-built block of flats'. The exception of s 12 applies where part of a flat is let even though the flat happens to be in a purpose-built block of flats. The question of whether there is a purpose-built block of flats is tested as at the date of the original design and construction of the building. If, at that date, there was no purpose-built block of flats, a later conversion of a building into flats will not take a tenancy granted by a resident landlord out of the exception.[76]

RESIDENCE REQUIREMENT

The residential occupation by the landlord[77] must be continuous at all times since the grant of the tenancy and in another dwelling house in the same building.[78] A person is treated as occupying a dwelling house if he fulfils the same conditions as are required by RA 1977, s 2(3) for a statutory tenant.[79] What amounts to sufficient occupation is a question of fact and degree. In one case, the fact that the landlord did not sleep on

---

72 *Bardrick v Haycock* (1976) 31 P & CR 420, CA.
73 *Griffiths v English* [1982] 1 EGLR 86, CA; also *Guppy v O'Donnell* (1979) 129 NLJ 930.
74 *Wolff v Waddington* [1989] 2 EGLR 108, CA.
75 RA 1977, Sch 2, para 4. 'Flat' means a dwelling house which (1) forms part only of a building, and (2) is separated horizontally from another dwelling house which forms part of the same building.
76 *Barnes v Gorsuch* (1981) 43 P & CR 294, CA.
77 Which includes one of two or more joint landlords: *Cooper v Tait* (1984) 48 P & CR 460, CA. In the case of the assured tenancy exclusion, this principle has been adopted by legislation (Housing Act 1988, Sch 1, para 10(2)).
78 Under the Housing Act 1988, Sch 1, para 10(1)(c) the expression 'residence' is replaced by a stricter requirement of occupation by the landlord as his 'only or principal home'.
79 RA 1977, Sch 2, para 5.

the premises did not prevent his residing there, as he lived there during the day and kept personal belongings in the subject premises.[80]

PERIODS OF DISREGARD OR SUSPENSION

The requirement of continuous residential occupation is relaxed[81] so as to permit the transfer inter vivos and on death of a resident landlord's interest for interim periods of between 28 days in the case of, notably, sales of a resident landlord's reversion, and, in the case of a transfer to trustees as such, for a period of up to four years[82] without loss of the exemption. The effect of the disregard periods in both these cases is that no order for possession can be made against the tenant during a disregard period save on grounds applicable to a regulated (ie a protected or statutory) tenancy.[83] Once the relevant period ends, two things may happen. First, the tenancy may not by then have been determined: if so the tenant becomes a protected tenant. Secondly, the non-resident landlord to be or the trustees may have validly determined the tenancy: if so, vacant possession may be obtained after the period of disregard.[84]

In addition, where a resident landlord dies and his interest becomes vested in his personal representatives acting as such after his death, the residence requirement is deemed to be satisfied for two years from the vesting of his interest in these persons.[85] In essence, the personal representatives are taken to be in the same position as the deceased resident landlord would have been, if alive, for the two-year period at issue. Thus if the tenancy expires or is ended by notice to quit during the two-year period, possession may be recovered from the tenant without any need to establish a statutory ground for possession while the extension period is continuing, as well as after it has ended. But should the two-year extension period run its course and possession has not been recovered by the personal representatives during it, the tenancy will then become protected or statutory as the case may be.[86]

---

80 *Palmer v MacNamara* [1991] 1 EGLR 121, approved in *Uratemp Ventures Ltd v Collins* [2001] UKHL 43, [2002] 1 All ER 46. In *Jackson v Pecic* (1989) 22 HLR 9, however, a landlord out of occupation for three years was not 'resident'.
81 By RA 1977, Sch 2, paras 1 and 2.
82 If landlord A dies and his heir B dies, say, after 23 months, his personal representatives having taken advantage of the two-year suspension period, qv, C, B's heir, has up to a further 24 months in which to become a resident landlord.
83 RA 1977, Sch 2, para 3.
84 *Landau v Sloane* [1982] AC 490; *Williams v Mate* (1982) 46 P & CR 43, CA.
85 RA 1977, Sch 2, para 2A.
86 *Landau v Sloane* [1982] AC 490. If a beneficiary under the will of the landlord takes up residence during the two-year period, even without a formal assent in their favour, then provided the new landlord satisfies the residence condition, the tenancy will not be protected or statutory: *Beebe v Mason* [1980] 1 EGLR 81, CA.

(iii) Miscellaneous

The following further exclusions from protection under the Rent Acts may be noted.[87]

Exclusions by type of tenancy. A tenancy which is granted at a *low rent* is not within the protection of the Rent Acts.[88] Such tenancies are given protection on expiry by the regime applying to long residential leases. *Farm business tenancies* within the Agricultural Tenancies Act 1995 granted to the person responsible for the control of the management of the holding cannot be protected or statutory tenancies.[89] A tenancy is not protected by the Rent Acts if under it the dwelling house is bona fide let at a rent which includes payments in respect of *board*[90] or *attendance*. To prevent the landlord providing 'attendance' or services which are more of a burden to tenants than a benefit, the amount of rent fairly attributable to the attendance, having regard to the value of the attendance to the tenant, must form a substantial part[91] of the whole rent.[92]

Crown landlords. A tenancy is not protected at any time when the landlord's interest belongs to Her Majesty in right of the Crown. This exclusion also applies where the landlord is a government department or where the landlord's interest is held in trust for Her Majesty for the purposes of a government department (RA 1977, s 13(1)(a)).[93] The operation of RA 1977 as between tenants and sub-tenants is unaffected by RA 1977, s 13. Sub-tenancies held indirectly from the Crown, where the mesne landlord is not the Crown, may be protected or statutory (RA 1977, s 154).

Public sector and social landlords. If the immediate landlord's interest is held by one of a number of bodies as listed in RA 1977, ss 14-16, such as local authorities, development corporations, a registered or co-operative housing association, the Housing Corporation and charitable housing trusts, the tenancy is not protected. It may be secure. Should the landlord assign his reversion to a non-exempt landlord, the tenancy will come within RA 1977, unless excluded for some other reason.

87   There is a regulatory power to exclude by order all tenancies of dwelling houses in a particular area from being regulated tenancies (RA 1977, s 143(1)).
88   RA 1977, ss 5 (pre-1 April 1990 tenancies) and 5(1A) (tenancies granted after then).
89   RA 1977, s 10.
90   'Board' is not defined in RA 1977. Daily provision of continental breakfast and no other meals suffices: *Otter v Norman* [1989] AC 129, [1988] 2 All ER 897, HL.
91   The value or benefit to the tenant of the service is the key: 10% is the lower end of the scale and 20% the upper end: *Nelson Developments Ltd v Taboada* [1992] 2 EGLR 107.
92   RA 1977, s 7(1) and (2). Tenancies within this provision would be restricted contracts. The services or 'attendance' must be personal to the tenant and not provided to all tenants in common (*Nelson Developments Ltd v Taboada* [1992] 2 EGLR 107). These might include the provision of a resident housekeeper who cleans the tenant's rooms, and who provides clean linen: *Marchant v Charters* [1977] 3 All ER 918, [1977] 1 WLR 1181, CA.
93   If the interest of the immediate landlord is held by one of these bodies, the tenant cannot be a statutory tenant (RA 1977, s 13(1)(b)). If the interest of the Crown is managed by the Crown Estate Commissioners, RA 1977, s 13(2) allows the tenancy to be protected or statutory.

Miscellaneous. Lettings to students by a specified educational institution are not, by RA 1977, s 8, protected tenancies in principle. Neither are tenancies of licensed premises (RA 1977, s 11).

Land let with a dwelling house. The Rent Acts protect a tenant in the occupation of his home,[94] and not in relation to land holdings which may also contain a house. Where a dwelling house is let together with land other than the site of the dwelling house,[95] the tenancy falls outside the Rent Acts (RA 1977, s 6). However, land or premises let together with a dwelling house are treated as part of the dwelling house, unless the land is agricultural land exceeding two acres (RA 1977, s 26).[96] In this way, a protected or statutory tenancy may exist consisting of the home of the tenant with a garden, a garage or other outbuildings, without security being lost on account of the additional land or premises. The tenancy is a composite entity: the house and the other premises or land.[97]

III RENT REGULATION

Introduction

Although the parties to a Rent Act tenancy, are free to agree on any rent they like for the premises, it is likely that a rent will be registered for the dwelling house concerned. In that case the maximum amount of rent which the landlord is entitled to recover from a statutory tenant is the registered rent. Any excess payable under the tenancy over that sum is irrecoverable from the tenant.[98]

However, if the dwelling house specified for the purpose of a registered rent is not the same as that currently let to the current protected or statutory tenant (referred to as the 'regulated tenant' for the purpose of fair rents), then the previous registered rent cannot apply to the new tenancy. There may have been a re-letting to a different tenant of different accommodation, or to the same tenant of different accommodation (as where under a new tenancy there are more, or fewer rooms). However, it was held that a change from an unfurnished to a furnished letting did not render the previous

---

94   *Uratemp Ventures Ltd v Collins* [2001] UKHL 43, [2002] 1 All ER 46.
95   It appears that 'let together with' does not require that both the dwelling house and the land are necessarily held under a single lease: *Mann v Merrill* [1945] 1 All ER 708. Indeed, the land and dwelling house can apparently be held from different landlords: *Jelley v Buckman* [1974] QB 488, [1973] 3 All ER 853, CA.
96   If at the date of the hearing the land concerned was used only in connection with the dwelling house then the Rent Acts applied both to the land and the house: *Bradshaw v Smith* [1980] 2 EGLR 89, CA. If the land was originally used as agricultural land, thus outside the Rent Acts, it cannot fall within them merely because at a later stage the tenant gave up the original use of the land: *Russell v Booker* [1982] 2 EGLR 86, CA.
97   *Langford Property Co Ltd v Batten* [1951] AC 223, [1950] 2 All ER 1079, HL. A dominant purpose test applies, however. If the dwelling house is an adjunct to the land, it is outside the Rent Acts: see *Feyereisel v Turnidge* [1952] 2 QB 29, [1952] 1 All ER 728, CA.
98   RA 1977, s 45. The same rule applies to protected tenancies (RA 1977, s 44).

registered rent inapplicable to the premises.[99] The landlord may in such cases seek the registration of a new rent.

The landlord alone or the tenant alone, or both jointly, may apply to the Rent Officer[100] to register a fair rent.[101] There is a minimum life (in principle) of two years from the date of registration for a registered rent.[102]

Once a fair rent has been registered, it must be entered by the Rent Officer in an area register.[103] Registration of a fair rent takes effect as from its date of registration by a Rent Officer or, as the case may be, from the date of a Rent Assessment Committee's decision.[104]

Effect on regulated or fair rents of deregulated comparables

Subject to what is said about the specific provisions of RA 1977, s 70, 'fair rents', which the courts regard as essentially open market rents with some adjustments as prescribed by law, are often if not usually assessed by use of the comparables method, on the basis of evidence of comparable rents in a locality chosen by a Rent Officer or Rent Assessment Committee. The courts made a number of rulings, having regard to the fact that as from 15 January 1989, landlords have been letting residential houses and flats under assured or assured shorthold tenancies, and so at often high market rents: a good deal higher than some registered fair rents.[105] In the locality of a house or flat occupied by a statutory (or protected) tenant under the Rent Acts, there may well

99   *Rakhit v Carty* (1990) 22 HLR 198, CA; see also *Cheniston Investments Ltd v Waddock* [1988] 2 EGLR 136, CA.
100 From whose decision there is a right to appeal to a Rent Assessment Committee.
101 RA 1977, s 72(1). The procedure is laid down in RA 1977, Sch 11, Pt I. The landlord alone may apply for a different rent within the last three months of the two-year period (RA 1977, s 67(4)).
102 RA 1977, s 72(1).
103 RA 1977, s 66. The registered rent includes payments for services and furniture, if any (RA 1977, s 71: see *Firstcross Ltd v Teasdale* (1982) 47 P & CR 228); but not payments made to a company which was not the agent of the landlord for service provision: *Eaton Square Properties Ltd v Ogilvie* [2000] 1 EGLR 73.
104 RA 1977, s 72(1). No further single application for a registered rent may be allowed within the two-year period from the taking effect of a registered rent or its confirmation (RA 1977, s 67(3) and (5)). This is subject to reconsideration of the rent in the circumstances set out in RA 1977, s 67(3), notably, a change in the condition of the dwelling house, including any improvements or major repairs transforming an unfit house into a fit house (as in *R (on the application of Haysport Properties Ltd) v Rent Officer of the West Sussex Registration Area* [2001] EWCA Civ 237, [2001] 2 EGLR 63: concerned with repairs costing some £3,829 after a repair notice). See also *London Housing and Commercial Properties v Cowan* [1977] QB 148, [1976] 2 All ER 385 (once reconsideration is allowed, all relevant circumstances may then be taken into account, not just the one triggering the reconsideration).
105 Notably *Spath Holme Ltd v Chairman of Greater Manchester and Lancashire Rent Assessment Committee* (1995) 28 HLR 107, CA and *Curtis v London Rent Assessment Committee* [1997] 4 All ER 842, CA. See Rodgers [1999] Conv 20.

be comparable rents from properties let on assured or assured shorthold tenancies. This will expose statutory or protected tenants to potentially steep rent increases, a result which, having regard to the limited means of some such tenants, could put at risk the security of tenure conferred on them by RA 1977, so undermining the whole object of the Act.

However, the best evidence of a fair rent, with the assured tenancies scheme in full flood, is likely to be assured or assured shorthold tenancy rents for premises in the locality. If these are available, then there would be no need for a Rent Assessment Committee to look at fair rent comparables. If a Committee had deregulated rents to hand as comparables, it could only prefer to make use of registered rent comparables if it could advance good reasons for disregarding assured tenancy comparables, still less could a Committee decide to apply a percentage discount to the rent it had ascertained.[106] It was held that, whatever might have been the case in the past, the best evidence of rents was no longer given by registered rent comparables, all the more so since the number of the latter would diminish with the passage of time. Committees were said, as a limited concession,[107] to be entitled to make suitable adjustments for differences between the 'close market comparables' afforded by deregulated rents and the subject properties. As required by law there would, it was accepted, have to be a discount from deregulated comparable rents on account of scarcity.[108]

The harshness of the results of these rulings caused the government to intervene. It produced a Consultation Paper,[109] which expressed concern at steep and disproportionate rent inceases. The government thought that hardship was being caused to tenants, seeing that many of them were on fixed incomes or elderly: the government said that of 128,000 tenancies with a registered rent, only about one-fifth of the tenants concerned were working. The government used its powers under legislation,[110] and promulgated delegated legislation capping fair rent increases.[111] However, the Court of Appeal ruled that the order was made outside the statutory powers of the relevant legislation, which they said was limited to counter-inflation measures,[112] with the result that the capping order was quashed. It took a decision of

106 As in *Northumberland & Durham Property Trust Ltd v London Rent Assessment Committee* [1998] 3 EGLR 85, where the relevant decision was quashed as a result.

107 By Keene J in *Northumberland & Durham Property Trust Ltd v London Rent Assessment Committee* [1998] 3 EGLR 85.

108 *District Estates Ltd v Chairman of Merseyside and Cheshire Rent Assessment Committee* [1997] NPC 39.

109 'Limiting Fair Rent Increases' (1998) DETR; see Madge 148 (1998) NLJ 950; Murphy *Estates Gazette* 19 September 1998 142.

110 LTA 1985, s 31.

111 Rent Acts (Maximum Fair Rent) Order 1999, SI 1999/6, in force from 11 February 1999. The result of the capping formula as explained in the House of Lords in *R v Secretary of State for the Environment, Transport and the Regions, ex p Spath Holme Ltd* [2001] 1 All ER 195, is to limit rent increases to increases in the RPI for the relevant period, plus a further percentage amount, with first registrations, and more generous extra allowances after then.

112 *R v Secretary of State for the Environment, Transport and the Regions, ex p Spath Holme Ltd* [2000] 1 EGLR 167.

the House of Lords to re-instate the statutory instrument in question.[113] The House of Lords regarded the relevant legislation as conferring a general reserve power, not limited to anti-inflation measures. It was exercisable if the Minister reasonably judged, as he did in this instance, that it was necessary or desirable to protect tenants from hardship caused by increased or excessive rents. Their Lordships looked at the possible human rights impact of the capping order. The EHCR jurisprudence, however (as seen elsewhere in this book), does allow national governments a right to strike a balance on policy grounds between the rights of individuals (in our case landlords, to higher rents) and the community. Here, as will have been noticed elsewhere in the field of private landlord and tenant, the courts seem to be adopting a cautious approach to the impact of the Human Rights Convention.

Determination of a fair rent

RA 1977, s 70(1) provides that in determining a fair rent under a regulated tenancy, regard is to be had to all the circumstances, but not to personal circumstances. It is permissible for inflation to be taken into account in such manner as the Rent Officer or Rent Assessment Committee deem reasonable, provided cogent reasons are given.[114] Statute directs that three particular matters must be taken into account:

1 the age, character, locality and state of repair of the dwelling house (RA 1977, s 70(1)(a));
2 the quantity, quality and condition of any furniture provided for use under the tenancy (RA 1977, s 70(1)(b))[115] and
3 any premium or sum in the nature of a premium, which has been or may be lawfully required or received on the grant, renewal, continuance or assignment of the tenancy (RA 1977, s 70(1)(c)).

(i) Disregards

The following matters are to be disregarded in assessing a fair rent.

Scarcity. Any element of scarcity in the relevant neighbourhood, by assuming that the number of persons seeking to become tenants of similar dwelling houses in the locality on terms (other than as to rent) is not substantially greater than the number of such dwelling houses in the locality which are available for letting on such terms (RA

---

113 *R v Secretary of State for the Environment, Transport and the Regions, ex p Spath Holme Ltd* [2001] 1 All ER 195.
114 *Metropolitan Property Holdings Ltd v Laufer* (1974) 29 P & CR 172; *Wareing v White* [1985] 1 EGLR 125, CA; *R v London Rent Assessment Panel, ex p Chelmsford Building Co Ltd* [1986] 1 EGLR 175.
115 *R v London Rent Assessment Panel, ex p Mota* (1987) 20 HLR 159 (furniture 'provided' is available to the tenant, even if not used by him).

1977, s 70(2)).[116] Scarcity is distinct from matters such as specific amenities or any inherent advantages in the particular dwelling house, which matters may be taken into account.[117] It has been held that it was appropriate at least in marginal cases to look at what reasonable alternatives were available to potential tenants. If demand exceeded supply but there was no scarcity of accommodation in the wide area where tenants could reasonably take alternative accommodation, no deduction should be made owing to scarcity: but if there was a shortage of accommodation in the wider area, matters would be different.[118]

Disrepair. Any disrepair or other defect attributable to a failure by the tenant or any predecessor in title of his to comply with the terms of the regulated tenancy (RA 1977, s 70(3)(a)).[119]

Improvements. Any improvement, including the replacement of any fixture or fitting, carried out, otherwise than in pursuance of the terms of the tenancy, by the tenant under the regulated tenancy or any predecessor in title of his (RA 1977, s 70(3)(b)).[120]

Furniture. If any furniture is provided under the regulated tenancy, any improvement to it by the tenant or any predecessor in title of his; and any deterioration in the condition of the furniture due to any ill-treatment by the tenant and any person residing or lodging with him or any sub-tenant of his (RA 1977, s 70(3)(e)).

(ii) Repairs and services

Repairs. A landlord's failure to enforce a tenant's covenant to repair cannot be taken into account and the premises must be valued as at the date of the determination.[121] A low rent may be registered where the state of disrepair is not the fault of the tenant.[122]

---

116 According to *Forebury Estates Ltd v Chiltern Thames and Eastern Rent Assessment Panel* (2000) 33 HLR 718, local authority housing registers of applicants for accommodation are not wholly irrelevant to determining scarcity, but such lists had to be treated with caution.

117 *Metropolitan Property Holdings Ltd v Finegold* [1975] 1 All ER 389, [1975] 1 WLR 349.

118 *Queensway Housing Association v Chiltern, Thames and Eastern Rent Assessment Committee* (1998) 31 HLR 945.

119 See *Sturolson & Co v Mauroux* (1988) 20 HLR 332, CA. This disregard does not extend to a tenant's failure to comply with some lesser obligation, eg to use furnished premises in a tenant-like manner, which neglect may properly be taken into account: *Firstcross Ltd v Teasdale* (1982) 47 P & CR 228.

120 Ie a predecessor in title to the tenant in the premises, as opposed to a person who improves them and then obtains a lease: *Trustees of Henry Smith's Charity v Hemmings* (1982) 45 P & CR 377.

121 *Metropolitan Properties Co Ltd v Wooldridge* (1968) 20 P & CR 64.

122 *McGee v London Rent Assessment Panel Committee* [1969] RVR 342 (unexplained fire); but it was held not to be obligatory to register a nil rent merely because the house was subject to a closing order: *Williams v Khan* (1980) 43 P & CR 1, CA.

Services. Services provided under covenant by the landlord are matters which should be taken into account where appropriate.[123] Since the basis of valuation is the value of the service to the tenant, if a service is insufficiently provided, however, any allowance made for it will be reduced.[124] The cost of services to the landlord may be taken into account, and, if it is, depreciation of his equipment which provides services and for his profit must be included in any allowance,[125] and in respect of the cost of replacement, based on original cost.[126]

IV   GROUNDS FOR POSSESSION

Restrictions on recovery of possession

A tenant within RA 1977 may only be evicted from the dwelling house concerned following proceedings in the county court taken by the landlord. The landlord is bound by the restrictions of RA 1977, s 98,[127] although if the tenant concedes that s 98 does not apply, the court may order possession without reference to it.[128] The landlord can only obtain possession against the tenant if he proves one or more statutory grounds. Most cases for re-possession will nowadays be concerned with statutory tenancies, and the court is entitled to assume that a Rent Act tenancy will be statutory rather than protected.[129]

RA 1977, s 98 distinguishes between the rules applicable where suitable alternative accommodation is available to the tenant, 'discretionary' grounds for possession, which are subject to an overriding discretion in the court to refuse an order if it thinks it unreasonable to make the order, despite the landlord's proving the ground concerned, and finally 'mandatory' grounds for possession, where the overriding discretion of the court is absent.

---

123 *R v Paddington North and St Marylebone Rent Tribunal, ex p Perry* [1956] 1 QB 229, [1955] 3 All ER 391.
124 *Metropolitan Properties Co v Noble* [1968] 2 All ER 313, [1968] 1 WLR 838.
125 *Perseus Property Co Ltd v Burberry* [1985] 1 EGLR 114.
126 *Regis Property Co v Dudley* [1958] 1 QB 346, [1958] 1 All ER 510, CA. In this and any like case, the landlord's figures ought to be considered but do not mandatorily have to be accepted: *R v London Rent Assessment Panel, ex p Cliftvylle Properties Ltd* [1983] 1 EGLR 100.
127 *Appleton v Aspin* [1988] 1 All ER 904, [1988] 1 WLR 410, CA.
128 *Barton v Fincham* [1921] 2 KB 291; *Syed Hussain v AM Abdulla Sahib & Co* [1985] 1 WLR 1392; but if the tenant does not concede his case, an order cannot be made without the landlord proving a ground and compliance with RA 1977, s 98(1) where appropriate: *R v Newcastle upon Tyne County Court, ex p Thompson* [1988] 2 EGLR 119.
129 *Wareing v White* [1992] 1 EGLR 271 (no notice to quit being necessary owing to the statutory restrictions on re-possession).

(i) Discretionary grounds: introduction

By RA 1977, s 98(1), the court must not make an order for possession of a dwelling house let on a protected or statutory tenancy unless the court considers it reasonable to make such an order and either:

1   the court is satisfied that suitable alternative accommodation is available for the tenant or will be available for him when the order in question takes effect; or
2   the court is satisfied that the landlord has established one of the Cases (or grounds) for possession set out in RA 1977, Sch 15, Pt I, which are referred to as 'discretionary grounds'.

The court's overriding discretion not to order possession despite the proof of alternative accommodation or of a 'discretionary ground' should operate as follows. The onus of convincing the court that it is reasonable to order possession is on the landlord.[130] The judge must deal with reasonableness as a specific issue, including examining matters of a domestic and general character.[131] The judge is bound to take account of all the relevant circumstances at the date of the hearing in a broad way, giving whatever weight he thinks right to the various factors in the situation.[132] Even where a ground itself involves a requirement of reasonableness, the general issue of reasonableness must be separately considered.[133] Once the judge has heard the relevant evidence, it will ordinarily be assumed that he directed his mind to the overall issue of reasonableness.[134] If for some reason the judge has not done so, the Court of Appeal has exercised its own discretion.[135] However, the Court of Appeal will not interfere with any proper exercise of discretion,[136] even if it might have acted differently to the judge.

The judge must consider all the relevant circumstances in relation to both the landlord and the tenant, the premises and the interests of the public.[137] It was therefore open to a judge to refuse to order possession, he having taken into account the personal attachment of the tenant to her existing flat, where she had lived for 35 years.[138] Anything which may cause hardship to either party is relevant.[139] The conduct of the parties is relevant, such as an expressed intention to continue a breach of covenant.[140]

---

130 *Smith v McGoldrick* [1977] 1 EGLR 53, CA.
131 *Chiverton v Ede* [1921] 2 KB 30; *Redspring Ltd v Francis* [1973] 1 All ER 640, [1973] 1 WLR 134, CA.
132 *Cumming v Danson* [1942] 2 All ER 653 at 655; *Dawncar Investments Ltd v Plews* [1994] 1 EGLR 141, CA.
133 *Shrimpton v Rabbits* (1924) 131 LT 478 at 469 (Case 9).
134 See *Minchburn Ltd v Fernandez* [1986] 2 EGLR 103, CA (where the judge related reasonableness solely to the specific, not the general, issue of reasonableness).
135 As in *Roberts v Macilwraith-Christie* [1987] 1 EGLR 224.
136 *RF Fuggle Ltd v Gadsden* [1948] 2 KB 236, [1948] 2 All ER 160.
137 *Cresswell v Hodgson* [1951] 2 KB 92.
138 *Battlespring Ltd v Gates* [1983] 2 EGLR 103, CA.
139 *Williamson v Pallant* [1924] 2 KB 173.
140 *Bell London and Provincial Properties v Reuben* [1947] KB 157, [1946] 2 All ER 547.

It is easier to establish reasonableness when suitable alternative accommodation is available for the tenant than when it is not.[141] If the suitable alternative accommodation is part of the house which the tenant currently occupies exclusively, so precluding him from living with persons of his own choosing, it may be unreasonable to order possession.[142]

(ii) Mandatory grounds: introduction

If the landlord would be entitled to recover possession because the matter falls within one of the mandatory grounds for possession (RA 1977, Sch 15, Pt II), the court must make an order for possession. The court has, in such cases, no overriding discretion to refuse to make an order for possession on the ground that it is not reasonable to do so, once the landlord has made out the facts of a mandatory Case to its satisfaction and has proved a genuine case.[143]

Suitable alternative accommodation: statutory definitions

Subject to the overriding discretion of the court to refuse to order possession despite proof of the availability of suitable alternative accommodation, which discretion must be separately considered,[144] the landlord may satisfy the onus of proving that suitable alternative accommodation is available to the tenant by producing a certificate of the local housing authority that they will provide such accommodation for the tenant by a date specified in the notice: it is conclusive evidence for the purpose of establishing this ground.[145]

In the absence of such a certificate, accommodation, whether offered by the landlord himself, or available otherwise, in either case at the date of the hearing,[146] will be deemed by statute[147] to be suitable if it consists of either:
1   premises comprising a separate dwelling so as to be let on a protected tenancy (other than one on which the landlord might recover possession under one of the mandatory repossession grounds); or
2   premises to be let as a separate dwelling on such terms as will, in the opinion of the court, afford to the tenant the same security of tenure as under a protected tenancy, other than such a tenancy with the right to mandatory repossession.

141 *Cumming v Danson* [1942] 2 All ER 653.
142 *Yoland Ltd v Reddington* [1982] 2 EGLR 80.
143 *Kennealy v Dunne* [1977] QB 837, [1977] 2 All ER 16.
144 *Hill v Rochard* [1983] 2 All ER 21, [1983] 1 WLR 478, CA; *Battlespring Ltd v Gates* [1983] 2 EGLR 103, CA.
145 RA 1977, Sch 15, Pt IV, para 3.
146 *Nevile v Hardy* [1921] 1 Ch 404.
147 RA 1977, Sch 15, Pt IV, paras 4 and 5.

There are additional conditions imposed by RA 1977, where the accommodation is not based on a local authority certificate. It must be reasonably suitable to the needs of the tenant and his family as regards proximity to place of work,[148] and either:

1 similar as regards rental and extent to the accommodation afforded by any local housing authority for persons whose needs as regards extent are, in the opinion of the court, similar to those of the tenant and of his family; or

2 reasonably suitable to the means of the tenant and to the needs of the tenant and his family[149] as regards extent and character.[150]

If any furniture was provided for use under the protected or statutory tenancy in question, furniture must be provided for use in the (new) accommodation which is either similar to that so provided or is reasonably suitable to the needs of the tenant and his family.

The courts interpret the requirement that the accommodation is to be suitable objectively, without making concessions to personal tastes of a particular tenant, but taking into account adverse objective factors. Thus, the fact that the accommodation offered was unsuitable for the tenant to entertain business acquaintances and had no garden for the tenant's child was relevant,[151] as was the fact that the proposed accommodation would not enable the tenant to carry out his profession as an artist because it lacked a studio.[152] So too has the fact that it would not accommodate the tenant's furniture.[153] The current house or flat held under the current tenancy minus one room may be suitable, depending on the needs of the tenant.[154]

148 See *Yewbright Properties Ltd v Stone* (1980) 40 P & CR 402, CA (where a tenant's difficulty in travelling from the proposed accommodation to various places of work was held relevant).

149 'Family', by analogy with statutory tenancies, does not include friends (*Kavanagh v Lyroudias* [1985] 1 All ER 560, CA) or a resident housekeeper (*Darnell v Millwood* [1951] 1 All ER 88, CA). However, 'family' would now include a single-sex partner in a long-lasting relationship: *Fitzpatrick v Sterling Housing Association* [1999] 4 All ER 705, HL.

150 RA 1977, Sch 15, Pt IV, para 5(1). The expression 'extent and character' enjoins the court to have regard to the tenant's objective housing needs, as opposed to his own personal wishes: *Hill v Rochard* [1983] 2 All ER 21, [1983] 1 WLR 478, CA; *Siddiqui v Rashid* [1980] 3 All ER 184, [1980] 1 WLR 1018 (loss of friends or culture due to move not relevant); *Montross Associated Investments v Stone* Legal Action, March 2000, p 29 (view from current flat, overlooking Hyde Park, not a relevant factor because 'needs' means 'needs for housing'). 'Character' does entitle the court to compare the environment of the tenant in the current and the new proposed accommodation, so that unsuitable was proposed accommodation in a busy road with a hospital and fish and chip shop nearby, when the tenant currently lived in a quiet flat: *Redspring Ltd v Francis* [1973] 1 All ER 640, [1973] 1 WLR 134, CA.

151 *De Markozoff v Craig* (1949) 93 Sol Jo 693.

152 *MacDonnell v Daly* [1969] 3 All ER 851, [1969] 1 WLR 1482, CA.

153 *McIntyre v Hardcastle* [1948] 2 KB 82, [1948] 1 All ER 696; but not that the new accommodation did not have a garage: *Briddon v George* [1946] 1 All ER 609, CA.

154 *Mykolyshyn v Noah* [1971] 1 All ER 48, [1970] 1 WLR 1271. If the tenant has sub-let part of the premises, it would be hard for him to claim that a new tenancy of the reduced accommodation now occupied was not suitable: see eg *Parmee v Mitchell* [1950] 2 KB 199, [1950] 2 All ER 872, CA. Shared accommodation is not, however, suitable: *Bernard v Towers* [1953] 2 All ER 877, [1953] 1 WLR 1203, CA.

Discretionary grounds for possession

The court may order possession, absolutely or conditionally, in favour of a landlord who proves that the matter falls within one or more of the following 'cases', subject to its overriding discretion (RA 1977, s 98(1)) to refuse possession. If the court makes an order for possession, it may exercise, on the tenant's or his spouse's application,[155] extensive discretionary powers to adjourn the proceedings. It may also stay or suspend the execution of the order for possession, either at the date the order is made or at any time until it is executed.[156] The principal discretionary grounds are as follows.[157]

(i)   *Case 1: breach of obligation*

Where any rent lawfully due from the tenant has not been paid or any obligation of the tenancy has been broken or not performed.

The broad policy of this Case is to require a statutory tenant to observe all the terms and conditions of the original contract of tenancy: a breach or non-performance of any obligation would therefore remove the statutory restriction on the landlord's right to recover possession.[158]

As far as rent goes, no order can be made if rent is tendered before commencement of the proceedings;[159] if rent is paid after the commencement of proceedings, an order can be made, and in practice, even if arrears are still unpaid at the time of the hearing, the court will rarely make an absolute order unless the arrears are substantial or there are other special circumstances, such as the tenant's bad record for non-payment.[160] Where a tenant withheld rent because of a reasonable complaint of a landlord's breach

---

155   RA 1977, s 100(4A) and (4B).
156   RA 1977, s 100(1) and (2). The court, save in the case of exceptional hardship to the tenant, or where this would otherwise be unreasonable, must impose conditions as to the payment by the tenant of arrears of rent or mesne profits, and may impose such other conditions as it thinks fit (RA 1977, s 100(3)). The court declines to order an indefinite or even a very long suspension, because the landlord must eventually be paid: *Taj v Ali* [2000] 3 EGLR 35, CA (where a suspension ordered had the result that the rent would take over 55 years to pay off: possession was ordered on appeal). The court cannot impose as a condition of suspending a possession order the payment of sums which are not rent against a statutory tenant: see *Raeuchle v Laimond Properties Ltd* [2000] L & TR 345, CA.
157   RA 1977, Sch 15. In addition, Case 4 applies where the condition of furniture provided for use under the tenancy has deteriorated owing to the neglect of the tenant or any resident, sub-tenant or lodger of his; Case 10 relates to a sub-letting by the tenant on an excessive rent.
158   *Cadogan Estates Ltd v McMahon* [2000] 4 All ER 897, [2000] 3 WLR 1555, HL.
159   *Bird v Hildage* [1948] 1 KB 91, [1947] 2 All ER 7.
160   *Dellenty v Pellow* [1951] 2 KB 858, [1951] 2 All ER 716; the exact amounts owed must be discovered: see *Crompton v Broomfield* [1990] EGCS 137, CA.

of covenant to repair, it was not reasonable to order possession.[161] A statutory tenant by succession is not liable for arrears of rent owed by his predecessor at the time of his death.[162]

As far as the word 'obligation' is concerned, this is the equivalent of the expression 'condition', when used in a tenancy as a description of an act of bankruptcy, with the result that a statutory tenant who was made bankrupt by a firm of travel agents had committed a breach of tenancy obligations within Case 1, entitling the landlord to seek possession of the premises.[163]

On the overriding question of reasonableness of granting an order for possession, the court will take into account the fact that the tenant has remedied the breach at the time of the hearing or that he is willing to give an undertaking in respect of it. Case I applies both to breaches of a continuing and of a once and for all nature. It applies to a breach of covenant against business user[164] and to sub-lettings, as opposed to an occupation by lodgers, without the landlord's consent.[165] It is a natural inference, in this connection, that a statutory tenant may occupy the premises with his family or extended family as licensees, without committing a breach within Case I.[166]

A landlord cannot rely on a breach that he has waived, but the common law doctrine of waiver cannot strictly apply to a statutory tenancy; but the landlord may lose the right to rely on this ground by continued acceptance of the rent in knowledge of the breach without qualification and undue delay in commencing proceedings.[167]

(ii) Case 2: nuisance, etc

> Where the tenant or any person residing or lodging with him or any sub-tenant has been guilty of conduct which is a nuisance or annoyance to adjoining occupiers, or has been convicted of using the dwelling house, or allowing it to be used, for immoral or illegal purposes.

This ground for possession remains unaltered, in contrast to the extension of its scope in the case of assured and secure tenancies. A statutory tenant who indulged in anti-social conduct such as racial abuse or threats of violence to a neighbouring tenant might still fall within Case 2, however, in view of the use of the word 'annoyance', which has a wider meaning than nuisance. Any behaviour which is likely materially to affect the peace of mind or physical comfort of an ordinary person is an annoyance:

---

161 *Televantos v McCulloch* [1991] 1 EGLR 123.
162 *Tickner v Clifton* [1929] 1 KB 207.
163 *Cadogan Estates Ltd v McMahon* [2000] 4 All ER 897, [2000] 3 WLR 1555, HL.
164 *Florent v Horez* (1983) 48 P & CR 166, CA.
165 *Roberts v Macilwraith-Christie* [1987] 1 EGLR 224, CA.
166 *Blanway Investments Ltd v Lynch* (1993) 25 HLR 378, CA.
167 *Oak Property Co Ltd v Chapman* [1947] KB 886, [1947] 2 All ER 1; *Henry Smith's Charity Trustees v Willson* [1983] QB 316, [1983] 1 All ER 73, CA.

indeed, it may be inferred without evidence from adjoining occupiers.[168] 'Adjoining' means 'neighbouring', but the premises of the complainant need not necessarily be physically contiguous to or even on the same floor as the offending tenant.[169] Conviction of immoral or illegal user is sufficient for this ground to be relied on, without evidence of nuisance or annoyance, and if the purpose of the tenant's user of the premises is illegal or immoral, a single offence is sufficient.[170] If an offence is committed on the premises accidentally, when the user itself is capable of being lawful, this is not enough to infringe Case 2.[171] Where the tenant was convicted of being in unlawful possession of cannabis resin, the drugs having been found on the premises, the Court of Appeal held that possession without knowledge did not constitute using the dwelling for illegal purposes; though presumably it would have been otherwise if it had been used for storing the drugs.[172] Even if a nuisance has abated, it may be reasonable for an order for possession to be made.[173]

(iii) Case 3: deterioration by waste or neglect

Where the condition of the dwelling house has deteriorated owing to acts of waste by, or the neglect or default of, the tenant, any sub-tenant or any lodger, and if caused by a sub-tenant or lodger, the court is satisfied that the tenant has not, before the making of the order in question, taken all reasonable steps to remove him.

'Waste' includes unauthorised alterations to the premises such as putting in new doors, enlargement of rooms, etc and also demolishing any part of the premises.[174] Likewise, failure by the tenant to take reasonable precautions to look after the premises causing deterioration to them, such as deterioration due to want of firing and airing in winter[175] or due to frost damage, will presumably suffice within this ground. Where the tenant allowed the garden to grow uncontrolled for a growing season, possession was ordered but the order was suspended for a year to allow her to comply with her obligations.[176]

168 *Frederick Platts & Co Ltd v Grigor* [1950] 1 All ER 941n: eg substantial business user of the tenant's residential flat: *Florent v Horez* (1983) 48 P & CR 166, CA.
169 *Cobstone Investments Ltd v Maxim* [1985] QB 140, [1984] 2 All ER 635, CA; Lyons [1985] Conv 168; nor is the sub-tenant of the tenant himself included as an 'occupier'; *Chester v Potter* [1949] EGD 247.
170 *S Schneiders & Sons v Abrahams* [1925] 1 KB 541.
171 See *Waller & Son Ltd v Thomas* [1921] 1 KB 301 (sale, out of hours, of intoxicating liquor).
172 *Abrahams v Wilson* [1971] 2 All ER 1114.
173 *Florent v Horez* (1983) 48 P & CR 166, CA.
174 *Marsden v Edward Heyes Ltd* [1927] 2 KB 1, CA.
175 *Robertson v Wilson* 1922 SLT (Sh Ct) 21.
176 *Holloway v Povey* [1984] 2 EGLR 115, CA.

(iv) Case 5: tenant's notice to quit

Where the tenant has given notice to quit, and in consequence of that notice, the landlord has contracted to sell or let the dwelling house, or has taken any other steps as a result of which he would be seriously prejudiced if he could not obtain possession.

This ground may be relied upon where the tenant gives an undertaking that he will give up possession, though not strictly in terms of a notice to quit; it does not apply to surrender.[177] Where a contractual tenant gave a notice to quit, and after its expiry changed her mind, the Court of Appeal held that the tenant was thereupon a statutory tenant, and that since, on the facts, the landlord only intended to sell and had not contracted to sell, he could not rely on this ground.[178]

(v) Case 6: assignment or sub-letting

Where, without the consent of the landlord, the tenant has assigned or sub-let the whole of the dwelling house or sub-let part of the dwelling house, the remainder being already sub-let. This applies for most regulated tenancies, and to assignments or sub-lettings since 8 December 1965.[179]

Case 6 is available to the landlord whether the tenancy is contractual or statutory, and whether or not there is a covenant against assignment or sub-letting in the head tenancy.[180] Even if there is a sub-tenant who is 'lawful' within RA 1977, s 137, the court may order possession against the sub-tenant under Case 6.[181] The policy of Case 6 is evidently to protect the landlord against the risk of finding a person unknown to him irremovably installed in his property.[182]

'Consent', however, need not be in writing, but may be implied, and must be given to a particular tenant,[183] and it will be sufficient if it is given at any time before the proceedings are issued.[184]

---

177 *Standingford v Bruce* [1926] 1 KB 466. Nor to an agreement to surrender: *De Vries v Sparks* (1927) 137 LT 441.
178 *Barton v Fincham* [1921] 2 KB 291.
179 Special rules exist for other tenancies, in particular the relevant date for furnished tenancies being 14 August 1974.
180 *Regional Properties Co Ltd v Frankenschwerth and Chapman* [1951] 1 KB 631, [1951] 1 All ER 178, CA; also *Pazgate Ltd v McGrath* [1984] 2 EGLR 130, CA.
181 *Leith Properties Ltd v Byrne* [1983] QB 433, [1982] 3 All ER 731, CA.
182 *Hyde v Pimley* [1952] 2 QB 506 at 512; [1952] 2 All ER 102 at 105.
183 *Regional Properties Co Ltd v Frankenschwerth*, supra.
184 *Hyde v Pimley* [1951] 1 KB 631, [1951] 1 All ER 178, CA.

(vi) Case 8: dwelling required for landlord's employee

Where the dwelling house is reasonably required for occupation as a residence for an employee or prospective employee either of the landlord or of some tenant from him, provided that the existing tenant was formerly a service tenant of the landlord or a previous landlord, but has ceased to be employed by him and the dwelling house was let to him in consequence of that employment.

This ground may be relied upon even though another house is available for the employee.[185] Where the dwelling is required for a prospective employee, he must have entered into a contract of employment which is conditional upon housing being provided, and started work by the date of the hearing unless reasonably prevented from doing so by reason of his absence on holiday or through illness.[186] In such a case, it might be reasonable to make a suspended order in case he should give notice. The employment must be full-time, but although the former employee *ex hypothesi* must have been a service tenant,[187] it is not necessary that the person for whom the dwelling is required should take it in that capacity; and it will be sufficient if he is merely a service occupier.[188]

(vii) Case 9: dwelling reasonably required for landlord

Under this ground for possession, the landlord must prove that the dwelling house is reasonably required for occupation as a residence for himself, or any adult son or daughter of his, or his father or mother, or his father-in-law or mother-in-law.

The policy of this case is to allow the landlord to recover possession of the dwelling house for the use of his or his spouse's immediate family.[189] The need for a landlord to pass between the Scylla of a reasonable requirement for possession and the Charibdis of greater hardship, as imposed by Case 9 on landlords' wishes to recover possession,[190] may be contrasted with the absence of both requirements from the owner-occupier ground applicable to Case 11 (and indeed to the equivalent ground for assured tenancies).

---

185 *Lowcock & Sons Ltd v Brotherton* [1952] CPL 408.
186 *R F Fuggle Ltd v Gadsden* [1948] 2 KB 236, [1948] 2 All ER 160.
187 As opposed to a licensee: see *Matthew v Bobbins* [1980] 2 EGLR 97, CA.
188 *UBM Ltd v Tyler* (1949) 99 L Jo 723. As to the payment of compensation under Case 8 (and Case 9) where a landlord obtains an order for possession by misrepresentation or concealment of material facts, see RA 1977, s 102.
189 *Potsos v Theodotou* [1991] 2 EGLR 93, CA.
190 These include a purchase condition whose aim is to prevent the landlord buying the house over his head and then evicting him: *Fowle v Bell* [1947] KB 242, [1946] 2 All ER 668, CA.

(viii) *Case 9: reasonably required*

There must be a genuine need at the time of the hearing: something more than desire but something much less than absolute necessity.[191] The onus of proof of 'reasonably required' is on the landlord.[192] He does not have to show that he requires possession at once, provided that it is reasonably required in the ascertainable future.[193] 'Reasonably required' would include proximity to work[194] and need not necessarily involve a genuine need for the whole house.[195] The fact that the person for whom the dwelling is required already has a house is clearly relevant, but it is not conclusive.[196] However, Case 9 does not apply if a landlord's intention to reside is uncertain, as where it was not clear that she might not wish to let the property at a profit.[197] If the reversion is held by two or more joint landlords, Case 9 may be claimed only if both or all the landlords are able to prove an intention to reside in the dwelling house.[198] Trustees or personal representatives cannot claim possession under Case 9 for the benefit of a beneficiary[199] but they may rely on it if able to show that they themselves intend, without breach of trust, to reside in the house.[200]

(ix) *Case 9: greater hardship*

The court cannot order possession under Case 9 alone if satisfied that, having regard to all the circumstances, including specifically the question whether other accommodation is available to the landlord or the tenant, greater hardship would be caused by granting the order than by refusing it.[201]

In considering greater hardship, the judge must take into account all the relevant circumstances, including the financial means of both parties,[202] and whether, if any other accommodation is available to the tenant, it is Rent Act-protected.[203] If the landlord has no alternative accommodation of his own, this is a relevant factor,[204] as is the fact that he has another, suitable, house.[205] The judge must consider hardship to all

191 *Kennealey v Dunne* [1977] QB 837, [1977] 2 All ER 16, CA.
192 *Epsom Grand Stand Association Ltd v Clarke* (1919) 35 TLR 525, CA.
193 *Kidder v Birch* (1982) 46 P & CR 362, CA.
194 *Jackson v Harbour* [1924] EGD 99.
195 *Kelley v Goodwin* [1947] 1 All ER 810, CA.
196 *Nevile v Hardy* [1921] 1 Ch 404.
197 *Ghelani v Bowie* [1988] 2 EGLR 130, CA.
198 *McIntyre v Hardcastle* [1948] 2 KB 82, [1948] 1 All ER 696, CA.
199 *Parker v Rosenberg* [1947] KB 371, [1947] 1 All ER 87, CA.
200 *Patel v Patel* [1982] 1 All ER 68, [1981] 1 WLR 1342, CA (personal representatives also parents of infant beneficiaries).
201 RA 1977, Sch 15, Pt III, para 1. The onus of proof of greater hardship falls on the tenant: *Sims v Wilson* [1946] 2 All ER 261, CA.
202 *Kelley v Goodwin* [1947] 1 All ER 810.
203 *Sims v Wilson* [1946] 2 All ER 261, CA; *Baker v McIver* (1990) 22 HLR 328, CA.
204 *Coombs v Parry* (1987) 19 HLR 384; *Baker v McIver* (1990) 22 HLR 328, CA.
205 *Chandler v Strevett* [1947] 1 All ER 164, CA.

who may be affected by the grant or refusal of an order for possession: relatives, dependants, lodgers, guests and the stranger within the gates, but should weigh such hardship with due regard to the status of the persons affected and their 'proximity' to the tenant or the landlord, and the extent to which, consequently, hardship to them would be hardship to him.[206] The judge must also have regard to the longer-term effects of a possession order, as the short-term effect is always to cause some hardship to the tenant.[207] Where there is an error of law, and the Court of Appeal has sufficient evidence to resolve the issue of greater hardship, it will do so; otherwise, a remit must take place.[208] However, the mere fact that the Court of Appeal might have arrived at a different result to that of the judge is not sufficient ground for interfering with his decision.[209]

Mandatory repossession

The landlord of a protected or statutory tenant may recover possession 'mandatorily', notably where he let the dwelling house or flat as an owner-occupier: a term which carries no necessary requirement that the landlord is a freeholder.[210] If the landlord makes out this, or any other mandatory ground for possession then the court must, by RA 1977, s 98(2), order possession, but the onus of proof falls on the landlord as regards the basic facts of, and compliance with, a given ground, but there is no express requirement in s 98(2) that it must be reasonable to make an order for possession, and no such requirement can be implied.[211]

Should the court make an order for possession the giving up of possession is not to be put off to a date later than 14 days after the order is made, unless exceptional hardship to the tenant would be caused, and in any event the giving up of possession cannot be put off beyond six weeks from the making of the order.[212]

The principal mandatory ground worth noting here is that relating to an owner-occupier landlord.[213] This ground is also present in a slightly narrower form in relation to assured

---

206 *Harte v Frampton* [1948] 1 KB 73 at 79.
207 *Manaton v Edwards* [1985] 2 EGLR 159, CA.
208 *Alexander v Mohamedzadeh* [1985] 2 EGLR 161, CA.
209 *Hodges v Blee* [1987] 2 EGLR 119, CA.
210 *Mistry v Isidore* [1990] 2 EGLR 97.
211 *Kennealy v Dunne* [1977] QB 837, [1977] 2 All ER 16, CA; *Whitworth v Lipton* (1993) 26 HLR 293, CA.
212 Housing Act 1980, s 89(1).
213 Other mandatory grounds listed in RA 1977, Sch 15, Pt II include Case 12 (landlord purchased a home for retirement, notified the tenant of this fact and now requires home for the stated purpose); off-season lettings of a dwelling house to be let on holiday lets in season (Case 13); recovery of possession against a tenant holding a protected shorthold tenancy granted under Housing Act 1980, ss 52-55 (Case 19); lettings to members of the armed forces (Case 20). These grounds emphasise the fact that for some time before the abrogation of the Rent Acts for new tenancies, many landlords, no doubt, would only be prepared to let under a contract of tenancy which envisaged one of these grounds or the owner-occupier ground.

tenancies.[214] The owner-occupier ground may be relied on by one of joint landlords.[215] One of the advantages of this ground, which has been altered in the case of assured tenancies,[216] was that there is no requirement within the Rent Act ground for possession that the landlord must occupy the house or flat as his or her only or principal home once possession has been regained: all that was required was use of the premises as an intermittent residence.[217] The ground may be summarised as follows.

> The 'owner-occupier' who let the house or flat on a protected tenancy had occupied it at some time, which does not have to be immediately beforehand, prior to the letting, as his residence. The landlord must give a written notice no later than, in principle, the commencement of the tenancy, that possession might be recovered under Case 11.

However, this requirement may be dispensed with by the court if it is just and equitable to do so. In principle, subject to a court dispensation power, the house or flat concerned must not have been let save under the owner-occupier case, so allowing, however, a string of such lettings. The court must be satisfied that one of a number of conditions is complied with. Of these, the principal condition is that the dwelling house is required as a residence for the owner or any member of his family who resided with him when he last occupied the dwelling house as his residence.[218]

The dispensation power, which exists also in relation to the similar ground applying to assured tenants, is exercised on broad principles. The court examines all relevant circumstances.[219] For example, it was exercised where the landlord honestly believed that due notice had been given: the notice was sent, but never in fact received by the tenant.[220] However, if at the time of the letting the landlord did not intend to make use

---

214 Housing Act 1988, Sch 2, Pt I, ground 1.

215 *Tilling v Whiteman* [1980] AC 1, [1979] 1 All ER 737, HL.

216 Owing to the requirement of the Housing Act 1988, Sch 2, Pt I ground 1 that the landlord (or one of joint landlords) requires the dwelling house as his or his spouse's only or principal home.

217 *Naish v Curzon* [1985] 1 EGLR 117; also *Davies v Paterson* (1988) 21 HLR 63 (both concerning landlords who visited the UK often enough to be able to claim successfully that they were owner-occupiers); but much depended on the county court ruling: see *Mistry v Isidore* [1990] 2 EGLR 97 and *Ibie v Trubshaw* (1990) 22 HLR 191 (where a landlord living mainly abroad failed).

218 Provision is also made for recovery after the owner's death of possession of the dwelling house by a member of his family resident with him at the time of his death; also for recovery of possession by a dead owner's successor in title who requires the dwelling house to live in or to dispose of it with vacant possession; recovery is also enabled for legal mortgagees whose mortgage was granted before the commencement of the tenancy; also where the dwelling house is no longer reasonably suitable to the needs of the owner having regard to his place of work and he requires to dispose of it and acquire a more suitable dwelling house (so covering relocation following a change of employment).

219 *Bradshaw v Baldwin-Wiseman* (1985) 17 HLR 260, CA.

220 *Minay v Sentongo* (1982) 45 P & CR 190, CA. The dispensation power was also, exceptionally, exercised where the landlord gave an oral notice and the tenant knew the landlord to be an owner-occupier: *Fernandes v Pavardin* [1982] 2 EGLR 104, CA.

of the owner-occupier ground for possession, he or she cannot later change their mind and ask the court to dispense with the relevant notice.[221]

Statutory tenancies

Statutory tenancies arise automatically as from the termination of the previous protected tenancy.[222] A succession scheme exists so that the surviving spouse or certain other relatives of the statutory tenant may succeed to the tenancy. However, as from 15 January 1989, this scheme has been curtailed and this type of statutory tenancy will die a lingering death.

(i)   Statutory tenancy on expiry of protected tenancy

A protected contractual tenancy, fixed-term or periodic, automatically becomes a statutory tenancy if and so long as, from the termination of the previous protected tenancy, the tenant occupies the dwelling house as his residence (RA 1977, s 2(1)(a)). The statutory tenancy will continue unless it is terminated in possession proceedings (subject to the various statutory restrictions) or unless the tenant ceases to comply with the statutory residence requirement.

If the tenant gives notice to quit but subsequently remains in occupation after the notice has expired, he becomes a statutory tenant, but the landlord may be able to terminate his occupation in proceedings.[223] If the previous protected tenancy has been forfeited, a statutory tenancy arises under RA 1977, s 2(1)(a), but the landlord may then establish a ground for possession which corresponds to the breach which was the basis of the forfeiture, and he then regains possession if he complies with the statutory restrictions.[224] If a protected tenant goes bankrupt, no statutory tenancy can arise.[225] Where a landlord was induced to grant a protected tenancy, which had since expired, by a fraudulent misrepresentation of the tenant, the landlord could rescind the contractual tenancy, as fraud unravels everything, and no statutory tenancy could arise.[226]

The precise nature of the rights of a statutory tenancy is hard to define, as a creature of statute, but it has been held to confer a purely personal right of continuing occupation

---

221 *Bradshaw v Baldwin-Wiseman* (1985) 17 HLR 260, CA.
222 Where two persons held a protected tenancy, but one of them alone occupied the property on its termination, that person alone was entitled to become the statutory tenant: *Lloyd v Sadler* [1978] QB 774, [1978] 2 All ER 529, CA.
223 Under RA 1977, Sch 15, Pt I, Case 5.
224 *Tideway Investment and Property Holdings v Wellwood* [1952] Ch 791, [1952] 2 All ER 514, CA.
225 *Smalley v Quarrier* [1975] 2 All ER 688, [1975] 1 WLR 938, CA. If a statutory tenant goes bankrupt, this is not ipso facto a ground for possession: *Sutton v Dorf* [1932] 2 KB 304.
226 *Killick v Roberts* [1991] 4 All ER 289, CA.

of the dwelling house, provided the tenant continues to comply with the residence requirement of RA 1977, s 2(1)(a); he has no estate in the land concerned.[227] Thus a statutory tenant who sub-lets the whole house or flat concerned loses their status as statutory tenant automatically, by ceasing to comply with the statutory residence requirement.[228] There are, nevertheless, some proprietary attributes of a statutory tenancy, such as a right to possession or a status of irremovability,[229] until such time if any as the court orders possession against the statutory tenant under RA 1977, s 98. A statutory tenant has also the right to treat any person entering without his permission as a trespasser.[230]

A statutory tenancy may be assigned, under a statutory procedure, by a statutory tenant to another person with the (formal) agreement of the landlord.[231] Where no formal agreement had been made, but the landlord's agent had represented to the tenant that she and her daughter now held a joint (statutory) tenancy, the landlord was estopped from going back on his word, seeing that the mother had, as a result of the representation, given up her priority housing status.[232] This shows the remarkable operation of equity, since it would probably not be possible for the statutory tenant by agreement with the landlord to transfer that tenancy to herself and her daughter jointly.

(ii) Succession to statutory tenancies

There is a scheme for succession to a statutory tenancy on the death of the statutory tenant. Its operation was curtailed in relation to deaths on or after 15 January 1989 and for the sake of simplicity the following deals only with those rules.

DEATH OF ORIGINAL TENANT

The rules differentiate between the position of a surviving spouse, who has the privilege of succession to a statutory tenancy, and of a family member, who succeeds, if at all, to an assured periodic tenancy by succession under the less secure assured tenancy regime of the Housing Act 1988.[233]

227 *Jessamine Investment Co v Schwartz* [1978] QB 264, [1976] 3 All ER 521, CA; *Metropolitan Properties Ltd v Cronan* (1982) 44 P & CR 1, CA. But a statutory tenant held an interest within the Insolvency Act 1986, s 182 to seek a vesting order where a head tenancy had been terminated following the head lessee's insolvency: *Re Vedmay Ltd* [1994] 1 EGLR 74.

228 *Haskins v Lewis* [1931] 2 KB 1, CA; *Skinner v Geary* [1931] 2 KB 546, CA. If a statutory tenant sub-lets part of the house or flat, security is retained as a rule: *Berkeley v Papadoyannis* [1954] 2 QB 149, [1954] 2 All ER 409, CA.

229 Which enabled a statutory tenant in equity to resist a claim for possession by a mortgagee who wished to remove the tenant rather than enforce the mortgage: *Quennell v Maltby* [1979] 1 All ER 568, [1979] 1 WLR 318, CA.

230 *Keeves v Dean* [1924] 1 KB 685 at 694, CA.

231 RA 1977, Sch 1, para 13.

232 *Daejan Properties Ltd v Mahoney* [1995] 2 EGLR 75, CA.

233 Such a tenancy is, however, an assured and not an assured shorthold tenancy even if it arises under the post 27 February 1997 regime: Housing Act 1988, Sch 2A, para 7.

A *surviving spouse* of the original tenant is entitled to succeed to the statutory tenancy, provided that the claimant occupies the dwelling house as his residence. A person living with the original tenant (eg as his cohabitee) as his or her wife or husband is treated by legislative extension as a surviving spouse.[234] Until this change in the law, a cohabitee would have had to claim as being a member of the deceased tenant's 'family'.[235] However, a single sex partner living with the tenant in a long-term homosexual relationship at the date of his death could not claim a succession as a surviving spouse, as the statute makes use of a 'gender-specific' expression, which necessarily excludes such claimants.[236]

A *member of the family* of the deceased statutory tenant cannot take the tenancy by succession if there is a surviving spouse. Subject to that, the family member claimant cannot obtain a succession unless he or she has resided in the dwelling house immediately before the original tenant's death and for a minimum period of two years immediately before then.[237] The family member, whether the succession is a first or a second succession, the latter following the death of a successor surviving spouse, obtains an assured tenancy by succession, whose terms are governed by statute, and which are in principle the same as those of the tenancy held by the predecessor immediately before his death, except that the tenancy is converted by the Housing Act 1988, s 39(5) and (6) from being a statutory tenancy into an assured periodic tenancy by succession. This assured periodic tenancy by succession is an estate in land, but it is probable that the burdens of the previous statutory tenancy would continue to bind the successor tenant, but not the original rent, if the rent for the previous tenancy was fixed on assumptions which do not apply to the fixing of a rent under an assured tenancy. Hence, where a registered rent had been calculated without paying any regard to the tenant's breaches of repairing covenant, it was held that a rent assessment committee were entitled, in determining the open market rent, to reduce the rent in order to take the breaches of covenant of the predecessor tenant into account.[238]

DEATH OF FIRST SUCCESSOR

If on the death of the first successor, the first successor was still a statutory tenant,[239] the succession of any claimant is to be to an assured periodic tenancy of the dwelling

---

234 RA 1977, Sch 1, para 2(2). If there is more than one such person, the claimant is to be decided by agreement, or by the court in default of agreement: RA 1977, Sch 1, para 2(3).
235 As in eg *Dyson Holdings Ltd v Fox* [1976] QB 503, [1975] 3 All ER 1030, CA.
236 *Fitzpatrick v Sterling Housing Association Ltd* [1999] 4 All ER 705, HL. *Harrogate BC v Simpson* (1984) 17 HLR 205 (which has the same result for secure tenancies) was approved on this point.
237 RA 1977, Sch 1, para 3.
238 *N & D (London) Ltd v Gadsdon* [1992] 1 EGLR 112.
239 This will be impossible if the first successor was a member of the original tenant's family and the death of the original tenant took place on or after 15 January 1989, whereupon the succession will be to an assured tenancy by succession, which is a single succession.

house by succession.[240] A person who was a member of the original tenant's family immediately before that tenant's death and also a member of the first successor's family immediately before the first successor's death, is entitled to claim an assured periodic tenancy by succession. The claimant must have resided in the dwelling house with the first successor at the time of, and for the period of two years immediately before the first successor's death.[241]

(iii) Further principles applicable to succession

Where a claimant had a permanent home elsewhere, the claim to succeed to a statutory tenancy failed, and the residence of the claimant in the tenant's home was found to be transient, given that the claimant continued to maintain her other home.[242] The residence must simply be in the same house as the tenant, so that it need not necessarily be shown that the claimant was part of the latter's household.

The term 'family' is interpreted in the popular sense and is not confined to blood relatives: it includes adopted children, and also those accepted into the tenant's family.[243] More interestingly, a divided House of Lords has now ruled by a narrow majority that a person who is a same sex partner of a deceased statutory tenant is entitled in principle to claim a succession as a member of that person's family.[244] To the majority, the word 'family' did not, having regard to the progressive development of public and professional opinion at home and abroad, connote a legal relationship. It could refer to a member of the relevant family unit or a member of a broadly recognisable de facto family nexus.[245] If a single sex partner could show mutual interdependence, sharing of living accommodation and mutual love, commitment and support, the surviving partner could qualify as a family member. Long residence is, however, insufficient by itself.[246] Occupation by a friend as a convenience would not suffice. A person treated by the tenant as her 'nephew', and who formed part of her household, failed in a succession claim.[247] This result may depend on its special facts.

240 RA 1977, Sch 1, para 5.
241 RA 1977, Sch 1, para 6. If there is more than one claimant, the question is either resolved by agreement or the court.
242 *Swanbrae Ltd v Elliott* (1986) 19 HLR 86, CA.
243 *Brock v Wollams* [1949] 2 KB 388, [1949] 1 All ER 715, CA.
244 *Fitzpatrick v Sterling Housing Association Ltd* [1999] 4 All ER 705. The claimant succeeded in this case owing to the long term, caring nature of the relationship. Compare *Brashi v Stahl Associates Co* 544 NYS 2d 784 (1989), cited by Lord Slynn at 715.
245 To the minority, however, there was no *de jure* relationship to which a homosexual relationship was equivalent (*Fitzpatrick v Sterling Housing Association Ltd* [1999] 4 All ER 705 at 739 per Lord Hutton); Lord Hobhouse considered that, apart from this point *Carega Properties SA (formerly Joram Developments Ltd) v Sharratt* [1979] 2 All ER 1084, [1979] 1 WLR 928, HL, bound the House of Lords to rule against the claimant.
246 *Sefton Holdings Ltd v Cairns* [1988] 2 FLR 109, CA (almost 50 years insufficient).
247 *Carega Properties SA (formerly Joram Developments Ltd) v Sharratt* [1979] 2 All ER 1084, [1979] 1 WLR 928, HL, as did a resident housekeeper: *Darnell v Millward* [1951] 1 All ER 88.

Terms and conditions of statutory tenancies

By RA 1977, s 3(1), so long as he retains possession, a statutory tenant is bound to observe and is entitled to the benefit of all the terms and conditions of the protected tenancy existing immediately beforehand, so far as consistent with the provisions of RA 1977. It is a condition of a statutory tenancy (RA 1977, s 3(2)) that the tenant must afford to the landlord access to the dwelling house and all reasonable facilities for executing any repairs which he is entitled to execute.

RA 1977, s 3(1) imports into the statutory tenancy all express obligations which run with the land and, indeed, any covenant which is of any benefit to the parties as such, for example, for the provision of personal services to the tenant.[248] Therefore, express and implied repairing obligations of either party are carried into the statutory tenancy, as are landlords' statute-implied repairing obligations under LTA 1985, ss 11-16 and his obligations under the Defective Premises Act 1972. So as not unduly to burden the landlord, purely personal covenants which are collateral to the protected tenancy are not carried into a statutory tenancy, but an obligation to pay £40 towards redecoration on quitting was held capable of running with the land and so of binding a statutory tenant.[249]

Statutory tenants are subject to special consent rules in relation to improvements: absolute prohibitions on these are banned, and the landlord cannot unreasonably withhold his consent to an improvement. If he does withhold his consent, he must prove that he had reasonable grounds for doing so.[250]

Termination of statutory tenancies

A statutory tenant retains his status only, by RA 1977, s 2(1)(a), 'if and so long as he occupies the dwelling house as his residence'. There are now discussed three ways in which the status of statutory tenant may be lost by non-compliance with the residence requirement,[251] and each of these is examined in what follows.[252] In such cases it is not necessary for the landlord to prove a statutory ground for possession.

---

248 *Engvall v Ideal Flats Ltd* [1945] KB 205, [1945] 1 All ER 230, CA.
249 *Boyer v Warbey* [1953] 1 QB 234, [1952] 2 All ER 976, CA.
250 Housing Act 1980, ss 81-83.
251 In addition, a statutory tenancy may be surrendered at common law; also, a statutory tenant is entitled to put an end to his or her statutory tenancy by a written notice of a length sufficient to end the previous contractual tenancy (RA 1977, s 3(3)), subject to a minimum period of four weeks (Protection from Eviction Act 1977, s 5). If the contractual tenancy was fixed term a three month notice to terminate the statutory tenancy is required (RA 1977, s 3(3)).
252 The onus of proof in each case is on the landlord: see eg *Roland House Gardens Ltd v Cravitz* (1974) 29 P & CR 432, CA.

(i) Occupation by tenant's spouse or ex-spouse

Where the tenant ceases permanently to occupy the dwelling house, occupation by his wife has been held to be sufficient for the purposes of RA 1977, s 2(1)(a), and the tenant remains statutory tenant, even if the parties are separated.[253] This will not apply if the house was never the matrimonial home.[254] Therefore, where a statutory tenant left, and eventually returned, leaving his wife in occupation of the house in between, he retained his statutory tenancy, in the absence of evidence of a surrender of it.[255]

If the parties are divorced, or judicially separated (in either case by court order) an occupation by that statutory tenant's ex-wife is not his occupation, and if he is out of occupation, with no intention to return, security is lost.[256] The same rule applies in the case of a statutory tenant's mistress.[257] The occupation of a wife is deemed to be that of the tenant; that of a divorced wife etc, cannot be so deemed, and the occupier is a mere licensee. In the case of wives, the court has power in divorce, nullity or judicial separation proceedings, to transfer a statutory tenancy to the wife.[258]

(ii) Permanent absence of tenant

Where a landlord proves that the tenant is permanently absent from the dwelling house with no intention to return, the tenant ceases to be a statutory tenant. A sufficiently prolonged absence, without any objective evidence of the necessary intention, such as the presence of the tenant's furniture, will enable the court to infer an abandonment of occupation, but it is open to the tenant to show an intention to return, backed by objective indicia such as the occupation of the house by his relatives (see below).[259] The question of intention to return is one of fact, but there must be a real hope of return coupled with a practical possibility of its fulfilment within a reasonable time.[260] Thus, where a tenant who moved out of her accommodation pending refurbishment did not, for some six months after the completion of the works, definitely indicate to the landlord that she intended to resume her residence there, her intention to return was held to be too contingent; she lost the statutory tenancy as a result.[261] In

---

253 *Brown v Draper* [1944] KB 309, [1944] 1 All ER 246, CA; *Hoggett v Hoggett* (1979) 39 P & CR 121; see now Matrimonial Homes Act 1983, s 1(6).

254 *Hall v King* [1988] 1 FLR 376, CA.

255 *Hulme v Langford* (1985) 50 P & CR 199, CA.

256 *Metropolitan Properties Ltd v Cronan* (1982) 44 P & CR 1, CA.

257 *Colin Smith Music Ltd v Ridge* [1975] 1 All ER 290, [1975] 1 WLR 463, CA, where the statutory tenant had, effectually, surrendered the tenancy.

258 Matrimonial Homes Act 1983, Sch 1. If the tenancy was subject to a suspended possession order, this infirmity will equally affect the tenancy transferred to the spouse: *Church Comrs for England v Al-Emarah* (1996) 72 P & CR D45, CA.

259 *Brown v Brash and Ambrose* [1948] 2 KB 247, [1948] 1 All ER 922, CA.

260 *Gofor Investments Ltd v Roberts* (1975) 29 P & R 366, CA.

261 *Robert Thackray's Settled Estates Ltd v Kaye* [1989] 1 EGLR 127, CA; Bridge [1989] Conv 450.

one case,[262] a tenant who was absent for seven years and who also held the freehold of other premises, was held to have lost his status of statutory tenant. However, a finding that a tenant had a genuine intention to return after 10 years enabled him to retain his statutory tenancy.[263] Moreover, there is a difference between cases where the tenant is voluntarily absent, and those where he is absent due to factors he cannot control, or where he is away for, say, an extended but finite absence.[264] In the latter instances, it may be easier for the tenant to retain security, as the court may more readily infer a genuine intention to return. For example, a tenant retained his statutory tenancy despite being in prison,[265] and also while detained in hospital due to insanity.[266] In all cases, as said, there must be some objective evidence of intention to return, such as retained furniture, or the presence of a relative in the premises to look after them, to back up the tenant's inward intention to return.[267]

(iii)   Two-home tenants

A third way in which security may be lost is if the landlord proves that the tenant has another home and he is using the house of which he is statutory tenant as a convenient resort only.[268] But the fact that the tenant has another home is, apparently, not enough of itself to deprive him of his statutory tenancy,[269] although it would be harder for an assured tenant to retain his tenancy owing to the statutory requirement of occupation as his only or principal home. Some generous results have been reached. A person may even occupy his own home for most of the time and the house held under a statutory tenancy more rarely or for a limited purpose: where this is so, it is a question of fact and degree whether the second house is occupied as his second home and, therefore, whether it remains held under a statutory tenancy.[270] Where, therefore, a tenant occupied a flat for some six years and then returned to his home abroad, making only occasional trips to the UK, he failed to retain his statutory tenancy as it was impossible to say that he occupied the flat as a home: his visits were too infrequent even by the generous two homes tenant standard.[271]

---

262 *Duke v Porter* [1986] 2 EGLR 101, CA.
263 *Gofor Investments Ltd v Roberts* (1975) 29 P & CR 366, CA; also *Brickfield Properties Ltd v Hughes* (1987) 20 HLR 108, CA (eight-year absence not sufficient to cost tenant security where he satisfied judge that he might well retire to the dwelling house concerned); Bridge [1988] Conv 300. The rule applying to assured tenancies is much stricter: even a comparatively short absence by the tenant can cost him his security: see *Ujima Housing Association v Ansah* (1997) 30 HLR 831, CA.
264 See eg *Richards v Green* [1983] 2 EGLR 104, CA.
265 *Maxted v McAll* [1952] CPL 185, CA.
266 *Tickner v Hearn* [1961] 1 All ER 65, [1960] 1 WLR 1406, CA.
267 See *Brown v Brash and Ambrose* [1948] 2 KB 247, [1948] 1 All ER 922, CA.
268 As in *Regalian Securities Ltd v Scheuer* (1982) 47 P & CR 362, CA.
269 *Langford Property Co v Tureman* [1949] 1 KB 29, CA.
270 *Hampstead Way Investments Ltd v Lewis-Weare* [1985] 1 All ER 564; Wilkinson (1985) 135 NLJ 357; PF Smith [1985] Conv 224.
271 *D J Crocker Securities (Portsmouth) Ltd v Johal* [1989] 2 EGLR 102, CA.

If, by contrast, the tenant holds two adjoining houses, originally from the same landlord, and lives in one and sleeps in the other (or divides his living activities in some other way between the two houses), it is a question of fact whether he, as RA 1977, s 2(1)(a) requires, resides in both houses as one complete unit, in which case he has security, or whether each unit is self-contained and occupied separately, in which case the tenant has no statutory tenancy in respect of either unit of habitation.[272]

V   PROTECTION OF SUB-TENANCIES

A group of rather difficult provisions exist to prevent a sub-tenant with a house or flat losing Rent Act protection simply on account of the termination of the head tenancy on which, at common law, the sub-lease depends for its existence. These fall into two groups: those dealing with repossession within RA 1977 against the sub-tenant (RA 1977, ss 137(1) and (2)) and a self-standing provision (RA 1977, s 137(3)).

Protection of sub-tenant where head tenant is dispossessed within RA 1977

So as to reverse the common law principle that the termination of a head tenancy entails automatically the ending of any sub-lease derived out of it, by RA 1977, s 137(1), the determination in proceedings for possession of a head tenancy of a dwelling house let to a protected or statutory tenant will not automatically determine any lawful sub-tenancy of the whole or any part. By RA 1977, s 137(2), where a head tenancy of a dwelling house is determined in possession proceedings by the court, any lawful sub-tenant of the dwelling house or any part is deemed to hold directly from the head landlord on the same terms as if the head 'statutorily protected tenancy' had continued.[273]

RA 1977, s 137(1) and (2) require that the sub-tenancy is lawful. A sub-letting in breach of an absolute prohibition against sub-letting in the head tenancy is outside the protection of these provisions.[274] Where a covenant allows only consensual sub-lettings for a term not exceeding six months in any year, any sub-lettings apart from these were taken to be unlawful, including a six-month periodic sub-tenancy.[275] While

---

272 *Wimbush v Cibulia* [1949] 2 KB 564, [1949] 2 All ER 432, CA; *Kavanagh v Lyroudias* [1985] 1 All ER 560, CA.

273 'Statutorily protected tenancy' is defined by RA 1977, s 137(4) as meaning: (a) a protected or statutory tenancy under the 1977 Act; (b) a protected occupancy or statutory tenancy under the Rent (Agriculture) Act 1976; (c) a tenancy of an agricultural holding within the Agricultural Holdings Act 1986; (d) a farm business tenancy within the Agricultural Tenancies Act 1995; and most long tenancies fall within RA 1977, s 137 by s 137(5).

274 *Oak Property Co Ltd v Chapman* [1947] KB 886, [1947] 2 All ER 1, CA.

275 *Henry Smith's Charity Trustees v Willson* [1983] QB 316, [1983] 1 All ER 73, CA; also *Patoner Ltd v Alexandrakis* [1984] 2 EGLR 124; and *Patoner Ltd v Lowe* [1985] 2 EGLR 154, CA. A strict approach thus applies.

the landlord may have waived an initially unlawful sub-letting by the time of the possession hearing, the strict common law principle of waiver does not apply as the landlord may have no choice (owing to the statutory protection scheme) but to accept the rent, and so a demand or acceptance of rent after the breach takes place will not ipso facto disentitle the landlord to claim possession against the sub-tenant. The question of whether the breach has been condoned is one of fact.[276]

RA 1977, s 137(3)

Where there is a sub-tenancy of a dwelling house which forms part only of the premises let as a whole under a superior tenancy which is *not* a statutorily protected tenancy, on termination of that superior tenancy, the sub-tenant will, in principle, retain such protection as RA 1977, s 137 offers him, by the statutory fiction that the dwelling house subject to the sub-tenancy is deemed to be let separately from the remainder of the premises at a rent equal to the just proportion of the rent under the superior tenancy (RA 1977, s 137(3)).[277] The purpose of the Rent Acts being to confer security of tenure on residential occupiers, this provision is considered to be self-standing. This is an important aspect to the provision in these days where most re-possession actions are likely to be against statutory tenants.

Further comments on RA 1977, s 137(1) and (2)

RA 1977, s 137(1) protects sub-tenants of Rent Act-protected tenants where the court orders possession against the head tenant on one of the discretionary grounds. If it orders possession on a mandatory ground, RA 1977, s 137(1) has no application, and any sub-tenancy falls with the head tenancy.

If the head tenant sub-lets the whole dwelling house at a time when he is statutory tenant, then, as the residence requirement of RA 1977, s 2(1) is not satisfied, the sub-tenancy cannot be statutorily protected and RA 1977, s 137 will not apply to it.[278] The same result follows, where for some other reason, such as the sub-tenant holding under a head tenant who is a resident landlord, there is no protected (sub-) tenancy. While a sub-letting of the whole dwelling house causes a statutory tenancy to cease, the sub-tenancy, if 'lawful', falls within RA 1977, s 137 but it is subject to RA 1977, Sch 15, Pt I, Case 6.[279] However, there must be some doubt as to whether a statutory tenant is entitled lawfully to sub-let, so as to create a term binding on the landlord, as he has no proprietary interest in the land.

276　*Henry Smith's Charity Trustees v Willson* [1983] QB 316, [1983] 1 All ER 73, CA.
277　This difficult provision originated in Housing Repairs and Rents Act 1954 ,s 41.
278　*Stanley v Compton* [1951] 1 All ER 859 at 863, CA. The date at which the status of the sub-tenant is decided is that of the determination of the head tenancy: *Jessamine Investment Co v Schwartz* [1978] QB 264, [1976] 3 All ER 521, CA.
279　*Henry Smith's Charity Trustees v Willson* [1983] QB 316, [1983] 1 All ER 73, CA

By RA 1977, s 137(2), where the head tenant's protected tenancy is determined, in proceedings based on discretionary grounds, by the landlord, any lawful sub-tenant continues to be a 'tenant' under RA 1977, and his position must be considered separately. He is still vulnerable to a discretionary order for possession under RA 1977, s 98(1) and Sch 15, Pt I.[280] Therefore, if the tenant has gone, the landlord will have to prove any such grounds separately against the sub-tenant. If a statutory head tenancy has been determined, as by forfeiture, RA 1977, s 137(2) deems any sub-tenant to hold as statutory tenant, to avoid the latter being given a more valuable right in the premises than his erstwhile landlord held.[281]

RA 1977, s 137(3)

Problems have arisen where the head lessee holds the premises for business purposes, thus outside RA 1977, and then sub-lets part of the premises to a sub-tenant who holds for residential purposes. RA 1977, s 137(3) comes into play. The provision is not a model of conspicuous clarity.[282] Thanks to recent rulings, in combined appeals by the Court of Appeal, RA 1977, s 137(3) prevents a sub-tenant losing the protection of RA 1977 merely on account of the termination, by surrender or otherwise, of the head lessee's non-protected tenancy.[283] Parliament was in their plain view concerned to protect a sub-tenant's home after the superior lease fell in.[284] Thus, say, a head tenant of a shop and flat above who sub-lets the flat on the face of it confers Rent Act protection on the sub-tenant of the flat, in respect of his home, who holds a separate letting of a 'dwelling house'. The focus is no longer to be on the question of whether the headlease falls within the Landlord and Tenant Act 1954, Pt II, to decide on the status of the sub-tenancy of any part of the premises. Instead, if in any doubt, the courts are to examine the purpose of the sub-letting, or the use made by the sub-

---

280 *Leith Properties Ltd v Springer* [1982] 3 All ER 731 at 736, CA; Martin [1983] Conv 155.

281 *John Lyon Grammar School v James* [1995] 4 All ER 740, CA.

282 *Maunsell v Olins* [1975] AC 373 at 385. Lord Reid stigmatised the provision as being 'unusually difficult' (at 382). It was there held that 'premises' did not apply to a person holding a sub-tenancy of a cottage on a farm.

283 *Wellcome Trust Ltd v Hamad* [1998] 1 All ER 657, [1998] L & TR 130; see Cafferkey [1999] Conv 232; also PF Smith (1998) 18 RRLR 109. For a convincing criticism of the previous decision of *Pittalis v Grant* [1989] QB 605, [1989] 2 All ER 622, which decision was held in *Hamad* to have been *per incuriam*, see Rodgers [1990] Conv 204.

284 Thus the Court of Appeal in the combined appeals referred to Scrutton LJ (the 'chief architect of the ... rent restriction system': per Harman LJ in *Parkin v Scott* (1965) 196 Estates Gazette 989) in *Hicks v Snook* (1928) 27 LGR 175, Scrutton LJ refuted an argument that a sub-tenant holding a flat could not retain Rent Act protection merely because there was a head letting of a shop in the same premises. They also cited from Denning LJ in *Feyereisel v Turnidge* [1952] 2 QB 29 at 37, placing emphasis on the requirement of a tenancy of a dwelling house and on personal security to a tenant in relation to his home. This turn of reasoning would now seem to have been approved by the House of Lords (*Uratemp Ventures Ltd v Collins* [2001] UKHL 43, [2002] 1 AC 301) albeit in the context of whether a single room was capable of being a 'dwelling house'.

tenant, if lawful, of their premises, in deciding whether RA 1977, s 137(3) applies.[285] RA 1977, s 137(3) is thus a free-standing provision, so that the sub-tenant can invoke directly the provisions of RA 1977, ss 1 and 2, and is not subject to the restriction applying to RA 1977, s 137(2), that the head tenancy must be protected or statutory.[286]

The interpretation of RA 1977, s 137(3) has been rendered consistent with the way the Housing Act 1988, s 18 (applying to assured tenancies) operates, because this provision contains no restrictions on the type of tenancy being held by the head tenant.[287] However, on one view, the rulings of the Court of Appeal place insufficient emphasis on the impact of the abolition as from 1980 of controlled tenancies, and so the limitation, as a possible result, of Rent Act protection to wholly residential head and sub-tenancies. It could, with equal force, be said that the decision is a welcome move away from the dichotomy between residential and business tenancies.

RA 1977, s 137 (3) (as will be appreciated from the foregoing) notionally splits up the premises, so that each part is taken to be let to the head tenant on separate tenancies.[288] Thus if T, a head tenant, sub-lets part of the premises to X, and the rental or rateable value of T's premises takes it outside Rent Act protection, X's sub-tenancy is caught, if X is a residential sub-lessee, provided X's part falls within these limits. If T has sub-let all parts of the premises, so depriving himself in any event of Rent Act protection, there is equally no reason why sub-tenants of parts should be denied protection of their individual parts of the premises. Clearly, as it has developed, RA 1977, s 137(3) may provide a formidable obstacle to landlords claiming possession against residential statutory sub-tenants who have not broken their tenancy obligations.

VI OTHER PROVISIONS

Two sets of provisions in RA 1977 modify the common law rights of the landlord with regard to distress and the taking of capital sums, and these are next noted.

Distress

No distress for rent of any dwelling house let on a protected or statutory tenancy is permitted except with the leave of the county court (RA 1977, s 147(1)) which has wide powers of adjournment and the like (RA 1977, s 100).

---

285 In effect, the result of the *Wellcome Trust Ltd v Hamad* [1998] 1 All ER 657, [1998] L & TR 130 appeals require the courts to read RA 1977, s 137(3) together with the proviso to RA 1977, s 24(3).
286 *Laimond Properties Ltd v Al-Shakarchi* (1998) 30 HLR 1099, CA.
287 As noted by Martin *Residential Tenancies* (2nd edn) p 196.
288 See *Laimond Properties Ltd v Al-Shakarchi* (1998) 30 HLR 1099, CA; [1999] Conv 248 (Martin).

Premiums

RA 1977 prevents the landlord, on the grant of a protected tenancy, from charging a premium to the tenant, and so evading the rent control provisions of the Act. It is an offence for any person[289] to require the payment of any premium (as widely defined in RA 1977, s 128(1)) in addition to rent, as a condition of the grant, renewal or continuance of a protected tenancy.[290] There are also provisions aimed at deterring the taking of a premium on assignment of a protected tenancy.[291] It is also an offence for any person (such as an agent) to receive such a premium in addition to rent (RA 1977, s 119(2)). While a lump sum in cash would amount to a premium, the prohibition appears also to include any consideration expressed in money conferring a benefit on the landlord and a detriment to the tenant.[292] There are no provisions to prohibit the taking of a premium on the grant of a statutory tenancy, as such tenancies arise under RA 1977. Certain rules restrict the sums a statutory tenant may require from an assignee in those cases where a statutory tenancy is assigned.[293]

289 Whether the landlord or eg his agent: see *Farrell v Alexander* [1977] AC 59, [1976] 2 All ER 721, HL; *Saleh v Robinson* [1988] 2 EGLR 126, CA.
290 Any term in a contract requiring the payment of a prohibited premium is void; and the court has powers to enable the tenant to recover the payment of such sums (RA 1977, s 125(1)).
291 RA 1977, s 120.
292 *Elmdene Estates Ltd v White* [1960] AC 528, [1960] 1 All ER 306, HL (where a prospective tenant was required to sell his house to a named third party connected to the landlord for less than its market value, as a condition of obtaining a protected tenancy).
293 RA 1977, Sch 1, Pt II, paras 12 and 14.

CHAPTER 15

Assured and assured shorthold tenancies

1   INTRODUCTION

Two forms of private-sector residential tenancy

The Housing Act 1988, Pt I created two forms of tenancy[1] for the private residential sector: assured and assured shorthold tenancies. When the scheme was originally conceived, unless the landlord elected to grant the tenant an assured shorthold tenancy, the tenancy was an assured tenancy. A fixed-term assured tenant may only be evicted from the house or flat concerned if the landlord is able to prove a statutory ground for possession even after the fixed term has expired. In the case of rent arrears, however, the landlord can in principle procure the removal of the tenant during a fixed-term assured tenancy. Because the government wished to deregulate rents, under an assured or assured shorthold tenancy, the landlord may charge the market rent for the premises. It is also generally easier to repossess the property let on an assured tenancy than on a Rent Act statutory tenancy, if only because the number of mandatory grounds for possession is larger in the case of an assured tenancy. At the same time an assured tenant has a much greater degree of security against eviction than have most assured shorthold tenants. For this reason, it causes no surprise that most private-sector residential tenancies appear to be the almost wholly insecure assured shorthold variety.

It now appears that the average length of occupancy by a private-sector residential tenant is about 15 months. Thus, in 1998/99, 41% of private tenants had been at their current address for less than one year, a further 25% less than three years and a further 10% less than five years.[2] Tenant insecurity is now a feature of the background to the relevant law. The reasons for this lie beyond the scope of this book. They may lie in the popularity with landlords of assured shorthold tenancies, but equally they may reflect

---

[1]   As opposed to a licence. It may be that the arrival of assured shorthold tenancies has reduced the incentives on owners to make use of licences.

[2]   DETR Housing Statistics Summary No 3 (1999).

the reality that in England and Wales, not a few private-sector tenants see renting as a stepping-stone to house purchase. At the same time, for many tenants from 'social landlords', such as housing associations, insecurity of tenure under the Housing Act 1988 (hereinafter HA 1988), which can be granted to them instead of the less insecure secure tenancies, could cause problems, especially when linked to high rents and tenant impecuniosity.

Some landlords have misused the freedom given to them by the current liberal legislative framework, as dramatically shown in a recent case.[3] In an assured tenancy, it was provided that the initial rent for the premises was to be £4,680 annually. However, there were to be rent reviews at annual intervals. As from the last review date the reviewed rent was to be £25,000 per annum. This term was not negotiated. The Court of Appeal rejected the idea that freedom of contract prevailed as between the landlord and tenant. Arden LJ thought that the rent clause did not in substance fix the rent but it was a provision enabling the landlord to recover possession outside the statutory possession scheme; it was a disallowed means of contracting out of HA 1988 and could not be enforced. The rent provision prevented the tenant from paying the genuine rent by providing for a sum which was never expected to be paid, and which sum was not rent at all.[4] This case does not disallow rent review provisions, but it requires that if parties to a private residential tenancy wish to end the tenancy, they may only do so within the limits of the statutory scheme.[5]

Apart from blatant attempts to evade the statutory framework, however, the balance of advantage shifted decisively in favour of landlords by changes made some eight years after the original assured tenancy scheme commenced. A tenancy which satisfies the criteria required to be an assured tenancy is, where entered into on or after 28 February 1997, presumed by statute to be an assured shorthold tenancy.[6] Such a tenancy requires landlords to seek an order for possession within a formal notice scheme on the simple ground that the tenancy has expired. Moreover, in accordance with a policy of deregulation, the formalities required to create an assured shorthold tenancy have been simplified. Thus, it is no longer a requirement that an assured shorthold tenancy should have a minimum fixed term of at least six months, although no order for or against any assured shorthold tenant can take effect until six months after the beginning of the tenancy.[7] However, a periodic assured shorthold tenancy is

---

3   *Bankway Properties Ltd v Pensfold-Dunsford* [2001] EWCA Civ 528, [2001] 2 EGLR 36. This tenancy was entered into in 1994, and so prior to the statutory presumption of the creation of an assured shorthold tenancy.

4   In *Bankway Properties Ltd v Pensfold-Dunsford* [2001] EWCA Civ 528, [2001] 2 EGLR 36 at paras 67-68, Pill LJ thought that the rent clause was inconsistent with the stated purpose of the parties to create an assured as opposed to an assured shorthold tenancy.

5   As was the case with the Rent Acts (see *Solle v Butcher* [1950] 1 KB 671) equity retains a power to rescind an agreement for an assured tenancy on the ground of a mutual misapprehension by the parties as to their respective rights: *Nutt v Read* (1999) 32 HLR 671.

6   HA 1988, s 19A.

7   HA 1988, s 21(5)(c). The 'beginning of the tenancy' seems to refer to the date of its commencement: *Sidebotham v Holland* [1895] 1 QB 378, CA.

now allowed. The landlord need not any longer precede the grant of an assured shorthold tenancy with a prescribed form warning notice.[8] While HA 1988 regulates certain terms of all assured tenancies, such as in relation to assignments, the parties are generally free to agree on the type of tenancy, the terms and the rent (subject to rights of reference of an excessive shorthold tenancy rent and in the landlord to increase the rent).[9] If the tenancy is for a term of less than seven years, the repairing obligations of LTA 1985, s 11 will however apply to the landlord.

General requirements

The following principles are common to assured and assured shorthold tenancies alike.[10] HA 1988, s 1(1) provides that an assured tenancy is a tenancy under which a dwelling house is let as a separate dwelling. The test involves considering the terms of the tenancy agreement itself, not merely the nature of the property and the use to which it is put,[11] although a dwelling house seems to connote a structure with some degree of permanent attachment to land. It has thus been held that a letting of a houseboat cannot fall within the HA 1988 scheme.[12]

Because there must be a tenancy, a licence to occupy which is not a sham is not capable of being an assured shorthold or assured tenancy.[13] The expression 'tenancy' includes a sub-tenancy (HA 1988, s 45(1)) and a sub-tenant may validly be granted an assured shorthold or assured tenancy even if the head tenancy is not assured or assured shorthold.

The requirement of a 'dwelling house' in HA 1988, s 1 does not now exclude from protection a single room. To fall within the Act, the tenant must 'move and have his being' in his room,[14] and treat it as his home. Thus an exclusive single occupier of a room in an hotel who lived and slept permanently there, and regarded it as his home,

8   Save where an assured tenancy ends and a new tenancy is granted to replace it to the same tenant: if it is to be a shorthold tenancy, then it must be preceded by a prescribed form notice (Housing Act 1996, Sch 7, para 4).
9   For an example of an 'ill-drafted' tenancy agreement which was held to create an assured tenancy (the date of the agreement being in 1994) with certain additional rights conferred on secure tenants by the Secure Tenants' Charter, see *North British Housing Association v Sheridan* [1999] 2 EGLR 138.
10   The statutory scheme is applied with modifications in points of detail to agricultural workers, notably as set out in HA 1988, s 25 and Schs 2A and 3. The 1988 Act scheme applies even though the rent is low. An agricultural worker condition must be complied with (HA 1988, Sch 3).
11   *Andrews v Brewer* (1997) 30 HLR 203, CA.
12   *Chelsea Yacht & Boat Co Ltd v Pope* [2000] L & TR 401, CA. The test to decide on the requisite degree of attachment to land is the same as governs fixtures.
13   Nor is a person who occupies a flat as an almsperson a tenant, since the occupation is a personal privilege, applying the principle recognised in *Street v Mountford* [1985] AC 809 of beneficial occupation with no intention to create legal relations: *Gray v Taylor* [1998] 1 WLR 1093, CA.
14   *Curl v Angelo* [1948] 2 All ER 189 at 190 (Lord Greene MR).

held an assured tenancy (having held tenancies of this and other rooms since 1988). The House of Lords held that it was not necessary that the tenant should be able to cook meals in his room. They took into account the fact that social and economic changes in the last 40 years meant that food could be bought from the many fast-food and similar outlets now available.[15]

If, however, the tenancy agreement grants a tenant in addition to the exclusive possession of his room, a right to shared use of other rooms, the question is then whether the room (or rooms) of which he has exclusive possession are his 'dwelling house' within HA 1988, or only part of it. In the latter case the tenancy cannot fall within HA 1988, s 1. The nature and extent of the right must be examined[16] and also the character of the other rooms. If the tenant has a right to occupy in common with and at the same time as the landlord a living room (such as a kitchen or bedroom) this is such an invasion of the latter's privacy that Parliament cannot have intended to confer security of tenure on the tenant.[17]

There have been problems in drawing the line between security and no tenancy arising from sharing of accommodation with the landlord who lives in the same premises as the tenant. In relation to the Rent Acts, it was held that a tenant who shared the kitchen, garage, cool-house, conservatory and bathroom with the landlord did not have a protected tenancy as the whole house was in substance shared.[18] If such an arrangement were made today, the tenancy would be excluded from the Protection from Eviction Act 1977 (Protection from Eviction Act 1977, s 3A).[19] By contrast, where a tenant held a tenancy of a flat on the top floor of a house and had exclusive use of the living room, kitchen and a bedroom, but shared a bathroom and toilet with the landlord, the tenancy was protected. The tenant had the exclusive use of living rooms. The use of the shared bathroom and toilet was not enough to take the tenancy out of protection. These latter rooms were used by each party when occasion required. They were not living rooms.[20] Where a landlord has let off one floor of a house to a tenant and occupies another floor in the same house, provided he satisfies a statutory residence test, he ought to be able to rely on the resident landlord exclusion from assured

---

15 *Uratemp Ventures Ltd v Collins* [2001] UKHL 43, [2002] 1 All ER 46.
16 As was the case with the Rent Acts. Thus in *Hayward v Marshall* [1952] 2 QB 89, CA the tenant had the right to draw water in the landlord's kitchen. This did not take the tenancy out of the protection of the Rent Acts. The right was akin to an easement.
17 Per Lord Millett in *Uratemp Ventures Ltd v Collins* [2001] UKHL 43, [2002] 1 All ER 46 at para 58. The nature of shared rights may be difficult to decide. In the Rent Act case of *Goodrich v Paisner* [1957] AC 65, the tenant had a right to use a bedroom in common with the landlord. The House of Lords construed this as a right to alternating use with the landlord of this room, reasonable conduct being assumed. As the law then stood, it had to be assumed that Parliament did not wish to take such tenancies as that in issue out of protection.
18 *Neale v Del Soto* [1945] KB 144, CA.
19 With the result that the landlord does not need to take court proceedings to enforce his right to repossession of the premises on expiry of the tenancy (Protection from Eviction Act 1977, s 3).
20 *Cole v Harris* [1945] KB 474, CA.

tenancy status,[21] in those cases where an assured shorthold tenancy has not been granted. That would seem to be so even if the landlord shares a bathroom and wc with the tenant, since these are not living rooms.

Two additional specific residence conditions apply. If at any time during the tenancy these are not satisfied, it cannot be assured or assured shorthold because HA 1988, s 1(1) states that only 'if and so long as' these conditions are satisfied, can the tenancy fall within the HA 1988 regime.[22] The first such condition is that the tenant, or each of the joint tenants (where applicable), is an individual (HA 1988, s 1(1)(a)). The second is that the tenant or at least one of a number of joint tenants occupies the dwelling house as his only or principal home (HA 1988, s 1(1)(b)). The test of occupation as the only or principal home of the tenant is stricter than the statutory tenant residence test under RA 1977, s 2. Where, therefore, an assured tenant gave up physical possession of his flat for about one year, but left furniture there, he was taken no longer to be occupying the flat. The tenant had sub-let it to others, a step seemingly fatal to retaining any statutory protection, albeit that he had an intention to return.[23] If a tenant abandons the property with no intention of returning, the landlord would be able to regain possession from the tenant without recourse to any ground for possession, unless the tenancy is claimed by the tenant's wife in divorce, nullity or judicial separation proceedings. In that case the court has power to transfer the tenancy to the tenant's wife.[24]

Only an individual may hold an assured tenancy, so that a residential tenancy held by a company is not capable of being assured, and if the company licenses a person to occupy the dwelling house, he will hold as a mere licensee. If a tenancy of residential property is granted to an individual and a company as joint tenants, neither party has any kind of assured tenancy, owing to HA 1988, s 1(1)(a), which requires that *each* joint tenant must be an individual. Provided that, in the case of a tenancy granted to two or more joint tenants, each tenant is an individual, the effect of HA 1988, s 45(3) is apparently that only one of a larger number of joint tenants needs at any one time to comply with the residence requirement of HA 1988, s 1(1)(b). Thus L grants an assured shorthold tenancy for one year certain to A, B and C as joint tenants, A resides alone in the premises for the first six months and B and C reside there for the second six. L cannot terminate the tenancy early merely because at no time in the year were A, B and C resident together in the property.

21 HA 1988, Sch 1, para 10.
22 The intention of HA 1988 s 1(1) is to limit protection more narrowly than does the Housing Act 1985, s 79 in the case of secure tenancies: *Waltham Forest Community Based Housing v Fanning* [2001] L & TR 1, [2001] L & TR 588.
23 *Ujima Housing Association v Ansah* (1997) 30 HLR 831, CA; see Whalan 142 (1998) Sol Jo 308.
24 Matrimonial Causes Act 1983, Sch 1, as extended by HA 1988, Sch 17, para 34.

II TENANCIES WHICH CANNOT BE ASSURED OR ASSURED SHORTHOLD TENANCIES

General principles

There is a statutory list of tenancies which cannot be assured or assured shorthold. If a tenancy falls within any of the following categories, it is precluded from being assured shorthold or assured. If a residential tenancy is within an excluded class of tenancy, then once the tenancy expires, the tenant has virtually no statutory protection of his occupation. However, if the tenancy is not an excluded tenancy, the Protection from Eviction Act 1977, s 3 will apply to the tenant, so that the landlord will have to enforce his right to possession in court proceedings if the tenant is not willing to leave of his own accord, but no grounds for possession would need to be shown.

The statutory exclusions

The principal statutory exclusions are as follows.[25] Note that because the assured tenancy scheme was introduced only as from January 1989, a tenancy which was entered into before, or under a contract made before, 15 January 1989 cannot be an assured or an assured shorthold tenancy.[26]

(i) Dwelling houses with high rental or rateable values

A tenancy entered into on or after 1 April 1990 (except where the dwelling house had a rateable value on 31 March 1990, in pursuance of a contract made before 1 April 1990) and under which the rent for the time being is payable at a rate exceeding £25,000 a year is outside HA 1988, Pt I.[27]

(ii) Tenancies at a low rent

A tenancy under which for the time being no rent is payable is excluded from HA 1988, Pt I, as is a tenancy entered into on or after 1 April 1990 and under which the rent

---

25 In addition to the exclusions discussed in the text there should be noted the following exclusions, which correspond to similar provisions applying to the Rent Acts: (a) tenancies of licensed premises (HA 1988, Sch 1, para 5); lettings to students (HA 1988, Sch 1, para 8 and Assured etc Tenancies Regulations 1998, SI 1998/1967); (c) Crown tenancies (HA 1988, Sch 1, para 11); (d) tenancies granted by certain public sector landlords such as local authorities, as well as by fully mutual housing associations (HA 1988, Sch 1 para 12); (e) tenancies to which Landlord and Tenant Act 1954, Pt II applies (HA 1988, Sch 1, para 4).

26 HA 1988, Sch 1, para 1. Also excluded from the assured or assured shorthold tenancy regime are protected tenancies within the Rent Act 1977, a housing association tenancy within RA 1977, Pt VI, a secure tenancy and a relevant tenancy of a protected occupier within the Rent (Agriculture) Act 1976 (HA 1988, Sch 1, para 13).

27 HA 1988, Sch 1, para 2. Rateable values are to be ascertained under Sch 1, Pt II.

payable for the time being is payable at a rate, in the case of a dwelling house situated in Greater London, of £1,000 or less a year, and elsewhere of £250 or less a year.[28]

(iii) Tenancies of agricultural land

A tenancy under which agricultural land, exceeding two acres, is let together with the dwelling house, is excluded from the assured tenancies rules.[29]

This exclusion must be read with HA 1988, s 2(1),[30] under which, where a dwelling house is let together with[31] other land:

1 if and so long as the main purpose of the letting is the provision of a home for the tenant (or at least one of a number of joint tenants) the other land is treated as part of the dwelling house; and
2 if and so long as the main purpose of the letting is not the provision of a home as above, the tenancy is not assured.

Therefore, if agricultural land exceeding two acres is let together with a dwelling house, the tenancy is outside HA 1988, Pt I. If a dwelling house is let together with other land, as an adjunct to the house, the tenancy will be assured only if and so long as the purpose of the letting is the provision of a home for the tenant or at least one joint tenant. In that case, the land is treated as part of the house (HA 1988, s 2(1)(a)). If the purpose of the tenancy is not to provide a home, the tenancy cannot be assured (HA 1988, s 2(1)(b)), as where a dwelling house and land are let for non-residential purposes. This may require the court to discover the purpose of the tenancy from the terms of the lease, or, if this is not possible, from the intentions of the parties and, it would appear, the circumstances at the date of the claim for possession.[32] Unlike RA 1977, s 26(1), there is no presumption that agricultural land under 2 acres let with a dwelling house is within HA 1988. If the letting is mainly for residential purposes, the tenancy will fall within HA 1988 even though subsidiary agricultural activities are carried out on the land.

(iv) Holiday lettings

A tenancy whose purpose is to confer on the tenant the right to occupy the dwelling house for a holiday is not an assured or assured shorthold tenancy.[33] A holiday letting is an excluded tenancy.[34] As a result, the Protection from Eviction Act 1977, s 3 does

---

28 HA 1988, Sch 1, paras 3 and 3A.
29 HA 1988, Sch 1, para 6(1). 'Agricultural land' is as defined by General Rate Act 1967, s 26(3)(a).
30 Which is subject to HA 1988, Sch 1, para 6 above (HA 1988, s 2(2)).
31 This expression presumably has the same meaning as in RA 1977, ss 6 and 26.
32 *Prout v Hunter* [1924] 2 KB 736; *Uratemp Ventures Ltd v Collins* [2001] UKHL 43, [2002] 1 All ER 46 at para 37.
33 HA 1988, Sch 1, para 9.
34 Protection from Eviction Act 1977, s 3A(7).

not apply to the tenant. It is therefore lawful for the landlord to recover possession, once the tenancy has expired, without an order of court. Where the landlord lets off-season, he may recover possession mandatorily,[35] provided he complies with a notice requirement and the letting is for a term certain not exceeding eight months.

(v)   Resident landlords

A tenancy granted by a resident landlord cannot be an assured or assured shorthold tenancy.[36] Certain conditions must, however, be complied with for a tenancy to fall within the present exemption. The resident landlord exemption allows a landlord to let part or parts of his house while being reasonably sure that he will be able easily to regain possession, without having to prove any statutory grounds, and without needing to resort even to the procedures of HA 1988, s 21, as from the expiry or determination of the tenancy at common law.

The conditions for application of the exemption are largely similar to those which apply under RA 1977, s 12. Similar rules to those in RA 1977, Sch 2 apply where the resident landlord sells his reversion to another person, or where, following the death of a resident landlord, his executors sell the reversion to a third party.[37]

Accordingly, reference should be made to the discussion of RA 1977, s 12 and Sch 2, which applies to the present exception, subject to the modifications below, and to its construction. This is particularly so, it is thought, with regard to the meaning of the word 'building'; and the operation in law of the statutory disregard periods (which are the same in length as for RA 1977, s 12).

Some technical rules differ from the position under the RA 1977 and these must be noted.

1   The resident landlord, described as an 'individual', must occupy the house or flat concerned as his only or principal home at the time the tenancy was granted.[38] If the landlord has another house where he resides permanently, it may be impossible for him to claim that, for the purposes of the exception, a convenience residence on occasions in the house or flat concerned is sufficient. If he has two residences and divides his time between the two, it will presumably be a question of fact and degree, whether the residence in the tenanted premises is in his 'only or principal home' for the purposes of this exemption.

2   The rule for joint tenants is that if the reversion is held by two or more persons as joint tenants, only any one of them need satisfy the residence requirement at the date of the grant of the tenancy.[39] The same applies to the requirement that the landlord must be a resident landlord throughout: it needs only to be satisfied by

---

35   HA 1988, Sch 1, Pt II, ground 3.
36   HA 1988, Sch 1, para 10.
37   HA 1988, Sch 1, Pt III.
38   As opposed to 'as his residence' in RA 1977, s 12(1)(b).
39   HA 1988, Sch 1, para 10(2).

any one of a number of joint landlords. If A and B are joint landlords and A is resident in the statutory sense at the date of the grant of a tenancy to X and later B becomes resident and A leaves, the tenancy remains within the exemption because the residence requirement at the date of the grant was satisfied by A and later by B.

3   Where a resident landlord dies and the executors vest the reversion within the two-year period in a further resident landlord, where the landlord is a joint landlord, of whom at least one must be an individual, the tenancy is not an assured shorthold tenancy nor assured provided that at least one of the joint landlords occupies the house or flat as his only or principal home.[40]

4   Where the reversion is held under a trust of land, while disregard periods apply during the occupation of a beneficiary, occupation by any one of a number of beneficiaries will qualify. If an occupying beneficiary dies, a two-year period of disregard runs from the date of his death until another beneficiary occupies, during which the tenancy is exempt from HA 1988, Pt I.[41]

III   RULES SPECIFIC TO ASSURED SHORTHOLD TENANCIES

General considerations

(i)   Introduction

Assured shorthold tenancies are the main form of assured tenancy as from 28 February 1997. The tenancy is presumed to be an assured shorthold unless one of a number of exceptions, notably those listed below, applies.[42] Where any one of these applies, the tenancy will be assured and so much more advantageous to the tenant. The main 'non-shortholds' are as follows.

1   Where a notice is served before the tenancy is entered into by the landlord on the tenant. It must state that the tenancy is not to be an assured shorthold tenancy. A notice may also be served to the like effect after the tenancy has been entered into.

2   Where the tenancy contains express provision to the effect that the tenancy is not an assured shorthold tenancy.

3   Where there is an statutory assured periodic tenancy to which, under HA 1988, s 39, a person whose predecessor held a RA 1977 statutory tenancy may succeed.[43]

4   Where, following the transfer of local authority housing containing secure tenancies, the tenancies in consequence losing their secure status, the tenants affected holding as assured tenants from their new landlord.

40   HA 1988, Sch 1, Pt III, para 17(1) and (2).
41   HA 1988, Sch 1, para 18(1) and (2) as amended by Trusts of Land and Appointment of Trustees Act 1996.
42   HA 1988, s 19A and Sch 2A.
43   Except that if the landlord could have recovered possession against a statutory tenant who succeeded to a contractual protected shorthold tenancy, the tenancy following it is an assured shorthold tenancy (HA 1988, Sch 2A, para 4).

5   Where an assured tenant is offered a new tenancy by the landlord. Although ordinarily, the new tenancy is to be assured, there is a provision under which if the tenant serves a prescribed form notice on the landlord stating that the replacement tenancy is to be an assured shorthold, then the present exception does not apply.[44]

If an assured, as opposed to an assured shorthold, tenancy is granted or conferred as a result of the operation of one of the above exceptions, it is not terminable merely on account of the fact that, whether it is fixed-term or periodic, it has expired, and once the initial fixed term does expire, the tenancy will be followed by a statutory periodic assured tenancy.

(ii) Advantages of assured shortholds

An assured shorthold tenancy allows the landlord all the advantages of an assured tenancy, such as the right to charge a market rent. The landlord can recover possession easily enough in most cases by making use of HA 1988, s 21, although he cannot ask for an order for possession to take effect before the expiry of six months from the beginning of the original tenancy.[45] If the assured shorthold tenancy has been granted for a fixed term, then no order for possession can be made until after the expiry date of the fixed term,[46] which date, owing to the previous requirement, is likely to be for a minimum period of six months.

There are few restrictions on the landlord's rights, which is emphasised by the fact that there is no statutory right for a shorthold tenant holding a fixed-term tenancy which has expired to renew. Nor has a tenant holding a fixed-term assured shorthold tenancy any statutory right, as was available to protected shorthold tenants,[47] to terminate the fixed term early by notice.[48] If the tenant is granted a periodic assured shorthold tenancy, the landlord cannot, however, ask the court to repossess the property for the first six months, but the tenant will face a statutory review of the rent under HA 1988, s 13, as the tenancy is periodic, subject to a right of reference under HA 1988, s 14.

44   HA 1988, Sch 2A, para 7(2). An assured tenancy in respect of which the agricultural worker condition (HA 1988, Sch 3) is fulfilled is also an assured and not, in principle, an assured shorthold tenancy (HA 1988, Sch 2A, para 9).
45   HA 1988, s 21(5). The procedural rules applying as from 15 October 2001 are in CPR 1998, Pt 55. See Webber (2001) 5 L&T Rev 102; see also below.
46   HA 1988, s 21(1).
47   Under the Housing Act 1980, s 53(1).
48   The then government resisted an Opposition amendment to include such a right on the ground that allowing the right would deprive the landlord of the expectation of a rent during an initial fixed term: *Hansard* HC Standing Committee G, 7 March 1996, col 256.

(iii) Definition and conditions of grant of assured shorthold tenancies

An assured shorthold tenancy has recognised being 'notably less advantageous to tenants than a tenancy protected by the Rent Acts'.[49] From 28 February 1997, an assured shorthold tenancy may be fixed-term or periodic.[50] Prior to the 1996 Act, all assured shorthold tenancies had to be granted for a term certain of not less than six months (HA 1988, s 20(1)(a)).[51]

Where an assured shorthold tenancy was granted before 28 February 1997, a preliminary statutory notice must have been served by the landlord before the tenancy was entered into (HA 1988, s 20(1)(c)). The penalty for non-compliance is that the tenancy is an assured tenancy. Landlords seem to have fallen foul of this provision so often that it was abandoned for that reason.[52] This abandonment took place in the face of the fact that 'the persons who were likely to be offered tenancies of such properties[53] were also likely to be unable to assess for themselves the full legal and practical consequences of taking them'.[54] A generous principle of construction applies to errors contained in HA 1988, s 20 notices. The test is, as with notices to exercise a break clause, whether the error was obvious or evident and whether a reasonable recipient would have been left in no reasonable doubt as to the terms of the notice, despite the error.[55] A HA 1988, s 20 notice need only convey to a tenant the substance of the prescribed form so that a notice which misinformed a tenant as to his rights was still valid.[56]

Where service of the preliminary warning notice in relation to a tenancy granted under the original scheme of HA 1988 had been left to the last minute before the tenancy was granted, difficulties arose. Thus, a tenant was given a prescribed form notice on the morning of 18 December, for a six-month tenancy as from that day and took possession

---

49 *Manel v Memon* [2000] 2 EGLR 40 at 42, CA. This case was concerned with a HA 1988, s 20 notice in relation to a pre-1997 tenancy which was not in the form prescribed and was too defective to be regarded as being in substantially the same form as the then prescribed form notice. For a different view, see *Naidu v Yanula Properties Ltd* [2002] EWCA Civ 719.

50 For a case where it would have been to a tenant's advantage to claim a monthly assured tenancy, not the six-month fixed-term objectively held to have been granted see *Mundy v Hook* (1997) 30 HLR 551, CA.

51 See *Goodman v Evely* [2001] EWCA Civ 104 (a pre-1997 tenancy).

52 See House of Lords Committee on Housing Bill 1996 *Hansard* 12 June 1996, col 1851. For an example of the technical problems caused by the preliminary notice rule see *Panayi v Roberts* [1993] 2 EGLR 51, CA; PF Smith [1993] Conv 301; *Yenula Properties Ltd v Naidu* [2001] 31 EG 100 (CS); also below.

53 Ie at the lower end of the market, a fact recognised in *Uratemp Properties Ltd v Collins* [2001] UKHL 43, [2002] 1 All ER 46 at para 10 (Lord Bingham).

54 *Manel v Memon* [2000] 2 EGLR 40 at 42, CA (Nourse LJ).

55 *York v Casey* [1998] 2 EGLR 25, CA; *Clickex Ltd v McCann* [1999] 2 EGLR 63, CA (where, however, the dates on a HA 1988, s 20 notice and the tenancy agreement were in 'complete conflict' and a 'perplexity rather than an evident error', so voiding the s 20 notice and deeming the tenant an assured tenant in a pre-1997 tenancy).

56 *Kasseer v Freeman* [2001] EWCA Civ 2024, [2002] 11 EG 156; also *Ravenseft Properties Ltd v Hall* [2001] EWCA Civ 2034 (error as to start date of an assured shorthold tenancy); and *White v Chubb* [2001] EWCA Civ 2034, [2002] 11 EG 156.

that afternoon. His claim to an assured tenancy on the ground that he did not have the full six-month term required by the Act was dismissed. The fraction of the first day that he was not in possession was to be ignored as being unimportant; the tenancy was, by the narrowest of margins, a shorthold tenancy.[57]

Although an assured shorthold tenant of a tenancy granted as from the commencement of the 1997 rules (SI 1997/225) has no right to a preliminary notice, he may by notice in writing request[58] the landlord[59] to supply him with a written statement of certain terms of the tenancy, if these have not been already evidenced in writing. It is a criminal offence for a landlord to fail without reasonable excuse to comply with the tenant's request for 28 days as from receipt of the notice (HA 1988, s 20A(4)). The terms that fall within this requirement are basic. They are:

1   the date the tenancy began or came into being;
2   the rent payable and the dates on which it is payable;
3   any term providing for an express rent review; and
4   if the tenancy is fixed term, its length (HA 1988, s 20A(2)).

The statement provided is not conclusive evidence of what was agreed (HA 1988, s 20A(5)) so that the tenant may always challenge its accuracy, as where he refers the rent as being excessive.

Recovery of possession

Once the initial fixed term of an assured shorthold tenancy has expired, or a periodic assured shorthold tenancy has run its first six months (HA 1988, s 21(1)), the landlord may regain possession of the premises once he satisfies a few simple formal conditions.[60] If a fixed-term assured shorthold tenancy has been granted, the landlord may exceptionally terminate it during the term certain under statutory grounds applicable also to assured tenants, notably that relating to rent, which ground is next considered in view of its importance.

57   *Bedding v McCarthy* [1994] 2 EGLR 40, CA. On the facts, the notice was held to have been given before the granting of the tenancy.
58   Under HA 1988, s 20A. One of the many 'performance standards' laid down in the Housing Corporation's Assured Tenant's Charter (1998) is the 'right' to a written tenancy agreement (p 5).
59   Where appropriate, this means any joint landlord (HA 1988, s 20(A)(7)).
60   The Assured Tenant's Charter (Housing Corporation, 1998) contains the statement (which is no more than an aspiration or expectation) that 'your landlord should make every effort to help you stay in your home, applying for repossession and for an eviction order only where there is no reasonable alternative' (p 6). This aspiration applies only to assured shorthold tenants from registered social landlords.

(i) Repossession for rent arrears under ground 8

The landlord of an assured shorthold tenant may obtain a mandatory order for possession against an assured shorthold tenant on the ground of rent arrears, under ground 8 of Sch 2 to HA 1988.[61] This is one of the two mandatory grounds under which an assured fixed-term shorthold tenancy may be terminated before the end of the contractual term of the tenancy: the other is ground 2, relating to mortgagees, discussed in relation to assured tenancies.[62]

As a condition precedent to invoking ground 8, the landlord must have served a HA 1988, s 8 notice on the tenant, which specifies the rent arrears and gives the amounts alleged to be owed. The notice must be in the prescribed form and must comply with a number of further requirements listed below in relation to assured tenancies, notably that proceedings must be stated in the notice to begin not earlier than two weeks from the date specified in the notice. A HA 1988, s 8 notice relying on rent arrears, whether or not in the prescribed form, must give full particulars to the tenant if it is to be valid.[63] Ground 8 provides as follows.

Both at the date of service of the HA 1988, s 8 notice relating to the proceedings for possession and at the date of the hearing:
1   at least eight weeks' rent is unpaid, where rent is payable weekly or fortnightly;
2   at least two months' rent is unpaid, where the rent is payable monthly;[64] or
3   at least one quarter's rent is more than three months in arrears, where the rent is payable quarterly;
4   at least three months' rent is in more than three months' arrears, where the rent is payable yearly.

'Rent' means rent lawfully due from the tenant.[65] Unless a notice under the Landlord and Tenant Act 1987, s 48 has been served on the tenant, prior to the service of a HA 1988, s 8 notice, ground 8 cannot be relied upon.[66] This potential trap for landlords has

61   If the landlord wishes to levy a distress on the premises as an alternative to use of ground 8, he must obtain the leave of the county court: HA 1988, s 19(1), which applies equally to assured tenancies.

62   HA 1988, s 7(6), which also requires that the terms of the tenancy make provision for termination on the ground in question. These are now contained in CPR 1998, r 55, which requires all proceedings to be commenced in the county court for the area in which the land is situated. The rules are summarised by Cross *Estates Gazette* 16 June 2001, p 158. He notes the extra workload which will fall on county courts thanks to the removal of almost all possession hearings from the High Court (only cases of eg factual complexity, or with important points of law are expected to be heard in the High Court).

63   *Mountain v Hastings* [1993] 2 EGLR 53, CA.

64   These periods are given as substituted by the Housing Act 1996, s 101 as from 28 February 1997 (SI 1997/225); the previous, longer, intervals were 13 weeks and three months respectively.

65   In *Bessa Plus plc v Lancaster* [1997] EGCS 42, CA, a landlord was held entitled to refuse a tender of rent from a local authority housing benefit department unless the third party was paying as the tenant's agent or on his account.

66   *Marath v MacGillivray* (1996) 28 HLR 484, CA; see Jones (1996) 146 NLJ 1517. Once a s 48 notice is served, the landlord can recover all accumulated rent arrears: ibid.

been alleviated because HA 1988, s 48 does not have to be complied with by means of a formal notice: a statement of the requisite information, say with a notice under HA 1988, s 8, suffices.[67] The amount of rent alleged to be due may be specified in the landlord's HA 1988, s 8 notice, but it suffices if he gives the tenant sufficient information to enable him to work out what is owed, as where a tenant who had paid no rent since a given date had been told that at that date he owed a specified sum.[68]

Ground 8 is mandatory: if rent arrears are proved within the above requirements, the court has no discretion to refuse to make an order for possession. The periods of rent arrears to be proved as a condition precedent to obtaining possession were shortened by the Housing Act 1996, as part of a policy of strengthening the position of the landlord of what will be presumed, in post-1996 Act tenancies, to be an assured shorthold tenancy. However, the rent must be in arrears in the prescribed sense both at the date of service of the HA 1988, s 8 notice and at the date of the hearing, and so, if the tenant repays all the arrears and (presumably) costs, between the date of service of the HA 1988, s 8 notice and that of the hearing, the landlord cannot regain possession on this ground, irrespective of the tenant's past record.

(ii) Repossession on expiry of tenancy

There is also a specific procedure for the recovery of possession against an assured shorthold tenant. This arises once the initial tenancy has come to an end (by expiry in the case of a term certain or by notice to quit in the case of a periodic tenancy) and no further assured tenancy, shorthold or not, exists for the time being, other than a statutory periodic tenancy which comes into being automatically as from expiry of the contractual term of an assured shorthold tenancy, but which is deemed to be a shorthold tenancy (HA 1988, s 21(1)(a)). The landlord must have given the tenant a written notice of not less than two months stating that he requires possession (HA 1988, s 21(1)(b)). The notice requiring possession may not only be given, once any term certain has expired; it may be given before or on the expiry date notwithstanding the fact that on the coming to an end of the fixed-term or periodic contractual tenancy a statutory periodic tenancy arises (HA 1988, s 21(2)). A landlord may time his termination notice so that it may expire on the contractual termination date of an initial term certain, provided it is served not less than two months before then.

If a valid s 21 notice is served on the tenant, it may also act as a notice to terminate the tenancy under a contractual break clause which requires one month's advance notice to the tenant, since once possession is obtained, the tenancy comes to an end.[69] In the

---

67 Or a notice under HA 1988, s 21, provided this notice supplies the landlord's name and address or the name and address of the landlord's agent: *Drew-Morgan v Hamid-Zadeh* (1999) 32 HLR 316, CA. An application for possession, however, does not amount to a notice within Landlord and Tenant Act 1987, s 48: *Drew-Morgan v Hamid-Zadeh* (1999) 32 HLR 316, CA.
68 *Marath v MacGillivray* (1996) 28 HLR 484, CA.
69 *Fawaz v Alyward* (1996) Times 15 July, CA.

case of a periodic assured shorthold tenancy, there is a further restriction. The court cannot order possession unless the landlord has specified, in his notice, the date when possession is required. This date must be the last day of a period of the tenancy. It must also be earlier than two months after the date the notice was given (HA 1988, s 21(4)).[70]

Provided the landlord has complied with the relevant notice requirements, the court, following the landlord's application, must make an order for possession, and has no discretion to refuse to make the order, if it is satisfied that the shorthold term has come to an end, and no further assured tenancy other than a shorthold tenancy, whether statutory or not, is in existence. So far these legislative provisions have escaped unscathed from human rights attacks. It has been held that the mandatory terms of HA 1988, s 21(4) do not conflict with the right to a person's family life, as set out in ECHR, Art 8. Some procedure had to exist to enable possession of the relevant property, at the end of the tenancy, to be recovered, and it was for Parliament and not the courts to rule on areas of legitimacy and proportionality.[71]

No order for possession may be made so as to take effect earlier than six months after the beginning of any assured shorthold tenancy granted as from 28 February 1997.[72] If the landlord has granted the tenant a new or 'replacement' tenancy of the same or substantially the same premises as those let under the first tenancy, the six-month period runs from the commencement of the first-mentioned tenancy.[73] Thus, if a tenant is granted a monthly periodic assured (shorthold) tenancy, and it is ended by valid common law notice to quit after three months, the tenant will have a further three months in the premises, if he wants them, as a statutory periodic tenant, unless he has, for example, fallen seriously into arrear with his rent.

Where possession is ordered, any statutory periodic tenancy coming into being on expiry of the initial term certain ends automatically (without further notice and regardless of the period) on the day the order takes effect (HA 1988, s 21(3)). There is no prescribed form of termination notice. Indeed, it appears that the specific notice procedures of HA 1988, s 21 are not to be subjected to a further requirement of service on the tenant of a notice under HA 1988, s 8.[74]

70 See *Lower Street Properties Ltd v Jones* (1996) 28 HLR 877, CA; also *F v Pazuki* Current Law (November 2000) No 384.

71 *Poplar Housing and Regeneration Community Association v Donoghue* [2001] EWCA Civ 595, [2002] QB 48.

72 HA 1988, s 21(5)(a).

73 HA 1988, s 21(5)(b).

74 *Panayi v Roberts* [1993] 2 EGLR 51, CA.

Shorthold tenancy rents

An assured shorthold tenant may refer the rent for the tenancy[75] to a Rent Assessment Committee (HA 1988, s 22(1)). This must be by an application in the prescribed form.[76] The Committee must then determine the rent which, in its opinion, the landlord might 'reasonably be expected to obtain'. The rent cannot be referred by the tenant of a new-style shorthold tenancy if more than six months have expired since the beginning of the tenancy (HA 1988, s 22(2)):[77] that period being the time during which the landlord cannot ask the court to implement an order for possession. If a rent has previously been determined under HA 1988, s 22, the tenant cannot in any case refer the rent (HA 1988, s 22(2)(a)).

The Committee cannot make a determination unless, by HA 1988, s 22(3), they consider that:
1   there is a sufficient number of similar dwelling houses in the locality let on assured tenancies (shorthold or not); and
2   the rent payable under the assured shorthold tenancy is 'significantly higher' than the rent which the landlord might reasonably be expected to be able to obtain under the tenancy, having regard to the level of rents payable under the tenancies in the locality of similar dwelling houses.[78]

A rent as determined takes effect from whatever date the Committee direct, but no earlier than the date of the application (HA 1988, s 22(4)(a)). Any excess rent over that determined is irrecoverable from the tenant as from the date the determination takes effect (HA 1988, s 22(4)(b)).[79] The landlord cannot serve a notice of increase of rent under HA 1988, s 13(2) until one year from the date of the determination taking effect (HA 1988, s 22(4)(c)).

If there is a scarcity of dwellings let on assured tenancies, the Committee cannot consider any application for a reduction in the rent, even if it is very high for that reason (HA 1988, s 22(3)(a)). This, it is said, contrasts with referrals of the rents of assured periodic tenancies, as a discount for scarcity might be proper, as there is no security of tenure for assured shorthold tenants.[80]

In any case, the limited right to refer is shown by the fact that the landlord will only have to face a determination if the tenant can prove that the rent is significantly higher than the landlord might reasonably obtain under the tenancy, regard being had to the general rent level in the locality (HA 1988, s 22(3)(b)). This is, therefore, a provision designed to counteract overcharging by landlords above that level which the Committee

---

75   In contrast to the position with fixed-term assured tenants, where such reference is impossible.
76   See Assured Tenancies (Forms) Regulations 1997, SI 1997/194, Form No 6.
77   As amended by Housing Act 1996, s 100(1).
78   By HA 1988, s 22(5). Housing Act 1996, s 14(4), (5) and (8) apply to a determination under HA 1988, s 22.
79   The information, procedural and publicity of determinations rules apply to assured shorthold tenancies as to any assured tenancy (HA 1988, ss 41 and 42).
80   Davey *Residential Rents* p 226.

find to be the general level of rents for comparable assured tenancies in the area. If the general rent level is forced up by the market in a given case, then it is more than arguable that a landlord could reasonably expect to obtain a rent reflecting the scarcity factor, against which a shorthold tenant is given no shield at all.

IV STATUTORY RULES GOVERNING SPECIFIC TERMS OF ASSURED TENANCIES

The following rules apply to assured shorthold and assured tenancies alike.

Prohibition on dispositions

Any periodic assured tenancy, but not a fixed-term tenancy, is subject to a specific statutory prohibition on assignments or sub-lettings of the tenancy, which applies instead of the general statutory rule.[81] By HA 1988, s 15(1), it is an implied term of any periodic assured tenancy and also of any statutory periodic tenancy that, except with the consent of the landlord, the tenant cannot:

1   assign the tenancy (in whole or in part); or
2   sub-let or part with the possession of the whole of any part of the dwelling house let on the tenancy.

The implied prohibition of HA 1988, s 15(1) does not apply, by HA 1988, s 15(3)(a), if there is a 'provision (whether contained in the tenancy or not) under which the tenant is prohibited (whether absolutely or conditionally) from assigning or sub-letting or parting with possession' or is permitted (absolutely or conditionally) to assign, sub-let or part with possession.[82]

Therefore, while the statutory prohibition on assignments, etc applies in all circumstances to a statutory periodic tenancy (as where a periodic tenancy arises under HA 1988, s 5, after the expiry of a previous fixed-term tenancy), it is apparently open to the parties to a periodic tenancy to exclude the terms of HA 1988, s 15. An express prohibition even in a narrower form than that of HA 1988 would seem on first principles wholly to exclude HA 1988, s 15, even though the terms of the statute may be wider than those of the express exclusion. Because statutory periodic tenancies are subject to the full force of HA 1988, s 15, which cannot be derogated from by the parties, if a previous fixed-term tenancy contained a narrower prohibition on dispositions than that of HA 1988, s 15, the landlord will benefit from the fact that the periodic tenancy arising after the fixed-term tenancy determines will be subject to a wider prohibition than any originally agreed.

---

81   HA 1988, s 15(2), excluding Landlord and Tenant Act 1927, s 19(1).
82   Nor does the statutory implied prohibition apply where a premium is required to be paid on the grant or renewal of the tenancy (HA 1988, s 15(3)(b)).

Repairs

It is an implied term of every assured tenancy that the tenant is bound to afford access to the landlord to the dwelling house concerned and all reasonable facilities for executing therein any repairs which he is entitled to execute (HA 1988, s 16). The landlord's agents and servants are not expressly entitled to access under HA 1988, s 16, which applies to work classified as repairs or subordinate renewal, but not full-scale renewals. There is nothing in HA 1988, s 16 to prevent the landlord from inserting into a fixed-term assured tenancy an access right in wider terms than those implied by HA 1988, s 16. Where this is so, it is presumed that such a term would be carried forward by HA 1988, s 5(3)(c) into any statutory assured tenancy arising after the termination of the former fixed-term tenancy.

Sub-tenancies

At common law, where a tenant sub-lets, and his own leasehold interest comes to an end by forfeiture or landlords' or tenants' notice to quit, any sub-tenancies granted by the tenant are determined by operation of law. In the case of a residential sub-tenant, proceedings may be required to evict him.

HA 1988, s 18 modifies the common law rule that a sub-tenancy is in principle dependent for its continued survival on an immediately superior leasehold interest. It applies only if the interest of the sub-tenant's immediate landlord is not such that the (sub-) tenancy could not be assured (HA 1988, s 18(2)). Thus, if the sub-tenancy was granted by a local authority landlord, the Crown or a resident landlord, HA 1988, s 18 is excluded and the common law rule applies. Thus the protection of a residential sub-tenant depends on the status of the landlord at the time of the grant and if the leasehold reversion becomes vested in a landlord who cannot grant assured tenancies, the protection of the provision is lost.

The protection of HA 1988, s 18(1) applies if, at any time, three conditions are satisfied. Where these are satisfied, the sub-tenancy continues in existence, despite the termination of the intermediate tenancy, held direct from the landlord of the person who granted the sub-tenancy. The conditions are:
1   a dwelling house is 'for the time being lawfully let on an assured tenancy' (which therefore includes a letting on an assured shorthold tenancy)
2   the landlord is himself a tenant holding a superior tenancy;
3   the superior tenancy has come to an end.

The requirement that the letting of the house or flat concerned must be 'lawful' disqualifies a sub-tenancy which was granted in breach of an absolute or qualified prohibition in his landlord's own lease from being preserved under HA 1988, s 18. Similar considerations would seem to apply as govern RA 1977, s 137.

The granting of reversionary tenancies as a means of avoiding HA 1988, s 18 is defeated by HA 1988, s 18(3). Thus, if the landlord, having granted a fixed-term tenancy, grants a reversionary tenancy to commence as from, or after, the date of the previous contractual tenancy (as defined: HA 1988, s 18(4)) ends by effluxion of time, and the fixed-term tenancy continues under HA 1988, s 5 as a statutory periodic tenancy, the reversionary tenancy is subject to the statutory periodic tenancy. A similar rule applies where the first-mentioned tenancy is periodic. Were it not for HA 1988, s 18(3), the superior tenancy mentioned in HA 1988, s 18(1)(c) would not have come to an end, so that the protection of the provision could not be claimed by any sub-tenant.

V REPOSSESSION RULES

General principles

An assured shorthold tenant has no statutory security once his contractual term has expired. The tenant may hold over as a periodic shorthold tenant but his landlord is entitled to ask the court for possession under the specific procedures of HA 1988, s 21, which have already been examined.

The following points should be noted with regard to the security of an assured tenant, as opposed to an assured shorthold tenant.

1   A fixed-term assured tenancy cannot in principle be terminated by the landlord before it expires (HA 1988, s 5(1)). If however the landlord has obtained a possession order against a fixed-term assured tenant on the ground of non-payment of rent, under ground 8, the court cannot grant relief to the tenant under the County Courts Act 1984, since no claim for forfeiture is being made: the landlord's claim for possession is being made solely under HA 1988.[83]

2   An assured tenancy may allow the landlord to exercise a contractual right to terminate it for a specified reason (eg redevelopment) before the end of the fixed term. HA 1988, s 5(1) preserves such a right. If such a break-clause is duly operated by the landlord, the fixed-term tenancy ends on the date specified in the landlord's notice and a statutory periodic tenancy comes into being. That tenancy is terminable solely in accordance with the proof by the landlord of one or more specified grounds for possession. So, in the case of exercise of a break-clause on the ground of redevelopment, the landlord would also need to prove that the requirements of ground 6 applied. There is a risk that if a contractual right to terminate is exercisable for breach of covenant, it may be held to be equivalent to a forfeiture clause, so rendering it not effective to put a premature end to the assured fixed-term tenancy (HA 1988, s 45(1)).

3   The tenant is entitled to remain in possession after the expiry of the fixed-term assured tenancy as a statutory periodic tenant (HA 1988, s 5(2)). The terms of this type of tenancy are governed by statute but they may be varied by the landlord

---

83   *Artesian Residential Investments Ltd v Beck* [1999] L & TR 278, CA. The court relied on the combined effect of HA 1988, ss 5, 45(1) and 7. Once a possession order is made, then ipso facto the assured tenancy terminates under HA 1988, s 5.

under a statutory procedure. If the tenant dies while holding a statutory periodic tenancy under HA 1988, provision is made under HA 1988, s 17 for a single succession to the tenancy. This may be by the tenant's spouse or sex partner (HA 1988, s 17(4)) if that person occupied the dwelling house concerned as his only or principal home.

4   The landlord may in cases of breaches of covenant by an assured tenant ask the court to put an end to the tenancy prior to its contractual expiry date, as by invoking mandatory grounds 2 (mortgagees' repossession), or 8 (rent arrears), or discretionary grounds other than 9 or 16, so including nuisances or anti-social behaviour by an assured tenant (HA 1988, s 7(6)).

5   Once a fixed-term assured tenancy has expired and has been followed by a statutory periodic tenancy, the latter may be terminated by the landlord proving facts within one or more grounds relating to breach of covenant by the tenant or other matters such as owner-occupation (HA 1988, s 7). We have already noted that these grounds apply to a fixed-term assured shorthold tenancy whose initial fixed term has expired, but the landlord would no doubt prefer to have recourse to HA 1988, s 21, in such a case, to remove a tenant who declined to leave voluntarily.

6   Any assured tenancy may be terminated by the tenant surrendering it (provided the surrender is accepted by the landlord) or by 'some other action' of his (HA 1988, s 5(2)(b)). It might be argued that conduct such as leaving the house or flat concerned, without paying rent, which might not necessarily amount to an implied surrender, could be treated as falling within this part of HA 1988, s 5(2)(b) by the landlord and so entitling him to possession without the need for proceedings.

Statutory periodic tenancy

A statutory periodic tenancy is an interim device. It bears the same general nature as the tenancy preceding it: if it was assured, the statutory periodic tenancy will be assured; if not, then the periodic tenancy arising is shorthold. It comes into being once the contractual term of the previous tenancy comes to an end by effluxion of time or notice to quit. The general principle is therefore that, as postulated by HA 1988, s 5, the terms of the statutory periodic tenancy are the same as those of the tenancy which immediately preceded it.[84] They may be varied by the landlord within the first complete year of the statutory periodic tenancy coming into being under HA 1988, s 6: a provision seemingly mainly apt for assured as opposed to assured shorthold tenancies.

The tenant may prevent the coming into being of a statutory assured tenancy, if the contractual tenancy was fixed term, by surrendering the latter. This statutory tenancy will continue until:

84   See *Laine v Cadwallader* [2001] L & TR 8, [2001] L & TR 77, CA (where, however, in an assured shorthold tenancy, a tenant's right to terminate the fixed-term tenancy was not carried into the statutory periodic tenancy but equally the landlord could only end the statutory periodic tenancy as laid down in HA 1988).

1 the landlord, if he can, obtains from the court an order for possession under HA 1988, s 21;
2 the landlord obtains an order for possession under a statutory ground for possession; or
3 a new assured or assured shorthold tenancy is granted to the tenant of the same or substantially the same dwelling house (HA 1988, s 5(4)).

Repossession by landlord against assured periodic or statutory tenants

(i) Basic rules

The following principles apply where the relevant tenancy is an assured periodic tenancy as opposed to an assured periodic shorthold tenancy. An assured periodic tenancy may only be ended if the landlord is able to prove one or more statutory grounds (HA 1988, s 7) and it cannot be brought to an end by a common law notice to quit: a special notice under HA 1988, s 8 must be served on the tenant. These rules put assured tenants in a more advantageous position than assured shorthold tenants. However, in theory, these principles would govern an assured shorthold tenancy during the initial six-month period when it cannot (save under ground 8) be ended by the landlord.

(ii) Notice procedure

A special notice procedure (HA 1988, s 8) applies to the contractual tenancy, and to the statutory periodic tenancy which follows it. If a HA 1988, s 8 notice is served when the dwelling house is let on a fixed-term tenancy, or in relation to events occurring during an expired fixed-term tenancy, it is effective even though the tenant holds or held under a statutory periodic tenancy (HA 1988, s 8(6)). This is to save the landlord the necessity of serving two notices.

The HA 1988, s 8 notice must be in the prescribed form.[85] If HA 1988, s 8 is ignored, or no prescribed form notice is served, or the notice, although not prescribed, is also not in a form substantially to the like effect, the court cannot entertain the possession proceedings (HA 1988, s 8(1)). The court has a power to dispense with the notice requirement if it considers it just and equitable to do so (HA 1988, s 8(1)(b)). Where on the facts the tenant had sufficient time in which to remedy the breach of covenant complained of, despite the absence of a HA 1988, s 8 notice, the power of dispensation was exercised. It was however pointed out that, as with the Rent Acts, each case would depend on its facts.[86] The dispensation power is not available in the case of

---

85 Assured Tenancies (Forms) Regulations 1997, SI 1997/194, Form No 3.
86 *Kelsey Housing Association v King* (1995) 28 HLR 270, CA. In a proper case, facts occurring after proceedings have started may be taken into account: ibid.

serious rent arrears (HA 1988, s 8(5)). As soon as a HA 1988, s 8 notice has been served, the landlord becomes entitled to bring possession proceedings, but there is also nothing in HA 1988 to prevent a landlord from inserting in the tenancy an undertaking to give a more generous notice period than that allowed by HA 1988, s 8.[87] The following requirements are imposed.

1   The landlord, or at least one joint landlord, must have served due notice on the tenant, and proceedings must be begun within the time-limits given in the notice (HA 1988, s 8(1)(a) and (3)).

2   The notice must specify the ground or grounds and particulars of it or them; the landlord may, with the leave of the court, alter or add to specified grounds which appear in a valid notice,[88] but, subject to that, if a ground and particulars are not specified in a HA 1988, s 8 notice, the court cannot order possession on that ground (HA 1988, s 8(2)).

3   The notice, as seen, must be in the prescribed form or a form substantially to the like effect and it must inform the tenant, by HA 1988, s 8(3):
    (a)   that the landlord intends to bring proceedings for possession on one or more grounds specified in the notice;
    (b)   proceedings will begin not earlier than a date specified in the notice which, generally, must be not earlier than two weeks from the date of service of the notice and not later than twelve months from the service of the notice.

4   If the notice specifies certain grounds[89] the date for beginning proceedings must not, by HA 1988, s 8(4), be earlier than two months from the date of service of the HA 1988, s 8 notice; and if, in this, the tenancy is periodic, as well as the two months requirement, the HA 1988, s 8 notice cannot specify a date for beginning proceedings any earlier than the earliest lawful date for determination of the tenancy by a common-law notice to quit. In all other cases except domestic violence, the specified date may be two weeks from the date of service of the notice.

Should the landlord rely on a notice which is not in the prescribed form, he is only entitled to claim that the notice is within the concession allowing for notices to be valid if substantially to the like effect if his notice closely follows the wording of HA 1988, s 8 and the relevant form, so as to avoid any danger of misleading the tenant. So, where a landlord served a non-prescribed form notice, followed by a written statement

87   *North British Housing Association Ltd v Sheridan* [1999] 2 EGLR 138, [2000] L & TR 115, CA. But equally, the court can be asked by the landlord to dispense with the requirement of a s 8 notice in any event.

88   It appears from *Mountain v Hastings* [1993] 2 EGLR 53, CA that if the notice is void, as where it is not in a form sufficiently like the prescribed form, this particular power cannot be exercised by the court.

89   Ie where the landlord was owner-occupier, a mortgagee seeks vacant possession, occupation for a minister of religion, redevelopment, devolution of periodic tenancy, suitable alternative accommodation and employee-tenant whose employment has ceased.

'ground 8, at least three months rent is unpaid', this notice was invalid, as not giving full particulars to the tenant.[90]

Where the tenant has the right under his tenancy to share some accommodation with other persons, but not the landlord, (ie where HA 1988, s 3 applies) the court cannot order possession of the shared accommodation unless it orders possession of the accommodation which the tenant occupies exclusively (HA 1988, s 10(2)). The court may, on the landlord's application, order the termination or modification of the tenant's right to occupy shared non-living accommodation (HA 1988, s 10(3)) except where the tenancy itself enables this to be done (HA 1988, s 10(4)).

VI GROUNDS FOR POSSESSION

In what follows we examine the statutory grounds for possession and are not concerned with the specific right of the landlord of an assured shorthold tenant whose tenancy has ended to resort to HA 1988, s 21 as a means of regaining possession of the premises.

Introduction

The court cannot make an order for possession of a dwelling house let on an assured tenancy, except on one or more of a number of grounds in HA 1988, Sch 2 (HA 1988, s 7(1)). The grounds for possession are divided into mandatory and discretionary grounds. In all cases, the onus of proving a ground is on the landlord. In the case of a mandatory ground the court must order possession if it is established (HA 1988, s 7(3)). If the dwelling house is let on an assured fixed-term tenancy, the court cannot make a possession order take effect on a mandatory ground before the end of the tenancy, unless ground 2 or ground 8 is made out (HA 1988, s 7(6)), and the terms of the tenancy make provision, by a forfeiture clause or in some other way, for the tenancy to be brought to an end on the ground concerned. It now appears that a clause in a tenancy agreement under which the landlord may bring the tenancy to an end and take the property back on specified grounds[91] is sufficient for HA 1988, s 7(6). This is so, even although it may not specify grounds under which possession maybe sought.[92]

90 *Mountain v Hastings* [1993] 2 EGLR 53, CA; *Kelsey Housing Association v King* (1995) 28 HLR 270, CA, where no notice was given but the requirement was dispensed with. On the facts, the tenants had had ample time by the date of proceedings to put right their abusive and threatening behaviour.

91 Ie that rent is unpaid for 14 days after it has become due and/or the tenant has broken any of his or her obligations in the tenancy agreement. See Brown and Malcolm (2001) PLJ 9.

92 *Artesian Residential Development Ltd v Beck* [1999] 2 EGLR 30, [1999] L & TR 278, CA. However, while HA 1988, s 7(6) requires forfeiture to be included in the tenancy terms, it does not allow the landlord to pursue forfeiture independently of HA 1988 possession provisions: *Artesian Residential Development Ltd v Beck* [1999] 2 EGLR 30, [1999] L & TR 278, CA at 286.

In other cases, where there is a fixed-term assured tenancy, the earliest date on which an order for possession will be able to take effect is a date after the contractual expiry date of the tenancy (HA 1988, s 7(7)). Where there is a periodic assured shorthold tenancy, no order for possession save in the case in particular of rent arrears can be made until the expiry of the first six months of the tenancy.

Once a mandatory ground has been made out the court has no overriding discretion to refuse an order for possession. By contrast, in the case of discretionary grounds, the court has powers of adjournment and the like conferred by HA 1988, s 9.[93] The court also, in the case of discretionary grounds, has an overriding discretion to refuse to order possession, since it may only make an order if it is reasonable to do so (HA 1988, s 7(4)). Similar principles apply to those governing the Rent Acts. Therefore, the issue of reasonableness must be given separate consideration by the court, and merely because it may be reasonable for a landlord to require possession, it does not follow that it is reasonable for the court to gratify his wish. If the judge takes all relevant factors into account, it may be assumed that the weight of any given factor is for him alone, and it would be reasonable to take into account personal,[94] environmental and domestic factors. Even apart from HA 1988, s 5(1), no power in an assured tenancy which would, if exercised, deprive the tenant of his tenancy for breach of obligation, can be enforced except following an order of the court.[95]

Grounds 1 to 5 inclusive in the mandatory grounds depend on prior notices from the landlord to the tenant, which may be presumably incorporated into the terms of the tenancy itself. Any notice must be in writing, and must, where there are joint landlords, be given by at least one of them.[96] In these grounds, the notices have to be given 'not later than the beginning of the tenancy': this means 'not later than the day the tenancy was entered into'.[97] Where a landlord gives a notice as required, the notice has effect in relation to any later tenancy which starts immediately after the ending of the earlier tenancy.[98]

Under HA 1988, s 12, where a landlord obtains an order for possession under a ground for possession and subsequently it is proved that the order was obtained by misrepresentation or concealment of material facts, the court must order the landlord

93   These resemble RA 1977, s 100.
94   As in *Drew-Morgan v Hamid-Zadeh* (1999) 32 HLR 316, CA (where it was held reasonable to order possession. Housing benefit had been received throughout the tenancy by a tenant who never paid the rent regularly).
95   *AG Securities v Vaughan; Antoniades v Villiers* [1990] 1 AC 417, HL; also *Bankway Properties Ltd v Pensfold-Dunsford* [2001] EWCA Civ 528, [2001] 2 EGLR 36 (rent provision, as discussed above, providing for automatic increase of rent to a level the tenant could not reasonably be expected to pay).
96   HA 1988, Sch 2, Pt IV, para 7.
97   HA 1988, Sch 2, Pt IV, paras 8 and 11, overriding HA 1988, s 45(2).
98   HA 1988, Sch 2, Pt IV, para 8(1). The tenancy must be the same as the immediately preceding tenancy, and the dwelling house must be 'substantially the same' (HA 1988, Sch 2, Pt IV, para 8(2)). This rule does not apply if the landlord serves a further written notice on the tenant that the ground concerned is not applicable: HA 1988, Sch 2, Pt IV, para 8(3).

to pay to the former tenant 'such sum as appears sufficient as compensation for the damage or loss sustained by that tenant as a result of the order'. The section does not give any further guidance, so it may be assumed that the quantum of an award is entirely at the discretion of the court: one wonders if it could legitimately order the landlord to pay to the tenant the value of the tenant's interest as sitting tenant, or his 'nuisance value'. One remedy which the tenant does not have, under HA 1988, s 12, is re-instatement in the premises.

Mandatory grounds for possession

With the alteration in the balance between assured and assured shorthold tenancies in favour of the latter type of tenancy in the Housing Act 1996, Pt III, Chapter II, it may be in the future that the main ground on which the landlord of a private-sector tenant will invoke as a means of putting an end to the tenancy during its initial fixed term will be ground 8. The principal mandatory grounds are here set out.[99]

(i) Ground 1: owner occupation

Not later than the beginning of the tenancy the landlord gave the tenant notice in writing that possession might be recovered on this ground[100] and:

1 at some time before the beginning of the tenancy,[101] the landlord seeking possession or, in the case of joint landlords, at least one of them, occupied the dwelling house as his only or principal home; or

2 the landlord seeking possession or, in the case of joint landlords, at least one of them, requires the dwelling house as his or his spouse's only or principal home *and* neither the landlord nor any one joint landlord (where appropriate) nor any person deriving title under the landlord who gave the notice acquired the reversion on the tenancy for money or money's worth.

Some points of construction arise out of this ground.

1 'At some time before the beginning of the tenancy' indicates that occupation by the landlord concerned need not necessarily have been immediately before the beginning of the tenancy: an occupation several years previously would

---

99 Other mandatory grounds are: ground 4, which relates to vacation lettings of student accommodation, and which is like RA 1977, Sch 15, Pt II, Case 14; ground 5, which is appropriate to houses let to a Minister of religion; and ground 7, which ensures that the sole way an assured tenancy devolves after the death of the tenant is by HA 1988, s 17. See *Shepping v Osada* [2000] L & TR 489, CA.

100 The court may dispense with the notice requirement if it is just and equitable to do so. See *Boyle v Verrall* [1997] 1 EGLR 25 (all relevant circumstances taken into account: the tenant failed to draw the landlord's attention to her mistaken non-service of a notice despite her known intention to do so and notice was dispensed with).

101 Ie not later than the day on which the tenancy is entered into (HA 1988, Sch 2, Pt, IV, para 11). It may be advisable for *any* private landlord letting on an assured tenancy to serve a ground 1 notice.

presumably suffice. The quality in which the landlord previously occupied is of no relevance, so that a previous occupation as a lessee or licensee suffices.

2   Once sufficient previous occupation is proved, the landlord does not have to prove that he requires to occupy the house personally, as with the owner-occupier grounds in RA 1977.

3   The previous occupation by the landlord must have been as his only or principal home. A tenant who could show that, at the relevant time, the landlord had a second home, which he treated as his principal home, might be able to defeat a claim based on para (a): but presumably in such a case, an alternative claim could be made under para (b).

4   Where the landlord was not previously an owner-occupier, he will have to rely on para (b) of ground 1, which is mandatory, unlike a similar discretionary ground in RA 1977(Case 9), but it is narrower with regard to the types of person whom the landlord can claim for.[102] Unlike Case 9, the strict joint landlord rule does not apply the present ground, as only one joint landlord need require occupation as a residence.

As is the case with the similar Rent Act ground for possession, it has been judicially recognised that this particular ground gives the court no discretion to refuse to order possession. The landlord need not show that his requirement of the house is reasonable: it need only be shown to be his bona fide intention to use the premises as a residence for him and his spouse.[103]

(ii) Ground 2: repossession by mortgagee

The dwelling house is subject to a mortgage or charge granted before the beginning of the tenancy,[104] and:

1   the mortgagee (or chargee) is entitled to exercise a power of sale conferred by the mortgage or by the Law of Property Act 1925, s 101; and

2   the mortgagee requires possession of the dwelling house to dispose of it with vacant possession; and

3   either notice was given as mentioned in ground 1 or the court is satisfied that it is just and equitable to dispense with the requirement of notice.

If the landlord has given a notice under ground 1, it will thus suffice for a mortgagee within ground 2. If not, the mortgagee must presumably either give a notice which states that possession might be required under ground 2, not later than the beginning of the tenancy, or invoke the court's dispensation power.

---

102 A reasonable requirement of occupation by certain members of the landlord's family is sufficient for Case 9.

103 *Boyle v Verrall* [1997] 1 EGLR 25, CA, applying the Rent Act decision of *Kennealy v Dunne* [1977] QB 837; also *Mustafa v Ruddock* (1997) 30 HLR 495, CA.

104 Defined, HA 1988, Sch 2. Pt IV, para 11, above.

(iii) Ground 3: out of season lettings

The tenancy is a fixed-term tenancy for a term not exceeding eight months and:
1   not later than the beginning of the tenancy[105] the landlord gave notice in writing to the tenant that possession might be recovered on this ground; and
2   at some time within the period of twelve months ending with the beginning of the tenancy,[106] the dwelling house was occupied under a right to occupy it for a holiday.

This ground is to enable a landlord who lets houses or flats on holiday lettings, which are not assured tenancies, to let on a fixed-term assured tenancy or series of fixed-term assured tenancies not exceeding eight months in all and recover possession mandatorily. If a notice is served as required before the first tenancy, and a second or subsequent tenancy is granted, the notice will be effective for that tenancy, if it is off-season, and the beginning of the tenancy is deemed to run from the beginning of the tenancy for which the notice was actually given.[107]

(iv) Ground 6: redevelopment by landlord

Under this ground, the landlord[108] or, if the landlord is a registered housing association or charitable housing trust, a superior landlord, intends to demolish or reconstruct the whole or a substantial part of the dwelling house or to carry out substantial works on the dwelling house or any part thereof or any building of which it forms part and:
1   the intended work cannot reasonably be carried out without the tenant giving up possession of the dwelling house because:
   (a) he is not willing to agree to a variation of the terms of his tenancy so as to give access or other facilities to permit the intended work to be carried out; or
   (b) the nature of the intended work is such that no such variation is practicable; or
   (c) the tenant is not willing to accept an assured tenancy of a reduced part of the dwelling house leaving the landlord in possession of so much of the dwelling house as would be reasonable to enable him to carry out the intended work and would give access and other facilities over the reduced part to permit the work to be carried out, or
   (d) the nature of the work is such that such a tenancy is not practicable; and

105 HA 1988, Sch 2, Pt IV, para 11, above, disapplying HA 1988, s 45(2).
106 Ie by HA 1988, Sch 2, para 11, the day on which the tenancy was entered into, disapplying HA 1988, s 45(2).
107 HA 1988, Sch 2, Pt IV, para 10. The same rule applies to ground 4, below.
108 Described as the 'landlord who is seeking possession' so as to enable one of joint landlords to rely on the ground.

2   either the landlord acquired his interest in the dwelling house before the grant of the tenancy[109] or his interest was in existence at the time of the grant and neither the landlord or any joint landlord nor any other person who has acquired the landlord's interest since the grant of the tenancy acquired it for money or money's worth; and

3   the assured tenancy did not come into being under a succession to a former statutory tenancy under, in particular, RA 1977.

The purchase condition will not prevent a landlord who acquires the reversion under a will or intestacy or by surrender for no consideration from relying on this ground. This ground enables a landlord or superior landlord with redevelopment plans to regain possession mandatorily of a dwelling house let on an assured tenancy for, presumably, a substantial period.[110] If the tenancy is fixed-term, however, because the court cannot make an order for possession take effect until the contractual expiry date of the tenancy, a landlord intent on redevelopment will not be able to evict the tenant until after that date. If the fixed-term tenancy contains a break clause entitling the landlord to determine it for redevelopment, then, by analogy with the Landlord and Tenant Act 1954, Pt II, the clause, if duly exercised, will be effective to determine the fixed-term tenancy, and an order for possession may thereafter be sought on ground 6.[111] Where the court orders possession under this ground, the landlord must pay the tenant his reasonable removal expenses (HA 1988, s 11(1)).

Ground 8, which deals with rent arrears, has already been discussed in relation to assured shorthold tenancies, even though it equally applies to an assured tenant.[112]

Discretionary grounds for possession

There are a number of grounds which, if they apply, enable the court to make an order for possession only at its discretion. The court may only evict the tenant if it considers it reasonable to do so (HA 1988, s 7(4)).[113] The following grounds are noted for the sake of completeness.

---

109 If the tenant (or any joint tenant) was in possession under an earlier assured tenancy, this means the grant of the earlier tenancy.

110 The policy of this ground is similar to that of Landlord and Tenant Act 1954, s 30(1)(f); a similar ground exists in relation to secure tenancies (Housing Act 1988, Sch 2, ground 10). In *Sugarwhite v Afriolic* [2002] 5 CL 4255 it was held that cases under LTA 1954, Pt II, s 30(1)(f) applied to ground 6.

111 Cf *Weinbergs Weatherproofs v Radcliffe Paper Mill Co* [1958] Ch 437, [1957] 3 All ER 663.

112 See however *Capital Prime Plus plc v Wills* (1998) 31 HLR 926 (where it is not shown whether ground 8 applies or a discretionary ground (ground 10) then the latter will be assumed to have been relied on and the court can suspend the possession order accordingly).

113 See *Drew-Morgan v Hamid-Zadeh* supra; also *Hounslow London BC v McBride* (1998) 2 L & TR Rev D 54 (where there was no express admission by the tenant that it was reasonable to make the order for possession, which was accordingly set aside).

The court has power to make an order for possession take effect before the expiry date of an assured fixed-term tenancy in the case of most discretionary grounds (HA 1988, s 7(6)) provided that the terms of the tenancy enable the landlord to terminate the tenancy on that ground, by forfeiture or otherwise (see further, above).

(i)   Ground 9: suitable alternative accommodation

Suitable alternative accommodation is available for the tenant or will be available for him when the order for possession takes effect.

This ground is similar in most material respects to the corresponding provision in RA 1977.[114] One new feature of the present ground is that where the landlord obtains possession, he is bound to pay the tenant's reasonable removal expenses (HA 1988, s 11(1)).

(ii)   Ground 10: rent lawfully due

Some rent lawfully due from the tenant is unpaid on the date on which the proceedings for possession are begun and is in arrears at the date of service of a HA 1988, s 8 notice, except where service of a s 8 notice is dispensed with.

The date of service of a HA 1988, s 8 notice within ground 10 is, however, at an earlier and distinct date from the date when proceedings in court are begun.[115] Thus rent has apparently to be in arrears on both dates for the landlord to succeed on this ground, even if he can overcome the overriding discretion of the court.

(iii)   Ground 11: persistent delay

Whether or not any rent is in arrears on the date on which proceedings are begun, the tenant has persistently delayed paying rent lawfully due.

Under this ground, the tenant's past record may be examined: even if he is currently punctual with his rent payments, if his past record is bad enough, the landlord may obtain possession.

(iv)   Ground 12: breach of obligation

Any obligation of the tenancy (other than as to rent) has been broken or not performed.

---

114 It is supplemented by HA 1988, Sch 2, Pt III.
115 *Shepping v Osoda* [2000] L & TR 489, CA.

The ground would, depending on the wording of the tenancy agreement, presumably allow an order for possession to be made against an anti-social tenant who, for example, indulged in racist or abusive behaviour towards other tenants, whereupon the chances of the discretion to refuse possession on the ground of reasonableness would seem slight. The courts might well adopt a strict approach in this type of case, much as they seem to be doing in relation to anti-social secure tenants. If an order could not be sought under ground 12, it could be sought under ground 14, where the courts adopt a strict approach.[116]

(v) Ground 13: waste, neglect, etc

The condition of the dwelling house or any of the common parts has deteriorated owing to acts of waste by, or the neglect or default of, the tenant or any other person residing in the dwelling house and, in the case of an act of waste by, or the neglect or default of, a lodger of the tenant or a sub-tenant, the tenant has not taken such steps as he ought reasonably to have taken for the removal of the lodger or sub-tenant.

While in most respects this ground corresponds to RA 1977, Sch 15,Case 3, ground 13 refers, in addition, which is new, to the common parts, so that if the tenant or those claiming under him actively injure a common staircase or damage the lighting in common passageways, for example, the landlord could invoke the present ground.

(vi) Ground 14: nuisance, annoyance, etc[117]

The tenant or any other person residing in the dwelling house has been guilty of conduct which was, or is likely to have been, a nuisance or annoyance to a person residing, visiting or otherwise engaging in a lawful activity in the dwelling house, or has been convicted of using the dwelling house or allowing it to be used for immoral or illegal purposes or an arrestable offence has been committed in, or in the vicinity of, the dwelling house.

The type of misconduct within this ground would be matters such as persistent racist abuse, or other anti-social conduct such as threatening behaviour to neighbouring tenants or members of their family, as well as acts of persistent nuisance (such as carrying out work on vehicles late at night on a regular basis).[118] As would be the case

---

116 See *West Kent Housing Association Ltd v Davies* [1998] EGCS 103 (judge's discretion in refusing to order possession overturned in face of clear evidence of nuisance conduct such as working late at night on motor vehicles and also of racist abuse of a child of neighbours).

117 Under ground 14A, specific landlords, notably charitable housing trusts, may procure the eviction of a husband or wife or partner who has driven out the other party by domestic violence, with special rules as to service of notices (HA 1988, s 8A).

118 As in *West Kent Housing Association Ltd v Davies* [1998] EGCS 103.

under ground 12, the courts would seem not very sympathetic to claims by the offending tenant that the discretion to refuse to order possession ought to be exercised in their favour, all the more so if the tenant has been convicted of a criminal offence.[119]

(vii) Ground 15: deterioration of furniture

The condition of any furniture provided for use under the tenancy has, in the court's opinion, deteriorated owing to ill-treatment by the tenant or any other person residing in the dwelling house and, in the case of ill-treatment by a lodger or sub-tenant, the tenant has not taken reasonable steps for the removal of the lodger or sub-tenant.

(viii) Ground 16: employee of landlord

The dwelling house was let to the tenant in consequence of his employment by the landlord or a previous landlord under the tenancy and the tenant has ceased to be in that employment.

The landlord seeking possession will have to prove either that the assured tenancy was granted by him to the tenant, as his former employee, or that the tenant was the former employee of any predecessor in title. The tenancy must be in consequence of the employment, but the tenant need not necessarily be occupying the house for the better performance of his duties. No doubt, if alternative accommodation is available for the tenant, it will be easier to persuade the court to order possession in its overriding discretion.

(ix) Ground 17: false statement inducing grant of tenancy

The tenant was the person, or one of them, to whom the tenancy was granted and the landlord was induced to grant the tenancy by a false statement made knowingly or recklessly by the tenant or a person acting at the tenant's instigation.

Since at common law it is possible for a landlord to rescind a statutory tenancy on the ground of fraudulent or reckless misrepresentation, the need for this ground may be doubted.

---

119 See *North British Housing Association Ltd v Sheridan* [1999] 2 EGLR 138, [2000] L & TR 115, CA.

VII   RENT PROVISIONS

General rules

One of the most important reasons for the enactment of the assured tenancies scheme was the fact that private-sector residential landlords would be able to grant new tenancies free of the shackles of rent controls, and so at whatever rent the landlord of a particular house or flat could extract from the tenant.

HA 1988, s 13 applies where a periodic assured or, as from 28 February 1997, a periodic assured shorthold tenancy, is granted, as also where an assured or assured shorthold tenancy granted for a fixed term expires.

(i) Fixed-term tenancies

Under a fixed-term tenancy, the parties may agree on any rent they like, which cannot be referred, and the tenancy may include legitimate rent reviews.[120] Subject to that, if the landlord wishes to increase the original rent, he will have to await the end of the fixed-term tenancy and the automatic coming into being of a periodic tenancy following the assured shorthold tenancy or of a statutory periodic tenancy following the assured tenancy. On that event, he will be able to proceed with a notice of increase. In the case of a statutory periodic tenancy, the general requirements as to the service of a notice apply, but the landlord does not have to delay the start of the period for the proposed new rent for one year from the commencement of the periodic tenancy, which he must do where he granted a periodic tenancy (HA 1988, s 13(2)(b)). All he must do is to serve his notice during the final year of the fixed-term assured tenancy, giving a minimum period for the coming into effect of the new rent, which will depend on the intervals at which rent is payable under the tenancy (HA 1988, s 5(3)(d)). Further increases in rent will be governed by the provisions which apply to periodic tenancies.

(ii) Periodic tenancies

The landlord may increase the rent of a periodic or statutory periodic assured tenancy or of an assured shorthold tenancy (as a variety of assured tenancy) by a notice under HA 1988, s 13. If there is a rent review provision in a periodic tenancy, however, it will govern rent increases to the exclusion of the statutory procedure (HA 1988, s 13(1)(b)). The statutory procedure is without prejudice to the right of either party to vary the rent by agreement (HA 1988, s 13(5)). It allows for an annual increase in rent.

---

120 As opposed to the term considered in *Bankway Properties Ltd v Pensfold-Dunsford* [2001] EWCA Civ 528, [2001] 2 EGLR 36.

The notice must be in the prescribed form,[121] proposing a new rent (HA 1988, s 13(2)). The new rent may take effect as from a 'new period of the tenancy specified in the notice': so if it is not specified, presumably, though the section does not so state, the notice is void. The minimum periods, below, run as from the date of service of the notice (HA 1988, s 13(2)(a)).

The 'minimum period', by HA 1988, s 13(2) and (3), from which the new rent begins, is not to begin earlier than:
1   in the case of a yearly tenancy, six months;
2   in the case of a tenancy where the period is less than a month, one month; or
3   in any other case, the period of the tenancy.

Each of the above runs from the date of service of the HA 1988, s 13 notice. In addition, no new rent period can begin except from the end of the first anniversary of the date in which the first period of the tenancy began (HA 1988, s 13(2)(b)), but this does not apply where a periodic tenancy follows a fixed-term tenancy, in which latter case the rent increase may be sought as from the expiry of the term certain. If the rent has been previously increased by a HA 1988, s 13 notice or a s 14 determination by a Rent Assessment Committee, no further notice of increase can be served until one year after the increased rent takes effect (HA 1988, s 13(2)(c)).

Once the period specified in the notice expires, unless the tenant has referred the notice to a Rent Assessment Committee, by an application in the prescribed form,[122] or the parties have agreed on a different rent, the new rent takes effect as specified in the notice (HA 1988, s 13(4)). The tenant must refer the notice, if he is going to do so, before the beginning of the 'new period' specified in the notice: if he does not, and a different rent has not been agreed, then he will have to pay the new rent, however steep an increase has been proposed. Whether this is a reasonable result, may be questioned, except that a periodic tenant who dislikes a new rent may always, by a notice to quit, determine his tenancy.

Determinations by Rent Assessment Committee

(i) General

Where a tenant refers a rent increase notice to a Rent Assessment Committee, which must be in a prescribed form application and before the beginning of the period from which the new rent is to commence (HA 1988, s 13(4)) the Committee must consider the reference under HA 1988, s 14. Committees have powers to obtain information from both landlord and tenant (HA 1988, s 41). Specified information must be kept by the

---

121 Assured Tenancies Regulations 1997, SI 1997/194, Form No 4. However, an old form of notice in the now defunct 1988 regulations was upheld as substantially to the same effect as the 1997 form in *Tadema Holdings Ltd v Ferguson* (1999) 32 HLR 866, CA (the format of the required information having been changed but not its essential content).
122 *Assured Tenancies Regulations 1997*, SI 1997/194, Form No 5.

president of every rent assessment panel as to rents of assured and assured shorthold tenancies (HA 1988, s 42).[123] Both parties may, by written notice, withdraw a reference (HA 1988, s 14(8)). Rent does not include a service charge (HA 1988, s 14(4)),[124] but the Committee must consider, nevertheless, sums payable for furniture and also sums payable for services, repairs, maintenance or insurance or the landlord's costs of management whether or not these sums are separate from the sums payable for the occupation of the dwelling house concerned or are payable under separate agreements.[125]

The Rent Assessment Committee must then determine the rent at which they consider the dwelling house might reasonably be expected to be let in the open market by a willing landlord under an assured tenancy (HA 1988, s 14(1)). It seems that the words 'reasonably to be expected' do not require the rent of an assured tenancy to be capped to the £25,000 rental value limit (above which the tenancy cannot be an assured tenancy), as in principle a full market rent is to be paid under the HA 1988 scheme of things.[126] It was noted that no landlord could reasonably be expected to let the premises at less than the market rent, when the only advantage of an assured tenancy would be then to the tenant. Otherwise the tenant would gain a double benefit: security of tenure and a rent cap.

HA 1988, s 14(1) requires the following assumptions to be made in fixing the new rent:
1   the tenancy is periodic with the same periods as the current tenancy;
2   it begins at the beginning of the period from which the new rent is payable, specified in the notice;
3   the terms are those of the current tenancy (other than as to rent); and
4   notices under HA 1988, Sch 2, grounds 1 to 5 have, where relevant, been given to the tenant.

The rent determined by a Rent Assessment Committee takes effect as from the beginning of the period specified in the landlord's HA 1988, s 13 notice, and so retrospectively, unless the Committee are satisfied that the application of this rule would cause undue hardship to the tenant, in which case a later date may be substituted by them, which cannot be any later than the date of their determination of the rent (HA 1988, s 14(7)). Thus the landlord is not to be deprived of any rent increase sanctioned by a Committee by a tenant's reference.

---

123 Assured Tenancies etc (Rent Information) Order 1988, SI 1988/2199; and a new rent may be proposed to take into account the tenant's liability to council tax (HA 1988, s 14A and SI 1993/654).

124 As defined by the Landlord and Tenant Act 1985, s 18.

125 As to rates borne by the landlord or a superior landlord, the determination is made as if these were not so borne (HA 1988, s 14(5)).

126 *R v London Rent Assessment Panel, ex p Cadogan Estates Ltd* [1997] 2 EGLR 134. The case concerned an assured tenancy for a fixed-term of just under one year expiring in 1995, at a rent well below the market level, the landlords then asking for a rent of nearly five times that amount from the start of the statutory periodic tenancy.

(ii) Statutory disregards

While the rent must be determined as a market rent, the Committee must make the following disregards (HA 1988, s 14(2)):

1 any effect on rent of there being a sitting tenant;
2 any increase in the value of the dwelling house or flat attributable to certain improvements carried out by the person who, at the time he carried them out, was the current tenant. Any improvement must have been carried out otherwise than under an obligation to the immediate landlord, or carried out under an obligation to the immediate landlord, following a consent to the improvement. Moreover, the improvement cannot be disregarded unless it was either carried out during the current tenancy, or unless the conditions are satisfied which closely resemble those imposed by the Landlord and Tenant Act 1954, s 34(2) (HA 1988, s 14(3)); and
3 any reduction in the value of the dwelling house attributable to a failure by the tenant to comply with the terms of the tenancy. Where a person became an assured tenant by succession under HA 1988, s 39, a Rent Assessment Committee could properly disregard a failure by his predecessor to comply with the terms of his tenancy, thus greatly reducing the rent payable, the premises being out of repair, as HA 1988, s 14(2)(c) applied only to the defaults of the current tenant.[127]

---

127 *N & D (London) Ltd v Gadsdon* [1992] 1 EGLR 112. This is because it was held that HA 1988, s 39 vests a new estate in the new tenant.

CHAPTER 16

Secure tenancies

I INTRODUCTION

General aspects

The Housing Act 1985 (hereinafter HA 1985) regulates the relationship of 'secure tenants' and public-sector or 'social' landlords, notably local authorities or housing action trusts. From 1989, however, new lettings by housing associations are on assured tenancies, so lessening the impact of secure tenancies.[1] The secure tenancies rules have been supplemented by an extra-legal Charter.[2]

The future of secure tenancies in their current form is uncertain. This is because the Law Commission is currently engaged on a programme of reform, whose current state is discussed in ch 13. The ultimate contours of the scheme remain to be seen. It is possible that a form of long-term tenancy will emerge for the social housing sector as a whole.

Introductory tenancies

The Housing Act 1996, Pt V enables local authorities and housing action trusts to elect to grant introductory, periodic, tenancies rather than secure tenancies. Introductory tenancies last for an initial or 'trial' period of one year. The period of one year runs from the date of entering into the tenancy or if later, the date when the tenant is first entitled to possession (Housing Act 1996, s 125(2)).[3] During this year, the

1   See Mullen, Scott, Fitzpatrick and Goodlad 62 (1999) MLR 11.
2   Secure Tenant's Charter (1998) (Housing Corporation), charged by Housing Act 1996 with certain supervisory functions in relation to social landlords. The Charter sets out a list of basic tenant rights and performance indicators, such as a right to a written tenancy agreement (p 6) and to a 'responsive repairs service' (p 11). It also summarises complaints procedures for aggrieved tenants (pp 18-20).
3   Periods under which a tenant granted an introductory tenancy had held under an assured shorthold tenancy from a registered social landlord count, in principle, towards the one-year trial period (Housing Act 1996, s 125(3)).

tenancy is prevented from being a secure tenancy.[4] Once the trial period comes to an end, the tenancy becomes a secure tenancy (Housing Act 1996, s 125(1)). This will not apply if the landlord has begun possession proceedings before the end of the one-year trial period and obtains possession during or outside the first year of the tenancy (as envisaged by Housing Act 1996, ss 127 and 130), or if one of the events in Housing Act 1996, s 125(5) apply, notably that a person or body other than a local housing authority or housing action trust becomes landlord.

Since an introductory tenancy has the potential to become, at the end of the initial year, a secure tenancy, it has some resemblances to a secure tenancy. A succession is allowed to the tenancy on the death of the original tenant by a member of his family subject to similar conditions to those applicable to secure tenancies (Housing Act 1996, ss 131-134). The express assignment of an introductory tenancy is prohibited with certain exceptions (Housing Act 1996, s 134).

If the local authority does not deem the tenant suitable for the grant of a secure tenancy, as where the tenant's conduct has been anti-social, it may seek possession without having to prove that a ground for possession exists, which would have to be done in the case of a secure tenancy. The landlord must however bring an introductory tenancy to an end by obtaining an order for possession from the court (Housing Act 1996, s 127(1)) and not, say, by means of a notice to quit. The landlord is bound to comply with a preliminary notice procedure, or possession cannot be ordered (Housing Act 1996, s 128(1)). Thus, a notice must set out the landlord's reasons for seeking possession (Housing Act 1996, s 128(3)) which enables the tenant to request him to review his decision to seek possession (under Housing Act 1996, s 129). A tenant dissatisfied with reasons given by an authority for its decision may challenge these by seeking a review by them.[5] A landlords' notice must specify a date for the beginning of proceedings, which must be no earlier that that of a common law notice to quit (Housing Act 1996, s 128(4)). A landlord may seek possession during the trial period. Provision is made for a case where possession is sought during that period and then the one-year initial period expires without an order having been made: during the whole period in question, the tenancy remains an introductory tenancy (Housing Act 1996, s 130(2)). It the requirements of a formal nature are satisfied, then the court is positively required to make an order for possession: the court has very little room for 'navigation' between the Scylla of Housing Act 1996, s 127 and the Charybdis of Housing Act 1996, s 128 (assuming the review procedure had been correctly

---

4   HA 1985, Sch 1, para 1A.
5   Introductory Tenants (Review) Regulations 1997, SI 1997/72. Where a tenant obtained a review after the commencement of possession proceedings, no second notice under Housing Act 1996, s 128 was required when the council concerned decided to press ahead with the proceedings: *Cardiff City Council v Stone* [2002] EWCA Civ 298. It might have been different if the position had altered in the period between the initial notice and the end of the review (eg a tenant having been in arrears with rent remedied matters).

undertaken).[6] Such a review may be undertaken after the date specified for proceedings in a s 128 notice.[7]

The security offered by an introductory tenancy is limited. It is deemed important to ease the removal of those introductory tenants whom the landlord considers to be anti-social, partly in the landlord's own interest, partly in the interest of other tenants in the vicinity. Provision is made for the loss of introductory status if any landlord other than a local authority or a housing action trust holds the landlord's interest (Housing Act 1996, s 125(5)). However, it seems that the introductory tenancy regime is not inconsistent with the ECHR, Arts 6 or 8. In the first place, housing policy is an area in which a wide margin of policy appreciation is left to domestic governments. Secondly, although the fact that the review process is not carried out by an independent tribunal if taken in isolation would infringe Article 6 (fair trial/proceedings requirement), the process as a whole did not do so. Thirdly, while it was true that the introductory tenancy scheme interfered with Article 8 (respect for home), the interference was justified. There was a balancing social policy: the need to take swift action against anti-social tenants as well as a need to prevent rent arrears from accruing.[8]

II SCOPE OF SECURE TENANCY PROVISIONS

By HA 1985, s 79(1) 'a tenancy under which a dwelling house[9] is let as a separate dwelling is a secure tenancy' at any time when the landlord condition and the tenant condition are satisfied. A tenancy may move into or out of the Act as and when either condition is satisfied or not applicable. This principle was applied with unfortunate results to a council landlord, whose business lessee, in breach of covenant, sub-let part of the premises on a weekly tenancy as a residential flat. The council obtained a surrender of the head lease without previously terminating any rights of the sub-lessee by notice, and the latter held a secure tenancy as a result.[10] Compliance with the statutory qualifying conditions important for the attaining of secure tenancy status, and only a secure tenant, save in those cases mentioned later in this Chapter, is entitled to exercise the 'right to buy' conferred by HA 1985, Pt *v*.

---

6 *Manchester City Council v Cochrane* [1999] L & TR 190, CA. The court cannot review the decision of a local authority to seek possession, it was held, owing to Housing Act 1996, s 130. The court deplored the absence of such a power.

7 *R v Salisbury DC* (2001) Times, 15 August .

8 *R v Bracknell Forest BC, ex p McLellan* (2001) 33 HLR 989, CA. Accordingly, the proportionality test was satisfied as regards ECHR, Art 8. Note was taken of the short duration of introductory tenancies. But ECHR, Art 8 applies even to non-secure tenancies and licences: *Sheffield City Council v Smart* [2002] EWCA Civ 04.

9 Which, as with RA 1977 and HA 1988, Pt I, may be a house or part of a house (HA 1985, s 112(1)); similarly, land let together with the dwelling house is within HA 1985 unless it is agricultural land exceeding two acres (HA 1985, s 112(2)).

10 *Basingstoke and Deane Borough Council v Paice* [1995] 2 EGLR 9, CA.

Landlord condition

The landlord condition relates to the type of landlord holding the interest out of which the tenancy is granted. This interest must, at all times, belong to a local authority, a new town corporation, an urban development corporation, or certain housing co-operatives (HA 1985, s 80(1)).[11] The landlord condition is satisfied if one of two joint landlords complies with it: both do not have to do so.[12] However, if the landlord's interest becomes transferred to a landlord who is outside those listed as satisfying the landlord condition of HA 1985, s 80, the tenancy ceases to be secure.

Tenant condition

The tenant condition requires, by HA 1985, s 81, that the tenant is an individual who occupies the dwelling house as his only or principal home. If all that the tenant has is a room in certain premises with the right to share kitchen and other facilities with others, he has no secure tenancy.[13] Two houses may be occupied at the same time as a home and actual physical occupation is not, it seems, always necessary to satisfy the tenant condition.[14] In the case of a joint tenancy, each of the tenants must be an individual and at least one of them must occupy the dwelling house as his or her only or principal home.

If any of these requirements ceases to be applicable, the tenancy ceases to be secure. So, too, where the landlord proves that the tenant has abandoned his occupation permanently, which occupation alone confers on him the statutory right to security. Thus, where a tenant had abandoned the premises permanently, and the landlords peaceably re-entered, changing the locks, security was lost.[15] A secure tenant who was imprisoned but who intended to return on release, was held to retain his occupation because he left his furniture on the premises as well as an occupying licensee.[16] Similarly, a tenant who had spent various periods in a nursing home on account of illnesses was found to have retained a sufficient intention to return. She had kept furniture on the premises, which were occupied by her relatives, presumably under licence.[17] The tenant condition may be lost by an intention to yield up the tenancy, even if the actual transaction concerned is ineffective, as where a tenant ceases to

---

11   Until 15 January 1989, most housing associations were able to grant secure tenancies; but these bodies are not longer within the landlord condition, and may only grant assured tenancies.

12   *R v Plymouth City Council, ex p Freeman* (1987) 19 HLR 328, CA.

13   *Central YMCA Housing Association Ltd v Saunders* (1990) 23 HLR 212.

14   *Crawley Borough Council v Sawyer* (1987) 20 HLR 98, CA.

15   *R v London Borough of Croydon Council, ex p Toth* (1987) 20 HLR 576, CA.

16   *Notting Hill Housing Trust v Etona* [1989] CLY 1912.

17   *Hammersmith & Fulham LBC v Clarke* (2000) 33 HLR 881, CA. The court referred to and seemingly followed Rent Act cases, notably *Brickfield Properties Ltd v Hughes* (1987) 20 HLR 108. There would seem to be no analogy with the stricter test applying to assured tenancies, where it appears that even a brief period of non-occupation will deprive the tenant of security.

hold a secure tenancy because of an ineffective assignment to another person.[18] The essential test seems in all of this to be that of the intention of the tenant. Evidence as to this before and after the tenancy is said to have terminated is relevant.

If the tenant has, at the date of the letting, a tenancy under which he may both carry on a significant amount of business user and also reside on the premises, he cannot hold a secure tenancy.[19] Moreover, a secure periodic tenancy is a personal right of occupation (much as is a statutory tenancy under the Rent Acts) so that it cannot be an asset forming part of the estate of a bankrupt.[20]

Secure licences

HA 1985, s 79(3) provides that the security provisions apply to a licence to occupy a dwelling house (whether granted for a consideration or not) as they apply to a tenancy. By HA 1985, s 79(4) this rule does not apply, and there is no security, where there is a licence granted as a temporary expedient to a person who entered the dwelling house as a trespasser (whether or not before the grant, another licence to occupy that or another dwelling house had been granted to him).

HA 1985, s 79(3) is narrow in scope, although it certainly brings a licence which confers exclusive possession within the secure tenancies rules.[21] It appears that HA 1985, s 79(3) has not altered the general law. It requires that the occupier is let a separate dwelling, which means a self-contained unit of habitation, exclusively possessed, as opposed to some rooms exclusively occupied as well as some additional living accommodation which the occupier must share with others.[22] A further example: where a single homeless person occupied a hostel room, and his 'licence to occupy' provided that he might have to change his allotted accommodation without notice, he held a licence outside HA 1985, s 79(3) as he lacked the requisite exclusive possession, which was retained by the landlord who, in the circumstances, needed it genuinely so as to control and supervise the hostel inmates.[23] Similarly, short-term arrangements in the form of licences from a developer, with a view to providing temporary accommodation, before the developer commenced redevelopment, were outside HA 1985, s 79(3).[24] On the other hand, where a council granted a licence of a self-contained flat, in premises awaiting redevelopment, to an occupier, and retained a duplicate set of

---

18 See *Westminster City Council v Peart* (1991) 24 HLR 389, CA.
19 *Webb v Barnet London Borough Council* (1988) 21 HLR 228, CA: hence, a cesser of business activities at the date of the hearing made no difference.
20 *City of London Corpn v Bown* (1989) 22 HLR 32, CA. Thus it will lie outside the Insolvency Act 1986, s 306.
21 *Family Housing Association v Miah* (1982) 5 HLR 94, CA; also *Kensington and Chelsea Royal Borough Council v Hayden* (1984) 17 HLR 114, CA.
22 *Parkins v Westminster City Council* [1998] 1 EGLR 22.
23 *Westminster City Council v Clarke* [1992] 1 All ER 695, HL.
24 *Shepherd's Bush Housing Association v HATS Co-operative* (1991) 24 HLR 176.

keys, but the occupier had apparently exclusive possession, she held a secure tenancy as the basic requirements of HA 1985, s 79(3) were satisfied.[25]

Tenancies which cannot be secure

HA 1985, Pt IV lists a group of tenancies which cannot be secure; and if a tenancy is excluded from Part IV, the tenant cannot, not being a secure tenant, exercise the RTB conferred by HA 1985, Pt V.

(i)   Long leases

A long tenancy, defined as a tenancy granted for a term certain exceeding 21 years whether or not terminable before the end of the term by a tenants' notice or by forfeiture is not secure.[26]

(ii)   Premises occupied in connection with employment

If the tenant is the employee of, in particular, a local authority, and where his contract of employment requires him to occupy the dwelling house for the better performance of his duties, the tenancy is not secure. 'Requires' means that it is a term of the tenant's contract of employment that he is, as an employee, required to occupy the premises for the better performance of his duties.[27] Once a dwelling house has been let on a tenancy within this exclusion, it may be re-let on a non-secure tenancy to any person for a period or periods not exceeding three years.[28] By this means, it is possible for a local authority to let employee accommodation for short periods to non-employees without falling within the security apparatus or the RTB provisions of HA 1985.

The policy of this principle is that if a tenancy of employment tied accommodation were held to become secure as soon as the employment ended, the landlord would lose the accommodation for use of future employees. It might also have to act harshly against any former employees in the accommodation.[29] However, the status of a tenancy

---

25   *Family Housing Association Ltd v Jones* [1990] 1 All ER 385, CA. The principle envisaged in this case that the landlord does not have to have an estate in land to confer a tenancy was approved by the House of Lords in *Bruton v London and Quadrant Housing Trust* [2000] 1 AC 406.

26   HA 1985, Sch 1, para 1 and s 115(1). Also excluded are tenancies with a right to perpetual renewal (HA 1985, s 115(1)(b)).

27   *Brent London BC v Charles* (1997) 29 HLR 876 (employee of sports centre whose contract of employment was later varied to require him to act as resident keyholder of the centre). See also *Coleman v Ipswich BC* [2001] EWCA Civ 852 (employee of council required to live in lodge because duties in relevant park better performed by a live-in employee than by one who resided away from the premises).

28   HA 1985, Sch 1, para 2(1) and (4).

29   *Greenfield v Berkshire County Council* (1996) 28 HLR 691, CA.

is not necessarily fixed as not secure, even if the conditions for exclusion are then satisfied, immutably at its commencement. If circumstances of the tenant alter, it may become secure.

The reverse principle also applies: the employment exception may apply to a tenant who originally was not required by his contract of employment to occupy in the required sense, but whose contract is later varied so as to incorporate such a requirement.[30] The court may imply a term that the employee is in occupation for the better performance of his duties, as where a school caretaker's terms of employment required him to live in school accommodation where possible, and he was allowed by the landlord authority to occupy a house near the relevant school.[31] Likewise, where a caretaker was contractually required to be on call for security reasons, deliveries, supervising contract workers and other duties, it was held to be essential for him to live near the school, in nearby council-provided accommodation, which fell within the present exemption, even though there was no clear statement in the caretaker's contract of employment that his accommodation was job-tied.[32] By contrast, where, at the date of a notice to quit, the tenant (a former school caretaker) had been made redundant some 14 months earlier, and had been allowed to remain in the house pending the availability of tied accommodation with his new employers, all connection with his former employment was held to have been severed. He therefore obtained a secure tenancy even though his tenancy, when it began, was not secure.[33]

If the occupation in that particular property is not essential for the better performance of the duties of the employee, the exemption is not applicable, so that a head teacher whose employment terms did not expressly require his residence in a specific house was outside the exemption, as no requirement to that effect needed to be implied to give business efficacy to that particular contract.[34] Where the exemption does not apply, the tenant will be able to exercise the RTB and remove the house concerned from the local authority's housing stock.

(iii) Land acquired for development

A tenancy is not secure if the dwelling house is on land which has been acquired for development and the dwelling house is used by the landlord, pending development of the land, as temporary housing accommodation.[35] This exception, whose policy is to avoid land awaiting redevelopment being sterilised and removed from the housing stock in the interim, does not impliedly require that the landlord be the person who

---

30 *Elvidge v Coventry City Council* [1994] QB 241, CA.
31 *South Glamorgan County Council v Griffiths* (1992) 24 HLR 334, CA.
32 *Surrey County Council v Lamond* [1999] L & TR 213, CA.
33 *Greenfield v Berkshire County Council* (1996) 28 HLR 691, CA.
34 *Hughes v London Borough of Greenwich* (1992) 24 HLR 605, HL.
35 HA 1985, Sch 1, para 3(1); see *Lillieshall Road Housing Co-operative Ltd v Brennan* (1991) 24 HLR 195, CA.

acquired the land for development, so that where a housing association held a flat under an agreement with a government department for use as temporary housing, and the former body granted a temporary weekly licence to occupy, the association was entitled to repossess for rent arrears and the agreement fell within the exception.[36]

(iv) Accommodation for homeless persons

A tenancy granted to certain classes of homeless persons is not secure for the first 12 months from notification of a decision on homelessness or threatened homelessness, unless before the expiry of the 12 months, the landlord notifies the tenant that the tenancy is to be regarded as secure.[37] The relevant date for the purpose of this exclusion runs from the date of written notification of the decision of the authority whether the occupier is intentionally homeless, and an oral notification will not, having regard to the importance of such decisions to homeless persons, suffice.[38]

A person who is let into exclusive occupation under this exclusion occupies as a tenant and not a licensee, and so HA 1985, s 79(3) cannot apply, converting it into a secure tenancy, as the tenancy was not secure when granted (though it may subsequently become so).[39] In any event, HA 1985, s 79(3) did not convert a non-exclusive licence to occupy into a tenancy so as to enable the occupier to claim a secure tenancy.[40]

(v)   Temporary accommodation for persons taking up employment

A tenancy is not secure for one year from its grant, unless before the expiry of that year the tenant has been notified by the landlord that the tenancy is to be regarded as a secure tenancy, if it is granted to a person not previously resident in the local housing authority's district, and who, prior to the grant of the tenancy, obtained employment or an offer thereof in the district or in the area of any district surrounding it. The tenancy must be granted to enable the person to meet his need for temporary accommodation in the district or its surrounding area in order to work, and to enable him to find permanent accommodation there. The landlord must notify the tenant in writing of the circumstances of the application of this exception.[41]

---

36   *Hyde Housing Association v Harrison* [1991] 1 EGLR 51, CA; Fox LJ pointed out that the identity of the acquirer was left at large by HA 1985, Sch 1, para 3, and the fact that there might be an overlap with HA 1985, Sch 1, para 6 was treated as immaterial.
37   HA 1985, Sch 1, para 4.
38   *R v Swansea City Council, ex p Hearn* (1990) 23 HLR 284, CA.
39   *Eastleigh Borough Council v Walsh* [1985] 2 All ER 112, [1985] 1 WLR 525, HL.
40   *Kensington and Chelsea Royal Borough Council v Hayden* (1984) 17 HLR 114, CA.
41   HA 1985, Sch 1, para 5.

(vi) Short-term arrangements

If the dwelling house has been leased to the landlord itself, by a landlord who cannot grant secure tenancies, with vacant possession, for use as temporary housing accommodation and the head lessor is able to obtain vacant possession from the landlord on the expiry of a specified period or when required by it (say pursuant to a break clause in the head lease) and the head landlord has no interest in the dwelling house other than as lessor or mortgagee, the tenancy is not secure.[42] It appears, so as to avoid unnecessary technicalities, that if the person granting the tenancy or licence to the immediate occupier in terms reserves himself the right to vacant possession, this exemption will still apply; and moreover, where a licence was terminable on seven days' notice, this requirement was sufficient to enable recovery within this exclusion.[43] Where a licensee was permitted to occupy premises in circumstances which in fact fell within this exclusion, it was held that he had no security on the termination of his licence, even though the exclusion is in terms confined to tenancies.[44] Were it otherwise, a licensee would be in a better position than a tenant.

(vii) Temporary accommodation pending works

A tenancy is not a secure tenancy if the dwelling house has been made available to the tenant or to a predecessor in title of his for occupation by him while works are carried on a dwelling house previously occupied as his home, and the tenant or, seemingly, any, predecessor was not a secure tenant of that dwelling house at the time when he ceased to occupy it as his home.[45]

(viii) Other exclusions

Tenancies or licences of the following classes in particular cannot be secure: farm business tenancies,[46] licensed premises,[47] student lettings,[48] business tenancies within the Landlord and Tenant Act 1954, Pt II,[49] and licences to occupy almshouses.[50]

---

42 HA 1985, Sch 1, para 6.
43 *Tower Hamlets London Borough Council v Abdi* [1993] 1 EGLR 68, CA.
44 *Tower Hamlets London Borough Council v Miah* (1992) 24 HLR 199, CA.
45 HA 1985, Sch 1, para 7. The aim of this is presumably to stop a claim to security merely on account of the enforced temporary move.
46 HA 1985, Sch 1, para 8, as substituted by the Agricultural Tenancies Act 1995, Sch, para 30. The dwelling house must be occupied by the person responsible for the control of the farming or management of the holding, as the tenant, or as his servant or agent.
47 HA 1985, Sch 1, para 9.
48 HA 1985, Sch 1, para 10. Specific notification rules apply.
49 HA 1985, Sch 11: this is akin to RA 1977, s 24(3) and HA 1988, Sch 1, para 4.
50 HA 1985, Sch 1, para 12. Tenancies granted to asylum seekers cannot be secure (HA 1985, Sch 1, para 4A).

III   ASSIGNMENTS, LODGERS AND SUB-LETTINGS

Assignments

A secure tenancy agreement may contain an express prohibition on the assignment of the tenancy, but HA 1985, Pt IV contains specific and seemingly, to the extent of the application of the statute, overriding rules as to assignments. A secure periodic tenancy cannot be assigned except in the circumstances set out in HA 1985 (HA 1985, s 19(1)).[51]

According to a majority of the House of Lords, the secure tenancy scheme would be open to abuse if the tenant were able to deal freely with his or her tenancy: hence, a wide view was taken of assignments under HA 1985, s 91. These included a deed of release executed by one joint tenant in favour of another, on the former leaving the premises, so as to vest the tenancy in the remaining tenant.[52] The 'esoteric concept' that a joint tenant has nothing to transfer to the other, as each owns the whole, was dismissed by Lord Nicholls as 'remote from the realities of life'. Thus HA 1985, s 91 applies where one of two tenants drops out. The underlying effect of the transaction was to vest the tenancy in one of the two former joint tenants. What may lie behind this broad-brush approach, which neglects the fact that the tenant condition may be satisfied by the occupation of one of two or more joint tenants as their only or principal home, is that otherwise, a house let to joint tenants might, after the departure of one of them, become over-occupied, when the landlord might wish to rehouse the remaining tenant elsewhere, and make more efficient use of the accommodation for others waiting to be housed.[53]

There are three exceptions to the statutory prohibition on express assignments. While to be valid at common law, an assignment within these exceptions must apparently, owing to technical reasons, be by deed,[54] it may be that the courts would accept as valid an informal or equitable assignment, to save the parties the unnecessary trouble and expense of drawing up a deed.[55]

---

51   A secure fixed-term tenancy granted as from 5 November 1982 cannot in principle be assigned, which includes, on a wide view, an assignment by operation of law, there is no secure tenancy to pass to a bankrupt secure tenant's estate for the benefit of his creditors: *City of London Corpn v Bown* (1989) 22 HLR 32, CA.

52   *Burton v Camden London BC* [2000] 1 AC 406, [2000] 1 All ER 943. However, as noted by Lord Millett the wording of HA 1985, , s 91 does not in terms refer to a release and can only be applied to it by doing violence to the language of HA 1985.

53   HA 1985, Sch 2, ground 16 enables repossession (at court discretion) where the accommodation is too extensive, but is limited to a case where the occupying tenant has been declared entitled to succeed to the secure tenancy.

54   *Crago v Julian* [1992] 1 All ER 744, CA.

55   *Westminster City Council v Peart* (1991) 24 HLR 389, CA (where the point was left open); but such assignment would need to comply with Law of Property Act 1925 s 53(1)(c), and so be in writing, save where a resulting, implied or constructive trust had been created on the facts.

1 Assignments under the Matrimonial Causes Act 1973, s 24 (HA 1985, s 91(3)(b)).[56] Such a permitted assignment causes the statutory succession provisions to operate if the other party to the marriage was a successor (HA 1985, ss 91(3) and 88(2)). The relationship between the Matrimonial Causes Act 1973, s 24 and the express terms of a secure tenancy held by one sole tenant has not been examined in recent authorities. While the court would presumably be prepared to exercise its powers to transfer the tenancy under the Matrimonial Causes Act 1973, s 24 if the tenancy did not in terms prohibit assignments, it has been said that it would not exercise its jurisdiction if the order would be defeated by an express prohibition on assignments in the tenancy agreement,[57] perhaps because, as was said, the court had the same power only as the tenant would have had to assign the tenancy.[58] However, if a secure tenancy is jointly held by a couple whose marriage ends in divorce, the court has the statutory power to order the transfer of the tenancy to the sole name of the spouse still in occupation.[59] Where it is held by one party only to the marriage, it is thought that the court could not order a transfer of the tenancy to the spouse who was not a secure tenant. It has, in particular, been held that a surrender by the secure tenancy holding spouse enables possession to be recovered from a non-tenant spouse still in occupation of the house or flat.[60] This would mean that, presumably, there would be nothing to transfer to the non-tenant spouse, who could not satisfy the statutory requirement of residential occupation and who could not be said (as was the case under the Rent Acts) to be occupying the premises through their tenant spouse.

2 An assignment to a person who would be qualified to succeed to the tenancy had the tenant died immediately prior to the assignment (HA 1985, s 91(3)(c)). The statutory succession provisions are operated by an assignment of this type and, on the death of the person to whom the tenancy has been assigned, there may be no further succession

---

56 Where a suspended possession order was made and the tenant failed to comply with its terms, from that moment, the tenancy ended and there was nothing for Matrimonial Causes Act 1973, s 24 to operate on: *Thompson v Elmbridge Borough Council* [1987] 1 WLR 1425, CA. The tenant became a 'tolerated trespasser' as to which see below.

57 *Thompson v Thompson* [1975] 2 All ER 208, CA, approved in *Newlon Housing Trust v Alsulamein* [1998] 4 All ER 1, HL: hence, a periodic tenancy no longer in existence because it has been determined by a valid notice to quit served by one of two spouses who were joint tenants cannot be transferred under Matrimonial Causes Act 1973, s 24 as there is nothing to transfer. A joint periodic tenancy can be ended by a notice to quit served by one of two joint tenants: *Hammersmith and Fulham London BC v Monk* [1992] 1 AC 478, [1992] 1 All ER 1, HL, as applied to secure tenancies by *Harrow London BC v Johnstone* [1997] 1 All ER 929, [1997] 1 WLR 459, HL (where a notice to quit served by a joint tenant wife was also not a contempt of a non-molestation order made against her). It will be appreciated that notices to quit (or surrenders) given by one spouse are often the prelude to that person being re-housed and their estranged spouse then being evicted from the home concerned.

58 *Hale v Hale* [1975] 2 All ER 1090, CA: in this case, the tenancy contained no prohibitions and the court exercised its power to order a transfer to the tenant's ex-wife after a divorce.

59 Matrimonial Homes Act 1983, Sch 2.

60 *Sanctuary Housing Association v Campbell* [1999] L & TR 425, CA; also *Hackney London BC v Snowden* [2001] L & TR 60, CA.

(HA 1985, s 88(1)(d)). Therefore, a secure tenant may use this exception as a way of preventing or pre-empting disputes as to who is entitled to succeed after his death by assigning to his spouse or resident family member. Such an assignment renders the tenancy secure in the hands of the successor-assign (provided this person is qualified to succeed, such as the tenant's husband or wife or son or daughter). The present exception overrides any term of the tenancy prohibiting assignments; but, curiously, if the tenancy prohibits assignments, the landlord may proceed against the successor for the previous tenant's assignment contrary to covenant.[61] Where a claimant relied on cohabitation in order to claim that a purported assignment to her by the secure tenant of the tenancy of a flat fell within the present exemption, it was held that the relevant date for determining whether the parties lived together as husband and wife was the date of the assignment, and so the 12-month period required for residence by a family member ran back from that date. On the facts, the parties had at best intermittently cohabited (as the claimant, the tenant's ex-wife, retained a secure tenancy of a different flat throughout the relevant period).[62]

3 Assignments by way of exchange (HA 1985, s 91(3)(a)). A secure tenant may, under HA 1985, s 92, assign the tenancy, whether it is fixed term or periodic, by way of exchange with another secure tenant, or with an assured tenant.[63] The statutory succession provisions only operate if the tenant receiving an assignment of a tenancy was a successor in relation to the tenancy he himself assigned (HA 1985, s 88(3)).

The tenant must obtain the written consent of the landlord (HA 1985, s 92(2)).[64] However, failing to ask for or obtain consent will not of itself invalidate the assignment by exchange, as there are two transactions, the assignments and the consent of the landlord to each of these.[65] Consent may be withheld only on the grounds set out in HA 1985, Sch 3. A consent withheld on any other ground is treated as given (HA 1985, s 92(3)). The landlord cannot rely on any HA 1985, Sch 3 ground unless, within 42 days from the tenant's application for consent, he has served a notice on the tenant specifying the ground and giving particulars of it (HA 1985, s 92(4)). The landlord cannot subject his consent to any conditions (HA 1985, s 92(6)).[66] These grounds may be summarised as follows.

1   The tenant or proposed assignee is obliged to give up possession of the dwelling house concerned under a court order, or will be so obliged at a date specified in the order.

61   *Peabody Donation Fund v Higgins* [1983] 3 All ER 122, [1983] 1 WLR 1091, CA.
62   *Westminster City Council v Peart* (1991) 24 HLR 389, CA.
63   The fact that an agreement to assign by exchange relates to a periodic tenancy makes no difference: *Sanctuary Housing Association v Baker* [1998] 1 EGLR 42, CA. The landlord is not a necessary party to the assignment: ibid.
64   No doubt because the secure tenancy rules are self-contained, the procedures of the Landlord and Tenant Act 1988 do not apply in this case (Landlord and Tenant Act 1988, s 5(3)).
65   *Sanctuary Housing Association v Baker* [1998] 1 EGLR 42, CA.
66   Where the tenant is in arrears with rent or has broken the terms of his tenancy, this is not a ground for refusing consent, but the landlord may impose a condition requiring repayment of the arrears or remedy of the breach concerned (HA 1985, s 92(5)).

2   Proceedings for possession of the dwelling house of which the tenant or proposed assignee is secure tenant have begun on one or more of grounds 1 to 6 of HA 1985, Sch 2; or a HA 1985, s 83 notice, which is still in force, has been served on either party which specifies one or more of these grounds.

3   The accommodation afforded by the dwelling house is substantially more extensive than is reasonably required by the proposed assignee.

4   The extent of the accommodation afforded by the dwelling house is not reasonably suitable to the needs of the proposed assignee and his family.

5   The dwelling house forms part of or is within the curtilage of a building which is held mainly for purposes other than housing purposes and consists mainly of accommodation other than housing accommodation, or is situated in a cemetery, and was let to the tenant or his predecessor as an employee of the landlord, a local authority or other specified landlord.[67]

6   The landlord is a charity and the proposed assignee's occupation of the dwelling house would conflict with its objects.

7   The dwelling house has features which make it substantially different from others, and is suitable for occupation by a disabled person; or the landlord is a housing association or housing trust which lets to persons whose non-financial circumstances make it specially difficult for them to satisfy their need for housing; and in either case, if the assignment were made, there would no longer be a disabled or disadvantaged person residing in the dwelling house.[68]

8   The dwelling house is subject to a management agreement managed by a housing association, where at least half the tenants are subject to the agreement and members of the association but the assignee is not willing to become a member of the association.

Lodgers and sub-lettings

Specific statutory rules are provided to deal with the taking in of lodgers and sub-lettings. First, it is a statutory (implied) term of every secure tenancy that the tenant may allow lodgers to reside in the house or flat in question (HA 1985, s 93(1)(a)). By contrast, no secure tenant may, except with the landlord's written consent, sub-let or part with the possession of part of the house or flat.[69] Should the tenant part with the possession or sub-let the whole of the 'dwelling house', or sub-let part and then the remainder, the tenancy ceases to be secure and cannot subsequently become secure, as where the sub-tenancy is terminated (HA 1985, s 93(2)). Therefore, on termination of the head (and, where HA 1985, s 93(2) applies, non-secure) tenancy, the sub-tenancy is equally not secure as against the head landlord, applying common law principles already discussed.

67   Ie a housing corporation, a housing action trust, a new town corporation, an urban development corporation or the governors of an aided school.

68   Similarly there is a ground (ground 9) which applies where the dwelling house is one of a group of premises for letting by the landlord to 'special needs' tenants.

69   These rules apply to the exclusion of LTA 1988 (LTA 1988, s 5(3)).

A secure tenant who, for some intermittent periods, had ceased to occupy a flat, had not parted with possession in favour of the premises in the permanent and illegal sense required by HA 1985, s 93.[70] On the other hand, where a secure tenant left his one-bedroomed home temporarily, and a couple occupied it exclusively, under what was held to be an oral tenancy, paying a deposit, and rent, and holding the keys, the tenant was in breach of HA 1985, s 93 and lost his secure tenancy, even though he may not have intended the result objectively arrived at from the grant of exclusive possession.[71]

The landlord, if asked, is bound not to withhold unreasonably his consent (HA 1985, s 94(2)).[72] The landlord must show that consent was not unreasonably withheld if his decision is challenged. He may give his consent following any action (as for a declaration by the tenant), so reversing the common law (HA 1985, s 94(4)). If the tenant applies in writing for consent, if the landlord refuses consent, it must give the tenant a written statement of the reasons for the refusal, and if he neither gives nor refuses consent within a reasonable time, consent is taken to have been withheld (HA 1985, s 94(6)).[73]

IV   STATUTORY SUCCESSION SCHEME

Introduction

HA 1985, Pt IV allows for a single succession to a secure fixed-term or periodic tenancy by a person qualified to succeed, who is either the secure tenant's spouse or a resident family member. However, where a landlord agreed to grant a new secure tenancy to a deceased intestate tenant's widow, the statutory succession scheme was not operated, and on her own death the secure tenancy could be transmitted to a member of her family.[74]

A *secure periodic tenancy*[75] devolves under statute as follows. After the death of the secure tenant, if there is a person qualified to succeed, the tenancy vests by operation of law, under HA 1985, s 89(1), in that person. Should there be more than one such person, as where there is both a spouse and a resident family member, preference is to be given to the tenant's spouse. If there should be no spouse, but two or more family

---

70   *Hussey v London Borough of Camden* (1994) 27 HLR 5, applying *Lam Shee Ying v Lam Shes Tong* [1975] AC 247.

71   *Brent London BC v Cronin* (1997) 30 HLR 43, CA.

72   Two factors are listed as material for the purpose, viz, the likelihood of overcrowding or the effect of works which the landlord proposes to carry out on the accommodation to be offered to the proposed sub-tenant (HA 1985, s 94(3)).

73   By analogy with LTA 1988, the 'reasonable time' allowed to the landlord is likely, save in exceptional cases of complexity, to be a few weeks at most.

74   *Epping Forest District Council v Pomphrett* (1990) 22 HLR 475, CA; none of the 'triggers' in HA 1985, s 88 of the succession scheme applied.

75   A similar provision is made for secure fixed-term tenancies by HA 1985, s 90. The tenancy is secure until it vests under the succession provisions in the successor, as a secure tenancy, or, if there is no such person, the tenancy ceases to be secure when it is vested or disposed of elsewhere or as soon as it is known that when so vested etc it will not be secure.

members in competition for the succession, since only one person may succeed to the tenancy solely, the preference is to be by agreement or, failing agreement, by selection of the landlord (HA 1985, s 89(2)).

Should there be no person qualified to succeed, and the tenancy is then vested or otherwise disposed of in the administration of the tenant's estate, the tenancy ceases to be secure, and cannot become secure subsequently.[76]

Persons who may succeed

A person is qualified to succeed if he occupied the dwelling house as his only or principal home at the time of the tenant's death and is either the tenant's spouse or another member of the tenant's family (HA 1985, s 87). The family member must reside with the tenant throughout the 12 months ending with the tenant's death. However, this 12-month period may be interrupted temporarily, without costing the claimant a right to succeed. Whether a period of interruption is temporary is a question of fact. Hence, a person who resided with his grandmother for all but 10 weeks of a year, living for the 10 weeks with his spouse in a friend's home, did not lose his right to succeed.[77]

The expression 'family' is defined in HA 1985, s 113(1) as including a person living with the tenant as husband or wife, the tenant's parent, grandparent, child, grandchild, brother, sister, aunt, nephew or niece. Moreover, although at first instance a stepchild was treated as a child for statutory purposes,[78] this decision was rejected in a later decision, where a foster child was held not entitled to claim a succession.[79] A minor is entitled to succeed even though a minor cannot hold a legal estate: after all, HA 1985 gives secure tenancy status to certain licensees under HA 1985, s 79(3), and nothing therefore precludes his holding an equitable tenancy interest.[80] Moreover, since a single-sex partner of a statutory tenant is in principle entitled to claim to succeed to an assured tenancy by succession as a member of his or her 'family', there would clearly be a right to succeed to a secure tenancy in similar circumstances by such a claimant.[81] As with statutory tenancies, it would be necessary for the claimant partner to show that there had been a long-standing, close, loving and faithful, monogamous homosexual

---

76   HA 1985, s 89(3) and (4), subject to a limited exception in favour of disposals under property adjustment orders under the Matrimonial Causes Act 1973, s 24.

77   *Camden London Borough Council v Goldenberg* (1996) 28 HLR 727, CA.

78   See *Reading Borough Council v Ilsley* [1981] CLY 1323.

79   *Hereford City Council v O'Callaghan* [1996] CLY 3831. It appears that the list of persons of HA 1985, s 113 is exclusive: *Michalck v London Borough of Wandsworth* [2002] EWCA Civ 271.

80   *Kingston-upon-Thames BC v Prince* [1999] L & TR 175, CA. See Mills and Joss (2001) 5 L&T Rev 53. A Rent Act decision relied on was *Portman Registrars v Mohammed Latif* [1987] CLY 2239.

81   *Fitzpatrick v Sterling Housing Association Ltd* [1999] 4 All ER 705; see Thompson [2000] Conv 153; Cretney and Reynolds (2000) 116 LQR 181. A same-sex partner was, however, not held to be the 'spouse' of the deceased tenant, as opposed to a family member, approving *Harrogate BC v Simpson* (1984) 17 HLR 205, CA on this point.

relationship as a condition precedent to succession to the tenancy. Whether a person who had cared for a secure tenant with whom that carer had resided for a long time, but with whom their relationship was platonic, could now claim a succession to a secure tenancy on the death of the tenant is a question that cannot be answered on the current state of the authorities.[82]

'Reside with' means to spend a significant part of one's time with the person concerned,[83] and may now involve living permanently with that person for a long time, even though common sense prevails and short absences may make no difference: in one case a 10-week absence did not break the occupation continuity required by HA 1985.[84] The statutory residence rule does not impliedly involve the further requirement that the claimant to a succession should have resided in the same dwelling house with the tenant for the full 12-month period: thus, where a secure tenant and his brother, having lived in the same premises for two-and- a-half years, moved to a different house, both properties being held on secure tenancies, and the tenant died within 10 days of the move, the House of Lords upheld the brother's claim to succeed: he had resided with the deceased for well over double the statutory period and it made no difference that the residence was in different premises.[85]

Position after death of successor

After the death of any successor to a secure tenancy, there is no further succession under the statute and the tenancy ceases to be secure. The word 'successor' is defined by HA 1985, s 88(1)(a) as including a person in whom the tenancy vested under a statutory succession. The succession provisions are operated where a joint secure tenant becomes the sole tenant.[86] They are also operated if the tenancy arose after the ending of a fixed-term secure tenancy and that first tenancy had been granted to another tenant, or to that person and another person jointly (HA 1985, s 88(1)(c)), and

82   The conclusion in *Carega Properties SA (formerly Joram Developments) v Sharratt* [1979] 2 All ER 1084, [1979] 1 WLR 928 (where a young man lived with a 74-year old widow for some 18 years in a platonic relationship failed to claim her statutory tenant as her successor) might indicate that a sexual relationship is a *conditio sine qua non* to a succession claim. While there may not have been a sufficient element of caring in that case, its result seems hard to reconcile with the ratio of the *Fitzpatrick* decision.
83   *Peabody Donation Fund Governors v Grant* [1982] 2 EGLR 37; otherwise, no doubt, the term 'reside with' bears a similar meaning to that under the RA 1977 scheme.
84   *Camden London BC v Goldenberg* (1996) 28 HLR 727, CA. The facts were nevertheless minutely examined: thus the claimant's postal address remained unaltered, and he could not afford alternative accommodation on a permanent basis. His 'house-sit' elsewhere did not therefore disqualify him.
85   *Waltham Forest London Borough Council v Thomas* [1992] 2 AC 198.
86   *Bassetlaw District Council v Renshaw* [1991] 2 EGLR 254, CA: for this rule to operate, the tenant must have been first a joint tenant and then a single tenant under the *same* tenancy: thus where T held a joint tenancy with X, which X terminated by notice to quit, and T was granted a new tenancy, and later died, a succession to the *second* tenancy was still possible.

also where the tenant became a secure tenant by an assignment,[87] and where the tenant becomes tenant by vesting in him of the tenancy on the death of the previous tenant (HA 1985, s 88(1)(d) and (e)), and finally where the tenancy had previously been an introductory tenancy and he had succeeded to it on the death of the original tenant (HA 1985, s 88(1)(f)).

V REPOSSESSION BY THE LANDLORD

General rules

HA 1985, Pt IV restricts the extent to which the landlord is entitled to terminate a secure fixed-term tenancy, and in the case of both this type of tenancy and secure periodic tenancies, requires that the landlord obtains an order for possession from the county court[88] on one or more statutory grounds. While it is understood that secure fixed-term tenancies may be much less common than secure periodic tenancies, a note of the specific rules governing the former is called for, for the sake of completeness.

Once a secure fixed-term tenancy comes to an end, a periodic tenancy arises under HA 1985, s 86(1).[89] The periodic tenancy arising on the determination of the fixed-term tenancy is on the terms of HA 1985, s 86(2) and, in particular, the rental periods are the same as those for which rent was payable under the previous tenancy. The other terms of the tenancy are those of the former tenancy, provided these are compatible with those of a periodic tenancy, and excluding forfeiture provisions. This statutory periodic tenancy is terminable only in accordance with the procedures of HA 1985.

If the landlord should decide to take proceedings for possession against a secure fixed-term tenant, rather than awaiting the ending of the term and then terminating the periodic tenancy arising, he cannot rely on any forfeiture clause, genuine or disguised,[90] to put an end to the tenant's right to occupy the house or flat. He must serve a statutory notice on the tenant under HA 1985, s 83, which notice will, however, apply to any statutorily arising periodic tenancy arising once the fixed-term tenancy has come to an end (HA 1985, s 83(6)).

Possession will only, however, be ordered by the court if the landlord is able to prove one or more of the statutory grounds which must be established against secure tenants

87 Subject to the exceptions mentioned in HA 1985, s 88(2) and (3), relating to assignments under property adjustment orders or by exchange, where the succession provisions are operated by the assignment only if the assignor was a successor.
88 The reformed procedure (following Lord Woolf's Report 'Access to Justice'(1996)) lies outside the scope of this book. See however Madge (1999) New Law J 1408; Sparkes *A New Landlord and Tenant* ch 13; there are new speedy procedures in the case of anti-social tenants (SI 2001/256).
89 This is automatic, unless the tenant is granted another fixed-term or periodic tenancy of the same dwelling house to begin when the first tenancy ends.
90 As considered in, eg *Clays Lane Housing Co-operative Ltd v Patrick* (1984) 49 P & CR 72, CA.

(HA 1985, s 82(1)(b)). The court cannot, indeed, order possession as a result of the operation of any forfeiture clause in the fixed-term tenancy, but if it would, but for HA 1985, have ordered possession under common law principles already discussed, it must terminate the fixed-term tenancy on the date specified in its order (HA 1985, s 82(3)). In this event, the statutory periodic tenancy arises under HA 1985, s 86. The powers of the court to grant relief to the tenant (but not to a sub-tenant) apply to proceedings under any forfeiture clause, as does the general doctrine of waiver (HA 1985, s 82(4)).

Termination of periodic tenancies

By HA 1985, s 82(1), a weekly or other periodic tenancy, whether arising under the Act or originally granted to the tenant, cannot be brought to an end by a landlord's notice to quit.[91] The landlord must obtain an order for possession (in the county court (HA 1985, s 110)) and the tenancy ends on any date specified in that order.

The landlord must, if he wishes to recover possession, serve a statutory notice on the tenant, who is thus entitled to advance warning of pending possession proceedings and as to the claims he will face. The court may dispense with the need to serve a statutory notice if it is just and equitable to do so (HA 1985, s 83(1)(b)). Any notice must, with the exception of proceedings based on ground 2 (HA 1985, s 83(4)), state a date after which proceedings may be begun.[92] A notice ceases to be in force 12 months after that date (HA 1985, s 83(4)). The specified date is of critical importance since the county court cannot allow the landlord to bring a claim for possession until after the specified date has passed where the notice remains in force (HA 1985, s 83A(1)).[93] Moreover, the specified date cannot be sooner than the earliest date the tenancy could be brought to an end by a common law notice to quit, though it may presumably correspond with that date. The protection given to a weekly or monthly secure tenant by this latter rule is not great although statute entitles him to a minimum four weeks' notice (see ch 17, below).

In accordance with the warning function assigned to termination notices, such notices must specify and give particulars of the ground on which the court will be asked to make an order for possession of a dwelling house let under a secure tenancy (HA 1985, s 83(2)). Otherwise the court cannot entertain the proceedings. 'Giving particulars' seems to require that landlords give some details of the alleged breaches, such as the amount of rent allegedly in arrear, or as to alleged items of disrepair, otherwise the

---

91 The landlord must put an end to the periodic tenancy by a notice which complies with the requirements of the Protection from Eviction Act 1977, as well as the common law rules (inference from HA 1985, s 83(3)).

92 Any notice must be in the prescribed form: SI 1987/755 as amended. In the case of ground 2 proceedings, the notice must specify the date at which the landlord wishes the tenant to give up possession (HA 1985, s 83(2)).

93 Substituted for HA 1985, s 83 by Housing Act 1996, s 147(1) as from 12 February 1997: SI 1997/66.

notice risks being invalid.[94] A HA 1985, s 83 notice is, perhaps resembling statutory forfeiture notices, a warning shot across the bows of the tenant, warning him that unless he rectifies the alleged breaches, he faces dispossession.[95] In any case, where the court may refuse possession in its general discretion (as with grounds based on allegations of tenant misconduct), a tenant may therefore improve his chances of resisting an order for possession by discontinuing the offending conduct as from receipt of the HA 1985, s 83 notice. If his record has in the past been bad, this would presumably be one factor to be taken into account in assessing whether the court would exercise its discretion to refuse possession; but a remedied breach at the time of the proceedings being heard cannot presumably afford the landlord a ground for possession.

The above rules as to notices have no application to tenants' notices to quit: if a tenant serves a notice to quit, he cannot later rely on the security provisions,[96] and the same principle would appear to apply if one of a number of joint tenants serves a notice to quit, without having consulted his co-tenants, as the joint tenancy would be at an end after expiry of this notice (as to which see above). If, moreover, a secure tenant permanently leaves the premises, whether or not owing rent, he loses security, having ceased to comply with the statutory residence requirement imposed by the tenant condition.[97]

Grounds for possession: general

The court cannot make an order for possession against a secure tenant except on proof by the landlord of one or more grounds for possession as laid down in HA 1985, Sch 2. If a ground is not specified in the landlord's statutory notice, the court cannot make an order for possession based on that ground (HA 1985, s 84(3)).[98] This particular provision states that 'the grounds so specified may be altered or added to with the leave of the court'. The power has been widely construed. The court may alter a specified ground, and add a new ground, and also, though the particulars of a ground are not in terms mentioned by HA 1985, s 84(3) in its former or altered form, it may even alter or add to these latter, as they may be said to be part and parcel of a ground. The protection of the tenant seems to lie in the discretion of the court and the power of the Court of Appeal to review the exercise of that discretion by a lower court.[99] The court

94 *Torridge District Council v Jones* [1985] 2 EGLR 54, CA.
95 All the allegations against the tenant must be put to him, having regard to the ECHR: *Sheffield City Council v Hopkins* [2001] EWCA Civ 1023, [2002] 1 P & CR D7.
96 *Greenwich London Borough Council v McGrady* (1982) 81 LGR 288, CA.
97 *Preston Borough Council v Fairclough* (1982) 8 HLR 70, CA; also *R v Croydon London Borough Council, ex p Toth* (1987) 20 HLR 576, CA.
98 As substituted by the Housing Act 1996, s 147(2). The court cannot make an order for possession requiring the tenant to give up possession before any date specified in a HA 1985, s 83 notice (HA 1985, s 84(4) as substituted).
99 *Camden London Borough Council v Oppong* (1996) 28 HLR 701, CA.

cannot, however, order possession to take effect any earlier than the date specified in the landlord's HA 1985, s 83 notice (HA 1985, s 84(4)).

Grounds 1 to 8 are subject to an overriding requirement that it must be reasonable to make an order for possession (HA 1985, s 84(2)(a)). The court exercises this overriding discretion in much the same way as it might under RA 1977. The court's overriding discretion is not limited to circumstances connected with the ground relied on for seeking possession.[100] The courts do not take a restrictive view of this legislation, and all relevant circumstances have to be taken into account as at the date of the hearing, taking a broad, common sense view, giving weight to the various relevant factors.[101] It is a material factor that, for example, a tenant, or a member of the tenant's family or household, is continuing with conduct that amounts to a nuisance or annoyance at the date of the hearing, so showing no wish to mend his ways.[102] However, the mere fact that a term of the tenancy agreement may have been broken, although no doubt a relevant matter, is not the sole factor, so that a judge was entitled to conclude that it was not reasonable to order possession against a tenant who had taken no active part in a fire caused by visitors to his flat, although the terms of his tenancy had been broken.[103] Thus it is appropriate for the court to take into account the effects of a possession order on the tenant.[104] These effects include the fact that the tenant will be rendered homeless by the possession order.[105]

Grounds 9 to 11 are subject to a requirement that when the order takes effect, suitable alternative accommodation will be available to the tenant and his family (HA 1985, s 84(2)(b)).[106] These grounds are, however, mandatory in the sense that there is no overriding discretion to refuse possession, if the alternative accommodation condition and the basic requirements of the ground have been proved. So as to protect such persons, the court cannot make an order for possession under HA 1985, s 84(2)(b) if a member of the tenant's family living in the premises, such as his estranged wife, has not been joined as a party to the proceedings.[107]

---

100 *Sheffield City Council v Hopkins* [2001] EWCA Civ 1023, [2002] 1 P & CR D7. Hence, in a case of rent arrears, proof of anti-social conduct would be relevant to the exercise of the overriding discretion.

101 *Haringey London Borough Council v Stewart* [1991] 2 EGLR 252, CA.

102 *Woking Borough Council v Bistram* (1993) 27 HLR 1, CA; also *Newcastle upon Tyne City Council v Morrison* [2000] L & TR 333, applying *Cumming v Danson* [1942] 2 All ER 653 (a case on RA 1977, s 98).

103 *Wandsworth LBC v Hargreaves* (1994) 27 HLR 142, CA.

104 *Bristol City Council v Mousah* (1997) 30 HLR 32, CA.

105 *Croydon London BC v Moody* (1998) 31 HLR 738; but the court cannot require the local authority to set out its proposals to re-house a tenant whom it is seeking to evict: *Watford BC v Simpson* (2000) 32 HLR 901 (otherwise repossession proceedings might be choked off, except to the extent that suitable alternative accommodation was available for, say, an anti-social tenant, a situation dismissed in *Simpson* at 905 as absurd).

106 HA 1985, Sch 2, Pt IV; see *Enfield Borough Council v French* (1984) 83 LGR 750, CA.

107 *Wandsworth London Borough Council v Fadayomi* [1987] 3 All ER 474 (where a consent order for possession made where the tenant's wife had not been allowed to intervene was set aside). The principle as to consent orders is applicable to the whole of HA 1985, s 84 and is by analogy with the Rent Acts.

Grounds 12 to 16 are subject to *both* the overriding discretion of the court to refuse possession on the ground that it would not be reasonable to order it and to proof by the landlord of the alternative accommodation condition (HA 1985, s 84(2)(c)).

Once the court has duly made an order for possession within the statutory scheme, it will ordinarily be taken to have complied with the requirements of ECHR Articles 6 (right to a fair and public hearing) and 8 (right to respect for one's home).[108] Thus, a tenant's right to retain possession had been decided at the relevant hearing of the landlords' possession claim. There was no need for a separate hearing to determine the human rights aspect of the matter. Thus Article 6 was complied with in a public and fair hearing. In relation to Article 8, the possession proceedings were lawful and were a legitimate and proportionate response, having regard to the level of rent arrears, to non-payment of rent by a council tenant. Thus Article 8 was also complied with. The issue of proportionality was duly considered within the scope of HA 1985. It did not require a separate set of proceedings to dispose of that matter.[109] These conclusions seem to be in accordance with the policy of making efficient use of court time and avoiding multiplicity of proceedings.

'Discretionary' grounds

(i) Ground 1: tenant's breach of covenant

Rent lawfully due from the tenant has not been paid or an obligation of the tenancy has been broken or not performed.

Under this ground, the court is to take into account all relevant circumstances as they exist at the hearing: thus where a tenant in serious rent arrears[110] made no proposals as to his paying these off, it was held correct, exceptionally, not to suspend an order for possession.[111] The court will not refuse to order possession merely where the tenant has, following past notices seeking possession, eventually found the moneys owed: a history of arrears and poor payment is relevant to the question of proof of breach of this ground for possession.[112]

Where the tenant breaks a condition of his tenancy agreement, he cannot argue, it seems, that only if the conduct amounts to a nuisance or annoyance is the court able to order possession against him.[113] Keeping drugs on the premises or supplying these,

---

108 *Southwark LBC v St Brice* [2001] EWCA Civ 1138, [2002] 1 WLR 1537; also *Michalck v London Borough of Wandsworth* [2002] EWCA Civ 271.
109 *Southwark LBC v St Brice* [2001] EWCA Civ 1138, [2002] 1 WLR 1537.
110 Payment of water rates, though these may be collected by a third party, is an 'obligation of the tenancy' triggering this ground if they are unpaid by the tenant: *Lambeth London BC v Thomas* (1997) 30 HLR 89, CA.
111 *Haringey London Borough Council v Stewart* [1991] 2 EGLR 252, CA.
112 *Paddington Churches Housing Association v Sharif* (1997) 29 HLR 817, CA.
113 *Sheffield City Council v Green* [1993] EGCS 185, CA.

even if it is not the tenant personally who is the keeper or supplier, is a sufficient breach of obligation to bring ground 1 into operation.[114]

(ii) Ground 2: nuisance, etc

The tenant or a person residing in or visiting the dwelling house has been guilty of conduct which was, or is likely to have been, a nuisance or annoyance to a person residing, visiting or otherwise engaged in a lawful activity in the vicinity of the dwelling house, or has been convicted of using the dwelling house or allowing it to be used for immoral or illegal purposes or an arrestable offence committed in, or in the locality of, the dwelling house.[115]

The nefarious conduct does not have to be at the relevant 'dwelling house'; which it would have to be at common law, if only because of the policy of ground 2, which is to ensure orderly conduct between those living on an estate.[116] The term 'annoyance' therefore means something which materially affects the peace of mind or physical comfort of ordinary sensible people.[117] Ground 2 covers nuisance by noise, and also it is not confined to matters emanating from the house or flat held by the tenant. It can include, therefore, in view of the wide language of ground 2, referring specifically to 'neighbours', abusive and foul language directed at neighbouring tenants over a long period.[118] It is necessary but also sufficient to show that the persons concerned are sufficiently close to the source of the anti-social conduct to be adversely affected by it. After all, social landlords are responsible for the quality of life of public-sector tenants: many of them, as was judicially recognised,[119] are likely to be vulnerable and needy, and unable to move away from a housing estate where their neighbour or some obstreperous family member living with that neighbour is making their life a misery. Hence the stringent approach both of Parliament and the courts to anti-social council tenants and their households.

For example, where the son of a tenant had, with his friends, been engaged for some time in a course of racial abuse towards neighbouring tenants, it was open to the county court to find that the tenant allowed her son to misconduct himself so as to make her responsible for a nuisance or annoyance under this ground.[120] It would have

---

114 *Bristol City Council v Mousah* (1997) 30 HLR 32 (where the premises were used to supply crack cocaine).

115 Special rules apply to HA 1985, s 83 notices in the case of this ground (HA 1985, s 83(3)) notably, owing to the policy of the new ground, that the notice is to state that possession proceedings may be begun immediately.

116 *Northampton Borough Council v Lovatt* (1997) 30 HLR 875, CA.

117 *Chorley Borough Council v Ribble Motor Services Ltd* [1996] EGCS 110, CA.

118 *Woking Borough Council v Bistram* (1993) 27 HLR 1, CA; *Northampton Borough Council v Lovatt* (1997) 30 HLR 875, CA.

119 In *Northampton Borough Council v Lovatt* (1997) 30 HLR 875, CA.

120 *Kensington and Chelsea Royal London BC v Simmonds* (1996) 29 HLR 507, CA; also *Newcastle upon Tyne City Council v Morrison* [2000] L & TR 333 (a series of violent incidents, amounting to a 'reign of terror', including death threats and arson, for some six years putting neighbours and the community in fear for their safety, perpetrated by the tenant's two teenage sons).

been intolerable, it was said, if neighbouring tenants had no relief merely owing to the fact that a tenant next door could not control his or her household. Thus the courts take a strict approach. Only exceptionally, it seems, will the courts refuse possession of proof of this type of conduct, even if the tenant personally is not a troublemaker.[121] Thus, where a tenant failed to do anything about her grandchildren, who sprayed graffiti in communal areas of an estate, allowed them to hurl abuse and cast stones at other residents and the like, this anti-social conduct having gone on for many years, a suspended possession order was made, and it was no answer to the order to say that the tenant herself had not been responsible for the behaviour in question.[122]

(iii) Ground 2A: domestic violence by partner[123]

Under this ground, introduced because of the policy of enabling landlords to remove unsocial tenants from the premises, the landlord is enabled to recover possession from a tenant or his partner where the tenant or his partner has left because of the violence of one to the other or to a child residing with the person leaving immediately before that person left. The court must be satisfied that the partner who left is unlikely to return and also that the accommodation offered by the house or flat is more extensive than is reasonably required by the person remaining there.[124] The violence must be the real, effective cause for the departure.[125]

(iv) Ground 3: deterioration in condition of dwelling house

The condition of the dwelling house or of any of the common parts has deteriorated owing to acts of waste by, or the neglect or default of the tenant or a person residing in the dwelling house and, in the case of an act of waste by, or the neglect or default of a lodger of the tenant's or a sub-tenant of his, the tenant has not taken such steps as he ought reasonably to have taken to remove the lodger or sub-tenant.[126]

---

121 *Newcastle upon Tyne City Council v Morrison* [2000] L & TR 333.
122 *Portsmouth City Council v Bryant* (2000) 32 HLR 906, CA. (It is worth noting that the fact that the government has promulgated a speedy procedure, supra, in the case of anti-social conduct shows a continuing problem to exist: ground 2 had already been tightened up by the Housing Act 1996, s 144). Also *Lambeth London BC v Howard* [2001] EWCA Civ 468, (2001) 33 HLR 636.
123 Inserted by the Housing Act 1996, s 145 from 12 February 1997: SI 1997/66. Special requirements as to the service of a HA 1985, s 83 notice apply in this case, notably, service of a copy of the notice on the partner who has left.
124 As with ground 2, a special rule applies to HA 1985, s 83 notices served by the landlord (HA 1985, s 83A(3)) notably that if the leaving partner is not the tenant, the landlord has served a copy of the notice on that person or has taken all reasonable steps to do so.
125 *Camden London BC v Mallett* (2000) 33 HLR 204.
126 Subject to the omission of the words 'before the order in question', these words are the same as RA 1977, Sch 15, Case 3.

(v) Ground 4: deterioration in condition of furniture

The condition of furniture provided by the landlord for use under the tenancy, or for use in the common parts, has deteriorated owing to ill-treatment by the tenant or a person residing in the dwelling house. In the case of a lodger or sub-tenant, the tenant has not taken such steps as he ought reasonably to have taken for the removal of the lodger or sub-tenant.[127]

(vi) Ground 5: inducement to grant tenancy

The landlord was induced by the tenant, as the person, or one of them, to whom the tenancy was granted, to grant the tenancy by a false statement made knowingly or recklessly by the tenant or a person acting at the tenant's instigation.

This ground reflects a wider principle. After all, it is a ground for rescinding a statutory tenancy in equity that the tenant has induced the landlord to grant the protected tenancy from which it is derived by a fraudulent statement.[128] The Court of Appeal refused to take into account in the overriding discretion to refuse to order possession that the tenant would not have to be re-housed, having made himself intentionally homeless by his fraudulent statement which admittedly induced the grant of his tenancy.[129]

(vii) Ground 6: premium paid on permitted assignment

The tenancy was assigned under HA 1985, s 92 by 'exchange' to the tenant or to a predecessor in title who is a member of his family, and a premium[130] was paid in connection with that assignment or the previous assignment.

(viii) Ground 7: dwelling house within building used for non-housing purposes

The dwelling house forms part of a building[131] which[132] is held mainly for purposes other than housing purposes and consists mainly of accommodation

---

127 These words correspond to Rent Act 1977, Sch 15, Case 4.
128 *Killick v Roberts* [1991] 4 All ER 289, CA.
129 *Lewisham London BC v Adeyemi* [1999] EGCS 74; *Lewisham London BC v Akinsola* (2000) 32 HLR 414, CA. Also *Shrewsbury and Atcham BC v Evans* (1997) 30 HLR 123, CA (only exceptionally, where a tenant lied on an application form for public housing, would the court consider the effect of homelessness on the tenant, if evicted; in addition, the gravity of the fraudulent claims was expressly taken into account).
130 As widely defined so as to include capital payments and any other pecuniary consideration in addition to rent.
131 Or is within its curtilage, as to be understood in the narrow sense discussed above.
132 Or, to the extent that the landlord holds part of the building, as where it is sub-divided, that part.

other than housing accommodation. The dwelling house was let to the tenant or a predecessor in title of his in consequence of the tenant or predecessor being in the employment of the landlord or the employment of certain bodies[133] and the tenant or a person residing in the house has been guilty of conduct such that, having regard to the purpose for which the building is used, it would not be right for him to continue in occupation of the dwelling house.

(viii) Ground 8: temporary occupation during works

The dwelling house was made available for occupation by the tenant (or a predecessor in title of his) while works were carried out on the dwelling house previously occupied by him as his only or principal home. The tenant or predecessor held a secure tenancy of the other property at the date he ceased to occupy it (owing to the works). The tenant or predecessor accepted the tenancy of the dwelling house of which possession is sought on the understanding that he would give up occupation when, on completion of the works, the other dwelling house was again available for occupation under a secure tenancy. The works have been completed and the other dwelling house is available for re-occupation.

Grounds where possession must be ordered on proof of suitable alternative accommodation

(i) Ground 9: overcrowding

The dwelling house is overcrowded, within HA 1985, Pt X, in such a way as to render the occupier guilty of an offence.

(ii) Ground 10: redevelopment

The landlord intends, within a reasonable time of obtaining possession of the dwelling house:
(a) to demolish or reconstruct the building or part of the building comprising the dwelling house, or
(b) to carry out work on that building or on land let together with, and thus treated as part of, the dwelling house,

and cannot reasonably do so without obtaining possession of the dwelling house.[134]

---

133 Notably, a local authority, new town corporation, housing action trust and the governors of an aided school.
134 Under ground 10A, possession may be recovered mandatorily if the dwelling house is within the area of a redevelopment scheme under HA 1985, Sch 2, Pt V.

The landlord is expected to prove the same definite and settled intention under this ground as would apply to the Landlord and Tenant Act 1954, s 30(1)(f). Thus, where the only evidence of work said to be required to a cottage adjacent to a countryside park, so as to incorporate it into the latter, was oral evidence by an officer of the local authority concerned, rather than any relevant minutes of the authority, which would have been better evidence, it was held that the evidence was not sufficient to meet the statutory requirement, but, even if it had been, the authority had not produced evidence to show that the work could not be done without possession of the cottage.[135] It will be noted that the tenant lacks the protection of any equivalent to the Landlord and Tenant Act 1954, s 31A.

(iii) Ground 11: landlord is a charity

The landlord is a charity and the tenant's continued occupation of the dwelling house would conflict with the objects of the charity.

'Discretionary' grounds where suitable alternative accommodation must be available

Where any of the following grounds applies, the landlord must overcome both the overriding discretion of the court and show that suitable alternative accommodation will be available for the tenant when the order for possession takes effect (HA 1985, s 84(2)). It is convenient to discuss briefly the requirements as to suitability which must be shown by the landlord.

The general criteria which the landlord must prove to the satisfaction of the court as to the suitability to the needs of the tenant[136] are similar to those which govern RA 1977. The types of tenancy which qualify for suitability, if the first hurdle is passed, as suitable, are: lettings as a separate dwelling under a secure tenancy or an assured tenancy, in which latter case the tenancy must not be an assured shorthold tenancy or an assured tenancy subject to recovery of possession on any of the five relevant mandatory grounds.[137]

(i) Ground 12: mainly non-housing accommodation and premises reasonably required for landlord's employee

The dwelling house forms part of, or is within the curtilage of, a building (or part) which is held mainly for non-housing purposes and consists of mainly non-housing accommodation, or is situated in a cemetery. It was let to the tenant or a predecessor in title of his in consequence of either or both being in the landlord's

135 *Wansbeck District Council v Marley* (1987) 20 HLR 247, CA.
136 HA 1985, Sch 2, Pt IV.
137 HA 1985, Sch 2, Pt IV, para 1.

employment, or that of certain bodies, such as a local authority, new town corporation, or the governors of a grant-aided school. The relevant employment has ceased and the landlord reasonably requires the dwelling house for occupation as a residence for some employee of his, or of one of the bodies listed (such as a local authority) with whom a contract of employment has been entered into conditional on such housing being provided.

(ii) Ground 13: special features to dwelling house

The dwelling house has features which are substantially different from those of ordinary dwelling houses and which are designed to make it suitable for occupation by a physically disabled person who requires accommodation of the kind provided by the dwelling house and:
(a) there is no longer such a person residing in the dwelling house; and
(b) the landlord requires it for occupation (whether alone or with members of his family) by such a person.

(iii) Ground 14: lettings to tenants whose circumstances are difficult

A housing association or housing trust landlord lets housing only to tenants whose circumstances (other than merely financial) make it especially difficult for them to satisfy their need for housing. The house or flat must have no such tenant residing there or he must have received an offer of accommodation from the local housing authority for a tenancy of premises to be let under a secure tenancy, and the landlord requires the subject property for occupation by a tenant of the kind they let housing to.

(iv) Ground 15: special needs tenants

The dwelling house is one of a group of properties which it is the practice of the landlord to let for occupation by persons with special needs. A social service or special facility is provided in close proximity to the group of dwelling houses in order to assist persons with special needs. There is no longer a person with such needs residing in the particular dwelling house, and the landlord requires it for occupation, alone or with family members, by a person having such special needs.

(v) Ground 16: accommodation too extensive

The ground provides that the accommodation in the dwelling house is more extensive than that reasonably required by the tenant, but only applies where the tenant obtained the dwelling house by succession under HA 1985, s 89, and had succeeded as a family member of the deceased secure tenant.[138] Apart from matters to be taken into account in the general discretion of the court, this ground specifies specific matters, notably the age of the tenant and the period he has occupied the dwelling house as his only or principal home.

Possession orders

(i)   General matters

In relation to the discretionary grounds, HA 1985, s 85 confers on the county court wide powers of adjournment, staying or postponement in relation to any order for possession. The court may, under HA 1985, s 85(1), adjourn the proceedings for such period or periods as it thinks fit. Under HA 1985, s 85(2), the court may, if it makes an order for possession, stay or suspend execution of the order, or postpone the date of possession, for such period or periods as it thinks fit. This wide power is exercisable at any time up to the date of execution of the order. If the court exercises its powers under HA 1985, s 85(1) or (2), it must impose conditions on the tenant for the payment of rent arrears or in respect of mesne profits, and may impose such other conditions as it thinks fit (HA 1985, s 85(3)). This provision has been examined in depth by the House of Lords.[139]

It was held, adopting the analysis in an earlier decision,[140] that although under HA 1985, s 85(2) the court could order possession, this was not necessarily final, owing to the power of s 85(2) to postpone or suspend the date for possession. That date was the crucial one for the tenant. The power of postponement, for example, was exercisable even after the date for possession specified in the court's order, and so even after the tenancy had terminated, thanks to HA 1985, s 85(2). HA 1985, s 85(3)(a) supported this view. It referred to the imposition of a condition as to the payment of mesne profits. The court could revive a defunct tenancy if the relevant condition was complied with. However, once a possession order has been made, even if suspended on conditions, the tenant changes in status and becomes a 'tolerated trespasser'.

It has been recognised, since this ruling, that public sector landlords are extremely conscious of the hardship that could be caused to tenants if they were to insist on their strict rights to possession. It was also the stated practice of the Court of Appeal to be merciful to tenants when they go into arrears. The court would thus give them a realistic opportunity to pay off the arrears even though this might take a considerable period of time.[141] The courts have a wide discretion when considering an application

---

138 Notice of proceedings for possession must have been served under HA 1985, s 83 more than 6 but less than 12 months after the date of the previous tenant's death, or the ground is not applicable.

139 *Burrows v Brent London Borough Council* [1996] 4 All ER 577, [1996] 1 WLR 144.

140 *Greenwich London Borough Council v Regan* (1996) 28 HLR 469 (Millett LJ).

141 *Lambeth London BC v Henry* [2000] 1 EGLR 33 at 34. It was not, however, open to a tenant who did not appear when the order for possession was made, to challenge the appropriateness of the order some eight years later.

to suspend a possession order, and consider all relevant circumstances as they exist at the hearing date, such as the past payment history of the tenant, as well as the tenant's past conduct (for example, whether the tenant has conducted himself in an anti-social manner to neighbouring tenants, whose interests are relevant).[142] No one factor or interest is relevant, as shown by a decision to suspend a possession order for 12 months in order to prevent the tenant from returning to a life of crime, giving the tenant the chance to lead an honest life of benefit to the local community.[143] The effect of ECHR Art 8 on these powers has been said to be minimal. However, it re-enforces the importance of making an order for possession (which will deprive a person of his or her home) only where a clear case is made out.[144]

On the other hand, the courts see suspended possession orders as a means of giving landlords some leverage over tenants as regards eventual compliance with suspension conditions, notably as to repayment of rent arrears over some agreed time-scale. Hence the importance of the doctrine of tolerated trespassers, the full ramifications of which remain to be clarified. The discretion of the court under HA 1985, s 85(2) to suspend or postpone possession comes to an end, and with it the status of tolerated trespasser, once a warrant for possession has been executed.[145]

(ii) Setting aside warrant for possession

Once a warrant for possession has been issued against a secure tenant, as may be imagined owing to the need to avoid endless litigation, it may only be set aside on narrow grounds, as where the judgment on which the order for possession is itself set aside, or the warrant has been obtained by fraud, or there has been an abuse of the

---

142 *Islington London BC v Reeves* [1997] CLY 436; also *Canterbury City Council v Lowe* [2001] L & TR 14, 33 HLR 583, CA (where the effect of making a suspended order on neighbouring tenants was expressly taken into account in overturning a county court decision to suspend possession, where the defendant had indulged in serious anti-social misconduct).

143 *Greenwich London BC v Grogan* (2000) 33 HLR 140, CA.

144 *Gallagher v Castle Vale Action Trust Ltd* [2001] EWCA Civ 23. (2001) 33 HLR 810. The court, according to Sedley LJ, must consider whether an order for possession is permitted by law to protect other's rights and freedoms (eg from anti-social conduct). The court must also address the issue of proportionality. This may evidently involve weighing up the tenant's rights to a home against the needs of the community for housing where the tenant is at fault. Despite this, the Court of Appeal has declined to interfere with a county court refusal to suspend a possession order that was not obviously made on incorrect grounds: *Richmond-upon-Thames Churches Housing Trust v Smith* [2001] EWCA Civ 973.

145 *Governors of Peabody Donation Fund v Hay* (1996) 19 HLR 145, CA; *Tower Hamlets London BC v Azad* (1997) 30 HLR 241, CA. A tenant who fails to make representations when an order for possession is being suspended, for example, as to the conditions, could be at risk if the landlord later seeks immediate possession for non-compliance with the conditions.

process of the court or oppression in the execution of the warrant.[146] Oppression refers not just to oppressive conduct by the landlord, but can include any state of affairs which is oppressive to the tenant, as where the tenant has been given misleading information by a member of the court staff.[147] Where, therefore, a tenant had thought that she need take no further action, owing to a note written at the bottom of a report from the housing officer of the landlord, which related to the question of the tenant's entitlement to housing benefit, and then lost her tenancy, there was held to have been oppression. It would have been wrong for the landlord authority to have insisted, in these circumstances, on their strict legal rights arising out of their possession order.[148] However, if the tenant has committed a self-induced error which has caused the tenant to misapprehend the landlord's intentions, this cannot amount to oppression in the required sense, as there is no fault by the landlord or the court. It was also said that once the grounds for setting aside a possession warrant are not proved, the court has no residual or inherent power to set aside the eviction.[149]

(iii) Tolerated trespassers

A former secure tenant against whom an absolute or suspended order for possession had been made is, we have seen, best described as a tolerated trespasser.[150] The old tenancy is then in limbo. No new tenancy could be inferred merely, for example, because the tenant agrees as a condition of suspension to repay rent arrears on some agreed pattern of repayments.[151] Under HA 1985, s 85(2)(b), at any time before a warrant for possession is executed, the tenant (as well as the landlord) may apply to the court to put off further the date for possession. This application might follow an agreement between the landlord and tenant for repayment of rent arrears. Indeed, the court usually imposes conditions, which, if complied with, allow the tenant or landlord to apply again to the court for a discharge of the suspended possession order (as where rent arrears have been paid off). The local council in the case where the concept of tolerated trespasser was recognised by the House of Lords was entitled, owing to the tenant's failure to comply with an arrangement entered into days before an order for possession was due to be enforced, to procure the tenant's eviction by executing the original

---

146 See, eg *Camden London BC v Akanni* (1997) 29 HLR 845; *Hammersmith & Fulham London BC v Lemeh* [2000] L & TR 423, CA; *Barking and Dagenham LBC v Saint* (1999) 31 HLR 620 (where had the tenant, who was then in prison, known of the warrant at the time it was executed, he could have successfully applied to suspend it); also *Lambeth London BC v Hughes* (2000) 33 HLR 350 (applicant misled).

147 *Hammersmith & Fulham London BC v Lemeh* [2000] L & TR 423, CA.

148 *Southwark London BC v Sarfo* (1999) 32 HLR 602, CA.

149 *Jephson Homes Housing Association v Moisejevs* [2001] L & TR 202, CA (where the relevant cases were reviewed).

150 *Burrows v Brent London Borough Council* [1996] 4 All ER 577, [1996] 1 WLR 1448.

151 *Burrows v Brent London Borough Council* [1996] 4 All ER 577, [1996] 1 WLR 1448 at 1457 and 588 per Lord Jauncey, who said that HA 1985, s 85(4) was inconsistent with the creation of a new tenancy as a discharge of a possession order would work only if the old tenancy had not been superseded by a new tenancy.

order for possession by warrant issued over two years after the order. Had their Lordships decided that the parties had impliedly agreed to a new tenancy, local authorities might become unwilling to make concessionary arrangements in favour of tenants whose personal circumstances had changed for the worse.[152] This would be because with any implied new tenancy, new possession proceedings would have to be commenced against the tenant.

There have been subsequent developments as, confronted with many tenants (who may well be dependent on housing benefit or in the process of claiming it) in a perilous position owing to persistent failure to pay rent, the courts have been refining the notion of a tolerated trespasser.[153] Once an order for possession is made, ending the secure tenancy, the landlord can enforce it,[154] unless it is suspended on terms, whereby the landlord can continue to take rent from the erstwhile tenant, who is now a tolerated trespasser from the acceptance of, strictly, mesne profits.[155] It is also apparently open to the landlord to agree to accept payments of arrears at a lower rate than that specified in the (suspended) possession order, which evidently amounts to a change in the terms of the suspension.[156] Erstwhile tolerated trespassers are apparently entitled, if the court unconditionally discharges an order for possession, to bring an action against the landlord for breaches of covenant to repair imposed by statute, as the tenancy is then revived, the limbo period of tolerated trespassing is retrospectively ended.[157] Tolerated trespassers are also entitled during the limbo period to bring an action in nuisance against the landlord.[158] It seems that owing to the fact that the tolerated trespasser has exclusive possession, this lawful possession suffices to found an action in nuisance. Since a tolerated trespasser is not a secure tenant the right to buy cannot be exercised by him.

(iv) Abandonment of possession by tenant

The statutory restrictions on making an order for possession assume that the tenant is a secure tenant and has not lost that status, as by ceasing to comply with the tenant

---

152 [1996] 4 All ER 577, 583 [1996] 1 WLR 1448, 1454, (Lord Browne-Wilkinson).

153 See Cafferkey [1998] Conv 39; Nichol [2000] JHL 69.

154 As in *London Borough of Brent v Knightley* (1997) 74 P & CR D7 (where repayment conditions in a suspended possession order were not complied with, hence the possession order came into effect ending the tenancy retrospectively, so that there had been nothing to succeed to).

155 *Lambeth London BC v Rogers* [2000] 1 EGLR 28: unless the parties agree as to the grant of a new tenancy, which was not proved there, nor in *Hackney London BC v Porter* (1996) 29 HLR 401, CA, both showing that any such inference is not lightly being made.

156 As in *Greenwich London BC v Regan* (1996) 28 HLR 469; see Bright (1997) 113 LQR 217.

157 *Lambeth London BC v Rogers* [2000] 1 EGLR 28; but not if the tenant has not sought an order reviving the tenancy, where the terms of possession were that possession would not be enforced so long as rent arrears were paid off at a fixed weekly rate and that the order would cease to be enforceable once the arrears were paid off in full: *Marshall v Bradford Metropolitan DC* [2001] EWCA Civ 594, [2001] 19 EG 140 (CS).

158 *Pemberton v Southwark London BC* [2000] 2 EGLR 33, CA.

condition of residence. If, for example, he concedes that he has abandoned possession, the court may make a consent order for possession on the ground that the tenant no longer occupies the dwelling house as his only or principal home. While clear evidence is required, it would be hard for the tenant to persuade an appellate court to revoke such an order if he had originally admitted that the protection of HA 1985, Pt IV did not apply.[159]

VI   SECURE TENANTS' IMPROVEMENTS AND REPAIRS

HA 1985, Pt IV provides specific rules for the consent of the landlord to improvements by secure tenants, as well as a limited scheme for improvements compensation after the secure tenancy ends, and provides enabling provisions for secure tenants' repair schemes. These rules may thus be noted.

Improvements

Special consent rules apply to improvements[160] by secure tenants.[161] By HA 1985, s 97(1), it is a term of every secure tenancy that the tenant will not make any improvement without the written consent of the landlord. Consent cannot be unreasonably withheld: if it is, it is treated as given (HA 1985, s 97(3)). If the tenant applies in writing for a consent, the landlord must give a written statement to the tenant of his reasons for refusing it, if applicable, and is treated as withholding consent if he does not consent or refuse consent within a reasonable time (HA 1985, s 98(4)). The onus of proving the reasonableness of a withholding of consent is on the landlord (HA 1985, s 98(1)).[162] However, the landlord has a power, when giving consent, to impose a reasonable condition (HA 1985, s 99(1)), and failure to comply with such a condition is treated as a breach of the secure tenancy obligations (HA 1985, s 99(4)). The landlord must show that any condition is reasonable (HA 1985, s 99(3)) and the imposition of an unreasonable condition is equivalent to refusing consent (HA 1985, s 99(2)).

Limited provision is made for compensation to be paid to a former secure tenant, or, if appropriate, another 'qualifying person'[163] such as his successor, where the secure

---

159   *Bruce v Worthing District Council* (1993) 26 HLR 223, CA.
160   As widely defined so as to include not only alterations or additions to the dwelling house but also, eg additions or alterations to landlords' fittings and external decorations (HA 1985, s 97(2)), neither of which might constitute an improvement at common law, as well as the provision of services, eg central heating, which would; cf ch 7 above.
161   The rules of the Landlord and Tenant Act 1927, s 19(2) do not, therefore, apply: HA 1985, s 97(4).
162   As to the matters to be taken into account by the court in determining reasonableness, see HA 1985, s 98(2).
163   As defined in HA 1985, s 99B(2).

tenancy comes to an end and was held, at that time, of a local authority landlord.[164] The improvement will not qualify unless the landlord or its predecessor must have given written actual, or deemed, consent. The scheme is supplemented by regulations.[165]

Repairs

Under HA 1985, s 96[166] regulations have been made[167] which apply to most secure tenants holding from local authority landlords, so that secure tenants of such bodies as housing associations are outside the scheme. This is a repair scheme under which minor repairs may be required to be carried out following a tenant's notice. The work must then be put out to a private contractor by the authority. There are default provisions available to the tenant who may require the landlord to procure the work to be done by a different contractor, and if the latter defaults, there is a provision for compensation to the tenant, with a right of set-off in the landlord if the tenant owes rent arrears.

Miscellaneous

No doubt most secure tenants hold their premises under a written tenancy agreement. If so, the terms of the agreement may only be varied within the limits of HA 1985, s 102, superseding the common law. These methods include agreement between the landlord and tenant or under HA 1985, s 103, which allows the landlord to vary the terms of a secure periodic tenancy by notice.[168] HA 1985, Pt IV contains a number of provisions about management matters, such as a requirement that everybody letting under secure tenancies is to publish information about the express terms of its tenancies and the RTB (HA 1985, s 104), as well as a requirement of consultation about certain matters of housing management (HA 1985, s 105),[169] housing allocation (HA 1985, s 106), and there is a provision limiting the right of landlords of secure tenants to recover heating charges (HA 1985, s 108).[170]

---

164 Thus, if the reason for the cesser of secure tenancy status is that the landlord condition is not satisfied, as where the reversion passes to a private landlord, the compensation rules may apply (HA 1985, s 99A(8)), inserted by LRHUDA 1993, s 122.

165 Secure Tenants of Local Authorities (Compensation for Improvements) Regulations 1994, SI 1994/613.

166 As substituted by LRHUDA 1993, s 121.

167 Secure Tenants of Local Authorities (Right to Repair) Regulations 1994, SI 1994/133, as extended to introductory tenancies by SI 1997/73.

168 But cf *Palmer v Metropolitan Borough of Sandwell* (1987) 20 HLR 74, CA (holding that statements in a booklet which differed from terms of tenancy did not bind landlord).

169 Each tenant does not have individually to be informed, but arrangements must be provided so that the relevant body of tenants are informed or can inform themselves: *R v Brent London BC, ex p Morris* (1997) 30 HLR 324, CA.

170 Note that the special provisions about assignments repairs, improvements and management *do not apply* where the landlord is a housing co-operative association (HA 1985, s 109).

VII   THE RIGHT TO BUY

Introduction

The Right to Buy (RTB) is conferred on secure tenants and certain others.[171] The policy of the RTB legislation is to enable tenants who exercise the right to buy to enjoy the ordinary fruits or advantages of home ownership, including a rise in the value of their property.[172]

When first introduced, the RTB had considerable importance numerically: about 200,000 dwellings were originally sold off each year, but since then these numbers have diminished somewhat (to around 40,000).[173] The RTB enables tenants to take out of the public housing stock the house or flat in which they live. It thus enables the person exercising the right to acquire the freehold of the house or a long lease of a flat as the case may be. It is exercisable against public-sector landlords such as local authorities. In addition, a right to acquire (which generally operates in the same way as the RTB) has been made available to tenants who hold from registered social landlords, provided however that the dwelling concerned was provided with public funds.[174] Secure tenants are entitled to exercise the RTB, as well as a tenant who holds an assured tenancy from a registered social landlord, which was a secure tenancy converted to an assured tenancy.[175] If a person is a qualifying successor to a secure tenancy, that person can exercise the RTB, as may a person succeeding to a tenant whose tenancy, which became assured on transfer to a registered social landlord, carries a preserved RTB. A tenant who holds from a registered social landlord whose tenancy was granted as from 15 January 1989 holds an assured tenancy, to which the RTB is not attached. Even if a tenant holds from such a landlord under a pre-January 1989 non-assured tenancy, if the landlord holds charitable status, the tenancy cannot be secure, and the RTB is not exercisable.

The legislature has placed but few formal obstacles to a secure tenant claiming the right, which has been judicially recognised as having the deliberate purpose of inducing secure tenants to buy their homes.[176] This generosity is shown by the following matters: the narrow scope of the exemptions to the RTB, the entitlement of the tenant to a generous discount and, the fact that, while he is under an obligation to repay it if he re-sells or re-assigns, the obligation is of short duration (three years from the acquisition of his title). Moreover, it is provided that any provision in a lease held by the landlord which prohibits or restricts the grant of a lease under the RTB is void, so

---

171 See passim Driscoll (1999) 143 Sol Jo 408, 445, 468 and 493.
172 *R v Braintree DC, ex p Halls* [2000] 3 EGLR 19 at 22 (Laws LJ).
173 'Secure Tenants Right to Buy' (1998) (DETR) para 9.
174 Housing (Right to Acquire) Regulations 1997, SI 1997/619; Housing Act 1996 s 16.
175 Thanks to HA 1985, ss 171A-171H. This is the preserved right to buy. The procedures are governed by Housing (Preservation of Right to Buy) Regulations 1993, SI 1993/2241 as amended.
176 *Dickinson v Enfield London Borough Council* [1996] 2 EGLR 88, CA.

protecting the RTB of the secure (sub-) tenant.[177] Although a secure tenant is required to serve his notice claiming the RTB in a prescribed form, 'a notice served by a tenant ... is not invalidated by an error in, or omission from, the particulars which are required by regulations ... to be contained in the notice'.[178]

Nevertheless, it has been said that because the provisions of HA 1985, Pt V give a secure tenant considerable benefits and result in corresponding disadvantages to the landlord, its provisions should, where appropriate, be construed strictly. In particular, a person claiming the right to buy but who, on investigation, has in fact lost it during one of the stages to obtaining the grant of the freehold or a lease, is precluded from pursuing his claim any further.[179] By contrast, once the right to buy is fully established, and a binding contract has been entered into, the tenant is entitled to an injunction under HA 1985, s 138(1) to enforce the landlord's duty to convey him the property. The court will not refuse the remedy on the ground of general considerations of hardship.[180]

Conditions for right to arise

If a tenancy is excluded from being secure, the RTB is also incapable of arising (HA 1985, s 118(1)). Where one of two joint secure tenants had served a notice to quit on the landlord, this put an end to the RTB as the secure tenancy on which it depended and to which it was incidental had been terminated.[181] A warning was however issued by one member of the Court of Appeal that the court, if asked after or immediately prior to a divorce petition, was entitled to make use of its inherent powers to prevent the secure tenancy and the RTB to which it is attached from being destroyed by a unilateral notice to quit. In the case of a house, where the landlord is the freeholder, the right is to acquire the freehold. If the premises are a flat, the RTB is to obtain a long lease, as is the case where the landlord of a house does not own the freehold HA 1985, s 118(1)).

If the secure tenancy is joint, the RTB belongs to the tenants jointly or to such one of them as may be agreed (HA 1985, s 118(2)). The requirement of residential occupation of the house or flat (which is a condition precedent to secure tenancy status) is relaxed because a joint tenant who does not reside in the house or flat as his only or principal home may still exercise the RTB. However, in the case of an agreement that one (or more) of a number of joint tenants is to exercise the RTB, at least one of these persons must satisfy the statutory residence requirement (HA 1985, s 118(2)).

---

177 HA 1985, s 179.
178 HA 1985, s 177(1).
179 *Muir Group Housing Association Ltd v Thornley* (1992) 25 HLR 89, CA.
180 *Taylor v Newham London Borough Council* [1993] 1 WLR 444.
181 *Bater v Bater* [1999] 4 All ER 944, CA. The notice had been given by the wife secure joint tenant to her husband following a divorce.

A qualifying period of residence is imposed on the tenant[182] as a condition precedent to the RTB arising (HA 1985, s 119(1)). It need be satisfied, where relevant, by only one joint tenant (HA 1985, s 119(2)). The statutory period to be taken into account for the purpose of this condition is two years.[183] Although this concept also relates to the amount of permitted discount on sale (see below), it is best dealt with here. Thus, for example, a period of occupation as a secure tenant or as a spouse of a secure tenant (if they were living together at that time) counts as a qualifying residential period, if, before the date of service of the tenant's notice of claim to exercise the RTB, the tenant was a public sector tenant.[184]

Where RTB does not arise

There are a number of cases in which the RTB does not arise in any event and these may be summarised as follows. The first two sets of exclusions relate to the status of the landlord (as where he has been grant-subsidised out of public monies), or to specific houses or flats where their sale under the RTB would be undesirable in the general interest. The last exclusion may be explained on the ground that the landlord against whom the RTB is exercisable is the secure tenant's immediate landlord.

(i) Status of landlord

The landlord is a charitable housing trust or a housing association, or is a co-operative housing association or is a housing association which at no time has received grants under specified legislation.[185] The RTB does not arise where the landlord holds a tenancy from the Crown, even if it would be sufficient, but for the exemption, to support the grant of a long lease to the tenant.[186]

(ii) Certain types of houses or flats

A small class of premises are excluded from the RTB owing to policy considerations.

1 Letting in connection with tenant's employment: where the dwelling house 'forms part of, or is within the curtilage of' a building or that part held by the landlord which

---

182 Who must be an individual and who must comply with the residence condition, see below.
183 In accordance with HA 1985, Sch 4.
184 As defined in HA 1985, Sch 4 para 6(1).
185 HA 1985, Sch 5, paras 1 and 2 respectively; as to the meaning of 'housing trust' see *Hounslow London Borough Council v Hare* (1990) 89 LGR 714 (provisions of a will created a housing trust in required sense, by providing gifted premises to a local authority to house old people).
186 HA 1985, Sch 5, para 12. However, the exemption does not apply where the landlord is entitled to grant a lease under HA 1985,without the agreement of the appropriate authority, eg the Crown Estate Commissioners, as where such authority notifies the landlord that as respects the Crown's interest, consent will be granted to the grant of a lease under the RTB.

building is held mainly for non-housing purposes and consists mainly of accommodation other than housing accommodation, or is situated in a cemetery. The accommodation must have been let to the tenant in 'consequence of the tenant or his predecessor' being in the landlord's employment.[187] The word 'curtilage' might extend the amount of exempt premises, were it not for the fact that it appears that a restrictive meaning must be applied, namely, the ordinary meaning, which refers to a small area forming part of the house and attached to it: hence, a cottage let to a college lecturer which was within but on the edge of the college grounds, and fenced off from the rest of the grounds, albeit with pedestrian access to them, was not within the 'curtilage' of the college buildings and the RTB was not excluded.[188]

2 Certain houses for the disabled: where the dwelling house has 'features which are substantially different from those of ordinary dwelling houses and are designed to make it suitable for occupation by physically disabled persons'.[189] It appears that the exemption is to be narrowly construed, as contemplating structural design features not found in ordinary dwellings, wherever situated, such as a ramp, lift or other mechanical contrivance, rather than the fact that, in one case, the house had a specially-designed, additional, ground-floor wc owing to the fact that the secure tenants' daughter suffered from spina bifida, and so had difficulty mounting stairs.[190]

3 Certain houses for pensioners: this exemption relates to a house or flat which is one of a group of dwellings which are particularly suitable, having regard to their location, size, design, heating systems and other features, for occupation by elderly persons, and which it is the practice of the landlord to let for occupation by persons aged 60 or over, or to those and physically disabled persons. However, so as to restrict the exemption, special facilities must be shown to be provided wholly or mainly to assist those persons.[191]

187 HA 1985, Sch 5, para 5; or in that of a local authority and certain other bodies such as, notably, the governors of an aided school.
188 *Dyer v Dorset County Council* [1989] QB 346, CA; also *Barwick and Barwick v Kent County Council* (1992) 24 HLR 341, CA (where a house situated near a fire station did not fall within the curtilage of the main fire station building; adjacent garages would have fallen within the 'curtilage' of the latter building).
189 HA 1985, Sch 5, para 7. The narrowness of this exemption is shown by the requirement that the house or flat must be one of a group of dwellings which it is the practice of the landlord to let for occupation by physically disabled persons and a special service or special facilities must be provided in close proximity so as to aid or assist those persons.
190 *Freeman v Wansbeck District Council* (1984) 82 LGR 131, CA.
191 HA 1985, Sch 5, para 10, as amended. The relevant facilities are defined in HA 1985, Sch 5, para 10(2). There is also an exemption in HA 1985, Sch 5, para 11, as substituted by LRHUDA 1993, s 106(2), which relates to individual dwelling houses for elderly persons, but which relates only to lettings on or after 1 January 1990.

(iii) Landlord's reversion insufficient

The RTB cannot arise unless the landlord owns the freehold, or has a leasehold interest which suffices to enable him to grant a lease within HA 1985, Pt V for a term exceeding 21 years in the case of a house and for a term of not less than 50 years in the case of a flat.[192]

Where RTB cannot be exercised

So as not to allow undesirable or financially insecure tenants to exercise the RTB, it cannot be exercised if the tenant is obliged to give up possession of the house or flat concerned under a court order for possession or will be so obliged at a specified date (HA 1985, s 121(1)). Thus, where a landlord was seeking possession against a secure tenant, who was claiming the RTB, but who had not completed the process, the House of Lords held that the tenant could not invoke a statutory duty to complete (HA 1985, s 138), which, as pointed out, is not unqualified, so as to avoid prior consideration by the court of the possession claim, which was the best way to proceed in all the circumstances.[193] Nor can the RTB be exercised where the tenant has a bankruptcy petition pending against him, a receiving order pending against him, or in two similar cases (HA 1985, s 121(2)).

Tenant's claim to exercise right to buy

There are at least four stages to the exercise of the RTB. The first stage is the tenant's claim to exercise the right. The last stage is the grant of the relevant interest, and the intermediate stages are the establishment of the right and the agreement, or in default, determination, of the terms of the grant.[194]

A secure tenant who wishes to exercise the RTB must do so by a written notice served on the landlord (HA 1985, s 122(1)).[195] The claim notice is to be in the prescribed form, or in a form substantially to the like effect.[196] The RTB is not, however, 'exercised' (within HA 1985, s 121) once and for all when the tenant serves his notice of claim. On the contrary, it is 'exercised' at each of a number of separate steps, and may be lost at

---

192 HA 1985, Sch 5, para 4. The measurement of the leases commences as from the date of the tenant's notice of claim to exercise the right to buy.
193 *Bristol City Council v Lovell* [1998] 1 All ER 775, [1999] L & TR 66. It is at the discretion of the court as to whether to give precedence to the possession claim or to the RTB claim: see *Tandridge DC v Bickers* [1999] L & TR 21 (where the sequence of events and the seriousness of allegations in the possession proceedings were relevant).
194 *Muir Group Housing Association Ltd v Thornley* (1992) 25 HLR 89.
195 The notice may be withdrawn at any time by a further written notice (HA 1985, s 122(3)).
196 The prescribed form is Form No 1 in the Housing (Right to Buy) (Prescribed Forms) Regulations 1986, SI 1986/2194, as amended.

each hurdle leading to the conveyance or grant of a new lease, because, after all, the secure tenancy is continued until the latter event.[197] The RTB may extend to any land let together with the dwelling house treated as part of the dwelling house, and may be included in the notice of claim, unless it is agricultural land exceeding two acres (HA 1985, s 184(1)).[198]

Where the tenant has members of his family (widely defined in HA 1985, s 186(1)) who are not secure tenants but who occupy the dwelling house as their only or principal home, up to three of these may be included by him in the notice of claim (HA 1985, s 122(1)).[199] However, the benefit of this extension is limited since although the tenant may insist, no matter what the landlord's wishes, in including in his claim notice his spouse or a family member, such as his cohabitee, who has been residing with him throughout the 12-month period ending with the giving of the notice, in the case of any other family member, the landlord must consent to the inclusion of that person (HA 1985, s 123(2)). Where a secure tenant validly required by notice that her daughter should be included in the RTB with her, and died before the completion of the purchase, the daughter, as deemed sole tenant, was as much entitled to require completion under HA 1985, s 138 (below) as would her mother have been, if still alive.[200] By contrast, where a sole secure tenant, who had claimed the RTB, died before she was able to execute a conveyance, the RTB had been lost to her daughter, since a binding contract had already been concluded.[201]

Should the identity of the secure tenant change, prior to any contract of sale,[202] but after the giving of a notice claiming the RTB, otherwise than under an exchange permitted by HA 1985, s 92, the new tenant is in the same position as if he had given the notice and in all other respects[203] as the tenant who gave the notice of claim (HA

---

197 *Enfield London Borough Council v McKeon* [1986] 2 All ER 730, CA; hence, there is nothing in HA 1985, Pt V against a landlord claiming repossession of the house or flat during the statutory buy-out procedures, as has already been noted.

198 Land outside HA 1985, s 184(1) may be included in the tenant's claim to the RTB if he serves a separate, revocable, written notice on the landlord and it is reasonable in all the circumstances for the land to be included (HA 1985, s 184(2) and (3)).

199 The effect of such inclusion, if valid, is that for the purposes of the RTB the tenant and the included family members are treated for RTB purposes (including therefore the conveyance of the property) as joint tenants (HA 1985, s 123(3)).

200 *Harrow LBC v Tonge* (1992) 25 HLR 99, CA; the effect of death on the RTB is reviewed by Brierley [1995] Conv 114.

201 *Bradford Metropolitan City Council v McMahon* [1993] 4 All ER 237, CA; it appears that no notice had been served under HA 1985, s 136(1) by the daughter at the stage the notice to claim has been served, and none could have been served, it appears, once the binding contract had been concluded.

202 As will appear, once a binding contract of sale is entered into, this ends the secure tenancy and it cannot thereafter be succeeded to: see *Cooper v City of Edinburgh District Council* (1991) 23 HLR 349, HL.

203 Including, therefore, the amount of the discount allowed to the new claimant: see *McIntyre v Merthyr Tydfil District Council* (1989) 21 HLR 320, CA.

1985, s 136(1)).[204] A similar rule applies where the identity of the landlord is passed to another landlord after the service of notice of claim on the former landlord (HA 1985, s 137(1)). However, where the new landlord is an exempt landlord (such as a charitable housing trust) then, as the RTB ceases to be exercisable, both sides to the claim must, so far as possible, take steps to see to it that the position is restored to the pre-claim circumstances (HA 1985, s 137(2)).

Procedures after claim notice

After a secure tenant has served a RTB claim notice, the landlord must serve a written notice of reply on the tenant, within four weeks, unless the two-year residence period of the tenant included a period of residence under another landlord, in which case the period is eight weeks (HA 1985, s 124(1) and (2)). The notice is in the prescribed form,[205] or in a form substantially to the like effect, and it must either admit the RTB or deny it. If the latter, the reasons for the non-existence of the RTB, in the landlord's opinion, must be given.[206]

Where the landlord, as it is understood is often the case, admits the RTB, or it is otherwise established, as in proceedings, the landlord must serve a notice of the purchase price under HA 1985, s 125, within 8 or 12 weeks, depending on whether the right is to a freehold or long lease (HA 1985, s 125(1)). This notice must, among other things, set out all matters relevant to the eventual conveyance or grant of a long lease, which pertain to the premises, such as a description of the dwelling house and the price to be paid in the landlord's opinion,[207] including, notably, the amount of the discount to which the tenant is entitled (HA 1985, s 125(2)).[208] Where, in the case of the grant of a lease to the tenant, the landlord would be enabled, in the terms of his notice, to recover from the tenant either service charges or contributions to improvements, the notice must contain estimates and certain other information about these charges (HA 1985, s 125(4)).[209]

---

204 The same result follows where the tenant who gave a notice of claim when holding a fixed-term secure tenancy holds a secure periodic tenancy under HA 1985, s 86 after the expiry of the former tenancy (HA 1985, s 136(2)(b)); and in either case, the original notice of claim would be applicable to any subsequent changed secure tenant (HA 1985, s 136(7)) although in all cases, if the original tenant did not claim to exercise the RTB for family members, his successors cannot alter the notice of claim in that respect (HA 1985, s 136(6)).

205 Housing (Right to Buy) (Prescribed Forms) Regulations 1986, SI 1986/2194, Form No 2.

206 Where a landlord's notice has been served and the tenant changes, the new tenant is bound to serve a notice under HA 1985, s 125D, notably within 12 weeks of his becoming a secure tenant (HA 1985, s 136(2)).

207 The tenant must be informed in HA 1985, s 125 notice of his right to require the price to be determined by the district valuer under HA 1985, s 128 (HA 1985, s 125(5) as substituted).

208 In addition, the notice must set out the value of the house at the date of the notice of claim (HA 1985, s 122(2)), certain tenants' improvements to be disregarded in determining that value (within HA 1985, s 127).

209 The required information about these matters is set out in HA 1985, ss 125A and 125B. The notice must also describe any structural defect known to the landlord affecting the premises

Following service of the landlord's purchase price notice, the tenant must[210] serve a written notice on the landlord stating either that he intends to pursue the claim to the RTB or that he withdraws it (HA 1985, s 125D).[211]

Price of house or flat

The price payable for the house or flat is governed by HA 1985 and not by the voluntary agreement of the parties, and is made up to two elements:
1 its value as determined in accordance with HA 1985, s 127;
2 less the discount to which the tenant is entitled (HA 1985, s 126).

The most important rule is that the value of the house or flat, determined as at the date of the notice of claim to the RTB, so that subsequent increases or falls are left out of account, is that the value is the 'price which at that time it would realise if sold on the open market by a willing vendor' but upon certain statutory assumptions (HA 1985, s 127(1)). So as to prevent the secure tenant from paying for the effect of his own improvements, the effect of these is to be disregarded (HA 1985, s 127(1)(b)).[212] The assumptions differ as between conveyances of the freehold and grants of a lease.

In the case of a freehold conveyance, the main assumptions are that the vendor is selling for an estate in fee simple with vacant possession and that neither the tenant nor a resident member of his family wanted to buy (HA 1985, s 127(2)). In the case of the grant of a lease, the main assumptions are that a lease is being granted with vacant possession (see further below) and at a ground rent not exceeding £10 per annum, otherwise they are similar to those for the conveyance of a freehold (HA 1985, s 127(3)).

The discount due to the tenant is a percentage applied to reduce the purchase price, by reference to the periods to be taken into account under HA 1985.[213] In principle, the discount is 32% plus 1% for each complete year by which the qualifying period exceeds two years, with a maximum of 60%, in the case of a house. In the case of a flat, the

---

(HA 1985, s 124(4A), as to which see *Payne v Barnet London BC* (1997) 30 HLR 295, CA (from which it seems that the purpose of the provision is informative in warning the tenant as to his maximum potential liability and does not impose a new duty of care on landlords: see also *Blake v Barking and Dagenham London BC* [1996] EGCS 145).

210 On penalty of receiving a landlord's default notice under HA 1985, s 125E requiring the service of a HA 1985, s 125D notice within 28 days or the deemed withdrawal of the RTB.

211 He may alternatively serve a notice that he claims to exercise the right to acquire on rent to mortgage terms under HA 1985, s 144 (HA 1985, s 125D).

212 See *Dickinson v Enfield London Borough Council* [1996] 2 EGLR 88, CA. The disregard extends to improvements made by any person who was a secure tenant before the secure tenant (whether, therefore, under that or a different tenancy, unless the applicant tenant has a secure tenancy by exchange) and to those made by a member of the applicant tenant's family who, immediately before his secure tenancy was granted, held a secure tenancy of the same dwelling house (HA 1985, s 127(4)). Any failure by any of these persons to keep the premises in good internal repair is, to any extent relevant, disregarded.

213 HA 1985, s 129(1), referring to HA 1985, Sch 4.

lowest and highest percentages are 44 and 70% (HA 1985, s 129(2)).[214] However, the maximum discount has been subjected to a ceiling by statutory instrument, the cap varying with the location of the premises (thus it is from £38,000 in London and the South East to, for example, £22,000 in the North East).[215]

A conveyance of the freehold or lease must contain a covenant binding on the secure tenant, which in principle lasts for three years from the disposal,[216] to repay the discount if he makes certain types of disposal, notably if he reconveys the freehold or assigns the lease, and in certain other cases,[217] although disposals to the former secure tenant's spouse or to a resident family member are not caught, nor are disposals under property adjustment orders in divorce proceedings (HA 1985, s 160).[218] The question has been raised as to whether a tenant who completes a purchase under the RTB as nominee for another person, for whom he declares himself a trustee has made a disposal caught by these provisions.[219]

HA 1985 says little about the position once all the terms have been agreed or determined by the parties other than that the landlord is then under a duty to complete (HA 1985, s 138(1)). If the tenant fails within a reasonable time of receiving a landlord's offer to reply to it, the RTB lapses, as where a tenant failed for one year to reply to such an offer and had moved to other premises.[220]

Completion

As with private-sector enfranchisement schemes, an unwilling landlord against whom the RTB has been established has in principle no choice but to sell or grant a lease of the property concerned, and on terms as laid down in HA 1985. It is recognised that sales under the RTB are not the result of a contract.[221] Parliament has made provision to force the hands of landlords who cannot put up valid possession claims. Once the

---

214 These percentages may be varied up or down by regulations (HA 1985, ss 129(2A) and 129(2B); and where a previous discount has been given, see HA 1985, s 130).
215 Housing (Right to Buy) (Limits on Discount) Order 1998, SI 1998/2997. In addition, it appears that there is a cost floor on discounts, so that no discount can reduce the purchase price below what it cost to build the premises (see Driscoll (1999) 143 Sol Jo 408 at p 445, referring to a Ministerial determination of 1999).
216 And which takes effect as a legal charge on the house or flat: HA 1985, s 156(1).
217 HA 1985, s 155(1); the 'relevant disposals' are listed in HA 1985, s 159(1). The amount to be repaid is reduced by one-third for each complete year elapsing after the RTB was exercised (HA 1985, s 155(2)).
218 See *R v Rushmoor Borough Council, ex p Barrett* [1988] 2 All ER 268, CA.
219 See Pawlowski (1998) 2 L & T Rev 127, who also discusses possible avoidance of this provision by means of a tenant contracting to sell the property, acknowledging receipt of the purchase price at exchange but putting off completion for three years.
220 *Sutton London Borough Council v Swann* (1985) 18 HLR 140, CA.
221 *Rushton v Worcester CC* [2001] EWCA Civ 367 (so that failure to notify a tenant of structural defects in her house was not actionable under the Misrepresentation Act 1967, although the duties of HA 1985 had been broken).

RTB has been established by a secure tenant, as soon as all matters relating to the grant have been agreed or determined, the landlord is bound to grant to the tenant the fee simple absolute, in the case of a house, of which the landlord holds the freehold. He is similarly bound to grant a lease of the house if he does not own the freehold or the property is a flat (HA 1985, s 138(1)).[222] The statutory duty is 'enforceable by injunction' (HA 1985, s 138(3)).[223] However, the statutory duty is, according to the House of Lords, limited by the fact that at all times from the service of a claim notice until the completion of the whole of the RTB procedure, the tenant must continue to be a secure tenant, and so cannot necessarily force the issue by asking for an injunction to force a landlord to transfer a freehold to him when possession has been claimed by the landlord.[224] Once the conveyance or lease has been made, pursuant to HA 1985, Pt V, the secure tenancy comes to an end (HA 1985, s 139(2)).[225]

HA 1985 makes specific provision, in the form of a landlord's first and second notice to complete, so as to require the tenant to complete, once all relevant outstanding matters have been agreed or determined.[226] Notices to complete should be in writing but this is subject to the operation of estoppel. Where a local government officer indicated to the tenants that their RTB would be treated as continuing, despite a dispute over two notices, so that the tenants desisted from taking immediate proceedings, the landlords were subsequently estopped from disputing the validity of the notices.[227] HA 1985 allows the tenant to serve an initial and a further notice of delay on the landlord where he has failed to serve a notice under HA 1985, ss 124 or 125 or where he considers that delays of the landlord are preventing him from expeditiously exercising his RTB (HA 1985, s 153A). In such a case, provided the delay notice is operative, HA 1985, s 153B enables the rent payable to be treated as going to the purchase price of the house or flat.

The courts have concluded that the reference in HA 1985, s 138(1) to a 'secure tenant' requires that the tenant must be a secure tenant not only at the date of his claim notice, but throughout the whole period running from then, during negotiations and ending

---

222 While landlords may be entitled, for the sake of administrative convenience, to use standard-form leases, the court reserves the power to strike out unreasonable terms, such as a reservation to a local authority of a right to deal with any land or building near the flat as it thought fit: *Guinan v Enfield London Borough Council* [1996] EGCS 142, CA.

223 It is not avoided where the tenant has failed to pay rent or other payments such as service charges, due from him as tenant, for a period of four weeks after being lawfully demanded, although the landlord is not bound to comply with his duty to convey or lease until the whole of the sums due have been paid (HA 1985, s 138(2)).

224 *Bristol City Council v Lovell* [1998] 1 All ER 775. In support of this limitation to HA 1985, s 138, Lord Clyde at 788 pointed out that a landlord cannot be forced to convey the estate in question if, in effect, he is not paid for it.

225 Subject to the application of LPA 1925, s 139 to any sub-tenant.

226 HA 1985, ss 140 and 141. A relevant outstanding matter includes removal of on of two claimant parties from an RTB application: *Sembanjo v Brent London BC* (2001) Times, 4 January.

227 *Milne-Berry v Tower Hamlets London BC* (1997) 30 HLR 229, CA.

with the date of the conveyance.[228] Thus, where a sole secure tenant had, before any completion date had been agreed, sub-let the whole premises, the RTB was lost.[229]

Terms of conveyance or lease

The terms of the conveyance or lease are not as negotiated between the parties, but, as might be expected in a scheme such as this, which is weighted in favour of the secure tenant, those terms are laid down in HA 1985, Sch 6 in detailed provisions which, in the case of the grant of the fee simple, are designed to secure to the tenant the full benefit of that grant. Thus, the tenant is entitled to the benefit of LPA 1925, s 62, as well as to rights of support, passage and related matters which are, as far as possible, as equivalent to the rights he enjoyed with the property as secure tenant.[230] The title to the freehold, and to any lease, whether for not less than 40 years or not, is to be registered, even if the title to the land at that time had not been registered (HA 1985, s 154).

The same policy of maximising benefits for the acquiring secure tenant is seen in the case of leases. So, if at the time of the grant the landlord's leasehold interest is not less than a lease for a term of which more than 125 years and five days are unexpired, the appropriate term is a term of not less than 125 years.[231] Similarly, rights enjoyed in common by the former secure tenant with other tenants are to be inserted in the lease granted under HA 1985 to the same extent.[232] So as to protect the loss of the new lease by the landlord's neglect to comply with his own obligations to his superior landlord, the landlord is under an implied obligation to pay his own rent and to discharge his own leasehold obligations.[233] Since the legislature aims to favour the free transfer of leases granted under these rules, generally speaking, terms purporting to prohibit or restrict the assignment or sub-letting of the lease are void.[234]

In the case of the grant of a long RTB lease, however, the landlord is under a covenant to keep in repair[235] the structure and exterior both of the flat itself and of the building

---

228 *Jennings v Epping Forest District Council* (1992) 25 HLR 241, CA; also *Bradford Metropolitan City Council v McMahon* [1993] 4 All ER 237, CA.
229 *Jennings v Epping Forest District Council* [1993] 4 All ER 237, CA.
230 HA 1985, Sch 6, para 2. Similarly, the tenant is entitled to the grant of any rights of way within the landlord's power to grant that are necessary for the reasonable enjoyment of the dwelling house (HA 1985, Sch 6, para 3).
231 HA 1985, Sch 6, para 12(1). Otherwise, the appropriate lease is in principle for a term expiring five days before the term of the landlord's own lease (HA 1985, Sch 6, para 12(2)).
232 HA 1985, Sch 6, para 13.
233 HA 1985, Sch 6, para 15.
234 HA 1985, Sch 6, para 17 (1).
235 To which there is linked an implied duty to rebuild or reinstate the premises in the case of damage by fire or other insurable risk (HA 1985, Sch 6, para 14(3)).

in which it is situated and to make good any defect affecting that structure.[236] Although the tenant is under an implied covenant, which may be varied by the parties, to keep the house in good repair or the interior of the flat in such repair, as the case may be,[237] the width of the landlord's own obligation is such that it could easily extend to the complete rebuilding of the building containing the flat even if the cause were to be an inherent defect unknown at the date the premises were constructed, or at the date of the lease being granted. However, the landlord is entitled to insert service charges clauses in the new lease so as to enable him to recover from the tenant a 'reasonable part' of the costs incurred in complying with his repairing, rebuilding and insuring obligations.[238] While HA 1985 contains various controls (akin to those which apply to private sector tenants) on the recovery of variable service charges, so that the tenant is not faced with unpredictable levels of future charges, these controls may be avoided by a service charge which is initially fixed and which is subject only to an indexed escalation clause, so as to protect the landlord from the consequences of, for example, rising building costs.[239]

Rent to mortgage scheme

There may be some secure tenants who would like to exercise the RTB a house or flat but who have not sufficient resources to be able to afford more than an initial deposit.[240] This possibility was foreseen at the time the legislation was introduced, and a right to a mortgage was introduced. So as further to widen the access of this class of tenant to the right to buy, Parliament has abolished the right to a mortgage and replaced it with a 'rent to mortgage' scheme.[241]

The essence of the scheme is as follows. The tenant must first serve a notice of claim to the RTB, and his notice of exercise must still be in force at the time he claims the rent to mortgage right (HA 1985, s 143(1)). Once the tenant has by notice claimed to exercise the right to rent on mortgage terms, and receives a landlord's notice admitting the claim, the tenant has 12 weeks from service of the landlord's reply notice to inform the landlord that he opts to exercise the right to buy, or to proceed with the rent to mortgage scheme, or to withdraw entirely from both (HA 1985, s 146A).

---

236 HA 1985, Sch 6, para 14(2). The county court may authorise the exclusion or modification of these duties (HA 1985, Sch 6, para 14(4)). The duty extends to any property over which the tenant has rights under HA 1985, Sch 6, and the landlord is also bound to ensure, so far as practicable, that services provided by him are maintained at a reasonable level.
237 HA 1985, Sch 6, para 16.
238 HA 1985, Sch 6, para 16A.
239 *Coventry City Council v Cole* [1994] 1 All ER 997, CA.
240 However, a secure tenant who has received housing benefit at any time in, notably, the last 12 months ending with the day of serve of notice exercising the rent to mortgage right cannot in fact claim that right (HA 1985, s 143A).
241 HA 1985, Pt V, ss 143-151 as amended.

Should the tenant in fact be able to pay most of the purchase price out of his own resources, either outright, or where the rent payable would be the equivalent of notional mortgage repayments by instalments, the right to rent to mortgage is excluded.[242] However, if the tenant is entitled to proceed with the exercise of a right to rent to mortgage, the rules envisage that, once he pays his initial deposit, the whole of the remaining price of the house or flat concerned is left outstanding. Subject to the same conditions as apply to the RTB, the tenant obtains a conveyance of the house or a lease of the flat concerned (HA 1985, s 150).

Since the tenant has not paid the whole purchase price, he is entitled to leave the balance of the price outstanding, and the conveyance (or lease) must include a covenant to repay the outstanding amount where the house or flat is disposed of to a person who is not the spouse of the secure tenant or is left in the secure tenant's will or is transferred in divorce proceedings. This covenant binds him and his successors in title.[243]

242 The statutory formulae for calculating these limits are in HA 1985, s 143B and appropriate regulations.
243 HA 1985, Sch 6A, para 1; however, the secure tenant and his successors in title may repay the amount outstanding at any time, following a notice procedure (HA 1985, Sch 6A, para 2). This contingent liability to repay must be secured by a mortgage (HA 1985, s 151B).

CHAPTER 17

Protection from illegal eviction and other rights of residential tenants

I GENERAL INTRODUCTION

Statute does not merely provide security of tenure to certain residential tenants. Parliament has provided a battery of rules aimed at combatting particular types of abuse by landlords of their superior bargaining strength in the residential sector. These specific rules may be termed information rules (about rent books and the like), anti-eviction rules, and buy-out enabling provisions.

Statute gives residential tenants, who pay the rent weekly, and who may be specially vulnerable, the right to information about the rent payable and the terms of their tenancy, by requiring the landlord to provide a rent book. Both residential tenants and licensees are entitled, even if they may not have any security of tenure, to a notice to quit both for a minimum four-week period, and in a prescribed form, so preventing the landlord from serving an oral notice or a written notice which might be unclear as to the date for quitting. Parliament has enacted two codes which give statutory protection against illegal eviction and harassment, one of which imposes criminal penalties on the landlord, and the more recent of which provides for a specific (and penal) statutory method of calculation of damages for illegal eviction. This is designed to rob the landlord of any profit he may have made from his illegal eviction, as where a landlord evicts a Rent Act-protected or statutory tenant and replaces him with an assured tenant. With the arrival of assured shorthold tenanies, the amount of damages recoverable by tenants has lessened overall, as the value of their tenancy is much less than that of a Rent Act tenant, due to the much greater security of the latter.

Long lessees of flats may invoke the Landlord and Tenant Act 1987 (hereinafter LTA 1987), Part I of which allows them to claim and exercise a statutory right of first refusal if the landlord sells, mortgages or otherwise disposes of his freehold interest. LTA 1987, Pt III provides for a compulsory buy-out of the landlord, notably where he has seriously and persistently neglected his repairing obligations, to the detriment of the value, and so the marketability, of individual flats. LTA 1987 was passed as a result of the deliberations of the Nugee Committee.[1] They reported on management problems in the case of certain long leasehold flats. These included gross neglect by landlords to comply with their repairing obligations or failure to collect service charges and so build up a fund to pay for repairs and related work. LTA 1987, Pt 1 is technical and to some extent it may have been overtaken by collective enfranchisement of flats (as to which see ch 18, below).

II   INFORMATION RULES

Provision of rent book

Where a tenant has the right to occupy premises as a residence in consideration of a rent payable weekly, the landlord must, by LTA 1985, s 4(1), provide a rent book or similar document.[2] 'Tenant' includes a statutory tenant and a person with a contractual right to occupy the premises (LTA 1985, s 4(3)). Therefore, the statutory duty applies to occupation of a residence at a weekly rent whether under a common-law tenancy, or statutorily protected tenancy including protected or assured tenancies, secure tenancies and also under licence.

The rent must be payable weekly, or the duty does not apply. The length of the tenancy need not necessarily be weekly, so that if a tenant holds under a monthly tenancy with the rent payable weekly, the duty applies; if it happens that the rent is payable monthly, it does not. If there is a term of years and the rent is payable weekly, then the duty to provide a rent book applies. The operation of the duty is thus fortuitous and it is difficult at first blush to see why the present obligation is confined to tenancies with a rent payable weekly, as opposed to those where the rent may be monthly or quarterly.

A rent book must state the name and address of the landlord (LTA 1985, s 5(1)). If the tenancy is a protected or statutory tenancy or an assured tenancy then particulars must be given of the rent and of the matters prescribed by regulations.[3]

Prescribed form of notice to quit

By Protection from Eviction Act 1977, s 5(1), no notice by a landlord or a tenant to quit any premises let as a dwelling is valid unless it is in writing and is given not less than

---

1   Analysed by Hawkins [1986] Conv 14.
2   This duty does not, by LTA 1985, s 4(2), apply where the rent includes a payment in respect of board where the value thereof forms a substantial proportion of the whole rent. Any failure to comply with the various statutory duties is an offence (LTA 1985, s 7).
3   Rent Books (Forms of Notice) Regulations 1982, SI 1982/1474 as amended.

four weeks before the date on which it is to take effect. Moreover, the notice, if served[4] by either side, must contain prescribed information.[5] By Protection from Eviction Act 1977, s 5(1A), the same rule applies to periodic licences; but not to a licence which is expressed to be terminable with the licensee's employment.[6] It does not apply to excluded tenancies or licences, or to tenants at will.[7] It now appears that it is open to the landlord and tenant to waive the requirements of Protection from Eviction Act 1977, s 5. Therefore, it was open to a tenant who was threatened with domestic violence by her husband to serve a four-day notice on her landlords, which they accepted. The provision was enacted for the sole benefit of the tenant.[8]

III PROTECTION AGAINST UNLAWFUL EVICTION, HARASSMENT AND EVICTION[9]

Unlawful eviction

By the Protection from Eviction Act 1977, s 1(2) it is an offence if any person unlawfully deprives a residential occupier of his occupation of the premises or of any part thereof, or for that person to attempt to do so.[10] It is a defence if the person evicting the occupier proves that he believed, and had reasonable cause to believe, that the residential occupier had ceased to reside in the premises. To amount to an offence, a deprivation of occupation must have the character of eviction: an exclusion from premises for a day and a night was outside the Protection from Eviction Act 1977, s 1(2).[11] However, it seems that an offence may be constituted even though the eviction may not be permanent, if there is an intention to deprive the occupier of his occupation by eviction.[12] The person accused has a defence if he is able to prove that he believed with reasonable cause that the residential occupier had ceased to reside on the premises.

The wide term 'any person' means that the Protection from Eviction Act 1977, s 1 applies both to landlords and licensors, which is no doubt deliberate. The term

---

4   In *Wandsworth London Borough Council v Atwell* [1995] EGCS 68 it was held that where a tenancy agreement did not expressly incorporate LPA 1925, s 196, the landlord could serve a notice to quit by leaving it at the tenancy address and failed to prove service, the tenant being absent from the premises.
5   Notices to Quit (Prescribed Information) Regulations 1988, SI 1988/2201.
6   *Norris v Checksfield* [1991] 4 All ER 327, CA.
7   *Crane v Morris* [1965] 3 All ER 77, [1965] 1 WLR 1104, CA.
8   *Hackney London BC v Snowden* [2001] L & TR 6, [2001] L & TR 60, CA.
9   For a comprehensive analysis of the criminal law principles applicable see ATH Smith *Property Offences* ch 16.
10   Civil remedies remain available to a residential tenant who is unlawfully evicted or harassed: Protection from Eviction Act 1977, s 1(5).
11   *R v Yuthiwattana* (1984) 80 Cr App Rep 55.
12   ATH Smith *Property Offences* para 16-10, noting that if L evicts T in that sense and then repents, he could still be convicted under Protection from Eviction Act 1977, s 1. There is, indeed, no provision in s 1 comparable to that of HA 1988, s 27(7), allowing for mitigation of a damages award if the landlord repents and re-admits the tenant to occupation.

'residential occupier' is defined (Protection from Eviction Act 1977, s 1(1)) as a person occupying the premises as a residence, whether under a contract, statute or rule of law. It therefore includes tenants, licensees, lodgers and statutory tenants under RA 1977, assured and excluded tenants under HA 1988 and secure tenants. It seems, though the point is not settled, that the protection of the Protection from Eviction Act 1977, s 1 may extend to the tenant's wife, where she does not hold the tenancy jointly with him, as her occupation is through that of her husband. If there is no intention to create any interest in the land, and no continuing right of occupation, then the Protection from Eviction Act 1977, s 1 as a whole seems not to apply. Where a person was allowed to occupy a house for two-week period until a specified date, on a wholly informal basis, it was held that the individual concerned was not a residential occupier.[13]

Damages for occupier

A residential occupier (a term to be understood as for the Protection from Eviction Act 1977, s 1) has a right to claim damages in two cases, by HA 1988, s 27. The expression 'residential occupier' includes both tenants and contractual licensees, so that a licensee occupying an hotel room on a long-term basis who was evicted on one day's notice recovered a substantial award of statutory damages.[14] The purpose of the legislation has been said to be to deprive the landlord of any profit that his wrongful eviction has released, but the Act does not intend to fine the landlord.[15] For this reason, the valuation exercise required to deprive the landlord of his profit from the illegal eviction must be calculated on actual valuation evidence and not in the abstract.[16]

The first case is where a landlord (referred to as the 'landlord in default') or any person acting on his behalf unlawfully deprives the occupier of his occupation of the whole or part of the premises (HA 1988, s 27(1)). 'Landlord' is defined (HA 1988, s 27(9)(c)) as the person who, but for the occupier's right to occupy, would be entitled to occupation of the premises and any superior landlord under whom he derives title. This definition was held to include, on a beneficial construction, a landlord-purchaser entitled in equity to the immediate reversion pending completion.[17] It also appears to extend to the wife of a landlord who occupies parts of the premises through her husband as his licensee.[18] However, there must exist a right to occupy before a person (such as the daughter of the landlord) is considered to be a 'landlord' for statutory purposes.[19] The

---

13   *West Wiltshire County Council v Snelgrove* (1997) 30 HLR 57, CA; see Morgan [1999] Conv 43.
14   *Mehta v Royal Bank of Scotland* [1999] L & TR 340, CA.
15   *Melville v Bruton* [1996] EGCS 57, CA; it was said that with the increasing use of assured shorthold tenancies, the incentive on landlord to use illegal evictions might decrease.
16   *King v Jackson* [1998] 1 EGLR 30, CA.
17   *Jones v Miah* [1992] 2 EGLR 50, CA: the fact that, as against the vendor, the landlord, pending completion, held only a revocable licence made no difference.
18   *Sullman v Little* 1993 Current Law Week, Issue 29, p 2 (Cty Ct).
19   *Francis v Brown* (1997) 30 HLR 143, CA.

words 'any person acting on behalf of the landlord in default' do not extend the scope of the Act to agency and employment by the landlord. A person employed to evict the tenant or to manage the property in such a way as to procure his departure was thus not liable with the landlord as a joint tortfeasor. The statutory language made it clear that the landlord alone is liable.[20]

The second case applies where these persons are guilty of an attempt unlawfully to deprive the occupier of his occupation, or are guilty of knowing harassment. As a result of one of these, the occupier is, within the Act, likely to give up occupation of the premises as a residence and in fact does so (HA 1988, s 27(2)). The acts of harassment are described as acts calculated to interfere with the peace or comfort of the residential occupier or members of his household, or persistent withdrawal or withholding of services. The acts must be done with an intent akin to that required for the offence of harassment. The sort of conduct here envisaged might include intimidation of the kind that is also capable of constituting a breach of the implied covenant for quiet enjoyment.

The remedy provided in HA 1988, s 28 (depriving the landlord of any profit made by the eviction) is draconian. In some cases, it may impose a penalty. However, HA 1988, s 27(2)(b) is not limited to a case where the landlord's conduct had been established to a high degree, and where this made the tenant's position so intolerable that he was driven out of the property.[21] Each element of HA 1988, s 27(2)(b) must be proved by the tenant, which may not be an easy task. However, a tenant whose landlord had introduced a new tenant into the complainant's bedroom when he was away on holiday was held to have fallen foul of this provision. The use of the flat had been so much curtailed that the tenant was induced to leave the flat entirely. His peace and comfort were directly and predictably caused by the landlord's acts.[22]

If the former occupier is reinstated as residential occupier before proceedings to enforce the liability are finally disposed of, there is no statutory liability (HA 1988, s 27(6)(a)).[23] This is also the case where the court, at the request of the occupier, orders his reinstatement (HA 1988, s 27(6)(b)). Re-instatement has been held not to consist in handing the tenant back a key to a lock which did not work and allowing her to resume occupation of a totally wrecked room; if the tenant does not wish to be re-instated, it is difficult to see how HA 1988, s 27(6) can apply.[24] The court, by HA 1988, s 27(7), may reduce the damages to such amount as it thinks appropriate, if:

1 prior to the event concerned, the conduct of the occupier or a person living with him is such that it is reasonable to mitigate the damages for which the landlord is liable; or

2 before proceedings were begun, the landlord offered reinstatement and it was unreasonable for the occupier to refuse it, or, if offered alternative accommodation

---

20 *Sampson v Wilson* [1996] Ch 39, CA.
21 *Abbott v Bayley* [1999] L & TR 267.
22 *Abbott v Bayley* [1999] L & TR 267. See also *Miller v Eyo* [1998] NPC 95 (where the landlord, with no right to do so, personally moved into the premises).
23 See *Murray v Aslam* (1994) 27 HLR 284, CA.
24 *Tagro v Cafane* [1991] 2 All ER 235, CA.

before that offer, that it was unreasonable to him to refuse the offer if he had not obtained the accommodation.

The court must look at the tenant's conduct (under HA 1988, s 27(2)(a)) in the light of the surrounding facts. Its conclusion will depend on the circumstances of the case.[25] Thus a landlord was entitled to invoke this provision to reduce damages against a tenant who failed unjustifiably to pay rent.[26] A council landlord who accepted notice to quit from a wife, who held a joint secure tenancy with her husband, for a shorter period than that required by the tenancy agreement was still able to invoke HA 1988, s 27(2)(a). This was owing to the fact that the husband co-tenant had been indulging in domestic violence, so that his eviction from the premises, although contrary to HA 1988, was precipitated by his own conduct.[27]

Damages are payable 'in respect of his loss of the right to occupy[28] the premises in question as his residence' (HA 1988, s 27(3)). Liability is in the nature of a tortious liability, and is additional to any other liability in contract or tort (HA 1988, s 27(4)). But damages cannot be awarded for the same loss both under HA 1988, s 27 and under common-law liability (HA 1988, s 27(5)). This has been taken to mean that the claimant may pursue two claims, but that the lesser sum awarded will be deducted from the larger sum.[29] The person liable has a statutory defence similar to that as under the Protection from Eviction Act 1977, s 1 (HA 1988, s 27(8)). In addition to statutory damages, the courts seem to be disposed where appropriate to award aggravated damages if the conduct of the landlord warrants this,[30] but since exemplary damages and statutory damages fulfil the same function, the latter cannot be awarded where the former are claimed.[31]

Damages are based, by HA 1988, s 28(1), on the difference in value, as at the time immediately before the residential occupier ceased to occupy the premises as his residence, between:

1   the value of the landlord's interest[32] on the assumption that the occupier has a continuing right of occupation; and
2   the value of the landlord's interest on the assumption that the occupier ceased to have that right.

Valuations for the purpose of assessing damages are to be based on objective criteria set out in HA 1988, s 28(3), which are: that the landlord is assumed to be selling his

---

25   *Regalgrand Ltd v Dickerson* (1996) 29 HLR 620 at 625 (Aldous LJ).
26   *Regalgrand Ltd v Dickerson* (1996) 29 HLR 620.
27   *Wandsworth London BC v Osei-Bonsu* [1999] 1 EGLR 26 (hence the award to the husband was reduced from £30,000 to £10,000).
28   This term expressly includes, by HA 1988, s 27(9)(b), any restriction on the right of any person to recover possession of the premises.
29   *Mason v Nwokorie* [1994] 1 EGLR 59, CA.
30   *Fairweather v Ghafoor* [2001] 2 CL 421.
31   *Francis v Brown* (1997) 30 HLR 143, CA.
32   Ie the landlord's interest in the building (HA 1988, s 28(2)), not just the part occupied by the occupier, if less extensive.

interest on the open market to a willing buyer, that neither the occupier nor any member of his family[33] wishes to buy, and that any substantial development (defined by HA 1988, s 28(6)) or demolition of the building is unlawful.

The comparisons are between the value of the landlord's interest as subject to the tenant's right to occupy and with vacant possession, owing to the aim of the Act. It is to rob the landlord of any illegitimate profit made from an illegal eviction. The valuations must be factual and not notional. Otherwise the landlord would be paying a fine.[34] So where a set of valuations had been reached assuming vacant possession, ignoring the fact that the evicted tenant had only an assured shorthold tenancy[35] and that there remained other tenants in the premises, an award of damages of £15,000 was reduced to £500 on appeal.[36] In one case, a tenant had given notice prior to the illegal eviction; the landlord had in effect jumped the gun, by evicting her illegally some six days before she would have lawfully been entitled to do so. The award of £11,000, statutory damages, or 20% of the vacant possession freehold value, was held to be 'manifestly wrong'. The tenant had a six-day entitlement to occupy: however, £1,500 was accepted as a proper award for the unavoidable breach of the common law quiet enjoyment covenant.[37] However, where a valuer with local knowledge concluded that a business tenancy held by a landlord who had illegally evicted a residential tenant should be valued on the basis that it 'could go on virtually for ever', even though theoretically it could be terminated on one month's notice, an award of £31,000 damages, though high, was not disturbed on appeal.[38] It was held correct in law for a judge to value the landlord's interest on the basis of what he paid for his interest with vacant possession, and then to take into account the value of each individual tenant's interest.[39]

Harassment

Under the Protection from Eviction Act 1977, s 1(3) it is an offence, if any person with intent to cause the residential occupier (as defined above) of any premises either:

1 to give up the occupation of the premises or any part thereof; or
2 to refrain from exercising any right or pursuing any remedy in respect of the premises or part thereof -

---

33 As defined in HA 1985, s 113, applied by HA 1988, s 28(5).
34 See however *McSpadden v Keen* (unreported) noted by Clarke (1999) 3 L & TR 140 (where a substantial award was held justified where the landlord refused to comply with orders to re-admit the tenant and tried to defeat the tenant's claim by sale of the premises).
35 As opposed to an assured tenancy, where there is a greater degree of tenant security. In *King v Jackson* [1998] 1 EGLR 30, CA, there was some dispute as whether the tenancy was assured or assured shorthold.
36 *Melville v Bruton* [1996] EGCS 57, CA.
37 *King v Jackson* [1998] 1 EGLR 30, CA.
38 *Tagro v Cafane* [1991] 2 All ER 235, CA; however, it appears that the landlord did not challenge the evidence which formed the basis of the valuation.
39 *Jones v Miah* [1992] 2 EGLR 50, CA.

does acts likely to interfere with the peace or comfort of the residential occupier or members of his household, or persistently withdraws or withholds services reasonably required for the occupation of the premises as a residence. The expression 'residential occupier' in this context appears not to include a licensee,[40] and certainly does not include a person in informal occupation for a fixed period of time where there is no intention to create legal relations.[41] An act of harassment may constitute an offence under s 1(3) even if it is not an actionable wrong, if done with the purpose or motive of causing a residential occupier to give up his occupation.[42]

The accused has a statutory defence if he or she can prove an honest and reasonable belief that the victim was not a residential occupier. If such a defence is put forward, the Crown must prove that the accused specifically intends to harass a person whom the accused knew or believed to be a residential occupier, as opposed to a trespasser, such as a squatter. The offence is not based on strict liability.[43]

It is an offence under the Protection from Eviction Act 1977, s 1(3A) for the landlord (defined in Protection from Eviction Act 1977, s 1(3C)) of a residential occupier or his agent to:
1 do acts likely to interfere with the peace or comfort of the residential occupier of members of his household; or
2 persistently to withdraw or withhold services reasonably required for the occupation of the premises as a residence,

and in either case he knows or has reasonable cause to believe that the conduct is likely to cause the residential occupier to give up the occupation of the whole or part of the premises or to refrain from exercising any right of pursuing any remedy in respect of the whole or part of the premises.[44]

The penalties for harassment are the same as for unlawful eviction (see above) and, similarly, civil remedies in respect of it are expressly preserved (Protection from Eviction Act 1977, s 1(5)). For example, there may be a contractual action for breach of the covenant, express or implied, for quiet enjoyment; and an occupier may even be granted a mandatory injunction to ensure access to and occupation of the premises, pending trial of the main action.[45]

40 *R v Blankley* [1979] Crim LR 166 (despite the wording of the Protection from Eviction Act 1977, s 1(1) which seems to include contractual licensees).
41 *West Wiltshire County Council v Snelgrove* (1997) 30 HLR 57, CA.
42 *R v Burke* [1990] 2 All ER 385.
43 *R v Phekoo* [1981] 1 WLR 1117; [1981] Conv 377 (Wasik).
44 Under the Protection from Eviction Act 1977, s 1(3B) if the person proves that he had reasonable grounds for his actions, he is not liable; see also *R (on the application of McGowan) v Brent Justices* [2001] EWHC Admin 814, (2001) 166 JP 29 (defendant's acts cumulatively breached Protection from Eviction Act 1977, s 1(3A)).
45 *Luganda v Service Hotels Ltd* [1969] 2 Ch 209, [1969] 2 All ER 692, CA.

Restriction on re-entry without due process of law

The Protection from Eviction Act 1977, s 2 provides that, where any premises are let as a dwelling on a lease which is subject to a right of re-entry or forfeiture, it is unlawful to enforce that right save by proceedings in court, while any person is lawfully residing in the premises or part of them.

Prohibition on eviction without due process of law

Under the Protection from Eviction Act 1977, s 3(1), where any premises have been let as a dwelling under a tenancy which is *not* a statutorily protected tenancy (defined in Protection from Eviction Act 1977, s 8(1)) or an excluded tenancy[46] and:

1 the former tenancy has come to an end, but
2 the occupier continues to reside in the premises or part of them,

then it is unlawful for the owner to enforce against the occupier his right to regain possession of the premises, otherwise than by proceedings in court. The term 'occupier' is widely defined (Protection from Eviction Act 1977, s 3(2)) so that it means any person lawfully residing in the premises at the termination of the former tenancy; and, by Protection from Eviction Act 1977, s 3(2A), the above restriction is extended to a restricted contract under RA 1977 which creates a licence. By the Protection from Eviction Act 1977, s 3(3), the general prohibition of Protection from Eviction Act 1977, s 3(1) applies where an owner has the right to recover possession after the death of a statutory tenant under RA 1977 or the Rent (Agriculture) Act 1976, as the case may be.

These rules apply to residential licences, provided that the licence is not excluded but whether entered into before or after the commencement of HA 1988, Pt I (Protection from Eviction Act 1977, s 3(2B)).[47]

The Protection from Eviction Act 1977, s 3 does not apply to any excluded tenancy or licence. The result is to render it easier for landlords to recover possession of residential premises which are shared with the occupier by himself or his family. This is because no security is enjoyed as an excluded tenancy cannot be assured, since the landlord must be resident, and the Protection from Eviction Act 1977, s 3 is also not applicable. Eviction without a statutory requirement of legal process is possible in the case of excluded tenancies and licences.

By the Protection from Eviction Act 1977, s 3A(2) and (3) a tenancy or licence is excluded if, under its terms:

---

46 This includes, for example, a protected tenancy under RA 1977, but not a statutory tenancy. Thus, where a landlord obtained an order for possession against a statutory tenant, the protection of Protection from Eviction Act 1977, s 3 applied until the court bailiff duly executed the court's order: see *Haniff v Robinson* [1993] 1 All ER 185.
47 But an occupier of an hotel room, lacking exclusive possession of his room, was not within Protection from Eviction Act 1977, s 3(2B): *Brillouet v Landless* (1995) 28 HLR 836, CA.

1   the occupier shares any accommodation with the landlord or licensor and, immediately before the grant and when the tenancy or licence ends, the landlord occupied as his only or principal home the shared accommodation, or that plus other accommodation;[48] or

2   the occupier shares any accommodation with a member of the landlord's or licensor's family (as defined in Protection from Eviction Act 1977, s 3A(5)) and, immediately before the grant and also when the tenancy ended, the family member occupied as his only or principal residence premises of which the whole or part of the shared accommodation formed part, and, immediately before the grant of the tenancy etc and when it ends, the landlord occupied as his only or principal home premises in the same building. If the building is a purpose-built block of flats (defined as for the resident landlord exclusion from assured tenancies) the tenancy, etc is not excluded. An occupier 'shares' accommodation if he has the use of it in common with another person (Protection from Eviction Act 1977, s 3A(4)). Certain other types of tenancy or licence are excluded from the 1977 Act, such as a right to occupy the premises for a holiday or gratuitously (Protection from Eviction Act 1977, s 3A(7)) even though there may be no sharing.

If the landlord flouts the Protection from Eviction Act 1977, s 3, as where he resorts to forcible or peaceable re-entry without a court order, or where, after 9 June 1988, following an order of the court, he forcibly ejects the tenant, he will face a potentially heavy liability in damages under HA 1988, s 27.[49]

IV   LONG TENANT'S RIGHT OF FIRST REFUSAL

Introduction

LTA 1987, Pt I[50] confers on qualifying tenants of residential flats a right to a first refusal where the landlord disposes of his interest in the premises. The aim of this legislation is to allow such tenants to buy out the transferring or the new landlord. However, the attainment of this object is weakened by the sheer complexity of the Act, a problem compounded by subsequent amendments. LTA 1987, Pt I has been stigmatised as ill-drafted, complicated and confused.[51] In a more recent case, it was said that the legal profession appeared to be the main beneficiaries of this Act, which had also been said to allow no room, by reason of the complexity of its provisions, for arguments based on common sense.[52] It was to be regretted that these provisions did not provide as

---

48   Accommodation within these rules does not include storage areas, passages, corridors or other areas of access, nor staircases.

49   As in *Haniff v Robinson* [1993] 1 All ER 185, where an award of £28,300 damages for forcible ejection of a statutory tenant, computed under HA 1988, s 28, was upheld.

50   For critiques of the Act, see Percival (1988) 51 MLR 97; Rogers [1988] Conv 122; PF Smith (1992) 12 LS 41.

51   *Denetower Ltd v Toop* [1991] 3 All ER 661, 668, CA.

52   *Belvedere Court Management Ltd v Frogmore Developments Ltd* [1996] 1 All ER 312, 331 (Sir Thomas Bingham MR).

many answers as they raised problems.[53] The following is a necessarily brief resume of the main operation of this legislation.

Scope of Part I

The statutory right of first refusal applies only to tenants holding long leases of residential flats occupied for residential purposes, as opposed to business or assured tenancies. In particular, the premises must consist of the whole or part of a building containing two or more flats held by qualifying tenants. To prevent a minority of tenants buying out the landlord, the number of such flats must exceed half the total number of flats in the premises (LTA 1987, s 1(2)). Essentially, a qualifying tenant is a tenant of a flat holding under a long lease (LTA 1987, s 3). Where an estate had been registered under two titles, the claim of the long lessees of one block of flats in the estate could nevertheless be dealt with on its own merits, as the expression 'premises' referred to that block and not to the whole estate.[54]

The most frequent type of disposal which will trigger the right of first refusal is, no doubt, a sale, grant of a reversionary lease (for perhaps a longer period than that of the leases of individual tenants of the flats) or a mortgage by the landlord. Certain types of disposal fall outside LTA 1987, Pt I, notably disposals under a will or gifts to a member of the landlord's family (LTA 1987, s 4). The policy of these exclusions seems to be that voluntary disposals for a substantial money consideration, especially as these might be deliberately intended to evade the statutory right of first refusal, are to be caught but not those which are involuntary or for no or no substantial consideration.

Outline of Operation of LTA 1987, Pt I

The scheme of LTA 1987, Pt I[55] is to force a landlord who makes a disposal of the whole premises caught by the Act,[56] such as a sale to a purchaser which has been an associated company of the landlord for over two years,[57] to in effect give a first refusal to long-residential tenants. The tenants, if there are over 50% who wish to take advantage of the Act, nominate a person to act for them, who then exercises the right of first refusal. LTA 1987 as amended has been designed to force the hand of landlords, as the following two main aspects of the operation of the legislation show.

---

53 *Belvedere Court Management Ltd v Frogmore Developments Ltd* [1996] 1 All ER 312.
54 *Kay Green v Twinsectra Ltd* [1996] 4 All ER 546, CA.
55 See Fox-Edwards *Estates Gazette* 7 September 1996, p 138.
56 It has been argued that a lease of a commercial part of premises with residential tenants in other parts who could claim LTA 1987, Pt I could be caught by the Act: Budge *Estates Gazette* 15 February 1997, p 141.
57 To counteract schemes such as that in *Michaels v Harley House (Marylebone) Ltd* [1997] 2 EGLR 44, LTA 1987, s 4(2)(l) catches disposals of a company associated with the landlord for up to two years from the disposal date. The disposal date within LTA 1987, Pt I is the date of the completion of the contract: *Mainwaring v Henry Smith's Trustees* [1996] 2 All ER 220, CA.

1 Landlords who fall within LTA 1987 are required by LTA 1987, s 5 to serve an 'offer notice' on tenants who qualify within LTA 1987, Pt I (essentially long-residential tenants of flats). It suffices if the notice is served on 90% of all the qualifying tenants or all but one if there are less than 10. This notice specifies the price of the premises. The landlord can decide on the method of sale, which may in particular be by contract, auction (LTA 1987, ss 5A and 5B),[58] or option (LTA 1987, s 5C).[59] The Act provides time-limits for each set of procedures. In the case of contracts, for example, the qualifying tenants must be given not less than two months from the offer notice to accept; it suffices if over 50% do so. The qualifying tenants who wish to participate must then nominate a nominated person, who acts as purchaser, within one month of acceptance. The landlord must send out the contract, within one month of service on him of the nomination notice, to the nominated person (LTA 1987, s 8A). Within two months of this being done, the nominee purchaser is required to offer an exchange of contracts. Alternatively he may withdraw by notice from the contract. In the case of an offer of exchange of contracts, the landlord has seven days to complete from receipt of the nominated person's contract (LTA 1987, s 8A(6)). However, the landlord may give a notice of withdrawal, in which case he is not forced to proceed, but cannot dispose of the relevant interest in the premises for a 12-month period from the date of service of his withdrawal notice (LTA 1987, s 9B).

2 The offer notice procedure cannot in principle be avoided, for if, without reasonable excuse, the landlord sells to a third party without having first served an offer notice under LTA 1987, s 5 on the tenants in question, he commits a criminal offence with a level 5 fine (LTA 1987, s 10A). Indeed, within two months of the disposal in question the new landlord is required to inform all the tenants of the fact of the assignment. He must also within the same time scale inform all qualifying tenants of their rights under LTA 1987, Pt I, otherwise he commits a criminal offence attracting a level 4 fine.[60] This gives four months, running from the date the tenants have been informed of the disposal, to the requisite majority of qualifying tenants (more than 50% of them) to ask for details of the relevant disposal by notice served on the new landlord under LTA 1987, s 11A, to which notice the landlord must respond within the short period of one month. Following that, more than 50% of the qualifying tenants have the right to force the new landlord to sell to them on the same terms as he acquired the interest in question (LTA 1987, s 12B).[61] The price[62] is the same as under the original transaction but if

---

58 As to which see Murphy *Estates Gazette* 30 August 1997, p 44.
59 As to which see Frost [1999] Conv 107.
60 Housing Act 1996, s 93; LTA 1985, ss 3 and 3A.
61 An accurate list of the names and addresses of more than 50% of the qualifying tenants authorising service of the notice is required: *El Naschie v The Pitt Place (Epsom) Ltd* (1998) Times, 27 May, CA.
62 And indeed the other terms. Thus where tenants prior to disposal held rights to amenity gardens, these had to be continued into the disposal to them under LTA 1987, s 12 in its original form: *Twinsectra Ltd v Jones* [1998] 2 EGLR 129: the court has to look to the original disposal from the landlord to the new landlord and restores the tenants to the position they would have been it but for that transaction.

the value has increased and the parties cannot agree, then the Leasehold Valuation Tribunal determines the price (LTA 1987, s 13).[63]

V RTM

Introduction

Long leaseholders are given no fault right to take over the management of long leasehold blocks by CLRA 2002, Pt II, Chapter 1. The new right is the right to manage (RTM). The right is available without the tenants having to pay any compensation, as envisaged by the government when it put forward the idea in 2000.[64]

The main principles of the scheme are similar to those applying to collective enfranchisement of flats in its latest form. Hence, the following is a summary of the main features of RTM. This scheme may be a stepping-stone to collective enfranchisement, but it involves the landlord being a member of the RTM company which takes over the management of the flats concerned, whereas collective enfranchisement buys out the landlord completely.[65] The RTM may cease in a number of circumstances. These include an agreement to end the right to management by the RTM company between it and the landlord, as well as where the RTM company is wound up or a receiver or manager of its undertaking is appointed (CLRA 2002, s 105). However, in principle the RTM cannot be contracted out of in any lease (CLRA 2002, s 106). Requirements as laid down in the CLRA 2002 for such matters as service of notices or observance of obligations can be enforced on the application of any person interested, such as a tenant, the landlord or the RTM company, by the county court (CLRA 2002, s 107).

Qualifying rules

RTM applies to self-contained (ie in principle structurally detached) buildings which contain two or more flats occupied by qualifying tenants (CLRA 2002, s 72(1)). The total number of flats held by long lessees must be not less than two-thirds of the total number of flats contained in the premises (CLRA 2002, s 72(1)). There are a number of limited exceptions to RTM.[66] RTM is exercisable by an RTM company, which is a

---

63 See *Groundpremium Property Management Ltd v Longmint Ltd* [1998] 1 EGLR 131 (the Tribunal must not value the premises de novo but must rule on the price payable for the property set out in the purchase notice).

64 Commonhold and Leasehold Reform Draft Bill and Consultation Paper (2000) Pt II, Section 3, para 10.

65 If the RTM is acquired, then the right of tenants compulsorily to buy out the landlord under LTA 1987, Pt III is excluded by CLRA 2002, Sch 7, para 9.

66 Notably that if the internal floor area of any non-residential part exceeds 25% of the internal floor area of the premises taken as a whole (CLRA 2002, Sch 6, para 1). There is an exception where the landlord is resident, in converted, as opposed to purpose-built premises with not more than four units. The residence must be throughout at least the last 12 months as his only

private company limited by guarantee (CLRA 2002, s 73(2)).[67] The members of an RTM company are essentially the qualifying tenants of the flats in the premises (CLRA 2002, s 74). Qualifying tenants are, in principle, tenants of a flat under a long lease (CLRA 2002, s 75(2)).[68] The main type of long lease is a lease granted for a term certain exceeding 21 years (CLRA 2002, ss 75(2) and 76(2)). Certain other types of lease are within the RTM scheme, notably leases terminable on death or marriage[69] and leases granted under the right to buy under HA 1985, Pt V (CLRA 2002, s 76(2)).

Where RTM is exercised, the RTM company steps into the shoes of the landlord. Hence, a number of statutory obligations are transferred from the landlord to the company, such as the repairing obligations of the landlord under LTA 1985 s 11, landlords' obligations with regard to 'relevant defects' in premises, and landlords' obligations to consult tenants about service charges.[70] An RTM company is entitled to service of a landlord's offer notice under LTA 1987, Pt I.[71]

Claim to exercise RTM

In general terms the RTM company claims to acquire the RTM by means of a claim notice served on the landlord, any managing company of his, or, if relevant, on any manager appointed under LTA 1987, Pt II (CLRA 2002, s 79).[72] If at the date the notice is given there are two qualifying tenants then both must be members of the RTM Company (CLRA 2002, s 79(4)). Otherwise the membership of the RTM company must include tenants who are qualifying tenants in at least half the total number of flats in the premises (CLRA 2002, s 79(5)).[73] The notice must specify the premises and state

or principal home by him or an adult member of his family as defined (CLRA 2002, Sch 6, para 3). If the immediate landlord of any qualifying tenant is a local authority the RTM is excluded (CLRA 2002, Sch 6, para 4). This exclusion does not apply where the immediate landlord is a registered social landlord such as a housing association, so reflecting the wishes of the government at the time of consultation: Commonhold and Leasehold Reform Draft Bill and Consultation Paper (2000) Pt II, Section 3, para 19.

67 Details as to the content of the memorandum and articles of association of the company will be a matter for regulations (CLRA 2002, s 74(2)). Use of a company was the chosen means of bringing about the RTM, so that it would be consistent with collective enfranchisement: Commonhold and Leasehold Reform Draft Bill and Consultation Paper (2000) Pt II, Section 3, para 26.

68 Joint tenants of a long lease together constitute the qualifying tenant (CLRA 2002, s 75(7)).

69 Subject to the exception in CLRA 2002, s 77(1).

70 CLRA 2002, Sch 7, paras 2–4.

71 CLRA 2002, Sch 7, para 7.

72 This and indeed all notices within the RTM procedure must be in writing and may be sent by the (ordinary) post (CLRA 2002, s 111).

73 A copy of the notice must be given to each qualifying tenant at the date it is served (CLRA 2002, s 79(8)). Thus a qualifying tenant who is not a member of the RTM company is informed as to the intention to acquire the RTM. A copy of the notice must also be given to the landlord and, if relevant, a manager appointed under LTA 1987, Pt II (CLRA 2002, s 79(6)).

the grounds on which it is claimed that they fall within the Act. Various other details must be given, notably the full name of each qualifying tenant of a flat within the premises who is a member of the RTM company, as well as sufficient particulars to identify that person's lease (CLRA 2002, s 80(2)-(4)).[74] A minimum period of one month must be given in the notice in which the landlord or other person can respond with a counter-notice (CLRA 2002, s 80(6)). A date of at least three months after this date must be given on which the RTM company intends to acquire the RTM premises (CLRA 2002, s 80(7)). The name and registered office of the RTM company must be given (CLRA 2002, s 80(5)). It is envisaged that claim notices will be in a form to be prescribed by regulations. A claim notice cannot be served unless the RTM company has invited any qualifying tenant who has not agreed to become a member of the RTM company to participate in the claim notice (CLRA 2002, s 78).[75] Within the time specified in the claim notice the landlord or other person such as a manager appointed under LTA 1987, Pt II may respond with a counter-notice (CLRA 2002, s 84). This either admits the right to acquire the RTM, or alleges that for some specific reason as set out in CLRA 2002, Pt II Chapter 1, such as that more than 25% of the premises are used for business purposes, or that there are insufficient qualifying tenants as members of the RTM company, there is no RTM at that date.

Acquisition of RTM

Where, as is assumed to be usual, there is no dispute about entitlement to the RTM, it is acquired at the date specified in the claim notice (CLRA 2002, s 90(2)). Moreover, there is deemed to be no dispute if no counter-notice is served or, if a such a notice is served, it admits the RTM (CLRA 2002, s 90(3)). Once an RTM company has acquired the RTM, but not beforehand, it has rights to obtain information from the landlord, the landlord's managing company (if any) and a manager appointed under LTA 1987, Pt II. This is to information which the person possesses or controls and which the company reasonably requires him to provide on connection with the RTM (CLRA 2002, s 93(1)).[76] Service charges which are not committed to expenditure, in the hands of the landlord or other person, such as his manager, must be paid to the RTM company (CLRA 2002, s 94).

74 However, as with much of this type of tenant-slanted legislation, it is provided that a claim notice is not invalid because required particulars are inaccurate (CLRA 2002, s 81(1)). There is also a provision to prevent challenges to claim notices based on a qualifying tenant who is a member of an the RTM company ceasing to qualify later (CLRA 2002, s 81(2)).

75 A claim notice may be withdrawn by further notice at any time before the RTM company acquires the RTM (CLRA 2002, s 86). There is deemed withdrawal if the RTM company has not applied to the leasehold valuation tribunal to settle a disputed claim to the RTM within two months from the date of the counter-notice (CLRA 2002, s 87).

76 Provision is made to cover contracts relating to the management of the premises which are running at the date of the acquisition of the RTM: thus the RTM company must be informed of these by the 'manager party' (the existing manager) under CLRA 2002, s 91.

Exercise of RTM by RTM company

The RTM company takes over from the landlord functions under all long leases in the premises with respect to services, repairs, maintenance, improvements, insurance and management from the landlord or the landlord's managing company as the case may be (CLRA 2002, s 96(4) and (5)). However, the landlord retains the right to forfeit leases, and is not shut out from the management of any lease which is not held by a qualifying tenant, as where a flat is held on a short lease or a business tenancy (CLRA 2002, s 96(6)). But in such cases the RTM company would still have to manage the common parts of the premises. Obligations falling on the RTM company in relation to repairs and other management functions are also owed to the landlord (CLRA 2002, s 97(1)). The landlord or his managing company or a manager appointed under LTA 1987, Pt II may still insure the whole premises at his own expense (CLRA 2002, s 97(3)) and may by agreement with the RTM company continue to exercise certain management functions (CLRA 2002, s 97(2)). The RTM will cover the whole building in which there are qualifying tenants, with 'appurtenant property', such as any garage, outhouse, garden, yard or appurtenances belonging to, or usually enjoyed with, the building or part or flat (CLRA 2002, ss 72 and 112).

The RTM company will deal with consents, in connection with assignment, underletting, charging, parting with possession and the making of improvements (CLRA 2002, s 98). However, the landlord remains involved. The RTM company cannot give consent (or as it put 'grant an approval') in the case of the covenants just mentioned without having given 30 days' notice in writing to the landlord. In the case of other matters requiring landlord approval the period of notice is 14 days (CLRA 2002, s 98(4)). This period gives the landlord time to object and if there is a disagreement with the RTM company which cannot be resolved, then the matter has to be resolved by a leasehold valuation tribunal (CLRA 2002, s 99(1)). However, the landlord may only object[77] if he could have refused consent to the transaction under the general law (CLRA 2002, s 99(2) and (3)).

Tenant covenants (other than re-entry or forfeiture functions) are in principle enforceable by the RTM company (CLRA 2002, s 100). However, there is a somewhat unusual provision, which derogates from the principle that the RTM company takes over management from the landlord. The government justified this derogation on the ground that the landlord retains an interest in the premises and yet has been shut out from the right to see to it that covenants are observed: hence the absolute nature of the duty.[78] The RTM company has no discretion as to which breaches to report to the landlord and which not to report to him. The RTM company is under a statutory duty to keep under review whether tenant covenants of leases in any part of the premises (including seemingly tenant covenants by any tenants who do not hold long leases)

---

77   Objection is by a written notice to the RTM company and the tenant in question in particular (CLRA 2002, s 99(4)).

78   Commonhold and Leasehold Reform Draft Bill and Consultation Paper (2000) Pt II, Section 3, paras 78-79.

are being complied with. The RTM company must then report breaches to the landlord, within three months from the day the failure comes to its attention (CLRA 2002, s 101(3)). If, in particular, the failure has been remedied then the duty to report to the landlord does not apply (CLRA 2002, s 101(4)). Nor does the duty apply if the landlord has informed the RTM company that he does not wish to have breaches of a particular kind reported to him (CLRA 2002, s 101(4)). The government thought that not all landlords would wish to be informed of every minor breach of covenant.[79]

VI   OUTLINE OF OTHER MISCELLANEOUS RIGHTS OF LESSEES

Long-residential tenants in blocks of flats (or a majority of them) have a statutory right to buy out the landlord on the basis of fault: where the landlord has in particular broken its repairing, maintenance, insurance or management obligations in relation to the premises. In this case the breaches must be likely to continue.[80] These tenants also have the right to buy out the landlord where the court has appointed a manager under LTA 1987, Pt II, which appointment is in force at the date of the buy-out application and has been in force for two years.[81] A statutory notice procedure must be followed by the tenants concerned in order to make use of this right (LTA 1987, s 27), and the landlord must have failed to comply with the notice.

The county court is empowered by LTA 1987, Pt IV as amended by CLRA 2002, ss 162-163 on the application by one or by a group of such long-residential lessees on various grounds, where the lease fails to make satisfactory provision in relation to a list of matters.[82] These include the repair and maintenance of the flat or building containing it. Also the service charge provisions of the lease. This list may be added to by statutory instrument.

---

79   Commonhold and Leasehold Reform Draft Bill and Consultation Paper (2000) Pt II, Section 3, para 80.
80   LTA 1987, s 29(2). 'Management' now includes improvement: LTA 1987, s 24(11) as amended by CLRA 2002, Sch 9, para 8.
81   LTA 1987, s 29(3).
82   An RTM company holding the RTM may also exercise the right to apply for a lease variation: CLRA 2002, Sch 7, para 10.

CHAPTER 18

Long leasehold enfranchisement

I   INTRODUCTION

Note of protection where a long lease expires

It has for some time been the policy of Parliament to provide special legislative rules applicable to long residential tenancies. Any long residential tenancy granted before 1 March 1990, as well as any long tenancy granted after that date which reaches its expiry date after at 15 January 1999, is governed by the new modified assured tenancy scheme.[1] In essence, the long tenancy is continued unless the landlord can terminate it on one of a number of statutory grounds or unless the landlord serves a notice proposing an assured tenancy on the tenant.

Principles of enfranchisement

The necessity for some protection of long residential lessees whose leases were coming to an end raises the question of why long leases of residential houses or flats had been granted as from the latter part of the nineteenth century. It will be appreciated, however, that it is not in principle possible to enforce covenants to repair or other positive covenants, such as to pay for repairs, against any successor in title to freehold land burdened with that type of covenant.[2] Hence, developers of residential flats may have preferred, prior to the advent of commonholds, to grant long leases of the units.

By the latter part of the twentieth century, Parliament was not slow to realise the political advantages in enacting legislation allowing for the enfranchisement or purchase

---

1   Local Government and Housing Act 1989, Sch 10. An assured tenancy proposed cannot be an assured shorthold tenancy (HA 1988, Sch 2A, para 6). Once the landlord proposes an assured tenancy, he can also ask for an interim monthly rent payable during statutory continuation (Local Government and Housing Act 1989, Sch 10, para 6).
2   *Rhone v Stephens* [1994] 2 AC 310, HL.

out, against the landlord's will, of his freehold interest in the premises, and we now have two major (and complex) statutes which enable long lessees of houses and of flats to acquire the freehold, and any intermediate leases, for themselves. These Acts (LRA 1967 (applicable to houses) and the Leasehold Reform, Housing and Urban Development Act 1993, Pt I (applicable to flats)) also provide for extensions of the lessee's interest where it is not desired to purchase the freehold.

The enfranchisement legislation could be said to be adverse to the interests of landlords, since they cannot ultimately refuse to convey the freehold or grant a new long lease to a claimant lessee or lessees who have established their right within the relevant Act. Equally, some long lessees seem to take the view that the presence of the landlord's freehold interest is at best a nuisance and at worst a source of difficulty, especially where there is a poorly-maintained block of long leasehold flats, or where a leasehold interest has diminished in length below the point where it can be used as security for a mortgage, so rendering it almost unassignable.

A still more recent twist to the resolution of the conflicting interests of the parties was exposed by amending legislation, applicable from 15 January 1999, aimed at discouraging failed end of tenancy applications to enfranchise houses or flats as a means of avoidance of a market rent. As from that date, the rent payable under a long tenancy which continues after expiry under statute is a market rent. If, however, prior to the reform, enfranchisement was claimed at the very end of the lease, not only is the tenancy continued on an interim basis: the old ground rent continued to be payable for the time being. The new rules apply where an enfranchisement claim is made during the last two years of the leasehold term but it fails. Broadly, the landlord is entitled to statutory compensation, designed to give him the difference between the ground rent and a market rent for the period concerned.[3] This aspect deserves mention if only to illustrate the complexity of the legislation applicable in this field.

Recent developments

Owing to the fact that the government thought the then current system for long leasehold enfranchisement of flats too complex, it proposed reforms.[4] These have now been enacted in the form of amending legislation.[5] It is intended to ease the path to enfranchisement for long lessees, as conversion to commonhold is not likely to be an option for most of them. As will appear, a requirement that at least two-thirds of long leaseholders must participate in the enfranchisement process has been done away

---

3   Housing Act 1996, s 116 and Sch 11, in force 1 October 1996: SI 1996/2212.
4   *Commonhold and Leasehold Reform Draft Bill and Consultation Paper* (2000) Cm 4383. See also Driscoll (1998) 148 New Law J 1855; Marcus Estates Gazette 12 December 1998, p 78. The reform proposals were preceded by a DETR Consultation Paper of 1998, which these articles considered. Driscoll thought that there were about 1 million long-leasehold houses and some 900,000 long-leasehold flats in England and Wales in 1998.
5   CLRA 2002, Pt 2, Chapter 2.

with. The former residence requirement has disappeared.[6] The resident landlord exclusion has been narrowed. The amount of floor area which can be occupied for business purposes without preventing enfranchisement has been increased from 10 to 25% of the surface area of the building as a whole. However, the government have retained an unhappy principle that the freeholder is entitled, when the purchase price is calculated, to participate in the marriage value resulting from the lessee obtaining a long lease and ridding himself with others in the building of the freehold interest. However, there is no marriage value, by legislative fiction, where the long leases currently held by the participating lessees exceed 80 years at the time of the buy-out.[7]

The subject of enfranchisement as a whole cannot be mentioned without mentioning the fact that it may be claimed that ECHR, Art 1 is infringed by enfranchisement legislation. However, what is likely to rescue enfranchisement legislation from supposed human rights incompatibility is the fact that domestic legislatures are taken to have wide margins of appreciation in housing, landlord and tenant, and social policy matters. Thus, in the context of assured shorthold tenancy possession procedures, it was recognised recently by the Court of Appeal that the policy implications in housing matters were complex. The court must treat legislative decisions in that field with particular deference.[8] Indeed, even when the issue of compatibility was referred to Strasbourg, it was held that the enfranchisement legislation of 1967 did not offend ECHR, Art 1. The 'margin of appreciation' of the domestic legislature was referred to, as was a public interest criterion. The long leasehold system was also, it appears, deemed to be unjust.[9] However, there are checks and balances in both sets of enfranchisement legislation: notably when it comes to the issue of 'marriage value' payable from the enfranchising lessee to the freeholder. These aspects strengthen the ability of enfranchisement to withstand future attacks by landlords on it under HRA 1998, s 3, at the price of imposing additional financial burdens on lessees, who have to pay twice over for their homes: once on purchase of their lease and once upon enfranchisement.

Brief comparison with commonholds

Looking at collective enfranchisement of long leases broadly, what the successful long lessees obtain as a result of their buy-out in their block is the ability to grant

6   According to the Commonhold and Leasehold Reform Draft Bill and Consultation Paper (2000) Cm 4383, para 7, this requirement had proved to be a major obstacle to enfranchisement, due to second home occupation, sub-letting and the high turnover of flats.
7   The figure originally proposed in the Consultation Paper was 90 years (Commonhold and Leasehold Reform Draft Bill and Consultation Paper (2000) Cm 4383, paras 10 and 76). The government resisted any attempt to get rid of the freeholder share of marriage value where the length of the long lease had fallen below 80 years. Collective enfranchisement was said to be a type of compulsory purchase. The freeholder should get the same price as he would if selling voluntarily to the leaseholder (HL Debates, 22 October 2001, col 872).
8   *Poplar Housing and Regeneration Community Association Ltd v Donoghue* [2001] EWCA Civ 595, [2002] QB 48, para 69.
9   *James v United Kingdom* (1986) 8 EHRR 123.

themselves long leases of, say, 999 years each without having to pay a premium. A brief contrast is invited with the position of those holding commonhold units, once CLRA 2002 and associated regulations come into force. First, commonhold land is registered as a freehold estate. Commonhold units are run by a commonhold association. However, the consent of all registered long leaseholders (viz, those holding leases for a term of more than 21 years, thus including those who have not participated in enfranchisement) is required. In practice, it may well be that this 100% hurdle will be unattainable. The commonhold association must be set up to run the commonhold units and it is not a matter of contract: it will be appreciated that in the case of long leases, management arrangements vary. There is to be a standard form[10] for the basic working of the commonhold association. Thus, there is required to be a 'commonhold community statement'. This statement must regulate the use of the common parts, which the commonhold association, as freeholder of the common parts, is responsible for repairing and insuring. Unit-holders are entitled to dispose of their units by sale but they are significantly subject to an implied covenant of title with any unit mortgagee. This requires a unit-holder 'fully and promptly [to] observe and perform all the obligations' under the commonhold community statement.[11] On the other hand, there are no forfeiture provisions entitling the commonhold association to rid itself of seriously defaulting or anti-social unit-holders.[12] These would be present no doubt in most long leases, but the remedy of forfeiture is disliked and was considered inappropriate in relation to a freehold interest in land. Nor has a commonhold association any right, as might have a landlord, to control assignments of a commonhold unit to persons whose credit worthiness was dubious or who had a record of anti-social conduct. A major limitation on the right of a unit-holder to grant a lease of his unit is, however, that only short leases, probably those only for a term of up to seven years, so as to link up with revised registration requirements, will be allowed in residential commonhold land.[13] This draconian provision[14] was seemingly aimed to prevent a mix of occupiers who are long lessees of units and commonholders, but its supposition that all commonholders must be resident and actively involved in management matters, and that long leaseholders of units will take no interest in the matter, seems difficult to reconcile with the realities of modern life. The tenor of the commonhold legislation is, perhaps necessarily, restrictive of absolute freehold ownership notions in other ways. While the tenure of commonhold units is freehold and the terms on which unit-holders hold commonholds will be the same from Bath to Newcastle, it is not to be supposed that a unit-holder in day-to-day terms will gain any more 'freedom' in respect of his

---

10 Ie in the form as envisaged by CLRA 2002, ss 31-33 and Sch 3. The association is a company limited by guarantee.
11 CLRA 2002, Sch 5, para 7 amending LP(MP)A 1989, s 5.
12 Regulations are envisaged to govern the enforcement of commonhold community statement 'house rules' (CLRA 2002, s 37).
13 CLRA 2002, ss 17 and 19. The exact length allowed will be prescribed in regulations.
14 In the individualistic French rules (as to which see Hill [1985] Conv 337; also PF Smith in *Property Law, Current Issues and Debates* (2001), ch 7, pp 17-146) such a prohibition is unheard of.

unit than would have a long leaseholder under a well-drawn long lease.[15] Indeed, the focus of disputes is likely simply to be transferred from the vertical to the horizontal, as seems to happen in France.[16]

II ENFRANCHISEMENT OF LONG LEASES OF HOUSES UNDER LRA 1967

Introduction

The Leasehold Reform Act 1967 (hereinafter LRA 1967)[17] gives a tenant[18] under a long lease of a house at a low rent, either the right to acquire the freehold or an extended lease. The policy of the Act is to allow tenants to resort to the statutory machinery against an unwilling landlord, who is forced to convey the freehold to the tenant (provided he holds it) provided the tenant complies with LRA 1967 in all respects, on terms laid down by the Act.[19] The landlord may be able to stop the process by proving that the conditions of LRA 1967 do not apply, or that the tenant has served incorrect notices, for example, but cannot resist the ultimate acquisition by the tenant of the freehold solely on the ground that he does not wish to part with his interest.

LRA 1967 is limited to houses because of the fact that it is not currently possible to enforce the running of positive covenants against freehold land.[20] LRA 1967, s 1 confers on 'a tenant[21] of a leasehold house, occupying the house as his residence, a right to acquire on fair terms the freehold or an extended lease of the house and premises' where the following conditions are satisfied:

1   the tenancy is a long tenancy;[22] and
2   at the relevant time (ie when the tenant gives notice under LRA 1967 of his desire to have the freehold or to have an extended lease, as the case may be), he has been a tenant of the house under a long tenancy, and occupying it as his residence, for the last two years or for periods amounting to two years in the last ten years.

---

15   For consideration of the wider issues see Van der Merwe in *Property Law, Current Issues and Debates* (2001), ch 5, pp 87-100.
16   It is the present writer's understanding that a significant proportion of disputes about 'property' matters concern co-ownerships of flats. See also *Le Monde* 14-17 March 1984 (there is no reason to think that matters have changed radically since then).
17   References to LRA 1967 are to the legislation as amended, most recently by the CLRA 2002.
18   Including a tenant whose landlord's forfeiture action had been dismissed, so re-instating him: *Hynes v Twinsectra Ltd* [1995] 2 EGLR 69, CA.
19   The determination of Parliament to promote enfranchisement of houses is shown by the treatment of devices such as 'Prince of Wales clauses', which were designed to avoid LRA 1967, but which have now been nullified, seemingly, by the combined effect of LRA 1967, ss 1B and 3.
20   A fact judicially recognised in *Duke of Westminster v Birrane* [1995] QB 262, CA, noted [1995] Conv 166.
21   And, thanks to LRA 1967, s 6A, his personal representatives.
22   If the other conditions are met for enfranchisement, the tenancy does not, as from the commencement of CLRA 2002, s 141, need to be at a low rent.

Financial limits

In principle, the house must fall within the relevant financial limits on the appropriate day, or the right to enfranchise is blocked. So as to ease the path of tenants, a house whose value, as so measured, is too high to qualify for enfranchisement will still be within LRA 1967 if these limits are the sole reason why the tenant cannot exercise his statutory rights (LRA 1967, s 1A).

Where the tenancy was entered into before 1 April 1990, the financial limits are based on ascertaining the rateable value of the house on the appropriate day.[23] Where a long tenancy was entered into on or after 1 April 1990, rateable value limits do not apply and the value of the premises is calculated by a formula based on the premium paid as a condition for the grant of the tenancy and on its length when granted (LRA 1967, s 1(1)).

'Tenant'

There must be a 'tenancy', which is defined by LRA 1967, s 37 as including a legal or equitable tenancy, but not a tenancy at will or a mortgage term.[24] 'Tenant', however, is not, as such, defined, but is given specific meanings in various provisions of the Act. Under LRA 1967, s 1(1) it is 'the tenant' who must satisfy the condition as to occupation and who has the right to claim the rights under the Act. Normally they will be the same person, but not necessarily. Under LRA 1967, s 5, a tenant who has established a right under LRA 1967 by giving a notice of intention, may assign that right together with the tenancy, and the assignee will be entitled to enforce that right without himself having to satisfy the condition as to occupation. The High Court has ruled that the statutory right to enfranchise cannot be assigned separately from the tenancy. Otherwise, it was said, the tenant could accidentally, by assigning his statutory right first, then his tenancy, deprive himself of the valuable right to enfranchise which he wished to vest in his successor in title.[25]

Trustees of land have the same rights as a beneficiary under the trust of land would have had if he had been the tenant (LRA 1967, s 6); and the widow (and certain other members of a deceased tenant's family), who succeeds to the tenancy, will be treated as having been the tenant during any period before the tenant's death when she was resident in the house during which the tenant was in occupation of the house as his residence (LRA 1967, s 7). Members of the tenant's family who so qualify include his

---

23   These differ depending on the rateable value of the dwelling house on a number of different days, eg where a tenancy had been rated on or after 1 April 1973, the limits are £750 except in Greater London and £1,500 in Greater London.

24   Mortgage term means a subsisting term, not one sold to the tenant under the mortgagee's power of sale: *Re Fairview, Church Street, Bromyard* [1974] 1 All ER 1233, [1974] 1 WLR 579.

25   *South v Chamberlayne* [2001] 43 EG 190. Parliament could not, it seemed, have wished to confer so great a windfall benefit on the landlord.

or her spouse, parents-in-law, son, daughter, son-in-law, daughter-in-law, stepchildren, illegitimate and adopted children and their respective spouses.

A sub-tenant may qualify for rights under LRA 1967 unless his sub-tenancy was unlawfully granted out of a superior tenancy, which was not itself a tenancy at a low rent, and that breach has not been waived (LRA 1967, s 5(4)).

'Long tenancy'

By virtue of LRA 1967, s 3(1) this means a tenancy (or sub-tenancy unless created out of a tenancy which was not itself a long tenancy) granted for a fixed-term exceeding 21 years,[26] whether or not it was terminable within that time by notice (ie a break-clause exercisable by either party), by re-entry, forfeiture or otherwise, except on death or marriage with special provisions in this latter case. Where a long lease provided that it should cease in certain events, including the lease not being held by a member of a certain housing association, it was held still to be within LRA 1967, s 3(1) as 'terminable' therein including (a) determination by act of the parties and (b) determination by a specified event prior to the term date.[27]

A tenancy continuing under the Landlord and Tenant Act 1954, ss 3 or 24 is within the definition (LRA 1967, s 3(5)),[28] but not a statutory tenancy under that Act. Where the original tenancy was not for more than 21 years (with a covenant for renewal without premium but not for perpetual renewal) and by one or more renewals the total term exceeds 21 years, LRA 1967 applies as if from the outset there had been a long tenancy (LRA 1967, s 3(4)). Where the tenant takes a new tenancy of the property (or part of it) at the end of a long tenancy at a low rent, the later tenancy (and any later tenancy) will be deemed to be a long tenancy irrespective of its terms (LRA 1967, s 3(2));[29] and where the tenant takes a new long tenancy (whether or not by virtue of LRA 1967, s 3(2)) of the property, or part of it, on the coming to an end of a long tenancy, the Act will apply, as if there had been a single tenancy beginning with the earlier tenancy and expiring with the later tenancy (LRA 1967, s 3(3)).[30] Where the tenant holds parts of a house (any of which may include other premises occupied with the house) under separate tenancies from the same landlord, the separate parts and other premises will be treated as being under a single tenancy corresponding to the duration of the tenancy comprising the house (LRA 1967, s 3(6)).

26 See *Roberts v Church Comrs for England* [1972] 1 QB 278, [1971] 3 All ER 703.
27 *Eton College v Bard* [1983] Ch 321, [1983] 2 All ER 961, CA.
28 As is a long tenancy continued as an assured tenancy under Local Government and Housing Act 1989, Sch 10.
29 LRA 1967, s 3(2) applies also to assigns of the tenant: *Austin v Dick Richards Properties Ltd* [1975] 2 All ER 75, [1975] 1 WLR 1033, CA.
30 See *Bates v Pierrepoint* (1978) 37 P & CR 420, CA (two leases granted in 1961 and 1973 at same rent treated as single term).

'House'

The policy of LRA 1967 is to allow the enfranchisement of separate dwellings, such as detached houses, and of houses which are vertically separated, such as terraced houses, but not to allow for the purchase of the freehold in horizontally divided premises such as flats.[31] The key word is 'house' and the Court of Appeal has emphasised that the expression 'building', as used in conjunction with the word 'house', is to be construed in a flexible and non-technical way.[32] A house to which the Act applies is thus defined by LRA 1967, s 2(1) as including any building designed or adapted for living in and reasonably so called.[33] Thus buildings which are not structurally detached, or are not solely designed or adapted for living in,[34] or are divided horizontally into flats or maisonettes, can all fall within enfranchisement of 'houses'. This generous view has been recently followed by the Court of Appeal in relation to a substantial terraced residential building connected to a mews cottage by means of a basement.[35] However, in arriving at this view the courts are doing no more than applying the overriding policy of LRA 1967: to allow tenants to buy out their freeholder on compliance with the (now eased) statutory tests and procedures. Thus, under LRA 1967, s 2(1):

1   where a building is divided horizontally, the flats or other units into which it is so divided are not separate 'houses', though the building as a whole may be; and

2   where a building is divided vertically the building as a whole is not a 'house' though any of the units into which it is divided may be.

LRA 1967, s 2(1) recognises that not every building is within the enfranchisement rules, even though the building could be lived in, otherwise office or factory buildings with some living accommodation could be caught.[36]

A house which is not structurally detached, and of which a material part lies above or below a part of the structure not comprised in the house, is excluded from the above definition by LRA 1967, s 2(2). By this provision, LRA 1967 ensures that, for example, a long tenant who holds a lease of a house and a basement, the latter being underneath neighbouring freehold premises, cannot enfranchise, since a material part of the whole premises lies under other premises.[37] However, it may be that, having regard to the human rights implications (specifically, the right to respect for one's home), the word

---

31   Enfranchisement of leasehold flats is provided for by LRHUDA 1993, Pt I considered below.

32   *Malekshad v Howard de Walden Estates Ltd* [2001] EWCA Civ 761, [2002] QB 364.

33   See *Malpas v St Ermin's Property Co Ltd* [1992] 1 EGLR 109 (building which looked like a house, but with two separate front and back doors, where each floor occupied by different families, a house reasonably so called). Several freestanding buildings were not a 'house reasonably so called', since 'building' is used in LRA 1967, s 2(1) in the singular: *Dugan-Chapman v Grosvenor Estates* [1997] 1 EGLR 96.

34   See *Lake v Bennett* [1970] 1 QB 663, [1970] 1 All ER 457 where part of the building had been converted into business premises.

35   *Malekshad v Howard de Walden Estates Ltd* [2001] EWCA Civ 761, [2002] QB 364.

36   *Tandon v Trustees of Spurgeons Homes* [1982] AC 755, [1982] 1 All ER 1086, HL.

37   As in *Duke of Westminster v Birrane* [1995] QB 262, CA.

'material' is likely not to be construed as limiting a right to enfranchise merely on account of a minor horizontal overlap between the tenant's house and other premises.[38]

'Structurally detached' means detached from any other structure: where part of a tenant's rooms were above garages sub-let by him, the rooms fell outside LRA 1967, s 2(1) since they were not detached from the rest of a structure not comprised in the house.[39] A house above an archway which gave access to mews behind was held not to be structurally detached.[40]

Because the essential requirement of LRA 1967, s 2 is that these should be a building, which is designed or adapted for living in, and which can be called a house by a reasonable man, a purpose-built shop with living accommodation above it may fall within the notion of 'house' as tenants of such premises are fully within the intendment of LRA 1967; and the question is not just one of fact. Thus, a mixed-user building which may reasonably be called a house (and this is a question of law) falls within LRA 1967 unless exceptional circumstances are shown.[41] A building consisting of two floors, with a flat on each floor, there being access between the two floors, which was used as a single dwelling, was held to be a 'house'.[42] The statutory residence test (disapplied once CLRA 2002, s 138 comes into force) and the requirements of LRA 1967, s 2(1) are, however, distinct. The tenant must show that he satisfies the residence requirement and that he has a building designed or adapted for living in, and that it must be reasonable to call that building a house.[43]

'Premises'

Where the qualifying conditions have been satisfied, a claim under the Act may be made in respect of the 'house and premises'. 'Premises' means any garage, outhouse, garden, yard and appurtenances which are let to the tenant with the house and are occupied with, and used for the purposes of, the house[44] or any part of it by him or by another occupant (LRA 1967, s 2(3)). A strip of land at the back of a house was not part of the premises, where it was let separately and was not closely connected with the

---

38 *Malekshad v Howard de Walden Estates Ltd* [2001] EWCA Civ 761, [2002] QB 364.
39 *Parsons v Viscount Gage (Trustees of Henry Smith's Charity)* [1974] 1 All ER 1162, [1974] 1 WLR 435, HL.
40 *Cresswell v Duke of Westminster* [1985] 2 EGLR 151, CA.
41 *Tandon v Trustees of Spurgeons Homes* [1982] AC 755, [1982] 1 All ER 1086, HL.
42 *Sharpe v Duke Street Securities NV* [1987] 2 EGLR 106, CA.
43 *Duke of Westminster v Birrane* [1995] QB 262, CA (the fact that the tenant claimed not to use the basement concerned residentially was irrelevant as it formed part of the premises demised to him, so that he could not enfranchise).
44 Ie as part of the same transaction as the original lease, as opposed to having been granted at a later date, as with a subsequently granted tenancy of a garden: see *Burr v Eyre* [1998] 2 EGLR 92.

lease of the house;[45] the term 'appurtenances' includes land let with the house; what falls within that is a question of fact.[46]

In addition to premises which the tenant occupies, there may be other premises under the tenancy which, because he does not occupy them, he is not entitled to claim. LRA 1967, s 2(4) entitles the landlord to require that they be treated as part of the house and premises. Conversely, LRA 1967, s 2(5) entitles him to have excluded from the house and premises any part of them lying above or below other premises (not consisting only of underlying mines or minerals). As regards underlying minerals, the landlord can require them to be excluded, if proper provision is made for the support of the house and premises.

'Occupying'

Occupation of the house by the tenant was, until CLRA 2002, a condition to be satisfied not only at the time when he serves his claim notice, but also throughout the qualifying period of two years or two years out of the last ten years. Occupation 'in part only' was sufficient, and this requirement was held by the Court of Appeal to have been satisfied by the tenant occupying a basement flat, the remaining three floors being sub-let unfurnished as separate flats.[47] The part occupied, however, must be viewed in relation to the whole, for under the definition of 'house', the building must be what could reasonably be called a house. Moreover, under LRA 1967, s 1(3)(a), a tenant cannot acquire rights under the Act by occupying a house let with land or premises to which the house is ancillary. The occupation condition had normally to be satisfied by the tenant personally, and accordingly, under LRA 1967, s 37(5), no company or other artificial person, nor any corporation sole is capable of occupation.[48] Where the tenant is temporarily absent, he will not for that reason cease to be in occupation; prolonged absence with no intention to resume physical occupation, or absence due to legal inability to do so, disqualified the tenant.[49] It is no longer necessary for a tenant to occupy the house as his residence, nor as his only or main residence.[50]

45 *Gaidowski v Gonville and Caius College, Cambridge* [1975] 2 All ER 952, [1975] 1 WLR 1066, CA.

46 *Methuen-Campbell v Walters* [1979] QB 525, [1979] 1 All ER 606, CA (paddock not within LRA 1967, s 2(3) on facts, though a valuable amenity).

47 *Harris v Swick Securities Ltd* [1969] 3 All ER 1131.

48 If the occupation by the tenant is as bare trustee for a company but with its permission, then, though he has the legal estate as against the landlord, he is not within LRA 1967, s 2(1) as he does not have the right to occupy as a residence; the 1967 Act does not extend to a company: *Duke of Westminster v Oddy* [1984] 1 EGLR 83, CA.

49 *Poland v Earl Cadogan* [1980] 3 All ER 544, CA.

50 Since LRA 1967, s 1 has been amended and partly repealed by CLRA 2002, s 138 and Sch 14.

Limitations on rights under LRA 1967

In addition to the cases, mentioned above, of tenants who cannot acquire any rights under the Act, eg tenants of agricultural holdings, companies, corporations sole, etc, there are a number of special cases where the rights under LRA 1967 are either excluded entirely or are restricted, even though all the conditions above have been satisfied.

1 Special categories of landlord. Tenants of the National Trust cannot enfranchise (LRA 1967, s 32). Specific but narrow exemptions, the details of which lie outside this book, deal with special landlords, who cannot be the subject of enfranchisement, either because of their privileged position (such as the Crown: LRA 1967, s 33), or for policy reasons, as with reservation of development and other rights by local authorities (LRA 1967, ss 28 and 29), or where the landlord is, subject to certain conditions, a charitable housing trust (LRA 1967, s 1(3A)), because charities often enjoy exemptions of this kind. If a landlord cannot be traced, there is a special rule that, after a claim procedure, the court deals in effect with the enfranchisement process (LRA 1967, s 27). Tenancies granted by local authorities, or registered housing associations, at a premium are, subject to conditions, outside LRA 1967.[51]

2 Loss of rights by the tenant. Any claim by a tenant is void under LRA 1967, s 22 and the Third Schedule, if he has already given notice to terminate the tenancy (eg by notice to quit, or a notice under Landlord and Tenant Act 1954, ss 5, 26 or 27), or if he has been granted a new tenancy under Landlord and Tenant Act 1954. Conversely, such a notice is of no effect if it is given whilst a claim under LRA 1967 subsists. Secondly, a tenant loses his rights under LRA 1967 if within two months of being given notice to terminate by the landlord, he does not himself give notice of his intention to claim enfranchisement or an extension under the Act. Thirdly, he may serve a notice under LRA 1967, s 9(3)[52] within one month of the price being fixed stating that he is unable or unwilling to take the freehold at that price; he will thereupon be liable for the landlord's costs, and will not be entitled to make another claim to enfranchise within the next three years. Thirdly, a tenant's rights may be lost by forfeiture, but after notice of a claim has been given, forfeiture proceedings may be commenced only with the leave of the court, and leave will not be granted unless the court is satisfied that the claim was not made in good faith,[53] ie in order to avoid forfeiture.[54]

3 Landlord's claim for possession. Where the tenancy is extended, or the tenant claims an extension, the landlord may apply to the court for possession under LRA 1967, s 17(1) (not more than one year before the term date of the original tenancy) on

---

51   Housing Act 1980, s 140 and Housing (Exclusion of Shared Ownership Tenancies) etc Regulations 1982, SI 1982/62.

52   The tenant may instead claim an extension. As from the commencement of CLRA 2002, s 143, this claim would appear not to rule out a subsequent claim to enfranchise.

53   LRA 1967, Sch 3, para 4(1).

54   See *Central Estates (Belgravia) Ltd v Woolgar; Liverpool Corpn v Husan* [1972] 1 QB 48, [1971] 3 All ER 647.

the grounds that he intends to redevelop the whole, or a substantial part, of the premises; in certain circumstances, the tenant will then have a right to claim enfranchisement. Also, where the tenant has claimed enfranchisement or an extension, the landlord may apply to the court for possession under LRA 1967, s 18 on the ground that he reasonably requires possession for occupation either by himself or an adult member of his family. The court shall not make an order for possession under LRA 1967, s 18 if having regard to all the circumstances of the case, including the availability of other accommodation for the landlord or the tenant, the court is satisfied that greater hardship would be caused by making an order than by refusing an order for possession. The landlord cannot seek possession on this ground if he acquired his interest in the house after 18 February 1966. In both cases, the tenant is entitled to compensation.

The enfranchisement process

Where the necessary conditions are satisfied, and the tenant has duly notified the landlord of his desire to acquire the freehold, the landlord is bound to make, and the tenant to accept, a conveyance of the freehold of the house and premises at a price to be fixed in accordance with the Act (LRA 1967, s 8).

The tenant's notice[55]

The tenant's notice of intention may be served[56] on the landlord at any time, provided that all the conditions have been satisfied. Notice may be served even though the original contractual tenancy has come to an end, as with a tenancy continuing under the Landlord and Tenant Act 1954, s 3. If the house has been beneficially occupied by two joint tenants under a trust for sale, one joint tenant having left, the sole remaining occupying joint tenant is not entitled to serve a LRA 1967, s 8 notice alone, in his capacity as a trustee of land (as envisaged by LRA 1967, s 6(3)), unless he has obtained the authority of his co-joint tenant to serve the notice on his or her behalf. Thus, where a husband and wife held a long lease under a trust for sale as beneficial joint tenants, the wife having left the premises permanently, a LRA 1967, s 8 notice served by the husband alone was invalid.[57] An inaccuracy in a tenant's notice does not invalidate it.[58]

55 For provisions where the tenant is a sub-tenant, see LRA 1967, Sch 1, identifying the 'reversioner' as the person with whom the sub-tenant deals.
56 In the form prescribed by the Leasehold Reform (Notices) Regulations 1997, SI 1997/640. Under LRA 1967, s 6A (inserted by CLRA 2002, s 141, rights under the 1967 Act are conferred on the personal representatives of a deceased tenant who at his death had the right to enfranchise or to an extended lease. Notice of intention must be given not later than two years after the grant of probate or letters of administration).
57 *Wax v Viscount Chelsea* [1996] 2 EGLR 80 (Cty Ct).
58 LRA 1967, Sch 3, para 6(3). However, failure to give a statement as to the period of the tenant's occupation (a fact known only to the tenant) invalidates the notice: *Speedwell Estates Ltd v Dalziel* [2001] EWCA Civ 1277, [2002] 02 EG 104.

Once validly served, the tenant's notice creates a binding contract of sale (in effect).[59] Time runs, for limitation purposes, for 12 years from the service of the LRA 1967, s 8 notice.[60] The tenant may, after service of a LRA 1967, s 8 notice, abandon or contractually release the right to enfranchise; but mere failure to pursue a disputed claim following a s 8 notice is not sufficient for this purpose, because any release has to be mutual, and arise out of mutual contract, representation or estoppel.[61] LRA 1967 contains detailed procedural rules as to LRA 1967, s 8 (and other notices) required to be served by the tenant.[62]

The price

(i) Houses with rateable values below £1,000 or £500

The level of rateable values, for the purposes of price determination, is that at the date of service of the tenant's notice.[63] The general principles on the calculation of the price are laid down in LRA 1967, s 9(1). The price is the amount which at the date of the notice, the house and premises might be expected to realise, if sold in the open market by a willing seller, with the tenant and members of his family residing in the house, not buying or seeking to buy. The following statutory assumptions must be made (LRA 1967, s 9(1)):

1   that the vendor is selling an estate in fee simple subject to the tenancy; that the Act did not confer a right to acquire the freehold; that the tenancy was extended by the tenant for 50 years subject to the landlord's right to resume possession under LRA 1967, s 17 (for redevelopment purposes);
2   that, apart from the incumbrances for which the tenant would be liable until the determination of the tenancy, it is being sold subject to the same rent charges as in the sale to the tenant; and
3   that it is being sold subject to the same rights and burdens as in the sale to the tenant.

---

59   The terms are governed by Leasehold Reform (Notices) Regulations 1997, SI 1997/640.
60   *Collin v Duke of Westminster* [1985] QB 581, [1985] 1 All ER 463, CA.
61   *Collin v Duke of Westminster* [1985] QB 581, [1985] 1 All ER 463, CA.
62   LRA 1967, Sch 3, para 6 especially. See eg *Dymond v Arunden-Timms* [1991] 1 EGLR 109, CA (notice void owing to misrepresentation of material facts); also *Speedwell Estates Ltd v Dalziel* [2001] EWCA Civ 1277, [2002] 02 EG 104 (serious omissions of material information such as particulars of the tenant's occupation of the house avoided a notice even though the landlord knew the position).
63   LRA 1967, s 9(1) and (1A)(i). See *Rosen v Trustees of Camden Charities* [2001] L & TR 24. It was noted that s 9(1A) provides a different valuation regime for the more expensive premises brought into the scheme of the 1967 Act after it had been originally passed. A concept of 'marriage value' is included, except where the term unexpired of the lease at the date of the claim notice exceeds 80 years. A landlord was, owing to the fixing of valuations at the notice of claim, unable to put forward a higher value based on what he paid for his interest at an auction held some time earlier: *Bello v Oakins* [2000] RVR 207.

The general principles of valuation which result from the above assumptions are that there is a hypothetical sale in the open market by a willing seller of the freehold reversion upon a lease which is deemed to be extended for 50 years under LRA 1967, s 14. In addition, the following factors govern the ascertainment of the value of the reversion:

1   the value of the present rent;
2   the value of the ground rent for the site only;[64]
3   the value of the right to resume possession under LRA 1967, s 17 for redevelopment purposes;
4   the value of the freehold reversion in possession at the end of the (deemed) 50 years' extension lease; and
5   the length of the existing term.[65]

No allowance is to be made under LRA 1967, s 9(1) valuations for 'marriage value', that is, the benefit to the landlord of other adjacent or neighbouring sites owned by him, even though enfranchisement will preclude him from comprehensive redevelopment which would enhance the value of each individual site.

By contrast, if the tenant is able to enfranchise only as a result of the recent relaxations in the relevant conditions, namely, the extensions to the financial limit tests or the rental value tests, the valuation of the house is to be under LRA 1967, s 9, in which case any marriage value is to be taken to be 50 % (LRA 1967, ss 9(1C) and (10)).[66] LRA 1967 rules are thus rendered, to that extent, consistent with the rules for enfranchisement of leasehold flats.

(ii)   Houses with rateable values above £1,000 or £500[67]

In this case the principles differ somewhat. First, there is no assumption that the tenant is granted a 50-year extension lease; and secondly, LRA 1967, s 9(1A) involves, in particular, the following special assumptions in calculating the price payable:

1   there is a deemed continuation of the tenancy under the Landlord and Tenant Act 1954, Pt I;[68]
2   it is to be assumed that the vendor is selling the freehold subject to the tenancy, but that the Act did not confer a right to acquire the freehold or an extended lease,

---

64   See *Official Custodian for Charities v Goldridge* (1973) 26 P & CR 191, CA.
65   See *Gallagher Estates Ltd v Walker* (1973) 28 P & CR 113, CA.
66   CLRA 2002, s 146. Under CLRA 2002, s 146, where the unexpired term of the tenant's lease at the date of the notice of claim exceeds 80 years the marriage value is taken as nil. These rules correspond to those applying to collective enfranchisement of leasehold flats.
67   These rules also apply where on 31 March 1990 the house had no rateable value limit and its value is above the statutory valuation formula: Reference to Rating etc Regulations 1990, SI 1990/434, para 9.
68   The same is required to be assumed in the case of a long tenancy continued under the Local Government and Housing Act 1989.

and, where the tenancy has been extended under LRA 1967, that the tenancy will terminate on the agreed date;[69]

3 that the tenant is assumed to have no liability to carry out any repairs, maintenance or redecorations at any time; and

4 the price must be treated as diminished by any increase in the value of the house and premises due to an improvement carried out by the tenant or his predecessors in title at their own expense.

Otherwise the general assumptions to be made are the same as those laid down in LRA 1967, s 9(1) for the lower rateable values. In valuing the price, however, an allowance may be made for 'marriage values'[70] so that an allowance may be made for the higher bid which the sitting tenant would make (as compared to any investor) due to the extra value to him of buying the reversion.

(iii) Miscellaneous

In the event of any dispute as to the price payable, it being initially supposed that the parties are to agree to it, the price must be determined by the leasehold valuation tribunal, which has jurisdiction also to determine any ancillary questions such as the terms of the conveyance (LRA 1967, s 21).

The tenant has the right to resile by notice to the landlord once the price has been determined (LRA 1967, s 9(3)) but this ends his rights under the relevant notice and no further rights may be claimed under the 1967 Act for 12 months (LRA 1967, s 9(3)).

The conveyance

The landlord's obligation under LRA 1967, s 8(1) is to convey to the tenant the house and premises in fee simple, subject to the tenancy and incumbrances on the leasehold interest created by the tenant (eg sub-tenancies, mortgages etc), but otherwise free from incumbrances. Incumbrances attaching to the freehold (eg rights of beneficiaries under a trust of land) are to be overreached, and for that purpose, the tenant is, in any event, to be treated as a purchaser for valuable consideration. Rights binding upon the land, such as easements and restrictive covenants, cannot be defeated, except by virtue of the general law, and the liability of the tenant is expressly preserved in relation to burdens originating in tenure and burdens in respect of the upkeep or regulation for the benefit of any locality of any land, building, structure, works, ways or water courses.[71]

69 LRA 1967, s 9(1A) as amended by Housing and Planning Act 1986, s 23, reversing *Mosley v Hickman* [1986] 1 EGLR 161, CA.

70 See *Norfolk v Masters, Fellows and Scholars of Trinity College Cambridge* (1976) 32 P & CR 147 (LT) subject now to CLRA 2002, ss 145 and 146.

71 While the tenant acquires any intermediate interest superior to his (LRA 1967, s 5(4) and Sch 1), if he holds the freehold already, he is not given the right to acquire intermediate leasehold interests: *Gratton-Storey v Lewis* [1987] 2 EGLR 108, CA.

Unless the tenant agrees otherwise, or they are excluded to protect the landlord's existing interest in tenants' incumbrances, the rights under LPA 1925, ss 62 and 63, will be implied in the conveyance (LRA 1967, s 10(1)). Additionally, the tenant is entitled to have the benefit, so far as the landlord is capable of granting them, of easements that he had under the tenancy (including rights of support, light and air, the passage of water or gas, sewage, drainage, and the use of maintenance of electricity, telephone or television cables); and conversely the burden of such easements may be imposed on the tenant for the benefit of other land (LRA 1967, s 10(2)). Rights of way necessary for the reasonable enjoyment of the house by the tenant (or of other property retained by the landlord) are to be included in the conveyance (LRA 1967, s 10(3)), as are user obligations for the purpose of ensuring that existing covenants remain enforceable, of indemnifying the landlord in respect of any breaches, or of enhancing the value of the house of the tenant or land of the landlord (LRA 1967, s 10(4)).[72]

The tenant is liable for the landlord's legal and other professional fees incurred in verifying the tenants claim, having the house valued and executing the conveyance (LRA 1967, s 9(4)). The landlord has a lien in respect of the purchase price, his costs, arrears of rent and any other sums due under the tenancy up to the date of the conveyance (LRA 1967, s 9(5)).

Lease extensions

The tenant's right to claim a single extension of his lease for 50 years under LRA 1967, s 14 is dependent upon all the conditions having been satisfied and the service of a valid notice of intention by the tenant.

The 50-year extension runs from the date on which the existing tenancy would have come to an end (ie the term date). In effect, the new tenancy will be substituted for any rights of continuation under the Landlord and Tenant Act 1954, Pt I. RA 1977 does not apply to an extended lease (LRA 1967, s 16(1A)). Nor is it an assured tenancy or an assured agricultural occupancy within HA 1988, Pt I.[73] The tenant is liable to pay the landlord's legal and other professional fees and costs incurred in verifying the tenant's claim, executing the lease, and valuing the house and premises for the purpose of fixing the rent (LRA 1967, s 14(2)), and the landlord is not bound to execute the lease until such costs have been paid, together with any arrears of rent or other sums due under the existing tenancy (LRA 1967, s 14(3)).

Where he would otherwise have had the right, the tenant may claim enfranchisement at any time before the term date of his existing tenancy, even though he first claimed an

---

72 See *Langevad v Chiswick Quay Freeholds Ltd* [1999] 1 EGLR 61, CA (the subsection is not limited to user covenants and extends to all restrictive covenants). LRA 1967 contains no limitation to covenants for user as opposed to development, and as noted by the Court of Appeal, the language of LRA 1967, s 10(4) is the same as that of Land Charges Act 1972, s 2(5), which has always been considered to include restrictive covenants.
73 LRA 1967, s 16(1A).

extension. As from the commencement of CLRA 2002, s 143, a tenant who has obtained an extension tenancy is not precluded from claiming enfranchisement once his original lease term has expired. Thus a serious anomaly in the law has at last been removed.[74]

Terms of the extended tenancy

LRA 1967, s 15(2) provides in effect that the rent payable under the extended tenancy shall be a modern ground rent for the site only, to be determined not more than 12 months before the new rent becomes payable. A rent review clause exercisable after 25 years, on notice, may be inserted, if the landlord so requires. In fixing the rent, regard must be had to any changes in the property to be comprised in the new tenancy, or in the terms of the new tenancy; further, costs of services, repairs, maintenance, etc may be added (LRA 1967, s 15(3)).

The other terms of the tenancy will generally be the same as under the existing tenancy, except in so far as they need to be modified as a result of changes in the property, etc (LRA 1967, s 15(1)). Options to purchase and options to renew contained in the existing lease or in a collateral agreement will not be included, however, nor any right to terminate the tenancy before the term date other than for breach of covenant (LRA 1967, s 15(5)). Either party may under LRA 1967, s 15(7) require the modification or exclusion of any terms under the existing tenancy that it would be unreasonable to include unchanged in view of changed circumstances since they were imposed. The landlord's right to resume possession under LRA 1967, s 17 must be reserved (LRA 1967, s 15(8)).

III RIGHT OF LONG LESSEES OF FLATS TO COLLECTIVE ENFRANCHISEMENT OR TO NEW LONG LEASE

General principles

LRHUDA 1993, Pt I[75] confers two rights on long lessees of flats: a right to collectively buy out the freehold and all intermediate leasehold interests, and a right, on an individual basis, to a new long lease.[76]

There seem to have been a number of reasons behind the enactment of this legislation. There has for some time been dissatisfaction with the rights and remedies available to long leaseholders of flats, at all events where they are saddled with a neglectful or absentee landlord, to the detriment of the repair and general well-being and so to the value on the market of the long leases of each flat-owner. The Court of Appeal have

---

74 Hague *Leasehold Enfranchisement* (1999) para 7-02 regards the extended lease as at that time as a 'hybrid and unsatisfactory estate'. Perhaps as from the new rules it may be seen as a stepping-stone to full enfranchisement rights.

75 References to LRHUDA 1993 are to the legislation as amended, most recently by the CLRA 2002, Pt 2, Chapters 2 and 3.

76 See Clarke [1994] *Conv* 223; PF Smith [1994] 12 PM 34; Bright [1994] *Conv* 211.

indicated that LRHUDA 1993, Pt I must be construed fairly, and with a view, if possible, to making it effective to confer on tenants the advantages which Parliament must have intended them to enjoy.[77] The legislation is, after all, tenants' legislation and recognition of this principle by the judiciary may ease some of the technical complexities surrounding it.

Outline of collective enfranchisement scheme

The scheme of LRHUDA 1993 is to enable the long lessees of residential flats who are qualifying tenants, to rid themselves of their freeholder, against his will, provided they can surmount the various procedural obstacles of the Act. The expression 'freeholder' is now to be understood as, where appropriate, a term of art, where the freehold to one or more flats is owned by a different person to he who owns the freehold of the rest of the block.

A procedure must be followed, which is started by forming an RTE company. This is a company limited by guarantee. The tenants who are members of it may alone exercise the statutory rights. There follows the preparation and service of a notice of claim by the tenants who wish to participate, since not all lessees are obliged to do so. Each lessee entitled to do so must be invited to do so even if not originally a member of the RTE company concerned. There follows a procedure for the giving of information by and to the freeholder. The cost of service of various notices and of setting up the RTE company falls on the participating tenants. The limited power of resistance of a freeholder who cannot point to one or more of the exemptions in LRHUDA 1993 is shown by the fact that, as with the enfranchisement of houses, he cannot refuse to reply to a tenant's claim notice. If he fails to serve a counter-notice, or if in any event, the parties cannot agree about the terms of the acquisition, these must be settled by a leasehold valuation tribunal. The price for the freehold is to be settled in accordance with statutory rules.

LRHUDA 1993, once its procedures have been followed, presupposes the continued operation of the leasehold system as between the flat-owners after the buy-out. After the buy-out, the freehold is in substance held by the participating lessees. Two tiers of flat lessees may thus arise: those who participate in a buy-out and who control the freehold, and those who did not so participate. This did not seem to worry Parliament; and individual flat-lessees who do not participate in collective enfranchisement may at any time demand of their new freeholder a right to a new long lease, so mitigating the otherwise undesirable consequences of such discrimination between different classes of flat lessee.

---

77 *Cadogan v McGirk* [1996] 4 All ER 643; *Martin v Maryland Estates Ltd* [1999] L & TR 30, CA.

Basic conditions for enfranchisement

The right to collective enfranchisement is exercisable by *qualifying tenants* who hold long leases of flats (LRHUDA 1993, s 1(1)). No flat is to have more than one qualifying tenant at any one time (LRHUDA 1993, s 5(3)) but where the lease is held by joint tenants, they together constitute the tenant for the purposes of Part I (LRHUDA 1993, s 5(4)(b)). However, the right cannot be exercised in pluralist form: a tenant holding a long lease of two or more flats cannot claim or exercise the right to collective enfranchisement, even if they might have so qualified had they held one single lease (LRHUDA 1993, s 5(5)).

In order to qualify, a tenant must be the tenant of a flat under a *long lease* (LRHUDA 1993, s 5(1)). The expression 'long lease' is defined as a lease for more than 21 years certain, whether or not terminable before expiry.[78] However, a business tenancy is excluded from the right to collective enfranchisement.[79] A flat lessee whose lease qualifies for the right to collective enfranchisement is not subject any longer to a residence qualification (LRHUDA 1993, s 13(2) as amended).

There are a small number of narrow *exclusions* from the right to collective enfranchisement.

1   Small premises, which contain not more than four units, with a *resident landlord* are outside the right (LRHUDA 1993, s 4(4)).[80]
2   There is no right to collective enfranchisement if the tenant holds a lease which itself had been created out of a superior lease in *breach of covenant*, unless the superior lease in question was itself a long lease at a low rent (LRHUDA 1993, s 5(1)(c)).

Since LRHUDA 1993, Pt I only applies to residential flats, it does not apply if more than 25% of the internal floor area of any structurally detached premises is occupied for *non-residential purposes* (LRHUDA 1993, s 4(1)).[81]

---

78   LRHUDA 1993, s 7(1), which includes four other types of lease, notably, a lease granted under the right to buy conferred on secure tenants.
79   LRHUDA 1993, s 5(2)(a), as defined by LRHUDA 1993, s 101(1); also excluded, so emphasising the privileged position of such bodies, is a lease granted by a charitable housing trust in pursuance of its charitable housing purposes (LRHUDA 1993, s 5(2)(b)) as are premises whose freehold includes track of an operational railway (LRHUDA 1993, s 4(5), inserted by CLRA 2002, s 116).
80   'Resident landlord' is widely defined in LRHUDA 1993, s 10(5) as amended; in addition, to fall within this narrow exemption, the premises must not be in or included in a purpose-built block of flats, and there is a minimum 12-month residence requirement. This exemption does not apply to the right to a new long lease.
81   In computing the 25% figure (applying as from the commencement of CLRA 2002, s 115) any common parts of the disputed premises are left out of account and also, parts used or intended to be used in conjunction with a flat or flats such as garages or parking and storage areas are treated as residentially occupied (LRHUDA 1993, s 4(2))). The original figure was a mere 10% which would have excluded many flats above a row of shops.

Premises within LRHUDA 1993, Pt I

While the object of Parliament throughout this legislation is to make the exercise of the right to collective enfranchisement as easy as possible for lessees, the definition of the premises which qualify is complex, because it is the policy of LRHUDA 1993, Pt I to extend this right not only to, say, lessees in a single block of flats, but also to those holding flat leases in part of a building which may be considered as separate from the rest of the building, even though it shares a common roof or foundations with the rest of the building. There are therefore three conditions which must be satisfied before the right may apply to particular premises.

1   The premises must be a *self-contained building or part of a building* (LRHUDA 1993, s 3(1)). The building must be structurally detached, as with a single independent block of flats (LRHUDA 1993, s 3(2)). The requirement of being self-contained is satisfied if the building has been vertically divided and the rest of the building is such that it could be redeveloped independently of the remainder of the building (LRHUDA 1993, s 3(2)(a)). However, in this, it must be shown that services provided by means of pipes, cables or other fixed installations are provided independently of the same services provided for other occupiers of the remainder of the building (LRHUDA 1993, s 3(2)(b)(i)).[82] As originally enacted, LRHUDA 1993, s 3 required that the freehold must be owned by the same person, so making it possible for a freeholder to sell the freehold in one or more flats to, say, a company controlled by him. This would preclude collective enfranchisement. This loophole has now, it seems, been plugged.[83] LRHUDA 1993 has therefore been amended throughout so as to allow collective enfranchisement to be exercised against one or more persons owning different freehold interests in the building concerned.

2   The premises must contain at least *two flats* held by qualifying tenants (LRHUDA 1993, s 3(1)(b)). Thus, a tenant with a flat above a shop is excluded from the right to collective enfranchisement, but not from that to a new long lease.

3   The total number of flats held by qualifying tenants must be at least two-thirds of the total number of flats contained in the premises over which the present right is claimed (LRHUDA 1993, s 3(1)(c)). This means that at least the required number of flats must be held on long leases for the right to collective enfranchisement to be available.

Outline of main procedures

The following is a brief consideration of the statutory procedures, to be followed before the freehold is bought out from an unwilling freeholder. The persons who wish

---

82   This condition is alternatively satisfied if the services could be provided without involving the carrying out of works likely to result in a significant interruption of any such services for occupiers of the remainder of the building (LRHUDA 1993, s 3(2)(b)(ii)).

83   Housing Act 1996, s 107 and Sch 10 (making consequential amendments to LRHUDA 1993) as from 1 October 1996: SI 1996/2212.

to exercise the right to acquire the freehold will need to inform themselves as to who is the freeholder (or, if need be, who are the various holders of freehold interests[84]) and the holders of any of leasehold interests in the premises, and provision is made in LRHUDA 1993, Pt I for the service of appropriate notices designed to obtain that information (LRHUDA 1993, s11).[85] The RTE company[86] must be constituted by the tenants who wish to buy out the freehold and it must procure, at their expense, a valuation of the property that the tenants wish to acquire, as well as any ancillary premises as well as of any specified leasehold interests (LRHUDA 1993, s 13(6)).[87] After the completion of this unavoidable first step, LRHUDA 1993 provides for the procedure leading to the conveyance of the freehold, by means of a series of notices.

(i) Notices

1 Claim notice. The notice of claim is served under LRHUDA 1993, s 13. Before this notice is served by an RTE company, it must give each qualifying tenant who has not up to then become a member of the company a notice inviting them to participate in collective enfranchisement.[88] No notice can now be served by the RTE company unless the qualifying tenants hold not less than half of the total number of flats at the 'qualifying date' (ie the date of the notice of claim (LRHUDA 1993, s 1(8)).[89] There is a list of formal matters which a LRHUDA 1993, s 13 notice should contain,[90] such as a specification of the premises which are to be acquired, as well as any appurtenant

---

84 In such a case, all freeholders are subject to the enfranchisement process (LRHUDA 1993, s 9(2A) and may be identified by LRHUDA 1993, Sch I, Pt 1A, added by Housing Act 1996, Sch 10, para 15.

85 For further details, see Matthews and Millichap, paras 3.1-3.7. They note that there is no direct sanction against a freeholder for non-response to information notices; but indicate that in their view, where title is registered, an application to the (now open) Land Registry might do just as well from the lessee's point of view.

86 Which is defined by LRHUDA 1993, ss 4A-4B (added by CLRA 2002, s 122). The company is a private company limited by guarantee. Members are qualifying tenants of the relevant flats. One RTE company can act for one or more relevant sets of premises.

87 The valuation so made must conform to LRHUDA 1993, Sch 6.

88 LRHUDA 1993, s 12A (added by CLRA 2002, s 123). The notice gives a minimum 14-day period for the tenant concerned to join the company and with it, the buy-out. Once the latter takes place, the freehold is conveyed only to participating company members (LRHUDA 1993, s 4B(3)) as defined in LRHUDA 1993, s 4B(4)). An assignee of a long lease has a 28-day right to join in the buy-out (LRHUDA 1993, s 4B(5)).

89 LRHUDA 1993, 13(2) as amended. This represents an easement of the rules. Prior to CLRA 2002, residence requirements were imposed and the minimum number of qualifying tenants giving the notice was higher.

90 However, so as to ease the path of tenants, any inaccuracy in the relevant particulars or any misdescription of the relevant property do not of themselves invalidate a LRHUDA 1993, s 13 notice (LRHUDA 1993, Sch 3, Pt III, para 15(1)); but a failure to enclose a plan of the property which rendered a s 13 notice invalid as a failure to comply is not an inaccuracy: *Mutual Place Property Management Ltd v Blaquiere* [1996] 2 EGLR 78. Equally, inaccuracies in a plan did not invalidate a notice in *Crean Davidson Investments Ltd v Earl Cadogan* [1998] 2 EGLR 96.

property (such as garages), which is likewise claimed.[91] Since details of each tenant serving the notice must be given the landlord will be able to see if he is able to reduce the number of tenants below the requisite minimum numbers, so as to defeat a LRHUDA 1993, s 13 notice and so a claim, on that occasion, to the right to collective enfranchisement. The claim notice must also inform the freeholder of the identity of the RTE company, as it is to this latter person that the freeholder's own notice in response is to be given. The claim notice must specify such matters as the purchase price for the premises to be acquired, which will have been discovered by the survey. There is no longer any residence requirement on tenants of long leases of flats before they can exercise the right to collective enfranchisement.[92]

2 Persons disqualified to serve initial notice. There is a statutory list of persons, whose participation would be obviously undesirable and so who cannot participate in service of a LRHUDA 1993, s 13 notice of claim, such as a tenant who might otherwise qualify but who has given notice to terminate his long lease, and likewise, a tenant against whom there are pending forfeiture proceedings.[93]

3 Freeholder's response. Any freeholder should, within the time stated in the LRHUDA 1993, s 13 notice,[94] serve a counter-notice on the RTE company (LRHUDA 1993, s 21(1)). If he fails to do so, the court has default powers on the application of the RTE company to determine the terms of the acquisition.[95] LRHUDA 1993 has been recognised as imposing a strict procedural timetable, which landlords cannot obstruct by refusing to serve a counter-notice. Safeguards exist for landlords in the fact that the tenants' proposals should be realistic.[96] A counter-notice must do one of three things. It may admit the right of the tenants to participate in collective enfranchisement; it may deny the right for reasons stated or it may indicate that the landlord intends to redevelop the premises, and to apply for a court order under LRHUDA 1993, s 23 that therefore the right to collective enfranchisement is not possible.[97] Where the notice admits the right to collective enfranchisement, it must then state which of the tenants' proposals in the initial notice it accepts and which it does not, putting forward alternative proposals in

91   If it is proposed to acquire any intermediate leasehold interests, these must be specified in the notice (hence the importance of the information notices already referred to).
92   Owing to CLRA 2002, s 120 and Sch 14 amending LRHUDA 1993, s 13(2).
93   LRHUDA 1993, Sch 3, para 2 and 3. See *Martin v Maryland Estates Ltd* [1999] L & TR 30, CA. By contrast, once a notice of claim is served, and is current, no landlord's or tenant's notice to terminate the lease has any effect on the claim (LRHUDA 1993, Sch 3, para 5).
94   Ie not less than two months of the date of the service of the tenant's notice of claim.
95   LRHUDA 1993, s 25(1), provided the application is within six months of the last date for the giving of the freeholder's notice. The terms will be those as set out in the initial notice under LRHUDA 1993, s 13.
96   *Willingale v Globalgrange Ltd* [2000] L & TR 549.
97   The landlord may use this means of defeating a claim only if two-thirds of the relevant long leases are due to expire within five years of the date of service of the initial notice (LRHUDA 1993, s 23(2)(a)). The landlord must also show that the work intended is akin to that required by Landlord and Tenant Act 1954, Pt II, s 30(1)(f).

the latter case (LRHUDA 1993, s 21(3)). Thus the freeholder may reject the price and also the premises suggested for acquisition and suggest alternatives.[98]

If any landlord would, thanks to the exercise of the right of collective enfranchisement, be left with property which would, in particular, cease for all practical purposes to be of use and benefit to him then he may in his counter-notice require that this property is included in the premises to be acquired by the nominee purchaser on behalf of the participating tenants (LRHUDA 1993, s 21(4)).

Following the service of the above notices, the parties may be able to agree on the terms of the acquisition. If they cannot, or cannot agree on some of them, then either side may apply to the leasehold valuation tribunal to resolve the disputed terms, within two months of the giving of a freeholder's counter-notice (LRHUDA 1993, s 24(1)).[99] Once the terms of an acquisition have been agreed or determined by the Tribunal, the court has power to make a vesting order of the freehold in favour of the RTE company.[100]

(ii) Price of freehold

The price of the freehold and of any intermediate leasehold interests is determined by a statutory formula[101] and not by the agreement of the parties. The main rule is that the price payable by the RTE company for the freehold and also for intermediate leasehold interests is the open market price payable as between a willing landlord and a willing tenant. There are a number of assumptions, so that it is assumed that the nominee purchaser acquires the freehold incumbered by the existing leases: otherwise, presumably, the price would rise greatly in some cases. Tenants' improvements to any flat held by a participating tenant are to be left out of account. If there is more than one freeholder concerned, as where flying freeholds on flats A and B are held by one person and the rest of the building is owned in freehold by a different person, the RTE company must pay a separate price for the freehold of these parts, calculated in accordance with a specific formula.[102]

An important concession to the freeholder and, where relevant, to intermediate leaseholders, is that they are entitled to share in the marriage value of the premises.

98 The freeholder also may require the lease-back of part of the premises from the RTE company, eg mandatorily where any flat is held on a secure tenancy and where the freeholder is his landlord (LRHUDA 1993, s 36 and Sch 9).

99 The terms include the purchase price (LRHUDA 1993, s 124(8)): see *Moore v Escalus Properties Ltd* [1997] 1 EGLR 200. If no application is made on time to the tribunal, the whole procedure is deemed to have been withdrawn (LRHUDA 1993, s 29(2)).

100 LRHUDA 1993, s 24 as amended. There is a strict time limit of two months from the final agreement of all terms or the Tribunal decision as the case may be (LRHUDA 1993, s 24(6)). See *Penman v Upavon Enterprises Ltd* [2001] EWCA Civ 956, [2001] 25 EG 158 (CS).

101 LRHUDA 1993, s 32 and Sch 6 as amended by Housing Act 1996, s 109 and CLRA 2002, ss 127 and 128.

102 LRHUDA 1993, Sch 6, para 5A, inserted by Housing Act 1996, Sch 10, para 18(5).

This means the increase in value resulting from the fact that the person acquiring will be able to obtain a new long lease without paying any premium and for an unlimited length of time. Moreover, a separate price must be paid for each intermediate leasehold interest. But there is now deemed to be no marriage value where, at the date of the claim notice, each lease held by a participating tenant member of an RTE company exceeds a term of 80 years.[103] In addition, it is taken that the freeholder's share of the marriage value is to be 50% in all cases except that just mentioned.[104]

(iii) Completion

The whole procedure of collective enfranchisement is followed, once the price has been determined and the other terms agreed or determined, by a conveyance to the RTE company of the freehold of the specified premises or part of any other property (LRHUDA 1993, s 34(1)). The relevant fee simple absolute is stripped of all intermediate leasehold interests, if any. Thus the company can grant very long lease terms to its participating members. Moreover, the effect of the conveyance is in principle to discharge the property from any mortgage (LRHUDA 1993, s 35). The conveyance must conform to the statutory rules.[105] After due conveyance, the RTE company will apply for registration of title to the Land Registry.

New long leases

There may be a number of long lessees of flats who are not able to participate in collective enfranchisement, because they are excluded from it, or because there are insufficient other lessees interested in exercising that right. At the same time, it appears that a residential long lease which has an unexpired term of less than 60 years is difficult to assign or to mortgage. At all events, the legislature has enacted a right to obtain a new, and individual, long lease. The procedures for the exercise of this right, with due modifications, are not dissimilar to those which govern collective enfranchisement. The right is exercised as against the landlord, ie a freeholder or a long leaseholder whose reversion is sufficient to enable him to grant a new long lease (LRHUDA 1993, s 40(1)).[106] If successfully exercised, the lessee obtains a substituted

---

103 CLRA 2002, s 128, prospectively amending LRHUDA 1993, Sch 6, para 4. The government flatly refused to do away with the concept of freeholder, etc marriage value completely.

104 LRHUDA 1993, Sch 6, para 4(1) as amended by CLRA 2002, s 127.

105 LRHUDA 1993, Sch 7. This is for example to ensure, so far as possible, that the RTE company, and so the acquiring lessees, enjoy the same rights of support, access and so on as were enjoyed up until the conveyance with the premises. The conveyance must contain the statement required by SI 1993/3045.

106 If a claim to collective enfranchisement is made before or after a claim to an individual new long lease is made, the former claim suspends the latter, which is then to be disposed of once the collective buy-out has succeeded or failed (LRHUDA 1993, s 54).

lease at a peppercorn rent for the term of his current unexpired lease plus 90 years (LRHUDA 1993, s 56(1)). The right to a new long lease may be exercised again, after expiry of the new term. The new lease is paid for by a premium calculated in accordance with LRHUDA 1993.

The tenant, if his claim succeeds, obtains a new lease of a 'flat', which expression bears an extended statutory definition (LRHUDA 1993, s 62(2)), and so includes any garage, outhouse, gardens, yard and appurtenances 'belonging to or usually enjoyed with' the flat. Unlike the position with LRA 1967, s 2(3), where any appurtenance, for example, must be within the curtilege of the house,[107] owing perhaps to the difficult questions of degree which might otherwise arise, in the case of new long leases of flats, it suffices if the appurtenant property is within the premises of which the flat forms part.[108] Hence, the tenant of a second-floor flat was entitled to have included in his new long lease a box attic room situated on the sixth floor of the building.

The right to an individual long lease is conferred on a 'qualifying tenant' holding a long lease.[109] The claimant must have been a qualifying tenant for the last two years (LRHUDA 1993, s 39(2)). The residence test has been done away with once the relevant parts of the CLRA 2002 come into force. As with collective enfranchisement, the process is commenced by the tenant making preliminary inquiries (LRHUDA 1993, s 41). This may then be followed by a tenant's notice under LRHUDA 1993, s 42. This notice is given to the landlord and to any third party to the lease. However, a notice served in certain cases is of no effect, in particular, if it is given after the tenant has by notice terminated the lease of the flat,[110] or if it is given more than two months after a landlord's notice to terminate the lease.[111] In addition, if the landlord is able to show to the satisfaction of the court that, where the tenant's lease is due to terminate within five years from the service of his notice of claim, he intends to redevelop the whole or a substantial part of premises in which the flat is contained, he can defeat the exercise of the right to a new long lease.[112]

---

107 *Methuen-Campbell v Walters* [1979] QB 525, [1979] 1 All ER 606, CA.

108 *Cadogan v McGirk* [1996] 4 All ER 643.

109 These expressions are defined as for collective enfranchisement (LRHUDA 1993, s 39(3)(b)). The right to a long lease may also be exercised by a deceased qualifying tenant's personal representatives (LRHUDA 1993, s 39(3A), added by CLRA 2002, s 132).

110 Or where the tenant is obliged to give up possession of the flat under a court order: LRHUDA 1993, Sch 12, para 3.

111 Under Landlord and Tenant Act 1954, Pt I or Local Government and Housing Act 1989, Sch 10, as the case may be: LRHUDA 1993, Sch 12, para 2.

112 By specifying this intention in his counter-notice (LRHUDA 1993, s 47(1)). The conditions are specified in LRHUDA 1993, s 47(2) and are akin to those applicable to collective enfranchisement. If the landlord's application to court fails, the court must order him to serve a fresh counter-notice on the tenant (LRHUDA 1993, s 47(4)) so recommencing the statutory procedure.

The claim notice[113] must give certain details, such as sufficient particulars of the flat to identify the property in question, as well as such particulars of the tenant's lease as identify it. The notice must also specify the premium he is prepared to pay for the new lease as well as his proposals for the other terms of the new lease.[114] It appears that the proposals must be realistic.[115]

Once served, the notice continues to run until the right to a new lease is established, or the claim is withdrawn, or the claim fails (LRHUDA 1993, s 42(8)). If a notice is given and then withdrawn, no further notice may be given with respect to that flat for a further 12 months from the date of withdrawal (LRHUDA 1993, s 42(7)).[116] The effect of a LRHUDA 1993, s 42 notice is that the rights and obligations arising from the notice of both parties enure for their benefit and that of their successors in title 'as rights and obligations arising under a contract for leasing freely entered into between the landlord and tenant' (LRHUDA 1993, s 43(1)). Thus, the tenant is treated, from that time, as being entitled, in equity, to the grant of a new long lease, provided he complies with such requirements as the payment of a premium.[117]

Once a LRHUDA 1993, s 42 notice has been given, the existing lease cannot be terminated during the currency of the claim and for three months after then by effluxion of time, or by a notice from the tenant's immediate landlord, or by termination of any superior lease.[118]

The landlord is entitled, as from the giving of the tenant's claim notice, to gain access to the flat concerned for valuation purposes (LRHUDA 1993, s 44) and he must, within the time-limit allowed by the tenant's notice, serve a counter-notice (LRHUDA 1993, s 45). The purpose and, as modified for the lease renewal scheme, contents, of this

113 The claim notice must be registered (LRHUDA 1993, s 97) as a notice or caution or it will not bind an assignee of the reversion: *Melbury Road Properties 1995 Ltd v Kreidi* [1999] 3 EGLR 108 (the case dealt with LRA 1925). No rights arising under a constructive trust could, it was held, be implied in favour of the lessee on the slender materials at issue.
114 The date for service of the landlord's counter-notice must be specified (LRHUDA 1993, s 42(3)(f)), which must be not less than two months after the giving of the notice (LRHUDA 1993, s 42(5)). It appears from *Viscount Chelsea v Hirshorn* [1998] 2 EGLR 90 and *Keepers and Governors of John Lyon School v Secchi* [2000] L & TR 308, CA, that the two-month period is strictly construed.
115 *Viscount Chelsea v Morris* [1999] L & TR 154.
116 As noted by Matthews and Millichap, para 4.24, a purchaser of a flat subject to a LRHUDA 1993, s 42 notice ought to take an assignment of the benefit of this notice (and so profiting from LRHUDA 1993, s 43(1)).
117 But if the lease is assigned without the benefit of the notice, the notice is automatically withdrawn (LRHUDA 1993, s 43(3)).
118 LRHUDA 1993, Sch 12, para 5(1). Similarly, by LRHUDA 1993, Sch 12, para 6, during the currency of a claim, forfeiture proceedings against the lessee require the leave of the court, which is only to be granted if the notice was given for the purpose of averting a forfeiture.

notice are similar to those of the landlord's counter-notice in the case of collective enfranchisement.[119]

(i) Steps to obtaining new lease

If the landlord's counter-notice does not admit the right of the tenant, he may prevent the exercise of the right going further by applying to the court for a declaration to that effect (LRHUDA 1993, s 46(1)) but if the application is dismissed, the landlord's counter-notice will be declared to be of no effect and he will be required to serve a further counter-notice (LRHUDA 1993, s 46(4)).[120]

However, if the landlord accepts the right to a new long lease but disputes some of the terms, or the landlord proposes terms which the tenant does not accept, and they cannot resolve their differences, then either party may apply to a leasehold valuation tribunal to resolve them (LRHUDA 1993, s 48(1)).[121] The application must be made within two months of the giving of the landlord's counter-notice (LRHUDA 1993, s 48(2)). The landlord cannot evade the granting of a new long lease by failing to serve a counter-notice, for, in this case, the tenant may apply to the court to determine the terms of the new long lease (LRHUDA 1993, s 49).

(ii) Terms of new lease

The new lease is for a substituted term of 90 years from the expiry date of the existing lease, and at a peppercorn rent (LRHUDA 1993, s 56(1)).[122] A premium must be paid as calculated in accordance with the Act, so as to take into account any diminution in the value of the landlord's interest in the flat, based on market values subject to statutory assumptions. The landlord is entitled to a 50% share[123] in the marriage value,[124] but to nothing if the unexpired residue of the lease at the date of the claim notice exceeds 80

---

119 Thus, the counter-notice an 'integral' part of the proper working of the scheme (*Burman v Mount Cook Land Co* [2001] EWCA Civ 1712, [2002] 1 All ER 144) must admit the claim, or state that the landlord denies it, for stated reasons, or, in either case, that he intends to apply for an order under LRHUDA 1993, s 47 because of his intention to redevelop any premises in which the flat is situated.

120 However, applications relating to redevelopment are saved from this provision (LRHUDA 1993, s 46(5)).

121 See *Hordern v Viscount Chelsea* [1997] 1 EGLR 195.

122 Any prohibition in a superior lease which prohibits absolutely or in a qualified way the granting of a new long lease is overridden (LRHUDA 1993, s 56(5)).

123 Thanks to CLRA 2002, s 135 amending prospectively LRHUDA 1993, Sch 13 para 4. The amendment is beneficial to lessees, since it was not always the case that a mere 50% share had been awarded: see eg *Goldstein v Conley* [1999] 1 EGLR 95.

124 LRHUDA 1993, Sch 13 as amended, Part III of which provides for the payment by the tenant of compensation to the holders of any intermediate leaseholds affected by the grant of the new lease.

years. The tenant has to pay the rent due up to the date of the new lease (LRHUDA 1993, s 56(3)).

The other terms of the new lease are the same as those of the existing lease which it replaces.[125] If the terms of the old lease did not contain any provision for variable service charges, or indeed for any service charges, the terms of the new lease must provide for the payment of such charges and for suitable enforcement provisions (LRHUDA 1993, s 57(2)).[126] Were it not for this provision, the landlord could not, it appears, have asked the court to insert a new or revised service charges clause in the new lease, as such a modification might only have been capable of being imposed on an unwilling tenant if the landlord offered some compensations. Either party may require the other to modify the terms of the existing lease in so far as is necessary to do so to remedy a 'defect' in the existing lease or in view of changes occurring since the commencement of the existing lease which affect the suitability of the provisions of the lease (LRHUDA 1993, s 57(6)). It seems that, so far, the word 'necessary' is treated as limiting the power of the landlord to vary the terms of a lease and it will not suffice to show that it might be convenient, or in accordance with modern practice, to revise the disputed term.[127] The new lease is not subject to any statutory security of tenure provisions but it may be further renewed at any time (LRHUDA 1993, s 59(1)).

125 Subject to any modifications as specified in LRHUDA 1993, s 57(1), eg that the new lease is of the flat only and not of other premises in the former lease.
126 The parties may otherwise agree (LRHUDA 1993, s 57(6)).
127 *Waitt v Morris* [1994] 2 EGLR 224 (where a new suggested term about notification of mortgagees by the landlord prior to forfeitures was rejected).

Business tenancy renewal rights

CHAPTER 19

Introduction to statutory business tenancy renewals

The relationship of landlord and tenant of business premises is governed by the general law until the contractual tenancy expires, or the landlord serves a notice to quit or otherwise terminates the tenancy at law. Thereafter, the Landlord and Tenant Act 1954, Pt II applies, and it is only possible to regain possession as laid down by this legislation. The tenant is given a conditional right to renew his tenancy.

The following is a summary of the main substantive effects of the Landlord and Tenant Act 1954.[1]

1 Business tenants are given security initially by the continuation, despite termination of the contractual term, of the tenancy (Landlord and Tenant Act 1954, s 24).

2 Continuation is on the same terms as the contractual tenancy. It may be prevented or terminated only as provided in the Landlord and Tenant Act 1954.

3 The landlord may prevent, or set in motion, the termination of continuation by a statutory notice procedure (Landlord and Tenant Act 1954, s 25). If he wishes to regain possession where the tenant is unwilling to give it up, he may do so only on the grounds in Landlord and Tenant Act 1954, s 30. This procedure generally overrides the common law methods. Certain of these are specially preserved (Landlord and Tenant Act 1954, s 24(2)) notably forfeiture and tenants' notice to quit.

4 If the landlord has not served a Landlord and Tenant Act 1954, s 25 notice, the tenant may request by notice a new tenancy (Landlord and Tenant Act 1954, ss 26 and 24(1)(b)). If the landlord has served a s 25 notice, the tenant may (if negotiations between the parties fail completely or on specific matters) apply to court for a new tenancy (Landlord and Tenant Act 1954, ss 24(1)(a) and 29(2)). In both cases the

---

1 The specific procedure for business tenancy renewals is likely to be revised by statutory instrument, following the so-called 'Woolf reforms' and is now in CPR 1998, Pt 56. The text of the relevant following chapters notes the impact of these anticipated changes.

landlord may resist the new tenancy on one of a number of grounds as set out in the Landlord and Tenant Act 1954, Pt II, s 30.

In the event that the court orders a new tenancy it follows guidelines in Landlord and Tenant Act 1954, ss 32-35.

I   COMPENSATION FOR IMPROVEMENTS

A tenant who quits the holding at the termination of a business tenancy may be entitled to compensation for qualifying improvements.[2] This aspect is dealt with by the Landlord and Tenant Act 1927, Pt I.[3] In this connection, a business tenant is only entitled to claim for compensation for an improvement made by him or by a predecessor in title[4] which adds to the letting value of the property.[5] The tenant must also comply with a statutory procedure for making his claim (Landlord and Tenant Act 1927, s 1). In essence, the scheme operates as follows. The tenant must require the landlord to certify that the improvement was duly carried out. He must claim compensation within strict time-limits. No improvement will qualify for compensation, however, unless the tenant has notified the landlord if his intention to make it (Landlord and Tenant Act 1927, s 3(1)), following which the landlord can object within three months, any disputes to be resolved by the court. The court may grant a certificate, which allows the tenant to carry out the improvement in accordance with plans and specifications submitted to it (Landlord and Tenant Act 1927, s 3(4)), if it is satisfied that the improvement will add to the letting value of the holding at the termination of the tenancy. The court must also be satisfied that the improvement is reasonable and suitable to the character of the holding, and that it will not diminish the value of any other property belonging to, in particular, the landlord.[6] However, the landlord can block the compensation procedure[7] by offering to make the proposed improvement himself in return for a

---

2   There is no statutory definition of 'improvements' but it is confined to physical improvements such as new buildings (see *National Electric Theatres Ltd v Hugdell* [1939] Ch 553, [1939] 1 All ER 567) and does not include trade or tenant's fixtures.

3   There is an excellent summary of the law to 1989 in Law Com No 178 (1989) 'Compensation for Tenants' Improvements', paras 2.1-2.18.

4   Such as a sub-tenant: *Pelosi v Newcastle Arms Brewery (Nottingham) Ltd* (1981) 43 P & CR 18.

5   The two bases of compensation (Landlord and Tenant Act 1927, s 1(1)) are (a) the net addition to the value of the holding as a whole which results from the improvement or (b) the reasonable cost of carrying out the improvement at the termination of the tenancy (subject to specific deductions, notably where the item needs to be put into repair).

6   The court may at its discretion modify the plans and specifications of the tenant as it thinks reasonable.

7   The claim procedure is by written notice served on the landlord in accordance with the time-limits laid down in Landlord and Tenant Act 1954, s 47 (and see *Donegal Tweed Co v Stephenson* (1929) 98 LJKB 657: these limits are strictly enforced).

reasonable rent increase. This aspect of the law is seen as a major defect of the rules.[8] Even if the tenant satisfies the basic qualifying requirements of the Landlord and Tenant Act 1927, because he can only claim compensation on quitting the holding, if he seeks renewal of his tenancy under the Landlord and Tenant Act 1954, Pt II, no compensation claim can be entertained. In 1989, the Law Commission recommended, after a thorough review of the law, that the statutory scheme should be done away with.[9] Curiously, seeing that it appeared that the statutory compensation procedure had fallen into disuse,[10] this proposal remains to be enacted some 13 years after it was first made.

II THE REFORM AGENDA

Reform of some of the details of the Landlord and Tenant Act 1954, Pt II is thought to be imminent at the time of writing this book. An overview of the reforms is taken here. In 1992, the Law Commission recommended a number of improvements to the workings of the Landlord and Tenant Act 1954, Pt II.[11] The Report did not propose a fundamental overhaul of the Act but it listed a number of reforms which are significant, if technical.[12] It bore in mind three general principles. First, the need to maintain the present fair overall balance between landlord and tenant. Secondly, a wish to retain present renewal procedure (with adjustments of detail). Thirdly, the need not to require the taking of court proceedings as a routine part of the procedure.[13]

The Report did not, however, call into question a basic rule[14] that when the court orders a new tenancy, it should not revise the terms of the contractual tenancy against the wishes of either party unless the party claiming change proves that the change is justified and reasonable. As this is a heavy onus of proof, the usual assumption is that

---

8   They may also be avoided by imposing an obligation to re-instate the premises at the end of the lease as well as by in terms requiring the tenant to carry out a specific improvement. In any event, many lessees would not wish to make long-term physical improvements to benefit their landlords and only invest in improvements on the basis that these will pay for themselves during the tenancy. See Law Com No 178 (1989) 'Compensation for Tenants' Improvements', paras 3.12 and 3.13.

9   Law Com No 178 (1989) 'Compensation for Tenants' Improvements', para 3.23. The various arguments for and against are set out at paras 3.15-3.21. Transitional rules would have been made use of. The parties would still be able to make their own contractual arrangements for compensation. The authorisation of improvements under the Landlord and Tenant Act 1927, s 3(4) would be retained under these proposals. As to this see Aylott and Wall (2001) PLJ 2.

10   Law Com No 178 (1989) 'Compensation for Tenants' Improvements', para 3.3.

11   Law Com No 208 (1992) 'Landlord and Tenant: Business Tenancies: A Periodic Review of the Landlord and Tenant Act 1954 Part II' (1992) HC 224.

12   For a critique of Law Com No 208 (1992) 'Landlord and Tenant: Business Tenancies: A Periodic Review of the Landlord and Tenant Act 1954 Part II'; as to Landlord and Tenant Act 1954 generally see Haley (1993) 13 LS 225.

13   Law Com No 208 (1992) 'Landlord and Tenant: Business Tenancies: A Periodic Review of the Landlord and Tenant Act 1954 Part II', para 1.9.

14   *O'May v City of London Real Property Co Ltd* [1983] 2 AC 726, [1982] 1 All ER 660, HL.

the principal terms of the contractual tenancy will not be revised without the agreement of both parties.[15] The main recommendations of the Law Commission were as follows. Most of these have been accepted, with some adjustments, by the government.

1   An individual and the company he controls should be treated as the same entity for the purposes of the renewal procedure. This recommendation was made to overcome a principle that if an individual tenant incorporates, he loses the right to renew the lease if the company so formed occupies the premises.[16] It is understood that this reform will be put into effect by the government by Statutory Instrument. However, entirely new business entities will not qualify for statutory renewal.

2   Companies controlled by one individual should be treated as members of groups of companies for the purposes of the Landlord and Tenant Act 1954.[17]

3   The tenant should retain his right to renew under the Landlord and Tenant Act 1954 even if the premises are occupied by a company controlled by the tenant, or the individual occupying the premises controls the tenant company.[18]

4   Where the landlord is a company, it should be able to oppose a new tenancy even though the property is to be occupied by the company for business purposes and the business is to be carried on by the individual who controls the company, or another company in the same group.[19]

5   Where an individual acquires control of a landlord company within five years of the date of the tenant's application to the court for a new tenancy, he should not be able to oppose the application under the Landlord and Tenant Act 1954, s 30(1)(g) where the tenancy existed when he assumed control. This would extend the protection of the five-year rule (Landlord and Tenant Act 1954, s 30(2)) to corporate control.[20]

6   The contracting out procedures would be revised, so that certain formalities would have to be observed by both parties for any agreement to contract out of the right to renew to be effective.[21] However, if these new formalities were followed, with the idea of ensuring that the tenant had full information as to his position, contracting out would become possible without the need, as at present, to seek the approval of the county court.

15   Law Com No 208 (1992) 'Landlord and Tenant: Business Tenancies: A Periodic Review of the Landlord and Tenant Act 1954 Part II' para 3.32-3.33.
16   Law Com No 208 (1992) 'Landlord and Tenant: Business Tenancies: A Periodic Review of the Landlord and Tenant Act 1954 Part II' para 2.7.
17   Law Com No 208 (1992) 'Landlord and Tenant: Business Tenancies: A Periodic Review of the Landlord and Tenant Act 1954 Part II' para 2.8.
18   Law Com No 208 (1992) 'Landlord and Tenant: Business Tenancies: A Periodic Review of the Landlord and Tenant Act 1954 Part II' para 2.9.
19   Law Com No 208 (1992) 'Landlord and Tenant: Business Tenancies: A Periodic Review of the Landlord and Tenant Act 1954 Part II' para 2.10.
20   Law Com No 208 (1992) 'Landlord and Tenant: Business Tenancies: A Periodic Review of the Landlord and Tenant Act 1954 Part II' para 2.11.
21   Thus the tenant would have to declare in the agreement that he read and understood the terms of the prescribed form agreement and statement (Law Com No 208 (1992) 'Landlord and Tenant: Business Tenancies: A Periodic Review of the Landlord and Tenant Act 1954 Part II' paras 2.14-2.16 and 2.20).

7   The statutory information procedures needed revision. The Law Commission suggested that both parties would be placed under a duty to give information to each other within the last two years of the term of the lease, a breach of which duty would be actionable in damages. The duty would bind any assignee, to the exclusion of the original landlord or tenant who served the notice. The information covered would include a statement as to whether the tenant occupies the whole or part of the property for business purposes. It would also include details of any sub-letting, in the case of tenants, and, as regards landlords, as to whether he is a freeholder or mortgagee and the identity of any reversioner of a severed part of the reversion.[22]

8   A landlord who serves a Landlord and Tenant Act 1954, s 25 notice terminating the tenancy would have to include his proposals for a new tenancy. The tenant would not have to serve a counter-notice, once a s 25 notice had been served on him. Both parties should be entitled to apply for renewal of the tenancy. The tenant would no longer be forced, as at present, to wait for two months from service of a s 25 notice, before applying for a new tenancy.[23]

9   There would be a number of reforms of the interim rent scheme.[24]

10   The maximum length of the term allowed to be ordered would go up to the more convenient figure of 15 years.[25]

Compensation for disturbance should in future be payable where the landlord withdraws his action to terminate the lease, which is not the case at the moment. On the other hand, it would be calculated for each part of the property occupied by the tenant, if he occupied different parts for a different length of time.[26]

The government intends, as we have seen, to implement this programme, with a number of modifications, by delegated legislation. Its response to the Law Commission Report was contained in a Consultation Paper.[27] The government have no plans to change the essence of the current legislative framework, but they did say that it had concerns that the legislation was not always easy or straightforward to operate. In the government's Consultation Paper, the Law Commission idea of a 'health warning' where the parties

22   Law Com No 208 (1992) 'Landlord and Tenant: Business Tenancies: A Periodic Review of the Landlord and Tenant Act 1954 Part II' paras 2.24-2.32.

23   Law Com No 208 (1992) 'Landlord and Tenant: Business Tenancies: A Periodic Review of the Landlord and Tenant Act 1954 Part II' paras 2.34-2.39.

24   Law Com No 208 (1992) 'Landlord and Tenant: Business Tenancies: A Periodic Review of the Landlord and Tenant Act 1954 Part II' paras 2.61-2.75.

25   Law Com No 208 (1992) 'Landlord and Tenant: Business Tenancies: A Periodic Review of the Landlord and Tenant Act 1954 Part II' paras 2.76-2.79.

26   Law Com No 208 (1992) 'Landlord and Tenant: Business Tenancies: A Periodic Review of the Landlord and Tenant Act 1954 Part II' paras 2.81-2.84.

27   'Business Tenancies Legislation in England and Wales: The Government's Proposals for Reform' (2001) DETR. For an examination of the Consultation Paper, see Hewitson [2002] *Conv* 261.

propose to contract out of the Landlord and Tenant Act 1954, was largely adopted.[28] The Consultation Paper also accepted other ideas of the Commission. Among other reforms, the government wished in future to treat an individual and a company as being equivalent for the purposes of renewal rights, or assessing rights to oppose the grant of a new tenancy.[29] The position as to surrenders of leases by agreement will be cleared up.[30] The statutory renewal procedures will be speeded up, so that in particular landlords who wish to terminate a business tenancy but who were not opposed to renewal should set out their proposals for a new tenancy in their statutory termination notice, which is not required at present.[31] Some technicalities in the renewal procedure are to be removed. For example, landlords of any parts of premises could collectively operate renewal procedures, with mirror procedures for tenants as against joint landlords.[32] Tenants as well as landlords would, under these proposals, be able to apply for an interim rent.[33] The government agreed with the Law Commission idea of rounding up the maximum length of renewed tenancies by court order to 15 years.[34]

28 'Business Tenancies Legislation in England and Wales: The Government's Proposals for Reform' (2001) DETR, para 8. The government at that stage thought that the tenant ought to receive the 'health warning' at a time when his decision might be affected by it, not at the later date of signing the lease. Thus 14 days' notice would ordinarily be required ('Business Tenancies Legislation in England and Wales: The Government's Proposals for Reform' (2001) DETR, para 10). These particular proposals are discussed by Joyce *Estates Gazette* 5 May 2001, p 166.

29 'Business Tenancies Legislation in England and Wales: The Government's Proposals for Reform' (2001) DETR, para 13. The government also approved of the proposals of the Law Commission supra as information notices by both parties (para 20) and would adopt their proposals to simplify renewal procedures (para 26).

30 'Business Tenancies Legislation in England and Wales: The Government's Proposals for Reform' (2001) DETR, paras 21-24. The government proposals follow the Law Commission proposals with the added idea of a tenant 'health warning' notice.

31 'Business Tenancies Legislation in England and Wales: The Government's Proposals for Reform' (2001) DETR, paras 25-29. A 'health warning' to the tenant to the effect that the proposals were not binding would be needed.

32 'Business Tenancies Legislation in England and Wales: The Government's Proposals for Reform' (2001) DETR, para 30. Landlords would also be able in future to start termination proceedings without renewal (para 35). In such a case rights of compensation under Landlord and Tenant Act 1954, s 37 would be preserved (para 57). If one party had begun proceedings the other would be prevented from doing so (ibid).

33 'Business Tenancies Legislation in England and Wales: The Government's Proposals for Reform' (2001) DETR, para 50.

34 'Business Tenancies Legislation in England and Wales: The Government's Proposals for Reform' (2001) DETR, para 56.

Chapter 20

Application of the Landlord and Tenant Act 1954, Pt II

I   TENANCIES PROTECTED BY THE LANDLORD AND TENANT ACT 1954, PT II

The Landlord and Tenant Act 1954, s 23(1) provides that Pt II 'applies to any tenancy where the property comprised in the tenancy is or includes premises which are occupied by the tenant and are so occupied for the purposes of a business carried on by him or for those and other purposes'.

Tenancy

There must be a *tenancy* before LTA 1954, Pt II (this Act is hereinafter referred to as LTA 1954) applies. The expression 'tenancy' is defined by LTA 1954, s 69(1) as including a tenancy created either immediately or derivatively out of the freehold, by lease or underlease, and also includes an agreement for a lease or underlease or by a tenancy agreement or under any enactment, including Part II. Thus it makes no difference whether the agreement for a tenancy is by deed, written or oral.

Genuine licences to occupy are excluded from LTA 1954, Pt II.[1] Thus, where in a recent case, an agreement describing itself as a licence for the management of a car park imposed on the licensee an obligation not to impede in any way the officers, servants or agents of the licensor in their exercise of rights of possession of the premises, and also obliged the licensee to keep 40 parking spaces for occupiers and employees of the licensor's land, the end result was held to be to create a genuine licence to occupy.[2]

---

[1]   See further the discussion in ch 3, above. A good example of a genuine licence was an agreement under which an occupier could be moved from one unit to another without terminating the agreement: *Dresden Estates Ltd v Collinson* (1987) 55 P & CR 47, CA. There could obviously be no exclusive possession in such a case.

[2]   *National Car Parks Ltd v Trinity Development Co (Banbury) Ltd* [2001] L & TR 33, [2001] L & TR 457.

This decision forms part of a line of cases in which genuine reservation of control of the premises and denial of exclusive possession in substance will prevent an occupier claiming a tenancy and statutory renewal rights.[3] Although an agreement which is a tenancy or sub-tenancy in disguise cannot be clothed with licence terminology so as to evade LTA 1954, Pt II,[4] the courts do not approach agreements which state that they are licences and which contain no terms consistent with conferral of exclusive possession, such as entry rights, with the same suspicion with which in the part they have approached certain types of residential occupation agreements.

Express or implied tenancies at will are also excluded from LTA 1954, Pt II.[5] Where it is not clear whether the parties have agreed on a tenancy, the presence of Part II security if a tenancy is granted impliedly is a relevant factor in assessing the parties' intentions: where a person was granted a series of extensions to his current tenancy, which excluded LTA 1954, ss 22 to 28, pending negotiations for a new tenancy, which failed, it was held that even though, in the interim, rent was paid and accepted, the occupier was, from expiry of his old agreement, merely a tenant at will and outside Part II: he was not a periodic tenant by implication of law.[6]

Occupation: the premises and the holding

LTA 1954, Pt II confers statutory renewal rights only on a business tenant who is in occupation of the 'holding' for the purposes of his business, which may include ancillary purposes, such as his residence. The Act distinguishes between the premises as designated by the contractual tenancy and the 'holding'. It continues the whole contractual tenancy as from the common law expiry date under LTA 1954, s 24(1). However, renewal under LTA 1954, Pt II is only possible for a tenant who is in personal occupation of the 'holding'. By LTA 1954, s 23(3), the 'holding' is the part of the property comprised in the contractual tenancy, excluding any part not occupied by the tenant for the purposes of his business.

It is therefore important to bear in mind that, to obtain the benefit of continuation under the Act as well as statutory renewal rights, the tenant must satisfy the occupation test of LTA 1954, s 23(1) and also occupy the 'holding', personally or through a

3   The line of cases runs from *Shell-Mex and BP Ltd v Manchester Garages Ltd* [1971] 1 All ER 841, [1971] 1 WLR 612, CA (where there was a clause under which the licensee undertook not to impede 'in any way' the officers servants or agents of the licensor company in the exercise of the company's rights of possession or control of the premises). See also eg *Esso Petroleum Co Ltd v Fumegrange Ltd* [1994] 2 EGLR 90, CA.
4   As in *Dellneed Ltd v Chin* [1987] 1 EGLR 75 (concerned with an agreement which in reality amounted to much more than a mere management agreement and conferred on the occupier valuable sub-tenancy rights).
5   *Manfield & Sons Ltd v Botchin* [1970] 2 QB 612, [1970] 3 All ER 143; *Hagee (London) Ltd v Erikson and Larson* [1976] QB 209, [1975] 3 All ER 234, CA (express); *Wheeler v Mercer* [1957] AC 416, [1956] 3 All ER 631, HL (implied).
6   *Cardiothoracic Institute v Shrewdcrest Ltd* [1986] 3 All ER 633, [1986] 1 WLR 368; also *Javad v Aqil* [1991] 1 All ER 243, CA.

servant or agent. Therefore, if the tenant has sub-let the whole of the premises to a sub-tenant, he no longer occupies a 'holding' for business purposes and cannot claim renewal rights under LTA 1954, Pt II. This is because the policy of Part II is not to protect a mesne landlord's rental income, but to confer renewal rights on an occupying business tenant. In our example, the occupying sub-tenant may claim renewal from the head landlord in respect of his 'holding' (owing to the combined operation of LTA 1954, ss 23(3) and 44.

In addition, difficulties may arise where the tenant has sub-let part of the property and retains part. In such a case, depending on the facts, the tenant would only occupy for renewal purposes a 'holding' which amounted to the parts he occupied at the date of the court order for a new tenancy (which is the relevant date). The sub-tenant could claim renewal for the parts he occupied for business purposes at that date. It may be that the tenant has sub-let most of the premises: in such a case only the sub-tenant may claim renewal if the tenant could not run a business solely in the retained parts. In one case, a tenant sub-let most of a market trading area to sub-tenants. He retained an office in the premises and provided services to the sub-tenants. Since it was held that LTA 1954, Pt II does not permit the simultaneous occupation by two persons of a 'holding', the sub-tenants were held to occupy their 'holdings' to the exclusion of the tenant and could alone exercise renewal rights.[7]

Occupation: existence in fact

Turning now to the existence of the occupation requirement for continuation and renewal purposes, the question is ultimately a question of fact and degree and no hard and fast rule may safely be laid down.[8] The Court of Appeal has emphasised that LTA 1954, s 23 shows that occupation for business purposes is essential, and that this provision recognises that the occupation may change from time to time while a tenancy continues.[9] Dealing with cases where a dispute arises whether a tenant, who has not sub-let any part of the premises, is in occupation, as well as where it is a sub-tenant who claims to be in occupation, a continuity or thread of occupation must exist, but it is not necessary for the tenant to be continuously in physical occupation: thus, premises capable only of seasonal occupation may fall within LTA 1954, Pt II.[10] Similarly, the fact that the tenant had temporarily abandoned occupation but intended to resume it if granted a new tenancy,[11] or that he temporarily abandoned occupation after a fire, with

---

7   *Graysim Holdings Ltd v P&O Property Holdings Ltd* [1996] AC 329, [1995] 4 All ER 831, HL.

8   As recognised by Lord Nicholls in *Graysim Holdings Ltd v P&O Property Holdings Ltd* [1996] AC 329, [1995] 4 All ER 831, HL.

9   *Esselte AB v Pearl Assurance plc* [1997] 1 EGLR 73.

10   *Teasdale v Walker* [1958] 3 All ER 307, [1958] 1 WLR 1076, CA (where the tenant was not in occupation, having made a fictitious management agreement with a third party).

11   *I & H Caplan v Caplan (No 2)* [1963] 2 All ER 930, [1963] 1 WLR 1247.

the intention of resuming it, leaving certain fittings and fixtures,[12] did not prevent the tenant from retaining the right to apply for a new tenancy.[13] The thread of continuity was held to have been broken where the tenants ceased their business activity at the premises, began it at other premises and merely wished, if so allowed by the Gaming Board, to resume it at the subject premises if granted a new tenancy.[14] Likewise, a tenant who, some ten days before the contractual expiry date of the tenancy, had removed all its equipment from the premises, had ceased to 'occupy' for statutory purposes on expiry of the tenancy and the tenancy did not continue under LTA 1954, s 24(1), owing to the requirement, read into s 24(1), of continuing occupation by the tenant at the expiry date.[15]

Sometimes, a tenant cannot be said, owing to his nature, to be in personal occupation, as where he is a company. Thus if an individual tenant incorporates, and the company comes to hold the tenancy, at present, the right to renewal is lost, for reasons mentioned elsewhere. The government regard this as unfortunate, and have proposed treating an individual and any company they control as being equivalent. In particular, the right to renew would be extended to a company under the control of an individual where the company occupied the premises concerned.[16] In such a case, and with unincorporated associations, occupation by the tenant's employees (such as managers) or agents suffices, if they maintain a sufficient degree of management and control over the premises, which is itself a question of fact and degree. For example, the Board of Governors of a hospital were capable on the facts of complying with the requirement.[17] So was a Secretary of State, owing to the day-to-day control exercised over the premises (employee flats).[18] Where a local authority's servants regularly exercised control over the premises (a piece of land used for the purposes of leisure and recreation) and carried out work on the land from time to time, it was held that the occupation requirement was satisfied.[19] Should the premises be only occupied by the tenant's servants, only if this is a necessary part of their contractual duties will such occupation be ancillary to the occupation of the tenant, and so within LTA 1954, Pt II.[20] In all of these cases,

12   *Morrison Holdings Ltd v Manders Property (Wolverhampton) Ltd* [1976] 2 All ER 205, [1976] 1 WLR 533, CA.
13   But in *Webb v Sandown Sports Club Ltd* [2000] EGCS 13 the thread of continuity was lost by a tenant who found alternative premises, ceased trading and removed almost all of his stock from the premises. Later visits to the premises after then were consistent with his overriding intention to quit.
14   *Aspinall Finance Ltd v Viscount Chelsea* [1989] 1 EGLR 103.
15   *Esselte AB v Pearl Assurance plc* [1997] 1 EGLR 73.
16   Business Tenancies Legislation in England and Wales: The Government's Proposals for Reform (2001) DETR.
17   *Hills (Patents) Ltd v University College Hospital Board of Governors* [1956] 1 QB 90, [1955] 3 All ER 365, CA; also *Groveside Properties Ltd v Westminster Medical School* [1983] 2 EGLR 68.
18   *Linden v Department of Health and Social Security* [1986] 1 All ER 691, [1986] 1 WLR 164.
19   *Wandsworth London Borough v Singh* [1991] 2 EGLR 75, CA.
20   See *Groveside Properties Ltd v Westminster Medical School* (1983) 47 P & CR 507, CA; *Methodist Secondary Schools Trust Deed Trustees v O'Leary* [1993] 1 EGLR 105.

the court looks through the occupation of the servants, managers or agents to the tenant itself, which differentiates the position from the exclusive occupation by a sub-tenant.

By contrast, where the tenant carried on the business of proprietor of lock-up garages and sub-let most of them, retaining merely a nominal presence on the land, he failed to satisfy the occupation test as the degree of control he exerted was insufficient on the facts.[21] Although a tenant who let most of the premises as furnished rooms was held to be in occupation, as a resident director of the tenant was on the premises, having a sufficient degree of control,[22] this case would now seem to depend on its special facts.[23]

Partial business user of whole premises

Where the tenant uses business premises for residential purposes, or residential premises for business purposes, the question arises whether LTA 1954, Pt II continues to apply. A number of principles are relevant. If the premises are let on a tenancy to which Part II initially applies, it ceases to do so if the premises are no longer occupied by the tenant for any business purposes.[24]

If, however, premises have been let for residential purposes, and thus fall within RA 1977 (or HA 1988, Pt I) but during the tenancy, significant business user begins and is continued, the tenancy ceases to qualify for residential protection and is then brought within LTA 1954, Pt II, apparently even if the landlord does not consent to the change of user.[25] If any business user is merely incidental to the residential user, the relevant residential code will continue to apply to the tenancy.[26]

If the user of the premises intended at the commencement of the tenancy is a wholly business user, but later, the user becomes part business and part residential, LTA 1954, Pt II will continue to apply to the tenancy.[27] However, if the tenant of business premises, without the landlord's knowledge or consent, discontinues all business activity but resides on the premises, he cannot for this reason alone claim to be protected by either residential code.[28]

---

21 *Trans-Britannia Properties Ltd v Darby Properties Ltd* [1986] 1 EGLR 151, CA.
22 *Lee-Verhulst (Investments) Ltd v Harwood Trust* [1973] QB 204, [1971] 3 All ER 619, CA; also below.
23 After *Graysim Holdings Ltd v P&O Property Holdings Ltd* [1996] AC 329, 337G–338A, [1995] 4 All ER 831, 837–838, HL.
24 *Henry Smith's Charity Trustees v Wagle* [1989] 1 EGLR 124, CA.
25 *Cheryl Investments Ltd v Saldanha* [1979] 1 All ER 5, [1978] 1 WLR 1329, CA.
26 *Gurton v Parrott* [1991] 1 EGLR 98, CA.
27 *Cheryl Investments Ltd v Saldanha* [1979] 1 All ER 5, [1978] 1 WLR 1329, CA.
28 *Pulleng v Curran* (1980) 44 P & CR 58, CA.

Personal occupation

There are three specific statutory modifications to the requirement of personal occupation by a tenant as a condition precedent to obtaining statutory renewal.

1   LTA 1954, s 41(1) provides that where a tenancy is held on trust,[29] beneficial occupation by all or any of the beneficiaries under the trust for business purposes is to be treated as equivalent to occupation by the tenant.

2   LTA 1954, s 41A enables, subject to a number of conditions, two or more joint tenants (eg partners in a firm) in whom the tenancy is vested to apply for a new tenancy where the same partnership no longer exists.

3   LTA 1954, s 42(2) provides that where a tenancy is vested in one member of a group of companies (as defined in LTA 1954, s 42(1)), occupation by any member of the same group of companies is to be treated as equivalent to occupation.

Business

The statutory definition of 'business' (LTA 1954, s 23(2)) is wide and non-exclusive as it is stated to include a trade, profession or employment and also any activity carried on by a body of persons whether corporate or unincorporate. Despite this, the words 'trade, profession or employment' have been held to be exhaustive of the meaning of 'business' in relation to an activity carried on by a single person, and in one case it was consequently held that a tenant who took in lodgers carried on no trade.[30] Because the definition requires an activity, a mere casual user such as dumping or storing waste on the premises concerned is not within it,[31] but an activity is not sufficient: thus the gratuitous running of a Sunday School by an individual was outside LTA 1954, Pt II.[32] It appears that a spare-time activity that does not reap a commercial profit, even if it could be described as a business activity, will not bring the tenancy within LTA 1954, Pt II.[33]

On the other hand, the width of business activities capable of falling within LTA 1954, s 23(2) is considerable and they include use for offices, shops, garages, warehouses, factories, laboratories, hotels, cinemas, a doctors' or dentists' surgery and members' clubs.[34] Moreover, because the words of definition of 'business' are not exhaustive in the case of a body corporate, the non profit-making running of a hospital by a board of

29   As in *Morar v Chauhan* [1985] 3 All ER 493, [1985] 1 WLR 1263, CA.
30   *Lewis v Weldcrest Ltd* [1978] 3 All ER 1226, [1978] 1 WLR 1107, CA.
31   *Hillil Property and Investment Co Ltd v Naraine Pharmacy Ltd* (1979) 39 P & CR 67, CA.
32   *Abernethie v AH & J Kleiman Ltd* [1970] 1 QB 10, [1969] 2 All ER 790; but not in the case of a body corporate: *Parkes v Westminster Roman Catholic Diocese Trustee* (1978) 36 P & CR 22, CA (a case on LTA 1954, s 30(1)(g)).
33   *Lewis v Weldcrest Ltd* [1978] 3 All ER 1226, [1978] 1 WLR 1107, CA.
34   As to the latter see *Addiscombe Garden Estates Ltd v Crabbe* [1958] 1 QB 513, [1957] 3 All ER 563, CA.

governors fell within LTA 1954, Pt II,[35] as did the provision of offices for Crown servants.[36]

While business user is a condition precedent to renewal, the occupation condition must also be satisfied by the tenant. Hence, a property company tenant ran a business of sub-letting residential flats in a block, retaining only the common parts, but was not in 'occupation' and could not renew.[37] This result, according to the House of Lords, illustrates a general and fundamental principle that the business for which the tenant is in occupation must not be terminated by the process, at the date of the court order for a new tenancy, of ascertaining the holding. Since the only occupiers in that case were the sub-tenants, and the tenant could not run his business of sub-letting flats from the retained parts, he was denied renewal by the very nature of Part II itself.[38]

A business carried on in breach of a general prohibition of use for business purposes covering the whole premises is outside LTA 1954, Pt II unless the immediate landlord or his predecessor in title consented to the breach, or the immediate landlord acquiesced (LTA 1954, s 23(4)).[39] This exclusion does not apply to a business carried on despite a prohibition of use for the purposes of a specified business, or of its use for purposes of any but a specified business (LTA 1954, s 23(4)).

II TENANCIES EXPRESSLY EXCLUDED FROM PROTECTION

A number of tenancies are prevented by LTA 1954, Pt II from being protected, notably because they are within a different statutory code or because the tenancy does not qualify, or due to the character of the tenant.

Agricultural holdings

A tenancy of an agricultural holding is excluded from LTA 1954, Pt II, as is a tenancy which would be such a tenancy but for the fact that it is excluded by the Agricultural Holdings Act 1986, s 2(3); a tenancy of agricultural land which has been approved by the Minister is likewise excluded, as is a farm business tenancy within the meaning of the Agricultural Tenancies Act 1995 (LTA 1954, s 43(1)(a)).

---

35 *Hills (Patents) Ltd v University College Hospital Board of Governors* [1956] 1 QB 90, [1955] 3 All ER 365, HL.
36 *Town Investments Ltd v Department of the Environment* [1978] AC 359, [1977] 1 All ER 813, HL.
37 *Bagettes Ltd v GP Estates Co Ltd* [1956] Ch 290, [1956] 1 All ER 729.
38 *Graysim Holdings Ltd v P&O Property Holdings Ltd* [1996] AC 329, [1995] 4 All ER 831.
39 See *Bell v Alfred Franks & Bartlett Co Ltd* [1980] 1 All ER 356, [1980] 1 WLR 340, CA; *Methodist Secondary Schools Trust Deed Trustees v O'Leary* [1993] 1 EGLR 105.

Mining leases

A tenancy created by a mining lease[40] is excluded from LTA 1954, Pt II (LTA 1954, s 43(1)(b)). Thus, a tenant who had the right to extract sand and gravel fell outside the Act.[41]

Residential tenancies

Exclusively residential tenancies are excluded from LTA 1954, Pt II.[42] See the discussion above as to the position where a tenant uses the premises partly for business and partly for residential purposes.

Tenancies of on-licensed premises

With certain exceptions, notably tenancies of restaurants and hotels with a licence to sell intoxicating liquor on the premises and where a substantial proportion of the business consisted of transactions other than the sale of alcohol,[43] a tenancy of on-licensed premises granted before 11 July 1989 was excluded from LTA 1954, Pt II (LTA 1954, s 43(1)(d)). This has altered. A tenancy entered into on or after 11 July 1989 of premises licensed for the sale of intoxicating liquor on the premises is within LTA 1954, Pt II.[44]

Service tenancies

A tenancy granted by reason of the fact that the tenant was the holder of an office, appointment or employment from the grantor thereof and continuing only so long as the tenant holds the post, or terminable by the grantor on his ceasing to hold it, or coming to an end at a time fixed by reference to the time when the tenant ceases to hold it, is excluded from LTA 1954, Pt II (LTA 1954, s 43(2)). A tenancy granted after 1 October 1954 (when Pt II commenced) is only excluded from Pt II if the tenancy was granted by an instrument in writing which expressed the purpose for which the tenancy was granted.

---

40 As defined by Landlord and Tenant Act 1927, s 25(1), applied by LTA 1954, Pt II, s 46.
41 *O'Callaghan v Elliott* [1966] 1 QB 601, CA.
42 If the tenancy is an assured tenancy, it cannot be within LTA 1954, Pt II: see HA 1988, s 1 and Sch 1, para 4; likewise with a protected or statutory tenancy within RA 1977, s 24(3).
43 See *Grant v Gresham* [1979] 2 EGLR 60, CA; *Ye Old Cheshire Cheese Ltd v Daily Telegraph plc* [1988] 3 All ER 217, [1988] 1 WLR 1173.
44 Landlord and Tenant (Licensed Premises) Act 1990, s 1(1). Landlord and Tenant (Licensed Premises) Act 1990, s 1(2) and (3) enabled a tenancy of on-licensed premises granted before 11 July 1989 or on or after 11 July 1989 under a contract entered into prior to that date to be terminated prior to 11 July 1992: such tenancy subsisting after that date will fall within LTA 1954, Pt II.

Short tenancies

By LTA 1954, s 43(3), LTA 1954, Pt II does not apply to a tenancy granted for a term certain not exceeding six months unless:

1   the tenancy contains provision for renewing the term or for extending it beyond six months from its beginning; or
2   the tenant has been in occupation for a period which, together with any period during which any predecessor in title in the carrying on of the business carried on by the tenant was in occupation, exceeds twelve months.

Periodic tenancies are not mentioned in LTA 1954, s 43(2) and they are capable of falling within LTA 1954, Pt II.

III   TENANCIES IN WHICH LTA 1954, PT II IS EXCLUDED BY AGREEMENT

In a number of cases, of which the two mentioned are the most important, LTA 1954, Pt II cannot apply.

Exclusions authorised by the court

At the time this book went to press, the county court is empowered (LTA 1954, s 38(4)(a)) on the joint application of the intending landlord and tenant in relation to a term certain which would otherwise be within LTA 1954, Pt II, to authorise an agreement excluding in relation thereto LTA 1954, ss 24-28. According to the Law Commission,[45] there are 'many cases where the landlord would be willing to let on a temporary basis and the tenant would be willing to accept such a tenancy'. They cited a landlord who has obtained possession and intends to sell, demolish or reconstruct the premises but cannot do so immediately. He would not wish to grant a tenancy which attracted statutory security.

However, the Law Commission expressed the view that the safeguard of court approval of contracting-out agreements was not working. They considered that few courts examined the parties' bargain with much care.[46] They therefore recommended that in future special formalities would have to be adopted to operate the contracting-out provisions. The formalities would be in the form, in effect, of 'health warnings' such as a statement in the prescribed form explaining in plain English the general nature of the tenant's statutory rights and the consequences of his giving them up. There would also be a declaration by the tenant that he understood the terms of the agreement and the statement.[47] The government have indicated that they are minded to implement these proposals with the adjustment that the tenant would have his 'health warning'

45   Law Com No 17 (1969), paras 32 and 33.
46   Law Com 208 (1992), 'Landlord and Tenant: Business Tenancies: A Periodic Review of the Landlord and Tenant Act 1954, Part II', para 2.16.
47   Law Com 208 (1992), para 2.20.

notice at least 14 days before signing the tenancy concerned.[48] Once this reform has been carried through, approvals of contracting out by the court will cease to be required.

Agreement for a new tenancy

Where the landlord and tenant agree, in writing (LTA 1954, s 69(2)), for the grant to the tenant of a future tenancy of the holding, or of the holding with other land, on terms and from a date specified in the agreement, the current tenancy is to continue until that date but no longer, and LTA 1954, Pt II does not apply to the future tenancy (LTA 1954, s 28). This provision applies only to an unconditional enforceable contract.[49] The 'landlord' referred to is, in most cases, the tenant's immediate landlord; if the latter is not 'the landlord', within LTA 1954, s 44 for the purposes of Pt II, the 'landlord' in question is a superior landlord: if so, the agreement would be capable of being specifically enforced against him.[50]

IV   TENANCIES WHICH HAVE COME TO AN END

In certain cases, the contractual or continuing tenancy has come to an end by permitted common law or certain other means within LTA 1954, leaving the tenant with no security.

Notice to quit

The giving of a valid notice to quit by the tenant will terminate his periodic tenancy at common law and will remove any protection he might have under LTA 1954, Pt II. To ensure that the notice is given voluntarily, LTA 1954, s 24(2)(a) precludes the tenant from giving an effectual notice to quit until he has been in occupation in right of the tenancy for at least one month.

Surrender

If the tenant voluntarily surrenders the tenancy, he loses any security he might have had under LTA 1954, Pt II. If the instrument of surrender[51] is executed, or, where appropriate, the instrument was executed in pursuance of a prior agreement, before the tenant had been in occupation in right of the tenancy for one month, the surrender will not deprive the tenant of security under LTA 1954, Pt II.[52]

48   Consultation Paper (2001) supra, paras 5-10.
49   *RJ Stratton Ltd v Wallis Tomlin & Co Ltd* [1986] 1 EGLR 104, CA.
50   See *Bowes-Lyon v Green* [1963] AC 420, HL, where differences of opinion as to the correct 'landlord' within LTA 1954, s 28 were expressed.
51   This does not include a notice pursuant to an option to purchase: *Watney v Boardley* [1975] 2 All ER 644, [1975] 1 WLR 857.
52   An agreement caught by this provision may be authorised by the court where LTA 1954, s 38(4) applies.

Forfeiture

A tenancy within LTA 1954, Pt II may be terminated by forfeiture of the tenancy or of a superior tenancy (LTA 1954, s 24(2)). If there is a pending application for relief in respect of a forfeited tenancy, the Act continues to apply to the tenancy, since relief applications are part of the process of forfeiture.[53]

Termination by tenant

By LTA 1954, s 27(1), a tenant holding under a tenancy for a term of years certain to which LTA 1954, Pt II applies may give his immediate landlord, not later than three months before the date at which the tenancy would come to an end by effluxion of time, a notice in writing that he does not desire the tenancy to be continued. Such notice will, unless given before the tenant has been in occupation in right of the tenancy for one month, prevent continuation under LTA 1954, s 24 in relation to that tenancy. A continuing tenancy for a term of years certain may be brought to an end on any quarter day by not less than three months' notice in writing given by the tenant to the immediate landlord, subject to the one-month occupation restriction just mentioned (LTA 1954, s 27(2)).

A number of points have arisen in relation to this provision and its relationship to the occupation conditions of LTA 1954, ss 23(1) and 24(1). If a business tenant is no longer in occupation of the premises at the contractual expiry date of the tenancy, he is not impliedly required to serve any notice under LTA 1954, s 27(2) to put an end to continuation: no continuation arises if he is out of occupation at such expiry date.[54] The Court of Appeal ruled that statutory continuation did not apply where a tenant had in the past been in occupation but was not at the expiry at common law of the tenancy. LTA 1954, s 24(1) reproduces in shorthand form the conditions of LTA 1954, s 23(1). Thus, a tenant who had abandoned possession before the contractual expiry date did not have to pay any rent as from then. By necessary inference, if a landlord serves a LTA 1954, s 25 termination notice on a tenant, who ceased to occupy the property at such date, the tenant may quit without formality and is not liable for rent or under the covenants of the tenancy until any later expiry date of the s 25 notice.[55] However, it is thought that the right of a business tenant to serve a LTA 1954, s 27(2) notice to terminate during continuation, whether or not he has received a LTA 1954, s 25 notice from his landlord, is not affected.[56]

53 *Meadows v Clerical, Medical and General Life Assurance Society* [1981] Ch 70, [1980] 1 All ER 454. Likewise, LTA 1954, s 24(2) will not exclude LTA 1954, s 24(1), and continuation, where a vesting order could have been made under LPA 1925, s 146(4): *Cadogan v Dimovic* [1984] 2 All ER 168, [1984] 1 WLR 609, CA.

54 *Esselte AB v Pearl Assurance plc* [1997] 1 EGLR 73, CA.

55 *Cheryl Investments Ltd v Saldanha* [1979] 1 All ER 5, at 13, [1978] 1 WLR 1329 at 1338, as cited in *Esselte AB v Pearl Assurance plc* [1997] 1 EGLR 73, CA.

56 In *Long Acre Securities v Electro Acoustic Industries Ltd* [1990] 1 EGLR 91 the tenant, having received a LTA 1954, s 25 notice, was able to cut short the date of expiry of that notice by

The Government have been looking at this issue. They propose to amend LTA 1954, s 27. It would be made explicit that a tenant wishing to end the tenancy at the end of the contractual term can do so by serving at least three months' notice before the end of the contractual term, or by vacating the premises by the end of the contractual term. In this way, the tenant would be able to cut off his potential liability to pay rent. In addition, LTA 1954, s 27(2) would be amended so as to permit the tenant to serve a three months' notice to end on any day.[57]

Tenant's failure to comply with s 29(2)

Where the landlord serves a notice to terminate the tenancy under LTA 1954, s 25, the tenant is required by LTA 1954, s 25(5) to notify the landlord within two months whether or not, at the date of termination, he will be willing to give up possession of the premises.[58] If the tenant fails to comply strictly with the two-month time-limit then, waiver by the landlord and estoppel apart, the tenant will lose any right, thanks to LTA 1954, s 29(2), to apply to the court for a new tenancy. The effect of the LTA 1954, s 25 notice will be to put his rights under the current tenancy to an end.

Tenant's failure to comply with LTA 1954, s 29(3)

The court cannot, by LTA 1954, s 29(3), entertain any application for a new tenancy unless the application is made not less than two nor more than four months after a landlord's LTA 1954, s 25 notice or a tenant's request for a new tenancy under LTA 1954, s 26 is given. These time-limits are procedural, being for the benefit only of one party, and the landlord may waive them expressly or impliedly, if so minded.[59] The court cannot extend these time-limits either way.[60] The Law Commission recommended that this particular requirement should be done away with. Under their proposals, where the landlord serves a notice to terminate a business tenancy, the tenant would no longer be required to serve a counter-notice. In these circumstances, they saw no reason why the landlord or tenant should have to wait for two months after service of the landlord's termination notice before applying to court.[61] The government wishes

---

means of a LTA 1954, s 27(1) notice; but was held, it now seems erroneously, liable for rent for a few months into what would have been a continuation if he had not abandoned the premises a few days into such continuation.

57   Consultation Paper (2001), supra, paras 39-40. There would be no obligation on tenants to serve notice. The aim of the reform seems to be consumerist: to make tenants fully aware of their rights under LTA 1954, s 27 (para 38).

58   No special form of notice is required from the tenant: *Lewington v Trustees of the Society for the Protection of Ancient Buildings* (1983) 45 P & CR 336, CA.

59   *Kammins Ballrooms Co Ltd v Zenith Investments (Torquay) Ltd* [1971] AC 850, [1970] 2 All ER 871, HL.

60   *Dodds v Walker* [1981] 2 All ER 609, [1981] 1 WLR 1027, HL.

61   Law Com No 208 (1992), supra, para 2.60.

to adopt this proposal. It indeed proposes to allow the parties to apply to court at any time before the date specified in a landlord's LTA 1954, s 25 notice or a tenant's LTA 1954, s 26 request.[62]

---

62 Consultation Paper (2001), supra, paras 41-42. The parties would also be entitled to extend time-limits for applications to court by agreement (para 43). However, once the tenant has requested a new tenancy, he would not be able to apply for a new tenancy to the court until the landlord had served a counter-notice (para 45).

CHAPTER 21

Restrictions on contracting out

Although the LTA 1954, Pt II confers only qualified security of tenure on business tenants, because of the ability of the landlord to oppose the grant of a new tenancy, especially if he wishes to redevelop the premises or to occupy them for the purposes of his own business, in principle it is not possible at present for the tenant voluntarily to contract out of the Act but reforms are anticipated.

I   SECURITY OF TENURE

Any agreement (whether contained in the instrument creating the tenancy or not) is rendered void by LTA 1954, s 38(1) in so far as it purports to preclude the tenant from requesting or applying for a new tenancy, or provides for the termination or surrender of the tenancy in the event of his making such application or request or for the imposition of any penalty or disability on the tenant in that event.[1] 'Purports' in LTA 1954, s 38(1)[2] means 'has the effect of precluding the tenant' and so caught an agreement for a tenancy under which the tenant agreed to give up possession by a certain date, thus precluding him from applying for a new tenancy under LTA 1954, Pt II.[3] Where a tenant held on a lease with a fully qualified prohibition on assignments which provided that, if the tenant wished to assign, he must first offer the landlord a surrender of the lease, LTA 1954, s 38(1) rendered the agreement to surrender void:[4] as with the previous case, if the agreement had been carried out (in fact the tenant withdrew from it) the

---

1   See *Stevenson & Rush (Holdings) Ltd v Langdon* (1978) 38 P & CR 208 (payment of all landlord's costs clause a penalty).
2   Which has been characterised as a declaratory anti-avoidance provision in *Nicholls v Kinsey* [1994] 1 EGLR 131, CA.
3   *Joseph v Joseph* [1967] Ch 78, [1966] 3 All ER 486, CA.
4   *Allnatt London Properties Ltd v Newton* [1981] 2 All ER 290, affd on this aspect [1984] 1 All ER 423, CA.

tenant would in fact have been precluded from applying for a new tenancy. Similarly a letter stating that the tenant would quit within 28 days, released from rent arrears, was caught by LTA 1954, s 38(1) as part of a contract for a surrender enforceable in equity.[5] However, LTA 1954, s 38(1) is limited to agreements to surrender, and was held not to apply to an actual surrender of a tenancy pursuant to a consent order in repossession proceedings.[6] Nor does LTA 1954, s 38(1) invalidate surrender-back clauses in covenants against assignments.[7]

The above prohibition has no effect on the ability of the tenant to give a notice to quit the holding or a notice that he does not desire to continue the tenancy.[8] The tenant may also validly execute an advance instrument of surrender, but LTA 1954, s 24(2)(b) precludes this from being executed before the tenant has been in occupation in right of the tenancy for one month or under an agreement entered into before such occupation. However, once the government implements reforms, this particular rule will cease to apply.

At the time this book went to press, the county court was empowered by LTA 1954, s 38(4)(a) to authorise, on the joint application of the parties,[9] agreements to be granted for a term of years certain[10] which exclude LTA 1954, ss 24-28. It also had power, under LTA 1954, s 38(4)(b), to authorise agreements for the surrender of the tenancy on such date or in such circumstances as may be specified in the agreement and on such terms as may be specified. The agreement must be contained in or endorsed on the instrument creating the tenancy or other instrument specified by the court. It has been claimed that the county court will invariably approve LTA 1954, s 38(4) applications by business persons who act with legal advice.[11] The purpose of the court's approval was held to be to enable the court to be satisfied that the prospective tenant understands that he is foregoing the protection of LTA 1954, Pt II, ss 24-28.[12]

It is anticipated that once the government promulgates the relevant delegated legislation, LTA 1954, s 38(4) will be repealed. In its place, the landlord will ordinarily be required

5   *Tarjomani v Panther Securities Ltd* (1982) 46 P & CR 32.
6   *Hamilton v Sengray Properties* (6 March 1987, unreported), CA.
7   *Allnatt London Properties Ltd v Newton* [1981] 2 All ER 290: the tenant was refused a declaration that he was entitled, for so long as LTA 1954, Pt II applied to the tenancy, freely to assign it.
8   See LTA 1954, Pt II, ss 24(2)(a) and 27.
9   Cf *Cardiothoracic Institute v Shrewdcrest Ltd* [1986] 3 All ER 633, [1986] 1 WLR 368, where a tenant holding over under interim extensions, paying rent, had no security as it was intended that the parties would resort to LTA 1954, s 38(4) but failed to do so.
10 In *Re Land and Premises at Liss, Hants* [1971] Ch 986, [1971] 3 All ER 380, accepted in *EWP Ltd v Moore* [1991] 2 EGLR 4, CA, 'term of years certain' was held to include, in the context of LTA 1954, Pt II, a term of six months certain. Query where a tenancy includes a landlord's or tenant's break-clause.
11 *Hagee (London) Ltd v AB Erikson and Larson* [1975] 3 All ER 234 at 236, CA.
12 *Metropolitan Police District Receiver v Palacegate Properties Ltd* [2000] 1 EGLR 63, CA. It was also held that the court had no power to investigate the fairness of bargains under LTA 1954, s 38.

to give the tenant a 14 days' advance 'health warning' notice. This will explain the consequences to the tenant of excluding security of tenure.

II RIGHTS TO COMPENSATION

The right to compensation conferred by LTA 1954, s 37 may be excluded or modified by agreement (LTA 1954, s 38(3)). Where, during the whole of the five years immediately preceding the date on which the tenant was to quit the holding, the business has been carried on by the occupier on the holding or part of it, any agreement whether contained in the tenancy agreement or not and whether made before or after the termination of the tenancy, which purports to exclude or restrict compensation under LTA 1954, s 37 is void to that extent. If during those five years there was a change of occupier of the premises, the person who was the occupier immediately after the change was a successor to the business, an agreement as above purporting to exclude or restrict compensation is likewise void (LTA 1954, s 38(2)). In that LTA 1954, s 38(2) is not directed at agreements as to accrued rights to compensation, an agreement as to the amount of any compensation under LTA 1954, s 37 which is made after the right thereto has accrued is not invalidated (LTA 1954, s 38(2)).

Chapter 22

Continuation and termination of business tenancies

A tenancy to which LTA 1954, Pt II applies is not to come to an end unless terminated in accordance with the provisions of Pt II (LTA 1954, s 24(1)). This is the principle of statutory continuation of a business tenancy, but three common law methods of termination, where applicable, are preserved from the principle that continuation is only terminable within LTA 1954, Pt II (LTA 1954, s 24(2)). Those methods are: a tenant's notice to quit; surrender; and forfeiture. However, if the tenant is not in occupation in the sense required by LTA 1954, s 23(1) at the contractual expiry date of the tenancy then there is no continuation of the tenancy under LTA 1954, s 24(1), since a past, as opposed to a present, occupation will not suffice to trigger the operation of LTA 1954, s 24(1).[1] Thus, if a tenant permanently abandons his occupation of business premises before the contractual expiry date, he may quit without having to serve a LTA 1954, s 27(1) notice on the landlord. If he continues to occupy at and for a time, after such expiry date, but then abandons occupation permanently, it is not clear whether he would have to serve a LTA 1954, s 27(2) notice of termination on the landlord.

The LTA 1954, Pt II enables a continuing tenancy, which is a holding device, to be brought to an end by a landlord's notice of termination under LTA 1954, s 25 or a tenant's request for a new tenancy under LTA 1954, s 26. The service of these notices is an essential step in a procedure which leads either to the termination of the current tenancy or its renewal by negotiation or by the court.[2]

---

1   *Esselte AB v Pearl Assurance plc* [1997] 1 WLR 891, CA. If, therefore, the tenant, having applied for a new tenancy after a landlord's LTA 1954, s 25 notice, changes its mind and leaves occupation before the contractual term date, it is not in principle liable for rent after that date: *Single Horse Properties Ltd v Surrey County Council* [2002] EWCA Civ 367, [2002] 19 EG 150.

2   The court procedure is governed, as from 15 October 2001, by CPR 1998, Pt 8. See Webber (2001) 145 Sol Jo 902. All proceedings are in principle in the county court. Of special note is the stay procedure which allows for either party to obtain a stay of up to three months, to allow for negotiations. This may have been instituted to meet criticisms that the procedural deadlines for business tenancy renewals were too severe and may have encouraged litigation.

LTA 1954 contains a provision which enables either the landlord or the tenant to obtain information about the other party following a notice (LTA 1954, s 40). The reason for this is that in order to serve a valid notice to terminate, the landlord must know whether the tenant is in occupation for business purposes. The tenant must know who is the competent landlord. The current provision allows the landlord to request information by a prescribed form notice asking the tenant to inform him whether he is in occupation for the purposes of a business (as required by LTA 1954, Pt II, s 23).

The Law Commission recommended improving this provision by enabling the notice to ask whether the premises were occupied by a company controlled by the tenant.[3] Likewise, landlords can at present ask for details of any sub-letting. The Law Commission proposed to add in an ability to request whether there is in any sub-tenancy an operative agreement that the renewal provisions of the LTA 1954, Pt II do not apply. The tenant has a right to seek from his reversioner information as to whether he is the freeholder, and if not, who, to the best of his knowledge and belief is his immediate landlord. The Commission proposed improving this provision by enabling the tenant to seek information as to who is the reversioner of any other part of the property. The government are intent on implementing these recommendations.[4]

I STATUTORY CONTINUATION

But for LTA 1954, s 24(1), the contractual term of a business tenancy would expire by effluxion of time. LTA 1954, s 24(1) continues the contractual term of a tenant in occupation at that date indefinitely,[5] despite its having reached its common law expiry date, unless or until it is terminated in accordance with LTA 1954, Pt II.

A continuation tenancy is an extension of the contractual term with a statutory variation as to the mode of termination.[6] The current tenant therefore has an estate in the land, not merely a personal right to occupy, and is subject to the burdens and benefits of the contractual tenancy. A right to remove tenant's fixtures extends into continuation.[7] Any liability of an original tenant to pay rent, if it is expressed to last for the term of the

---

3   The whole revised package is in Law Com No 208 (1992), supra, paras 2.24-2.33.

4   Consultation Paper 'Business Tenancies Legislation in England and Wales: the Government's Proposals for Reform' (2001) DETR, paras 19-20.

5   By LTA 1954, s 65(2), a sub-tenancy continued beyond the term of a superior tenancy, is kept alive for the duration of its term, and is then deemed to have been surrendered under LPA 1925, s 139(1), so that the sub-tenant holds directly under the head landlord.

6   See eg *Weinbergs Weatherproofs Ltd v Radcliffe Paper Mill Co* [1958] Ch 437; *Cornish v Brook Green Laundry Ltd* [1959] 1 QB 394, [1959] 1 All ER 173, CA; *GMS Syndicate Ltd v Gary Elliott Ltd* [1982] Ch 1, [1981] 1 All ER 619.

7   *New Zealand Government Property Corpn v HM & S Ltd* [1982] QB 1145, [1982] 1 All ER 624, CA; as do rights of way enjoyed under the contractual tenancy: *Nevill Long & Co (Boards) v Firmenich & Co* (1983) 47 P & CR 59, CA.

lease, does not extend into any period of continuation, where the original tenant has assigned the term before its contractual expiry date. The contractual obligations of the original tenant are not independently continued by LTA 1954, s 24(1). Thus, if the original tenant is to be liable,[8] clear words of extension of his contractual liability under the lease into statutory continuation are required.[9] Moreover, it was not possible for a landlord who had terminated the contractual term before its expiry date of 2000, pursuant to a break-clause, to invoke a rent review during continuation, where the term was assumed for review purposes to run until 2000.[10] (In any case, a landlord is entitled to seek an interim rent under LTA 1954, s 24A during continuation.) In the absence of clear words, however, a guarantor's liability in respect of rent arrears does not, in principle, extend into continuation.[11]

A landlord's notice to quit or notice to determine the contractual tenancy are effectual to put an end to the contractual term, if otherwise valid, and continuation will commence as from the date of the expiry of the notice.[12] The landlord may serve a statutory notice to terminate the continuing tenancy under LTA 1954, s 25; or he may serve a single notice, which will, if it complies both with LTA 1954, s 25 and common law rules, suffice to terminate the contractual tenancy and continuation under LTA 1954, Pt II.[13]

Where, during continuation, a tenancy ceases to be a business tenancy, it may be determined by the landlord, subject to the terms of the contractual tenancy, on not less than three nor more than six months' written notice (LTA 1954, s 24(3)(a)). If the landlord gives a notice to quit to a periodic tenant who enjoys no security of tenure (and so no continuation rights) under LTA 1954, Pt II, the operation of the notice is not affected by the fact that after the giving of the notice, the tenancy becomes one to which Pt II applies (LTA 1954, s 24(3)(b)). But for this provision, the tenant might try to occupy the premises for business purposes during the currency of a notice and then claim the benefit of statutory continuation.

---

8   As to the effect of the Landlord and Tenant (Covenants) Act 1995 on such liabilities, see ch 5 above.

9   *City of London Corpn v Fell* [1994] 1 AC 458, [1993] 4 All ER 968, HL. Where an original lessee was, under an express clause, liable to pay rent into continuation, this liability did not as a matter of construction extend to a liability to pay an interim rent fixed under LTA 1954, s 24A between the landlord and the assignee.

10 *Willison v Cheverell Estates Ltd* [1996] 1 EGLR 116, CA.

11 *Junction Estates Ltd v Cope* (1974) 27 P & CR 482; *A Plesser & Co v Davis* [1983] 2 EGLR 70.

12 *Weinbergs Weatherproofs Ltd v Radcliffe Paper Mill Co* [1958] Ch 437.

13 *Keith Bayler Rogers & Co v Cubes* (1975) 31 P & CR 412; also *Aberdeen Steak Houses plc v Crown Estate Comrs* [1997] 2 EGLR 107 (single notice served under LTA 1954, s 25 and a break-clause).

II   TERMINATION BY THE LANDLORD

Notice under LTA 1954, s 25

The landlord may terminate a tenancy to which LTA 1954, Pt II applies solely by giving the tenant a statutory or LTA 1954, s 25 notice[14] to terminate the tenancy.[15] If the landlord serves a valid notice, it cannot be withdrawn; if his notice is invalid, and the tenant does not waive the defect, the landlord may withdraw the invalid notice and serve a new, valid, notice.[16] The requirement of a notice applies to all periodic tenancies and tenancies for a fixed term exceeding six months, whether the tenancy is continuing or not.[17] The following requirements apply to the landlord's notice.

1   It must be both in writing and in the prescribed form,[18] or in a form substantially to the like effect. In particular, the notice must require the tenant,[19] within two months after it is given, to notify the landlord in writing whether or not he is willing to give up possession (LTA 1954, s 25(5)). If the tenant fails to serve a counter-notice on time, he generally loses his right to apply to the court for a new tenancy (LTA 1954, s 29(2)) unless the landlord is estopped by his conduct from taking the point.[20] If the tenant replies in time, however, the effect is to enable him to apply under LTA 1954, s 24(1) for a new tenancy. No special form is prescribed for the tenant's LTA 1954, s 25(5) notice, which must, as a matter of form, state

---

14   Thus a common law notice is ineffectual: *Commercial Properties Ltd v Wood* [1968] 1 QB 15, CA.

15   Service of both LTA 1954, ss 25 and 26 notices (and all notices under LTA 1954, Pt II) is governed by Landlord and Tenant Act 1927, s 23 (LTA 1954, s 66(4)), so that a notice sent by recorded delivery or registered post is deemed to have been received in the ordinary course of the post, whether the recipient sees it or not but the presumption of due service is rebuttable. See *Italica Holdings SA v Bayadea* [1985] 1 EGLR 70; *Lex Service plc v Johns* [1990] 1 EGLR 92, CA.

16   *Smith v Draper* [1990] 2 EGLR 69, CA. An exception to the rule that a valid LTA 1954, s 25 notice cannot be withdrawn is provided by LTA 1954, Sch 6, para 6, which applies where a competent landlord has served a s 25 notice on the tenant and within two months thereof, a new landlord becomes the competent landlord.

17   It may be disputed whether the occupier is a tenant or a licensee. In *Wroe v Exmos Cover Ltd* [2000] 1 EGLR 66, CA, the owners served a s 25 notice on the occupier on the basis that they had to assume he was a tenant. This did not of itself represent by conduct that the owners would not oppose the grant of a new tenancy on a specified ground in this notice.

18   Landlord and Tenant Act 1954 Part II (Notices) Regulations 1983, SI 1983/133, notably Form 1.

19   Where there is more than one tenant, such as trustees, the notice serving tenant may be taken, provided the notice so states, or the context makes this apparent, to act on behalf of the others: see *Hackney London BC v Hackney African Organisation* [1999] L & TR 117, CA (the court declining to read too much into the relevant requirements).

20   As in *JT Development Ltd v Quinn* [1991] 2 EGLR 257, CA. Equally, a tenant who serves a counter-notice on the landlord may find that he is estopped by having done so from contesting the formal validity of the landlord's LTA 1954, s 25 notice. See *Keepers and Governors of the Free Grammar School of John Lyon v Mayhew* [1997] 1 EGLR 88, CA.

unequivocally the tenant's intentions.[21] The government now intend to get rid of the requirement that the tenant serves a counter-notice on the ground that it is superfluous and indeed a trap.[22] This would get rid of a requirement which, it is said, has often been complied with only as a matter of form.[23]

2   Although it is best to follow strictly the most up to date prescribed form available,[24] a notice which omits certain immaterial details, such as notes to the prescribed form, will be upheld.[25] Likewise an otherwise correct notice in which the space for the date and signature was left blank, was valid.[26] The tenant will suffer no loss from such trifling deviations, provided the notice conveys the substance of what is required.[27] If a reasonable tenant is not misled by the notice, despite its defects, then the notice will be upheld in spite of errors as to dates.[28] Where, however, a notice failed to state the correct name and address of the competent landlord, (a vital piece of information for any tenant) it was held invalid,[29] and this result would seem to have survived the advent of the new, generous, validity test. Likewise invalid was a notice which failed to state the names of all the joint landlords.[30] This information is necessary for the correct service of the tenant's notices, but no reasonable tenant could be expected to know the names of all the competent landlords. Similarly, again showing that not too much detective work or intuition can be reasonably expected of a reasonable recipient, a tenant who received two documents, one a LTA 1954, s 25 notice and one in similar form, opposing a new tenancy on no specified grounds, could not treat the two documents together as a valid LTA 1954, s 25 notice. A reasonable recipient could not be expected to ignore one of the two documents or to read them as one, especially as they were inconsistent, as one of the two documents stated that a new tenancy application would not be opposed.[31] Perhaps the new, liberal 'reasonable recipient' test is causing as many problems as did the old, more formal test.

---

21   See eg *Lewington v Trustees of the Society for the Protection of Ancient Buildings* (1983) 45 P & CR 336; *Mehmet v Dawson* [1984] 1 EGLR 74, CA.

22   Consultation Paper 'Business Tenancies Legislation in England and Wales: the Government's Proposals for Reform' (2001) DETR, para 32.

23   Law Com No 208 (1992), para 2.38. As noted in para 2.37, the counter-notice can act as a trap, as failure to serve it denies the tenant the right to apply for a new tenancy.

24   Cf *Snook v Schofield* [1975] 1 EGLR 69 (outdated form which did not materially depart from LTA 1954 valid).

25   *Tegerdine v Brooks* (1977) 36 P & CR 261, CA.

26   *Falcon Pipes Ltd v Stanhope Gate Property Co Ltd* (1967) 117 NLJ 1345; also *British Railways Board v AJA Smith Transport Ltd* [1981] 2 EGLR 69.

27   See eg *Barclays Bank v Ascott* [1961] 1 WLR 717. In *Sabella Ltd v Montgomery* [1998] 1 EGLR 65, the cumulative effect of individual omissions was to invalidate a LTA 1954, s 25 notice, even though any one of these alone might not have done so.

28   *Mannai v Eagle Star Assurance* [1997] AC 749; *Sabella v Montgomery* [1998] 1 EGLR 65.

29   *Morrow v Nadeem* [1987] 1 All ER 237, [1986] 1 WLR 1381, CA.

30   *Pearson v Alyo* [1990] 1 EGLR 114, CA; also *Yamaha-Kemble Music (UK) Ltd v ARC Properties Ltd* [1990] 1 EGLR 261.

31   *Barclays Bank plc v Bee* [2001] EWCA Civ 1126, [2002] 1 WLR 332, CA. See Haley [2002] Conv 292.

3   The notice must specify the date on which the current tenancy is to come to an end: the date of termination (LTA 1954, s 25(1)). The date so specified must not be earlier than the date on which, in the case of a fixed-term tenancy, it would have expired by effluxion of time (LTA 1954, s 25(4)).[32] In the case of a periodic tenancy, the specified date must be no earlier than the earliest date on which the tenancy could have been brought to an end by a notice to quit served by the landlord on the giving of the LTA 1954, s 25 notice (LTA 1954, s 25(3)(a)). However, it is not necessary for the date of termination to fall on the correct expiry date at common law,[33] no doubt because, as seen, the statutory method of termination is the sole permissible means of ending a business tenancy.

4   The landlord (which expression includes one of two or more joint landlords)[34] may give a LTA 1954, s 25 notice not less than six nor more than twelve months before the specified termination date (LTA 1954, s 25(2)).[35] Where the tenancy requires a period of notice above six months, the time-limit is altered from twelve months to the period equal to the period required under the tenancy plus six months (LTA 1954, s 25(3)(b)).

5   A notice of termination must state whether or not the landlord would oppose an application to the court for a new tenancy and, if so, on what grounds he will rely (LTA 1954, s 25(6)).[36] The landlord will, in proceedings, be limited to the grounds stated in his LTA 1954, s 25 notice,[37] which cannot later be changed.[38] The paragraphs of LTA 1954, s 30(1) (which are the grounds of opposition to a new tenancy, discussed in ch 23, below) need not be set out in full.[39] If, after service of a s 25 notice, the reversion is assigned, the successor in title may rely on, but will be bound by, the grounds specified in the notice. The government wish to alter the law, so that in future landlords would have to indicate their key proposals for a new tenancy in a s 25 notice which did not oppose the grant of a new tenancy.[40]

A LTA 1954, s 25 notice must generally relate to the whole demised premises, and this may be of importance where the tenant occupies premises which are not physically contiguous, as with an office-floor and ground-floor storage facilities.[41] A s 25 notice

32   See *Re Crowhurst Park, Sims-Hilditch v Simmons* [1974] 1 All ER 991, [1974] 1 WLR 583.
33   *Hogg Bullimore & Co v Co-operative Insurance Society Ltd* (1984) 50 P & CR 105.
34   *Leckhampton Dairies v Artus Whitfield Ltd* (1986) 130 Sol Jo 225.
35   See *Hogg Bullimore & Co v Co-operative Insurance Society Ltd* (1984) 50 P & CR 105.
36   Law Com No 208 (1992), para 2.34, recommended that if the landlord does not intend to oppose an application for a new tenancy, he should in his LTA 1954, s 25 notice set out his proposals for a new tenancy. It is understood that this recommendation will be implemented.
37   *XL Fisheries v Leeds Corpn* [1955] 2 QB 536, CA.
38   See *Betty's Cafes Ltd v Phillips Furnishing Stores Ltd* [1957] Ch 67, [1957] 1 All ER 1, CA; *Hutchinson v Lamberth* [1984] 1 EGLR 75, CA.
39   *Biles v Caesar* [1957] 1 All ER 151; also *Philipson-Stow v Trevor Square Ltd* [1981] 1 EGLR 56.
40   Consultation Paper 'Business Tenancies Legislation in England and Wales: the Government's Proposals for Reform' (2001) DETR, paras 27-29, with the additional consumerist requirement of a tenant health warning to the effect that the landlord's proposals were not binding on the tenant. The original proposal is in Law Com No 208 (1992), para 2.34.
41   See *Herongrove Ltd v Wates City of London Properties plc* [1988] 1 EGLR 82.

will be invalid unless it relates to the whole of the holding, and not just to part of it.[42] Therefore, if the reversion has been severed since the grant of the tenancy, it may be impossible for any valid s 25 notice to be served, since neither landlord may serve a notice to terminate which applies to the whole holding.[43] Where there were held to be two leases in one document, a LTA 1954, s 25 notice served in respect of the whole premises demised by one of the leases was upheld.[44] The government considers that the current law requires amendment so that in future landlords holding a split reversion should be entitled collectively to operate renewal procedures and vice versa.[45]

It is understood that the government will change the law so as to allow landlords to commence proceedings to terminate a business tenancy without renewal. Such proceedings could not be terminated without the tenant's consent. If the proceedings, fail, the court will be able to order a new tenancy and to settle its terms.

Competent landlord

A LTA 1954, s 25 notice must be served by a 'landlord' within LTA 1954, s 44(1), and this person may not necessarily be the tenant's immediate landlord. LTA 1954, s 44(1) imposes three requirements on the nature of the landlord's interest before the landlord is a competent landlord within LTA 1954, Pt II.[46]

1   The landlord's interest must be in reversion expectant (whether immediately or not) on the termination of the tenancy.
2   The interest must be either the fee simple or a tenancy which will not come to an end within 14 months by effluxion of time. If the interest is a qualifying tenancy, the mesne landlord must have given no notice by which his interest will come to an end within 14 months or any further time it may be continued under LTA 1954, ss 36(2) or 64.
3   The landlord's interest must not itself be an interest on a reversion expectant (immediately or not) on an interest which fulfils those conditions.

These provisions are apparently aimed at disentitling a mesne landlord with no substantial interest in the premises from taking any direct part in the proceedings, where there is a business sub-tenant in occupation of the holding in question. They are not free from difficulty. Where the interest of an intermediate landlord is continuing under LTA 1954, Pt II, he remains a 'competent landlord' for the purpose

---

42 *Southport Old Links Ltd v Naylor* [1985] 1 EGLR 66, CA; also *M&P Enterprises (London) Ltd v Norfolk Square Hotels Ltd* [1994] 1 EGLR 129.
43 As in *Dodson Bull Carpet Co Ltd v City of London Corpn* [1975] 2 All ER 497, [1975] 1 WLR 781 (tenancy of two properties not determinable by s 25 notice from landlord of severed part of reversion).
44 *Moss v Mobil Oil Co Ltd* [1988] 1 EGLR 71, CA.
45 Consult Consultation Paper 'Business Tenancies Legislation in England and Wales: the Government's Proposals for Reform' (2001) DETR, para 30.
46 What is said here applies with equal force to notices served on the landlord by the tenant.

of service of LTA 1954, ss 25 and 26 notices.[47] This applies whether or not the mesne landlord has granted a reversionary lease to the sub-tenant of part of the premises.[48] Once the head landlord has served a LTA 1954, s 25 notice on the intermediate landlord, who applies for a new tenancy, the latter ceases to be a 'competent landlord' and so, if his own tenant (of part of the whole premises) desires to request a new tenancy, he should serve any relevant notice on the head landlord. If he serves notices on the mesne landlord, he risks losing the right to apply for a new tenancy as time begins to run against him under LTA 1954, s 29(3). In one case, where the mesne landlord had served a LTA 1954, s 25 notice on his tenant (of part of the premises) and had subsequently requested a new tenancy from the head landlord, so ceasing to qualify as a 'competent landlord', the mesne landlord was under a duty to his tenant to correct the misrepresentation involved in his earlier s 25 notice that he was the 'competent landlord'. Since he had not, the (sub) tenants were entitled to apply for a new tenancy.[49]

4   A head landlord may terminate both the tenancy and any sub-tenancies derived out of it where the tenant is protected by LTA 1954, Pt II.[50]

III   TENANT'S REQUEST FOR A NEW TENANCY

The request

A tenant holding under a tenancy granted for a term of years certain exceeding one year, whether or not continued under LTA 1954, s 24(1), or for a term of years certain and thereafter from year to year, is entitled to apply for a new tenancy under LTA 1954, s 26 (LTA 1954, s 26(1)).[51] The LTA 1954, s 26 procedure cannot be used by a tenant who has already been given a LTA 1954, s 25 notice by his landlord; nor where the tenant has given a notice to terminate under LTA 1954, s 27 and a landlord cannot serve a s 25 notice if the tenant has already made a request for a new tenancy under LTA 1954, s 26 (LTA 1954, s 26(4)). In other words, the procedures under LTA 1954, ss 25 and 26 are mutually exclusive. Thus, if a landlord decides to leave serving a s 25 notice until the last minute, the tenant can, as things stand, pre-empt the landlord by serving a LTA 1954, s 26 request for a new tenancy. This will mean that, provided the notice expires after the maximum 12-month period, the tenant can obtain the benefit of 12 months' occupation at the old rent. The Law Commission disapproved of such tactics and proposed to combat them by adjusting the date from which interim rent

---

47   *Cornish v Brook Green Laundry* [1959] 1 QB 394, [1959] 1 All ER 373, CA.
48   *Bowes-Lyon v Green* [1963] AC 420, HL.
49   *Shelley v United Artists Corpn* [1990] 1 EGLR 103, CA.
50   LTA 1954, Sch 6, paras 6 and 7; *Lewis v MTC (Cars) Ltd* [1975] 1 All ER 874, [1975] 1 WLR 457, CA (competent landlord may determine business sub-tenancy before mesne tenancy expired).
51   See *Watkins v Emslie* [1982] 1 EGLR 81, CA.

under LTA 1954, s 24A is payable.[52] A tenant for a fixed term which does not exceed one year and periodic tenants have no right to request a new tenancy under LTA 1954, s 26, although they may apply for a new tenancy if the landlord serves on them a LTA 1954, s 25 notice of termination. The tenant's request must comply with a number of requirements.

1   It must be in the prescribed form.[53] It must be served on the 'competent landlord' within LTA 1954, s 44(1).[54]

2   The notice must specify the date on which the proposed tenancy is to begin, which must be not more than twelve nor less than six months after the date specified in the request (LTA 1954, s 26(2)). If this date is stated in error, the mistake can be overlooked provided that a reasonable recipient would have been in no doubt as to the correct date. Thus a landlord whose tenant broke their tenancy under a break-clause, so triggering a renewal claim under statute, by a notice giving the wrong date, was held bound to accept the notice. In all the circumstances, a reasonable recipient would have realised so plain a mistake, and would have read in the correct date.[55] The date specified in a LTA 1954, s 26 request must not be any earlier than the date on which the current tenancy would otherwise have expired by effluxion of time or could have been brought to an end by notice to quit given by the tenant (LTA 1954, s 26(2), proviso). The statutory reference to effluxion of time relates to fixed-term tenancies exceeding one year; that to notice to quit to periodic tenancies. Hence, a tenant holding a 20-year fixed-term business tenancy granted in June 1985 would not have been able to break the tenancy in June 1995, a right preserved by LTA 1954, s 24(2), and at the same time serve a LTA 1954, s 26 request for a new tenancy.[56] The court did not wish to confer on a tenant who validly broke his tenancy at common law some ten years ahead of time the right to obtain a new tenancy on more favourable terms in times of recession.

3   The tenant must, in his request, set out his proposals as to the property to be comprised in the new tenancy and as to the rent payable thereunder and as to the other terms of the new tenancy, otherwise his request is of no effect (LTA 1954, s 26(3)). These requirements have been construed, where relevant, as of pure form. Thus a tenant was held entitled to serve a LTA 1954, s 26 request with the relevant specifications even though he did not in fact apply for a new tenancy. Instead, he wished all along simply to protect his rights to statutory compensation on quitting. There was, it was said, no express requirement of an intention to claim

---

52 Law Com No 208 (1992), para 2.64. The revised date would be the earliest date that could have been specified in a s 26 request.

53 Landlord and Tenant Act 1954 Part II (Notices) Regulations 1983, SI 1983/133, Form No 8.

54 No doubt the tenant will make use of the registered post or the recorded delivery service, for if he does not, and uses the ordinary post, the notice is received only when actually delivered to the landlord: see *Railtrack plc v Gojra* [1998] 1 EGLR 63, CA.

55 *Garston v Scottish Widows Fund & Life Assurance Society* [1998] 3 All ER 596, CA.

56 *Garston v Scottish Widows Fund & Life Assurance Society* [1998] 3 All ER 596, CA.

a new tenancy.[57] The property to be comprised in the new tenancy need not necessarily be the whole premises held under the current lease. Indeed, where a tenant has sub-let part of the premises, it seems that he cannot properly claim renewal for that part, as it no longer forms part of the 'holding' within LTA 1954, s 23(3). If he has sub-let the whole, retaining only common parts, he seemingly cannot claim renewal at all.[58] The tenant should specify the length of the proposed new tenancy, as this is one of the 'terms' required by LTA 1954, s 26(3). Where a tenant failed to specify a term, but held under a seven-year term, it was held that he had impliedly requested a seven-year new tenancy by requesting that the other terms of the new tenancy should be the same as those of the current tenancy.[59]

Once the tenant has applied for a new tenancy, the current tenancy terminates immediately before the date specified in the request for the beginning of the new tenancy (LTA 1954, s 25(5)) subject to interim continuation (LTA 1954, s 64). Where, therefore, a tenant requested a new tenancy with a date specified in June 1971, but did nothing further until early 1973, at which time the landlord obtained an order for possession, his existing tenancy was held to have terminated immediately before the date specified in 1971. His application failed as he was no longer a tenant.[60] In principle, the time-limits laid down in LTA 1954, s 26 are strict. The tenant, moreover, must apply to the court, following a request, within the four months specified by LTA 1954, s 29(3), which run from the date of his request. If he fails to comply with this limit, he cannot make a second request under LTA 1954, s 26, having purportedly withdrawn the first, since LTA 1954, s 25(5) terminates his current tenancy. It makes no difference that he may have followed up his second request with an application to the court which is on time.[61]

Landlord's counter-notice

The prescribed form of a tenant's request for a new tenancy makes it clear that the landlord has the right to oppose the request. This he may do by serving a counter-notice on the tenant within two months of the making of the request for a new tenancy (LTA 1954, s 26(6)). The landlord's notice must state on which of the grounds given by LTA 1954, Pt II, s 30 the landlord will oppose the application. No prescribed form of notice is required for this particular notice.

57   *Sun Life Assurance plc v Thales Tracs Ltd* [2001] EWCA Civ 704, [2002] 1 All ER 64, CA. It was pointed out that entitlement to compensation under LTA 1954, Pt II, s 37 ought not to depend on the question of which party initiated the statutory notice procedures. No words could be read into the Act unless unavoidably necessary.

58   *Graysim Holdings Ltd v P&O Property Holdings Ltd* [1996] AC 329, [1995] 4 All ER 831, HL.

59   *Sidney Bolsom Investment Trust Ltd v E Karmios & Co (London) Ltd* [1956] 1 QB 529, [1956] 1 All ER 536, CA.

60   *Meah v Sector Properties Ltd* [1974] 1 All ER 1074, CA.

61   *Polyviou v Seeley* [1979] 3 All ER 853, CA; also *Stile Hall Properties Ltd v Gooch* [1979] 3 All ER 848, CA.

Time-limits

LTA 1954, s 26 imposes various time-limits on the tenant as a condition precedent of his making a valid request, but these are imposed for the sole benefit of the landlord, who may, if he so wishes, waive them by accepting an otherwise procedurally invalid notice.[62] In addition, the landlord may be estopped by conduct from insisting on a strict compliance with the statutory time-limits. Thus, a tenant served a LTA 1954, s 26 request which did not comply with these time-limits, but the landlord initially indicated that it would not oppose a new tenancy and gave no counter-notice under LTA 1954, s 26(6), but subsequently, having applied for an interim rent took the invalidity point.[63] The two grounds for upholding the tenant's request were, first, that the landlord accepted the notice; secondly, that he had in any case affirmed the tenancy by asking for an interim rent. By contrast, where, following a LTA 1954, s 26 request, the tenant applied too soon to the court, and the parties conducted abortive negotiations, the landlord had not impliedly represented to the tenant that he would not oppose a new tenancy, and the tenant lost his right to apply under LTA 1954, s 26.[64]

IV INTERIM RENT

Introduction

The landlord may apply to the court, if he has given a LTA 1954, s 25 notice or following a LTA 1954, s 26 tenant's request for a new tenancy, for the determination of a 'rent which it would be reasonable for the tenant to pay' during continuation under LTA 1954, s 24. The court has a discretion to fix what is known as an 'interim rent' (LTA 1954, s 24A(1)). The purpose of LTA 1954, s 24A is to prevent a tenant, in times of inflation, spinning out the steps required by the LTA 1954, Pt II, so as unfairly to prolong the continuation of the old rent. The interim rent is deemed to be payable either from the date on which the proceedings were commenced,[65] or the date specified in the landlord's notice or the tenant's request, whichever is the later (LTA 1954, s 24A(2)). In determining a rent under LTA 1954, s 24A, the court is bound to have regard to the rent payable under the terms of the tenancy. Otherwise LTA 1954, s 34(1) and (2) apply to the determination as if a new tenancy from year to year of the whole of the property comprised in the tenancy were granted to the tenant by order of the court (LTA 1954, s 24A(3)). Therefore an interim rent is an open market rent, taking into account the disregards required by LTA 1954, s 34, for a hypothetical new yearly tenancy on the same terms as the existing tenancy, so far as compatible with a yearly

---

62 *Kammins Ballrooms Co Ltd v Zenith Investments (Torquay) Ltd* [1971] AC 850, [1970] 2 All ER 871, HL.
63 *Bristol Cars Ltd v RKH Hotels Ltd* (1979) 38 P & CR 411, CA.
64 *Stevens & Cutting Ltd v Anderson* [1990] 1 EGLR 95, CA.
65 See *R v Gravesend County Court, ex p Patchett* [1993] 2 EGLR 125 (L applied in February and T discontinued proceedings in July, unaware of L's application; court could not later backdate L's application for the purposes of securing an interim rent).

tenancy.[66] The effect of the requirement that the court must have regard to the existing rent is that the court may at its discretion determine an interim rent which is less than the full market rent.[67]

Discounts from interim rent

The courts may, at their discretion, permit a discount from the interim rent so as to shield the tenant from too steep a jump in the rent from its old level. The question of whether any allowance may be made, and, if so, as to its amount, is at the discretion of the court, and the Court of Appeal will only interfere with the exercise of a county court judge's discretion if it is obviously wrong.[68] However, in one case a county court decision was held to be erroneous in law because the judge had paid insufficient attention to the fact that at the contractual termination date, a major company was leaving the precinct concerned. This had adversely affecting the value of the tenant's unit. Thus, a 3.275% reduction in the interim rent for the tenancy from year to year by way of a cushion was insufficient, and it was increased to 10%.[69] Subject to issues as to errors of law, the amount of any reduction is a question of fact. A 50% reduction has been allowed, exceptionally.[70] More modest reductions of the order of 6-10% have properly been made.[71]

Other matters

It is implicit in LTA 1954, s 24A(3) that the interim rent is to be a market rent throughout the whole period for which it is payable: thus, where proceedings were delayed for some three years and the interim rent was fixed at 300% above the old rent, the decision was upset on appeal, since for the earlier part of the three-year period, the rent was above the market level.[72] But where a tenant had enjoyed the benefit of a low rent in times of inflation, his advantage was not perpetuated, so as to cause injustice to the landlord and no discount was conferred.[73]

Regard must be had to the state of the premises, at the time when the relevant period starts: if they are then out of repair, in breach of a landlord's covenant, the court may

---

66 As notably in *Woodbridge v Westminster Press Ltd* [1987] 2 EGLR 97.

67 *English Exporters (London) Ltd v Eldonwall Ltd* [1973] Ch 415, [1973] 1 All ER 726; also *Ratners (Jewellers) Ltd v Lemnoll* [1980] 2 EGLR 65; *UDS Tailoring Ltd v BL Holdings Ltd* [1982] 1 EGLR 61.

68 *Halberstam v Tandalco Corpn NV* [1985] 1 EGLR 90, CA; *Khalique v Law Land plc* [1989] 1 EGLR 105, CA.

69 *French v Commercial Union Life Assurance Co Ltd* [1993] 1 EGLR 113, CA.

70 *Charles Follett Ltd v Cabtell Investment Co Ltd* (1987) 55 P & CR 36, CA.

71 As in *Janes (Gowns) Ltd v Harlow Development Corpn* [1980] 1 EGLR 52.

72 *Conway v Arthur* [1988] 2 EGLR 113, CA; also *French v Commercial Union Life Assurance* [1993] 1 EGLR 113.

73 *Department of the Environment v Allied Freehold Property Trust Ltd* [1993] 2 EGLR 100 (Cty ct).

determine a differential interim rent, so that the landlord only recovers the full amount if and when he remedies his breaches.[74] Once the application for an interim rent has been made, the fact that the tenant later withdraws his application does not affect the jurisdiction to order an interim rent.[75] The fact that the reversion is assigned once an application for interim rent is made also makes no difference and the new landlord obtains the benefit of it.[76]

Reform

The Law Commission proposed a number of reforms to the principles of interim rent, which was first introduced in 1969. First, they recommend that the tenant, as well as the landlord, should be able to apply for an interim rent. They accepted that as long as commercial rents rise, such applications are not likely, but say that the reform would show the law as even-handed.[77] Secondly, they proposed moving the date from which interim rent is payable where the renewal procedure begins with a tenant's request for a new tenancy, to the earliest date which could have been specified in the tenant's notice, not as at present, the latest date.[78] The government indicated that they have accepted both of these proposals.[79] It is understood that these will be implemented by delegated legislation. The Commission also had proposals about the amount of interim rent.[80] In particular, if the tenant was going to have a new tenancy under LTA 1954, Pt II, they recommended that the interim rent was to be equal to the rent payable under the new tenancy, if granted, as from the start of that lease. The current formula would apply in other cases in principle. The government have indicated that they wish the amount of interim rent to be based on market values prevailing when the interim rent first became payable. In a rising market, this would produce a lower interim rent than the new tenancy rent. In a falling market the interim rent would produce a higher figure than the new tenancy rent.[81]

74 *Fawke v Viscount Chelsea* [1980] QB 441, [1979] 3 All ER 568, CA.
75 *Michael Kramer & Co v Airways Pension Fund Trustees Ltd* [1978] 1 EGLR 49; *Artoc Bank and Trust Ltd v Prudential Assurance Co plc* [1984] 3 All ER 538, [1984] 1 WLR 1181; *Benedictus v Jalaram Ltd* [1989] 1 EGLR 251, CA.
76 *Bloomfield v Ashwright Ltd* (1983) 47 P & CR 78, CA.
77 Law Com No 208 (1992), para 2.63. There would, they thought, have to be provision to extend back the date for payment of interim rent to the earliest date the landlord could have served a LTA 1954, s 25 notice, to combat abuse where the landlord would get a higher rent than payable on an interim basis. Hence, this principle would, said the Commission, only apply if the tenant applied for interim rent (para 2.65).
78 Law Com No 208 (1992), para 2.64: see further the treatment of LTA 1954, s 26 requests above. The backdating effect would be applied only where the landlord applied for interim rent (para 2.65).
79 Consultation Paper 'Business Tenancies Legislation in England and Wales: the Government's Proposals for Reform' (2001) DETR, paras 46-51.
80 Law Com No 208 (1992), paras 2.67-2.71. As to the recommended forum for interim rent applications see paras 2.72-2.75.
81 Consultation Paper 'Business Tenancies Legislation in England and Wales: the Government's Proposals for Reform' (2001) DETR, para 53. In the anticipated delegated legislation, it is

V   TENANT'S RIGHT TO APPLY TO THE COURT FOR A NEW TENANCY

If the tenant considers that the landlord has uncontestable grounds of opposition, he may decide to quit and not to apply to the court for a new tenancy under LTA 1954, s 24(1). In that event, the current tenancy will come to an end on the date specified in the landlord's LTA 1954, s 25 notice or the tenant's LTA 1954, s 26 request for a new tenancy. If the tenant decides to quit after receiving a landlord's counter-notice relying on LTA 1954, s 30(1), grounds (e)-(g) having applied for a new tenancy, and seeks leave to withdraw his application, leave will generally be given unconditionally in the absence of intervening prejudice to the landlord. If the landlord withdraws his opposition, he cannot in these circumstances avoid paying compensation to the tenant.[82]

The parties may negotiate, after the service of the various statutory notices and counter-notices, for the grant of a new tenancy by agreement out of court: but the tenant should beware of allowing the time-limit laid down by LTA 1954, s 29(3) of not less than two[83] nor more than four months after the original notice was served to pass: if he does so, and fails to apply to court within the prescribed time-limit, he will be unable to apply unless the court exceptionally agrees to extend the time-limits.[84] The government is likely to allow the parties to apply to court at any time to extend the time-limit for making an application to court.[85] If the parties agree on all the terms of a new tenancy, the current tenancy is continued until the new tenancy commences (LTA 1954, s 28). If the tenant applies to the court under LTA 1954, s 24(1) for a new tenancy, but before the hearing the parties agree on the grant of a new tenancy, the tenant may withdraw his application. Alternatively, the parties may ask the court to order a new tenancy on the terms agreed.

---

expected that the government will allow the courts to adjust the amount of interim rent where, for example, the terms of the new tenancy (other than as to rent and duration) differ from those of the period for which interim rent is payable and would have a substantial effect on the rental value of the tenancy.

82   *Lloyds Bank Ltd v City of London Corpn* [1983] Ch 192, [1983] 1 All ER 92; also *Fribourg & Treyer Ltd v Northdale Investments Ltd* (1982) 44 P & CR 284.

83   Two months means just that: the period ends on the corresponding date in the relevant month: *EJ Riley Investments v Eurostile Holdings Ltd* [1985] 3 All ER 181, [1985] 1 WLR 1139, CA.

84   As in *Saloman v Akiens* [1993] 1 EGLR 101, CA, where correspondence in negotiations for a new tenancy following a LTA 1954, s 25 notice was 'subject to contract'.

85   Consultation Paper 'Business Tenancies Legislation in England and Wales: the Government's Proposals for Reform' (2001) DETR, paras 41-45. In addition, once the landlord had given a LTA 1954, s 25 notice, the tenant would be entitled to apply to the court without delay but if the tenant had served a LTA 1954, s 26 request, he could not apply to court until the landlord had served a counter-notice or until two months from the service of such counter-notice had expired.

CHAPTER 23

Grounds of opposition

A landlord who cannot terminate a business tenancy by one of the permitted common law or other methods is entitled to defeat tenant renewal and to regain possession of the premises if he is able to establish one of a number of statutory grounds of opposition. He must inform the tenant in his LTA 1954, s 25 notice or LTA 1954, s 26(6) counter-notice of which, if any, ground he intends to rely on, and then prove the ground at the hearing. The court must dismiss the application if it is satisfied that the landlord has established any ground stated in his notice (LTA 1954, s 31(1)). 'Landlord' includes any successor in title, so that the latter may rely on his predecessor's notice, if he is landlord at the date of the hearing.[1] The statutory grounds, with the exception of that relating to alternative accommodation, fall into two classes. Some relate to breaches of tenants' obligations, which, if proved, enable the landlord to evict the tenant without having to pay him 'disturbance' compensation. Others entitle the tenant to compensation, if established, as the price for the landlord to obtain possession.[2] The largest number of reported cases centres, as might be imagined, around the grounds entitling the landlord to repossession in order to redevelop the premises or to occupy them for his own business. The existence of these various grounds emphasise the

1   *Betty's Cafes Ltd v Phillips Furnishing Stores Ltd* [1957] Ch 67, CA; *Marks v British Waterways Board* [1963] 3 All ER 28, CA.
2   However, if alternative accommodation is available, below, the tenant does not need such compensation and so is not given it. The government proposes to extend the right to compensation where it already applies to cases where the landlord successfully opposes a new tenancy on the ground that it is the intention of a company controlled by him to occupy the premises. It also proposes to extend compensation where there is no renewal following successful proceedings by the landlord to end the tenancy but where no fault is involved by the tenant (ie under LTA 1954, s 30(1)(e) to (g)). See Consultation Paper 'Business Tenancies in England and Wales; the Government's Proposals for Reform' (2001) DETR, para 57; also Law Com No 208 (1992), para 2.81. The latter reform was proposed owing to the proposal that a landlord should be able to start termination proceedings to end the tenancy without renewal.

overriding rights of the landlord and the qualified nature of the statutory renewal rights. Indeed, the courts have said more than once that LTA 1954 grounds of opposition must, as with the rest of the Act, be construed sensibly. A fair balance must be held between the interests of landlord and tenant.[3] Thus neither LTA 1954, s 30(1)(f) nor s 30(1)(g) in particular, the most litigated grounds, are intended to create a series of artificial hoops through which the landlord must jump before he satisfies the required intention.[4] As a result of this relatively benign approach as far as landlords are concerned, there is for example a relatively low level of proof with regard to landlords' intentions to occupy the premises for the purposes of their own business.[5]

LTA 1954, s 30(1)(a): breach of repairing obligations

where under the current tenancy the tenant has any obligations as respects the repair and maintenance of the holding, that the tenant ought not to be granted a new tenancy in view of the state of repair of the holding, being a state resulting from the tenant's failure to comply with the said obligations.

The breach must exist at the date of service of the notice. It is not enough for the landlord to prove that the tenant is in substantial breach of a repairing obligation: he must satisfy the court that the breach is so serious that the tenant 'ought not', in the court's discretion, to be granted a new tenancy because the court may grant a new tenancy despite the breach.[6] An undertaking by the tenant to remedy the breach would be taken into account by the court in the exercise of its discretion.[7] The question is whether it would be unfair to the landlord, having regard to the tenant's part conduct, to grant the latter a new tenancy: where the past breaches, which will be taken into account, were serious and the tenant had neglected his covenant to repair, a new tenancy was refused.[8]

LTA 1954, s 30(1)(b): persistent delay in paying rent

the tenant ought not to be granted a new tenancy in view of his persistent delay in paying rent due under the current tenancy.

3   See eg *Dolgellau Golf Club v Hett* [1998] L & TR 217, CA.
4   *Palisade Investments Ltd v Collin Estates Ltd* [1992] 2 EGLR 94 at 97, CA.
5   See eg *Gatwick Parking Services Ltd v Sargent* [2000] 2 EGLR 45, CA; Haley [2000] Conv 456. A legitimate landlord's claim can defeat an equally legitimate tenant renewal expectation and turn it into a compensation claim. It is not without significance that neither the Law Commission (Law Com No 208 (1992), paras 3.25-3.29) nor the DETR ('Business Tenancies Legislation in England and Wales: the Government's Proposals for Reform' (2001)) proposed any change in the law affecting landlords' grounds of opposition except those consequent on company incorporation or those flowing from the proposal that landlords should in future be able to ask for a possession order without the grant of a new tenancy.
6   *Nihad v Chain* (1956) 167 Estates Gazette 139.
7   *Lyons v Central Commercial Properties Ltd* [1958] 2 All ER 767, 775, CA.
8   *Lyons v Central Commercial Properties Ltd* [1958] 2 All ER 767, CA.

'Persistent delay' means a course of conduct over a period of time. The court will have regard to the frequency and extent of the delays,[9] and the steps the landlord was obliged to take to secure repayment and the question of how the landlord may be secured in any new tenancy against future breaches of this covenant.[10] Once persistent delay has been proved by the landlord, the tenant may persuade the court to grant him a new tenancy if, for example, he has a good explanation for the delay and can demonstrate that it was exceptional.[11] Thus, where a county court judge was satisfied with a tenant's explanation for persistent delays in paying rent over two and a half years, payments having thereafter been prompt, the Court of Appeal declined to interfere with his decision, on such a question of fact, to order a new tenancy.[12]

LTA 1954, s 30(1)(c): other substantial breaches

the tenant ought not to be granted a new tenancy in view of other substantial breaches by him of his obligations under the current tenancy, or for any other reason connected with the tenant's use or management of the holding.

The seriousness of any alleged breach will thus be considered,[13] and the question of whether the breach is or is not continuing in nature is relevant. In the case of a remediable breach, the court will take into account whether it has been remedied and whether the breach has in any case been waived. LTA 1954, s 30(1)(c) is based on fault generally, going beyond any breaches of obligation. The landlord may thus rely on the fact that the tenant's continued user of the holding would constitute a breach of a planning enforcement order.[14] In its discretion (para (c) being a discretionary ground in view of the words 'ought not') the court has regard to all relevant circumstances, and the general conduct of the tenant.[15] The landlord's interest must be shown to be prejudiced and where a county court judge did not indicate which matters he took into account, apart from the tenant illegally keeping his van on a grass verge, the case was remitted.[16] However, only if the county court's decision is vitiated by an error of law will the Court of Appeal interfere, as where there was no evidence to support a finding that rooms in a basement flat had been converted into a laundry.[17]

---

9   *Hopcutt v Carver* (1969) 209 Estates Gazette 1069, CA. See also *Hazel v Akhtar* [2001] EWCA Civ 1883, [2002] 1 P & CR D34 (where landlords were estopped by conduct from insisting without notice on prompt payment, since their predecessors had accepted delayed payment).
10 *Rawashdeh v Lane* [1988] 2 EGLR 109, CA.
11 *Betty's Cafes Ltd v Phillips Furnishing Stores* [1957] Ch 67, CA.
12 *Hurstfell Ltd v Leicester Square Property Co Ltd* [1988] 2 EGLR 105, CA.
13 See eg *Norton v Charles Deane Productions Ltd* (1969) 214 Estates Gazette 559.
14 *Turner and Bell v Searles (Stanford-le-Hope) Ltd* (1977) 33 P & CR 208, CA.
15 *Eichner v Midland Bank Executor and Trustee Co Ltd* [1970] 2 All ER 597, [1970] 1 WLR 1120; *Hutchinson v Lamberth* [1984] 1 EGLR 75.
16 *Beard v Williams* [1986] 1 EGLR 148, CA.
17 *Jones v Jenkins* [1986] 1 EGLR 113, CA.

LTA 1954, s 30(1)(d): suitable alternative accommodation

the landlord has offered and is willing to provide or secure the provision of alternative accommodation for the tenant. The terms on which the alternative accommodation is available are reasonable having regard to the terms of the current tenancy and to all other relevant circumstances. The accommodation and the time at which it will become available must be suitable for the tenant's requirements (including the requirement to preserve goodwill), having regard to the nature and class of his business and to the situation and extent of, and facilities afforded by, the holding.

The landlord must have made an offer in good faith, which he is still able and willing to honour. Despite the use of the present tense in LTA 1954, s 30(1)(d) the offer need only be made before the issue is joined in pleadings, and need not be made before the service of a LTA 1954, s 25 notice.[18] If the offer is of part only of the accommodation, he must prove that the part in question is sufficient for the tenant's business purposes as at the date of the hearing. Paragraph (d) is not discretionary, so that if the landlord establishes it, the application must be dismissed.[19] Thereafter the tenant must accept the landlord's offer or run the risk of having to quit the premises with no compensation for disturbance.

LTA 1954, s 30(1)(e): possession required for letting or disposing of the property as a whole

the tenant ought not to be granted a new tenancy where the current tenancy was created by the sub-letting of part only of the property comprised in a superior tenancy and the landlord is the owner of a superior interest in reversion expectant on the termination of that superior tenancy; the aggregate of the rents reasonably obtainable on separate lettings must be substantially less than the rent reasonably obtainable on a letting of the property as a whole; and on the termination of the current tenancy the landlord requires possession of the holding for the purpose of letting or otherwise disposing of the property as a whole.

Where LTA 1954, s 30(1)(e) applies, a superior landlord has, under LTA 1954, s 44(1), become the competent landlord as against a sub-lessee of part of the premises. If, at the date of the hearing, the landlord is merely the immediate landlord of the tenant, para (e) cannot be invoked by him. The landlord's requirement of possession must arise on the termination of the current tenancy (that held by the tenant requesting a new tenancy) so that the landlord has to prove that the intermediate tenancy will come to an end by the termination date of the current sub-tenancy. It is, however, sufficient if the landlord proves that the intermediate tenancy will come to an end within the period specified as sufficient to entitle him to a LTA 1954, s 31 declaration. LTA 1954,

---

18   *M Chaplin Ltd v Regent Capital Holdings Ltd* [1994] 1 EGLR 249 (Cty ct).
19   *Betty's Cafes Ltd v Phillips Furnishing Stores Ltd* [1957] Ch 67 at 84, [1957] 1 All ER 1 at 8.

s 30(1)(e) is discretionary. The court would presumably take into account the fact that the landlord had consented to the sub-letting. Because of the requirement that the landlord must show that the total rents for the whole premises would be substantially higher if let as a whole then if it were re-let in parts, it was not sufficient for a landlord to prove only that the aggregate rents of parts of the premises were less, but not substantially less, than the total rent of the whole.[20]

LTA 1954, s 30(1)(f): landlord intends to demolish or reconstruct

on the termination of the current tenancy the landlord intends to demolish or reconstruct the whole or a substantial part of the premises,[21] or to carry out substantial work of construction on the holding or part, and he cannot reasonably do so without obtaining possession of the holding.

Landlord's intention The landlord[22] must have a clear and settled intention. If the proposed works require planning permission, the landlord must prove that there is a real chance, a prospect that is strong enough to be acted upon by a reasonable landlord, as opposed to a fanciful prospect, that permission will be obtained. He is not required to show on the balance of probabilities that he will obtain planning permission.[23] This light requirement emphasises the fact that renewal rights under LTA 1954, Pt II are relative and not absolute. However, a landlord who fails to show even that he has a reasonable prospect of obtaining planning permission for works can only be said to be contemplating and not genuinely intending the desired course of action.[24]

Often the required intention is proved by the existence of a works programme. Should the execution of this involve a technical illegality (as where the works might as planned contravene a conservation order) this will not prevent reliance on LTA 1954, s 30(1)(f) provided that the incidental illegality can be avoided, as by a different method of carrying out the works.[25] The intention must be proved at the time of the hearing.[26] In

---

20 *Greaves Organisation Ltd v Stanhope Gate Property Co Ltd* (1973) 228 Estates Gazette 725.
21 Ie land with or even without buildings on it: *Pumperninks of Piccadilly Ltd v Land Securities Ltd* [2002] 21 EG 142 (CS).
22 Or, in the case of joint landlords, the survivor, if one of them dies before the hearing: *Biles v Caesar* [1957] 1 All ER 151, [1957] 1 WLR 156, CA. 'Landlord' refers to the competent landlord within LTA 1954, Pt II, s 44. Thus a freeholder who also held a sub-lease from an intermediate landlord could take advantage of LTA 1954, s 30(1)(f): *Shiel v St Helens MBC* [1997] CLY 3266.
23 *Cadogan v McCarthy & Stone (Developments) Ltd* [2000] L & TR 249, CA.
24 *Cadogan v McCarthy & Stone (Developments) Ltd* [2000] L & TR 249, CA. For a case where the landlord failed to discharge the required onus of proof see *Coppin v Bruce-Smith* [1998] EGCS 55, CA.
25 *Parkside Investments Ltd v Colln Estates Ltd* [1992] 2 EGLR 94, CA (but the result in this case would have been different if the works could only have been carried out illegally).
26 *Betty's Cafes Ltd v Phillips Furnishing Stores Ltd* [1957] Ch 67, [1957] 1 All ER 1, CA; *Aberdeen Steak Houses Group plc v Crown Estate Comrs* [1997] 2 EGLR 107.

the case of a company, its resolutions may afford evidence of the requisite intention,[27] and in the case of a local authority, the requisite intention may be gathered from committee minutes or from its officers.[28] If the landlord gains possession and subsequently changes his mind, the tenant has no recourse against him.[29] The 'intention', whose existence is ultimately one of fact and degree,[30] must have moved out of the zone of contemplation into the valley of decision.[31] The landlord must show that his project is viable and has a reasonable prospect of being carried out. The court does not expect to examine all the details of the scheme provided such a prospect is shown,[32] once finance and other general arrangements, such as with a building contractor, have been made, even if not all the details of the latter two points have been settled.[33] It is not necessary to show that binding contracts have been entered into in connection with the work.[34] On the other hand, there must not be too many obstacles left for the landlord to clear. Where a planning permission for site clearance imposed onerous conditions, which the landlord was not able to comply with at the date of the hearing; he had also not selected a developer, without whose participation his development project would fail, and so the landlord failed under LTA 1954, s 30(1)(f).[35]

The landlord is entitled to choose his own method of work, even if a different scheme would not involve the tenant quitting the whole holding.[36] If the landlord intends, on regaining possession, as opposed to at some future date,[37] to sell his interest, he cannot satisfy LTA 1954, s 30(1)(f). Since he does not necessarily have to carry out the work personally, para (f) may be satisfied if the landlord definitely intends to grant a building lease to a developer.[38] The precise length of any building lease is not, in itself, a significant matter: in one case, para (f) was satisfied by a local authority landlord

---

27 *Betty's Cafes Ltd v Phillips Furnishing Stores Ltd* [1957] Ch 67, [1957] 1 All ER 1, CA.

28 *Poppetts (Caterers) Ltd v Maidenhead Corpn* [1971] 1 WLR 69, CA.

29 See *Reohorn v Barry Corpn* [1956] 2 All ER 742, CA (where the requisite intention was not proved).

30 *Fleet Electrics Ltd v Jacey Investments Ltd* [1956] 3 All ER 99, CA; *DAF Motoring Centre (Gosport) Ltd v Hatfield & Wheeler Ltd* [1982] 2 EGLR 59, CA.

31 *Cunliffe v Goodman* [1950] 2 KB 237 at 254, CA.

32 *A Levy & Son Ltd v Martin Brent Developments Ltd* [1987] 2 EGLR 93; *Peter Goddard & Sons Ltd v Hounslow London Borough Council* [1992] 1 EGLR 281, CA; also *Aberdeen Steak Houses plc v Crown Estate Comrs* [1997] 2 EGLR 107.

33 *Capocci v Goble* [1987] 2 EGLR 102, CA.

34 *Capocci v Goble* [1987] 2 EGLR 102, CA.

35 *Edwards v Thompson* [1990] 2 EGLR 71. However, owing to the prospect of a successful scheme being worked out, the tenant obtained a one-year tenancy.

36 *Decca Navigator Co Ltd v Greater London Council* [1974] 1 All ER 1178, [1974] 1 WLR 748, CA.

37 *Turner v Wandsworth London Borough Council* [1994] 1 EGLR 134, CA.

38 *PE Ahern & Sons Ltd v Hunt* [1988] 1 EGLR 74; *Spook Erection Ltd v British Railways Board* [1988] 1 EGLR 76, CA; *Aberdeen Steak Houses Group plc v Crown Estate Comrs* [1997] 2 EGLR 107.

which intended to grant a developer a four-year lease, once it had cleared and replanted the site.[39]

An intention to carry out work within LTA 1954, s 30(1)(f) need not be the primary purpose. Hence, neither the fact that the landlord intended, after demolition works, to incorporate the premises in an agricultural holding,[40] nor that he intended, after demolition, to rebuild the premises and occupy them himself,[41] precluded him from invoking para (f).

Although the requisite intention must be to carry out the work at termination of the tenancy, this refers to the time the landlord actually obtains possession, which may be a few weeks after the hearing.[42] Under LTA 1954, s 31(2), if the landlord fails under LTA 1954, s 30(1)(f) but would have succeeded at such later date (within one year of the date specified in the LTA 1954, s 25 notice or LTA 1954, s 26 request) as the court determines, the court may make a declaration to that effect. It is then not to order a new tenancy.[43] The landlord did not have to rely on para (f) where, the tenant having left the premises voluntarily for new temporary accommodation, thus giving the landlord possession, his premises had ceased to exist as a separate entity due to works of reconstruction.[44]

Since the court is supposed to make a finding as to which part of LTA 1954, s 30(1)(f) particular work relates,[45] it is necessary to examine the various items of work in an overall way. The courts do not adopt an item-by-item approach. If, taken as a whole, the work is, for example, structural or building work, it will satisfy para (f) even if it may contain individual items of work which, in isolation would not,[46] since the position as a whole is looked at.

'Demolition' in LTA 1954, s 30(1)(f) presents no difficulty, but 'substantial work of construction' in the second limb of para (f) is less simple and whether work falls within this category is a question of degree and impression.[47] To take two extreme contrasts, it includes the amalgamation of two shops by the substantial removal of a party wall and other major structural alterations,[48] but does not include the removal of material, in-filling and landscaping.[49] The nature and extent of the proposed work must be taken

39   *Turner v Wandsworth London Borough Council* [1994] 1 EGLR 134, CA.
40   *Craddock v Hampshire County Council* [1958] 1 WLR 202, CA.
41   *Fisher v Taylors Furnishing Stores Ltd* [1956] 2 QB 78, CA.
42   See also *Livestock Underwriting Agency v Corbett and Newsom* (1955) 165 Estates Gazette 469.
43   The tenant has 14 days from the making of the declaration to have the termination date of the tenancy put off by up to one year to the date indicated by the court (LTA 1954, s 31(2)).
44   *Aireps Ltd v City of Bradford Metropolitan Corpn* [1985] 2 EGLR 143, CA.
45   *Romulus Trading Co Ltd v Henry Smith's Charity Trustees* [1990] 2 EGLR 75, CA.
46   *Joel v Swaddle* [1957] 3 All ER 325, [1957] 1 WLR 1044, CA; *Romulus Trading Co Ltd v Henry Smith's Charity Trustees* [1990] 2 EGLR 75, CA.
47   *Cook v Mott* (1961) 178 Estates Gazette 637, CA.
48   *Bewlay (Tobacconists) Ltd v British Bata Shoe Co Ltd* [1958] 3 All ER 652, [1959] 1 WLR 45, CA.
49   *Botterill v Bedfordshire County Council* [1985] 1 EGLR 82, CA.

into account in order to decide if it involves 'substantial' work of construction. A plan
to build an extension over a period of nearly four months, at a cost of upwards of
£8,000, so considerably improving the premises, qualified.[50] The requirement that the
work is 'substantial' limits the landlord, since, if the work, taken as a whole, is not
building work, affecting the structure of a building, it will not qualify. Thus, work
involving the re-siting of a staircase, re-wiring, the installation of central heating, re-
roofing and redecoration, was not 'substantial work of construction'.[51] Similarly, the
word 'reconstruct' in the first part of para (f) requires there to be a substantial
interference with the structure of the premises and then a measure of rebuilding,
before work may qualify.[52]

LTA 1954, s 31A defences

To prevent the landlord from gaining possession of the whole premises where he only
intends to carry out work on part of the premises, or where the duration of the work to
the whole premises will be very short, the tenant has a defence under LTA 1954, s 31A.
The tenant must establish a defence under LTA 1954, s 31A but since it is related to
LTA 1954, s 30(1)(f) the court must consider this ground in the light of s 31A. The
tenant may put forward conditional arguments so that if para (f) were to be satisfied,
the tenant would then accept a tenancy of part of the holding.[53] Section 31A provides
that the court cannot hold that the landlord could not reasonably carry out the demolition
or other work without obtaining possession if:

1   the tenant agrees to the inclusion in the terms of the new tenancy of terms giving
the landlord access and other facilities for the carrying out of the work intended
and, given that access and facilities, the landlord could reasonably carry out the
work without obtaining possession of the holding and interfering to a substantial
extent or for a substantial time with the use of the holding for the purpose of a
business carried on by the tenant; or
2   the tenant is willing to accept a tenancy of an economically separable part of the
holding[54] and either LTA 1954, s 31A(1)(a) is satisfied with respect to that part or
possession of the remainder of the holding would be reasonably sufficient to
enable the landlord to carry out the intended work.

The expression 'work intended' in LTA 1954, s 31A(1)(a) refers to work which could
not be done by the landlord without obtaining possession (and not, therefore, work

50 *Morar v Chauhan* [1985] 3 All ER 493, [1985] 1 WLR 1263, CA.
51 *Barth v Pritchard* [1990] 1 EGLR 109; also *Joel v Swaddle* [1957] 3 All ER 325, [1957] 1
WLR 1044, CA.
52 *Percy E Cadle & Co Ltd v Jacmarch Properties Ltd* [1957] 1 QB 323, [1957] 1 All ER 148,
CA.
53 *Romulus Trading Co Ltd v Henry Smith's Charity Trustees* (No 2) [1991] 1 EGLR 95, CA.
54 See LTA 1954, s 31A(2): the aggregate of rents reasonably obtainable on separate lettings of
that part, after completion of the work, in addition to those from the rest of the premises,
must not, for LTA 1954, s 30(1) (b) to apply, be substantially less than the rent reasonably
obtainable from letting the whole premises.

which he is entitled to enter and carry out pursuant to an express term in the lease).[55] If the landlord's right of access is wide enough to enable him to complete the work, as where it refers to improvement, alteration and addition, and this is what the landlord intends to do, LTA 1954, s 31A(1)(a) will preclude him relying on LTA 1954, s 30(1)(f).[56] Should the work go outside the contemplation of an entry clause, as with total rebuilding, it is otherwise.[57] If the right of entry is wide enough to allow the landlord to do part of the work, but not the whole, the court must decide which part falls within and which without the clause. It must then, in relation to the work outside the clause, make rulings as to the effect of that work on the tenant's business and whether LTA 1954, s 31A(1)(a) applies.[58]

The court looks at the physical effects of the work, as opposed to their results from a business point of view.[59] Whether the proposed work will, within LTA 1954, s 31A(1)(a) interfere with the use of the holding 'to a substantial extent and for a substantial time' is a question of fact, and the duration, extent and nature of the work are all relevant factors, as is the nature of the tenant's business.[60] If the tenant's business will be closed or severely disrupted for more than a very few weeks, he cannot invoke LTA 1954, s 31A(1)(a). Where the works would last for two weeks, closing and vacating the premises, there was an insufficient interference with the tenant's business.[61] By contrast, where, owing to the works, the tenant's cafe would be closed for at least 12 weeks, the interference was very substantial, having regard to the type of business, and the tenant failed to make out a LTA 1954, s 31A(1)(a) defence.[62]

LTA 1954, s 30(1)(g): landlord's intention to occupy the premises

on the termination of the current tenancy the landlord intends to occupy the premises for the purposes or partly for the purposes of a business to be carried on there by him, or as his residence.

(i) Intention

The test for the sufficiency of the landlord's intention is similar to that applicable to LTA 1954, s 30(1)(f). It is objective, and requires proof by the landlord of his settled

---

55 *Heath v Drown* [1973] AC 498, [1972] 2 All ER 561, HL; see Wilkinson (1985) 135 NLJ 145.
56 *Price v Esso Petroleum Ltd* [1980] 2 EGLR 58, CA.
57 *Leathwoods Ltd v Total Oil Great Britain Ltd* (1985) 51 P & CR 20, CA; *Pumperninks of Piccadilly Ltd v Land Securities Ltd* [2002] 21 EG 142 (CS).
58 *Cerex Jewels Ltd v Peachey Property Corpn plc* (1986) 52 P & CR 127, CA.
59 *Redfern v Reeves* (1978) 37 P & CR 364, CA. As with LTA 1954, s 30(1)(f), the landlord is entitled to choose his method of work: if this requires possession of the whole, the tenant cannot invoke LTA 1954, s 31A by showing that an alternative scheme would involve possession of part only of the holding.
60 *Mularczyk v Azralnove Investments Ltd* [1985] 2 EGLR 141, CA.
61 *Cerex Jewels Ltd v Peachey Property Corpn plc* [1986] 2 EGLR 65, CA.
62 *Blackburn v Hussain* [1988] 1 EGLR 77.

and firm intention to occupy[63], to be carried out in the reasonable future. This may be within a reasonable time of the termination of the lease if the landlord first intends to carry out work.[64] Subject to bearing in mind that the requisite onus of proof on the landlord relates mainly to the genuineness of a landlord's intentions, the issue is often a question of fact.[65] In the case of a company landlord, evidence of its intention may be proved by a manager with authority delegated to him by the board of directors,[66] or it may be established by a resolution of the board of directors. Where relevant, a reasonable prospect of his obtaining any necessary planning permission must be shown by the landlord, as opposed to a fanciful prospect of his doing so.[67]

The relevant date is thus the date of the hearing[68] and it is not necessary to produce evidence that the relevant intention existed before them.[69] However, a landlord who intends to occupy even only for a short time prior to selling the premises will generally come within LTA 1954, s 30(1)(g).[70] A company (or other) landlord with the requisite intention does not have to show what particular part of the business it intends to transfer to the subject premises.[71] In any event, once a sufficient intention is shown by the landlord, he does not have to show that he intends to make physical use of the entire holding.[72] The courts do not impose very heavy burdens of proof on landlords. The landlord is not required to show that he will achieve a start to his business, still less that it is going to be successful after then.[73] According to one commentator,[74] the

---

63 *Europark (Midlands) Ltd v Town Centre Securities plc* [1985] 1 EGLR 88; *Mirza v Nicola* [1990] 2 EGLR 73, CA.
64 As in *London Hilton Jewellers Ltd v Hilton International Hotels Ltd* [1990] 1 EGLR 112, CA.
65 See eg *Cox v Binfield* [1989] 1 EGLR 97, CA (genuine but 'ill thought out' plans were held to be sufficiently genuine to satisfy the relevant test).
66 *Manchester Garages Ltd v Petrofina* (UK) Ltd [1975] EGD 69, CA.
67 *Gregson v Cyril Lord Ltd* [1962] 3 All ER 907, [1963] 1 WLR 41, CA; *Cadogan v McCarthy & Stone Developments Ltd* [2000] L & TR 249, CA; *Dolgellau Golf Club v Hett* [1998] L & TR 217, CA.
68 It is assumed, as with LTA 1954, s 30(1)(f), that, if the landlord proves a sufficient intention, this will be the same at the date of the hearing and the expiry of interim continuation: *Expresso Coffee Machine Co Ltd v Guardian Assurance Co* [1958] 2 All ER 692, [1958] 1 WLR 900; affd [1959] 1 All ER 458, [1959] 1 WLR 250, CA; *Chez Gerard Ltd v Greene Ltd* [1983] 2 EGLR 79, CA.
69 *J W Thornton Ltd v Blacks Leisure Group plc* (1986) 53 P & CR 223, CA. Thus a resolution of a company board was accepted as evidence of the required intention during the hearing: *London Hilton Jewellers Ltd v Hilton International Hotels Ltd* [1990] 1 EGLR 112, CA.
70 *Willis v Association of Universities of the British Commonwealth* [1965] 1 QB 140, CA.
71 *Mash & Austin Ltd v Odhams Press Ltd* (1957) 169 Estates Gazette 655; *Pelosi v Bourne* (1957) 169 Estates Gazette 656.
72 *Method Developments Ltd v Jones* [1971] 1 All ER 1027, [1971] 1 WLR 168, CA.
73 *Dolgellau Golf Club v Hett* [1998] L & TR 217, CA. Thus, a landlord who proved that he had a real intention to start his own golf club business, did not in that case have to produce detailed plans, permissions or consents. The court was not prepared to subject him to a minute examination of his finances.
74 Wilkinson (1998) NLJ, 6 November, p 1644.

courts have relaxed the test of intention.[75] The possibility of success needed only to be considered in relation to the genuineness of the landlord's intention.

Legislation imposes a solution in two cases where the person who is likely to occupy is not the person who gave the LTA 1954, s 25 or s 26(6) notice.

1 *Trusts.* By LTA 1954, s 41(2), if the landlord's interest is held on trust[76] then, because references to the 'landlord' include the beneficiaries, or any of them, LTA 1954, s 30(1)(g) may be invoked if either the landlord or any beneficiary intends to carry on a business on the premises.[77] However, any beneficiary claiming thus to invoke para (g) must be entitled to occupy solely under his trust interest and not otherwise, as under a lease granted by the beneficiaries to some, but not all of their number.[78]

2 *Groups of companies.* By LTA 1954, s 42(3)(a), where the landlord's interest is held by a member of a group of companies, an intended occupation by any member of the group includes intended occupation by any member of the group for the purposes of a business to be carried on by that member.[79]

There is a further special rule for companies in which the landlord has a controlling interest:[80] any business carried on by the company is to be treated, within LTA 1954, s 30(1)(g), as a business to be carried on by him (LTA 1954, s 30(3)); otherwise, however, the business will be treated as carried on by the company and not the landlord, owing to the general principle that a company is a separate entity from the landlord.[81]

(ii) Occupation

While the landlord must intend to occupy the whole premises, personally or through an agent,[82] or manager, at least where the landlord retains practically complete control over the running of the business,[83] he need not necessarily intend to use the whole for business purposes. Where the landlord intended, having obtained possession, to re-let the whole premises, LTA 1954, s 30(1)(g) was inapplicable, even though during the

---

75 The relatively low level of proof of intention is shown also by the approach of the Court of Appeal in *Gatwick Parking Services Ltd v Sargent* [2000] 2 EGLR 45. It should not be forgotten that it is the landlord's premises which are at issue.
76 See *Maurar v Chauhan* [1985] 3 All ER 493, [1985] 1 WLR 1263, CA.
77 See *Sevenarts Ltd v Busvine* [1968] 1 WLR 1929, CA.
78 *Meyer v Riddick* [1990] 1 EGLR 107, CA.
79 Two bodies corporate are taken as members of a group if and only if one is a subsidiary to the other or both are subsidiaries of a third body corporate (LTA 1954, s 42(1)).
80 As defined by LTA 1954, s 30(3) and applies if: (a) the landlord is a member of the company and able, without the consent of any other person, to appoint or remove the holders of at least a majority of the directorships; or (b) he holds more than half of the company's share capital, disregarding any shares held by him in a fiduciary capacity or as nominee for another person.
81 See *Tunstall v Steigmann* [1962] 2 QB 593, [1962] 2 All ER 417, CA.
82 See *Skeet v Powell-Sheddon* [1988] 2 EGLR 112, CA.
83 As in *Teesside Indoor Bowls Ltd v Stockton on Tees Borough Council* [1990] 2 EGLR 87, CA.

planned works of conversion, the landlord would be in temporary occupation.[84] It seems that para (g) is not available where the landlord intends to demolish existing buildings and to put new ones on the site.[85] This may be because it is not possible to occupy the holding with buildings which one is intent on demolishing. By contrast, where a site was vacant and the landlord intended to erect a building on part of it, the landlord could invoke para (g), as the intention of the ground is to hand back the landlord his land if he wishes to carry on his own business on it.[86]

(iii) The five-year rule

LTA 1954, s 30(1)(g) is subject to a qualification under LTA 1954, s 30(2). This precludes the landlord from invoking the ground:

1   if his interest or an interest which has merged in that interest and but for the merger would be the landlord's interest was purchased or created[87] within the five years preceding the date specified in the original LTA 1954, s 25 notice or LTA 1954, s 26 request; and

2   if throughout that period there has been a tenancy or succession of tenancies of the holding within LTA 1954, Pt II.

The object of LTA 1954, s 30(2) has been stated to be to prevent exploitation of the tenant by a landlord who acquires the reversion with the aim of forthwith evicting the tenant on expiry of a business tenancy. However, LTA 1954, s 30(2) does not defeat a landlord who has held a leasehold interest for a long period under a succession of long leases, even if his title has been renewed within the last five years.[88]

A landlord who has 'purchased', that is bought for money,[89] the freehold or a tenancy (by grant or assignment),[90] within the five-year period, cannot rely on ground (g), unless there was a time during that period when there was no business tenancy of the holding in being.[91]

---

84   *Jones v Jenkins* [1986] 1 EGLR 113, CA.
85   *Nursey v P Currie (Dartford) Ltd* [1959] 1 All ER 497, [1959] 1 WLR 273, CA.
86   *Cam Gears Ltd v Cunningham* [1981] 2 All ER 560, CA.
87   The interest is created on the date of execution of the lease and not the commencement date of the term, or that of taking possession if different: *Northcote Laundry Ltd v Frederick Donnelly Ltd* [1968] 2 All ER 50, [1968] 1 WLR 562, CA.
88   *VCS Car Park Management Ltd v Regional Railways North East Ltd* [2001] Ch 121.
89   *HL Bolton (Engineering) Co Ltd v T & J Graham & Sons Ltd* [1957] 1 QB 159, [1956] 3 All ER 624, CA.
90   But not by surrender without consideration: *Frederick Lawrence Ltd v Freeman, Hardy and Willis* [1959] Ch 731, [1959] 3 All ER 77.
91   For successful avoidance of LTA 1954, s 30(2) by the grant of a reversionary lease by the freeholders to sub-lessees see *Wates Estate Agency Services v Bartleys Ltd* [1989] 2 EGLR 87, CA.

CHAPTER 24

Dismissal of tenant's application

I   TERMINATION OF THE CURRENT TENANCY

The court is precluded by LTA 1954, s 31(1) from ordering a new tenancy to be granted if the landlord establishes any one or more of the grounds of opposition under LTA 1954, s 30(1) to its satisfaction. Otherwise, the court will order a new tenancy. Where a notice to terminate or a tenant's request for a new tenancy has been given, followed by an application to the court, the effect of the notice is to terminate the tenancy at the expiration of three months as from the date on which the application[1] is finally disposed of (LTA 1954, s 64(1)).[2] In one case, a tenant's application for a new tenancy was dismissed but some ten days before the date the right to occupation ended, the landlords' computer sent out a routine rent demand. The tenants paid the sum demanded but the landlords were not estopped by conduct from treating the lease as duly terminated.[3]

If the landlord fails to establish any of the grounds specified in LTA 1954, s 30(1)(d), (e) or (f) to the satisfaction of the court, but the court would have been satisfied as to any of those grounds if the date of termination specified in the landlord's notice or the date specified in the tenant's request for a new tenancy had been such later date as the court may determine, but which is no later than one year from the specified date:

---

1   This provision applies even to a tenant's application which contravenes the time-limits laid down in LTA 1954, s 29(3): *Zenith Investments (Torquay) Ltd v Kammins Ballrooms Co Ltd (No 2)* [1971] 2 All ER 901, [1971] 1 WLR 1032, with the result that in that case the tenancy ended when the tenants surrendered possession.
2   This latter expression is to be construed in accordance with LTA 1954, s 64(2).
3   *Legal & General Assurance Society v Motel Agencies Ltd* (1969) 212 Estates Gazette 159. This result is seemingly unaffected by the strict development of the common law of waiver (see eg *Central Estates (Belgravia) Ltd v Woolgar (No 2)* [1972] 3 All ER 610, CA) since a similar result arises in the case of Rent Act statutory tenancies (see *Trustees of Henry Smith's Charity v Willson* [1983] QB 316, [1983] 1 All ER 73, CA).

1   the court must make a declaration to that effect, stating which of the above grounds would have been satisfied and specifying the date so determined: it cannot order a new tenancy; and

2   if, within 14 days from the making of the declaration, the tenant requires this, the court is to make an order substituting the date specified in the declaration for that specified in the landlord's notice to terminate or the tenant's request for a new tenancy (LTA 1954, s 31(2)).

Where the court refuses an order for a new tenancy, and it is subsequently proved that the court was induced to refuse the grant, by misrepresentation or concealment of material facts, the court may order the landlord to pay the tenant such sum as appears sufficient compensation for damage or loss sustained by the tenant as a result of the refusal (LTA 1954, s 55(1)). It seems that if the landlord, in good faith, establishes a ground of opposition, and subsequently changes his mind, LTA 1954, s 55(1) will not avail the tenant.

II   DISTURBANCE COMPENSATION

A tenant who fails to obtain an order for a new tenancy[4] may qualify for compensation under s 37, if the landlord has established any of the grounds specified in LTA 1954, s 30(1)(e), (f) or (g), and no other ground within LTA 1954, s 30(1) had been made out by the landlord (LTA 1954, s 37(1)). He is also entitled to such compensation where no other ground was specified in his LTA 1954, s 25 notice or LTA 1954, s 26(6) reply, except for grounds (e), (f) or (g),[5] and no application was made for a new tenancy, or, if it was, it was withdrawn (LTA 1954, s 37(1)). Under LTA 1954, Pt II, s 38(2) if the tenant has occupied the premises for the five years immediately preceding the date on which he quits the holding, a clause contracting out of his right to compensation will be void.

Compensation is payable on the tenant quitting.[6] A tenant who found alternative premises and removed his stock by a given date (19 October) was held to have quit on that date and not before, so preserving his right to compensation.[7] There have indeed

---

4   Including a case where a tenant, having served a LTA 1954, s 26 request for a new tenancy, did not apply to court, as he knew that the landlord's LTA 1954, s 30(1)(f) application to court would succeed: *Sun Life Assurance plc v Thales Tracs Ltd* [2001] EWCA Civ 704, [2002] 1 All ER 64. The state of mind of the tenant was not relevant. Also, the right to compensation did not depend on motives. See also Haley [2002] Conv 192.

5   The government intends to extend the right to compensation to cover a successful opposition by a landlord on the ground that it is the intention of a company controlled by him that the company will occupy the property.

6   No period of occupation as a tenant at will counts: *London Baggage Co (Charing Cross) Ltd v Railtrack plc (No 2)* [2001] L & TR 19, [2001] L & TR 217.

7   *Webb v Sandown Sports Club Ltd* [2000] EGCS 13. On that date, the tenant had no intention to return.

been some complications as to the precise date of quitting. In one decision,[8] the Court of Appeal ruled that the termination date of the tenancy was the relevant date. That was on 11 August 1994, a date arrived at on the basis of interim statutory continuation, which had come to an end then, because the tenant had discontinued his application for a new tenancy three months before, wishing to retire from the restaurant trade. However, during the last 12 days of the tenancy period (from 29 July to 11 August 1994) the premises were closed and empty. The Court of Appeal treated this period as being equivalent to a short period of non-occupation akin to that owing to a holiday. It did not wish to insist that the business occupation must be for every day of the relevant period, as had been held in an earlier ruling,[9] which had held that even non-occupation for one day short of the 14-year period would cost the tenant higher-rate compensation. In a different dispute, however, the High Court ruled that the relevant date for the purposes of seeing whether the span of 14 years, which alone allows a tenant to obtain higher rate compensation, is satisfied must be the date of termination specified in the landlord's LTA 1954, s 25 notice.[10] The High Court distinguished the Court of Appeal ruling on the ground that the tenant there was treated as being in occupation in the sense laid down by s 23 of the 1954 Act Part II for the whole of the relevant period. The process of moving out was simply part of the occupation taken as a whole. The High Court also prayed LTA 1954, s 37(7) in aid for its strict view, which places a premium on timing of the date of quitting. But for Court of Appeal ruling, however, a tenant who could not start fitting out works, an essential aspect of occupation, for a few days into his tenancy without being at much at risk of losing compensation rights as one who could not arrange his move out of the premises on precisely the day the tenancy ended.

The amount of compensation is the product of the appropriate multiplier[11] and either (a) the rateable value of the holding or (b) twice the rateable value of the holding (LTA 1954, s 37(2)).[12] The rateable value of the holding is that as it appears in the valuation list in force at the time when the original notice or request was made: it makes no difference that, subsequently, the list may have been amended so as to reflect an increased rateable value as such amendment cannot be retrospectively applied.[13]

---

8   *Bacchiochi v Academic Agency Ltd* [1998] 2 All ER 241, [1998] 1 WLR 1313. See Bennion (1998) 148 NLJ 953 and 986; S Murdoch *Estates Gazette* 2 May 1998, p 130; PF Smith (1998) 18 RRLR 345.

9   *Department of the Environment v Royal Insurance plc* (1986) 54 P & CR 26.

10   *Sight and Sound Education Ltd v Books Etc Ltd* [2000] L & TR 146.

11   The multiplier is fixed at levels laid down by regulations, notably at one where the relevant date is on or after 1 April 1990: Landlord and Tenant Act 1954 (Appropriate Multiplier) Order 1990, SI 1990/363.

12   As calculated under LTA 1954, s 37(5) and (5A)-(5D): the latter being applicable where any part of the holding is domestic property as defined by Local Government and Housing Act 1989, s 66.

13   *Plessey & Co v Eagle Pension Funds Ltd* [1990] 2 EGLR 209.

The higher rate of compensation is only available if, by LTA 1954, s 37(3):

1 during the 14 years immediately preceding the termination of the current tenancy, premises being or comprised in the holding have been occupied for the purpose of a business carried on by the occupier or for those and other purposes;

2 if, during those 14 years there was a change in the occupier of the premises, the person who was the occupier immediately after the change was the successor to the business carried on by the person who was the occupier immediately before the change.

The words 'the premises comprised in the holding' in LTA 1954, s 37(3) refer to the particular premises which had been occupied by the tenant (or where relevant, any sub-tenant) for the purposes of his business. Provided that at least part thereof, such as one floor of a demised building, was occupied by the tenant for the purposes of his business for the continuous period of 14 years prior to the termination of the tenancy, he qualifies for the higher rate compensation, because the premises in question need only be 'comprised' in the holding.[14] The result of this case was that the tenant received greater compensation for the two floors occupied for the shorter period than he would have obtained if these had been let separately. The Law Commission thought this not a just result. They recommended that the rate of compensation ought to be calculated separately for each part of the property.[15] The government have indicated that they accept this proposal.[16]

The relevant date for assessing compensation is now unclear. It may be the date specified in a landlord's LTA 1954, s 25 notice or tenant's LTA 1954, s 26 request, or it may be the date when the tenancy expires at common law or after the end of interim continuation where a s 26 request, for example, is withdrawn.[17] In any event, no compensation under LTA 1954, s 37 may be claimed unless the tenant has first served a LTA 1954, s 29(2) notice of unwillingness to give up possession on the landlord.[18] On the other hand, once a landlord has served a counter-notice to a tenant's application which invokes grounds (e), (f) or (g), he cannot both recover possession and avoid the payment of compensation, because by serving a counter-notice he has presented the tenant with the choice of the doubtful possibility of a new tenancy and the certainty of LTA 1954, s 37 compensation.[19]

14 *Edicron Ltd v William Whiteley Ltd* [1984] 1 All ER 219, [1984] 1 WLR 59, CA.

15 Law Com No 208 (1992), paras 2.82-2.83. They also recommended that if a reversion was split between different landlords, compensation should be only recoverable from each of them separately (para 2.84).

16 Consultation Paper 'Business Tenancies Legislation in England and Wales: the Government's Proposals for Reform' (2001) DETR, para 58. Compensation would also be payable where the landlord succeeded in obtaining possession of the premises on no fault grounds or where the action of the landlord was withdrawn (para 57) (LTA 1954, s 30(1)(e)-(g)).

17 See *Bacchiochi v Academic Agency Ltd* [1998] 2 All ER 241, [1998] 1 WLR 1313 and also *Sight and Sound Education Ltd v Books Etc Ltd* [2000] L & TR 146, the latter praying LTA 1954, s 37(7) in aid.

18 *Re 14 Grafton Street, London W1* [1971] Ch 935.

19 *Lloyds Bank Ltd v City of London Corpn* [1983] Ch 192, [1983] 1 All ER 92.

CHAPTER 25

Court order of a new tenancy

I   POWERS OF THE COURT AS TO TERMS

Where the tenant has applied to the court for a new tenancy, the court is bound, by LTA 1954, s 29(1), to make an order for the grant of a new tenancy comprising such property, at such a rent and on such other terms as are provided in LTA 1954, Pt II, ss 32-35. The court cannot do this where:

1   the landlord successfully establishes one or more grounds of opposition under LTA 1954, s 30; or

2   the court is precluded by LTA 1954, s 31(2) from ordering a new tenancy.

If the parties reach an enforceable agreement on any of the matters specified in these provisions, the court's power to determine terms is limited to those not agreed.

Property to be comprised in the holding

The parties may agree on what is to constitute the holding; if not, LTA 1954, s 32(1) requires the court to designate the holding with regard to the circumstances existing at the date of the order. The tenant's application must relate only to the premises or part, occupied by him for business purposes. Where the whole or part of the premises, is, at the relevant date, occupied by a sub-tenant, the latter is entitled to renewal and not the tenant, in respect of the parts he occupies. The landlord may insist under LTA 1954, s 32(2), that all property comprised in the current tenancy be included in the new tenancy.[1] In addition, the court has the power, under LTA 1954, s 32(1A), to order a new tenancy in respect of the part of the premises of which the tenant has indicated[2] that he was willing to accept a tenancy. The tenant cannot be forced to accept the

---

1   Even if he cannot offer vacant possession of the property over and above the holding: *Re No 1, Albermarle Street W1* [1959] Ch 531, [1959] 1 All ER 250.

2   Under LTA 1954, Pt II, s 31A(1)(b). This would follow a LTA 1954, s 30(1)(f) application by the landlord.

landlord's offer of a tenancy of part only of the business premises where he cannot obtain the grant of a new tenancy of the whole and he will be given leave to withdraw his application.[3]

LTA 1954, s 32 distinguishes between property to be comprised in the new tenancy and 'rights enjoyed in connection with the holding', such as purely contractual rights (eg to erect advertising signs),[4] fixtures, easements and quasi-easements such as would pass under LPA 1925, s 62, unless expressly excluded. Such rights as were enjoyed by the tenant under the current tenancy will be included in the new tenancy except as otherwise agreed between the parties, or in default of agreement, as determined by the court.[5]

Duration (LTA 1954, s 33)

The court may order a new tenancy for any duration it thinks reasonable in all the circumstances: if it is a tenancy for a term of years certain, its duration cannot exceed 14 years (LTA 1954, s 35). The new tenancy begins on the coming to an end of the current tenancy. The Law Commission proposed that the current upper limit on a court-ordered new term should be adjusted to 15 years. This figure was divisible by both three and five and would fit in with modern rent review patterns.[6] The government have indicated that they agree with this change.[7]

The parties, by contrast, may agree on a tenancy of any duration they like: if so, the court has power to order a tenancy for that agreed term,[8] where other terms are in dispute. Thus, relative hardship may be a relevant factor, or that the landlord would in a matter of months be able to establish the ground specified in LTA 1954, s 30(1)(g) or (f).[9] The length of the current tenancy, the nature of the business, the age and the state of the property and its prospects of redevelopment are all material circumstances.[10]

Therefore, if the landlord is able to show a bona fide intention to redevelop, which is not capable of immediate realisation, the court may order a tenancy for a given period with a break clause on suitable terms. These can then enable him to terminate the lease

---

3   *Fribourg and Treyer Ltd v Northdale Investments Ltd* (1982) 44 P & CR 284.
4   *Re No 1 Albemarle Street W1* [1959] Ch 531 [1959] 1 All ER 250; *G Orlik (Meat Products) Ltd v Hastings and Thanet Building Society* (1974) 29 P & CR 126, CA.
5   Evidence is admissible to show the true extent of the intended demise if the parcels clause is incorrect: *I S Mills (Yardley) Ltd v Curdworth Investments Ltd* (1975) 235 Estates Gazette 127, CA.
6   Law Com No 208 (1992), para 2.79. They favoured keeping an upper limit on the relevant term if only as a focus for negotiations.
7   Consultation Paper 'Business Tenancies Legislation in England and Wales: the Government's Proposals for Reform' (2001) DETR, para 56; it is understood that the change will be implemented.
8   *Janes (Gowns) Ltd v Harlow Development Corpn* [1980] 1 EGLR 52.
9   See *Upsons Ltd v E Robins Ltd* [1956] 1 QB 131, [1955] 3 All ER 348, CA.
10 See eg *London and Provincial Millinery Stores Ltd v Barclays Bank Ltd* [1962] 1 WLR 510, CA.

and redevelop if and when able to do so.[11] Similarly, a landlord was given the right to break a new tenancy on six months' notice, where there was a real possibility that he might redevelop the site, during the ten years proposed by the tenant.[12] There is no inevitability that a break-clause will be inserted to suit the convenience or requirements of the landlord. Where the tenant intended to retire at a given date, the landlord was refused a break-clause exercisable for redevelopment at any time on six months' notice, having regard to the hardship caused to the tenant in possible relocation so close to his retirement date.[13] Equally, where the tenant requested a one-year term and the landlord sought a fourteen-year term, a one-year term was granted, giving the landlord time in which to find new tenants.[14] Essentially, the length of the term is at discretion. In one case, a tenant was given a longer lease than he would have liked.[15] Since the policy of LTA 1954 is not to give the tenant security if the landlord proves that he intends to occupy the premises himself in the near future, but could not at the date of the hearing, owing to the five-year rule, the effect of the latter was taken into account in determining the duration of a new tenancy.[16] To prevent long appeals prolonging a term, the court may well direct that the term should start from the final disposal of the application and end on a specified date.[17]

The discretion of the county court regarding the term is wide and generally the Court of Appeal will not interfere in the absence of error of law.[18] Special rules exist to order the grant of any necessary reversionary leases, where required, because the new tenancy extends beyond the immediate landlord's interest.[19]

Rent

(i) Generally

In the event of non-agreement as to the rent payable under the new tenancy, LTA 1954, s 34(1) provides that the court shall determine it as that at which, having regard to the terms of the current tenancy (other than those relating to rent), the holding might reasonably be expected to be let in the open market by a willing lessor. By LTA 1954,

11 *McCombie v Grand Junction Co Ltd* [1962] 2 All ER 65n, [1962] 1 WLR 581, CA; *Adams v Green* [1978] 2 EGLR 46, CA; *Amika Motor Ltd v Colebrook Holdings Ltd* [1981] 1 EGLR 62, CA.
12 *National Car Parks Ltd v Paternoster Consortium Ltd* [1990] 1 EGLR 99.
13 *Becker v Hill Street Properties Ltd* [1990] 2 EGLR 78, CA.
14 *CBS United Kingdom Ltd v London Scottish Properties Ltd* [1985] 2 EGLR 125.
15 *Re Sunlight House, Quay St, Manchester* (1959) 173 Estates Gazette 311.
16 *Wig Creations v Colour Film Services* (1969) 20 P & CR 870, CA (tenants obtained a three-year term, not the twelve-year lease they asked for).
17 *Chipperfield v Shell UK Ltd* (1980) 42 P & CR 136, CA.
18 *Upsons Ltd v E Robins Ltd* [1956] 1 QB 131, [1955] 3 All ER 348, CA.
19 Landlord and Tenant Act 1954, s 44 and Sch 6, para 2, which applies both where the parties agree on duration and where it is fixed by the court.

s 34(4),[20] the matters taken into account by the court in determining the rent include any effect (on the new tenancy) of the operation of the provisions of the Landlord and Tenant (Covenants) Act 1995. That Act, notably, enables the landlord if it is reasonable to do so, to pre-specify in a renewed business tenancy[21] that it is a condition of any assignment that the assigning tenant guarantees the immediate assignee's performance of his covenants. As noted below, such a condition cannot be claimed by the landlord unless it is reasonable for him to impose it.

LTA 1954, ss 34 and 35 both direct the court to have regard to the terms of the current tenancy; the court must first consider other terms before deciding on the new rent: if any new term is added or if any existing term is altered or excluded in the new tenancy, this may well have an effect on the new rent.[22] If a party seeks a departure from the terms of the current tenancy, the onus of justifying the departure is on him. Hence, the courts have refused both to relax a user clause where the effect would be to raise the rent[23] and to narrow a user clause where the effect would be to depress it.[24] Where the county court altered a covenant against assignment or underletting so as to incorporate a surrender-back clause after fixing the new rent, the case was remitted to enable reconsideration of the rent.[25]

LTA 1954, s 34(1) postulates an open market rent. This expression has been said to require the inclusion of a sufficient number of (notional) lessors and lessees to create the opportunity of comparing rents, enabling the forces of supply and demand to operate. There must be a willing lessor and a willing lessee (as might happen in a rent review matter) and a reasonable period in which to negotiate the new tenancy at arm's length. Any rent payable by a lessee with a special interest must, in accordance with general valuation principles, be disregarded. The landlord will no doubt seek to obtain the best rent for the premises on the terms offered and the tenant to persuade the landlord to accept the lowest rent possible.[26]

The new rent may be decided having due regard to expert evidence from a surveyor experienced in current values for comparable neighbourhood property,[27] taking into

20   Added by Landlord and Tenant (Covenants) Act 1995, Sch 1, para 3; a similar rule applies to LTA 1954, s 35 (Landlord and Tenant (Covenants) Act 1995, Sch 1, para 4).
21   It will be appreciated that a pre-1 January 1996 tenancy renewed under LTA 1954, Pt II counts as a 'new' tenancy within the Landlord and Tenant (Covenants) Act 1995.
22   *O'May v City of London Real Property Co Ltd* [1983] 2 AC 726 at 740, [1982] 1 All ER 660 at 665, HL (Lord Hailsham LC).
23   *Charles Clements (London) Ltd v Rank City Wall Ltd* [1978] 1 EGLR 47; also *Northern Electric plc v Addison* [1997] 2 EGLR 111.
24   *Aldwych Club Ltd v Copthall Property Co Ltd* (1962) 185 Estates Gazette 219.
25   *Cardshops Ltd v Davies* [1971] 2 All ER 721, [1971] 1 WLR 591, CA.
26   *Baptist v Ministers of the Bench and Trustees of the Honourable Society of Gray's Inn* [1993] 2 EGLR 136 (where an open market at Gray's Inn could operate despite the fact that the occupiers were all in the same profession).
27   The court is the ultimate arbiter of the weight of such evidence and in one case a re-hearing was ordered on appeal where excessive reliance had been placed on the evidence of one expert, the tenant not having his own expert: *Miah v Bromley Park Garden Estates Ltd* [1992] 1 EGLR 98, CA.

account the terms of the new tenancy.[28] On occasion, he may also take into account a firm offer of a rent to be paid in respect of the same premises with vacant possession.[29] However, the expert has to direct his main focus onto the statutory formula, which speaks of a willing tenant. Therefore, if the only permitted use of the premises is one specified purpose, such as an electricity sub-station, it must be assumed in making a valuation that any willing tenant would have to hold the premises on the same user terms.[30] The court will also not admit new evidence of rents for leases of allegedly comparable premises, where it has, on the basis of evidence already available to it, already exercised its discretion as to the amount of the new rent.[31] The rent of neighbouring property is relevant, however, only to compare the relative trading position of the premises.[32]

If there are no comparables, general rent increases in the area may be applied.[33] The matter is, at the end of the day, at the general discretion of the judge.[34] There is no general rule that the tenant is bound to disclose the trading accounts of his business[35] but they may be admissible with special types of premises whose profitability fluctuates, such as hotels, restaurants and so on, as a relevant indication of earnings capacity.[36] The tenant cannot set up his own breaches of covenant to repair in reduction of the rent under LTA 1954, s 34(1).[37] In contrast, the court has power, under LTA 1954, s 34(1), to order that the rent is not to commence, or is to commence at a lower rate, until repairs are carried out, where it is the landlord who is in breach of a covenant to repair under the contractual term.[38] Since an assessment of the rent is objective, LTA 1954, s 34 does not allow a rent below the market level to be fixed simply because the tenant cannot afford the new rent.[39] On the other hand, other factors relevant to the premises which might reduce the rent, such as the fact that, in times of recession, retailers may not be ready and willing to take leases of inferior sites without some substantial incentive, may be taken into account.[40]

(ii) Disregards from rent

It is provided (LTA 1954, s 34(1)) that four matters must be disregarded in assessing the rent for a new tenancy:

28 Cf *English Exporters (London) Ltd v Eldonwall Ltd* [1973] Ch 415, [1973] 1 All ER 726.
29 *Re 52-56 Osnaburgh Street* (1957) 169 Estates Gazette 656.
30 *Northern Electric plc v Addison* [1997] 39 EG 175.
31 *Khalique v Law Land plc* [1989] 1 EGLR 105, CA.
32 *Rogers v Rosedimond Investments (Blakes Market) Ltd* [1978] 2 EGLR 48, CA.
33 *National Car Parks v Colebrook Estates Ltd* [1983] 1 EGLR 78.
34 *Turone v Howard de Walden Estates Ltd* [1982] 1 EGLR 92, CA; *Oriani v Dorita Properties Ltd* [1987] 1 EGLR 88, CA; *Khalique v Law Land plc* [1989] 1 EGLR 105, CA.
35 *WJ Barton Ltd v Long Acre Securities Ltd* [1982] 1 All ER 465, [1982] 1 WLR 398, CA.
36 See *Harewood Hotels Ltd v Harrison* [1958] 1 WLR 108, CA.
37 *Family Management v Gray* [1980] 1 EGLR 46, CA.
38 *Fawke v Viscount Chelsea* [1980] QB 441, [1979] 3 All ER 568, CA.
39 *Giannoukakis Ltd v Saltfleet Ltd* [1988] 1 EGLR 73, CA.
40 *French v Commercial Union Life Assurance* [1993] 1 EGLR 113, CA.

1   Any effect on rent attributable to occupation by the tenant (or a predecessor in title) of the holding. Therefore, the tenant is not protected against the open market rent by the fact that he is a sitting tenant.[41]

2   Any goodwill attaching to the premises by reason of the business carried on by the tenant or any predecessor in title of his in the same business.

3   Any increase in value attributable to certain improvements carried out[42] by the person who was current tenant other than in pursuance of an obligation to his immediate landlord.[43] The following conditions apply to this, by LTA 1954, s 34(2):

    (a)   that the improvement was completed either during the current tenancy or not more than 21 years before the application for a new tenancy;

    (b)   that the holding or the part improved was at all times since completion of the improvement, subject to tenancies to which LTA 1954, Pt II applies; and

    (c)   that on the termination of any tenancy the tenant did not quit. As with rent review, it is not possible to treat the premises as though no improvement had ever been made, as a matter of valuation.[44]

4   In the case of licensed premises, the increase in value attributable to the licence, if its benefit is to be regarded as the tenant's.

(iii) Rent review clauses in new tenancy

The court has power, under LTA 1954, s 34(3), to include a rent review clause in the new tenancy on such terms as it thinks fit. This provision was passed (as an amendment to the LTA 1954, Pt II) to confirm a High Court ruling.[45] It has been decided that the court in the exercise of its discretion may, if the parties agree on the insertion of a rent review clause for the first time in the new tenancy, but not as to its terms, render the clause both upwards and downwards.[46] Thus, the court ordered that a new nine-year tenancy of shop premises should have such a clause every three years, where the original lease had been for a twenty-one-year term, without any rent review, on the

41   *O'May v City of London Real Property Co Ltd* [1983] 2 AC 726, [1982] 1 All ER 660. The list of statutory disregards is comprehensive: *J Murphy & Sons v Railtrack plc* [2002] 19 EG 148 (CS).

42   According to *Durley House Ltd v Cadogan* [2000] 1 WLR 246, 'carried out' means to carry out the work personally or to arrange for a third party to do so, provided in this case that the tenant supervises or finances the work.

43   If the improvement is carried out under a licence prior to the lease, the disregard will not apply: *Euston Centre Properties Ltd v H & J Wilson Ltd* [1982] 1 EGLR 128. If under a licence to improve, disregard is a question of construction: *Godbold v Martin the Newsagents Ltd* [1983] 2 EGLR 128.

44   Cf *Estates Projects Ltd v Greenwich London Borough* [1979] 2 EGLR 85.

45   *Stylo Shoes Ltd v Manchester Royal Exchange Ltd* (1967) 204 Estates Gazette 803. For a fairly recent example of the exercise of a discretion not to insert a rent review clause see *Northern Electric plc v Addison* [1997] 2 EGLR 111.

46   *Janes (Gowns) Ltd v Harlow Development Corpn* [1980] 1 EGLR 52 (where owing to a neighbouring development, a fall in rental values was quite possible); also *Boots the Chemists Ltd v Pinkland Ltd* [1992] 2 EGLR 98 (Cty Ct).

ground that an upwards-only clause would be unfair to the tenant, due to a continuing local recession.[47]

Where the contractual tenancy already contains an upwards-only rent review clause, the position is more open. In one case, the judge refused, in his discretion, to alter the terms of an upwards-only clause which he regarded as suitable for reproduction in the new tenancy.[48] There is no reason why the court should not alter the terms of an existing upwards-only rent review clause as they apply to the new tenancy, so as to allow for a downwards review, if it has a general unfettered discretion. If, however, the issue is governed by LTA 1954, Pt II, s 35, the court would have to incorporate the clause in an unaltered form in the new tenancy, unless persuaded by the tenant of the fairness and justice of altering its terms, with some compensation to the landlord. By reason of LTA 1954, s 35, there is power in the court to include a term dealing on a fixed or variable basis, with service charges.[49]

(iv) Date for new rent

As to the date from which the new rent is payable: if the parties agree on the commencement date for the new tenancy, they may provide that rent is payable from the date of commencement, even if this precedes execution of the lease.[50] If there is no agreement as to a commencement date, the relevant date is that of the hearing.[51]

Other terms

The court is enabled by LTA 1954, s 35, in the absence of agreement between the parties, to determine any other terms under the new tenancy, having regard to the terms of the current tenancy and to all relevant circumstances.

The courts are reluctant to impose, without good reason, new terms and the party seeking to do this must justify a change as fair, reasonable, and adequately compensated for. Thus, under a contractual tenancy, the landlords were responsible for all maintenance, repairs and services, without recourse to the tenants. On renewal, they sought to impose a term on the tenants providing for service charges in respect of these items, in return for a small cut in the overall basis of calculation of the rent payable. The House of Lords refused to force this proposal on the tenants as it was a

---

47 *Forbouys plc v Newport County Council* [1994] 1 EGLR 138 (Cty ct) (the possibility of an upwards review discounted any unfairness to the landlord); also *Amarjee v Barrowfen Properties Ltd* [1993] 2 EGLR 133.

48 *Charles Follett Ltd v Cabtell Investments Ltd* [1986] 2 EGLR 76. This aspect was not considered on appeal. Also *Blythewood Plant Hire Ltd v Spiers Ltd* [1992] 2 EGLR 103 (Cty Ct).

49 *Hyams v Titan Properties Ltd* (1972) 24 P & CR 359, CA.

50 *Bradshaw v Pawley* [1979] 3 All ER 273, [1980] 1 WLR 10.

51 *Lovely and Orchard Services Ltd v Daejan Investment (Grove Hall) Ltd* [1978] 1 EGLR 44.

significant, unjustified and inadequately compensated for change.[52] A change in the terms of the current tenancy will be allowed if essentially fair with adequate compensation to the party adversely affected by the change.[53] On this basis, the county court ordered that a shop tenant must in future contribute to a service charge referable to the whole of the parade concerned, having regard to the common features of the particular development.[54] But the court refused to insert a tenant's option to purchase the freehold in a new tenancy where the option in the current tenancy had expired.[55] Nor is the court able to enlarge the current holding by incorporating against the landlord's will, easements or rights over his own land not hitherto enjoyed by the tenant.[56] As to user clauses, see the text dealing with LTA 1954, s 34.

Where the residue of a business lease was assigned subject to a newly imposed term on assignment that the tenant would obtain guarantors of his obligations under the lease, the court could, on a ten-year new tenancy order, impose the like guarantee requirement, even though it would last for ten years rather than, under the contractual term, one year.[57] However, the court should not impose a term on the tenant requiring him to pay the landlord's costs of preparing the new tenancy.[58] Where the original leases of business premises contained break-clauses exercisable in the event of the landlord's wishing to redevelop, new leases were granted for fixed terms with break-clauses in each after five years.[59]

Nevertheless, the enactment of the Landlord and Tenant (Covenants) Act 1995 has produced a sea change in this part of the law. As already noted, the 1995 Act enables the landlord, if such a requirement is reasonable,[60] to require a tenant of a new tenancy to accept a term in the lease involving his signing an authorised guarantee agreement. This guarantee would be signed if and when the tenant assigns the tenancy, provided the landlord could then defend requiring the tenant to sign the guarantee as being a reasonable requirement. Thus while 'radical surgery'[61] can be done to a renewed

52   *O'May v City of London Real Property Co Ltd* [1983] 2 AC 726, [1982] 1 All ER 660.
53   *Gold v Brighton Corpn* [1956] 3 All ER 442, [1956] 1 WLR 1291, CA.
54   *Amarjee v Barrowfen Properties Ltd* [1993] 2 EGLR 133.
55   *Kirkwood v Johnson* (1979) 38 P & CR 392, CA.
56   *G Orlik (Meat Products) Ltd v Hastings and Thanet Building Society* (1974) 29 P & CR 126, CA.
57   *Cairnplace Ltd v CBI (Property Investment) Co Ltd* [1984] 1 All ER 315, [1984] 1 WLR 696, CA.
58   *Cairnplace Ltd v CBI (Property Investment) Co Ltd* [1984] 1 All ER 315, [1984] 1 WLR 696, CA. Otherwise the tenant would lose the protection of the Costs of Leases Act 1958, s 1.
59   *JH Edwards & Sons Ltd v Central London Commercial Estates Ltd* [1984] 2 EGLR 103. The landlords did not have any firm proposals: hence the measure of security given to the tenants. Cf *Leslie & Godwin Investments Ltd v Prudential Assurance Co Ltd* [1987] 2 EGLR 95.
60   The requirement of reasonableness was read into Landlord and Tenant (Covenants) Act 1995, s 16 by *Wallis Fashion Group plc v CGU Life Assurance Ltd* [2000] L & TR 520. This was because the requirement of an AGA had to be 'lawfully imposed'. Also it was unattractive to hold that a landlord could obtain a term which would entitle him to be unreasonable.
61   In the words of Neuberger J in *Wallis Fashion Group plc v CGU Life Assurance Ltd* [2000] L & TR 520 at 530.

tenancy (all renewals as of the present time now falling within the Landlord and Tenant (Covenants) Act 1995 as new tenancies), the landlord cannot insist on a guarantee agreement as of right. It makes no difference that this may conflict with what the landlord deems to be good estate management.

Reform

The Law Commission had no recommendations for reform of the rent-fixing formula of LTA 1954, Pt II, s 34. They said that the overall aim had been not to make a significant change in the balance between landlords and tenants.[62] They also declined to recommend any changes to LTA 1954, s 35. It did not, in their view, aim only to reflect market conditions. LTA 1954 tried to deal fairly with the two parties concerned. The Commission considered, having reviewed the matter, that the necessary combination of flexibility and stability existed. It was best managed by the use of the discretionary powers currently conferred on the courts.[63]

II EFFECT OF THE ORDER

Carrying out of the court's order

Even though the court makes an order for the grant of a new tenancy, on the application of the tenant, the tenant is not bound to take the tenancy and the parties may agree not to act on its terms. First, the tenant is entitled under LTA 1954, s 36(2) to apply to the court within 14 days for the revocation of the order, and the court is bound to revoke it.[64] In that event, the parties may agree, or the court may determine, that the current tenancy shall continue beyond what would otherwise have been its date of termination (ie the date specified in the original notice or a later date by virtue of LTA 1954, s 64) for such period as is 'necessary to afford to the landlord a reasonable opportunity for reletting or otherwise disposing of the premises which would have been comprised in the new tenancy'. This provision is necessary for the protection of a tenant who cannot afford the rent, for example, or accept the terms, as finally determined by the court. Where these were matters in dispute, he was not necessarily sure of their outcome when he made the application. The parties are free, by a written agreement (LTA 1954, s 69(2)), to modify or exclude any of the terms determined by the court which may suit neither of them.

The landlord is in principle bound to execute and the tenant bound to accept, a lease or agreement for a tenancy of the holding embodying the terms as agreed between

---

62 Law Com No 208 (1992), para 3.31.
63 Law Com No 208 (1992), paras 3.32-3.33.
64 There is no discretion in the court not to revoke: *Broadmead Ltd v Corben-Brown* (1966) 201 Estates Gazette 111.

them or determined by the court; and the tenant may be required by the landlord to execute a counterpart of the instrument. Default in execution is not only a contempt of court; compliance may be enforced by specific performance.[65] Until then, equity treats the parties as landlord and tenant.[66]

Termination of the current tenancy

The current tenancy will continue until the new lease or binding agreement for a new lease takes effect. Where the court determines the duration of the new tenancy under LTA 1954, s 33, that will commence on the date specified in the original notice, or a later date by virtue of LTA 1954, s 64. Where the parties have themselves agreed upon the duration of the new tenancy, however, there appears to be nothing in LTA 1954, s 33 to prevent them from agreeing to some other date, except possibly that if the agreed date were earlier, it is arguable that this would be a surrender of the current tenancy, which in turn would have to be authorised under LTA 1954, s 38(4)(b). Once there is a binding agreement for a new tenancy, the tenant loses all his rights under LTA 1954, Pt II in relation to the current tenancy.

65   *Pulleng v Curran* (1980) 44 P & CR 58.
66   *Greaves Organisation Ltd v Stanhope Gate Property Co Ltd* (1973) 228 Estates Gazette 725.

Agricultural tenancies

CHAPTER 26

Outline of old-style agricultural tenancies regime

I INTRODUCTION

Until the advent of statute, agricultural tenancies were governed by a mixture of the common law and customary rights. Statute intervened first to provide compensation for tenants who carried out improvements to the land or buildings comprised in the tenancy concerned and then quit the holding. The passing of the Agricultural Holdings Act 1948 ushered in a strict security of tenure regime, perhaps to match that of the Rent Acts. The 1948 Act was consolidated into the Agricultural Holdings Act 1986 (hereinafter AHA 1986). Before the passing of this Act, a succession scheme had been introduced as from 1976, but it was not long before the scheme had been curtailed as from 1984.[1]

The security of tenure and succession regimes were blamed by the then Conservative government for a reduction in the availability of farming land for letting,[2] even though the 1986 regime was not unduly easy to avoid, as by use of licences or short-term tenancies. Objection was also taken to the fact that if a farming tenant moved away from agricultural uses, he would be at risk of losing rights to compensation conferred by statute, not to mention loss of security of tenure. As from 1 September 1995, the Agricultural Tenancies Act 1995 came into force. From then on, farm business tenancies alone may be created in relation to agricultural land. The old regime is slowly dying out, as time passes. A brief note of its principal aspects is retained if only as a contrast to the new rules. The following points of contrast between the two regimes should be noted.

1 The succession scheme applies to an agricultural tenancy granted before 12 July 1984 and is governed by AHA 1986, ss 34-39 and 43-48 in particular. See Rodgers *Agricultural Law* ch 8 (and indeed passim as to the 1986 Act regime).
2 See the MAFF News Release dated 6 October 1993 in which not only were the security provisions of AHA 1986 condemned, but also the old regime as a whole was condemned as not allowing innovation and diversification.

1   AHA 1986, is capable of conferring on a yearly tenant a tenancy which can only be determined in accordance with strict notice procedures under the Act. By contrast, the Agricultural Tenancies Act 1995 confers no security of tenure on the tenant who holds a farm business tenancy once the tenancy has expired.

2   AHA 1986 contains specific rules as to the fixing of agricultural tenancy rents. These are invoked by the use of notices. The means of deciding a new rent is by arbitration if the parties cannot agree. There are legislative directions as to the amount of new rent and as to disregards. By contrast, the Agricultural Tenancies Act 1995 follows the current policy of deregulation in the setting of rents and of rent reviews.

3   The Agricultural Tenancies Act 1995 regime allows agricultural tenants to diversify from agricultural use to business use (as by farming part of the land and also allowing part of it to be used as a visitor attraction for tourists) without risking the loss of rights to statutory compensation. These rights could be lost under AHA 1986 rules to a tenant whose activities fell outside the statutory definition of agricultural user at some time after the tenancy commenced.

4   AHA 1986 lists 'new improvements' in respect of which compensation is in principle payable to the tenant. In relation to some of these, such as the making or planting of osier beds, or the making of water meadows, the prior consent of the landlord is required. In the case of others, which are more extensive, such as the erection, alteration or enlargement of buildings, or an improvement of permanent yards,[3] the consent of the Agricultural Land Tribunal is required. The Agricultural Tenancies Act 1995 retains the principle of compensation for improvements. One aim of these rules is to assist quitting tenants with their relocation expenses. While AHA 1986 allows disturbance compensation in some cases, notably following a landlords' notice to quit,[4] this is not a feature of the Agricultural Tenancies Act 1995.

II   OUTLINE OF MAIN SECURITY UMBRELLA OF AHA 1986

AHA 1986 applies to a contract of tenancy of an agricultural holding (as defined in AHA 1986, s 1(1)), which was entered into before 1 September 1995. Many types of uses for agricultural purposes fall within AHA 1986, such as horticulture, fruit growing, seed growing, dairy farming and livestock breeding (AHA 1986, s 96(1)). If, however,

---

3   AHA 1986, Sch 7. 'New improvements' refers to improvements begun on or after 1 March 1948. Some 'new improvements' such as mole drainage or protection of fruit trees against animals do not require the prior consent of the landlord (AHA 1986, Sch 8, Pt I). Tenants under the 1986 Act rules are also entitled to compensation for 'tenant right' matters which are listed in AHA 1986, Sch 8, Pt II.

4   AHA 1986, ss 60 and 63. Compensation is excluded where the landlord is able to rely on AHA 1986, Sch 3, Cases C-G (AHA 1986, s 61(1)) as also where the Agricultural Land Tribunal consented to the notice to quit on certain grounds, notably bad husbandry. The aim of this compensation is evidently to reward a 'good' tenant on quitting.

the tenant decides to use the land, or even a substantial part of it, for a non-agricultural purpose such as tourism, security of tenure under the 1986 Act scheme is in principle lost.[5] The whole of the land must in principle be let for use as agricultural land (AHA 1986, s 1(2)). Security of tenure under AHA 1986 is also lost entirely if, having been let land for agricultural purposes, the tenant wholly or substantially abandons agricultural user during the tenancy. In such a case the strict notice procedures of AHA 1986, do not apply so as to limit the right of the landlord to repossess the land and premises in question.

The tenant must, to retain security, make use of the land for agricultural purposes in the course of his trade or business, which rules out security if the use is for personal or pleasure uses. The idea of use as a trade or business has been carried further by the Agricultural Tenancies Act 1995 regime when it poses as one of the tests for applying the 1995 Act that the tenant has to satisfy a business condition. The condition must, as will appear, be satisfied throughout the farm business tenancy. However, it appears that as long as some part of the land is farmed as a farm business tenant's trade or business, he may use other parts of the land for other purposes, which have nothing to do with farming, such as running a donkey centre for childrens' rides. This type of diversification is only possible under AHA 1986 to a very limited degree.[6]

AHA 1986 applies to pre-September 1995 lettings of land or agreements for letting land for a term of years or from year to year (AHA 1986, s 1(5)). Often the tenancies which come within the 1986 Act scheme will be tenancies from year to year, reflecting an old established practice. There are special rules for certain types of tenancy.[7] AHA 1986 is relatively easy to contract out of. A pre-September 1995 tenancy for a fixed term granted for more than one year but for less than two years lies outside AHA 1986 entirely.[8] However, curiously, in view of the relative simplicity of this particular means of contracting out of AHA 1986, the legislation makes provision for some devices which might otherwise fall outside its protective umbrella. Thus, a pre-1995 tenancy for less than from year to year is deemed to fall within AHA 1986, as are certain licences to occupy.[9] Agreements granting grazing or mowing rights during some

5   See *Russell v Booker* [1982] 2 EGLR 86, CA (mere residence not sufficient to amount to agricultural use); also *Wetherall v Smith* [1980] 2 All ER 530, CA; *Short v Greeves* [1988] 1 EGLR 1, CA (diversification away from original agricultural user not sufficiently great on facts to cost tenant security).
6   Thus in *Brown v Tiernan* [1993] 1 EGLR 1, the keeping of a mare for pleasure was allowed without loss of the 1986 security umbrella, but the line was harder to draw than it would be under the new rules.
7   For example, AHA 1986, s 3 provides for tenancies granted for two years or more.
8   *Gladstone v Bower* [1960] 2 QB 384, [1960] 3 All ER 353, CA; see also *EWP Ltd v Moore* [1992] 2 EGLR 4, CA (23-month tenancy not within AHA 1986; also fell outside protection for business tenancies as the land was agricultural land). A tenancy within the 1986 Act can be surrendered: *JS Bloor (Measham) v Calcott* [2002] 1 EGLR 1.
9   AHA 1986, s 2. In the case of licences to occupy, it is envisaged that only exclusive licences (an example being *University of Reading v Johnson-Houghton* [1985] 2 EGLR 113) are caught by AHA 1986, s 2(2)(b). If the owner has genuine overriding control or co-occupation rights, these take the agreement outside the Act: *Bahamas International Trust Co Ltd v*

specified period of the year as set out in the agreement fell outside the security umbrella of AHA 1986, unless the whole agreement was a sham.[10]

III   STATUTORY REGULATION AND SECURITY OF TENURE

Outline of statutory regulation of contract of tenancy

AHA 1986 contains a number of detailed provisions, which enable the tenant to secure a written tenancy agreement if there is none.[11] Regulations made under AHA 1986 deal with the incidence of liability for maintenance, repair and insurance of fixed equipment.[12]

The rent under a tenancy of an agricultural holding is fixed by agreement but if the parties cannot agree on rent, statutory machinery comes into play.[13] The landlord or tenant may refer the rent to an arbitrator. However, any new rent determined by him cannot take effect until 12 months after the date of the demand for arbitration. In principle, the rent as determined by arbitration has a three-year life.[14] The arbitrator is required to fix a new rent, which may be the same rent as currently payable, or at a reduced or increased level, in accordance with statutory guidelines. These require him to determine in effect a market rent: a rent at which the holding might reasonably be expected to be let by a prudent and willing landlord to a prudent and willing tenant. There are certain statutory disregards which must be made.[15]

    Threadgold [1974] 3 All ER 881, HL. The reservation of limited access rights does not deprive the occupier of security: see eg *Lampard v Barker* [1984] 2 EGLR 11, CA. An owner who had the right to alter the land which was the subject matter of the agreement had not conferred security on the occupier: *McCarthy v Bence* [1990] 1 EGLR 1, CA.

10   See *Chaloner v Bower* [1984] 1 EGLR 4. Where cultivation of the land was required by an agreement, AHA 1986, applied: *Lory v London Borough of Brent* [1971] 1 All ER 1042.

11   AHA 1986, s 6 and Sch 1.

12   SI 1973/1473 and SI 1988/281, made under AHA 1986, s 7(3) and deemed to be incorporated into every tenancy agreement unless the agreement makes express contrary provision: see *Burden v Hannaford* [1956] 1 QB 142, [1955] 3 All ER 401, CA. However, contracting out is not allowed in the case of oral tenancies. Modifications in a tenancy to these 'model clauses' may be varied following an application to an arbitrator (AHA 1986, s 8), who has wide powers to vary the terms of the tenancy and the rent payable. The regulations are discussed in, eg West and Smith's *Law of Dilapidations* ch 12.

13   AHA 1986, s 12(1).

14   AHA 1986, Sch 2, para 4(1).

15   AHA 1986, Sch 2, para 1. As to the approach in relation to open market rents see, eg *Aberdeen Endowment Trust v Will* 1985 SLT 23; also *JW Childers Trustees v Anker* [1996] 1 EGLR 1, CA. The current level of rent for comparable lettings must be taken into account by the arbitrator (AHA 1986, Sch 2, para 1(3)). Increases or decreases in the value of the holding due to in particular tenants' improvements or fixed equipment must be disregarded as well as certain other matters such as any increase in rental value caused by registered quota (AHA 1986, Sch 1, para 2). The landlord is entitled to an increase in rent owing to landlords' improvements carried out on the holding, following a notice procedure (AHA 1986, s 13).

Arbitrators have a significant role to play under the 1986 Act rules. Apart from their powers when a rent is referred to them, arbitrators have powers on a reference by either party to deal with such diverse matters as rent increases on account of landlords' improvements, variation of the terms as to permanent pasture, disputes as to the fair value payable by the landlord for tenants' fixtures and in relation to claims on the termination of a tenancy.[16] AHA 1986 also regulates other diverse aspects of the parties' relationship. These include a provision entitling either party at any time during the tenancy to require the making of a record of the condition of the fixed equipment on the holding and of the general condition of the holding.[17] A special set of rules applies to landlords' claims for damages for dilapidations after the tenancy has terminated.[18]

Outline of security of tenure rules

The essence of AHA 1986 security scheme is that it is ordinarily not possible for a landlord to put an end to the contract of tenancy, which would ordinarily be a yearly periodic tenancy, by means of a six-month notice to quit. Instead, the landlord is required to give a twelve-month minimum notice to quit.[19] To that notice, if it specifies no statutory grounds, the tenant is entitled to respond with a counter-notice served under AHA 1986, s 26. He has one month from the landlord's notice in which to do this. However, timely service of a counter-notice is essential. At the same time, AHA 1986, s 26 cannot be contracted out of: it is an overriding right, imposed in the interests of public policy, for the benefit of the tenant.[20] However, there is nothing to stop head

16 AHA 1986, ss 13(7), 14, 10(6) and 83 respectively. AHA 1986, s 84 and Sch 11 govern the procedure on an arbitration.

17 AHA 1986, s 22. The detailed regulation of special aspects of the parties' contract of tenancy does not stop there. There is a special rule as to compensation for damage by wild animals (AHA 1986, s 20) and a limitation on recovery of penal rent by distress (AHA 1986, s 24).

18 The landlord may claim under the contract of tenancy for the tenant's failure to farm in accordance with the rules of good husbandry (AHA 1986, s 71(3)). A claim may be made under AHA 1986, s 71(1) for breaches by the tenant of his implied obligation to farm in accordance with the rules of good husbandry. This claim is an alternative to the claim under the contract. The landlord may also claim under AHA 1986, s 72 for general deterioration of the holding. Claims under both AHA 1986, ss 71 and 72 must be preceded by an arbitration notice. The landlord may also claim damages at common law during the tenancy for dilapidations to particular buildings or fixed equipment, subject to the ceiling imposed by Landlord and Tenant Act 1927, s 18(1).

19 AHA 1986, s 25(1). There are a number of exceptions to this rule, notably, where the tenant is insolvent, or where the notice is given under a tenancy provision authorising the resumption of possession of the whole or part of the whole or part of the holding for a specified non-agricultural purpose. Also where after a rent has been referred, the arbitrator determines a rent increase. In this case, the tenant can serve a six-month notice to quit, whatever the tenancy may provide (AHA 1986, s 25(3)).

20 *Johnson v Moreton* [1980] AC 37, [1978] 3 All ER 37, HL. See also *Gisborne v Burton* [1988] 3 All ER 760, CA; Rodgers [1989] Conv 196, for a case where an attempt to evade AHA 1986, s 26(1) by means of the grant of a sub-tenancy failed.

tenants from declining to serve a counter-notice if they do not want to, even if this will entail that the landlord can then recover possession against a sub-tenant.[21] Where the landlord's notice specifies no statutory grounds the landlord has one month from service of his notice to apply to the Agricultural Land Tribunal for consent to the operation of the notice.[22]

The consent of the Agricultural Land Tribunal to an unspecified notice to quit may only be given if the landlord establishes one of five grounds. These are designed to allow repossession where the land could be put to better use by the landlord,[23] or where the landlord proposes to use the land for non-agricultural purposes,[24] but there is also a greater hardship ground.[25] However, these grounds are subject to an overriding principle that the Tribunal cannot in any case consent to the operation of the notice if a fair and reasonable landlord would not insist on possession.[26]

The landlord of a pre-1995 agricultural tenancy may preclude the tenant serving a counter-notice by serving a notice specifying one or more of a set of statutory grounds. It is implicit that if the landlord has made false statement in relation to a chosen statutory ground, the whole notice will become invalid owing to its being tainted by fraud.[27] There are a number of statutory grounds.[28] Ground or Case D has given rise to perhaps the largest number of reported disputes.

21 *Barrett v Morgan* [2000] 2 AC 264. In this case the tenants had agreed not to serve a counter-notice on the landlord.

22 AHA 1986, s 27(1). The one-month period is inflexible: *Parrish v Kinsey* [1983] 2 EGLR 13, CA.

23 As with the good husbandry ground (AHA 1986, s 27(3)(a)) and also the sound estate management ground (AHA 1986, s 27(3)(b)) as well as the agricultural research ground (AHA 1986, s 27(3)(c) and (d)).

24 AHA 1986, s 27(3)(f). The use must fall outside specified Ground B.

25 AHA 1986, s 27(3)(e). The Tribunal may take into account any poor performance by the tenant as a farmer (*R v Agricultural Land Tribunal for the South Eastern Area, ex p Parslow* [1979] 2 EGLR 1).

26 AHA 1986, s 27(2). For an example of the exercise of the discretion see *Jones v Burgoyne* (1963) 188 Estates Gazette 497.

27 *Rous v Mitchell* [1991] 1 All ER 676, CA; Rodgers [1991] Conv 144. In this context, a fraudulent statement includes one that is recklessly careless. It makes no difference that the tenant is not in fact deceived by the statement. Estoppel may also afford a defence to a notice relying on a specified ground: see *John v George* [1996] 1 EGLR 7, CA.

28 Apart from Case D they are: Case A (smallholdings), Case B (planning consent) as to which see *Floyer-Acland v Osmond* [2000] 2 EGLR 1; Case C (certificate of bad husbandry), Case E (irremediable breaches of a term or condition of the tenancy); Case F (tenant insolvency) and Case G (death of tenant).

Non-compliance with notice to pay rent or to remedy breaches (Case D)

Under Case D, at the date of the notice to quit, the tenant has failed to comply with a landlord's written notice[29] in the prescribed form[30] requiring him:

1 within two months of the service of the notice, to pay any rent due;[31] or

2 with a reasonable period specified in the notice, to remedy any breach capable of being remedied by him of the terms and conditions of the tenancy.

1 Rent. Once the tenant fails to pay all the rent due within two months of the landlord's notice to pay the notice to quit takes effect,[32] unless the two-month requirement has been waived by express or implied agreement.[33] However, the tenant may contest the notice by arbitration under AHA 1986, Sch 4. If he fails to do this, the notice, provided it is in the correct form,[34] will deprive the tenant of his tenancy. Equity does not intervene in this process, since the statutory procedure is not treated as being equivalent to forfeiture.[35]

2 Other Breaches. A notice to remedy other breaches must, as with a notice to pay rent, be in the prescribed form. It must state a period for remedying the breach in question which must be of at least six months in length.[36] Where works of repair maintenance or replacement are required, the tenant has one month from service of the notice in which to contest a reason stated in the notice by means of a written notice specifying the items in relation to which he denies liability and requiring arbitration.[37] The arbitrator has wide powers to modify or alter a notice to do work. He may extend the period in which the tenant is to carry out the work. But an original or modified notice to do work must be complied with in full. Substantial compliance is not enough.[38]

---

29 Where the premises held by the tenant include a dwelling, a Case D notice must be preceded by a notice under the Landlord and Tenant Act 1987, s 48, until which service no rent is due: see *Dallhold Estates (UK) Pty Ltd v Lindsey Trading Properties Inc* [1994] 1 EGLR 93, CA.

30 Ie as prescribed by Agricultural Holdings etc Regulations 1987, SI 1987/11.

31 Rent is not due, at least in Scots law, if the tenant is entitled to withhold it as where the landlord is in material breach of his own obligations: see *Alexander v Royal Hotel (Caithness) Ltd* [2001] 1 EGLR 6.

32 *Stoneman v Brown* [1973] 2 All ER 225, CA.

33 See, however, *Official Solicitor v Thomas* [1986] 2 EGLR 1, CA (envisaging that a landlord might if he wished accept a tender of a cheque but had not done so on the facts).

34 As to which see *Pickard v Bishop* (1975) 31 P & CR 108, CA and *Dickinson v Boucher* [1984] 1 EGLR 12, CA: a strict test is applied. The landlord must thus, eg state his name and address correctly, the rent due and the correct name and address of all joint tenants (as to the latter point see *Jones v Lewis* (1973) 25 P & CR 375, CA).

35 *Parrish v Kinsey* [1983] 2 EGLR 13, CA.

36 If more than one breach is alleged, a reasonable time in which to remedy each of them must be allowed by the landlord, or the notice will be bad: *Wykes v Davis* [1975] QB 843, [1975] 1 All ER 399, CA.

37 Agricultural Holdings (Arbitration on Notices) Order 1987, SI 1987/710, art 3.

38 *Price v Romilly* [1960] 3 All ER 429.

However, a tenant who has not complied with a Case D notice has the right to require the consent of the Agricultural Land Tribunal to the notice.[39]

---

39 AHA 1986, s 28. The tenant has one month from, notably, the arbitration award to require such consent. The powers of the Tribunal are set out in AHA 1986, s 28(5). They must consent to the notice unless it appears to them that a fair and reasonable landlord would not insist on possession, having regard notably to the extent of the tenant's failure to comply with the notice to do work.

CHAPTER 27

Farm business tenancies

I INTRODUCTION AND POLICY

General background

The common law rules governing tenancies of farmland and associated buildings have long been subjected to statutory controls. Yet, during most of the last century, the proportion of agricultural land farmed by tenants, as opposed to landowners, under various different arrangements has been in decline.[1]

With the avowed intention of deregulating the law, and of encouraging new lettings of farmland for agricultural and other more diversified uses, such as the provision of leisure facilities, Parliament has enacted ATA 1995.[2] The machinery of the Act is a break with most aspects of the previous statutory regime. It confers no security on an agricultural tenant and shifts the balance of advantage firmly into the landlord's favour in that respect. The new legislation is supposed to mark a change away from the making of detailed statutory provisions as to most aspects of the contractual relationship, once established within ATA 1995, between the parties to a tenancy of farming land. Parliament now favours freedom of contract. However, it has been said that the rules in relation to the establishment of a farm business tenancy, a pre-requisite to taking advantage of the new rules, may put off new entrants to tenanted farming, owing to their complexity.[3]

---

1   It appears that in 1991, for example, about one-third of agricultural land was held by tenants. Cardwell, [2000] Conv 229, thinks that this proportion had increased by 1999.
2   See further and passim, Sydenham and Mainwaring, *Farm Business Tenancies*; Evans *Agricultural Tenancies Act 1995*; Rodgers *Agricultural Law* (1998) chs 3 and 4. For a comparison with the US see Cardwell [2000] Conv 229.
3   See Gibbard and Ravenscroft *Reform of Agricultural Holdings* (1996) CELTS (University of Reading No 96/3), para 6.8.

A deregulated approach

That ATA 1995 follows a deregulation policy is illustrated by its approach to the contractual obligations of the parties to a farm business tenancy (other than as to rent review and compensation). These are left for the parties to insert into the tenancy and to the general law to resolve. Thus, ATA 1995 does not enable the tenant to refer the terms of a non-written agreement to arbitration, as does AHA 1986.

The freedom of contract approach is further shown by the fact that ATA 1995 has no specific statutory rules dealing with damages on account of tenants' dilapidations. The issue is left to the common law as adjusted by the Landlord and Tenant Act 1927, s 18(1). Model clauses as to repairs and maintenance in the form of delegated legislation, a feature of the old rules, are not part of the 1995 Act compulsory scheme of things.

The most dramatic illustration, however, of the deregulation promoted by ATA 1995 is that it confers no security of tenure on a farm business tenant. He has no automatic right to renewal of his tenancy. One reason for the lack of security has been said to be that 'the farming industry today does not need protection but rather deregulation and competition'.[4] The parties have an initial choice between the grant of a fixed-term tenancy, and a periodic tenancy. In the case of fixed-term tenancies which are granted for more than two years, statutory continuation applies.[5] However, this is not the case with fixed-term tenancies for shorter periods than this. As has been noted,[6] ATA 1995 will allow landlords to grant a tenancy for less than two years certain which will be excluded from statutory continuation, much as under the old regime such a tenancy escaped the protection of the security umbrella.

There is thus a contrast between the new rules and the right of the tenant of an agricultural holding within the old system to prevent, by service of a counter-notice, his landlord from terminating the tenancy by a general notice to quit. It is unlikely that any farm business tenant will enjoy a tenancy of the land for his life, or perhaps for any long period. It is possible that in relation to tenancies of 'bare land' ATA 1995 may lead to short terms and the adoption of farming practices to enable market rents to be paid, at the possible expense of the long-term interest of the land itself.[7]

ATA 1995 is not retrospective. There is nothing to prevent the landlord of a sitting tenant within AHA 1986 from offering his tenant a new farm business tenancy, in return for the surrender of his previous tenancy. Special deterrents against this type of replacement such as exist in the private residential sector were not deemed necessary, so emphasising the need for old-style tenants to be wary of offers of new land to be incorporated into their tenancy.

4   Sydenham and Mainwaring *Farm Business Tenancies*, p 5.
5   ATA 1995, s 5(1).
6   Rodgers *Agricultural Law*, para 4.04.
7   For these and other considerations see Bishop [1996] Conv 243; cf Gibbard and Ravenscroft *Reform of Agricultural Holdings* (1996) CELTS (University of Reading No 96/3), para 6.4. It appears from research cited in Cardwell [2000] Conv 229, that initial indications show terms of about four years.

Two planks of ATA 1995

The full-blown security of tenure provisions of AHA 1986, combined with its succession provisions, were blamed by the government for a fall in the amount of tenanted agricultural land in England and Wales. By 1994, one of the Ministers sponsoring the then Bill thought that only about one-third of such land was at that time rented, and much of that under short-term, non-secure, tenancies.[8] Moreover, it was feared that a farm tenant who diversified his initial farming business into other activities, during the tenancy, such as the provision of leisure facilities, might take the tenancy out of the protection of the new rules into that of LTA 1954, Pt II. Specific provision is made to cover this contingency, so as not to frustrate one of the main planks of the new Act. ATA 1995, passed with the agreement of the landlords' and tenants' representative organisations, creates a 'farm business tenancy'. The Act is not retrospective.[9] By ATA 1995, s 2(1), a tenancy which begins before the commencement of the Act, on 1 September 1995, cannot be a farm business tenancy.

Main objectives and principles of ATA 1995

It appears convenient to provide a summary of the main objectives and principles of ATA 1995.

1   A principal aim is to get rid of the *security of tenure* apparatus applicable to lettings of agricultural holdings. ATA 1995 requires a farm business tenancy to be determined by a notice to quit by either party. However, the Act imposes merely formal requirements as to the form and duration of a notice to quit, which, if valid, takes effect in the same way as would any common law notice, to determine the tenancy. There is no automatic right to renewal of a farm business tenancy, once such a tenancy is validly ended by the landlord.

2   ATA 1995 precludes any *succession scheme* applying to a farm business tenancy. The attainment of this objective was simple enough, by precluding AHA 1986 rules from applying to most tenancies granted on or after 1 September 1995.

3   The *constitution of farm business tenancies* is provided for in specific rules. Following an exchange of notices at the beginning of the tenancy, the parties may enter into a tenancy which initially envisages the undertaking of farming activities for the purposes of a trade or business, but which also allows the tenant who continues to run parts of the land concerned as a farm, to enter into major diversification away from agriculture, while ensuring that the tenancy does not cease to be a farm business tenancy for that reason alone.[10] The government believed that, without this safeguard for landlords, the tenant, by diversification, might risk bringing the a tenancy which was originally a farm business tenancy

8   Earl Howe *Hansard*, 28 November 1994, col 486, in second reading debate of the Agricultural Tenancies Bill.
9   It applies to land in which the Crown holds or has held an interest (ATA 1995, s 37).
10 As stated by the government spokesman in the House of Lords at the Committee Stage of the Agricultural Tenancies Bill, *Hansard*, 12 December 1994, col 1091.

within ATA 1995 into the (more stringent) protection of LTA 1954, Pt II, without the landlord's consent.[11]

4 The farm business tenancies legislation introduces a fresh statutory framework for compensation to farm business tenants for improvements carried out during the tenancy. The provisions seemingly provide for rapid compensation to the tenant so that he is able to have the funds to start a new farming business after having to quit his former premises, seeing that he has no security of tenure under the Act. A novel feature of the rules is that the tenant may claim compensation in respect of his having obtained a planning permission which was not implemented during his tenancy (ATA 1995, s 16). The basis of compensation is generally the increase attributable to the improvement in the value of the holding at the termination of the tenancy (ATA 1995, s 20(1)), which in itself does not represent a break with the previous rules.

Instead of providing lists of matters for which the tenant may claim compensation, with or without the landlord's consent,[12] ATA 1995 imposes a general requirement that no compensation may be claimed unless the landlord has given his written consent to the making of an improvement. The government resisted an amendment which would have required the consent of the landlord not to be unreasonably withheld. They said that a landlord of an agricultural tenant had a close personal interest in the land, its management and development.[13] The tenant is protected, however, by a new enabling provision which allows him to refer a refusal of consent or condition attached to a consent to arbitration.

5 ATA 1995 introduces altered statutory rules as to *the revision of rent payable under a farm business tenancy*, which rules may yield to the contrary intention of the parties, as where they provide in the tenancy for a fixed rent during the term. Subject to that, the rent may be reviewed in accordance with a formula, such as the Retail Prices Index, or, if the parties so agree, at specified intervals. Either party has the right to refer a rent to arbitration under the general law, in contrast to the position under AHA 1986, where arbitrations are within the umbrella of that Act.

6 ATA 1995 is essentially based, then, on deregulation principles. It provides a framework for the agreement of the parties and not a prescriptive set of rules. To take one good illustration of this: under ATA 1995, the parties are free to leave the issue of repairing liabilities to the common law principles and thus to express

---

11 *Hansard,* 12 December 1994, col 1090. However, it may be that the notice procedure is defective. After the grant of the tenancy, if the tenant then diversifies away from agricultural uses, it is said that the notice procedure cannot be used again in relation to that land: Rodgers *Agricultural Law*, para 3.14. This contention is based on the requirement of ATA 1995, s 1(4)(b) that, at the commencement of the tenancy, the land must be wholly or primarily agricultural.

12 Which method dates back at least to the Agricultural Holdings Act 1883, and was repeated in the Agricultural Holdings Acts 1923, 1948 and 1986. Listing is, however, a method which may involve regular updating.

13 Earl Howe, HL Committee *Hansard*, 13 December 1994, col 1233. If that is so, then it is curious that ATA 1995 does not impose a residence requirement on the tenant of a farm business tenancy.

agreement. They are not required by the Act to make use of model clauses as is the presumption where the previous regime applies.[14]

II DEFINITION AND SCOPE OF ATA 1995

Application of new rules

ATA 1995, Pt I establishes a farm business tenancy: a new form of tenancy where land is to be used for the purposes of agriculture.[15] AHA 1986 does not apply to any tenancy beginning on or after 1 September 1995. Equally, ATA 1995 is not applicable to tenancies which began before 1 September 1995 (ATA 1995, s 2(1)), which, if of an agricultural holding, may be governed by AHA 1986. A tenancy at will and a genuine licence to occupy fall outside ATA 1995.[16] There are a number of cases, specified where AHA 1986 applies to a tenancy of an agricultural holding created on or after 1 September 1995 (ATA 1995, s 4). The principal exceptions are as follows.[17]

1 Pre-Act contracts. ATA 1995 does not apply where a tenancy was granted by a written contract of tenancy entered into before 1 September 1995 which indicates that AHA 1986 is to apply to the tenancy (ATA 1995, s 4(1)(a)).[18] This exception might apply where, for some reason, the parties have contracted say in August 1994 for a tenancy under which possession is to be taken, and rent paid, only on or after 1 September 1995.

2 Preservation of established successions. A number of related matters are here covered. Thus, where a tenancy was obtained by succession under the curtailed succession scheme by virtue of a direction of an Agricultural Land Tribunal under AHA 1986, ss 39 or 53 (ATA 1995, s 4(1)(b)), ATA 1995 does not apply to it.[19] This exemption applies, therefore, where a direction is made for a succession either in favour of a person eligible to succeed to a tenancy of an agricultural holding within AHA 1986, or the person nominated by the tenant of such a holding applies for a Tribunal direction. It is also possible for the parties, in a written contract of tenancy entered into after

---

14 According to research quoted by Rodgers *Agricultural Law,* para 3.61, about 35% of farm business tenancies then being entered into in fact made use of the model clauses imposed by statutory instrument (SI 1973/1473 as amended) and 44% did not. What is not clear is whether the model clauses as incorporated into the former farm business tenancies were those of the original or amended regulations.

15 'Agriculture' is defined by ATA 1995, s 38(1) and is the same as that of AHA 1986, s 96(1).

16 Tenancies at will are excluded by ATA 1995, s 38(1). There is no anti-avoidance provision corresponding to AHA 1986, s 2(2)(b) but similar principles would presumably apply to ATA 1995.

17 See further Evans *Agricultural Tenancies Act 1995,* notes to ATA 1995, s 4.

18 Where an incoming tenant accepts a post-1 September 1995 tenancy of an agricultural holding as a result of the 'Evesham custom' that tenancy is subject to AHA 1986 (ATA 1995, s 4(1)(e)). That custom regulates the compensation of tenants of market gardens.

19 There is a related exception (ATA 1995, s 4(1)(c)) where a direction is made to one of a number of joint tenants under AHA 1986, s 39.

ATA 1995 commences, to contract into AHA 1986 statutory succession rules, where the parties agree on the name of the successor (ATA 1995, s 4(1)(d)).[20]

3 Variation of AHA 1986 tenancy. The aim of non-retrospectivity for farm business tenancies would have been at risk, where a tenancy of an agricultural holding to which AHA 1986 applied is varied after the commencement of ATA 1995, owing to the common law principle that should an existing tenancy be varied by, notably, adding land to the holding, in consideration of an increased rent, the effect of this transaction is seemingly to surrender the existing tenancy and to re-grant a new tenancy.[21] Although ATA 1995, s 4(1)(f) affirms this principle, it provides that the new tenancy is to be subject to AHA 1986, provided that the tenant had been the tenant of the holding 'or of any agricultural holding which comprised the whole or a substantial part of the land comprised in the holding' under a tenancy to which AHA 1986 applied.

Definition of farm business tenancy

There are two types of farm business tenancy (ATA 1995, s 1(1)). ATA 1995 leaves it to the parties to decide about the length of the tenancy: there is no upper or lower limit on duration. Both types of farm business tenancy are however subject to the 'business conditions'. However, if these conditions are satisfied, the tenancy[22] must either comply with the agriculture condition or the notice conditions.

Business conditions

The business conditions are as follows (ATA 1995, s 1(2)).
1 all or part of the land comprised in the tenancy must be farmed for the purposes of a trade or business, and
2 since the beginning of the tenancy,[23] all or part of the land so comprised has been so farmed.

Although it appears from ATA 1995, s 38(2) that references to the farming of land include references to the carrying on in relation to land of any agricultural activity, so referring back to the wide definition of 'agriculture' in s 38(1), the expression 'trade or business' is not defined in ATA 1995. It is therefore thought that, at least at the beginning of the tenancy, the whole or part of the land must be farmed as a business. It may well be that to satisfy the business condition, it is not necessary for the same

20 This principle is subject to the limitations of ATA 1995, s 4(2) so as to avoid overlapping with the remainder of the succession exceptions in ATA 1995, s 4(1).
21 See eg *Jenkin R Lewis v Kerman* [1971] Ch 477.
22 Which expression includes a sub-tenancy and an agreement for a tenancy or sub-tenancy but not a tenancy at will (ATA 1995, s 38(1)).
23 Ie since the day on which, under the terms of the tenancy, the tenant is entitled to possession under the tenancy (ATA 1995, s 38(4)) and not, therefore, the date of the contract, if possession is postponed.

part of the holding always to have been farmed for the purposes of a trade or business: the overriding requirement is that some part of the holding is at all times used for commercial farming.[24]

The business conditions must be satisfied throughout the tenancy, so that, since the tenant is required to farm at least part of the land throughout for the purposes of a trade or business, he would cease to have a farm business tenancy if such farming discontinued completely.[25] It remains to be seen, where the 'notice condition' applies, how much diversification away from farming would be allowed: presumably the question would be one of fact and degree. If all farming activity ceased, the tenancy would fall within LTA 1954, Pt II.

Agriculture condition

The agriculture condition is that the character of the tenancy must be 'primarily or wholly agricultural' having regard to:

1 the terms of the tenancy;
2 the use of the land comprised in the tenancy;
3 the nature of any commercial activities carried on on the land; and
4 any other relevant circumstances (ATA 1995, s 1(3)).

Nevertheless, should the tenant of a farm business tenancy where the notices envisaged immediately below were not exchanged discontinue wholly or substantially all agricultural activities then, even if this is without the landlord's consent, ATA 1995 would cease to apply to the tenancy. However, the tenant is precluded by ATA 1995, s 1(8) from claiming in breach of the terms of his tenancy, that he carries on only non-agricultural commercial activities on the land so as, for example, to bring the tenancy within the protection of LTA 1954, Pt II.

Notice conditions

If the notice conditions are complied with at the beginning of the tenancy[26] or the day on which the parties enter into any instrument creating the tenancy,[27] diversification from primary farming activities may safely take place, and the tenancy remains firmly within ATA 1995. It has been said that parties ought to ideally comply with the notice conditions so as to avoid uncertainty about the nature of the tenancy.[28]

24 See Sydenham and Mainwaring, p 18.
25 Subject to ATA 1995, s 1(7): if at the date of proceedings, for example, all or part of the land is farmed for the purposes of a trade or business, it is presumed that it had been so farmed since the beginning of the tenancy.
26 See ATA 1995, s 38(1) above.
27 Other than an agreement to enter into a tenancy at a future date (ATA 1995, s 1(5)(a)), so ruling out the creation of reversionary tenancies from the notice conditions but not the agriculture condition.
28 See Sydenham and Mainwaring, p 20.

The landlord and tenant must give each other a written notice, which must be a separate notice: it is not sufficient if the terms of the tenancy incorporate it (ATA 1995, s 1(6)).[29] The notices must be served in accordance with ATA 1995 (ATA 1995, s 36) as by delivery to the party concerned,[30] though in the case of service on the landlord, service on any managing agent of his is sufficient (ATA 1995, s 36(5)(a)).

The *contents* of the notice are as follows. The land to be comprised in the tenancy must be identified. The notice must state that the person giving the notice intends the tenancy to be and to remain a farm business tenancy (ATA 1995, s 1(4)(a)). Moreover, at the beginning of the tenancy, having regard to the terms of the tenancy and to any other relevant circumstances, the tenancy must have a character which is primarily or wholly agricultural (ATA 1995, s 1(4)(b)).

The tenant of a farm business tenancy where initial notices have been exchanged may diversify into non-farming business activities during the duration of his tenancy in principle, without a risk that ATA 1995 rules will not apply, provided that the tenancy was initially wholly or mainly agricultural, and that he continues to farm part of the land for the purposes of his trade or business (ATA 1995, s 1(2)(a)). However, such diversification must not be into activities in breach of the terms of the tenancy. If it is, then the tenancy ceases to be a farm business tenancy, on account of failure to comply with the 'business condition', unless the landlord or his predecessor consented to the breach or the landlord acquiesced in it (ATA 1995, s 1(8)). Thus, if the tenant wishes to open a leisure park and this is prohibited by the terms of the tenancy, in principle ATA 1995 would cease to apply to him and the landlord could regain possession untrammelled by the Act, by common law means. It may also be presumed that where a tenant runs a business on the land in breach of a planning enforcement order, this could be relied on by the landlord as a breach of ATA 1995, s 1(8), so entitling him to possession.

Where a fixed-term (but not a periodic) farm business tenancy is granted subject to the protection of the notice conditions, the landlord and tenant may subsequently vary the amount of land comprised in the tenancy, provided that any additions or subtractions are 'small in relation to the size of the holding and do not affect the character of the holding' without any need to serve fresh notices on each other (ATA 1995, s 3(2)). Were it not for this provision, it might have been held that the previous tenancy had been surrendered and a new tenancy re-granted which would have entailed the service of fresh notices so as to preserve the advantages of allowing diversification out of farming activities.[31]

---

29   In contrast to the position with, eg an owner-occupier notice under an assured tenancy.
30   It is specifically provided that transmission by fax or other electronic means is not sufficient service of a notice (ATA 1995, s 36(3)).
31   According to the government at the Committee Stage of the Bill in the House of Lords: *Hansard* 12 December 1995, col 1144.

III TERMINATION PROVISIONS OF ATA 1995

With the avowed aim of encouraging landlords to let more agricultural land, ATA 1995 does not confer any security of tenure on the tenant, save on an interim basis, after the expiry or termination of a fixed-term or periodic farm business tenancy. However, the legislation does not allow either party to a farm business tenancy to bring it to an end merely by serving a notice to quit valid at common law on the other party. Instead, it continues fixed-term farm business tenancies for a term of more than two years as tenancies from year to year.[32] The only way the landlord or tenant may prevent such continuation is by serving a notice of intention to terminate on the other party. In the case of a farm business tenancy from year to year, whether a periodic yearly tenancy or a continuing fixed-term tenancy for more than two years, the Act requires either party to give the other a notice to quit of at least twelve months before its stated termination date. These limited restrictions may be intended to allow the parties sufficient time either to negotiate a new tenancy or the tenant to find alternative accommodation and premises for his farm business and his family, if he lives on the premises.[33]

Tenancies for more than two years

A farm business tenancy for a term of more than two years, but not for any shorter term, is subject to statutory continuation by ATA 1995, s 5(1). Instead of terminating on its term date,[34] the tenancy continues from that date as a tenancy from year to year 'but otherwise on the terms of the original tenancy so far as applicable'. Either party has the right, under ATA 1995, s 5(1), to prevent statutory continuation by a written notice to the other party of his intention to terminate the tenancy. A notice of intention must be given at least 12 but less than 24 months before the term date. The effect of a valid notice under ATA 1995, s 5(1) is to terminate the farm business tenancy for a term of more than two years on the term date originally agreed, and to entitle the landlord to possession as from then, unless a new tenancy is agreed between the parties. Since, after a valid notice under ATA 1995, s 5(1) has been given, there is no continuing tenancy from year to year, no separate notice to quit is seemingly required from the party serving the s 5(1) notice under ATA 1995, s 6(1).

The statutory method of termination has effect notwithstanding 'any agreement to the contrary' (ATA 1995, s 5(4)). This seemingly precludes the parties from agreeing, by

---

32 Thus supplying the parties with an obvious means of avoiding statutory continuation (viz, the grant of a fixed-term tenancy for a term of less than two years in duration).

33 There is nothing in ATA 1995 to prevent the landlord including a forfeiture clause in a fixed-term farm business tenancy. According to Rodgers, paras 3.50-3.51, such clauses when used extend not only to breaches of covenant to pay rent or other breaches of tenant obligation, but also to the appointment of a receiver and the presentation of a winding-up petition in the case of a corporate tenant.

34 Ie the date fixed for the expiry of the term in the case of a fixed-term tenancy (ATA 1995, s 5(2)).

either a term in the tenancy itself or a subsequent variation to it, to surrender a fixed-term farm business tenancy for two years or more by, say, a two months' notice. If either the landlord or tenant fails to serve a notice of intention to terminate within the prescribed time-limits before the term date, the tenancy will continue under ATA 1995, s 6.

The special position of a farm business tenancy for more than two years is re-enforced by ATA 1995, s 7. By ATA 1995, s 7(1) 'any notice to quit the holding or part ... given in pursuance of any provision of the tenancy ... shall be invalid unless it is in writing and is given at least twelve months but less than twenty-four months before the date on which it is to take effect'. This particular requirement overrides 'any provision to the contrary in the tenancy'.[35] This wording contrasts with the words 'any agreement to the contrary' in ATA 1995, s 5(1) and might invite a narrow construction of them, so that the parties could, by a separate agreement to the tenancy provide for, say, a different length of notice to that laid down in ATA 1995, s 7(1).[36]

ATA 1995, s 7(1) is presumably directed at landlords' or tenants' options to break the tenancy following a unilateral notice. Should such a notice be required by the terms of the tenancy to be served six months in advance, the terms of the tenancy would be disregarded. It may be that nothing in ATA 1995, s 7(1) would prevent a landlord, in such a case, from serving a notice to determine under his break-clause which gave the tenant the minimum 12-month period of notice, if the only effect of the provision is to substitute a statutory period and form of notice for that agreed between the parties.

The relationship between ATA 1995, ss 5(1) and 7(1) is not free from difficulty where the tenancy is for a fixed term of over two years. It is thought that, if, for example, the landlord serves a valid notice to break a fixed-term tenancy for ten years, expiring in December 2005 to expire in December 2000, the 'term date' of the tenancy is, for the purposes of ATA 1995, s 5(1), December 2000, since the purpose of ATA 1995, s 7(1) is presumably to give the tenant a minimum period of notice which is of at least twelve months. The continuation provisions of ATA 1995 would seemingly, following the first part of ATA 1995, s 5(1), apply, as would those of ATA 1995, s 6(1). The landlord would seemingly need to serve a separate notice to quit on the tenant, complying with ATA 1995, s 6(1), and expiring in December 2001, as his break-clause notice ('to quit') could not be saved by ATA 1995, s 6(2), discussed below, not being a notice of intention 'which complies with' ATA 1995, s 5(1).

---

35   ATA 1995, s 7(1) does not apply to a tenant's counter-notice under LPA 1925, s 140(2) (ATA 1995, s 7(2) , and see below) or to a tenancy caught by LPA 1925, s 149(6) (ATA 1995, s 7(3)).

36   Cf also the wider language of LTA 1954, s 38(1), referring to contrary agreements the instrument creating the tenancy or not.

Length of notice to quit

A notice to quit by the landlord or the tenant of a farm business tenancy from year to year is subject to the limited protection conferred by ATA 1995, s 6. This imposes a minimum 12-month requirement on landlords' and tenants' notices to quit. These requirements apply 'notwithstanding any provision to the contrary in the tenancy'. A notice to quit the whole or part of the holding concerned will be invalid unless:

1   it is in writing;
2   it is to take effect at 'the end of a year of the tenancy'; and
3   it is given at least 12 months but less than 24 months before the date on which it is to take effect.

ATA 1995, s 6(1) applies to periodic tenancies from year to year and to continuing fixed-term tenancies of over two years, as well as to fixed-term tenancies of up to two years. However, it is provided that where a landlord or tenant gives a valid notice of intention to terminate under ATA 1995, s 5(1), in relation to a tenancy for a term of two years or more, provided it takes effect on the first anniversary of the term date, a notice to quit under ATA 1995, s 6(1) is not invalid merely because it is given before the term date (ATA 1995, s 6(2)). Thus, if L granted T a farm business tenancy on 1 January 1996 with a term date of 31 December 1999, he may decide to give T a notice of intention to terminate the tenancy in November 1998 (13 months before the term date, and so valid). L could at the same time, in November 1998, serve on T a notice to quit, complying with ATA 1995, s 6(1), which takes effect on 31 December 1999, that date being the end of a year of the tenancy. The notice to quit would not be invalid because it was served during the term certain.

Where a tenant of a farm business tenancy receives a notice to quit part of the land, because the reversion has been severed as between two or more landlords, he has the specific right under LPA1925, s 140(2) to give a one month notice to quit to the reversioner in relation to the rest of the land. Although the landlord's notice must comply with the minimum 12-month requirement of ATA 1995, s 6(1), a tenants' counter-notice under LPA 1925, s 140(2) is saved by ATA 1995, s 6(3) from having to do so.

IV   RENT REVIEW PROVISIONS

ATA 1995, Pt II provides for the review of the rent of a farm business tenancy. However, the parties are free to fix the initial rent for the tenancy at any level they like.

The statutory provisions may be contracted out of by the parties, but only in three cases. First, where the terms of the tenancy expressly state that there is to be no review of rent during the tenancy (ATA 1995, s 9(a)) but the rent is otherwise to remain fixed, as where it is reserved throughout. The second case where the statutory provisions do not apply is where, although the rent is, apart from any review, to remain fixed, the tenancy allows for the variation of rent at a specified time or times during the tenancy by or to a specified amount (ATA 1995, s 9(b)(i)). The third case is where, again subject to the rent otherwise remaining fixed, there is to be a rent review in accordance with a specified formula which is not upwards only ('does not preclude a reduction') and which does not require or permit the 'exercise by any person of any judgment or discretion in relation to the determination of the rent of the holding' (ATA 1995, s 9(b)(ii)). Thus a rent review formula, requiring the parties to agree on an open market rent, to a level which may be above or below the current level of rent, but which does not envisage any arbitration or determination by an expert, would seemingly operate to the exclusion of the statutory rules. By contrast, a formula which required the agreement of the parties to an increase only in the rent would not be excepted, and this provision of ATA 1995 is the first known manifestation of some legislative hostility to upwards-only rent review clauses.

Arbitration notices

The statutory machinery operates by entitling the landlord or the tenant to refer the rent to arbitration at regular intervals. Accordingly, both the landlord and tenant of a farm business tenancy may give a notice in writing to the other (called a 'statutory review notice') which requires that the rent payable for the holding is referred to arbitration under ATA 1995 (ATA 1995, s 10(1)). This provision overrides any agreement to the contrary (ATA 1995, s 9). The new rent is to be paid as from the 'review date', but specific provisions are made as to this date, so governing the minimum life of a rent review.

The review date must, in any case, be at least 12 months but less than 24 months from the date of giving of the 'statutory review notice' (ATA 1995, s 10(3)). The terms of the tenancy itself, if they provide for shorter periods, are overridden. Moreover, so giving primacy to the agreement of the parties, if they have agreed in writing (seemingly in the tenancy or by separate agreement) that the rent is to be varied as from a specified date or dates, or at specified intervals, the review date must be a date as from which the rent could be varied under the agreement (ATA 1995, s 10(4)).[37] Subject to this, the date as from which the new rent is payable, the review date:

1   must be an anniversary of the beginning of the tenancy,[38] or some other day of the year as agreed between the landlord and tenant, and

---

37   Likewise, if the parties have agreed in writing that the statutory review date is to be a specified date or dates, the review date must be one of those dates (ATA 1995, s 10(5)). Once again it will be seen that owing to the primacy of the agreement of the parties, the statutory three-year rule, which is carried over from AHA 1986 rule, is, in Rodgers' words, op cit, para 3.82, a 'fall-back' provision.

38   Where the tenant takes a new tenancy of part of the holding from a landlord of a split reversion, the expression 'beginning of the tenancy' refers to the original tenancy until the first occasion following the beginning of the new tenancy that an arbitration, etc under ATA 1995, s 10 takes effect (ATA 1995, s 11). Thus, if L1 grants T a tenancy for 10 years in 1998 and T is granted a new tenancy of a smaller holding by L2, who holds part of the freehold, in 2000, T cannot, seemingly, avoid a rent reference in 2001.

2   must be not before the end of three years beginning with the latest of four dates, notably, the beginning of the tenancy, or any date as from which a previous direction of an arbitrator as to the amount of the rent took effect (ATA 1995, s 10(6)).[39]

Where, therefore, the parties to a farm business tenancy of substantial length have agreed that the rent is to be reviewed at five-yearly intervals, this agreement prevails and no reference to arbitration under ATA 1995 may be made by either party at shorter intervals. Although the interval between reviews which applies in the absence of agreement for statutory purposes is three years, there is nothing in the Act to prevent the parties from agreeing on shorter intervals, even annually.

Arbitrations: further

Once a statutory review notice has been given under ATA 1995, the parties may agree on the new rent or, failing agreement, may appoint an arbitrator. If, within six months ending with the review date, they cannot agree even on a name, either party has the right under ATA 1995, s 12 to apply to the President of the RICS for the appointment of an arbitrator. Where the parties have agreed that the new rent is to be decided on some other basis, as by an expert,[40] but that person has not been appointed within the six months already mentioned, the same default provision applies, and either party may apply for the appointment of an arbitrator to the President of the RICS.

The amount of the rent referred to an arbitration is to be determined in accordance with ATA 1995, s 13. The policy of ATA 1995 to avoid the prescriptive approach of AHA 1986.[41] The policy of these provisions of the Act is seemingly to allow the rent for a farm business tenancy to reflect the law of supply and demand.[42] The new rent is payable as at the review date, and the arbitrator must determine what rent is properly payable in respect of the holding. He may increase or reduce the rent previously payable or direct that it is to continue unchanged (ATA 1995, s 13(1)). The arbitrator must ascertain the rent 'at which the holding might reasonably be expected to be let on the open market by a willing landlord to a willing tenant' taking into account all relevant factors, including in every case the terms of the tenancy (ATA 1995, s 13(2)). While the arbitrator is entitled to have regard to the intervals agreed between reviews, he is to disregard the criteria for the determination of any new rent. Any effect of the fact of the occupation of the tenant who is a party to the arbitration on the rent is to be disregarded

---

39   By ATA 1995, s 10(6), the other dates are: (i) the date as from which a previous determination of rent took effect, where made by a person appointed under an agreement of the parties who was not an arbitrator, but was, eg, an expert; and (ii) the date of a previous written agreement between the parties, since the beginning of the tenancy, as to the amount of the rent.

40   It will be seen that in allowing for the appointment of an expert rather than an arbitrator, ATA 1995 is more flexible than AHA 1986.

41   *Hansard* HL Committee on the Agricultural Tenancies Bill, 12 December 1994, col 1188.

42   See Sydenham and Mainwaring, p 45 (as opposed, it appears, to any profits made by the tenant from the land); also Rodgers, para 3.87.

(ATA 1995, s 13(4)(a)). Thus, any effect of the occupation of his predecessor in title under the current or even a previous tenancy might be taken into account.

So as not to give the tenant the benefit of his own wrongdoing, the rent is not to be fixed at a lower amount by dilapidation or deterioration of, or damage to, buildings or land caused or permitted by the tenant (ATA 1995, s 13(4)(b)). The words 'caused or permitted' not only seem to apply to deliberate breaches of repairing covenant, but to neglect amounting to waste. There again being no reference to the tenant's predecessor in title under the current or a previous tenancy, it could be argued that any effect on rent of dilapidations due to such predecessor's fault could be taken into account – unless the tenant is subject not only to an obligation to repair but to put or to keep in repair.

Disregard of tenant's improvements

So as to protect the tenant against having to pay a new rent inflated by his own improvements which have a lasting value, any increase in the rental value of the holding which is due to tenant's improvements[43] is to be disregarded (ATA 1995, s 13(3)). However, the following increases owing to such improvements are not to be disregarded, because the tenant is presumed to have been adequately compensated already for these.

1   Any tenant's improvement provided under an obligation imposed on the tenant by the terms of his present or any previous tenancy, and which arose on or before the beginning of the tenancy in question;
2   Any tenant's improvement to the extent that any allowance or benefit has been made or given by the landlord in consideration of its being provided; and
3   Any tenant's improvement to the extent that the tenant has received any compensation from the landlord for the improvement.

Increases in value resulting from improvements of a predecessor in title fall outside ATA 1995, ss 13(3) and 15, and so may, if their effect is not spent, presumably be taken into account, unless the parties otherwise agree.

Comparison with previous rules

The rules for rent review under ATA 1995 are largely a break with the previous system. Those applying to farm business tenancies envisage an arbitration under the general law as the principal dispute resolution. The fact that ATA 1995 allows the parties' agreement as to the intervals of rent review to prevail over the statutory three-year intervals, which are provided in default, is new: the previous principle was that there should be three-year reviews. A further novelty of ATA 1995 is that it enables the

---

43   The definition of 'tenant's improvement' in ATA 1995, s 15, below, applies (ATA 1995, s 13(5)).

parties, by agreement, to have their dispute as to a reviewed rent referred to an expert, rather than to an arbitrator. However, one party cannot refuse to agree to such a reference without risking the other from invoking the statutory default provision for reference to an arbitrator. Although the parties are thus free to agree as to the machinery of a rent review, neither of them can avoid a rent review itself taking place if the other requires it to do so. The fact that the new formula does not require in terms that the character, situation and locality of the holding, nor its produce or related earnings capacity (in contrast to the requirements of AHA 1986) be taken into account is a result of the new, flexible, approach of the Act, so as to make the tenant pay a market rent no matter what his profits or lack of them may amount to.

V COMPENSATION FOR TENANTS' IMPROVEMENTS

Introduction

ATA 1995, Pt III provides for a fresh set of rules governing compensation payable by the landlord to the tenant of an oral or written farm business tenancy, on the tenant quitting the holding. The general policy of these provisions is seemingly two-fold. The aim of Pt III was said to be to compensate tenants quickly (and one might add, in full) for any useful improvements to incoming new tenants, thus putting them in funds with which to establish a new business, and to provide for the rapid resolution of any disputes. The tenant has, accordingly, only four months from the date of his request for the landlord's consent within which to seek arbitration (ATA 1995, s 19(3)). The landlord's position is protected to some extent by the fact that compensation is only payable for relevant improvements for which the landlord's written consent[44] has been given (ATA 1995, s 17).[45]

The second strand of policy is that, since ATA 1995 was said by the government to allow for diversification away from traditional farming, it was essential not to attempt to prescribe a legal straitjacket of permitted improvements, requiring further amendment in time.[46] This, and the argument that one could not predict in advance which improvements a diversifying tenant might make,[47] may explain why lists of permitted improvements (which have appeared since at least 1883) are not present in ATA 1995. Moreover, which is new, the obtaining of an unimplemented planning permission by a farm business tenant counts as a tenants' improvement qualifying for compensation

---

44 Written consent was said by the government spokesman in the HL Committee to be required to ensure that there was evidence at the time of assessment of compensation that the tenant was entitled to claim it (*Hansard* 13 December 1994, col 1219): a point of obvious importance where the reversion has changed hands since the giving of consent.

45 The government resisted an attempt to make such consent subject to a test of reasonableness on the ground of the special character of agricultural tenancies: *Hansard* HL Committee, 13 December 1994, col 1223.

46 HL Committee, supra, col 1208.

47 See Sydenham and Mainwairing, p 67.

within ATA 1995, Pt III. If, however, the tenant has implemented a planning permission, this form of compensation is not available, seemingly because the tenant would be able to claim, where relevant, compensation for any improvements made to the holding as a result.[48]

Definition of tenant's improvement and amount of compensation

The tenant of a farm business tenancy is entitled to claim compensation under ATA 1995, Pt III in respect of any tenant's improvement. Claims for compensation are to be settled by arbitration (ATA 1995, s 22(1)) although the parties may avert this by settling the claim by agreement in writing.[49] A tenant's right arises on the termination of his tenancy, when he quits the holding, and the landlord[50] pays the compensation (ATA 1995, s 16(1)). However, there are certain absolute bars to compensation, notably, where the tenant removes any physical improvement, notably a fixture, under ATA 1995, s 8 (as to which, see ch 12, above). No compensation is payable for improvements which do not have the landlord's prior consent, and the tenant has only a two-month period from the termination of the tenancy in which to claim compensation, failing which, his right is lost (ATA 1995, s 22(2)).

ATA 1995, s 15 gives a wide definition of 'tenant's improvement'. Two types of improvement qualify for compensation.[51]
(a) Any physical improvement made on the holding by the tenant by his own effort or wholly or partly[52] at his own expense, or
(b) Any 'intangible advantage' obtained for the holding by the tenant by his own effort or wholly or partly at his own expense, which becomes attached to the holding.

The first limb of this provision would cover permanent improvements to the holding, such as the erection of a new building or the installation of equipment which the tenant does not or cannot remove on expiry of the tenancy. Paragraph (b) is designed to cover planning permissions obtained by the tenant but not implemented by him, which will benefit his successor in title or the landlord, as well as compensation for

---

48 HL Committee *Hansard* 13 December 1994, col 1232.
49 Which must not provide for compensation in a manner not in accordance with ATA 1995, Pt III (ATA 1995, s 26(1)).
50 The policy of preserving full compensation is shown by the fact that where the reversionary estate is vested in more than one landlord, the tenant is entitled to compensation as if the estate were not severed (ATA 1995, s 25(1)) but the amount of any compensation payable may be apportioned by the arbitrator as between the different landlords (ATA 1995, s 25(2)).
51 Compensation for 'routine improvements' (tenant-right matters such as growing crops, acts of husbandry and so on) is provided for in ATA 1995, s 19(10). The tenant may apply for compensation in this case even without the landlord's prior consent (ATA 1995, s 19(9)).
52 So as not to over-compensate a tenant, where he has received a grant out of public money for an improvement, the amount of any compensation is proportionately reduced (ATA 1995, s 20(3)).

loss of EU milk or other production quotas, as well as loss of business goodwill built up by the tenant.

So as to prevent the landlord from having to pay a large amount of compensation for an improvement which, say because it was specially suited for the particular outgoing tenant's needs, might be of little value to an incoming tenant, the amount of compensation for a tenant's improvement, other than one consisting of planning permission, is the amount equal to the 'increase in value attributable to the improvement in the value of the holding at the termination of the tenancy' (ATA 1995, s 20(1)). However, if the tenant has, by written agreement with the landlord, received a benefit in consideration of the improvement, such as a premium, there is to be a proportionate reduction in any compensation payable (ATA 1995, s 20(2)). In the case of an improvement consisting of planning permission, the amount of compensation is the amount equal to the increase 'attributable to the fact that the relevant development is authorised by the planning permission in the value of the holding at the termination of the tenancy' (ATA 1995, s 21(1)).

In view of the stated importance of the right to compensation at the termination of a farm business tenancy to a tenant, specific provisions preserve the tenant's right to claim compensation. So, the fact that the tenant may have remained in the holding during two (or more) farm business tenancies does not deprive him of his right to compensation in relation to an improvement he carried out during an earlier tenancy (ATA 1995, s 23(1)). The parties may, however agree on the payment of compensation on the termination of the relevant earlier tenancy (ATA 1995, s 23(2)).[53] Equally, where, following a severance of the reversion and the resumption of possession of part of the holding by the landlord of part, the tenant's right to claim compensation in relation to the part he quits is triggered as at that time (ATA 1995, s 24). The affected part of the holding is treated as if it were a separate holding.

Requirement of landlord's consent

The tenant is only able to claim compensation for an improvement (of any kind) where the landlord[54] has given his consent in writing to the provision of the improvement (ATA 1995, s 17(1)). The tenant must not have commenced the improvement before he seeks consent – or he loses any right to compensation, unless the improvement is a 'routine improvement'. Consent may be given unconditionally or on condition that the tenant agrees to a specified variation in the terms of the tenancy (ATA 1995, s 17(3)). The consent may be given in the instrument creating the tenancy, as where

---

53 Such agreement does not, in terms, have to be in writing but ATA 1995, s 23(3) precludes the tenant in such a case from claiming any further compensation at the termination of his last tenancy.

54 'Landlord' for this and any purpose under ATA 1995 includes a person holding a leasehold estate or a limited owner, such as a tenant for life (ATA 1995, s 32).

the tenant undertakes to make certain improvement, or elsewhere, as in a landlord's letter (ATA 1995, s 17(2)).

However, where the improvement consists of a planning permission, a specific rule applies. The landlord must have given his consent in writing to the making of the application (ATA 1995, s 18(1)). If that consent is refused, the tenant obtains no right to compensation (ATA 1995, s 19(1)). Otherwise, the tenant might presumably make an application for a change of use which might be inconsistent with the landlord's interests.

There is no requirement that the landlord is not to refuse his consent unreasonably, for reasons mentioned earlier. However, as a counterpart to this, if, except in the case of planning permission applications, the tenant is aggrieved by a refusal of consent, he may give a written notice to the landlord which demands that the question is referred to an arbitration (ATA 1995, s 19(1)). He may also serve such a notice where the landlord fails to give consent within two months of a written request by the tenant for consent, or where he objects to a variation in the terms of the tenancy (such as a rent increase) required by the landlord as a condition of consent.

So as to promote speed of dispute resolution, the tenant must give notice referring a landlord's refusal of consent or disputed variation within two months beginning with the day the landlord gives him notice (ATA 1995, s 19(3)). In the case of a failure of the landlord to give consent following a tenant's request, the tenant must give his arbitration notice within four months beginning with the day he gave his request to the landlord (ATA 1995, s 19(3)).[55]

Arbitrations as to compensation

Arbitrations over compensation fall into two classes, those which relate to disputes about landlords' consents, and those relating to the amount of compensation itself. Regarding the first of these categories, the arbitrator has a general power to consider whether, having regard to the terms of the tenancy and any other relevant factors, it is reasonable for the tenant to provide the improvement (ATA 1995, s 19(5)), but his powers are balanced against the policy of giving weight to the landlord's wishes while not allowing the tenant's compensation to be diminished. Thus, in particular, although an arbitrator has the power unconditionally to approve the provision of an improvement, he cannot make his approval subject to any condition, otherwise the amount of compensation could be reduced[56] and he has no power to vary any condition required by the landlord (ATA 1995, s 19(6)).

---

55   It is envisaged that, to prevent the landlord frustrating the compensation provisions, following a tenant's arbitration notice, the parties may reach an agreement, but if not, the tenant may apply to the President of the RICS for the appointment of an arbitrator (ATA 1995, s 19(4)).

56   This result, if permitted, would, in the government view, run against the key provision in the Act of full compensation: HL Committee *Hansard* 13 December 1994, col 1235.

As far as arbitrations over the amount of compensation are concerned, where the parties cannot settle the claim by a written agreement, and the tenant has claimed compensation before the end of two months as from the date of termination of the tenancy (ATA 1995, s 22(2)) either party has the right, within four months from the termination date of the tenancy, to apply to the President of the RICS to appoint an arbitrator (ATA 1995, s 22(3)). No doubt the arbitrator, in assessing the amount of compensation, is mainly concerned to find the amount of the increase in the value of the holding attributable to the improvement at the termination of the tenancy, as required by ATA 1995, s 20(1)).

VI MISCELLANEOUS PROVISIONS

There is a role assigned by ATA 1995 to arbitrations and the provision made for an alternative means of dispute resolution. There is an important, but not exclusive, role to arbitrations.[57] Any arbitrations are to be under the general law and not, as is the case under AHA 1986, pursuant to a specific set of rules applicable to agricultural holdings alone.

In disputes not concerned with statutory rent reviews, consents to improvements or compensation claims, all of which have specific rules, ATA 1995, s 28(1) provides that any dispute other than in these three matters which concerns the rights and obligations of the parties under the Act is to be determined by arbitration. Where a dispute of this kind has arisen, the landlord or tenant may give a written notice to the other specifying the dispute and stating that unless the parties have appointed an arbitrator by agreement, he proposes to apply to the President of the RICS to appoint an arbitrator (ATA 1995, s 28(2)). Although ATA 1995, s 28(2) requires that two months must elapse from the date of giving the notice before any such application is made, no time-limit is imposed by ATA 1995, s 28(3) for the making of the application to the President of the RICS. The application must be in writing (ATA 1995, s 30(2)).

---

57 This is because provision is made in ATA 1995, s 29 for joint references to a third party who is not an arbitrator, where the tenancy agreement expressly provides for this method of dispute resolution. However, as a safeguard, if only one party makes a reference the other has a four-week period in which to refer the dispute to arbitration.

Index